Cultural Encounters in India

Cultural Encounters in India

The Local Co-workers of the Tranquebar Mission, 18th to 19th Centuries

Heike Liebau

Translated from the German by
Rekha V. Rajan

SOCIAL SCIENCE PRESS

Published by
Esha Béteille
Social Science Press
69 Jor Bagh, New Delhi 110 003

Social Science Press gratefully acknowledges that
The cover photograph has been reproduced with friendly permission from the **Study Centre August Hermann Francke of the Francke Foundations Halle**. AFSt/M 2 B 5: 1 *Malabarian Catechist and Portuguese Soldier*, coloured drawing by an unknown artist, commissioned by the missionary, Nicolaus Dal, 1729.

The translation of this book was funded by Geisteswissenschaften International—Translation Funding for Humanities and Social Sciences from Germany, a joint initiative of the Fritz Thyssen Foundation, the German Federal Foreign Office, the collecting society VG Wort and the Boersenverein des Deutschen Buchhandels (German Publishers & Booksellers Association)

ISBN: 978-81-87358-72-5

Set in Plantin 10/12.5
Typeset by Eleven Arts, Delhi 110 035
Printed by Ravindra Printing Press
Delhi - 110 006

Contents

Acknowledgements

This book is a translation of the German edition 'Die indischen Mitarbeiter der Tranquebarmission (1706–1845). Katecheten, Schulmeister, Übersetzer.' which appeared in 2008 in Tübingen. I am thankful to the Translation Fund for Humanities and Social Sciences in Germany 'Geisteswissenschaften International' for its generous translation grant. Rekha Rajan, Professor for German Studies at JNU translated the book. Thanks to her great effort and translation experience, the book is now available to an English speaking audience in India and elsewhere. I am indeed grateful to her.

The book would not have been possible without the kind support and help of many individuals and institutions. I would like to express my sincere thanks to all of them. I am thankful to Dr Mueller-Bahlke, the director of the Francke Foundations, and the colleagues in the Study Centre August Hermann Francke, with Dr Britta Klosterberg as the head of the center, for their openness and support for my work. I am obliged to staff members of the Bibliothek des Berliner Missionswerkes, the Archiv der Brüderunität Herrnhut, the Royal Library, and the National Archives in Copenhagen, who provided me with the sources I needed. I also wish to express my gratitude to staff members of the Archive of the Society for Promoting Christian Knowledge in Cambridge, the Archive and Library of the Gurukul Theological College and Research Institute in Chennai, the Archive and Library of the United Theological College in Bangalore, the Sarasvati Mahal Library in Thanjavur, and the Tamil Nadu State Archive in Chennai for their support.

The Centre for Modern Oriental Studies (ZMO) in Berlin provided me with an excellent research environment and facilities to complete this work. Many colleagues at ZMO, especially those in the research group 'Actors of Change' (1996–2000), with whom I shared my ideas, were of great help. Besides, my thanks and appreciations also go to Robert E. Frykenberg (Madison Wisconsin), Daniel Jeyaraj (Liverpool), Vincent Kumaradoss (Chennai), Susan Alexander (Chennai), Andreas Gross (Chennai, Berlin), Adapa Satyanarayana (Goa), Anderas Nehring (Erlangen), Geoffrey Oddie (Sydney) and Indira Vishvanathan Peterson (Massachusetts). Special thanks go to Bishop Johnson Gnanabaranam (1933–2008) and his wife Eva-Maria Siebert-Johnson who helped with translations from Tamil and showed me some of the historical places. Prof. Maria Lazar from TBML College Porayar helped me to establish valuable contacts in Tranquebar itself.

I take this opportunity to thank Valentina Lori and Tiziana Ziesing from De Gruyter publishers, who took care of the process of publishing the translation. Jolita Zabarskaite, my student assistant at ZMO, has helped me with a lot with correcting footnotes and with compiling the index. I would like to express my profound gratitude to Esha Béteille, Radha Béteille, and Aaleya Giri from Social Science Press in Delhi for their interest in publishing the book and for their careful editing. And finally, my family members were of great support, especially my husband Kurt, who prepared the maps and diagrams for the book.

Needless to say that, despite all help, all remaining errors are mine.

Heike Liebau
December 2012

Approaches to an Intermediary Group

> ... if one wants to understand what was happening in the mission field then it is important to start with the convert's world rather than with the missionaries.[1]

A few days before he died Daniel Pullei (1740–1802), the Indian *dubash* of the Danish governor Peter Herman Abbestée (1728–94)[2] in Tranquebar narrated the circumstances of his life to his long-standing confidante and friend, the German missionary Christoph Samuel John (1747–1813). John transcribed this narrative and sent it to Europe with the remark that it was one of the 'most remarkable and rich' biographies.[3] Although Daniel Pullei died before he could complete the account of his life, his memories, as written down by C.S. John, provided an impressive testimony of the manner in which an Indian convert dealt with the Christian faith and its moral teachings in an environment shaped by Hinduism. As a Tamilian Christian Daniel Pullei had attended a mission school and had also served for some time in

[1]Oddie, Geoffrey A., 2000, 'India: Missionaries, Conversion and Change', in Kevin Ward and Brian Stanley (eds.), *The Church Mission Society and World Christianity 1799–1999*, 228–53, Curzon Press Ltd., Richmond, Surrey, 250.

[2] P.H. Abbesté was governor of Tranquebar from 1761 till 1775 and from 1779 till 1788. Cf. Larsen, Kay, 1940, *Guvernører, Residenter, Kommandanter og Chefer samt enkelte andre fremtrædende Personer i de tidligere Danske Tropekolonier*, Arthur Jensens Forlag, København, 18, 35f.

[3]In a letter to a co-worker of the Halle Orphan House dated 3 February 1802 John confirmed that he had talked at length with the Tamilian about his life during the latter's last days. NHB 59. St. 1012f.

the mission. Even after he had been appointed in the service of the Danish governor in Tranquebar and had shifted from the religious to the political sphere he maintained his good contacts with the mission.[4] As a Tamilian and as a Christian, as a member of the local court and in his function as an advisor to the Danish governor, as a churchwarden and as a prosperous citizen of the small South Indian town of Tranquebar Daniel Pullei combined many different, even conflicting identities. While narrating his story to his friend he revealed his personal strife, the inner conflicts and doubts in a matter-of-fact manner. He said that he often didn't know what to do, 'since he sometimes incurred the displeasure and calumny of the Europeans, but more often that of his country men when he could not or did not want to act according to their separate interests.'[5]

Daniel Pullei was one of those Indians who as a 'national worker' for the Danish-English-Halle Mission[6] acted as an intermediary between the Europeans and the local population in the early phase of the spread of colonial domination in South India. When the Danish king, Frederick IV (Rule from 1699–1730), set up a Protestant mission in Tranquebar in 1705 this town on the south-east coast of India had already been in the possession of different Danish trading companies for almost one century. The Danish-English-

[4] For Daniel Pullei see also pp. 285–9 of this study. Cf. also Liebau, Heike, 2001, 'Tamilische Christen im 18. Jahrhundert als Mitgestalter sozialer Veränderungen. Motivationen, Möglichkeiten und Resultate ihres Wirkens', in Petra Heidrich and Heike Liebau (eds.), *Akteure des Wandels. Lebensläufe und Gruppenbilder an Schnittstellen von Kulturen*, 19–44, Das Arabische Buch, Berlin. Liebau, Heike, 2012, "Alle Dinge, die zu wissen nötig sind.' Religiös-soziale Übersetzungsprozesse im kolonialen Indien', *Geschichte und Gesellschaft* (38): 1–29.

[5] AFSt/M 1 K 5: 16, Brief curriculum vitae of Daniel Pullei' by [Christoph Samuel John], ??. ??. Tranquebar, 1803. See also NHB 62. St., 166–81.

[6] The term Danish-English-Halle Mission (DEHM) refers firstly to the Lutheran aspect of the mission that was initiated by the Danish royal house and was concentrated on the territory of the Danish colony in Tranquebar and the surrounding regions. Secondly, the term includes the so-called English mission supported by the SPCK that spread on territory controlled by the English East India Company from 1728 onwards. Tranquebar remained the centre for both regions so that the term Tranquebar mission is used here for the entire Danish-English-Halle Mission. The term Danish-Halle Mission (DHM) that has been commonly used till now appears here only in reference to the early years of the mission or when referring explicitly to the Lutheran mission in Tranquebar and its districts.

Halle Mission—also known as the Tranquebar Mission—was active as the first Protestant mission in India between 1706 and 1845 in different parts of what is today the state of Tamil Nadu. From 1706, when the first missionary, Bartholomäus Ziegenbalg (1682–1719), landed in Tranquebar till the Danish trade settlement was handed over to the British colonial rulers in 1845 more than fifty—mainly German—missionaries were entrusted with the task of propagating Christianity among the Tamils.

Along with the missionaries sent out from Europe several hundred local employees worked for the mission. Collaboration with Tamilians was crucial for the survival of the mission. There are several reasons for this. Firstly, the missionaries themselves, whose numbers were never very large, could not cope alone with all the work linked with the schools and churches as well as with administration and correspondence. Secondly, while travelling, the missionaries not only needed porters, but also people familiar with the place, the people and the language and who were integrated in local networks. Especially in the early years these people were indispensable as advisors and interpreters. Finally, the missionaries also relied on their local informants for the geographical, historical and political information they required for writing their reports and scientific studies. These informants were often employees of the Mission.

Corresponding to the infrastructure of the Mission establishments and the requirements of the missionaries the group of local employees and supporters of the Mission included technical personnel (porters, cooks, washer men, bell-ringers, grave-diggers etc.), the mission helpers in a narrower sense (prayer-leaders, bible-women, assistants, teachers, catechists, country-preachers) as well as interpreters, language-teachers and informants. A section of the 'national workers' was placed under the direct control of the Mission and paid by the Mission. These were, as a rule, the mission helpers in the narrower sense and most of the technical personnel. The interpreters, language teachers and informants also included non-Christians who worked with individual missionaries and were paid individually for their services.

In certain cases the missionaries maintained a close contact with people who had been educated in mission schools and had subsequently gone on to work in other fields. This group of people was primarily instrumental in ensuring that the actual influence of the mission extended far beyond the mission stations, although its sphere of activity in the first half of the eighteenth century was essentially limited to the territory under Danish control. It was only later that their missionary activity could be extended beyond this region. Local people educated in mission schools were sent to other European establishments as accountants, interpreters, soldiers, teachers, domestic helpers or, also, as craftsmen, especially after 1777 when responsibility for the colony Tranquebar passed from the trading company to the Danish state.[7]

The Tamils who were associated with the Danish-English-Halle Mission over a period of 130 years are the focal point of this study. This group, by no means homogeneous with regard to their social background, their religious and caste affiliation, but also with regard to their function in the everyday work of the mission, will be studied against the backdrop of processes of social and religious change in South India. As co-workers and contact persons of a European missionary society these players had to bear the brunt of specific conflicts. In the framework of an encounter between different cultures they entered into religious and social commitments that were often in mutual conflict, and they also worked as intermediaries between the Europeans (missionaries) and non-Europeans (local population). This had its consequences for the lifestyle, the social status and the social actions of the Indian employees of the Danish-English-Halle Mission. Conversion to Christianity often meant that these converts had to find a compromise between the new faith and their earlier lives—a compromise that was practical for the needs of everyday life and suitable for dealing with different social classes. While this was a

[7] Nørgaard sees a marked orientation towards establishing the 'usefulness' of the mission during the period when Christoph Samuel John (1769–1813 in India) worked as a missionary in Tranquebar. The usefulness for European establishments consisted in educating the Indians according to Western standards while taking local requirements into account. The Indians, on the other hand, saw this as a possibility of improving their social status. Cf. Nørgaard, Anders, 1988, *Mission und Obrigkeit—Die Dänisch-hallische Mission in Tranquebar 1706–1845*, Gütersloher Verlagshaus Gerd Mohn, Gütersloh (=Missionswissenschaftliche Forschungen, 22), 190 and 198f.

difficult social process for every convert, for those who entered into the service of the mission it presented a far greater problem. For the local mission employees, the 'national workers', the passage to Christianity did not end with a documented and publicly announced change of faith sanctioned by the act of baptism. They were subsequently expected to pass on the new religious content with its norms and values in a credible and convincing manner to the people of the region.

This study will attempt to gain insights into the lives of the local, basically Tamil, mission employees from a social and—only in a limited fashion—from a religious perspective. These people were intermediaries in political and legal conflicts, as well as advisors and contact persons for the local population, but they were sometimes also persecuted and cast out. Those among them who developed their own understanding and thus critically accompanied and helped shape the missionary cultural encounter became—although they were not always aware of it—initiators of religious and social change. They constantly crossed religious and social boundaries and created new social and religious identities.[8]

As the first overseas Protestant mission the Danish-English-Halle Mission was in many respects, even with regard to the formation of a group of Tamil co-workers, a model for later missions. Urs Biterli's statement that the formation of an 'intermediary mixed-class' ('vermittelnde Mischlingsschicht') was carried out successfully in the missionary field only in the nineteenth century would have to thus be relativized.[9] More so, since the formation of this intermediary class in the Tranquebar Mission took on more distinct aspects than in later missionary societies.

In what follows the role of cultural, in this case predominantly religious, intermediaries in pre- and early colonial India will be examined through the example of the Indian co-workers of the DEHM. The history of this mission will be understood in the

[8] Liebau, Heike, 2001, 'Zwischen Hinduismus und Christentum. Veränderung sozialer und religiöser Bindungen im Süden des vorkolonialen Indien', in Henner Fürtig (Hg.), *Aneignung und Abgrenzung in der Globalisierung*, 107–18, Das Arabische Buch, Berlin.

[9] Cf. Bitterli, Urs, 1986, *Alte Welt—neue Welt. Formen des europäisch-überseeischen Kulturkontakts vom 15. bis zum 18. Jahrhundert*, C.H. Beck Verlag, München.

broadest sense as the history of cultural relations.[10] Based on its religious agenda Christian missions initially only planned a one-sided influence of Christians on non-Christian peoples with a view to converting the 'heathens' to Christianity. In this framework the missionaries were cast in the role of superior teachers and helpers, while those who were to be converted were, at best, to play the role of grateful converts. They were not understood as thinking and active adherents of the faith. In reality, missionary work always proved to be a complex, often long-lasting and direct encounter between representatives of different religions and cultures in the process of which new social and religious values and norms were negotiated. By naming one side of the encounter as active (missionaries) and the other as passive (missionized/converts) we ignore the complexity of mutual dealings between the groups. If we look at the local co-workers as servants of the European missionaries and players controlled by the mission, as objects or victims of an intercultural encounter whose actions can then only be viewed as the result of external influences, we fail to see the possible scope of the actions of individual mission co-workers. It also makes it more difficult to analyze mutual contacts in the sphere of Christian missionary activity and only provides a limited scope for questions regarding relations of communication, negotiation and exchange between the 'missionizing' and the 'missionized'.[11] In the course of missionary

[10] Bitterli understands cultural relations as 'a lasting and permanent relationship of mutual contacts on the basis of a power equilibrium or a stalemate. The condition for cultural relations was the play between demand and supply: its representatives on the European side were traders and missionaries.' (translated from German; all references from original German sources have been translated by Rekha-Rajan), Bitterli, *Alte Welt—neue Welt*, 42. Although he considers the work of the missionaries to be a classical example of cultural relations, Bitterli qualifies this by saying: 'nevertheless, cultural contact as fostered by the missionary was an extremely problematic undertaking. This is because the missionary—in contrast to the trader and the colonizer—sought to adopt a more sympathetic approach, but at the core he remained an exponent of European culture and was, in the final instance, dependent on the material support of church institutions and the colonial administration.' (translated from German), Bitterli, *Alte Welt—neue Welt*, 48f.

[11] 'European and indigenous discourses both played a role in the construction of modern India. European knowledge may have been hegemonic, but it was never absolute.' Bayly, Christopher Allan, 1996, *Empire & Information. Intelligence Gathering and Social Communication in India, 1780–1870*, Cambridge University

work many of the (local) 'missionized' became helpers or partners of the missionaries in their function as mission employees and were thus themselves 'missionizers', while the European missionaries learnt a lot from their Indian partners especially with regard to their understanding of local society, philosophy and literature. The concrete shape of relations between the Europeans and the local population was always dependent on the historical background of missionary activity, on the religious and social principles of the mission society, its methods of carrying out missionary work and the local conditions in the mission region.

The work of the Tranquebar mission falls in the period of the formation and consolidation of British colonial rule in India, which was accompanied by far-reaching social changes. The eighteenth century, which comprises the main part of the period under study, also constitutes a break in the history of missions. It spelt the decline of influence of the Catholic missions, while Protestant missions came into being, at first hesitantly in association with pietistic movements.[12] The Danish-Halle mission gave birth to 'the history of broad-based and continuous evangelical missionary work.'[13]

In the 1960s there was a shift in emphasis in socio-historical research from a predominant consideration of social structures and processes to a greater engagement with the role of social groups and classes as historical protagonists and as contributors to social transformations. With the development of the Annales School, the Subaltern Studies or the History from Below, history was no longer

---

Press, Cambridge [et.al.], 370. Interaction and dialogical processes in the formation of India's colonial society are also emphasized by Irschick, Eugene F., 1994, *Dialogue and History, Constructing South India, 1795–1895*, University of California Press, Berkeley; van der Veer, Peter, 2001, *Imperial Encounters. Religion and Modernity in India and Britain*, Princeton University Press, Princeton.

[12] Cf. Obst, Helmut, 1999, 'Missionsberichte aus Indien im 18. Jahrhundert: Eine Einführung in den missionsgeschichtlichen Kontext', in Michael Bergunder (ed.), *Missionsberichte aus Indien im 18. Jahrhundert. Ihre Bedeutung für die europäische Geistesgeschichte und ihr wissenschaftlicher Quellenwert für die Indienkunde*, 1–5, Verlag der Franckeschen Stiftungen, Halle (=Neue Hallesche Berichte, Quellen und Studien zur Geschichte und Gegenwart Südindiens, vol. 1).

[13] Gensichen, Hans-Werner, 1961, *Missionsgeschichte der neueren Zeit*, Vandenhoeck & Ruprecht, Göttingen (=*Die Kirche in ihrer Geschichte. Ein Handbuch*, ed. by Kurt Dietrich Schmidt and Ernst Wolf, vol. 4. Lieferung T.).

understood in a unidirectional fashion as the history of influential groups led by powerful ruling personalities. Historians increasingly directed their questions to the role of marginalized groups and lower sections of society in historical processes. Accompanied by a growing interest in mentality studies and the history of everyday life, as well as by new approaches in biographical and anthropological research these developments also promoted the turn to the so-called intermediary groups in history. Such groups always arose in specific historical situations when people with special characteristics and abilities were required to mediate between different interest groups. Political, economic and social developments influenced the need for such intermediaries and also determined their status in the concerned society.[14] Based on anthropological research the scientific studies of intermediary groups have, in the meantime, also gained significance in other disciplines.[15] The framework of

[14] There are always new incentives for the rise of such intermediary groups. For example, the rapid changes in information technology today favour the formation of information intermediaries whose task consists in collecting and collating the electronic flood of information for special user requirements. 'Network-based information intermediaries are mediators between information sources and information seekers ...' What is remarkable here is that the reference is not only to the people working as information intermediaries, but also to the technical execution of mediation within electronic networks. Cf. Rose, Frank, 1999, *The Economics, Concept, and Design of Information Intermediaries: A Theoretic Approach*, Physica Verlag, Heidelberg, New York, 209.

[15] The term was introduced by E. Wolf. Wolf, Eric R., 1956, 'Aspects of Group Relations in a complex Society: Mexico' *American Anthropologist*, New Series, 58 (6): 1065–78. Early studies were primarily directed at intermediaries between different social, economic, cultural and political sphere within a (Western) society. Originally, the term *broker* referred to a business agent or a marriage-broker, i.e. persons who took on the role of an intermediary in a concrete process of negotiation. In later historical, sociological and anthropological research the term 'broker' was used for people who mediated between the rural areas and metropolitan culture. Boissevain and other representatives of social anthropology reconstructed the networks of these groups and discovered their motives and interests. Boissevain sees these brokers as self-interested entrepreneurs and network specialists. Cf. Boissevain, Jeremy, 1974, *Friends of Friends: Networks, Manipulators and Coalitions*, St. Martin's Press, New York, 8, 148. Some studies were devoted to the analysis of 'classical' cultural intermediaries in European history such as writers, translators and publishers. Cf. Pelzer, Erich, 1998, *Die Wiederkehr des girondistischen Helden. Deutsche Intellektuelle als kulturelle Mittler zwischen Deutschland und Frankreich während der Französischen Revolution*, Bouvier, Bonn.

these studies was considerably extended by applying the concept to the colonial context in which processes of mediation not only took on translocal and global forms, but were also extended to include different spheres of life. The activation of existing and the formation of new intermediary groups followed different patterns depending on historical circumstances and the participating players, but it was a necessary accompaniment and a consequence of intercultural encounter and colonial conquests.

From the 1970s, at the latest, relevant historical studies on Indian history propounded the thesis that British colonial rule could not have been established without the participation of different groups among the local population. The eighteenth century which was long considered a period of decline and chaos was reevaluated as a historical stage that contained the seeds of development in a political, economic and cultural sense. With this the study of the Indian middle class and elites that took part in social transformation processes became relevant.[16]

[16] Burton Stein talks about the prosperous and influential segments of South Indian society who, towards the end of the eighteenth century, became an important instrument for enforcing the East India Company's system of control and who saw in this the possibility of personal gain. 'These respectable groups of South Indians were not passive agents in the system of control established by the Company in the late eighteenth century. They quickly received the opportunities for advancing their social and economic interests under the Company...' Cf. Stein, Burton, 1969, 'Integration of the Agrarian System', in Robert E. Frykenberg (ed.), *Land Control and Social Structure in Indian History*, 175–216, The University of Wisconsin Press, Madison, 203. Arasaratnam regards the indigenous trader-groups on the south-east coast of India who collaborated with the Europeans not primarily as dependents of the colonial power but as allies who influenced the process whereby trading bases were established and consolidated. Cf. Arasaratnam, Sinnappah, 1995, *Maritime Trade, Society and European Influence in Southern Asia, 1600–1800*, Variorum, Aldershot, Brookfield. C.A. Bayly comes to a similar conclusion for the process of creation of colonial rule in India as a whole. Here Indians appear as 'active agents not simply passive bystanders and victims in the creation of colonial India'. Cf. Bayly, C.A., 1990, *Indian Society and the Making of the British Empire*, Cambridge University Press, Cambridge [et al], 5; Bayly, C.A., 1983, *Rulers, Townsmen and Bazaars. North Indian Society in the Age of British Expansion 1770–1870*, Cambridge University Press, Cambridge [et al], 4. For Niels Brimnes too Indian groups are more than just players controlled by the Europeans. Through the example of the violent conflicts between representatives of castes of the right and of the left hand on the east coast of India in the eighteenth century he demonstrates the interaction between Europeans and Indians as a form of

Local groups of intermediaries operated between representatives of European trading companies, on the one hand, and producers or Indian merchants on the other. Since they were not directly and exclusively answerable to any authority they could act relatively independently. They had to have contacts, networks, economic structures, means of transport and storage facilities at their disposal. They also required knowledge of languages and experience in the way of life and work both of the European merchants as well as of the Indian producers and merchants. These positions of trade intermediaries (brokers) were traditionally occupied in South India by certain castes who for centuries had specialized in coastal trade.[17] Existing structures and networks often proved to be advantageous and stable for the European trade-settlements in India.[18] Whether it was a matter of obtaining permission from local rulers to establish a trade-settlement, a matter of military and political alliances, economic contacts or information about the country and its people, the mutual relationships and interdependency between the colonial power and the colonized population had a wide range, and in this

dialogue. Cf. Brimnes, Niels, 1999, *Constructing the Colonial Encounter, Right and Left Hand Castes in Early Colonial South India*, Curzon Press, Richmond. See also Förster, Stig, 1992, *Die mächtigen Diener der East-India Company: Ursachen und Hintergründe der britischen Expansionspolitik in Südasien, 1793–1849*, Steiner, Stuttgart.

[17] For example, *veḻḷāḷar*-brokers who, among other things, were active in the elephant trade were looked on as partners both by the Europeans and by the local rulers. Individual Indian merchants who were considered to be 'company merchants' maintained a close contact with Europeans over long periods of time. On the south-east coast it was mainly the *cheṭṭi* who were important representatives of intermediary groups and often also leading figures in trade associations. Cf. Arasaratnam, S., 1981, 'Social History of a Dominant Caste Society. The Vellalar of North Ceylon (Sri Lanka) in the 18th Century', *IESHR* 18 (3/4): 377–91; Arasaratnam, S., 1995, 'Indian intermediaries in the trade and administration of the French East India Company in the Coromandel. (1670–1760)', in Arasaratnam, *Maritime Trade*, X, 133–46; Arasaratnam, S., 1995, 'Indian commercial groups and European traders, 1600–1800: Changing relationships in Southeastern India', in S. Arasaratnam, *Maritime Trade*, III, 42–53.

[18] Das Gupta, Ashin, 1984, 'Indian Merchants in the Age of Partnership. 1500–1800', in Dwijendra Tripathi (ed.), *Business Communities of India. A Historical Perspective*, 27–39, SAGE, New Delhi, 30. For the African continent and the role of the Duala as trade intermediaries see: Austen, Ralph A. and Jonathan Derrick, 1999, *Middlemen of the Cameroon Rivers. The Duala and their Hinterland c. 1600–c. 1960*, Cambridge University Press, Cambridge.

process local groups of intermediaries periodically gained immense significance.[19] On the one hand, the agreements reached between European trading companies and local rulers cleared the path for European acquisition of territories on the coast to set up trade settlements while, on the other, it offered advantages to the local ruler in case of conflicts with other local powers. The European trading companies gained access to the local structures of production, exchange and trade. Initially, they did not seek to actively change or shape these structures. In addition, insufficient knowledge about the people and the place as well as of the language made the European employees of the East India companies particularly dependent on local support in the early phase of colonial conquest.[20]

The brokers who were involved in trade activity between European societies and local producers or merchants[21] had a

[19] Similar statements have also been made with regard to the African continent: 'For the smooth progress of cultural relations based on trade it was essential to have an intermediary class of Africans and persons of mixed descent who served as brokers, boatmen, interpreters or artisans. This intermediary class, which was located between two cultures and used a pidgin language, could, at times, gain so much significance that the interests of the European factory officials as well as those of the local government were endangered.' (translated from German), Bitterli, *Alte Welt–neue Welt*, 45.

[20] Eugene Irschick studies the process of interaction in the production of knowledge about local society through the example of the South Indian district Chingleput. He clearly shows how knowledge and perceptions about local conditions and about cultural identity were created and transformed and he describes the imbalance in the process of dialogue between the British colonial power and the local population. Irschick, *Dialogue and History*. C.A. Bayly looks at another kind of alliance in the form of colonial structures of surveillance and argues that British knowledge was fed by existing autonomous social networks and systems of communication, i.e. by Indian sources. Bayly, *Empire and Information*. Similarly, proceeding from the assumption that colonial structures could not have been established without the help of the indigenous population Ravi Ahuja reconstructs the role of labour and thus, that of the working classes in the rise of colonial structures in the Madras region in the second half of the eighteenth century. Ahuja, Ravi, 1999, *Die Erzeugung kolonialer Staatlichkeit und das Problem der Arbeit. Eine Studie zur Sozialgeschichte der Stadt Madras und ihres Hinterlandes zwischen 1750 und 1800*, Steiner, Stuttgart.

[21] S. Arasaratnam and C.A. Bayly have studied commercial intermediaries in the context of colonial India. Cf. Arasaratnam, *Social History of a Dominant Caste Society*; Arasaratnam, 1986, *Merchants, Companies and Commerce on the Coromandel Coast, 1650–1740*, Oxford University Press, New Delhi; Arasaratnam, 1989,

different range of tasks from those carried out by political brokers. The latter became significant in the framework of far-reaching territorial conquests, appropriation of land and territorial occupation that occurred later.[22] Since the 1970s research has turned to a study of these groups.[23] Studies on the South Indian *dubashes* are a major focus in research on political intermediaries in the context of South

---

'Coromandel Revisited: problems and issues in Indian maritime history', *IESHR* 26 (1): 101–10; Arasaratnam, *Maritime Trade*; Bayly, *Rulers, Townsmen and Bazaars*; Bayly, *Indian Society*.

[22] For the African continent the history of the Duala in Cameroon had been studied as a history of intermediary communities since representatives of the Duala always undertook the role of economic or cultural brokers under changing political conditions. 'Broker' is understood here as a term 'which links the literal function of historical middlemen with a more metaphorical sense of what means in contemporary Africa to beat once a client to external sources of power and wealth and a patron within a network of indigenous dependents.' Austen and Derrick, *Middlemen of the Cameroon rivers*, 3.

[23] Scott, James C., 1977, 'Political clientelism: a bibliographical essay', in Steffen W. Schmidt et al., *Friends, Followers and Factions: A Reader in Political Clientelism*, 483–505, University of California Press, Berkeley. In the field of social anthropology a volume of collected essays on political middlemen in Oceania deals primarily with various groups of administrative officials who mediate between overarching and subordinate political structures. By dealing with the phenomenon of intermediary groups the authors are looking for answers to broader questions of social and cultural change in different local societies. They argue that in certain situations political middlemen became cultural brokers and can thus be seen as transporters of ideas that could influence social and cultural change. Cf. Rodman, William L. and Dorothy Ayers Counts (eds.), 1982, *Middlemen and Brokers in Oceania*, The University of Michigan Press, Ann Arbor (=ASAO Monograph, No. 9). The question concerning the potential of intermediaries to change society under different conditions of cultural contact is the focus of a book brought out by the Zentrum Moderner Orient (ZMO), Berlin: 'Akteure des Wandels. Lebensläufe und Gruppenbilder an Schnittstellen von Kulturen'. The study focuses on a historical perspective of individual groups from different regional and social backgrounds who, under varying historical conditions and in different social areas, mediated between the Orient and the Occident. Through a comparison of these heterogeneous individuals and groups, who can be termed political, cultural or religious intermediaries, the authors arrive at the conclusion that these groups, born out of historical necessity, underwent a development and change. Whether consciously or unconsciously, these groups participated in varying degrees in social transformation. Cf. Heidrich, Petra and Heike Liebau (eds.), 2001, *Akteure des Wandels. Lebensläufe und Gruppenbilder an Schnittstellen von Kulturen*, Das Arabische Buch, Berlin (=Studien des Zentrums Moderner Orient, 14).

India. In the eighteenth century the role of the *dubash* had become particularly important as an intermediary between the Europeans and the local rulers.[24] The term *dubash* initially meant a person who spoke two languages (Hindi: *do bhāṣā*) and could therefore work as an interpreter. The employer expected absolute loyalty from the *dubash* as an intermediary in the political sphere. Depending on his personal knowledge and his capabilities, or on his diplomatic abilities, a *dubash* could achieve great prestige through his dealings with the negotiating sides. Apart from their European employees and assistants, European officials in important and decisive political positions had 'their' Indian *dubash* who not only needed to know different languages, but also had to have the ability to carry out negotiations and be capable of mediating local conditions to his European superiors. The *dubashes* were indispensable props of the colonial administration, but they were also a constant threat. Masked behind a public show of loyalty towards their foreign employers they often nurtured their own ideas which they hid from the Europeans.[25]

Whereas certain groups or castes seemed to be almost predestined for the role of economic or political intermediaries in colonial India, religious groups of intermediaries were selected or specially trained by the European mission societies. While in the early period of organized Christian missionary activity there were isolated incidents of *dubashes* (some failures) who offered their services to a mission, most mission societies quickly organized the training of their local intermediaries. Religious-cultural intermediary groups were not only different from intermediaries in other spheres with regard to the history of their formation and with regard to their social position (they were often members of lower castes or 'untouchables'), but they also exhibited certain distinctive features in the course of their development as a social group. The consolidation of England's position as a territorial power in India meant that better-trained men conversant in the languages and with knowledge of the region

[24] See, among others, Bayly, *Empire and Information*; Neild-Basu, Susan, 1984, 'The Dubashes of Madras', *Modern Asian Studies* 18 (1): 1–31. Arasaratnam, *Indian Intermediaries in the trade and administration*.

[25] Cf. Irschick, *Dialogue and History*, 35; Bayly, *Empire and Information*, 6; Ahuja, *Die Erzeugung kolonialer Staatlichkeit*, 57; Neild-Basu, 'The Dubashes of Madras'.

were required for administering and controlling the conquered regions. While, in this process, European employees of the Company increasingly replaced local workers,[26] the opposite development can be observed in the long term for religious intermediary groups in the colonial context. Here, a local elite was formed in the religious sphere since it was the local co-workers of the missions who, in the course of history, took over the tasks and the role of the European missionaries and gradually displaced them from their missionary role. The 'national workers' became 'national missionaries' who, by the beginning of the twentieth century, participated actively in the development of Christianity in India.

However, in relevant studies on church, mission or religious history this group plays only a marginal role. In addition, the focus is mostly on the dependence of local players on the European Christian missions and few attempts are made to study the contribution of this group to Christian missionary activity and social change.[27] In many studies Christian missionary activity is conceived of methodologically as a unilateral action directed towards the people who have to be converted by missionaries as bearers of Christian teachings, not as dialogue and encounter. In the course of the centuries-old history of Christian missionary activity the manner in which the gospel was propagated varied. It happened directly or indirectly, violently or peacefully, individually or through mass conversions, as a one-time act or spread over a longer period of time. In every case,

[26] Cf. Gründer, Horst, 1992, *Welteroberung und Christentum. Ein Handbuch zur Geschichte der Neuzeit*, Gütersloher Verl.-Haus Mohn, Gütersloh, 295. The privilege of studying India, which had been accorded till then to only a few scholars, gave way to a more broad-based study of the languages, religions and traditions of India by English officials in India. Michael Adas is of the opinion that the study of languages, religions and traditions changed from 'an enriching pastime for gentlemen with a taste for the exotic into a vital concern for India's new rulers'. Cf. Adas, Michael, 1989, *Machines as the Measure of Men, Science, Technology and Ideologies of Western Dominance*, Cornell University Press, Ithaca, London, 96. On the necessity of training English officials in regional studies see also: Kulke, Hermann and Dietmar Rothermund, 1998, *Geschichte Indiens von der Induskultur bis heute*, C.H. Beck Verlag, München, 305f.

[27] Cf., among others, Shobhanan, B. (ed.), 1996, *A History of the Christian Missions in South India*, Kerala Historical Society, Thiruvananthapuram. Sharma, Raj Bahadur, 1988, *Christian Missions in North India, 1813–1913. A Case Study of Meerut Division and Dehra Dun District*, Mittal Publications, Delhi.

missionary activity required constant mediation at the linguistic, cultural and religious levels. Particularly in the early period of their work in new regions Christian missionaries were dependent on the loyalty and support of the local population. The principal task of the local religious intermediaries who were employed and paid by the European missions was to spread Christian teachings and, to some extent, also European moral concepts among the people of their region. At the same time they taught the European missionaries about life in India. In accordance with their individual experiences, their personal motivations, social interests and intellectual capabilities they linked their religious tasks with social commitment and ideas for social change. Since the intercultural missionary encounter was an encounter of unequal partners in the context of European colonial rule, their ability to act remained limited, both theoretically and realistically. While it is true that the heterogeneous religious, social and caste identities of the 'national workers' was, in a sense, relativized by the fact of their employment with the mission and that their status in society was redefined, even within the mission they continued to remain a heterogeneous group.

Strictly speaking, religious intermediaries had a dual intermediary status: firstly between Europeans in the form of Christian missionaries and the local population, secondly between Christian Indians, on the one hand, and Hindus and Muslims, on the other. In addition, European missionaries themselves represented a cultural and religious intermediary group, so that what we have here are several levels of mediation that are interlinked. The missionaries represented European Christian revival or reform movements whose aim was to spread the Christian faith worldwide. The Indian mission workers represented, in the final instance, local endeavours for change. Each group acted in the interests of a certain clientele, but each was highly dependent on the other.

COLLECTIVE BIOGRAPHY, OR MOSAIC OF INDIVIDUAL BIOGRAPHIES?

In this study attention will be directed towards the subjective element of history, in this case, to a concretely defined group of religious players. These people, shaped by socio-political and cultural developments, influenced social processes with a varying degree of consciousness and varying intensity. Two interlinked methodological approaches enable us to make generalized statements about the self-perception, the motivations and the role of intermediary groups: firstly, an approach via the cultural and everyday history of the mission and, secondly, the approach via the individual lives of the local mission co-workers.

In recent decades historical studies have turned away from dealing with a history of structures and events towards a study of the problems of cultural and social history as well as history of mentalities. Since the 1980s themes from the everyday history of a society in general and from the lives of socially marginalized groups in particular have been providing questions for research in social history.[28] The rediscovery of the history of mentalities that can be traced back to the representatives of the Annales, Lucien Febvre and Marc Bloch, helped, for its part, in bringing collective action, collective views of society, in short, collective biographies into the focus of historical studies.[29] Historical anthropology and the history of mentalities place greater emphasis on the subjective element in their research. The human being is observed as a factor constituting history and as being shaped by history in order to show processes of development and to uncover motivations.

In the present study the focus is on daily life within a missionary context. For this it is not enough to engage with the methods and results of conversion. The direct reality of conversion is only a fraction of the mission reality in which daily encounters between missionaries and the local population, communication endeavors on

[28] Cf. Rotermund, Hermann, 1980, 'Alltagskultur–Kritische Literaturhinweise', in Wolfgang Fritz Haug and Kaspar Maase (ed.), *Materialistische Kulturtheorie und Alltagskultur*, 122–36, Argument-Verlag, Berlin; Dausien, Bettina and Kelle, Helga, 2005, 'Biographie und Kulturelle Praxis. Methodologische Überlegungen zur Verknüpfung von Ethnographie und Biographieforschung', in Bettina Völker, Bettina Dausien, Helma Lutz and Gabriele Rosenthal (eds.), *Biographieforschung im Diskurs*, 189–212, VS Verlag, Wiesbaden.

[29] See for instance: Schröder, Wilhelm Heinz, 1985, 'Kollektive Biographie in der historischen Sozialforschung. Eine Einführung', in Wilhelm Heinz Schröder (ed.), *Lebenslauf und Gesellschaft. Zum Einsatz von kollektiven Biographien in der historischen Sozialforschung*, 7–17, Klett-Cotta, Stuttgart (=Historisch-sozialwissenschaftliche Forschungen, 18).

both sides, negotiations by the missionaries with local and colonial authorities as well as with the European mission directors would all have to be taken into consideration. A reconstruction of the formal organizational structure and the manner of functioning of an overseas Christian mission station already throw up questions about economic, political and cultural contexts which go far beyond the religious core of missionary activity. In addition, differing religious and ideological symbols, different systems of order and interpretation determine the daily image of the Mission.

When dealing with everyday life in a limited social context and with the changes in mentality of a selected social group a historian runs the risk of losing sight of larger historical processes and of limiting him/herself to a descriptive account of the subject matter. This danger can only be countered by constantly relating the cultural and social questions regarding the daily life of the mission with the history of religion of the country and of the church, with the international missionary power structure and the development of local society as a whole.

An analytical perspective on the daily life of the mission over a long period of time provides insights into the development of a professional group or of a local elite and the changes in their attitude towards social developments and religious practices. Where there is insufficient (auto)biographical material the silent gestures of people and a description of their actions served as sources 'which tell us about the behaviour and the attitudes of as large a number of people as possible, of groups'.[30] While the 'national workers' of the Tranquebar Mission formed a quantitatively clearly defined group, they were, in several regards, a heterogeneous community which constantly changed and regenerated itself in the course of the period under study.

An analysis of the social contacts and hierarchies, of the conflicts and negotiations in the everyday life of the mission will be supplemented through an attempt to come closer to the perspectives of individual representatives of the group under study. This approach

[30] Sprandel, Rolf, 1987, 'Erfahrungen mit der Mentalitätengeschichte', in Ulrich Raulff (ed.), *Mentalitäten-Geschichte. Zur historischen Rekonstruktion geistiger Prozesse*, 97–113, Wagenbach, Berlin, 97, (translated from German).

is based on the impetus received from historical-biographical research.[31] The scientific study of 'conversion biographies' is particularly interesting since for the majority of people in the group under study personal conversion or, sometimes, the event of conversion in the family, going back at times to earlier generations, was the starting-point for far-reaching changes. Conversion was not only a turning point in their lives but also a symbol and expression of an often long-lasting process of a religious and social change of personality.[32]

Despite all similarities of the persons studied I have tried to understand their individual characters, identities and biographies as a basis for their diverse actions. Their actions were active as well as reactive, conscious or unconscious, intended or unintended. The group under study will be observed as a community of individuals who, in many ways, encountered similar challenges. However, they were sometimes shaped by very different social and religious traditions that were reflected in their actions and their status as Christians. A group picture, in a manner of speaking, will be sketched in which, however, the individuals remain visible because, despite their affiliation to the group of 'national workers', there are many self-contained, individual biographies that need to be studied. On the basis of biographical sketches of individual members of the group an attempt will be made to arrive at conclusions about common ideas and intentions. The change of personality and of individual identity experienced by the Indian workers of the DEHM as well as the

[31] Biographical research has thus become a legitimate means to study history of colonial India. See for instance: Arnold, David and Stuart Blackburn (eds.), 2004, *Telling Lives in India. Biography, Autobiography and Life History*, Indiana UP and Permanent Black, Bloomington; Brown, Judith, 2009, 'Life Histories and the History of Modern South Asia', *American Historical Review*, June 2009, 587–95; Brown, Judith M., 2011, *Windows into the Past, Life Histories and the Historian of South Asia*, Oxford University Press, New Delhi.

[32] It is interesting to note the statement that conversion only creates an ostensible break with the life lived prior to it and that there is, in fact, an attempt to maintain a certain continuity with important roots of social behaviour being retained even after conversion. Cf. Wohlrab-Sahr, Monika, 1998, 'Protestantische Ethik im islamischen Gewand. Habitusreproduktion und religiöser Wandel. Das Beispiel der Konversion eines Afroamerikaners zum Islam', in Ralf Bohnsack and Winfried Marotzki (ed.), *Biografieforschung und Kulturanalyse. Transdisziplinäre Zugänge qualitativer Forschung*, 183–201, Leske und Burdich, Opladen, 199.

self-perception of their intermediary role will be reconstructed. This does not give rise to a group- or collective biography. Rather, the formation and development of a religious-social occupational group will be described, illustrated with numerous individual biographies, or with biographical details.

The specificities of the sources, their fragmentary character, the absence of written reflections of the people under study about their own lives, the necessity of having to draw direct conclusions from reports of other persons (European missionaries) required the combination of methods of biographical research with those of prosopographical research. The state of the sources leads to the question to what extent one can draw conclusions about the motives of the person concerned when there are no explicit statements in this regard.[33] Just as the prosopographical method attempts to 'gain insights into the social structure of the village community by collecting all available data about the life history of individuals or families.'[34] I have attempted to complete the picture of the social group of religious intermediaries through the biographies of individuals. For this, all available material in the documents about the circumstances of the persons' lives and those of their families has been collected and analyzed.[35] In order to achieve the highest possible degree of authenticity in the survey of the group under study I have traced biographies over several generations. In the essential

[33] Eck, Werner, 1993, 'Überlieferung und historische Realität: Ein Grundproblem prosopographischer Forschung', in Werner Eck (ed.), *Prosopographie und Sozialgeschichte. Studien zur Methodik und Erkenntnismöglichkeit der kaiserzeitlichen Prosopographie*, 365–96, Böhlau, Köln [et al]. In contrast to prosopographical sources the missionary documents of the Danish-English-Halle Mission sometimes contain comprehensive descriptions of the group of Indian co-workers or reports about individual representatives of the group.

[34] Hagedorn, Dieter, 1993, 'Eignet sich die prosopographische Methode zur Erforschung sozialer Strukturen in den Dörfern des Römischen Ägypten?', in Werner Eck, *Prosopographie und Sozialgeschichte*, 351–63, Böhlau, Köln, Wien, Weimar, 352.

[35] Systematically gathered and regularly updated data like the information collected in the 'Orphans' Album of the Halle Orphanage' does not exist for this group. Cf. Jacobi, Juliane and Thomas Müller-Bahlke (eds.), 1989, *'Man hatte von ihm gute Hoffnung …' Das Waisenhausalbum der Franckeschen Stiftungen 1695–1749*, Verlag der Franckeschen Stiftungen Halle im Max Niemeyer Verlag, Tübingen. Jacobi, Juliane, 1993, 'Das erste Waisenalbum des Halleschen Waisenhauses (1695–1749)', *Jahrbuch für historische Bildungsforschung*, vol. 6: 7–26, Klinkhardt, Bad Heilbrunn, Obb.

characteristics of their social, their age and gender structure the group remains constant. The genres of the sources do not change for the period under study apart from some modifications with regard to the classification and weight-age given to individual documents in the overall context of the mission sources. This enabled a long term perspective along the lines of the questions in the individual chapters and, in the final instance, it made generalized statements possible about the changed role of Indian mission co-workers as well as about the emancipation of Indian Christians.

In terms of practical research the retrieval of concrete biographical and statistical data over a long period of time dictated work on this study. This initially meant the collection of all available data on each individual person. Sometimes, the identity of the person could only be ascertained properly after the material had been collected since, in some cases, Tamil names were used alongside the European baptismal names. At times, the person was also not mentioned by name at all, but only with regard to responsibility for a particular function.

Despite the fact that the history of the group under study here occurs within a specific, but changing cultural, political and socio-economic context that, therefore, needs to be constantly redefined, its ideal-type function as a religious intermediary group can be transferred to other regional and temporal conditions. The micro-historical perspective is relativized and opened out by the constant references to the historical background of the period under study and is thus extended to larger social contexts in pre- or early colonial society of South India. Although, regarding content, the topic is close to mission history, broader social processes are made more transparent and intercultural encounters are illuminated. The aim is to study the role of the Indian side in these processes. Biographical research is a means to study political and social history[36] provided that the comparison of biographies of different players allows us to draw conclusions about the structure of society. For the present study this means that the cultural and religious interaction between European missionaries and Indians should be viewed in connection

[36] Voges, Wolfgang, 1987, *Biographie und Gesellschaft. Methoden der Biographie- und Lebenslaufforschung*, Leske, Budrich, Opladen; Arnold, Blackburn, *Telling Lives in India*; Brown, *Windows into the Past.*

with the processes of social change brought about by the entry of Europeans into India. Following the premises of the history of mentalities and agency my attention will be directed towards the formation and change of ideas and behaviour within the religious-social group that is being studied here.[37]

USE OF MISSION SOURCES FOR SOCIO-HISTORICAL RESEARCH

'No single group of sources on a historical theme can claim to have absolute validity', says Adam Jones with regard to European sources on Africa, which are always perceived as having a Eurocentric bias, but of which it is then said that 'we cannot afford to do without such sources.'[38]

The sources for this study comprise an immense amount of material, but they are characterized by their predominantly religious character as well as by the missionary context. Whereas in the field of historical African studies missionary sources are no longer used only by mission and church historians, but also by historians, anthropologists, geographers and linguists,[39] studies on India even now seldom make use of this corpus. This is evidently not only because of abundantly available alternatives in the form of the source materials of the British colonial administration and the local administrations. If one considers the use of mission sources in research on Indian cultural history one would have to assume that the constantly reiterated suspicion of censorship of mission reports

[37] Cf. Raulff, Ulrich, 'Vorwort', in U. Raulff, *Mentalitäten-Geschichte. Zur historischen Rekonstruktion geistiger Prozesse*, 7–20. Wagenbach, Berlin, 15. As Bernd Hausberger argues, historical biographical research helps to use microhistory in order to do research on global history, in other words, it helps to incorporate an actor centered approach into studies on global history. Hausberger, Bernd (ed.), 2006, *Globale Lebensläufe. Menschen als Akteure im weltgeschichtlichen Geschehen*, Mandelbaum Verlag, Wien.

[38] Jones, Adam, 1990, *Zur Quellenproblematik der Geschichte Westafrikas 1450–1900*, Franz Steiner, Stuttgart (=Studien zur Kulturkunde, vol. 99), 25, 34, (translated from German).

[39] See Justin, W., 1996, 'The Nature of a Mission Community: The Universities' Mission to Central Africa in Bonde', in Robert Bickers and Rosemary Seton (eds.), *Missionary Encounters: Sources and Issues*, Routledge, London. 128–52.

by their editors gives rise to doubts about their authenticity and, thereby, about their academic value.

This also holds true for the use of materials from the Danish-English-Halle Mission. Although till now there has been no comprehensive and scientifically substantive study on the nature and extent of editorial changes made in Halle to documents sent from Tranquebar and other places, there are always references to the strict censorship measures adopted by August Hermann Francke (1663–1727) and successive directors of the Francke Foundations who were the editors of the mission reports. The authors often do not base their statements on the original sources, rather—to corroborate their suspicion—they use isolated passages from standard histories of the mission.[40] These critical remarks are by no means meant to

[40] Thus, Gita Dharampal-Frick, for example, backs up her assessment that the letters of the missionary, Bartholomäus Ziegenbalg, were not published 'without being strongly censored' by A.H. Francke with a quote of Francke's cited by Arno Lehmann: 'I tend to leave out odious matter from all the diaries when they are published' (translated from German). Apart from the fact that Arno Lehmann is not referring to August Hermann Francke in this context, but to a letter written by his son, Gotthilf August Francke, to Johann Finkenhagen in 1740, it is not clear what could be meant by the term *odiosa* (Lat.: annoying stories). This quote is the best example for the continued extrapolation of a statement in different contexts. Lehmann alone uses it in two places in his book, referring once to Fenger and the next time to an unnamed 'source from Copenhagen'. Daniel Jeyaraj also points to Fenger and Lehmann with the same quote. Nørgaard, who also uses this quote as proof of the strict censorship practised by the editors, takes recourse to the original document, a letter of 1744 that is is the National Archives in Copenhagen. Cf. Dharampal-Frick, Gita, 1994, *Indien im Spiegel deutscher Quellen der frühen Neuzeit (1500–1750). Studien zu einer interkulturellen Konstellation*, Niemeyer, Tübingen, 100, footnote 370; Lehmann, Arno, 1956, *Es begann in Tranquebar. Die Geschichte der ersten evangelischen Kirche in Indien*, Evangelische Verlagsanstalt, Berlin, 99 and footnote 28 in chapter 7, (quote from Fenger, J.F., 1845, *Geschichte der Tranquebarschen Mission nach den Quellen bearbeitet*, Gebhardt, Grimma, 170) and also p. 145; Jeyaraj, Daniel, 1996, *Inkulturation in Tranquebar. Der Beitrag der frühen dänisch-halleschen Mission zum Werden einer indisch-einheimischen Kirche (1706–1730)*, Verlag der Evangelisch-Lutherischen Mission, Erlangen, 21, footnote 115; Nørgaard, *Mission und Obrigkeit*, 4 and footnote 6. John Brockington carries over the allegation about censorship to the Danish mission board in Copenhagen without, however, citing concrete evidence. Cf. Brockington, John, 1992, *Hinduism and Christianity*, St. Martin's Press, New York, 168 and 197, footnote 3; Sita Ram Goel takes over examples and explanations for August Hermann Francke's censorship from an article by Hugald Grafe who, in turn, refers to Lehmann and Germann. Goel establishes a direct connection between Francke's statement that the missionaries

deny that missionary source material was, firstly, written for a specific purpose and, secondly, that it was characterized by the claim of Christian superiority and missionary zeal. The mission societies at home used the published reports as proof of their legitimacy, as their hallmark and as an important mean to gain sponsors. Given this framework it is only logical that certain issues could not be included in the published reports. Reports about the misconduct of missionaries, about disputes with regard to the method of work or about persistent failures and setbacks were only published prudently.[41] This, however, underscores the need to also work with the manuscripts, to compare the published reports with the original sources and to place the statements in their historical context.[42] Although the evaluation of

---

had not been sent out to spread 'heathen' teachings and Ziegenbalg's concession to Francke to freely edit the *Malabarian Correspondence* (correspondence between the missionaries and Tamilians during the years 1710–14)–a connection that did not exist in the manner portrayed. Cf. Goel, Sita Ram, 1996, *History of Hindu-Christian Encounters*, Voice of India, New Delhi, 25. Grafe, Hugald, 1999, 'Hindu Apologetics at the Beginning of the Protestant Mission Era in India', in Michael Bergunder (ed.), *Missionsberichte aus Indien im 18. Jahrhundert. Ihre Bedeutung für die europäische Geistesgeschichte und ihr wissenschaftlicher Quellenwert für die Indienkunde*, Verlag der Franckeschen Stiftungen, Halle, 69–93, here 72; Germann, Wilhelm (ed.) 1867, [Bartholomäus Ziegenbalg] *Genealogie der malabarischen Götter* [...] Edition of the original manuscript of 1713, Higginbothem et al., Madras, foreword, VII; Lehmann, *Es begann in Tranquebar*, 32; Lehmann, Arno, 1957, *Alte Briefe aus Indien, Unveröffentlichte Briefe von Bartholomäus Ziegenbalg 1706–1719*, (henceforth AB)), Berlin, 389f. The following works dispense, to a large extent, with the inclusion of original sources of the Tranquebar mission: Hudson, Dennis D., 2000, *Protestant Origins in India: Tamil Evangelical Christians, 1706–1835*, William B. Eerdmans Pub., Grand Rapids, (=Studies in the History of Christian Missions), 42–48, 160; Singh, Brijraj, 1999, *The First Protestant Missionary to India: Bartholomäus Ziegenbalg, 1683–1719*, Oxford, New Delhi, New York.

[41] Anders Nørgaard justifiably entertains doubts about the reliability of the *Halle Reports* when he examines the role of Benjamin Schultze (1689–1760) in the early years of the mission in Tranquebar. The concerns here were the tensions between Schultze and his colleagues, Schultze's alleged authoritarian style of leadership and his non-compliance with some of the decisions of the Mission Board in Copenhagen. Nørgaard, Anders, 1977, 'Missionar Benjamin Schultze als Leiter der Tranquebarmission (1720–1726)', *NZM* 33: 181–201.

[42] The works of Anders Nørgaard and Daniel Jeyaraj demonstrate this very clearly. Cf. Nørgaard, *Mission und Obrigkeit*; Jeyaraj, *Inkulturation in Tranquebar*, 13–23. Gensichen gives credit to Daniel Jeyaraj for being the first to have thoroughly examined the entire complex of editorship of the *Halle Reports* on the basis of comparisons with the manuscripts. Cf. Gensichen, Hans-Werner, 1999,

mission sources in research on India is still far removed from G.A. Oddie's findings that these documents are 'one of the most valuable sources for 'history from below'',[43] several more recent works on the history of the Tranquebar Mission have attempted to demonstrate the historical value of these sources.[44]

The most important basis and point of departure for my further investigations was the mission reports published in Halle since 1710.[45] The Halle Reports (HB) and the New History of the Evangelical

---

'Indienmission im Weltaspekt: Globale Perspektiven in den Halleschen Berichten', in Michael Bergunder (ed.), *Missionsberichte aus Indien im 18. Jahrhundert. Ihre Bedeutung für die europäische Geistesgeschichte und ihr wissenschaftlicher Quellenwert für die Indienkunde*, 30–43, Verlag der Franckeschen Stiftungen, Halle, here 31. The demand to compare published sources with the (handwritten) originals can be similarly made for all mission archives.

[43] Oddie, Geoffrey A., 1996, 'Missionaries as Social Commentators: The Indian Case', in Robert A Bickers and Rosemary E Seton, *Missionary Encounters: Sources and Issues*, 197–210, Curzon Press, Richmond, Surrey, here 198.

[44] Nørgaard, *Mission und Obrigkeit*, 290–99, gives a brief overview of archives in Germany, Denmark and England which contain material on the Tranquebar Mission. Information on the German archives in particular can be found in Liebau, Heike, 1993, *Die Quellen der Dänisch-Halleschen Mission in Tranquebar in deutschen Archiven. Ihre Bedeutung für die Indienforschung*, Das Arabische Buch, Berlin; Liebau, H., 1994, 'Missionsquellen als Gegenstand interdisziplinärer Forschungen', in Wilfried Wagner (ed.), *Kolonien und Missionen. Referate des 3. Internationalen Kolonialgeschichtlichen Symposiums 1993 in Bremen*, 380–92, Lit. Münster, Hamburg; Füllberg-Stolberg, Katja and Heike Liebau, 1997, 'Einige Überlegungen zur Nutzung missionarischer Dokumente für historische Forschungen in Asien und Afrika. Eine vergleichende Quellenkritik', in Heike Liebau and Dietrich Reetz (eds.), *Globale Prozesse und 'Akteure des Wandels' in der Geschichte. Quellen und Methoden zu ihrer Untersuchung*, 169–96, Das Arabische Buch, Berlin. Daniel Jeyaraj, *Inkulturation in Tranquebar*, 1–29, describes the theological and social background as well as the historical origin of important sources. He was the first to use and, partly also, to evaluate the Tamil sources. The Danish sources of the colonial administration, which constitute an important background for the history of the Danish-Halle Mission, have been used by Niels Brimnes for studying the conflicts between the right-hand and the left-hand castes. Cf. Brimnes, Niels, *Constructing the Colonial Encounter*.

[45] These are, in the first instance, the 108 Continuations of the early mission reports combined in nine volumes: *Der Königlich-Dänischen Missionarien aus Ost-Indien eingesandter ausführlichen Berichten*, Waysewnhaus, Halle, 1710–1772 (henceforth: HB–Hallesche Berichte); as well as the 95 parts (Stücke) of the later mission reports in eight volumes: *Neuere Geschichte der Evangelischen Missions-Anstalten zu Bekehrung der Heiden in Ostindien*, Waisenhaus, Halle, 1/1, 1770–8/95, 1848 (henceforth NHB—Neue Hallesche Berichte).

Mission Establishments (New Halle Reports, NHB) represent a unique published corpus of sources for the history of the Tranquebar Mission and there is nothing comparable in the history of Protestant missions. With the first extensive publications of the mission reports at the beginning of the eighteenth century August Hermann Francke established an editorial practice that his successors made all efforts to continue despite occasional shortfalls in reports from India.[46] For the present study on the Indian mission co-workers the published reports represent a rich corpus of sources. A comparison of the published versions with existing manuscripts seldom brought forth any major deviations. Wherever such deviations exist, or where manuscripts were not published, this has been pointed out.

A systematization of the rich source material can initially be undertaken with regard to its historical origins. Firstly, there are documents that arose directly in connection with the Danish-English-Halle Mission. This corpus contains:

- sources which emerged from the link between the mission and the Francke Foundations in Halle and which are stored in the mission archives of the Archives of the Francke Foundation (AFSt), Halle. These include correspondence, reports, diaries and scientific studies done by the missionaries as well as invoices and accounts;
- sources that emerged from the direct contact between the mission and the Danish royal house as well as the Danish mission board. These are to be found in the National Archives in Copenhagen (Rigsarkivet, RA) or in the Royal Library, Copenhagen (Kongelige Biblioteket, KB). The corpus contains correspondence, royal decrees, petitions, accounts, invoices, reports and thematic statements (pro memoria) by the missionaries on different aspects of missionary work;

[46] The editor of the NHB, Georg Christian Knapp (director of the Francke Foundations since 1799), filled these gaps with reports of different English missions: 'The news contained in this volume includes both the original letters of the missionaries as well as excerpts from reports of the English society and other published material: In the latest *Stücke,* however, the latter sources have been used more often since, in recent times, the missionaries themselves, due to various circumstances, have been more sparing with their written communications.' (translated from German), NHB, vol. 6, Preface III, IV.

- sources that arose out of the link between the mission and the *Society for Promoting Christian Knowledge* in London (Archives of the SPCK in Cambridge);
- sources sent by the missionaries of the Moravian Brethren who lived in their 'settlement' in Tranquebar from 1760 to 1800 (Archives of the Fratrum Unitas, Herrnhut, UH). These are mainly diaries of the Moravian missionaries who document their encounters with the Royal Danish missionaries from their perspective;[47]
- sources that were brought from Tranquebar to Germany in the second half of the nineteenth century by missionaries of the Leipzig Mission (Archives of the Evangelical-Lutheran Mission Society in Leipzig, AELM). This corpus consists of letters that were sent from Halle to India and which then returned to Leipzig.[48]

Secondly, documents with a broader historical background are of interest, i.e. materials of the Danish and British colonial administrations as well as those of the corresponding trading companies:

- sources of the Danish colonial administration in Tranquebar and of the Danish trading company (National Archives, Royal Library, Copenhagen);[49]
- documents of the British colonial administration of the Madras Presidency (British Library, Asia, Pacific & Africa Collections, London; Tamil Nadu State Archives, Chennai, TNSA);
- documents of the local rulers in South India, especially of the kingdom of Thanjavur (Sarasvati Mahel Library Thanjavur; Tamil Nadu State Archives, Chennai).

[47] The sources in the UH archives in Herrnhut have, till now, been seldom used for studies of the Tranquebar Mission. From their position as observers the Moravian missionaries viewed the work of the Danish-Halle Mission critically, and these sources could therefore be used to examine or relativize the statements of the Halle missionaries. Especially with regard to the biography of the catechist Rajanayakan (1700–1771) it was possible to gain new insights from these sources. Cf. Liebau, *Tamilische Christen im 18. Jahrhundert*. See also pp. 335–41 of this study.

[48] These sources have since been placed in the Archives of the Francke Foundations in Halle on a permanent loan.

[49] An overview of the material in Denmark is given by Hansen, C. Rise, 1980, *Sources of the history of North Africa, Asia and Oceania in Denmark*, The Danish National Archives, (Transl[ated] from Danish into Engl[ish]), München [et al] (=Sources of the history of North Africa, Asia and Oceania in Scandinavia, 1); (=Guides to the sources for the history of the nations, 3).

On the basis of their form these documents can also be classified under different categories:

Dairy Entries

The missionaries of the Danish-English-Halle Mission were required to report regularly and extensively about their activities. The readership was not limited to the co-workers of the Francke Foundations in Halle and the Mission Board in Copenhagen, but also included people and institutions of the public sphere and the academic field. In this mission that was significantly shaped by Halle pietism the regular maintenance of a diary did not depend on the individual choice of the missionary. Halle pietism preached piety through active edification. A person was not only supposed to demonstrate his divine faith externally by leading an ascetic life, but he was also required to repeatedly renew this faith through constant inner discipline and self-control.[50] The missionaries took it for granted that it was their duty to regularly maintain a diary, which, at the same time, was also a means for inner edification and reflection on their actions. The daily self-examination combined with the contemplation of their South Indian surroundings is reflected in detailed descriptions of experiences and observations. This not only helped towards self-discovery for the missionary, but also towards publicizing missionary activity and gaining donations and sponsors. Missionaries with a long experience of India regularly confirmed the usefulness of writing a diary. In an instruction for young missionaries written in 1784 Christoph Samuel John, for example, called on them to begin writing a diary even before their departure for India.[51]

[50] For the image of the Pietist personality cf. Hinrichs, Carl, 1971, *Preußentum und Pietismus*, Vandenhoeck & Ruprecht, Göttingen, 14f.; Brecht, Martin and Johannes van den Berg, (eds), 1993, *Der Pietismus vom siebzehnten bis zum frühen achtzehnten Jahrhundert*, Vandenhoeck & Ruprecht, Göttingen (=Geschichte des Pietismus, vol. 1); Brecht Martin and Klaus Deppermann (eds.), 1995, *Der Pietismus im achtzehnten Jahrhundert*, Vandenhoeck & Ruprecht, Göttingen (=Geschichte des Pietismus, vol. 2); Gäbler, Ulrich (ed.), 2000, *Der Pietismus im neunzehnten und zwanzigsten Jahrhundert*, Vandenhoeck & Ruprecht, Göttingen (=Geschichte des Pietismus, vol. 3); Schicketanz, Peter, 2001, *Der Pietismus von 1675 bis 1800*, Evangelische Verlagsanstalt, Leipzig (=Kirchengeschichtliche Einzeldarstellungen III/I).

[51] RA Miskol 9g. Pro Memoria for new missionaries by Christoph Samuel John, Tranquebar, 27 October 1784.

Besides the individual diaries there were also collective diaries in which—generally in an interval of six months—several missionaries reported the progress of work in their respective stations.

Indian co-workers of the mission were also expected to make daily notes of their activities. At regular intervals these notes, generally written on palm leaves, were read out in the presence of the missionaries and other co-workers in Tranquebar. The missionaries translated excerpts from these reports by the 'national workers'/'national assistants' for publication and inserted them in relevant sections of their own daily registers. In select cases the entire report of a journey or of a monthly working report by Tamil co-workers was translated.[52] The original manuscripts of the reports by individual Indian co-workers are today kept in the National Archives in Copenhagen.[53]

Correspondence

The extensive correspondence constitutes a further significant corpus of archival material. The culture of letter writing as a means of private and public communication, generally important

[52] In the HB these reports are contained in the diaries of the missionaries without any special mention. Often there is a reference to the arrival of a co-worker at the mission station and to the presentation of his report, which is then summarized in detail. In the early decades of the mission the reports of the catechist, Rajanayakan, were the only ones that were sometimes published separately. In the NHB the sections dealing with the work of the Indian 'assistants' appeared in the six-monthly reports from Tranquebar as separate paragraphs under the heading 'Reports of the National Assistants' or 'Work of the Assistants'. Thus, for example, a description of 'The City Catechist's, Philipp's, Journey to Tirutchinapalli' was published under this title as part of the report by the Tranquebar missionaries for the first half of the year 1771, dated August. Cf. NHB 8. St., 1003–95. In his daily register 1783/84 Christian Friedrich Schwartz (1750–1798) takes up parts of Sattianaden's (1750–1815) reports, in which the Tamilian speaks of himself in the third person. In the introduction to his diary Schwartz expressly points out to this practice. NHB 29. St., 576–89.

[53] Daniel Jeyaraj has done an initial classification of this corpus. 'The palm-leaf manuscripts stored in Copenhagen contain working reports of the catechists and their assistants. Although they are addressed to Halle they are, for unknown reasons, in Copenhagen. They provide useful insights into the daily work of the Tamilian co-workers of the mission.' (translated from German), Jeyaraj, *Inkulturation in Tranquebar*, 29 and 330–34.

in the eighteenth century,[54] was very pronounced in the context of the Tranquebar Mission. There are three different categories of correspondence: firstly, the official letters to the institutions in Europe supporting the mission, secondly, personal letters from individual missionaries to relatives, acquaintances and friends and, thirdly, scientific correspondence with European research bodies as well as with scholars and scholarly societies. As a rule, what was published was the correspondence with the Mission Board, with the directors of the Francke Foundations and editors of the mission reports, or with the Danish royal house. These official letters contained petitions, statistical reports as also problems and references to the physical and emotional condition of the mission workers. We would have to assume that only a small part of the private correspondence appeared in print, even though the letters were first sent to Halle and forwarded to the addressees from there. Similarly, correspondence with scholars and scientific bodies or institutions in Europe cannot be found in its entirety in the mission materials. A study of the individual biographies of the missionaries could yield interesting material in this regard.[55] In their scientific correspondence the missionaries replied to questions put to them by European scholars or they, in turn, put questions to the scholarly world in Europe. Letters from Indian co-workers of the Mission were also included in this correspondence. In print one would find only a German translation for the German-speaking readership; the files often also contain the corresponding Tamil originals. As a rule, these letters contained edifying self-reflection, descriptions of the correspondent's relationship to Christianity in general

[54] Cf. Dutu, Alexander (ed.), 1989, *Brief und Briefwechsel in Mittel-und Osteuropa im 18. und 19. Jahrhundert*, Hobbing, Essen (=Brief und Briefwechsel im 18. und 19. Jahrhundert als Quellen der Kulturbeziehungsforschung, vol. 1).

[55] For example, studies on the biography of the missionary Christoph Theodosius Walther. His treatise on the Indian calendar appeared in an edition of the works of Theophil Siegfried Bayer, a member of the Petersburg Academy of Sciences. Bayer, Theophil Siegfried, 1738, *Historia regni graecorum bactriani in qua simul graecarum in India coloniarum vetus memoris explicatur [...] accedit Christophori Theodosii Waltheri Doctrina Temporum Indica, cum paralipomenis*, Ex typogr. Acad. scient. Petersburg. There are also several letters from other missionaries in Bayer's papers. Cf. Glasgow University Library, Special Collection, Manuscript Documents, Reference Code: GB 247.

and to the Tranquebar missionaries in particular, expressions of gratitude to the supporting institutions and persons in Europe, but also reported about work undertaken and, occasionally, ideas and suggestions for the organization of missionary work. Important information was often concealed in these texts behind the set phrases of courtesy and piety, but the 'atmosphere' of the letters was often also as important as their contents.[56] The tenor of the letters written by the Tamil co-workers to the mission institutions in Europe varied. Often they were a succession of expressions of subordination, servitude and gratitude directed to the Mission Board, the directors of the Francke Foundations, the editors of the Halle Reports or particular patrons of the Mission. In addition, there were declamatory expressions of the will to work for the well-being and enlightenment of the 'heathens living in darkness and ignorance'. Such letters often ended with the correspondent signing off as 'Your servant'.[57] Other letters were more oriented towards the problems and practice of missionary work. Despite formal expressions of subordination they were self-assured and have evidently been written without the help of a missionary. This is the case, for example, when the first country preacher Aaron (1698–1745) wrote: 'On account of my limited understanding I am ignorant of the titles and expressions of respect that are due to you and beg you to kindly forgive me for this. I am also eager to

[56] Translations of some such Tamil letters appeared in the HB—marked as such in their own right—under the rubric 'Extracts from the letters of the missionaries…', ['Extracte aus Briefen der Herren Missionare…']. Cf. HB 57. Cont., 1409–16, letters 9–13; 60. Cont., 1903–12, letters 5–11. In the volumes of the NHB the letters of the Indian co-workers play a lesser role with greater importance being given to the reports of their work. This is in keeping with the original sources. Whereas for the 1730s and 1740s we find, comparatively speaking, numerous letters of the country-preachers, sources for the 1770s and 1780s contain detailed translations of the diaries of local catechists and preachers. The only exception is a collection of 132 letters written by the interpreter Daniel Pullei to his colleague Piragasa, which can be found in the National Archives in Copenhagen. These letters are primarily important because of their socio-historical contents. See also Liebau, *Tamilische Christen im 18. Jahrhundert*.

[57] HB 54. Cont., 1092f., letter dated 10 January 1741 from the newly-ordained country preacher Diogo (1704?-81) in Tranquebar to the Mission Board in Copenhagen.

know what further instructions you might have for me. May the Lord guide everything well. Aaron, Country preacher.'[58]

Thematic Treatises (essays)

The systematic reports or the scientific treatises of the missionaries on a particular topic or event are, to some extent, a contrast to the anecdotal nature of the diary entries. These essays were written, on the one hand, in response to enquiries from scholars and friends of the mission in Europe. On the other hand, they emerged from the interests of the individual missionaries or their desire to know more about the country. Alongside essays on religion, philosophy, languages and literature there are studies on aspects of the natural sciences or on the history and geography of India. Although it must be assumed that local co-workers and informants made major contributions to this kind of research, it is rarely possible to reconstruct their work. Not all of these essays were published. Many, however, did find their way into print in the context of the mission reports, while others appeared as separate publications.

Biographies, Obituaries

Biographies, which had to be submitted when applying for missionary service, or which were published on the occasion of ordination or on the death of a co-worker, constitute a basis for the reconstruction of biographical data and facts. They are decisive for this present study, which is highly biography-oriented. However, such biographies, especially in the first half of the eighteenth century, rarely provide chronological reports. Mention of particular years or other 'profane' dates appear to be unimportant for the authors. The focus of such, generally very emotional, portrayals are the person's path to

[58] HB 54. Cont., 1091f., letter dated 18 January 1741 from the country preacher Aaron in Porayar to the Mission Board (translated from German). The fact that Aaron dispenses with the correct salutations for the members of the Mission Board is proof of the awareness of his equal status not only with regard to the missionaries at home, but also with regard to the Mission Board in Copenhagen. Although he awaits orders from Copenhagen, he is fully aware of the importance of his own role in the implementation of these tasks. He does not sign the letter as 'your servant', but only with his name.

Christianity, to a religious awakening, their vocation and motivation for missionary service.[59] When a Tamil mission co-worker was taken into service or was promoted, the description of his life (written as a rule by missionaries) contained a certain amount of information. Although such descriptions are also in the nature of an evaluation, on the whole they contain more information about the person concerned than descriptions of edifying and enlightening experiences. Such documents were generally prepared very conscientiously in order to prove to the sponsors in Europe that the local co-workers selected were fit and capable, especially since these workers were partly financed through donations from European congregations. Whereas detailed biographical data about co-workers at lower levels, such as schoolteachers or Bible-women, is sparse, the source material becomes more abundant the higher the person is in the mission hierarchy.[60] Depending on the person's reputation and his position in the mission biographical sketches were published on his ordination or his death.

Statistics and Accounts

Research has hitherto taken scant notice of the annual statistics and accounts. These sources clearly document the situation of the Mission regarding finances and personnel. Compared over a long period of time, the figures enable us to draw conclusions about social changes and developments in local society. Whereas statistics

[59] This also holds true for the few autobiographical statements of Tamils, we have. The country preacher Diogo, for instance, wrote his biography—more in the nature of a description of his religious awakening—to one of the mission patrons in Europe who had presumably made a special donation in his name. HB 34. Cont., 1084–86.

[60] Henriette Bugge comes to the same conclusion with regard to the sources of the Danish Mission Society and the French *Société des Missions Ètrangères de Paris*: 'We know nothing about the lower group, the Bible women, the teachers and the catéchistes sédentaires. The source material is rather more eloquent and detailed when it comes to the group closest to the missionaries, the catechists (in the DMS) [*Danish Mission Society*, HL] and the native clergy (in the MEP) [*Société des Missions Ètrangères de Paris*, HL].' Bugge locates the reason for the differential treatment of local co-workers in the mission reports not only in the degree of closeness to the missionaries, but also in the degree of threat that the missionaries felt these co-workers represented. Bugge, Henriette, 1994, *Mission and Tamil Society. Social and Religious Change in South India (1840–1900)*, Curzon Press, Richmond, 81f.

on personnel of the Mission (figures on births, baptism and deaths, marriages, number of school children) were generally included in the annual publications,[61] the accounts, information about expenditure and income and the salaries for mission employees were not published. Here too, however, the polemical nature of the sources has to be taken into consideration: the selective nature of statistical data can only reflect a part of the mission reality and the occasional changes in selection criteria make it difficult to compare the data. Nonetheless, in the extent to which these documents are available for the Danish-English-Halle Mission, they constitute an informative source of facts that have hitherto been neglected. While gathering the data, however, it became evident that the compilation of statistics in the context of the Mission is a problematic venture. While the missionaries kept meticulous accounts, the guidelines and criteria for collating the data were not always recorded clearly leading to shifts and overlaps, which sometimes rendered the data incomprehensible.

This listing of the corpus of materials suggests another problem associated with the use of these documents. Along with the basic practical and methodological concerns of this study to undertake a socio-historical evaluation of sources that have hitherto been used mainly in the context of mission history or church history, another anomaly lies in studying a non-European community on the basis of sources created predominantly by Europeans. Formulated more pointedly: the task is to undertake an 'India centric' project with 'Eurocentric' sources. These are mainly documents whose authors, initiators and addressees were Europeans. This study is concerned, however, with reconstructing biographies of South Indian Christians and, on this basis, understanding the motivations for their actions, their views of society, their self-perception as well as their significance as a social and religious group in the historical and local context. These people, who often appear only indirectly in the sources,

[61] The first statistic on the personnel structure of the mission including the Tamil co-workers is contained in the 'Historische Nachricht von der Bekehrung unter den Heyden in Ost=Indien', 28 September 1712. In this document the missionaries compile the most important events and facts from 1705 to 1712. HB 6.Cont., 330f. Surveys of the personnel structure in varying detail were compiled regularly and published for all mission stations.

mostly as the observed, very seldom as those directly reporting, will be made to speak.

The fact that the study of an indigenous group of people is dependent, to a great extent, on the observations of European missionaries, leaves it open to the perils of subjective misjudgment. In order to counter this it is imperative to first undertake a critical analysis of the sources. A quantitatively small but important group of documents consists of letters, reports and biographies written by the Indian mission co-workers themselves. These documents are, for the most part, available in a translated version. This means that one of the missionaries prepared a literal or a substantive translation of the text, which was then sent—generally together with the original—to Europe. Some of the original documents, generally in a colloquial Tamil of the eighteenth century, have been preserved.

Thus, an adequate and informative source-base is available for dealing with the topic of local mission employees with concrete reference to the Tranquebar Mission. This does not hold true for every mission society. The mission method and the reporting practices were the crucial factors in dealing with and describing the work of the local employees. The practice of reporting in the Danish-English-Halle Mission differed fundamentally from that of other missions. Comparatively speaking, the material of the Danish-English-Halle Mission contains a large number of documents written by the South Indian mission employees.[62] However, there were also differences within the Mission. The reports were not similarly detailed from every station and in every year. Ultimately, how much was written about the local employees depended on different factors, not least on the concerned missionary himself. Through their earlier pedagogic work in the Francke Foundations in Halle the missionaries had gained experience in the practice of evaluation. We, therefore, see that the many reports and remarks about the Indian mission employees written by the European missionaries of the Tranquebar Mission are far removed from the one-sided negative stereotypes of the Tamilians.

[62] See the comparative critical study of sources by Füllberg-Stolberg and Liebau, *Einige Überlegungen zur Nutzung missionarischer Dokumente*.

STRUCTURE OF THE STUDY

This study consists of six chapters in which the mission is located in its historical and regional context and the daily life of the Mission—in a manner of speaking, from within—is highlighted from a different perspective each time. Taken together, these chapters yield a panorama that reflects the complex encounter of conflicting social groups.

The first chapter begins with a historical summary of the work of the Danish-English-Halle Mission on the Coromandel Coast in southeast India. Against the backdrop of the political, social and religious conditions in the kingdom of Thanjavur, the main area of work of the mission in the eighteenth and the first half of the nineteenth century, the work of the Tranquebar Mission will be dealt with as a component of the history of this region. Following this, the study will look at the religious principles of the mission and at the background and motivation of the missionaries. Their image of South India and their manner of dealing with the local society will be examined. Given the actual encounter with an alien society biographical ruptures were the order of the day and mission methods as well as goals were put to the test. Proceeding from these observations an attempt will be made to provide an answer to the question as to how the attitude of the Tamilians to the representatives of an alien religion developed. From the beginning the European missionaries intended to include local people in the work. Concrete ideas developed in the field and changed according to the situation and the demands and possibilities of the mission. The question is raised to what extent the actions of the 'national workers' led to new methods in dealing with this group of co-workers and how changes of the political regime affected the relationship between the missionary and the 'national worker'.

The second chapter contains a socio-historical analysis of the group under study. Proceeding from statements about the necessity—from the point of view of mission strategy—of recruiting local co-workers the manner in which the missionaries handled the local recruits is dealt with first. As intermediaries the 'national workers' had to fulfill certain requirements which included knowledge of the country and its languages, ability to communicate, access to networks, contacts, alliances and access to certain sections of society (castes, gender). A study of the methods through which local workers were recruited and trained and the analysis of their religious and social composition also allow us to draw conclusions about their motivation for working in the mission. In doing this we will not only look at the limited group of South Indians who were employed for different functions in the Mission. The focus will also be on local informants and on people who, having been educated by the Mission, went on to work in 'secular' fields. By extending the perspective to include these other groups of people it is possible to avoid a narrow view of the mission context alone while striving to place the issue within a broader social context. With regard to motivation the study takes a critical look at the sweeping generalization that is constantly reiterated, whereby the decision to convert is guided by material consideration and by the desire for social advancement ('Rice Christians'). It will be shown that the group under study was not compelled (either by material considerations or because of their caste identity, for example) to take on this role of an intermediary, but was qualified to do so mainly through education and/or life-experience.

The third chapter focuses on hierarchies and relationships of dependence within the mission as well as on processes of negotiation between European missionaries and the Indian co-workers. The problem of 'partnership' between Europeans and Indians in the eighteenth century is dealt with in this context. On the basis of a detailed examination of daily life in the mission in which local people were visible as servants of the missionaries (cooks, gardeners, porters), as teachers and informants of the missionaries, as assistants and as independent officials in the service of the Mission, forms of mutual material and non-material dependency are shown. The manner, the forms and the sum of payment made to the local co-workers clearly show limitations and hierarchies. The missionaries' dependence on their local helpers can be seen in the fact that the Tamils who accompanied them on travels functioned as a 'gateway' to the people, as instruments of legitimacy, as local experts in practical mission work or as informants for scientific studies. It is interesting to see how the local side influenced identity shifts in the missionaries. The 'native agents' passed on their knowledge and ideas about South Indian society, and it was only on this basis that the missionaries could carry out their scientific studies. The social background of the informants thus also coloured the image of India that the missionaries developed. This is followed by an analysis of the conflicting hierarchies within the group of local mission co-workers itself. What is examined here are the levels of responsibility, the distribution of functions, the description of these functions, the manner and amount of remuneration as well as the forms of accounting/reporting. The caste problem is closely linked with the question of hierarchies. Even after conversion caste identity remains a ground for discrimination or an argument for promotion. There was a direct connection between caste identity, place of work and catalogue of duties of an Indian co-worker. It is also useful to observe the familial relationships within the group of 'national workers'. Children of mission workers showed a marked tendency to enter into the service of the Mission and they often intermarried.

The fourth chapter deals with relations between the Christian converts and mission workers, on the one hand, and the local population, on the other. The complexity and ambivalence of loyalties and identities that characterized the position of many local mission employees is documented here. Firstly, it is an issue of religion, politics and law since South Indian employees were called on as intermediaries in conflict situations or even as prison ministers. Local individuals educated in the mission schools were employed as *dubashes*, or in other functions, by the Danish or the English trading company. Travels and visits to the congregations in the surrounding areas was an important aspect of missionary work carried out by the local co-workers. They were responsible for regular contact with the local population. Secondly, the manner of dealing with the caste question is also looked at here and the question posed as to how the issue of identity was influenced by the meeting of Christianity and caste. When we consider the fact that the protagonists viewed themselves as the chosen ones and were thus conscious of fulfilling a certain special role, the question of caste often created specific problems. In addition, the chapter looks at the connections between the mission employees and the different political authorities as well as between the Tranquebar Mission and other mission societies working in the same region.

The fifth chapter is dedicated to a central area of work carried out by the group under study—the educational system. Just as for the large majority of Christian mission societies, for the Tranquebar Mission too educational establishments represented important social spaces of intercultural encounter and communication. Education was part of the mission method, since the work with children and the youth not only helped in acquiring members for the local congregations, but also in training local mission employees and in anchoring Christianity in South Indian society. The chapter shows how the hierarchical organizational structures of the Mission were reproduced in the educational system. Although the mission schools were governed by the goals of the Mission, they had to be anchored in their social surroundings. This often meant that compromises had to be reached between European, i.e. Pietistic and Enlightenment, ideals of education and upbringing and the circumstances obtaining in South India. Over a period of more than a century the Danish-English-Halle Mission gave formative shape to the educational sector in the regions around Thanjavur and Madras. The main concern of educational work remained the propagation of the gospel. The large majority of Christians of the Tranquebar Mission, however, came from the lower sections of society and for them the access to education was a crucial precondition for social emancipation.

In the sixth chapter the position of women in the first Protestant mission in India is examined. Although the number of male mission workers of the DEHM far outnumbered that of female mission employees, the group of women in the service of the Mission is worthy of special note. While in later Protestant and Catholic missions women not only served as wives, but had official functions as missionaries, nurses or school teachers, the missionary wives of the Tranquebar Mission remained, as a rule, the 'assistants' of their husbands. Accordingly, they play only a marginal role in the sources. However, alongside their often extensive family responsibilities they were included in many ways in the work carried out by their husbands, whether in dealing with the correspondence or in the upbringing of Tamil children or children of Indo-European origin in missionary families. Some women carried on the work of their husbands after the latter's death. This is also true for the wives of the Tamil mission co-workers. Having accompanied their husbands during their lifetime, they often continued to do the work of the mission as widows and earned their living in this manner. Mainly employed as Bible women or as teachers they had special responsibility for the sensitive area of dealing with local women and children. Alongside cases where both the husband and the wife were officially involved in the daily life of the mission, there are some women about whom it is not known whether they were married or who their husbands were. The work of these female employees was very important for the mission since they provided access to sections of the society that were often closed to the male co-workers.

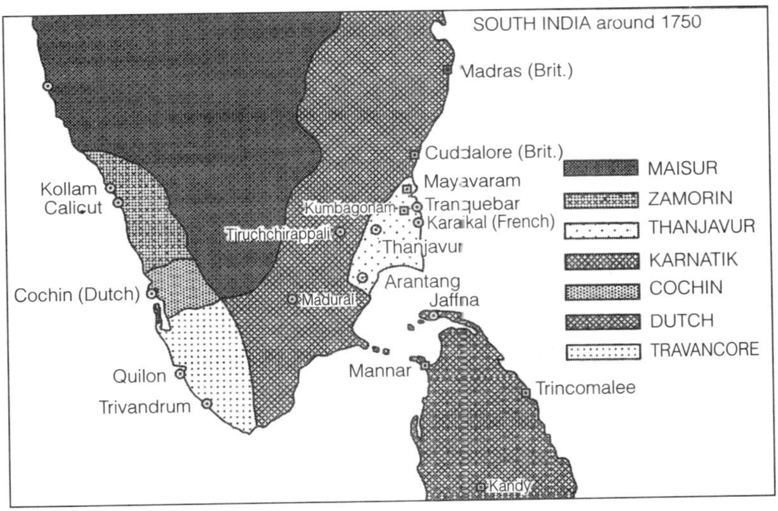

MAP 1 South India around 1750 (copyright Kurt Liebau)

CHAPTER ONE

History of the Tranquebar Mission

> The eighteenth century was an age of equilibrium between a small Europe and a large Asia.[1] Asia could be compared to Europe as long as Europe did not consider itself to be beyond comparison.[2]

Every Christian mission has several histories. Depending on the perspective and the research interest of the historian it is the history of the mission in its place of origin or, rather, the histories of missionary encounters in places where the mission society was active. If one foregrounds those responsible for the mission, their motives, their work and the results of their work, the histories of mission encounters can be perceived and reconstructed as part of the history of the missionizing society. If attention is directed at the society and people whose conversion was the aim of missionary activity, these encounters can be seen as a part of the history of the missionized. In this case one must ask how these people dealt with the mission, how their lives were impacted by missionary work but also how they used their changed identities to influence missionary work.

An important condition for such an approach is to view Christian mission as a reciprocal phenomenon in which the missionizing and the missionized are part of a process of communication in whatever form this may be. Since the end of the 1970s secular historians have been increasingly making use of mission sources for research on regional histories. In these works missionary activity is perceived as a multi-dimensional process of convergence and demarcation, and

[1] Osterhammel, Jürgen, 1998, *Die Entzauberung Asiens. Europa und die asiatischen Reiche im 18. Jahrhundert*, C.H. Beck Verlag, München, 375, (translated from German).

[2] Ibid., 378.

sometimes 'the pivotal role of the local "co-workers" becomes the focus of interest'.[3] Along with the exploration of mission history in the literal sense missionary sources are also used to study non-European Christian history or the history of the Church,[4] whereby especially adherents of a contextual history of Christianity take into account the connection between religion and society[5] and increasingly emphasize socio-historical methods. Thus, a study of mission history also brings the social history of a region into focus.

While it is true that research on mission history still predominantly studies the one-sided perception of the non-European world by European Christians, there have been, since the 1980s, analyses—in different forms and with different concerns—of missionary encounters as a translocal and intercultural phenomenon.[6] This also applies to the study of missionary work in India. For a long time the contact between European missionaries and the Indian population was studied exclusively from a European perspective. An important reason for this is that most of the relevant sources are stored in European archives and, as a rule, these documents are written in European languages. In his paper at the conference in Berlin on 'Mission history—Church history—World history' in 1994 Werner

[3] Koschorke, Klaus (ed.), 1998, *'Christen und Gewürze' Konfrontation und Interaktion kolonialer und indigener Christentumsvarianten*, Otto Harrassowitz Verlag, Göttingen, 27. See also Oddie, Geoffrey A., 1991, *Hindu and Christian in South-East India*, Curzon Press, London (=London Studies on South Asia 6); Kooiman, Dick, 1989, *Conversion and Social Equality in India: the London Missionary Society in South Travancore in the 19th Century*, Manohar Publications, New Delhi. For the African context cf. Luig, Ulrich, 1997, *Conversion as a Social Process: A History of Missionary Christianity among the Valley Tonga, Zambia*, LIT, Hamburg, 17.

[4] Klaus Koschorke sees the history of non-European Christianity as a new discipline; one, however, that has still not gained much importance in the German-speaking region. Cf. Koschorke, '*Christen und Gewürze*', 12.

[5] Koschorke, Klaus, 1992, 'Kontextualität und Universalität als Problemstellung der Kirchengeschichte', *Evangelische Theologie: Synkretismus und Inkulturation*, München, 52 (3): 209–24.

[6] Habermas, Rebekka, 2008, 'Mission im 19. Jahrhundert. Globale Netze des Religiösen', *Historische Zeitschrift*, 56: 629–79; Mettele, Gisela, 2009, *Weltbürgertum und Gottesreich. Die Herrnhuter Brüdergemeine als globale Gemeinschaft 1727–1857*, Vandenhoeck & Ruprecht, Göttingen (=Bürgertum Neue Folge, 4); Juneja, Monica, 2006, 'Mission Encounters and Transnational History. Reflections on the Use of Concepts across Cultures', in Gross, *Halle and the Beginning of Christianity in India*, Vol. III, 1025–45.

Ustorf stated that in recent publications mission historians had extended their research to the consequences of missionary presence in the relevant region and had brought the 'other side' into the focus of their studies.[7] However, he felt that this new understanding of missionary work as a reciprocal process of understanding the other was slow in establishing itself.

Within the substantial research on questions concerning religious and social change in the South-Asian sub-continent there has been an increase in the number of studies that specifically study Christian groups and the correlation between Christianity and society. These studies have been initiated and primarily carried out by representatives of Christian communities as well as by church and mission historians. Some of the studies focus on the role of Christian churches or missions in their social environment,[8] while other recent studies centre round the self-understanding of Indian Christians based on a study of prominent Indian Christian personalities.[9] Such studies arise out of the need to explore the formation and development of Indian Christianity. Some studies, oriented towards religious or social history, look at the interaction between Christianity and Hindu-dominated society, especially the phenomenon of caste and Christianity.[10] They represent a

[7] Werner Ustorf talks of 'another mission history' meaning developments that are not directly connected with traditional European mission history but which have their contexts and causes in local societies. Ustorf, Werner, 1996, 'Dornröschen oder die Missionsgeschichte wird entdeckt', in Ulrich van der Heyden and Heike Liebau (eds.), *Missionsgeschichte—Kirchengeschichte—Weltgeschichte: Christliche Missionen im Kontext nationaler Entwicklungen in Afrika, Asien und Ozeanien,* 23–38, Franz Steiner Verlag, Stuttgart.

[8] Sangma, Milton S., 1987–1992, *History of the American Baptist Mission in North-East India 1836–1950,* 2 vols, Mittal Publications, Delhi; Raghaviah, Jaiprakash, 1990, *Basel Mission Industries in Malabar and South Canara (1834–1914): A Study of its Social and Economic Impact,* Gyan Publishing House, New Delhi; Karotemprel, Sebastian, 1994, *The Impact of Christianity on the Tribes of North East India,* Sacred Heart Theological College, Shillong; Chatterjee, Ramakrishna, 1986, *Christian Missionaries and Labour Migration to Assam Tea Gardens in Colonial Times (Occasional Paper N⁰ 80),* Centre for Studies in Social Sciences, Calcutta; Eaton, Richard Maxwell, 1984, 'Conversion to Christianity among the Nagas, 1876–1971', *IESHR,* 21 (1):1–44.

[9] Seminal works in this context are those by Kai Baago and Robin Boyd. Baago, Kai, 1969, *Pioneers of Indigenous Christianity,* CLS, Madras; Boyd, Robin, 1994, *An Introduction to Indian Christian Theology,* ISPCK, New Delhi.

[10] Arasaratnam, Sinnappah, 1981, 'Protestant Christianity and South Indian Hinduism 1630–1730: Some Confrontations in Society and Beliefs', *ICHR,* 15 (1):

growing trend towards more comprehensive, problem-oriented, systematic studies of socio-historical questions in connection with the development of Christian communities in India.[11] More recent socio-historical studies regarding the question of religious identity-consciousness among Indian Christians find themselves increasingly committed to the conceptional approach defined by the project of the Church Association of India/Bangalore *(CHAI)* carried out since the 1970s to describe the history of Christianity in India as an integral part of the socio-economic history of the sub-continent and to focus on the self-conception of Indian Christians.[12] A longish section in the third volume of this series deals with the history of the Tranquebar Mission and, along with the religious context, the political and social conditions that influenced the development of the mission are also described.[13] Furthermore, there are also increasing attempts to analyze the work of individual mission societies, their integration in and their interaction with the local society as well as their role in changing this society. This is accompanied by the attempt to outline the identity markers of converts and their changed social

---

7–33; Popley, Herbert A., 1987, *K.T. Paul. Christian Leader,* CLS, Madras, (1938); Caplan, Lionel, 1989, *Religion and Power: Essays on the Christian Community in Madras*, CLS, Madras; Koilparampil, George, 1982, *Caste in the Catholic Community in Kerala: A Case Study of Caste Elements in the Inter Rite Relationship of Syrians and Latins*, Dept. of Sociology, St. Teresa's College, Cochin; Forrester, Duncan B., 1974, 'Indian Christian's Attitude to Caste in the Nineteenth Century', *ICHR*, 8 (2): 131–147; Forrester, Duncan B., 1975, 'Indian Christian Attitude to Caste in the Twentieth Century', *ICHR*, 9 (1): 3–21; Stein, Jürgen, 2002, *Christentum und Kastenwesen: Zum Verhältnis von Religion und Gesellschaft in Indien*, Lembeck, Frankfurt/Main.

11 Cf. Pankratova, Viktorija Aleksandrovna, 1982, *Christiane Keraly. Rol' v social' no-političeskoj žizni stata*, Nauka, Moskva; Mosse, David, 1994, 'Idioms of Subordination and Styles of Protest among Christians and Hindu Harijan Castes in Tamil Nadu', *Contributions to Indian Sociology*, 28 (1): 67–106.

12 The series 'History of Christianity in India' includes: Mundadan, Anthony Mathias, 1989, *History of Christianity in India, Vol. I: From the Beginning up to the Middle of the Sixteenth Century (up to 1542)*, CHAI, Bangalore; Thekkadath, Joseph, 1988, *History of Christianity in India, Vol. II. From the Middle of the Sixteenth Century to the End of the Seventeenth Century*, CHAI, Bangalore; Hambye, Édouard René, 1997, *History of Christianity in India, Vol. III: During the Eighteenth Century*, CHAI, Bangalore; Grafe, Hugald, 1990, *History of Christianity in India, Vol. IV, Part 2: Tamilnadu in the Nineteenth and Twentieth Centuries*, CHAI, Bangalore; Downs, Frederick Sheldon, 1992, *History of Christianity in India, Vol. V, Part 5: North East India in the Nineteenth and Twentieth Centuries*, CHAI, Bangalore.

13 Hambye, *History of Christianity in India, Vol. III*, 109–240.

mobility.[14] The authors proceed from an understanding of the role of Christianity as a mobilizing factor that leads to social change.[15]

In the case of the Tranquebar Mission[16] attempts to write a history (histories) of the mission also focused mainly on the European mission society and its missionaries. Academic interest in the Mission began directly after its work in India came to an end in the middle of the nineteenth century. Mission scholars, scholars of religion and church historians studied the history of the mission from various perspectives and with differing motives. Individual studies that went beyond the nature of edifying religious tracts, but which, to all intents and purposes, were meant to portray the exemplary function of the Mission or of individual missionaries, appeared already in the 1830s and 1840s.[17] Studies by representatives of mission societies that followed the Tranquebar Mission analyzed both its missionary work in the narrower sense as well as the scholarly work of the Halle missionaries in South India.[18]

[14] Cf., among others Kooiman, *Conversion and Social Equality in India*; Oddie, *Hindu and Christian in South-East India*; Bugge, *Mission and Tamil Society*.

[15] Hefner, Robert William (ed.), 1993, *Conversion to Christianity: Historical and Anthropological Perspectives on a Great Transformation*, University of California Press, Berkeley. See especially the introduction 'World Building and Rationality of Conversion', 3–44.

[16] The official names of Christian mission societies generally stem from the country of origin or the place of work, from the founder, or the religious background (Berlin Mission, Basel Mission, Hermannsburg Mission, Gossner Mission, Evangelical-Lutheran Mission at Leipzig). If it is a matter of concrete work at a particular place, the name of the place is added. As far as the mission dealt with here is concerned, two names are commonly used. One refers to its origin, the other to its place of work: Danish-English-Halle Mission or Tranquebar Mission. See footnote 6 in the introduction of this study as well as Liebau, Heike, 2006, 'Das Hallesche Waisenhaus und die Tranquebarmission', in Michael Mann (ed.), *Europäische Aufklärung und protestantische Mission in Indien*, 125–42, Draupadi Verlag, Heidelberg, here 127f.

[17] Fenger, *Geschichte der Tranquebarschen Mission* (Engl. edition: *History of the Tranquebar Mission: worked out from the original papers*, Evangelical Lutheran Mission, Tranquebar, 1863); Pearson, Hugh, 1835, *Memoirs of Life and Correspondence of Christian Frederick Swartz*, D. Appleton & Co, New York.

[18] See, especially, some articles by Wilhelm Germann (1840–1902), missionary in South India from 1865–1867: Germann, Wilhelm, 1865, 'Die Geschichte der tamulischen Bibelübersetzung', *MNOIM*, 17: 86–119; Germann, 1865, 'Die wissenschaftliche Arbeit unserer alten Tamulen-Missionare mit Berücksichtigung neuerer Leistungen', *MNOIM*, 17, 1: 1–27; Germann, 1886, 'Der Ausgang der Dänisch-Halleschen Mission in Indien', *AMZ*, 345–53. Other Leipzig missionaries

In the twentieth century scholarly interest in the Tranquebar Mission was relocated in the field of theology as well as in mission and church history.[19] Questions of scientific history were also taken up, but these studies were selective and often remained rudimentary.[20] Socio-historical and political aspects of Christian missionary work were seldom examined in the context of the Tranquebar Mission.[21] Very little has also been done in the last 150 years with

---

such as Georg Stosch (missionary from 1888–92) also repeatedly referred to the beginnings of the mission in the eighteenth century while reflecting on and analyzing their own work in the Tamil region. Stosch, Georg and Hilko Wiardo Schomerus, 1936, 'Die Bedeutung der dänisch-halleschen Mission', *Luthertum*, Leipzig, 11: 321–38.

[19] Handmann, Richard, 1903, *Die Evangelische Lutherische Tamulen Mission in der Zeit ihrer Neubegründung: Ein Beitrag zur Geschichte der Evangelischen Mission im 19. Jahrhundert*, Hinrichs, Leipzig; Lehmann, *Es begann in Tranquebar*; Gensichen, Hans-Werner, 1956, 'Die konfessionelle Stellung der dänisch-halleschen Mission', *EMZ*, 13: 1–19; Gensichen, 1956, *Tranquebar Then and Now*, CLS, Madras; Gensichen, 1962, 'Die deutsche Mission und der Kolonialismus', *Kerygma und Dogma*, 8: 136–49; Grafe, Hugald, 1967, 'The Relation between the Tranquebar Lutherans and the Tanjore Catholics in the First Half of the 18th Century', *ICHR*, 1: 41–58; Grafe, 1981, *Evangelische Kirche in Indien: Auskunft und Einblicke*, Verlag der Eveng.-Luth. Mission, Erlangen.

[20] Merkel, Franz Rudolf, 1921, 'Die Bedeutung der Mission für die Wissenschaft', *Mission und Wissenschaft*, in *HMK*, 17. This article surveys the scholarly achievements of missionaries in the study of non-European regions. The studies by missionaries in the fields of linguistics and religion are valued as a contribution to the development of Indic studies in Europe. Gaps in research, suggestions and related questions are mentioned, but the article also contains deprecatory statements such as the following: '[...] Gründler even wrote the tract 'Medicus Malabaricus' from Tamil works on medicine in the naïve assumption that he was enriching Western science.' 10; Nebe, August, 1932, 'Die Missionsärzte der Dänisch-Halleschen Mission', *Die ärztliche Mission: Blätter zur Förderung der deutschen missionsärztlichen Bestrebungen*, 4: 98–101; Lehmann, Arno, 1952/53, 'Halle und die südindische Sprach-und Religionswissenschaft', *WZ*, II, *Gesellschafts-und Sprachwissenschaftliche Reihe*, Heft 3: 149–156; Lehmann, 1955, 'Hallesche Mediziner und Medizinen am Anfang deutsch-indischer Beziehungen', *WZ*, V, *Mathematisch-Naturwissenschaftliche Reihe*, Heft 2: 117–32; Lehmann, 1959, 'Bibliotheca malabarica: Eine wieder entdeckte Handschrift', *WZ*, VIII, Heft 4/5: 903–906; Lehmann, 1960, 'Der deutsche Anteil an der Dravidologie', *Forschungen und Fortschritte*, 34(10): 307–309; Lehmann, 1968, 'German Tamil Studies', *WZ*, XVII, Heft 6: 139–45.

[21] Exceptions are for instance: Gensichen, Hans-Werner, 1977, 'The social impact of the early Protestant missions in South India', *The Church in a Changing Society: Conflict—Reconciliation or Adjustment?* (International Commission on Comparative Ecclesiastical History), Uppsala, 430–35; Nørgaard, *Mission und Obrigkeit*.

regard to biographical research on missionaries or Indian mission employees. The biographical studies on Christian Friedrich Schwartz (1726–1798)[22] or Johann Philipp Fabricius (1711–1791)[23] are, by now, in need of revision. Comprehensive individual biographies of personalities such as Benjamin Schultze (1689–1760), Christoph Theodosius Walther (1699–1740/41) or even Christoph Samuel John (1747–1813) are still not available. Bartholomäus Ziegenbalg is the only missionary of the Tranquebar Mission who enjoys the continuous attention of scholars.[24]

Parallel to the increasing study of missionary work as a form of intercultural encounter, new studies in the context of the history of the Tranquebar Mission have also moved away from a mission-oriented perspective and focus not only on the effects on Tamil society but partly also on the interaction between mission and society.[25]

[22] Pearson, *Memoirs of Life and Correspondence*; Germann, Wilhelm, 1870, *Missionar Christian Friedrich Schwartz: Sein Leben und Wirken*, Deichert, Erlangen; Page, Jesse, 1921, *Schwartz of Tanjore*, SPCK, London.

[23] Germann, Wilhelm, 1865, *Johann Philipp Fabricius: Seine fünfzigjährige Wirksamkeit im Tamulenlande und das Missionsleben des achtzehnten Jahrhunderts daheim und draußen*, Deichert, Erlangen.

[24] Germann, Wilhelm, 1868, *Ziegenbalg und Plütschau, Die Gründungsjahre der Tranquebarschen Mission*, Deichert, Erlangen; Beyreuther, Erich, 1952, *Bartholomäus Ziegenbalg: Aus dem Leben des ersten deutschen Missionars*, Evang. Verl.-Anst., Berlin; Settgast, Ann-Charlott, 1981, *Der Mann in Tranquebar: Ein Portät des Bartholomäus Ziegenbalg*, Evang. Verl.—Anst., Berlin; Singh, *The First Protestant Missionary to India*. In recent years Daniel Jeyaraj has published some of Ziegenbalg's works with extensive commentaries: Jeyaraj, Daniel, (ed.), 2003, *Bartholomäus Ziegenbalgs Genealogie der malabarischen Götter: Edition der Originalfassung von 1713 mit Einleitung, Analyse und Glossar*, Verl. der Franckeschen Stiftungen, Halle; Jeyaraj, Daniel, 2005, *Genealogy of the South Indian Deities: An English Translation of Bartholomäus Ziegenbalg's Original German Manuscript with a Textual Analysis and Glossary*, Routledge, Curzon, London, New York; Jeyaraj, Daniel, 2006, *A German Exploration of Indian Society: Ziegenbalg's 'Malabarian Heathenism': An Annotated English Translation with an Introduction and a Glossary*, The Mylapore Institute for Indigenous Studies et al., Chennai [et al].

[25] Cf. the efforts of Indira Peterson and Robert Frykenberg to examine the interplay between the mission society and South Indian society in the spheres of education, culture and science. Peterson, Indira Viswanathan, 1999, 'Science in the Tranquebar Mission Curriculum: Natural Theology and Indian Responses', in Michael Bergunder, *Missionsberichte aus Indien im 18. Jahrhundert: ihre Bedeutung für die europäische Geistesgeschichte und ihr wissenschaftlicher Quellenwert für die Indienkunde*,

The search for the Indian Christian past also includes attempts to study the development of local congregations or the biographies of eminent Indian Christians. With reference to the Tranquebar Mission the interest in the European 'fathers' of the Lutheran Church is accompanied by the desire to reconstruct the Indian contribution to this development.[26] Historical research has been conducted in a systematic and focused manner, among other places, in the Gurukul Lutheran Theological College and Research Institute, Chennai to study the Lutheran tradition in Tamil Nadu.[27] In preparation of the tercentenary of the first Protestant mission in India the Gurukul-college established a Lutheran Heritage Project. In co-operation with the Francke Foundations at Halle (Saale) workshops were conducted, some of which resulted in the publication of edited volumes.[28] In

---

175–219, Verlag der Franckeschen Stiftungen, Halle (=Neue Hallesche Berichte. Quellen und Studien zur Geschichte und Gegenwart Südindiens, Bd. 1); Peterson, Indira, 2003, 'Tanjore, Tranquebar and Halle: European Science and German Missionary Education in the Lives of two Indian Intellectuals in the Early Nineteenth Century', in Robert Eric Frykenberg (ed.), *Christians and Missionaries in India: Cross-Cultural Communication since 1500: With Special Reference to Caste, Conversion and Colonialism*, 93–126, W.B. Eerdmans, London; Frykenberg, Robert Eric, 1999, 'The Halle Legacy in Modern India: Information and the Spread of Education, Enlightenment and Evangelization', in Bergunder, *Missionsberichte aus Indien*, 6–29. My article on the development of the mission education system as illustrated by the Danish-English-Halle Mission follows a similar trajectory. Liebau, Heike, 2003, 'Über die Erziehung 'tüchtiger Subjekte' zur Verbreitung des Evangeliums: Das Schulwesen der Dänisch-Halleschen Mission als Säule der Missionsorganisation', in Artur Bogner et al. (ed.), *Weltmission und religiöse Organisationen Protestantische Missionsgesellschaften im 19. und 20. Jahrhundert*, 427–58, Ergon Verl., Würzburg.

[26] A biography of the Tamil poet Vedanayakam Sastri (1774–1864) was published in 1995. Sastri was educated in the schools of the Tranquebar Mission and he had worked for many years with the missionary Christian Friedrich Schwartz. The author of this biography is the grand-niece of the great-grandson of Vedanayakam Sastri. Appasamy, G.P., 1995, *Vedanayaka Sastriar: A Biography of the Suviseda Kavirayar of Thanjavur*, Madras. In 1997 a conference on the life and work of the first ordained pastor of the Danish-Halle mission, Aaron, took place in Madras. Cf. Jeyaraj, Daniel (ed.), 1998, *Ordination of the First Indian Pastor Aaron*, Lutheran Heritage Archives, Chennai.

[27] 'The Lutheran Heritage Archives at Gurukul is a research institute that aims to collect and preserve historical documents on Lutheran Churches in India. Its main focus is to highlight the manifold contributions of the Lutheran Missions and Churches in India.' K. Rajaratnam, 'Foreword' in Jeyaraj, *Ordination of the First Indian Pastor Aaron*, V.

[28] Thus, in 1997 a conference was organized in Halle on the significance of the Halle Reports published between 1710 and 1770. Cf. Bergunder, Michael (ed.),

the anniversary year 2006 a three-volume publication was brought out with German-Indian co-operation which comprehensively documents the current international research in the area.[29]

Despite all the changes in scholarly research on mission history in general and on the Tranquebar Mission in particular, many studies still have one thing in common: they are written from the perspective of the European founders of the mission with European-Christian concerns about missionary work in mind. The reasons for this and for other lacunae in research on the Tranquebar Mission can be found, on the one hand, in the narrow understanding of mission as part of religious and church history—an understanding that is evident in many studies and which does not allow one to consider mission history as part of the social history of a region.[30] On the other hand, access to the sources is important. Although mission archives are as accessible to a historian as the archives of other institutions, the structure and character of the sources do not necessarily suggest their use for research in social history. In addition, since the documents on the history of the Tranquebar Mission are largely in German, South Asian scholars often find it difficult to use them.[31]

1999, *Missionsberichte aus Indien im 18. Jahrhundert. Ihre Bedeutung für die europäische Geistesgeschichte und ihr wissenschaftlicher Quellenwert für die Indienkunde*, Verlag der Franckeschen Stiftungen, Halle (=Neue Hallesche Berichte. Quellen und Studien zur Geschichte und Gegenwart Südindiens, Bd. 1); In February 1998 a joint conference took place in Thanjavur on the occasion of the 200th death anniversary of Christian Friedrich Schwartz. Jeyaraj, Daniel (ed.), 1999, *Christian Friedrich Schwartz: His Contributions to South India*, Lutheran Heritage Archives, Chennai.

[29] Gross, Andreas et al. (eds.), 2006, *Halle and the Beginning of Protestant Christianity in India, Vol. I: The Danish-Halle and the English-Halle Mission. Vol. II: Christian Mission in the Indian Context. Vol. III: Communication between India and Europe*, Verl. der Franckeschen Stiftungen, Halle.

[30] Paul Jenkins also emphasizes this when he calls mission history a 'sub-domain of social history or, rather, the history of two societies'. Jenkins, Paul, 1991, 'Missionsgeschichte: Ein Manifest', *ZM*, 3: 8–18, here 8. Jenkins is, however, skeptical about the intention of this present work to view mission history as a part of the social history of a non-European society and use mission sources as one possible means to understand this history: 'There is still a marked tendency to bring in the easily accessible mission archives of Western countries for understanding historical processes and events in the Third World. This is guaranteed not to do justice to either of the two movements.' Jenkins, 'Missionsgeschichte', 9.

[31] In recent decades the interest of South Asian scholars in the German sources has increased. See, among others, the numerous works of Daniel Jeyaraj as well as

As far as the DEHM is concerned, the work with the German original manuscripts of the eighteenth century requires a special knowledge of 18th century language and script. The published mission reports[32] are comprehensive but have been censored. Indexes are mostly incomplete or non-existent. Collections of documents that have been published till now do not take a potentially broader scholarly interest into account. They focus on the work of individual personalities, mainly from the early period of the mission.[33] Even the most recent editions of source materials remain within the traditionally dominant study of the early Tranquebar Mission.[34] The comprehensive efforts of the Francke Foundations in recent years to digitalize and catalogue its source materials will not only make it easier to access these documents in the future, but will surely also lead to new editorial projects.[35]

A comprehensive and systematic study of the structure, formation, development and characterization of the group of Indian

---

Mohanavelu, C.S., 1993, *German Tamilology: German contributions to Tamil language, literature and culture during the period 1706–1945*, Saiva Siddhanta, Madras.

[32] For the full title see fn. 45 in the introduction of this volume.

[33] Philipps, Thomas J., 1719, *Thirtyfour Conferences Between the Danish Missionaries and the Malabarian Brahmans (or Heathen Priests) in the East Indies, concerning the Truth of the Christian Religion: Together with some Letters written by the Heathens to the said Missionaries*, printed for H. Clements [...] W. Fleetwood [...] and J. Stephens [,,,], London; Caland, Willem (ed.), 1930, *B. Ziegenbalg's kleinere Schriften*, Koninklijke Akademie van Wetenschappen, Amsterdam. te Amsterdam/Afd. Letterkunde; N.R. 29.2); Caland, Willem, 1926, *Ziegenbalg's Malabarisches Heidentum* (ed. and with indices by Willem Caland), Koninklijke Akademie van Wetenschappen, Amsterdam; Germann, *Genealogie der Malabarischen Götter*. A list of Ziegenbalg's letters is given in: Werther, Gottfried, 1956, 'Die Briefe von Bartholomäus Ziegenbalg (1682–1719)', *WZ, Gesellschafts—und Sprachwissenschaftliche Reihe*, 5: 221–26; see also Lehmann, *Alte Briefe* (AB).

[34] Cf., among others: Gründler, Johann Ernst und Bartholomäus Ziegenbalg, 1998, *Die Malabarische Korrespondenz: Tamilische Briefe an deutsche Missionare. Eine Auswahl*, (With an introduction and with explanations by Kurt Liebau), Thorbecke, Sigmaringen; Jeyaraj, *Bartholomäus Ziegenbalgs Genealogie der malabarischen Götter*; Jeyaraj, *Genealogy of the South Indian Deities*; Jeyaraj, *A German Exploration of Indian Society. Ziegenbalg's 'Malabarian Heathenism'*; see also fn 24 in this chapter.

[35] The archival material of the Danish-Halle Mission is available in an online database of the Archives of the Francke Foundations. http://192.124.243.55/cgi-bin/dhm.pl. The digital library of the Francke Foundations gives the reader access to the complete digitalized version of the Halle Reports. http://www.francke-halle.de/main/index2.php?cf=3_1_3_3_2

mission employees has remained a research desiderate. In most recent research on the Danish-English-Halle Mission we see first signs of an inclusion of local co-workers in the study. Even though, as a rule, the local employees still appear in the company of 'their' European missionaries, they are no longer merely the recipients of instructions, but persons whose actions could have, by all accounts, influenced the missionaries.[36]

In its approach this study builds upon the now emerging attempts to change the dominant perspective in studies of mission history. In other words, the mission is no longer viewed from the perspective of the missionizing, either the mission societies in Europe or the missionaries. The focus is on the 'missionized', whose history needs to be written, whose perspective and self-understanding needs to be reclaimed. As 'national workers' of the mission they also became part of the missionizing structure—not only with regard to the local society, but also with regard to the missionaries with whom they negotiated the mechanisms of their daily co-operation. Accordingly, the perspective shifts even in this chapter. The historical survey of the work of the DEHM does not replicate traditional mission history.

[36] Jeyaraj, Daniel, 1997, 'Die Ordination des ersten protestantischen Pfarrers Aaron in Südindien, 28.12.1733', *ZM*, XXIII (2): 105–25; Jeyaraj, *Ordination of the First Protestant Indian Pastor Aaron*; Liebau, Heike and Magret Liepach, 1994, 'Christliche Hindus—indische Christen? Die Nationalarbeiter der Dänisch-Halleschen Mission in Südindien im 18. Jahrhundert', in Joachim Heidrich (ed.), *Changing Identities: The Transformation of Asian and African Societies under Colonialism*, 307–22, Das Arabische Buch, Berlin; Liebau, 1997, 'Indische Angestellte in der dänischen Kolonialadministration während der sozialen Unruhen in Tranquebar und Umgebung im Jahre 1787', *Asien, Afrika, Lateinamerika*, 25: 111–26; Liebau, *Tamilische Christen im 18. Jahrhundert*; Liebau, 'Country Priests, Catechists and Schoolmasters as Cultural, Religious and Social Middlemen in the Context of the Tranquebar Mission', in Frykenberg, *Christians and Missionaries in India*, 70–92; Liebau, 'The Indian Pastors in the Danish-Halle and the English-Halle Mission', in Gross, *Halle and the Beginning of Protestant Christianity in India, Vol. II*, 719–34; Liebau, 'Indian Pastors 1733–1817 (Short biographies)', in Gross, *Halle and the Beginning of Protestant Christianity in India, Vol. III*, 1543–49; Liebau, Kurt, 1996, 'Die ersten Tamilen aus der Dänisch-Halleschen Mission in Europa. Vom Objekt zum Subjekt kultureller Interaktion?', in Gerhard Höpp (ed.), *Fremde Erfahrungen: Asiaten und Afrikaner in Deutschland, Österreich und in der Schweiz bis 1945*, 9–28, Das Arabische Buch, Berlin; Kent, Eliza F., 'Raja Clarinda—Widow, Concubine, Patroness: Women's Leadership in the Indian Church', in Gross, *Halle and the Beginning of Protestant Christianity in India, Vol. II*, 659–83.

Instead, the mission is portrayed as an integral part of and as a player in the history of South India.

THANJAVUR IN THE EIGHTEENTH CENTURY

The region in which the Danish-English-Halle Mission worked stretched like a net from the small port-town of Tranquebar to various parts of the Thanjavur kingdom on the east coast of South India, the so-called Coromandel Coast.[37] This 20–30 km wide coastal strip with its fertile soil and crossed by wide-bedded rivers flowing into the Bay of Bengal presented favourable conditions for agriculture and enabled two harvests annually.[38] The climatic conditions on the south east coast of India, the succession of dry seasons and monsoon rain, the natural system of rivers, irrigation facilities and water tanks created the necessary foundations for a settled cultivation of land. The main crop of the region was rice; its production and processing influenced all spheres of social life. As the primary crop rice was a significant economic factor; in addition, it had important ritual functions as a component of religious symbolism in the temple and in the households. Textile production was important and its importance was, for a while, significantly enhanced by the increased demand from Europe in the eighteenth century.[39] Among other things, calico, a stiff white cotton cloth, was produced.

Along with Bengal, the Malabar region and Gujarat, the Coromandel Coast was one of the most important trade regions of India.[40] However, in most of the coastal cities, as was the case

[37] From the point of view of an interconnected system of trade Arasaratnam defines the boundaries of the Coromandel Coast with Ganjam in the north, Ceylon in the south and the Bay of Madura and Tuticorin. Cf. Arasaratnam, *Coromandel Revisited*, 102.

[38] For geography and agriculture of South India see Singh, Gopal, 1976, *A Geography of India*, Atma Ram, Delhi (=A Geography of India, Delhi 1976); Ludden, David, 1990, *Peasant History in South India*, Princeton University Press, Princeton.

[39] Arasaratnam, *Indian Commercial Groups*, 44.

[40] Raychaudhuri, Tapan, 1962, *Jan Company in Coromandel*, Nijhoff, The Hague; Arasaratnam, *Merchants, Companies and Commerce*; Das Gupta, Ashin Das and Michael Naylor Pearson (eds.), 1987, *India and the Indian Ocean 1500–1800*, Oxford University Press, Calcutta, New York.

in Tranquebar, the large deep sea ships could not dock directly in the harbour but had to berth up to four miles into the sea. From there the goods were transported to the coast by Indian merchants, representatives of the *Karaiyar* caste, in coastal boats.[41] It was only in port-towns such as Cuddalore, Porto Novo or Karaikal which lay at the estuaries of large rivers that ships could dock directly in the harbour.[42] The main export of the kingdom of Thanjavur was rice, which was transported from Thanjavur to Ceylon, the Malabar Coast and Bengal, among other places. Besides this, the port of Nagapattinam was a base for trade with South East Asia.

At the beginning of the eighteenth century the kingdom of Thanjavur is estimated to have had about one million inhabitants.[43] Hindus constituted over 90 per cent of the population, more than 5 per cent were Muslims. Catholics made up perhaps 2 per cent of the population. In contrast to other Tamil regions there was a relatively higher representation of Brahmins on account of the historical migration from North India into the heartland of the Chola dynasty (approx. 6–7 per cent). Besides them, the *vaṉṉiyar* ('agricultural

[41] NHB 11. St., 1420 (description of 1743); the missionaries called these boats 'Sellingen'.

[42] Arasaratnam, Sinnappah, 1995, 'Factors in the rise, growth and decline of Coromandel ports circa 1650–1720', in Arasaratnam, S., *Maritime Trade, Society and European Influence in Southern Asia 1600–1800*, Variorum, Aldershot.

[43] For South India at the beginning of the seventeenth century Sanjay Subrahmanyam postulates a figure of 22 to 30 million inhabitants, concentrated mainly in the coastal area. Subrahmanyam, Sanjay, 1990, *The Political Economy of Commerce: Southern India 1500–1650*, Cambridge University Press, Cambridge, 15. If one scales down the census figures of 1881 (2.13 million in Thanjavur and 31.7 million in the entire Madras Presidency) and those of 1822 (13.5 million for the entire Presidency), one arrives at a figure of roughly one million inhabitants for the period around 1800. The devastating wars, especially in the second half of the eighteenth century, led to high population losses which Michael Mann estimates at around 400,000 inhabitants (40 per cent of the population). From this we can infer that the population of Thanjavur at the beginning of the eighteenth century was probably also around one million or a little less. Cf. Maclean, C.D., 1996, *Manual of the Administration of the Madras Presidency. Vol. 1 (1885)*, Asian Educational Services, New Delhi, 490f.; Mann, Michael, 2006, 'Südindien im 18. Jahrhundert: wirtschaftliche und politische Entwicklung', in Heike Liebau (ed.), *Geliebtes Europa, Ostindische Welt. 300 Jahre interkultureller Dialog im Spiegel der Dänisch-Halleschen Mission. Katalog der Jahresausstellung der Franckeschen Stiftungen zu Halle*, 41–51, Verlag der Fanckeschen Stiftungen, Halle, here 50.

workers') with roughly 30 per cent and the *veḷḷāḷar* ('farmers') with 17–18 per cent were the largest caste groups. In addition, there were roughly 15 per cent *paṟaiyār*.[44]

Historically speaking, the territory of the Hindu kingdom of Thanjavur encompassed the heartland of the earlier Chola Empire. After the downfall of this empire, which had, at one time, extended to Ceylon and South East Asia, the kingdom of Vijaynagar became its successor in 1336. The rulers of Vijaynagar sent out several military leaders to conquer South India. Following upon such conquests these leaders were installed as *nāyaka* to administer the newly won territories. They were responsible for maintaining law and order as well as for collecting taxes. In addition, they were obliged to maintain an army to support the incumbent ruler of Vijaynagar in his wars, especially against the Muslim rulers in the north. The domains of the *nāyaka* contained smaller administrative units, which were managed by so-called *pāḷaiyakkārar*, local military chiefs. On the one hand, there were often conflicts between the *pāḷaiyakkārar* and the *nāyaka* regarding the ownership of land and the question of power. On the other hand, the *pāḷaiyakkārar* maintained troops, which they had to place at the disposal of the *nāyaka* whenever required.[45]

The downfall of the Vijaynagar Empire began after its defeat in the battle of Talikota in 1565. The growing weakness of the central power in Vijaynagar was paralleled by the consolidation of power of the *nāyaka* as local regents at the periphery of the empire who were able to establish their sovereign dominions in the sixteenth and seventeenth centuries.[46] Thus, the dynasty of the *nāyaka* of Thanjavur began with Sevappa Nayak in 1532 (ruled 1532–80) and reached its zenith with Raghunatha Nayak (1600–34). Through innumerable wars against his neighbours, especially against the Muslim states of North India and the *nāyaka* of Madurai, but also against the Portuguese colonial rulers, Raghunatha Nayak tried in

[44] This calculation is based on the census of 1881. Cf. Maclean, *Manual of the Administration of the Madras Presidency*, Vol. II, 126

[45] Rajayyan, Kunjukrishnan Nadar, 1974, *History of Madurai (1736–1801)*, Madurai University, Madurai, 31f.

[46] Cf. Subrahmanian, N., 1994, *Social and Cultural History of Tamilnad [AD 1336–AD 1984]*, Ennes, Udumalpet.

vain to salvage the remains of the collapsing empire and to establish the supremacy of Thanjavur over the other *nāyaka*.[47] The rule of the *nāyaka* in Thanjavur came to an end in the second half of the seventeenth century. Vijayaraghava Nayak (1634–73), son of Raghunatha Nayak, was the last ruler of the *nāyaka* dynasty. On the whole, this period shaped the country both economically and culturally since most of these Hindu (Vaishnava) rulers had cultural, literary and scientific interests and were comparatively tolerant and open in religious matters. Music, architecture, sculpture and painting flourished.

The rule of the *nāyaka* in Thanjavur ended as a result of Vijayraghava Nayak's military conflicts with Chokkanatha Nayak (1659–82) of Madurai and a simultaneous attack on Thanjavur in 1674 by Muslim armies from North India. The country was conquered by Madurai and placed under the administrative rule of a referee. He was replaced in 1674 with a descendant of the *nāyaka* of Thanjavur with the help of the Marathas under their leader Ekoji Bhonsle (around 1630–84), who, after initial conquests in South India, began to display an interest in developments there. A year later, Ekoji himself became the ruler of Thanjavur and established the Maratha dynasty of the Raja of Thanjavur. After a victory in the battle of Valigandpura on 16 November 1677 Ekoji finally broke free of his brother Shivaji (1630–80) and had himself crowned as the first Raja of Thanjavur in 1678.[48] As a result of administrative reforms the country was divided into initially six and later seven districts: the central district Thanjavur and the six districts Mayavaram,[49] Kumbakonam, Tiruvadi, Vallam, Mannarkudi, Pattukottai.

The subsequent history of the kingdom of Thanjavur is embedded in far-reaching changes in the political map of South India after the decline of the Mughal Empire. Several independent or semi-independent kingdoms consolidated their power. The

[47] Cf. the somewhat older but comprehensive portrayal by Vriddagirisan, V., 1995, *The Nayaks of Tanjore*, (Annamalainagar 1942) Asian Educational Services, New Delhi.

[48] See Majumdar, R.C. (ed.), 1984, *The Mughal Empire*, Bharatiya Vidya Bhavan, Bombay (=The History and Culture of the Indian People), 272.

[49] Today Mayiladuthurai.

Mughal Empire, established in 1526, lost its position as the dominating empire after the death of the last emperor Aurangzeb (1658–1707). The influence of the once powerful central force diminished and was replaced by the consolidation of peripheral provincial administrations, limiting, in effect, the power of the Mughals in the eighteenth century to Delhi. Local representatives of the Mughals sometimes safeguarded their factual independence by recognizing the nominal authority of the Delhi emperors. In the south of the sub-continent the Nizam of Hyderabad, the Nawab of Arcot with the Carnatic kingdom and the rulers of Mysore and Travancore, among others, created their own spheres of influence which, at the beginning of the eighteenth century, were under the administrative control of Mughal governors. In the course of the eighteenth century these unstable constellations of power faltered and, with the weakening of the imperial centre, the shifting equations of power between the provinces were put to the test. Thanjavur was also affected by this.

After Ekoji's death his brother Shahji II (1684–1712) ruled the kingdom. Nominally, these Maratha rulers, like the *nāyaka* of Thanjavur since 1658, were dependent on the Mughal rulers in Delhi[50] and had to make annual payments of tribute to their representatives.[51] The wars against Madurai, that had already begun under the *nāyaka*, continued. With support from the ruler of Pudukkotai Madurai went to war against Thanjavur and against the *setupati* of Ramnad in 1700. Although Thanjavur suffered a military defeat the raja succeeded in signing a treaty of peace. As a result of the war the *setupati* became independent in 1702 and in return for the support he handed over Fort Arantangi and its surrounding territories to Thanjavur. In 1709 Thanjavur supported Madurai against the *setupati*, suffered a military defeat and had to return the

[50] Habib, Irfan, 1996, *An Atlas of the Mughal Empire: Political and Economic Maps with Detailed Notes, Bibliography and Index*, Oxford University Press, Delhi et al., 65. Cf. also Vriddhagirisan, *The Nayaks of Tanjore*, 165f.

[51] 'The King of Tanjore is sovereign insofar as he has to pay a sizeable tribute every year to the Great Mogul—a payment that is said to amount to 3,33,333 Reichstaler annually. The Diwan, as the general of the Great Mogul, who administers the Mogul district adjacent to the Tanjour kingdom further north on this coast, demands this payment annually.' (translated from German), HB 11. Cont., 878.

territories to him.[52] This war took place during a period of famine in the *setupati*'s region, which lasted till about 1713. During this time many starving people fled to Thanjavur and Madurai.

In 1712 Serfoji I (1712–28) took over the reins of government. In alliance with Madurai he tried to gain territories in the framework of the wars of succession in Ramnad from 1724 onwards. In the course of these conflicts, which continued till 1729, the *setupati* of Ramnad lost a large amount of territory. All the territory north of Pambar fell to Thanjavur. Two-fifths of the remaining territory went to the hitherto independent state of the Raja of Sivaganga.[53] By 1720 Thanjavur had also recaptured Arantangi that had been occupied in the interim period by Pudukkotai.

At the beginning of his rule Tuljaji I (1728–36) was successful in neutralizing the pressure applied by the Nizam of Hyderabad at the northern boundaries of his kingdom. He was thus free to support the declining kingdom of Madurai. His attempt in 1733 to defeat the *setupati* of Ramnad was unsuccessful. A subsequent joint attack by Thanjavur and Madurai against Pudukkotai was repulsed with help from Ramnad. The victors were then able to convince the Nawab of Arcot and Madurai to attack Thanjavur. Tuljaji I was only able to broker a peace with the promise of considerable funds. After wars of succession and civil wars the kingdom of Madurai became a part of the kingdom of the Nawab of Arcot/Carnatic in 1736. The Nawab was a vassal of the Nizam of Hyderabad and a representative of the Mughals. With his accession to the throne the rule of the *nāyaka* in Madurai came to an end.[54]

After the death of Tuljaji I in 1736 there was a three-year interregnum in Thanjavur, in the course of which the country sank into chaos and battles were fought between pretenders to the throne. During this time the Nawab of Arcot occupied the country and plundered it. In 1739 the new Raja of Thanjavur, Pratap Singh (1739–63), had to hand over the port-town of Karaikal to the French in return for their help. In 1740 the Marathas descended on South India and thus saved Thanjavur from an attack by the

[52] Subrahmanian, *Social and Cultural History of Tamilnad*, 126.

[53] Aiyar, R. Sathianatha and Sakkottai Krishnaswami Aiyangar, 2001, *History of the Nayaks of Madura*, (Madras 1924) Asian Educational Services, New Delhi, 229.

[54] Rajayyan, *History of Madurai*, 33f.

Nawab of Arcot on account of unpaid tributes. After the Marathas left the Nawab himself appeared at the head of a large army and laid siege to Thanjavur. With a payment of 700,000 rupees Pratap Singh was able to make the Nawab lift the siege. In the 1740s the battles for the former territories of the Madurai Nayaks influenced the political situation in Thanjavur. In 1740/41 the Nawab of Arcot suffered several defeats and his state faced disintegration because of the intrusion of the Marathas in the battles for Madurai. Using differences among the Marathas as well as among the pretenders to the title of Nawab the Nizam of Hyderabad, Asaf Jah, intervened and, in 1743, restored the kingdom of Arcot to its earlier extent.

From the second half of the eighteenth century the developments in Thanjavur were marked by the increasing rivalry between the British, the French and the Muslim elites of South India.

EUROPEAN PRESENCE IN SOUTH EAST INDIA

The Portuguese, who had been in Goa on the west coast of India since 1510 as conquerors and as a trading power, advanced to Nagapattinam in the Thanjavur kingdom during the reign of the first *nāyaka* Sevappa Nayak, thus strengthening their presence in this South Indian region.[55] In order to create counter-balances to the Portuguese monopoly the *nāyaka* of Thanjavur, who were always hostile to the Portuguese, opened their realm to other Europeans.[56] The European presence in Thanjavur increased primarily during the reign of Sevappa Nayak's grandson Raghunatha Nayak. Europeans set up their trading posts in places that had always functioned as ports and trading centres, or they established new settlements, factories and forts. Local rulers gave the Dutch almost exclusive rights to trade and commerce. Having signed a treaty in 1626 with the Zamorin of Calicut on the west coast of India, they ensured their rights over the former Portuguese possession of Nagapattinam

[55] For the history of the Portuguese in Tamil Nadu cf.: Stephen, S. Jeyaseela, 1998, *Portuguese in the Tamil Coast: Historical Explorations in Commerce and Culture (1507–1749)*, Navajothi Pub. House, Pondicherry.

[56] Arasaratnam, Sinnappah, 'The politics of commerce in the coastal kingdoms of Tamil Nadu 1650–1740', in S. Arasaratnam, *Maritime Trade*, II, 1–19, here 5.

on the southeastern coast in 1659.[57] In the eighteenth century the British and the French also entered the political arena in South India. Although the Dutch remained a strong trading power in the first half of the eighteenth century, the growing French role made it difficult for them to hold on to some of their possessions.[58] The British and the French also intervened in the conflicts surrounding the succession to the throne of the Nizam Asaf Jah who died in 1748. Whereas the War of the Austrian Succession (1740–48) had caused only minor skirmishes in India between these powers, the Peace of Aachen (18 October 1748) ensured that the French ended their occupation of Madras and returned it to the British. The French managed in ensuring power for those they supported in Hyderabad and Arcot and bound them through subsidy contracts. The surrender of the northern *sarkars* by the Nizam then led to the temporary supremacy of the French in southeast India. The British, for their part, countered the alliance between France, Hyderabad and Arcot through a pact with Mysore and Thanjavur. In 1749 the former Raja of Thanjavur, Sahuji (ruled 1736–39) tried to win back his throne from Pratap Singh with the help of the British and offered to hand over Devkottai in return for their help. By supporting Sahuji in Thanjavur the British intervened for the first time in an internal conflict in South India.[59] After capturing Devkottai in July 1749 the British neutralized Sahuji by setting him aside with an annuity. Pratap Singh, in the meantime, legalized the handing over of Devkottai through a treaty with the British and thus succeeded in winning them over to his side. Through this alliance with the rivals of the French Pratap Singh was able to withstand the attacks by the French and the Marathas in 1754 and 1758 respectively. However, in 1753 he lost all the districts of Ramnad, which Thanjavur had been able to annex through treaties or wars.

After the futile attempt to lay siege to the fort of Tiruchirapalli and given the lack of support from Europe the French were forced in 1754 to cede the northern *sarkars* to the British and to hand

[57] Arasaratnam, Sinnappah, 'Mare Clausum, the Dutch and Regional Trade in the Indian Ocean 1650–1740', in Arasaratnam, *Maritime Trade*, 73–91, here 73.

[58] Arasaratnam, Sinnappah, 'The Dutch East India Company and its Cormandel Trade 1700–1740', in Arasaratnam, *Maritime Trade*, VI, 325–46, here 325.

[59] Rajayyan, *History of Madurai*, 100.

over Arcot to the ally of the British. After this the decisive conflicts between the British and the French began. The Seven Years' War (1756–63) in Europe also led to military conflicts in Southeast India, which ended with enormous loss of territory for the French, while the British occupied the territory of the Nizam of Hyderabad.

The second half of the eighteenth century witnessed an increase in the importance of the kingdom of Mysore first under Haidar Ali (1722–82), who had risen from the rank of a *nāyaka*, and then under his son and successor Tipu Sultan (1749/ruled 1782–99). After the ruling Hindu dynasty in Mysore had been overthrown by Haidar Ali in 1761 this kingdom had fought several wars against neighbouring states. During these so-called Carnatic Wars, which began in 1763 and in which the British and the French fought for supremacy in South India, Mysore allied itself with the French. Earlier already, the French had had to accept severe blows from the British and their allies. At the beginning of the 1760s, when the French territories of Pondicherry and Karaikal were temporarily occupied by British troops, many French citizens and citizens of the cities had fled to the territory of the Danish trading company in the north, with whom the French had often co-operated.[60] Haidar Ali extended his dominions on the Malabar Coast and in the Deccan and established a strong centralized state. This provoked resistance from the Marathas and the Nizam of Hyderabad. In 1764 the Marathas attacked Mysore twice and defeated Haidar Ali. Despite this, Haidar Ali continued his conquests on the Malabar Coast and succeeded in deflecting a threatened attack by an alliance of the Marathas, the Nizam of Hyderabad and the Nawab of Arcot. With the help of different alliances Mysore fought against the consolidation of British rule in South India.

The first Anglo-Mysore War began in 1767 with the British invasion of Mysore. Haidar Ali countered this attack with a military force under the command of his son Tipu Sultan. As a result of this war status quo was re-established in 1769 and a pact was signed between Mysore and the British. Under Pratap Singh's successor,

[60] Krieger, Martin, 1998, *Kaufleute, Seeräuber und Diplomaten. Der dänische Handel auf dem Indischen Ozean (1720–1868)*, Böhlau, Köln (=Wirtschafts—und Sozialhistorische Studien 8), 134.

Tuljaji II (1763–87), Thanjavur was embroiled in these wars and in a series of further conflicts that ravaged the country and caused an enormous loss of lives. In the 1770s Thanjavur waged several wars against Ramnad and Sivaganga. In these conflicts the Nawab of Carnatic, Muhammad Ali Khan (ruled: 1750–95), supported the latter. Reacting to an alliance between Thanjavur and Mysore, the Nawab and his British allies attacked Thanjavur in 1771 and defeated the Raja of Thanjavur in September of that year. According to the peace treaty the Raja had to cede some territories to the Nawab, surrender two provinces along with their revenue to him and pay the Nawab 3.25 million rupees towards the costs of the war. Vallam Fort had to be destroyed. In 1773 the Nawab and the British again invaded Thanjavur territory for failure to comply with the treaty of 1771.[61] The raja was dethroned; the country was occupied and ruthlessly plundered by the Nawab and the British. In this period the tax burden was almost doubled.[62] In 1776 the Governor of Madras, Lord George Pigot (1719–77), was instructed to reinstate Raja Tuljaji II of Thanjavur.[63] However, the ruler of Thanjavur had to accept a distinct loss of sovereignty. The defence of the country was handed over to British troops; the raja was not allowed to enter into any alliances with other powers without British consent and could not support enemies of the British. In addition, Tuljaji had to hand over 277 villages in the Nagore district to the East India Company.

After the French king Louis XVI (1754/ruled: 1774–91) called for a war against England in 1778, the conflicts between the two European powers in India also intensified. In the second Anglo-Mysore War (1780–84) an anti-British alliance consisting of Mysore, the Marathas, the Nizam and the French initially fought against the British. From May to November 1780 Haidar Ali invaded regions east of the Carnatic with the aim of destroying the territories of his opponents.[64] Thanjavur was also devastated. The people were killed or

[61] Rajayyan, *History of Madurai*, 262f.

[62] Subrahmanian, *Social and Cultural History of Tamilnad*, 139.

[63] Rajayyan, *History of Madurai*, 271.

[64] Sarkar, Jadunath, 2001, 'Haidar Ali's invasion of the Eastern Carnatic, 1780', in Irfan Habib (ed.), *Confronting Colonialism: Resistance and Modernization under Haidar Ali and Tipu Sultan*, 21–34, Indian History Congress, New Delhi [First published in: Islamic Culture, XV (1941), 214–28].

driven out of the country by Haidar Ali's troops. In this way Thanjavur lost about 40 per cent of its inhabitants.[65] In order to run the state a repressive system of taxation was introduced. Simultaneously—with the consent of the British—Pudukkotai seized the opportunity to occupy the Thanjavur forts of Kilanilai, Pattukkottai and Arantangi. In 1782 a renewed attack by Mysore on Carnatic laid waste to the districts Sirkazhi, Kumbakonam and Mayavaram.[66]

The coalition between Mysore and its allies broke up in the course of the conflicts, increasingly leaving Mysore alone against the British. The second Anglo-Mysore War ended in March 1784 with the Treaty of Mangalore, which provided for the withdrawal of Mysore from Carnatic and the British from the Malabar. Haidar Ali died during this war on 7 December 1782; his eldest son, Tipu Sultan, 32 years old at that time, took over from him. In negotiations lasting several months after the war a mutual and comprehensive return of the territories as well as strict neutrality was agreed upon. In the same year the British passed the Pitt's India Act, and under the terms of this Act Company representatives were required to refrain from unnecessary interference in India's internal affairs and expected to maintain a politically neutral position.[67] From 1785–87 Tipu Sultan waged a war against his former allies, the Marathas and the Nizam (Mysore-Maratha War), in which the British intermittently supported the Marathas.

In the third Anglo-Mysore War from 1790–92 in which the British allied with the Marathas and the Nizam of Hyderabad to fight against Mysore while the French remained neutral, the British gained a victory over Tipu Sultan. Tipu now found it difficult to realize many of his more ambitious plans although he again managed to reach Pondicherry in January 1791. This war ended in February 1792 with the signing of the Treaty of Seringapatnam (Srirangapattanam), which provided for the return of all territories north of the river Krishna, formerly occupied by Mysore, to the Marathas; of the territories between the Krishna and the Tungabhadra to Hyderabad

[65] Mann, *Südindien im 18. Jahrhundert*, 50.

[66] Subrahmanian, *Social and Cultural History of Tamilnad*, 141.

[67] Cf. Ali, Belagodu Sheikh, 'Cornwallis and the Mysore-Maratha War 1786–1787', in Irfan Habib (ed.), *Confronting Colonialism: Resistance and Modernization under Haidar Ali and Tipu Sultan*, 65–68, Tulika, New Delhi, here 67.

and the transfer of territories around Salem and Dindigul, as well as a significant part of the Malabar Coast, to the British.

Tipu Sultan used the time between the end of the war in 1792 and the beginning of a new war in 1798 to strengthen his weakened political and economic power, to recoup the losses of the third Anglo-Mysore War and to prepare for new conflicts with the British. In 1799 he saw the possibility of a new war against the British and, therefore, sought alliances with France and Turkey. His efforts, however, were unsuccessful. The British reacted in 1799 with a march on Seringapatnam, the capital of Mysore, which was captured after a brief siege in which Tipu Sultan died. After the victory over Tipu Sultan on 4 May 1799 the British installed a Hindu dynasty in Mysore and handed over large parts of the country to Hyderabad.

When Tuljaji II's successor, Amar Singh (ruled 1787–98), assumed the throne Thanjavur's payments to the British were increased to such an extent that financial collapse of the state was imminent. Serfoji II (1798–1833), therefore, finally handed over the country to the British in 1799. Nominally, Serfoji II remained the raja of Thanjavur, but his power extended only to the cities of Thanjavur and Vallam. The British gave him subsidies in return. In 1801 Thanjavur became a part of the Madras Presidency.[68] By placing Hyderabad under a treaty of subsidies (1799) and by occupying the nominally independent Carnatic (1801) the consolidation of British rule in Southeast India was complete.[69]

THE DANES IN TRANQUEBAR

The first Danish East India Company was established in 1616 under King Christian IV (1588–1648) following the model of the Dutch East India Company (VOC). With this, Denmark hoped to be profitably active in maritime trade. Like other European powers

[68] Subrahmanian, *Social and Cultural History of Tamilnad*, 144f.

[69] Further literature on the history of South India: Kulke, Hermann and Dietmar Rothermund, 1982, *Geschichte Indiens*, Kohlhammer, Stuttgart et al.; Kulke, Rothermund, *Geschichte Indiens von der Induskultur bis heute*. Rajayyan, *History of Madurai*; Rajayyan, K.N., 1992, *History of Tamil Nadu 1565–1982*, Raj Publishers, Madurai; Rothermund, Dietmar, 1989, *Indische Geschichte in Grundzügen*, Wissenschaftliche Buchgesellschaft, Darmstadt; Irschick, *Dialogue and History*.

in the seventeenth century the country had trading settlements in different parts of the world and, as a European maritime power, it had, at different times, participated successfully in intercontinental as well as inner-Asian trade.[70] Whereas initially it was more in the nature of sporadic undertakings, Danish overseas trade was institutionalized and centralized with the establishment of the first trading company. The activities were regulated from Copenhagen and the links to the trade settlements around the Indian Ocean, on the west coast of Africa and in Greenland were maintained from there.

By acquiring the trading settlement in Tranquebar (Tarangambadi) Denmark was able to strengthen its position in the Indian Ocean trade, especially with China. Like other European trading settlements on the Coromandel Coast of India Tranquebar offered favourable conditions for maritime trade.[71] The agreement signed with the *nāyaka* of Thanjavur, initially for a period of two years and then re-negotiated, permitted the Danes to build a fort in Tranquebar, to have jurisdiction over its inhabitants and to introduce the Danish Krone as legal currency.[72] Apart from having to pay the *nāyaka* of Thanjavur an annual rent in return, there were no other permanent obligations. Despite the fact that the political and economic importance of the Danish settlement was far less than that of the French settlement in Pondicherry or of the British settlement in Madras, for the Danes Tranquebar represented an important intermediate station for trade with Southeast Asia.

[70] On Denmark's trade policies see Diller, Stephan, 1992, 'Tranquebar: Handelsplatz und Missionsstation (1620–1845)', *Forschungsforum (=Berichte der Otto-Friedrich-Universität Bamberg)*, Heft 4: 43–54; Diller, Stephan 1999, *Die Dänen in Indien, Südostasien und China (1620–1845)*, Harrassowitz, Wiesbaden; Krieger, *Kaufleute, Seeräuber und Diplomaten*.

[71] For the history of the town see Feldbæk, Ole, 1984, 'The Development of an Indo-European Town in Mughal India: Tranquebar in the Seventeenth and Eighteenth Centuries', in Kenneth Ballhatchet and David Taylor (eds.), *Changing South Asia: City and Culture*, 11–20, The Centre of South Asian Studies at SOAS, London.

[72] Schmitt, Eberhard, 1988, *Wirtschaft und Handel der Kolonialreiche. Dokumente zur Geschichte der europäischen Expansion* (Vol. 4), Beck, München, 235–37 (Agreement between Admiral Ove Giedde on behalf of King Christian IV and the King of Tanjore, dated 19 November 1620); A detailed analyzis of Ove Giedde's report addressed to the Danish king Christian IV, written 1622 is given by Esther Fihl: Fihl, Esther, 2009, 'Shipwrecked on the Coromandel: the First Indo-Danish contract, 1620', *Review of Development and Change*, XIV: 1–2.

Danish trade in India was not always successful. In 1650 the first trading company was disbanded for lack of capital which, for a while, led it to consider selling the colony of Tranquebar. Shipping traffic to Tranquebar was interrupted for more than two decades. It was only in 1688 that a ship could be equipped again for the journey to East India.[73] In 1670 a new *Ostindisk Kompagni* was established and good trade results were achieved during the period of its functioning.[74] At the beginning of the eighteenth century Denmark suffered considerable economic setbacks resulting from its participation in the Northern Wars (1700–21). This also affected support for the trading companies and, thus, in the first decades of the eighteenth century trading activity was sporadic.[75] In 1729 the East India Company was again dissolved in order to be re-established in 1732 as the Asiatisk Kompagni, which was furnished with privileges and customs concessions. It was only this third Asiatisk Kompagni, which—with brief interruptions and with varying success—was active in trade for more than a century (1732–1843).[76] Especially in the years after 1750 the Danes could use their successes in the China trade to consolidate their position in East India since active trade brought capital to the settlements.[77] The Danish trading company even tried to underscore their influence in south-east India vis-à-vis the French and the British by buying or leasing more villages from the Raja of Thanjavur.[78] Denmark's position in the turbulent political developments in South India was officially one of neutrality; in reality, however, it participated indirectly in the events through arms supplies to different sides. Well into the 1750s Denmark maintained close relations with the French. When the Danish crown took over responsibility for the territories

[73] Cf. Feldbæk, Ole, 1991, 'No Ship for Tranquebar for Twenty-Nine Years. Or: The Art of Survival of a Mid-Seventeenth Century European Settlement in India', in Roderich Ptak and Dietmar Rothermund (eds.), *Emporia, Commodities and Entrepreneurs in Asian Maritime Trade, c. 1400–1750*, 29–36, Steiner, Stuttgart (=Beiträge zur Südasienforschung, vol. 14), 36.

[74] For the development of Danish trade see also: Feldbæk, Ole,1986, *Danske Handelskompagnier 1616–1843*, Selskabet for Udgivelse af Kilder til Dansk Historie, København.

[75] Arasaratnam, *The Dutch East India Company and its Coromandel Trade*, 331.

[76] Krieger, *Kaufleute, Seeräuber und Diplomaten*, 12.

[77] Ibid., 14.

[78] Ibid., 135.

of the Company in 1777 trade with India and East Asia became a state undertaking. The area of the colony had almost doubled after the territorial expansions of 1670 and 1739 as well as through the lease of further villages from the Raja of Thanjavur in 1773, 1783 and 1788. Already in 1801 all leased lands had to be handed over to the new rulers, the British.[79] In 1799 Thanjavur was occupied by the British and was nominally incorporated in the British Empire in India. Tranquebar and its surrounding area officially remained Danish territory until 1845—except during the temporary British occupation in 1801/02 as well as between 1808 and 1815.

In order to establish himself as an absolutist monarch with regard to the influential businessmen active in Tranquebar, and in order to fulfill his 'duties' towards the subjects of his empire, the Danish king, Frederick IV, influenced by the revivalist movement of Pietism, established a Lutheran overseas mission in the South Indian trading settlement of Tranquebar. He entrusted the task of finding suitable missionaries to his court chaplain, Franz Julius Lütkens (1650–1712), who had studied at the University of Wittenberg and had formerly been superintendent at the Peter's Church in Berlin. Lütkens used his contacts to Pietistic circles in Berlin who proposed the names of two prospective theologians: Bartholomäus Ziegenbalg from Pulsnitz in Saxony and Heinrich Plütschau (1677–1752) from Wesenburg in Mecklenberg.[80] Both of them were ordained in November 1705 in Copenhagen and shortly thereafter they set off for Tranquebar aboard the 'Sophia Hedwiga'.

Ziegenbalg and Plütschau came as authorized personnel of the Danish royal house to the territory of the Danish trading company. The missionaries viewed this territory, which consisted of Tranquebar and some surrounding villages,[81] as their place of work. The representatives of the Danish Company, however, did not look upon the missionaries as support for the Danish presence in Tranquebar. On the contrary, their aim to spread Christianity, based as it was on intensive contact with the local population,

[79] Ibid., 136.

[80] For the Pietistic circles in Berlin see Mentel, Friedrich-Franz, 2001, 'Kirche, Schule, Mission. Die Wirksamkeit von Pietisten in Berlin (1701–1713)', *Jahrbuch für historische Bildungsforschung*, vol. 7., 109–130, Klinkhardt, Bad Heilbrunn/Obb.

[81] Krieger, *Kaufleute, Seeräuber, Diplomaten*, 132f.

appeared to be incompatible with the goals and the manner of functioning of a trading company. The culminating point in the confrontation between the mission and the authorities in Tranquebar was Ziegenbalg's arrest in November 1708 on the orders of the Danish commandant, Johann Sigismund Hassius (1664–1729), governor of the trading place from 1707 to 1718.[82] Particularly in the early years the relationship between the mission and the authorities was subjected to ups and downs.[83] Soon, however, both parties became aware of their mutual dependency. Just as the mission had to use the Company's infrastructure for their communications with Europe, the mediating work of the missionaries as well as the availability of local workers trained and educated by the mission were of great help to the local Danish authorities. The fact that in the third year of missionary work the 'Commandant in Tranquebar, Mr Hassius, contributed several thousand stones/and the Danish head-clergyman some money'[84] to build a church for the mission congregation was, however, not so much a sign of their appreciation for the work done by the missionaries, but rather an expression of these mutual dependencies. Without a mission church the converts in Tranquebar would have had to use the Danish church built for the employees of the Danish Company. After Governor Hassius left, the association between the mission and the Company on Danish territory on the Coromandel Coast was more visibly determined by the reciprocity between both these institutions. 'The mission had abandoned the radical-Pietistic views that had characterized the early phase of the mission and that had led to the endless conflicts with secular authority. It had now become "official" in the sense that in its dealings with this authority it used the norms that were valid in this sphere.'[85]

In the early period of the mission shipping transport between Copenhagen and Tranquebar was irregular, and the contact between the missionaries and Europe, therefore, lacked continuity and was undependable. In some situations this fact demanded a high degree of

[82] For more details see Nørgaard, *Mission und Obrigkeit*, 41.

[83] Nørgaard, *Mission und Obrigkeit*, 106f.

[84] HB 1. Cont., 66., letter from F.J. Lütkens to A.H. Francke. Copenhagen, 19 March 1709.

[85] Nørgaard, *Mission und Obrigkeit*, 114, (translated from German).

independence and decision-making on the part of the overseas mission employees. It also led to the fact that conflicts with the local Danish authorities, for example, were dragged out longer that was necessary since one had to wait months or years for instructions from Europe.

The co-operation between Halle as the spiritual centre and Copenhagen as the official seat and the organizational hub of the Tranquebar Mission was extended from 1710 onwards through intensive contacts with the Society for Promoting Christian Knowledge (SPCK) in London, that had been established in 1698 by Thomas Bray (1656–1730) and other English clerics. Its task was the (worldwide) spread of the Christian faith through education and through the distribution of Christian literature. Schools were established under the supervision of the SPCK not only in England and Wales, but the organization also viewed the support of overseas Christian missions as an important aspect of its work.[86] The Danish royal house tried to further consolidate its position as the initiator and promoter of the mission by setting up a Mission Board in 1714 with headquarters in Copenhagen. This was especially meant to underscore the position of the royal house vis-à-vis the trading authorities in Tranquebar who were representatives of Danish trading companies. The Mission Board, supported by Pietistic circles and the Church, officially administered matters concerning Danish overseas missions. It had decision making powers in financial and personnel matters and it worked on behalf of and in accordance with the guidelines and decrees issued by the king. In 1777 the Mission Board had to hand over its powers to the Crown, but retained its function as the link-institution to the mission. Once the Danish Mission Society was established in 1821 (which also carried out missionary work in India from 1860) there were two parallel institutions till the Mission Board was disbanded in 1859.[87]

In the early years the missionaries lived and worked almost exclusively in Tranquebar. Each missionary received a sum of 200 Reichstaler annually, provided by the Danish king, and with which they had to manage not only their living expenses but also the work

[86] For the history of this institution see Brunner, Daniel, 1993, *Halle Pietists in England—Anthony William Boehm and the Society for Promoting Christian Knowledge*, Vandenhoeck & Ruprecht, Göttingen.

[87] Stampe, L., 1964, 'Missionskollegiet', *Nordisk Missionstidsktift*, 75: 225–41.

of the mission.[88] In 1709 the missionaries bought land in Porayar and Tilaili, a few kilometers away from Tranquebar and also on Danish territory. After the initial difficulties and impediments, which had arisen chiefly out of the conflict with the local Danish authorities, small branches of the mission were established in these places.[89] For organizational purposes the mission, after a period of time, was divided into different congregations: the Tranquebar station comprised of the 'Malabarian city congregation', the 'Portuguese congregation' and the 'Malabarian rural congregation'. The rural congregation, for its part, was made up of the congregations from several mission districts that were named, as a rule, after the capitals of these particular regions. In 1716 there were Christians to be taken care of in the following districts: Mayavaram, Thanjavur, Mahadevpattnam and Marava.[90] In 1728 three mission districts are mentioned,[91] from 1729 to 1733 there are four rural districts,[92] while from 1734 onwards there are six.[93] Around 1740 the congregation of the Marava region was divided into the congregations of Tiruppalatturai

[88] HB 1. Cont., 65, letter from F.J. Lütkens to A.H. Francke, Copenhagen, 19 March 1709.

[89] The population of Porayar, the largest town in the Tranquebar district, would have been, at this point of time, at least as large as that of Tranquebar. One source even mentions double the number of inhabitants. Cf.: HB 2. Cont., 108, letter from Plütschau, Gründler and Bövingh in Tranquebar to Copenhagen, 6 February 1710; HB 3. Cont., 112, Ziegenbalg replies to questions about the mission, Tranquebar 27 August 1709; AB 154, Ziegenbalg's letter to Francke, 30 August 1710; HB 2. Cont., 79, Gründler's letter of 7 December 1709; HB 6. Cont., 245, 276f.

[90] HB 33.Cont., 870.

[91] 'The Malabarian rural congregation in the kingdom of Thanjavur consists of 143 persons. They are divided into three small groups according to the three places where these new Christians live, namely Mayaburam (or Mairom) on the borders of Tranquebar; Madewipadtnam, in the interior towards the north; and the capital Thanjavur towards the west.' (translated from German), HB, preface to the 26th Cont.; Cf. also HB, preface to Cont. 27.

[92] HB, preface to Cont. 29. The following districts are mentioned: 'Mayapuram, Thanjavur, Madewipadtnam, Wedarniom—along with the bordering Marrawer district'.

[93] In 1734 six districts are named: 'Mayapuram, Thanjavur, Madewipatnam, Tirupalaturei, Madagacudi, Marrawer district'. Cf. HB, preface to Cont. 38; Cf. also Niekamp, Johann Lucas 1740, *Kurtzgefaßte Mißions-Geschichte Oder Historischer Auszug Der Evangelischen Mißions-Berichte aus Ostiniden [Teil I] von dem Jahr 1705 bis zu Ende des Jahres 1736*, in Verlegung des Waysen=Hauses, Halle, 496.

and Kumbakonam.[94] From 1743 onwards the missionaries always divided the rural congregation into five districts.[95]

Already in 1709 Ziegenbalg had wanted to undertake a journey into the territory of the raja of Thanjavur,[96] and in January 1710 Johann Ernst Gründler (1677–1720) announced the intention of the missionaries to approach the king of Thanjavur. They abandoned this idea since they could not finance the valuable presents to the ruler that apparently had to accompany such a petition.[97] After these first attempts by Ziegenbalg and Gründler to establish contact with

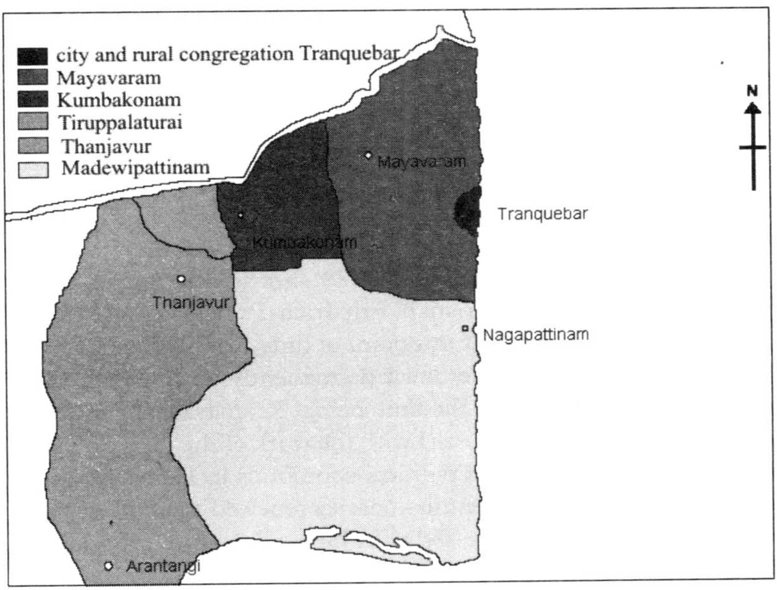

MAP 1.1 Division of the mission area in rural districts around 1745 (copyright: Kurt Liebau)

94 HB 58. Cont., 1513.

95 The names of these districts were: 'Mayapuram, Thanjavur, Madewipatnam, Tirpalaturei and Kumbakonam'. Cf. HB, supplement to Cont. 59, Cf. also NHB 2. St., 3 (for 1770); 11. St., 1407 (for 1773).

96 Lehmann, *Es begann in Tranquebar*, 214.

97 HB 2. Cont., 90, letter from Gründler, 6 January 1710; HB 2. Cont., 93f., letter from Gründler and Ziegenbalg, 16 January 1710.

Thanjavur had been dropped for various reasons, it was Benjamin Schultze who resumed these efforts in the 1720s. He was in close contact with Telungarasa (died 1736), a representative of the ruling family in Thanjavur (an uncle of the king), who visited him several times and corresponded with him.[98] Schultze himself, however, did not venture into Thanjavur territory since Serfoji I did not allow foreign missionaries to work in his kingdom.

The missionaries established initial contacts of a more permanent nature to the court of the Raja of Thanjavur indirectly through their catechist Rajanayakkan (1700–71) during the rule of Raja Tukkaji (ruled 1728–35). As an officer of the Thanjavur army Rajanayakkan had become personally acquainted with representatives of the Danish-Halle Mission in 1727 in Porayar during a military operation on Danish territory and had offered to work for the mission in Thanjavur. After initial doubts the missionaries decided to use this contact; they appointed Rajanayakkan as catechist and allowed him to proselytize in their name in the Thanjavur region. Rajanayakkan set up a school there and, for over 20 years, he was the 'vanguard' of the Tranquebar mission. In July 1728, shortly after Rajanayakkan had begun his work, Christian Friedrich Pressier (1697–1738) travelled to Thanjavur.[99] At this point of time, however, a European missionary could not settle down permanently on the territory of the raja of Thanjavur. For the time being, Rajanayakkan and other co-workers had to be entrusted with the work of the mission in this region. Under the changed political conditions in Thanjavur at the beginning of the 1750s the missionaries renewed their attempts to work there, this time successfully. In July and August 1753 Johann Christian Wiedebrock (1713–67) preached publicly for the first time in the city of Thanjavur.[100] With the start of missionary work in Thanjavur, outside the territory of the Danish Company, the mission

[98] Lehmann, *Es begann in Tranquebar*, 214, 239.

[99] Pressier went on Telungarasa's invitation. HB 26. Cont., 129f.

[100] HB 80. Cont., 1195–1208, Wiedebrock's travel diary, July-August 1753.

[101] Krieger, *Kaufleute, Seeräuber, Diplomaten*, 133. In 1756 the Danes occupied a village in the territory of the Raja of Thanjavur and set up positions of defense there, but they were driven away by the Raja's troops who, in turn, began a counter attack on Danish property. All this also made it more difficult for the mission to get permission to work in the Raja's territory.

was now directly involved in political events in the region. At the same time, the Danes intensified their efforts at expansion, since it became increasingly clear to them that they would have to expand their territory if they wanted to remain players in the power equations in South India. This led in the 1750s to — sometimes military conflicts between the Danes and the Raja of Thanjavur.[101]

Whereas the efforts to get permission for missionary work in the territory of the Raja of Thanjavur did not meet with any success for a long time, the work in the regions controlled by the British was very intensive. In 1717 Ziegenbalg and Gründler reported on their first activities in Madras and Cuddalore in co-operation with the SPCK.[102] Missionary work in Cuddalore began with the decision of the British authorities to set up a so-called charity school there, and they approached the Danish missionaries for schoolteachers.[103] Benjamin Schultze became the first missionary who officially went into the service of the SPCK. Others followed. Despite the formal transfer to another mission society, these missionaries remained in close contact with the Tranquebar Mission and the Francke Foundations. It was only in 1813 that the charter of the English East India Company allowed English mission societies to work in India. Till this point of time the SPCK supported other foreign mission societies in India or used their employees for concrete tasks.[104] In this way it could carry out its own projects, especially in the sphere of education.

While initially, only several schools were run in co-operation with the SPCK, with Schultze's entry into SPCK 1728 the picture began to change. From 1737, Johann Anton Sartorius (1704–38) and Johann Ernst Geister (in India: 1732–46, died: 1750) worked as missionaries for the British in Cuddalore. Since 1742 Johann Philipp Fabricius had also been working for the British, continuing the work done by Benjamin Schultze for the SPCK in Madras from

[102] HB 14. Cont., 164, letter from Ziegenbalg and Gründler, 5 December 1718.

[103] HB 14. Cont., 156, letter from Ziegenbalg and Gründler to Francke, 22 February 1718.

[104] 'The English Society for the Promotion of Christian Knowledge has let it be known that it would be interested in having co-workers, who have been trained for missionary work in Tranquebar and who could be spared, to set up good schools in the English territories in East India.' (translated from German), HB 14. Cont., 152.

1728 to 1742. A close co-operation began in the 1760s between Christian Friedrich Schwartz and the SPCK. The consolidation of the British position in South India in the 1760s was accompanied by a new surge in missionary activity. In 1768 Schwartz, along with the mission station he had established in Tiruchirappalli since 1762, was placed under the SPCK. The initiative for missionary work in Tiruchirappalli had emanated from Tranquebar. In the efforts to expand the regional base of the mission into the interior of the country and into regions south of Tranquebar, this place proved to be favourable.[105] In concurrence with the missionaries in Tranquebar, Schwartz, from the beginning, also worked for the British in Tiruchirappalli. Out of a feeling 'of gratitude and protection'[106] he did not want to refuse their requests, especially with regard to the spiritual care of soldiers in the British garrison. Schwartz was afraid that the SPCK would take over his identity completely and in several letters to the Mission Board he repeatedly referred to the fact that he still wanted to be considered a Danish missionary and be regularly relieved by a colleague from Tranquebar, or, indeed, return to Tranquebar entirely.[107] However, the Mission Board and the SPCK together came to a different decision: Schwartz was to be taken over by the SPCK; he was to be permanently stationed in Tiruchirappalli without being relieved, since he was the only missionary suitable for this post on account of his knowledge of English.[108] Schwartz acted judiciously, but he was dissatisfied and, even in 1771, three years after the takeover, he requested the

[105] In 1761, when Schwartz wished to stay on longer in Tiruchirappalli while his companions travelled on, no one had thought of establishing a permanent station here. HB 97. Cont., 124.

[106] RA Miskolark 9f, letter from Ch. F. Schwartz to the Mission Board, Tiruchirappalli, 10 July 1766.

[107] RA Miskolark 9f, letter from Ch. F. Schwartz to the Mission Board, Tiruchirappalli, 17 December 1766.

[108] RA Miskolark 9f, letters from Ch. F. Schwartz to the Mission Board, Tiruchirappalli, 26 October 1768 and 31 March 1768. In a letter from the Mission Board to all the missionaries in Tranquebar 24 November 1768, the decision is stated to be left to Schwartz. In the interim period his salary would be paid in equal parts by the Mission Board in Copenhagen and the SPCK in London. RA Miskolark 4, 1765–89.

Mission Board to still consider him a member of the Royal Danish Mission.[109]

In 1767 Christian Wilhelm Gericke (1742–1803) accepted an appointment by the English mission society in Cuddalore where he initially worked with Johann Zacharias Kiernander (1710–99) and Georg Heinrich Conrad Hüttemann (1728–81). From 1788 onwards Gericke worked in Vepery (Madras). Although the transfer to the SPCK meant that these missionaries were formally not a part of the Tranquebar mission of the Danish royal house and that they were now financed by the British, the close link between the stations of the Tranquebar Mission and the so-called English stations was always maintained. After 30 years of work as a Royal Danish missionary Johann Peter Rottler (1749–1836) entered the services of the SPCK in 1806 with the permission of the Mission Board.[110] While new missionaries (Europeans) were increasingly being appointed by the SPCK for the English stations, the Indian "national workers" were gaining importance in Tranquebar. By the beginning of the nineteenth century there were hardly any missionaries being sent out directly to Tranquebar.[111]

Although the last quarter of the eighteenth century already witnessed a decline of missionary work, with the beginning of the nineteenth century the Tranquebar Mission lost its standing even more. The political conditions in Europe and the effects of the Napoleonic wars on Germany led to a decrease in the amount of financial support to the mission from its well-wishers. Young people were now also less interested in going to India and, therefore, new missionaries could not be recruited on a continuous basis. When

[109] RA Miskolark 9f, letter from Ch. F. Schwartz to the Mission Board, Tiruchirappalli, 12 October 1771. The Mission Board welcomed the missionary's intention not to cut himself off entirely from the Danish mission. RA Miskolark 4, 1765–1789. Letter from the Mission Board to Ch. F. Schwartz, 29 October 1770.

[110] RA Miskolark 9i, letter from J.P. Rottler to the Mission Board, 11 October 1806.

[111] Ernst Philipp Heinrich Stegmann (1753–after 1808, sent out: 1796), Johann Daniel Mentel (sent out: 1780) and Lambert Christian Früchtenicht (1772–around 1806, sent out: 1798) returned to Europe for various reasons after a brief period in India. Peter Rubeck Hagelund (1756–88, sent out: 1785) and Lorentz Friedrich Rulfsen (1753–80, sent out: 1780) died shortly after their arrival in India.

the Danish factory was shifted from Tranquebar to Serampore in 1799 Danish ships did not berth very often in Tranquebar.[112] When Denmark entered the Napoleonic wars, Danish trade was further weakened and Danish territories around Tranquebar were occupied by British troops in 1801/02 and between 1808 and 1815. The maritime link between Tranquebar and Denmark was interrupted.[113] Officially, the Tranquebar Mission existed till the sale of the settlement in Tranquebar to the British in 1845. In 1843 already, the Danes had dissolved their East India Trading Company and, since the end of the 1830s there had been no Royal Danish Missionaries in Tranquebar.[114]

INTERCULTURAL ENCOUNTER AND PERCEPTIONS OF THE 'OTHER'

Against the backdrop of these historical conditions the daily encounters between the missionaries and the local population were characterized by their perceptions and efforts towards a reciprocal understanding, but also by flaws, conflicts and misunderstandings. Like the varying degrees of preparation for the confrontation with representatives of an alien religion and culture, the motives for the mutual association and the expectations from the encounter were also different.

At the beginning of the eighteenth century European merchants, civil servants, officers or missionaries were a common sight in South Indian port cities. While the population in the interior land, at that point of time, seldom had anything to do with Europeans, in the port cities or in places with European settlements different forms of encounter and co-operation had developed. For the Tamils, the Europeans were political partners, trade partners, commissioning principals or employers, or simply adventurers and all of them needed help from representatives of the local population. They were the 'Blancs'.[115] The conduct of the Europeans also determined how

[112] NHB 57. St., 781.

[113] Cf. Krieger, *Kaufleute, Seeräuber und Diplomaten*, 200.

[114] The last missionary, August Friedrich Cämmerer, died in 1837.

[115] The term 'Blancs' refers to the skin-colour of the Europeans. It was probably coined by the missionaries themselves as the German equivalent for the derogatory term used by the Tamils in imitation of the word 'Franks': 'Parengikarer, Parengi'

they were perceived by the local population. This image, developed by a section of the Tamilians, arose, first and foremost, out of encounters in their own society. Unfortunately, there is a great deal of conjecture and speculation involved in a reconstruction of this image of the Other since written records of the relationship between the two groups stem either from Europeans or from those Tamilians who served with the Europeans and, therefore, displayed an attitude of loyalty.[116]

One of the rare sources from the context of the Tranquebar Mission which can give today's readers an idea of how the Tamils perceived the Europeans is a correspondence carried out with the Tamilians by Bartholomäus Ziegenbalg and Johann Ernst Gründler from 1712 to 1714. Six years after beginning work in South India the missionaries sought a dialogue with the local society outside the framework of the mission. The aim of this exchange of thoughts was to find out more about the local society and about the attitudes of South Indians to religion, philosophy and to the Europeans in general. From the numerous replies that the missionaries received 99 letters were published in the mission reports under the title 'Malabarian Correspondence'.[117] In this unique dialogue Tamils

(Tamil: paraṉ—stranger, foreigner). Cf., among others, HB 97. Cont., 99; 98. Cont., 297, footnote.

[116] One of the authentic testimonials of the period is the diary of the Hindu Ananda Ranga Pillai (1709–61), son of a merchant-family and *dubash* of the French governors Joseph François Dupleix (1697–1763) and Georges Duval de Leyrit (governor 1754–58). Pillai's father and other family members had also served the French. From 1736 to 1761 Ananda Ranga Pillai maintained a private diary about his life as an employee of the French. His notes are a mix of observations and experiences regarding both his private life as well as his life in politics. He wrote about the life of Europeans in India, about corruption and intrigues, but also about political conditions as someone close to the French, dependent on them, but also as someone important to them. Cf. Pillai, Ananda Ranga, 1985, *The Private Diary of Ananda Ranga Pillai: a record of matters political, historical, social and personal from 1736 to 1761*, Vol. I., (Madras, 1904), Asian Educational Services, New Delhi.

[117] The first part of the 'Malabarian Correspondence' appeared in the 7th Continuation of the Halle Reports in 1714 and was announced with the additional remark: '[...] wherein the outer and the inner forms of their heathenism/along with their customs, ceremonies and sciences/and also the aversion to or the inclination for Christianity among them is discovered and described in great detail.' (translated from German), HB 7. Cont., 337–504, here: excerpt from the preface. The second part

got a chance to speak and also to express their criticism of their European contemporaries:

> We despise Christianity because the Christians slaughter and eat cows/because they do not wash themselves after evacuating their bowels/because they imbibe strong alcoholic drinks/and because, when someone dies, they do not perform any ceremonies to help the soul of the dead reach the place of salvation/also because they do not have any joyous marriage ceremonies. As for the rest, as far as the law of the Christians is concerned, it cannot be rejected. The Christians have a holy law, but no ceremonies. Our law is not only holy, but it also has ceremonies.[118]

This was the reply given by a Tamil correspondent to the question: 'What do the Malabarians think of the Christian religion and its laws?' The missionaries were horrified about the remarks made by their Tamilian correspondent about the life of Europeans in India; the image that the Tamilians had of Europeans was, after all, important for the success of missionary work.

In the second part of the correspondence, which was published in the Eleventh Continuation of the Halle Reports in 1717, the answer to the question about the most common sins of the Europeans in South India was even more sobering:

> As concerns what we Malabarians consider to be the greatest sins of Europeans living here, we must state that we are aware that they have their Ten Commandments and other teachings. However, no one follows these teachings in daily life. In addition, they drink so much as to lose their senses and lie around and talk like foolish people. Those who were best of friends begin to hate each other and beat each other up. They fight among themselves in such a horrid way that they even kill one another. While talking they frequently swear by god and by their souls. They fornicate, they gamble, and when they gamble they get into fights where one

appeared in the 11. Continuation; A selection of letters from Tamilians was published again in 1998. Cf. Gründler, *Die Malabarische Korrespondenz*.

[118] HB, 7. Cont., 340–42. First Letter of the Malabarian Correspondence. The Second Question. 'What do the Malabarians think of the Christian religion and its laws?' (translated from German).

> kills the other. They slaughter cows and eat their flesh. These are the sins that the Malabarians observe among the Blancs. They talk about it among themselves and also say that the Blancs are evil. They do nothing for travellers and pilgrims and do not perform any good deeds. Although they possess great wealth they do not give alms or use the wealth for good works. The rich are only concerned about living and eating well, about wearing nice clothes and decorating their houses; they do not help anyone, nor are they concerned about their poor neighbour. This is why we say that these are the greatest sins of the Europeans in East India. This is what I was asked to say.[119]

On a closer look it becomes clear that it was mainly superficialities and a hitherto unknown way of life that aroused the ire of the Tamilians and led to their rejection of the Europeans. The observers made a distinction between Christian teachings as the basis of the European way of life and the application of these teachings by the Europeans living in India. While the Christian teachings as such were not attacked, the criticism was directed all the more against those who represented these teachings. There was no distinction made between Europeans as representatives of Christianity and Europeans as representatives of particular nations. For the Tamilians the Europeans were Christians regardless of where they came from and what their function in India was.

This was indeed an unfavourable point of departure for the missionaries in Tranquebar who had been raised in the devoutness and strict self-discipline of Pietism and who saw themselves in a different light. They wanted to transmit a new faith which—to their minds—would, in the long run, require the observance of different rules of life and moral norms. For this, they had to be able to project themselves as models. Those Tamilians, however, who had dealt with Europeans, had already developed an ambivalent attitude towards them. Despite the fact that they worked with Europeans, many Tamilians were distrustful of and skeptical about them, sometimes to the point of rejection.

[119] HB 11. Cont., 942–45. The Second Part of the Malabarian Correspondence. The 34th Letter. 'What sins do the Malabarians perceive among the Blancs?' (translated from German).

MOTIVATION AND AIMS OF THE MISSIONARIES

The attitude of Christian missionaries to the country and to the people in the mission region differed, at least in theory, from the concerns of those who came to India as merchants, adventurers or diplomats. Despite the differences in the latter group regarding expectations and motivation, they were linked by the general striving for profit and advantages. The concern of the Christian missionaries consisted in bringing the 'true faith' to a country whose people, according to them, urgently needed this new faith. Ultimately, this was meant to overcome the 'condition of a lack of faith and a lack of morality' in which these 'heathens' lived. In order to achieve this goal they looked for possible ways of dealing with the religion of these people. The willingness to tolerate this religion temporarily did not change the fact that Christian missionaries of all confessions proceeded from the understanding that the non-Christian religion would finally have to be overcome.

Christian missionary efforts in India, undertaken by Europeans since the sixteenth century, have to be viewed in connection with the relevant historical expansion efforts of the European country concerned. Whereas in the sixteenth and seventeenth centuries the Portuguese and the Dutch dominated and pushed missionary work, the eighteenth century saw the French and the British enter the political stage in India. The latter, however, did not promote missionary work on a large scale initially. The political decline of Catholic powers in Europe and the ban on the Jesuits in 1773 led to a temporary decline in Catholic missionary work on a global scale.[120] With few exceptions, the Evangelical Church reacted slowly to these developments. It was only in the nineteenth century that it established larger mission societies that were neither merely partners of secular European powers nor their firm opponents.[121]

In order to understand why a young man in the eighteenth century would pledge his life to missionary service in India knowing

[120] Obst, *Missionsberichte aus Indien*; Gründer, *Welteroberung und Christentum*, 291.

[121] On the ambivalent role of Christian missions see, among others, Sanneh, Lamin, 1991, 'The Yogi and the Commissar: Christian Missions and the New World Order in Africa', in Wade Clark Roof (ed.), *World Order and Religion*, 173–92, State University of New York Press, New York.

that he would probably never return to Europe, we would have to look at the religious and ideological background of missionary work. In the case of the Tranquebar Mission the Pietistic circles in Halle initially played a crucial role in influencing those who were sent out as missionaries. As a part of the Archbishopric of Magdeburg, Halle fell in 1680 to the Electorate of Brandenburg-Prussia under the terms of the Peace of Westphalia. Along with efforts to expand their power and consolidate their rule by gaining and conquering new territories, the then Elector, Friedrich Wilhelm (ruled: 1640–88), and his successors displayed a pronounced interest in culture, education and science. In 1694, during the rule of Friedrich III (Elector since 1688; King of Prussia from 1701–13), the University of Halle was established as a rival institution to the University of Leipzig, which was controlled by conservative forces. Driven out of Leipzig, important scholars like Christian Thomasius (1655–1728) and August Hermann Francke had come to Halle and this contributed to the fact that for some decades the University of Halle was at the forefront of academic developments in German universities. With Thomasius and the philosopher Christian Wolff (1679–1754) the university became an important centre of early and high-Enlightenment and, within a short span of time, it became one of the greatest German Protestant universities.[122]

At the same time, the religious tolerance of the rulers of Brandenburg-Prussia allowed Halle to become an important centre of Pietism. German Pietism, which in its early phase should be viewed in close connection with the Enlightenment, was a heterogeneous movement within the Protestant Church and was especially important in the first half of the eighteenth century. One of the most important representatives of this movement was the university professor in Halle, August Hermann Francke. Influenced by and partly in co-operation with Philipp Jakob Spener (1635–1705) and Joachim Lange (1670–1744) Francke not only introduced innovations in the field of Bible studies, but also actively developed

[122] Brieger, Johann Georg, 1788, *Histcrisch-topographische Beschreibung der Stadt Halle im Magdeburgischen,* im Verlag und zum Besten der evangelischen Schulanstalt, Grottkau, (Reprint, Halle 1990), 150. Cf. Also Hinske, Norbert, 1989, *Zentren der Aufklärung. Vol I, Halle: Aufklärung und Pietismus*, Schneider, Heidelberg (=Wolfenbüttler Studien zur Aufklärung, Vol. 15).

the idea of a Protestant mission among the 'heathens'. Like Spener, Francke propagated the idea of Christian thought and action, where individual piety was combined with an active engagement in the world. According to Spener this could not be achieved through the precepts of the Church but through the religious conviction of the individual. The internal and emotional coming to terms with oneself and one's personal relationship to God along with a constant questioning of one's place on earth were meant to decisively influence the life of a Pietist.[123]

In 1695, in Glaucha near Halle, the pastor of Glaucha and professor of Oriental languages of the newly established university, August Hermann Francke, laid the foundation stone for what would be called after him the Francke Foundations.[124] Francke first opened a school for the poor, which was followed later by an orphan-house and other teaching establishments in which he sought to realize his pedagogic aims based on the idea of a new human being characterized by Pietistic devoutness. Francke's plans as an educator and as an entrepreneur with world-wide contacts in trade and science found the approval of the state of Brandenburg-Prussia, and this was expressed in the form of trade licenses, special rights of pre-emption, tax exemptions and donations of money.[125] Francke's contacts with the 'soldier king', Friedrich Wilhelm I (ruled: 1713–40) were more than the formal encounters between

[123] Cf. Denzler, Georg and Carl Anderson, 1993, *Wörterbuch der Kirchengeschichte*, Kösel, München, 469–72.

[124] Fries, Wilhelm, 1913, *Die Stiftungen August Hermann Franckes*, Waisenhaus, Halle, 8.

[125] There are different opinions about this 'proximity to the state' from a contemporary perspective. Carl Hinrichs speaks of a 'functional alliance' and he reiterates, in favour of Halle Pietism: 'The fact that Pietism was grateful for state protection does not mean that in its deepest religious being it did not believe in universal goals that went far beyond the intentions of the state.' (translated from German), Hinrichs, *Preußentum und Pietismus*, 18. Peter Schicketanz is more critical: 'In the course of these years Halle Pietism lost its ecumenical breadth to a growing effectiveness in Brandenburg-Prussia. The Francke Foundations became, more or less against the wishes of its founders, a Prussian educational institution for the Church and school, for orphanages and the military. Pietistic clergy were inducted in influential positions.' (translated from German), Schicketanz, Peter, 1972, *Der Briefwechsel Carl Hildebrand von Cansteins mit August Hermann Francke*, DeGruyter, Berlin (= Texte zur Geschichte des Pietismus III, 1).

a ruler and an important pedagogue and entrepreneur. The king was aware of the role of Francke's institutions and the value of his pedagogic abilities, and he tried to use this by asking Francke to train field-clergy for the army. He later offered him the post of director of the newly established military orphanage in Potsdam. Francke, concerned about pragmatic compromises between his ideals and the politics of the 'soldier king', trained young people in his institutions who later became field-clergymen; however, he declined the offer of the post in Potsdam.[126]

Although it did not exist for very long, the Collegium Orientale Theologicum, established in 1702 in Halle, was important for defining Francke's global plans and activities. The work of its members (primarily professors of the university at Halle) in the area of Bible studies was sought to be strengthened through a thorough knowledge of languages, both with regard to Hebrew as well as other Oriental languages. Along with the so-called Bible languages a series of other languages were included in the work of the collegium (among others also Polish and Russian). Salomon Negri (1670–1729) from Damascus taught Arabic at the Collegium Orientale. The practical work of the collegium consisted in the study of different languages, the systematic organization of language teaching for a university course in theology as well as the preparation of Bible editions in different languages. The collegium was most active between 1702 and 1705, but it existed officially till 1720.[127] After Francke's death in 1727 Johann Heinrich Callenberg (1694–1760) set up the Institutum Judaicum et Muhammedicum in 1728 in Halle, whose primary goal was the Protestant mission among the Jews, but which also extended its activities to the

[126] For this relationship see Schnitter, Helmut (ed.), 1994, *Gestalten um den Soldatenkönig: Biographische Skizzen*, Vol. I., Preußischer Militär-Verlag, Reutlingen, 144–58. Later rulers of Prussia were also well disposed towards the Francke Foundations and were willing to support it in times of crisis. Thus, Friedrich Wilhelm III (ruled: 1797–1840) arranged for regular donations of money to the Foundations. Cf. Baltzer, Justus (ed.), 1906, *August Hermann Francke*, Velhagen und Klasing, Bielefeld, Leipzig, XXVII.

[127] For the history of the Collegium Orientale see Podczeck, Otto, 1968, 'Die Arbeit am Alten Testament in Halle zur Zeit des Pietismus. Das Collegium Orientale theologicum A.H. Franckes', *WZ*, VII, *Gesellschafts—und Sprachwissenschaftliche Reihe*, Heft 5: 1059–78.

Muslims. Callenberg, who had studied in Halle since 1715 and had been decisively influenced by A.H. Francke, had learnt Arabic from Salomon Negri.[128]

Like August Hermann Francke who was a professor of Oriental languages at the university, the later directors of the Halle Orphan-House were also connected with the local university.[129] The Orphan-House maintained a close contact with the university, not only because its directors were generally also professors there, but also because students of the university worked as teachers in the Orphan-House and its establishments. From 1696 till 1749, 3788 students worked in the Foundations.[130] They taught according to the plans and instructions of the directors and also supervised groups of 10–30, sometimes more, children. Through this work as preceptors they earned some money while studying.[131] These contacts were useful for finding new missionary candidates. More than half the missionaries sent out had studied for some time in Halle or had been teachers either at the royal preparatory school or at one of the other schools in the Francke Foundations.[132] Some missionaries had studied

[128] Cf. Aring, Paul Gerhard, 1987, *Christen und Juden heute—und die 'Judenmission'? Geschichte und Theologie protestantischer Judenmission in Deutschland, dargestellt und untersucht am Beispiel des Protestantismus im mittleren Deutschland*, Haag und Herchen, Frankfurt am Main, 51.

[129] Francke's son, Gotthilf August Francke (1696–1769) was in the theological faculty of the university, from 1725 he was professor extraordinarius, from 1727 a full professor of theology and from 1767 a consistorial councilor. Gottlieb Anastasius Freylinghausen (1719–85) was professor extraordinarius of theology from 1753 and, from 1771 full professor of theology. Johann Ludwig Schulze (1734–99) became professor of philosophy in 1760, in 1765 professor of oriental languages and in 1769 full professor of theology. August Hermann Niemeyer (1754–1828) became professor extraordinarius for theology in 1779; in 1784 he was made full professor and inspector of the royal preparatory school. Brieger, *Historisch-topographische Beschreibung der Stadt Halle*, 129–32.

[130] Brieger, *Historisch-topographische Beschreibung der Stadt Halle*, 175.

[131] Müller-Bahlke, Thomas, 2000, 'Kinderleben in den Glauchaer Anstalten zu Franckes Zeiten. Entsagung auf Teufel komm raus?' in Penelope Willard (ed.), *Die Franckeschen Stiftungen zu Halle im Jahre 2000*, 18–30, Verlag der Franckeschen Stiftungen, Halle.

[132] Those who had studied in Halle were: Johann Christian Breithaupt (1719–82), August Friedrich Cämmerer (1767–1837), Nicolaus Dal (1690–1747), Petrus Dame (1731–1766), Johann Christmann H. Diemer (1745–92), Johann Philipp Fabricius (1711–91), Ernst August Georg Falcke (1784–1824), Johann Ernst Geister (died 1750), Christian Wilhelm Gericke (1743–1803), Johann Wilhelm Gerlach (1738–91),

in Leipzig,[133] Jena,[134] Copenhagen,[135] Marburg,[136] Tübingen[137] Göttingen,[138] Kiel,[139] Gießen,[140] Uppsala,[141] Strasbourg in the Alsace[142] and Wittenberg.[143] As a rule they had studied theology, and till the middle of the eighteenth century this was almost always the case. In the second half of the century subjects like physics, mathematics, medicine and other natural sciences also came up. Although a Seminarium Scholasticum for training missionaries had existed in Copenhagen since 1716, the missionaries for India still came from German religious circles, while those who trained at the Danish seminary were generally sent to the Danish mission in Greenland.[144]

The first missionaries trained in Halle had been brought up in a strict Pietistic tradition, or they had reached a deeply internalized Pietistic feeling through a subjective experience of edification.

Johann Ernst Gründler (1677–1720), Christlieb Augustin Jacobi (1791–1814), Joseph Daniel Jänicke (1759–1800), Christoph Samuel John (1746–1813), Jacob Klein (1721–90), Johann Zacharias Kiernander (1710–99), Friedrich Wilhelm Leidemann (1743–74), Wilhelm Jacob Müller (1734–71), Gottfried Wilhelm Obuch (1707–47), David Poltzenhagen (1726–56), Christian Friedrich Pressier (1697–1738), Samuel Gottlieb Richtsteig (1700–35), Wilhelm Tobias Ringeltaube (1770–1816), Johann Anton Sartorius (1704–1738), Benjamin Schultze (1689–1760), Christian Friedrich Schwartz (1726–98), Christoph Theodosius Walther (1699–1741), Johann Christian Wiedebrock (1713–67), Andreas Worm (1704–35), Daniel Zeglin (1716–80), Bartholomäus Ziegenbalg (1682–1719).

[133] Johann Ernst Gründler, Immanuel Gottfried Holzberg (1770–1824), Christlieb Augustin Jacobi, Christian Pohle (1744–1818), Johann Georg Philipp Sperschneider (1794—after 1846).

[134] Nicolaus Dal, Johann Ernst Geister, Johann Wilhelm Gerlach, Christian Friedrich Pressier, Johann Georg Philipp Sperschneider, Andreas Worm.

[135] Lauritz Peter Haubroe (1791–1830), Ole Maderup (1711–76), David Rosen (1791–1857), Lorenz Friedrich Rulfsen (1753–80), Peter Mandrup Due Wissing (born 1799).

[136] Ernst Philipp Heinrich Stegmann (1773–after 1808).

[137] Ernst August Georg Falcke, Johann Jacob Schöllkopf (1748–77).

[138] Ernst August Georg Falcke, Christoph Heinrich Horst (1761–1810).

[139] Johann Georg Bövingh (1676–1723), Lambert Christian Früchtenicht (1772–after 1806).

[140] Johann Philipp Fabricius.

[141] Johann Zacharias Kiernander.

[142] Johann Daniel Mentel (1755–96), Johann Peter Rottler (1749–1836).

[143] Johann Ernst Gründler, Carl Wilhelm Pätzold (1764–1817).

[144] Stampe, 'Missionskollegiet'.

As young thinking and believing Pietists they strove to live their lives in harmony with the higher values in which they believed, and in missionary work they saw the possibility of being true to their beliefs. It was common for the early workers of the Danish-English-Halle Mission to have had a theological-philological training. Although there was no institution in the Halle Orphan-House to directly train missionaries,[145] the fact that many who became missionaries had studied at the University of Halle and had worked in one of the schools of the Foundations shows that close links existed here.

The Danish royal house and the Mission Board in Copenhagen, the Francke Foundations in Halle and the Society for Promoting Christian Knowledge in London were the institutions that coordinated missionary work out of Europe and supported it both materially and spiritually. In addition, during the existence of the Danish-English-Halle Mission innumerable personal contacts between missionaries, scholars and patrons of the mission were established globally. Even if many of these arose from personal contacts and links and did not always lead to long-term institutionalized contacts, they contributed to the international networking of the organization. By using the transport and communication possibilities of the eighteenth century the missionaries tried, through such networks, to help in the worldwide spread of Christianity.

The missionaries sent out in the second half of the eighteenth century were often more influenced by the growing spirit of rationalism and enlightenment than by Pietism, which was steadily becoming weaker. Among other things, this meant that the frame of reference of religion and language was increasingly supplemented by the frame of reference of research and natural sciences, with which significantly more missionaries identified, although the quality and extent of this identification varied. Arno Lehmann regrets this development and sees it as a reason for the decline of the mission:

[145] The *East India Mission Institute* ('Ostindische Missionsanstalt') in the Francke Foundations, the central link between the Foundations and the India-mission, was primarily responsible for the correspondence with the missionaries, for collecting, managing and distributing money received as donations and also for preparing, publishing and distributing the mission reports and other religious texts of edification.

> [...] in Germany rationalism and enlightenment had appeared. It was a systematic attempt to make the views of natural man prevail upon the belief in revelation and Christian ethics, and to help these views to dominate. [...] A belief based on reason was meant to replace Christian faith. Pure reason was all that was supposed to matter. Even the universities were saturated with this spirit. Miracles were explained rationally. [...] Once the fire of Pietism died out, and the undoubtedly pious men in Halle lost their first love, the mission also had to suffer.[146]

The image of India among the missionaries varied. The first missionaries, Ziegenbalg and Plütschau, had believed, till shortly before their departure that they were sent to Africa and for this reason alone they could not prepare themselves for India. The groups that followed them in 1709 and 1719, however, had the possibility of familiarizing themselves with their place of work through the letters and diaries of their predecessors. For some of the later missionaries the published mission reports played a decisive role in their desire to enter missionary service. The growing academic development in Germany, for its part, made it possible to give these candidates an intensive introduction to the country. The ideas of the missionaries about Indian society were those of external observers from a foreign country, whose initial reactions to the new society could range from scepticism and rejection to admiration. The image of India among the Protestant missionaries in the eighteenth century was not an image created by self-centered colonial masters. Coming from different educational backgrounds many of them discarded the stance of distanced European observers and became mediators between Europe and India. Their European education was gradually expanded through knowledge and experience gained from the mission region. Alongside this growth in knowledge there was a noticeable change in the attitude of some missionaries to Indians as 'heathens', which became apparent in their manner of reporting. Their engagement with languages, religions and traditions could lead them to rethink their original opinions and, sometimes, to correct them.

A development of this kind can be seen very clearly in the

[146] Lehmann, *Es begann in Tranquebar*, 293f. (translated from German).

personality of the first missionary, Ziegenbalg. In 1706 he proudly wrote to August Hermann Francke:

> Yesterday we went for a walk into the interior and came upon a temple in which the wife of their great god Isparae (*isvara-siva*) is worshipped as a goddess; around the statue of this goddess there were porcelain figures of many gods. Full of divine zeal we knocked some down and broke the heads of others to show the poor people that these are only powerless and unworthy idols.[147]

A few years later the same missionary wrote the Genealogy of the Malabarian Gods and Malabarian Heathenism, which not only display a vast knowledge of local society but which are also marked by a high degree of respect for Indian thought and culture.[148]

If an attentive reader follows the diaries of individual missionaries over several years, he/she will notice the internal process of dealing with the mandate of the Christian mission, on the one hand, and the growing understanding for South Indian reality, on the other. In a letter of 2 February 1806 the missionary Daniel Schreyvogel (1777–1840) described this changed attitude based on experience and growth of knowledge in the following manner: 'Some of their customs initially seemed to me to be strange and foolish, but when I studied the origins of these customs more closely I found that there are good reasons for them.'[149]

Concessions in thought and changes in opinions about Indian society always operated, however, within the basic and immovable frame of reference of the superiority of Christianity. This, however, did not necessarily mean the superiority of a European way of life. The early German missionaries in South India, especially, saw their task as having to convince Indians about the necessity and the rightness of the Christian faith, but they did not necessarily combine this goal with the attempt to bring about changes in Indian society as a whole. Rather, in many ways, they came closer to local habits, sometimes secretly or unconsciously, as for example with regard to dress and food. Since the meals were, in any case, prepared by

[147] AB 45, (translated from German).

[148] Germann, *Genealogie der malabarischen Götter*.

[149] RA Miskolark 9i, letter from Daniel Schreyvogel, 2 February 1806.

local cooks, the compromise with food had to be made from the beginning. As far as dress is concerned, some missionaries recognized the advantages of traditional South Indian dress for the climatic conditions there, but in public they attached great importance to a European exterior. Missionaries who came out in public dressed like Indians were also likely to arouse the displeasure of the mission directors and of the Europeans living in India.[150]

Candidates for the mission generally did not apply for the job but were selected and recruited by those responsible for the mission, i.e. the Mission Board in Copenhagen or the Society for Promoting Christian Knowledge.

> The Mission Board in Copenhagen enacted by His Royal Majesty of Denmark and Norway is entirely responsible for the Royal Danish Mission in Tranquebar. The missionaries are voted for and accepted by it, it manages the Royal Fund graciously set up to pay the salaries of the missionaries who receive all their orders and instructions from this Board in the name of their royal employer. Ever since the praiseworthy Society for Promoting Christian Knowledge in England took some missionaries into their service and set up English missions, these workers in the English missions are under the orders of this pious society, view it as their employer and also receive their salaries from it.[151]

In 1780 it is said: 'The names of both the Danish and the English missionaries are generally proposed by the director of the Halle Orphan-House who has been given this mandate by the Mission

[150] Benjamin Schultze, who attempted to walk through Tranquebar in Indian clothes, was subjected to so much pressure that he was forced to conform to the 'norm' again. Nørgaard, *Mission und Obrigkeit*, 134f.; Christian Friedrich Pressier admitted in a letter 'to two of his former colleagues in Halle' in 1728: 'It is only in December that one can wear clothes made of European fabric; at other times it would be the greatest torture. We wear ordinary black summer or silk clothes if Chinese ships bring something. Since, at present, here outside Tranquebar I have no dealings with Europeans, I dress in white in the Indian manner at home and when I go out, which is very comfortable. Since I don't need shoes and socks, but wear slippers, I can walk unhampered through water like the other Indians. Otherwise one has to always have two servants to carry you across; however, when I go into town, namely on Fridays and Sundays, I go in black European clothes.' (translated from German), HB 27. Cont., 223.

[151] HB, preface to Continuation 107, (translated from German).

Board in Copenhagen and the English Society for Promoting Christian Knowledge.'[152]

Piety, steadfastness and endurance were important criteria for the selection and confirmation of missionaries. On 20 January 1784 Christoph Samuel John sent a memo (*Pro Memoria*) to Copenhagen in which he developed guidelines and criteria for the future selection of missionaries.[153] An important precondition for missionary work was, according to him: '[...] age, which should not be too close to the thirties or even beyond it'.[154] Younger people would not only find it easier to learn Tamil, but adapting to the climatic conditions in South India would also not be as difficult. As far as other things were concerned, a missionary should, according to him, possess 'a cheerful but mature temperament, be healthy and, particularly, have a good chest and voice'.[155] The ability and the willingness to communicate as well as a good physical constitution were necessary. People prone to depression would scarcely be able to fulfill the tasks required of a missionary in a foreign country. Along with physical and character traits John considered it extremely important to test the knowledge of a future missionary.[156]

Under the conditions of the eighteenth century the decision to go out and 'work among the heathens' was, in effect, a decision for a lifetime, since it was safe to assume that they would never be able to return to Europe. Apart from missionary work the missionaries

152 NHB 25. St., 5. 'Letter from the missionaries to the Learned Society in Batavia, dated Tranquebar, 14 October 1780, in which general information about the structure of the mission is given.'

153 The manuscript is in the archives in Copenhagen. Johann Peter Rottler supported his colleague's statements with his signature. RA Miskolark 9g, Pro Memoria for new missionaries from Ch. S. John [J.P. Rottler], Tranquebar 20 January 1784.

154 Ibid.

155 Ibid.

156 Although this did not apply to the Tranquebar Mission, the India missionaries of the later Leipzig mission were trained in indology. The rise of comparative linguistics at the beginning of the nineteenth century and, linked to this, the development of indology as an academic discipline in Germany gave future missionaries the possibility of India-specific training before they started missionary work. The training not only influenced the missionary's ideas and knowledge about the country, in other words his image of India, but also his questions about Indian religions and his expectations of Indian society. What was important in the final analysis was whether this knowledge would have an effect in the framework of Christian belief.

also had to shape their personal lives in a foreign country. In other words, they left behind their European life and began a second life as Europeans and Christians in India. Missionaries who returned to Europe, or even asked to be allowed to return, were exceptions in the Tranquebar Mission. It generally happened only on serious health grounds. The psychological pressure caused by the finality and irrevocability of their decision[157] was intensified by the fact that they mostly went alone and established a family only once they were in India. Under these conditions the hope of material advantages and wealth, or of getting a good position on one's return, hardly played a role.

BETWEEN HEGEMONY AND DIALOGUE

The main concern of all missionary work was the conversion to Christianity of as large a number of non-Christians as possible, to be demonstrated in the number of people baptized. Accordingly, the correlation between the propagation of the faith by the missionaries, on the one hand, and the reception of this faith by the local people, on the other, was an important indicator of the success of the mission. Depending on whether the propagation of the gospel was taken as a call to mission, and the new faith was accordingly forced onto the people without any compromise, or whether the act of baptism was preceded by a process of communication and agreement, conversion could be a short-term event or missionary work could lead to constant intercultural encounters.

In the case of the Tranquebar Mission the interest of the European missionaries in the local population resulted, first and foremost,

[157] Such thoughts were seldom so clearly expressed in the reports as was the case with Christoph Samuel John: 'The complete separation from the beloved fatherland and from near and dear ones is often a main consideration, even if not for the new missionary, then certainly for the relatives who, therefore, refuse to give their consent. I have already said what I think of an early return. A missionary becomes useful only after some years. But, if he has faithfully served the Lord for several years, then feels that his strength is declining, if he then longs for his fatherland and for some relief, this should not be denied him and the hope of seeing him again, God willing, would make some relatives more prone to give their consent.' (translated from German), Cf. RA Miskolark 9g, Pro Memoria for new missionaries from Ch. S. John [J.P. Rottler] Tranquebar 20 January 1784.

from the conviction that they had an 'obligation' to the people living 'in heathen darkness'. 'Heathenism' as the 'cause of all evils' was to be removed through Christianity. The missionaries believed that in the long term the conversion to Christianity would bring about far-reaching changes in the way the people in South India lived.[158] The most important element of identification for the German Protestant missionaries of the eighteenth century was not Europe with its civilizational and technological achievements, but rather the Christian faith, as representatives of which they encountered the 'Other'. Despite this, they were naturally Europeans with a comparatively high level of education; they were influenced by the level of development of the sciences in Europe as well as by the contemporary European image of the 'Other'. Shaped by specific religious experiences and the study of theology they had classified the 'Other' into certain categories and value-based frameworks long before their encounter with the non-European world.

In the course of their stay and work in India many missionaries led a life between adaptation and demarcation, between acceptance and rejection as well as between appreciation and contempt. They were simultaneously missionaries and researchers, teachers and pupils. In their dealings with the Indian converts there was an attempt to come together and to view the converts as equals, since they were now adherents of the same faith. This attempt was, however, overshadowed by the actual experience of distance towards the Tamil people who, even after receiving baptism, remained the Other for the missionaries, namely 'Malabarians'. On the whole, the direct contact between the missionaries and the local people involved numerous conflicts of an individual and social nature. Assimilation took place on both sides, but the protagonists were unwilling to give up their own traditions and their cultural roots.

[158] R. Wendt's statement that, particularly since the nineteenth century, Europeans in Asia attempted to 'modernize the continent in a kind of secular civilizing mission and to raise it to Western standards' (translated from German) does not immediately apply to the work of the Tranquebar Mission, although this mission naturally had to redefine itself, even with regard to these questions, in its relationship to British colonial power. Cf. Wendt, Reinhard, 1998, 'Allgemeine historische Perspektiven: Grundstrukturen des europäischen Interesses in Asien', in Koschorke '*Christen und Gewürze*', 259–73, here 264.

For the people living in the mission region the encounter with the 'Other' in the shape of the Christian mission could take on diverse forms and produce different results. Missionary work differed from other forms of intercultural encounter in that it was not a meeting of select and limited groups of people whose positions and concerns were comparable. For a missionary every person was factually a potential convert. In addition, missionary work in contrast to the work of other groups (trade, diplomacy) was not envisaged as an activity of exchange or negotiation. In return, the people were initially 'only' expected to accept this activity through their willingness to be baptized. Theoretically, the missionaries were meant to be the active protagonists who effected changes in the structures of belief of local society through their work. Christian missionaries, as a rule, were specifically prepared for the first direct contact with the 'Other'. Even the representatives of early Protestant missions were of the opinion that they were sufficiently equipped for the encounter through their religious beliefs, through the conviction that their actions were necessary and through vague ideas about the world of 'heathenism'. The difference between missionary work and the work of other Europeans overseas, such as diplomatic ambassadors or trade representatives, also lay in the fact that the former was not based on a one-time, short-term meeting, but was actually a long and continuous process of encounters.

Regardless of the differences in the intensity and quality of preparatory training, all missionaries faced the same problem on their arrival in India: learning the local language. The dominant language in the area where the Danish-Halle Mission worked was Tamil, one of the four main Dravidian languages spoken in South India. Besides Tamil, Portuguese offered a basis of communication, but its use excluded certain sections of the population. Although language teaching in Halle and the general attitude of Pietists to the study of foreign languages created favourable conditions, the direct possibilities for language training specifically related to different countries were limited. The missionaries in Tranquebar, therefore, applied themselves from the very beginning to learning Tamil. Besides Tamil, some of them spoke other local languages such as Telugu, Hindustani or Marathi. In addition, the missionaries generally had an excellent knowledge of Latin and, sometimes, also a basic knowledge of English or Portuguese. This favoured their position as mediators or figures of integration within social developments in South India. Even in the 1740s Portuguese, an important lingua franca in Southeast India in the eighteenth century, was used by some missionaries to start preaching in India. Thus, for example, Gottfried Wilhelm Obuch (1707–45) preached his first sermon to a native congregation in 1744 in Portuguese.[159] With their theological training from home and their locally acquired language skills the missionaries created the most important pre-conditions for actual mission work in the region.

In his memo regarding the desirable qualifications for new missionaries John had demanded a knowledge of languages but not, as one would expect, of the languages spoken in the mission region. Rather, he emphasized the knowledge of classical Bible languages and modern European languages.

> Latin retains its excellent value; however, reading and writing skills in Latin are not as necessary here as in Europe. If a missionary has these skills—wonderful! If he lacks them and concentrates more on Portuguese, English or French, these languages would be far more useful in mission matters than the former. Who would deny that an excellent knowledge of Greek and Hebrew are important and necessary both to understand the Holy Book better as well as to translate it into the Malabarian and the Portuguese. [...] If a new missionary, therefore, has an opportunity on the voyage to learn Portuguese, English, French or at least one of these languages, he will be happy to have done so once he is here.[160]

As against this, he forcefully warns the missionaries against learning Tamil in Europe because, in his opinion, there were no satisfactory possibilities for this at that point of time.

> On the other hand, I would not advise anyone to learn the Malabarian language prior to their arrival in this country. He will not find any one, either in Europe or on the ship, who would be able to teach him this language properly. To try and learn something from

[159] HB 61. Cont., 99.

[160] RA Miskolark 9g, Pro Memoria for new missionaries from Ch. S. John [J.P. Rottler], Tranquebar, 20 January 1784, (translated from German).

> books and grammars, or from an East Indian sailor, or even from a Malabarian who has not learnt the rules of the language in school, is unnecessary, indeed, even harmful. He will internalize mistakes, which he will find difficult or even impossible to correct.[161]

The knowledge of languages required for religious work not only gave the missionaries the possibility of a more wide-ranging communication, but it often also led to a scientific interest in the languages themselves. The constant changes and corrections in the translation of individual parts of the Bible, or of the Bible as a whole, became an essential basis for the daily work of the mission. In the eighteenth century two translations of the entire Bible by the missionaries of the Tranquebar Mission were published.[162] Besides this, parts of the Bible were translated into Telugu and Hindustani by Benjamin Schultze. The texts were prepared by the missionaries in close co-operation with language experts and writers and then printed directly in Tranquebar or in Halle. This work would not have been possible without the South Indian co-workers. Initially, the texts had to be copied laboriously and tediously on long, thin palm leaves and the letters had to be engraved onto these leaves with the help of a sharp object. From 1712 onwards a printing press with Latin letters, sent by the SPCK, was available in Tranquebar. In 1713, August Hermann Francke sent a press with Tamil letters to Tranquebar. Along with the equipment for the press a printer, a typesetter and an apprentice landed in Tranquebar in the persons of Johann Gottlieb Adler, his younger brother, Dietrich Gottlieb Adler, and Johannes Berlin. In subsequent years printing presses were also set up in other mission stations. Especially from the 1740s to the 1760s works sent by the missionaries as manuscripts by ship to Europe were also published in Halle.[163] Indians conversant with

[161] Ibid., (translated from German).

[162] Bartholomäus Ziegenbalg began the first translation shortly after his arrival, and parts of it were published from 1714 onwards. After Ziegenbalg's death (1719) Benjamin Schultze continued the work on the translation. In 1728 the entire Bible in its Tamil translation was published. The printing of the second Bible translation by Johann Philipp Fabricius was completed in 1796. Cf. Henry, Victor I., 1982, 'Tamil Translations of the Bible by the Danish-Halle Mission during the Eighteenth Century', *ICHR*, 16 (1): 72–85.

[163] For the development and significance of printing in the Danish-English-Halle mission see Liebau, Kurt, 'Buchdruck und Missionsbibliothek', in Liebau, *Geliebtes*

the language checked the translations done by the missionaries but it is difficult to determine their actual contribution to the translations. The work on Bible translations and the desire for the most accurate reproduction of the original content forced the missionaries to deal intensively with the semantic, religious and philosophical content of particular words. In order to have convincing arguments for their work of conversion they had to try and understand the religious thought of the South Indian population. This was difficult to the extent that Brahmins controlled this knowledge and their texts were mostly written in Sanskrit. The missionaries, however, hardly had any contact with this section of the local society. Apart from this, only a few missionaries learned Sanskrit.

The scientific pursuit of the literature, religion and culture of the mission region, but also the interest in problems of the natural sciences, contributed to the change in the outlook of the missionaries. Proceeding partly from personal interests and inclinations many missionaries began to pursue a branch of knowledge systematically. In this they went far beyond a simple collection of material and attempted initial analyses and interpretations in the fields of language studies, religious studies and climate science. Knowledge of the structure and functioning of Indian society was essential for successful missionary work. The caste system with its firmly entrenched social distinctions and religious norms required sensitive dealings with the people and made it difficult to use a broad-based form of missionary work that would appeal to everyone. Therefore, the missionaries had to learn about the position of the individual castes in the social hierarchy in order to use this to gain access to the people (often through a combination of missionary work and social work). With the growing influence of enlightenment in the second half of the eighteenth century the role of the natural sciences in the

---

Europa, Ostindische Welt, 105–20; Muthiah, Subbiah, 'Giving India the Printed Word', in Gross, *Halle and the Beginning of Protestant Christianity in India*, Vol. III, 1231–48; Liebau, Heike, forthcoming, 'Translocal networks of the Tranquebar Mission Press in 18th century South Asia', in Esther Fihl and A.R. Venkatachalapathy (eds.), *Grappling with Cultural Borders. Tranquebar—a place in South Asia,* (Orient Blackswan, New Delhi); For an overview of the development of print in Tamil Nadu see the excellent study by A.R. Venkatachalapathy 2011, *The Province of the Book*, Permanent Black, New Delhi.

missionary profession also increased. John advised every prospective missionary to study the literature of the natural sciences: 'Linne, Sander, Martinet, Bode and other excellent men will give him the most beautiful introduction to and an initial knowledge of this field and their works should not be missing in his travel library.'[164]

The social work of the mission in the fields of medicine and education also contributed to the success of missionary work. A person healed was often far more convincing than all sermons. Since 1730 (with interruptions) the mission not only had a European mission doctor, even some of the Indian employees were medical men. On their journeys the mission employees took along medicines with which simple illnesses could be cured. It was, however, mainly through the education system that the mission gained its profile even among non-Christians. During the course of their work in India the Danish-English-Halle missionaries established numerous schools that imparted religious and secular knowledge. The missionary education system was an area in which the 'Indian' and the 'European' existed in close proximity but were also, simultaneously, in close competition. In times of devastating famines caused by wars and natural disasters the people converged at the mission stations. When the Coromandel Coast was hit by a famine in 1732/33, which covered the entire Thanjavur kingdom and which led to a decline in handicraft production since the producers had little to invest in their work, many people turned to the missionaries.[165] The same happened in 1770 when, in addition to a steep rise in prices because of war or as a result of failed harvests, a shipload of rice from Bengal did not arrive and many people did not have much of a chance of survival.[166]

164 RA Miskolark 9g, *Pro Memoria* for new missionaries from Ch. S. John [J.P. Rottler], Tranquebar 20 January 1784, (translated from German); On the role of science in the Tranquebar Mission see the collection of articles: Liebau, Heike, Andreas Nehring and Brigitte Klosterberg (eds.), 2010, *Mission und Forschung. Translokale Wissensproduktion zwischen Indien und Europa im 18. und 19. Jahrhundert*, Verlag der Franckeschen Stiftungen, Halle.

165 Arasaratnam, *The Dutch East India Company and its Coromandel trade*, 340.

166 'The inflation of the previous year caused by the destructive war and, subsequently, exacerbated by the sinking of a ship from Bengal laden with 8000 sacks of rice is still continuing. Although the early harvest has begun, also many vessels from the north and from Pegu have arrived with rice and other grains, the rice is still not sold in public markets but only in one place on the shore for 2 Fan. for those

This occurred again in the famine years from 1811 to 1813 when prices fluctuated considerably.[167]

On their journeys into the interior the missionaries and the South Indian mission employees got the opportunity to carry out their own observations, but also to become known and to address larger groups of people, i.e. to be perceived. They wandered through the villages and preached everywhere in a central place. The people of the village, some of whom had never seen a European before, would gradually gather, initially mostly out of curiosity. These journeys would be repeated at regular intervals to the same places, some people would develop a deeper interest in the sermons and they would be provided with literature as a preparation for baptism or, in some cases, they would be invited to the central mission station for the preparation. Often the teachers of the village schools, in particular, would be addressed and urged to explain Christian ideas. Local mission assistants and catechists accompanied the missionaries on these journeys. When the mission was expanded to include rural districts, local co-workers were increasingly sent alone into the places with Christian congregations in order to preach, to participate in religious festivals and, simply, to announce the presence of the mission.

TRANQUEBAR—THE CENTRE OF THE ENCOUNTER

The encounter between the people of Tranquebar and the missionaries began in 1706. At this point of time foreigners, even Europeans, were already living in this port and trading city. After becoming Danish territory in 1620 the development of Tranquebar had been marked by the politics of the Danes. Bartholomäus Ziegenbalg's impression of the colony clearly reflects this. When asked the questions: 'When was the Danish colony in Tranquebar established? How strong is it? How far does its diocese or district extend?' Ziegenbalg replied:

---

who can come there.' (translated from German), NHB 3. St., 349, letter from J.C. Breithaupt to G.A. Francke, dated 22 January 1770.

[167] Ludden, *Peasant History in South India*, 220.

> The Danish colony at Tranquebar was established about 80 years ago: [...] Tranquebar was earlier a small place but, later, after the king of Denmark took it over through a contract with the then ruling Malabarian emperor and populated it with Europeans, it has gradually grown into a fine town equipped with a sturdy fort. According to the terms of the contract an annual sum of 2000 perdous have to be paid to the heathen king of Tanjour. The entire city is surrounded by a solid wall with ramparts and cannons. The fort is close to the sea, it has a moat and is surrounded by strong walls and ramparts. A fine citadel has been built in front of the landward gate. There are three Christian churches in the city, namely the Danish church called Zion, our own called Jerusalem and the Catholic church. There is also a large Moorish or Mohammedan church and the Malabarian heathens have five big temples. The inhabitants are made up of white Europeans, half-white Portuguese, yellow Moors and blackish-brown Malabarians who are in the majority.[168]

The detailed description of the lay-out, the population and the geographical features of the region around Tranquebar, which Ziegenbalg gave in 1709, is essentially identical with Kamma Struwe's description for the 1730s based on Danish files: Around 1730 there were 648 houses in Tranquebar, of which 476 were built of stone and 172 were huts with straw roofs. The roads were laid systematically. The South Indian and the European population lived separately since European settlements generally had an inner, so-called White town, and an outer, so-called Black town. The presence of the Europeans attracted Indian traders, craftsmen and representatives of the service sector. Four-fifths of the population was Indian—Hindus and Muslims, native Lutheran and Catholic Christians. There were about 50 European households of the Danish officials or German missionaries. The 'Portuguese' occupied an in-between position. The term was used for a local group of people of mixed Indian and European descent who spoke Portuguese. There were two churches, a mosque and twelve temples in Tranquebar. The second largest town, Tilaiali, comprised of 129 stone houses and 632 huts. In Porayar,

168 HB 3. Cont., 111–13, Ziegenbalg replies to questions from Europe about the social environment of the mission, (translated from German), Tranquebar, 27 August 1709.

the next largest town, there were three oil-mills, a church, a mosque and a temple. The region of Tranquebar, i.e. the city with some surrounding villages, was 32 km^2 large, had 3,000 households and a population of 10,000–15,000. This included farmers, craftsmen, merchants, temple priests and indigent daily-wagers.[169]

Because of the Danish presence in Tranquebar and also because of the comparatively favourable geographic and climatic conditions the town was the starting-point and the coordinating centre for the work of the missionaries in South India, and this lasted for the entire period of the existence of the DEHM. The first missionaries landed here in 1706 and even after further mission stations were established in other cities Tranquebar remained the central station of this mission society. From the beginning efforts were made to extend the reach of the mission. Whereas, initially, it was limited to the territory of the Danish trading settlement, in 1727 it was extended into the territory of the Thanjavur kingdom. Some of the less successful attempts were those made in 1756 on the Nicobar Islands and in 1760 and 1766 in Ceylon. During the period of existence of the Tranquebar Mission some missionaries, who had been educated in Halle and had come to India as Danish missionaries, entered the services of English societies and carried out missionary work in areas under British administration. Thus, there were mission stations in Madras (from 1726), in Cuddalore (from 1737 to 1783), in Nagapattinam (from 1783 to 1788) and in Calcutta (from 1758). The mission station in Tiruchirappalli began its work in 1762. Despite this development, for the Danish-Halle Mission and its successor, the Evangelical Lutheran mission of Leipzig, Tranquebar remained the main station.

[169] Cf. esp.: Struwe, Kamma, 1967, *Dansk Ostindien 1732–1776. Tranquebar under Kompagnistyre*, Fremad, København (=Johannes Brønsted (ed.): Vore gamle Tropekolonier. Vol. 6), 10f. For Tranquebar also see: Hjelm, Torben, 1988, *Fra det nu forsvundne Tranquebar. Billeder med en uddybende tekst, der beskriver historien om vor gamle handelskoloni, Tranquebar of logen Serampore samt Nikobar-øgruppen*, Strandberg, Copenhagen. Niekamp mentions 18,000 inhabitants for the city of Tranquebar and 30,000 for the entire region with the surrounding villages: Niekamp, *Kurtzgefaßte Mißions-Geschichte*, 6, 19. Fenger considers these figures to be a mere guess: Fenger, *Geschichte der Tranquebarschen Mission*, 21. For a more general overview cf.: Ludden, *Peasant History in South India*.

As the most important mission station Tranquebar represented an interim and overlapping social space from where the links to different places were coordinated and where important norms of the co-operation between European missionaries and Tamil employees were negotiated. The relationship between the missionaries and the 'national workers' was always marked by the ambivalence through which it functioned. On the one hand, the assistance of local people was necessary to support and shape missionary work, and, on the other, their presence was also required to legitimize this work not only to the local population but also to the missionary society in Copenhagen and to the directors in Halle. The missionaries viewed their Tamil co-workers first and foremost as Christians, thus distinguishing them from the other Indians, the 'heathens' (Hindus) or the 'Moors' (Muslims). But, although the 'national workers' were Christians like the missionaries, they always remained in the latter's view 'Malabarian' Christians or Christian 'Malabars'. They were only allowed a small degree of independence. Local workers were used in places where it was difficult for the missionaries to have access to potential converts, or where one expected to achieve greater success by using indigenous helpers. They accompanied missionaries on their journeys, bridged language barriers and enabled access to areas where Europeans found it difficult to go alone. In their work the 'national workers', consciously or unconsciously, adapted elements of the Christian doctrine to Indian experiences in order to understand the doctrine better and to make it more comprehensible to others. The attitude of the local population to the indigenous mission workers was also ambivalent. On the one hand, they were viewed as deserters and were rejected by their social groups.[170] On the other hand, there were situations in which they were suddenly perceived again as representatives of one's own caste to whom one could go for advice and support because of their education and influence.[171]

[170] Cf. Liebau, Heike and Magret Liepach, 1994, 'Christliche Hindus—indische Christen? Die Nationalarbeiter der Dänisch-Halleschen Mission in Südindien im 18. Jahrhundert', in Joachim Heidrich (ed.), *Changing Identities: The Transformation of Asian and African Societies under Colonialism*, 307–22, Das Arabische Buch, Berlin.

[171] Thus, for example, the interpreter of the Company, Daniel Pullei, acted as a mediator in the caste unrest of 1787 in Tranquebar, see Liebau, Heike, 1997,

The hitherto existing division of the history of the Tranquebar Mission in stages of development was primarily based on the perspective of European mission history. In 1740 already Johann Lucas Niekamp made a first attempt at periodization, at a point of time when the mission was particularly successful.[172] Niekamp's attempts to systematize the first 30 years of the mission were undertaken in order to filter important dates, high points and developmental tendencies from the annual reports and to thus enable interested friends of the mission to have easier access to this voluminous material. He divided the period under study into three stages: the first stage (1706–20) is characterized as the early phase of orientation in which the missionaries established themselves in South India and developed suitable methods for missionary work. The second phase (1720–26) was marked by the completion of the Bible translation, the establishment of contact with the kingdom of Thanjavur and the departure of the missionary Benjamin Schultze for Madras. The following stage (from 1727) opened with the activities of the catechist Rajanayakkan, who began the work of conversion in the Thanjavur territory and thus initiated the setting up of rural congregations, which was decisive for the further development of the mission.[173] Looking back at the entire history of the mission from 1706 to 1845 Arno Lehmann distinguished three broad developmental stages of the Mission, which he described in the following manner: The foundation is laid, The expansion, and Decline and building of new bridges. According to his periodization the second stage begins after the death of the two pioneering missionaries, Ziegenbalg and Gründler; the third stage begins in

---

'Indische Angestellte in der dänischen Kolonialadministration während der sozialen Unruhen in Tranquebar und Umgebung im Jahre 1787', *Asien, Afrika, Lateinamerika*, 25: 111–26.

[172] In his historical review of the history of the Tranquebar Mission Fenger assesses this in the following manner: 'If we look at the situation of the mission in 1740 we find that, at this point of time, the mission had more or less reached its zenith. However, this was not followed by a sudden decline since, for a number of years afterwards, the mission worked effectively. Indeed, in some regards the work was expanded, but there was no further development.' (translated from German), Fenger, *Geschichte der Tranquebarschen Mission*, 159f.

[173] Niekamp, *Kurtzgefaßte Mißions-Geschichte*.

the last quarter of the eighteenth century and does not end with the decline, but flows into the new beginning with the Leipzig mission in southeast India.[174] Anders Nørgaard bases his analysis of the relationship between the mission and the Danish authorities in Tranquebar on a periodization of the mission also in three broad stages, namely the founding period (1706–29), the established mission (1730–80) and the period of decline (1780–1845).[175]

Although the present study is thematically rather than chronologically oriented and does not attempt to establish a new periodization, certain important dates with regard to the theme have to be mentioned.

The early years of the mission were characterized by the search for a suitable strategy in dealing with South Indian co-workers. One can assume that from the very beginning the missionaries in South India realized the necessity of indigenous helpers, whereas the people in Europe viewed this process with a degree of scepticism. In the early years the missionaries were dependent on chance encounters. During this time there were a comparatively large number of people who came from Hindu families and, even as non-Christians, worked for the mission. Another group of people, from whose ranks 'national workers' could be recruited, were the Roman Catholic Christians who, because of inner conflicts, sometimes sought the encounter with the Tranquebar Mission.

On 30 October 1716 the missionaries established a special seminary in Tranquebar to train the local co-workers,[176] expecting that they would be loyal to the mission and display a special commitment towards the requirements of the mission. On the whole, however, only some of the 'national workers' actually came from this seminary. Many of them still came to the mission on their own, or in a roundabout manner. Often, the children of mission employees stepped into their father's footsteps. The spatial growth of the mission and the formation of Christian congregations in far-flung places meant, especially since the end of the 1720s, that more people were required to look after these congregations. In the person

[174] Lehmann, *Es begann in Tranquebar.*
[175] Nørgaard, *Mission und Obrigkeit.*
[176] Niekamp, *Kurtzgefaßte Mißions-Geschichte*, 984.

of Rajanayakkan, a Tamilian entered the arena of missionary work in 1727 and confidently offered his help in a region that became accessible to Europeans only much later.

The ordination of the Indian pastor, Aaron, in 1733 meant that for the first time European and Tamil personnel were formally placed on an equal footing. In practice, the Europeans remained the decision makers in all mission affairs. The constant and direct contact between missionaries and South Indian co-workers, as it existed in the beginning in Tranquebar and the surrounding areas, was no longer possible once the mission had expanded its base. However, even under these changed conditions, the South Indian co-workers did not have broader latitude or a greater responsibility since their work was still subjected to strict controls.

From the 1760s onwards there was an increase in the number of 'English' mission stations, which were looked after by missionaries who originally belonged to the Tranquebar Mission but became employees of the London-based SPCK. This process had started with Benjamin Schultze's work in Madras from 1728 onwards and continued with places like Cuddalore (from 1737), Thanjavur (from 1762) or Tiruchirappalli (from 1766).[177] Local personnel now had to be selected, trained and prepared for these regions as well.

At the beginning of the 1780s missionary work began to decline. The missionaries in India had become too old and very few new ones were sent out, that too at greater intervals. Of the 10 missionaries sent out between 1780 and 1797[178] only five served the mission for a longer period of time.[179] Two died early[180] and others returned to Europe for reasons of health (Mentel, Stegmann)

[177] For more information about the English stations see the articles included in: Gross, Andreas, *Halle and the Beginning of Protestant Christianity in India*, Volume I, Part III.

[178] Mentel, Rulfsen, Hagelund, Jänicke, Cämmerer, Pätzold, Ringeltaube, Stegmann, Holzberg, Früchtenicht.

[179] Cämmerer was in India from 1789 till his death in 1837. He died in Tranquebar as the last of the Danish-Halle missionaries. Holzberg stayed in India from 1797 till 1824. Jänicke came in 1787 and died in 1800. Pätzold arrived in India in 1792 and died there in 1817. Ringeltaube was in India, with breaks, from 1797 till 1821.

[180] Rulfsen died shortly after his arrival in Tranquebar. Hagelund worked in India for three years (1785–1788).

or on account of a breach of discipline (Früchtenicht). With the temporary closure of the University of Halle between 1797 and 1813 the fruitful co-operation between the Orphan-House and the university was interrupted. Not a single missionary was sent out during this period. Subsequently, seven more were sent out,[181] but there was none among them who was able to give a strong impetus to missionary work.[182] Because of these developments the daily work of the mission had to be carried out primarily by the South Indian co-workers. At the same time, the role of English mission societies grew at the beginning of the nineteenth century, and from 1813 onwards they began their work officially in many places in South India. In 1818 the Mission Board in Copenhagen requested the SPCK to take over the rural congregations in the Thanjavur region, which had 1300 members and 11 catechists.[183] In 1820 the rural congregations of Thanjavur were handed over. Many Christians also voluntarily went to English territories during this time.[184]

[181] Jacobi, Haubroe, Rosen, Schreyvogel, Sperschneider, Falcke, Wissing.

[182] Ernst August Georg Falcke came to Madras in 1822 and died there in 1824. Lauritz Peter Haubroe stayed in India from 1818 till his death in 1830. Christlieb Augustin Jacobi travelled to East India in 1813 and died in 1814 in Thanjavur. David Rosen came to India in 1819 and returned to Europe at the end of the 1830s. Daniel Schreyvogel (1777–1840) went to India in 1813 and died in Cuddalore where he is also buried. Johann Georg Philipp Sperschneider resigned from the English society on account of arbitrary payments a year after he had been sent out in 1819. Peter Mandrup Due Wissing came to India in 1827, was often ill and returned home in 1831.

[183] NHB, 69. St., 838. 'News of the Continued Efforts of the London Society for Promoting Christian Knowledge in England and East India. From their annual report of 1818', 835–39. According to Stampe this request had been made two years earlier by the missionaries Schreyvogel and Cämmerer, after John had turned to the British with the request for help in educational matters. Stampe, 'Missionskollegiet'.

[184] In 1836 Julius Berger estimated in a report to A.H. Niemeyer that the number of Christians in the Tranquebar region had decreased from 6000 to 1000. This was not only because of the low numbers of baptisms, but also by the migration of Christians to regions under British administration. NHB 84. St., 1213.

CHAPTER TWO

Local Mission Workers

> Thus the 'planting' of churches in various parts of the world from the beginning of the nineteenth century could never have been accomplished without the active initiatives of local people, who freely appropriated the Christian message for themselves and commanded that message both within their own societies and beyond. Thus, local people were as much missionaries as were the members of the mission society. They often were the driving force in the work of evangelization, Bible translation, creating education and health facilities, and building up and providing pastoral care for the community.[1]

The basic concern of organized Christian missionary activity in the eighteenth and nineteenth century was to transport ideas, principles of faith and the meaning of life associated with these into a society with other social, cultural and religious structures and to ensure that the former grew strong roots in this new society. Like the act of translation, for which the translator not only needs to know at least two languages but—for the translation to appear authentic—also the cultures linked with these languages, the mission—in order to carry out its mediating function—required people who had the knowledge and experience of different cultures and religions. Local helpers and intermediaries were necessary not only to propagate the Christian faith effectively, but also in dealings with the local population and for the social institutions of the mission. In the context of interaction between the local co-workers and the

[1] Ward, Kevin and Brian Stanley (eds.), 2000, *The Church Mission Society and World Christianity 1799–1999*, Grand Rapids, 7.

European missionaries, these two cultural intermediary groups initially engaged in a mutual exchange of knowledge and experience. On the one hand, the people conversant with the place and the society gave the missionaries the requisite information regarding the region and its languages, which the missionaries needed to know in order to adapt the methods and goals of the mission to local conditions. On the other hand, the 'national workers' acquired from the missionaries the religious knowledge that they had to pass on to the local population.

For both missionary groups the mission stations represented the most important zones of contact[2] and negotiation, where the process of exchange took place at various social levels. Like other Europeans living in India, the missionaries of the Tranquebar Mission also had their local domestic help for cooking, washing and cleaning. On their trips to surrounding areas the missionaries were accompanied by a large group of servants who looked after their safety and comfort. When Bartholomäus Ziegenbalg undertook a journey from Tranquebar via Cuddalore and Pondicherry to Madras in 1710 accompanied by the merchant from Zerbst, Anton Günther Wü[r]ger, who was living in India, six soldiers, ten palanquin bearers, five porters, a Tamilian writer, a cook and a groom for the horses were hired for this journey.[3] These attendants looked after the needs of the Europeans and made every effort to ensure that their surroundings were comfortable (as regards food and accommodation, for example). At the same time, however, they also helped the Europeans to understand the alien environment.

With the increasing expansion of the mission and with a growing number of social and religious establishments it became necessary to employ—in addition to these personal attendants of the missionaries—members of different professions to ensure the smooth running of the mission station. Gardeners, washermen, water-carriers and cooks were as much a part of this undertaking as a sexton or a gravedigger. It included doctors and teachers,

[2] Mary Louise Pratt defines a contact zone as a social space where representatives of different cultures act in an asymmetric way within a frame determined by hierarchies and power. Pratt, Mary Louise, 1992. *Imperial Eyes: Travel Writing and Transculturation,* Routledge, London, New York, 7.

[3] HB 2. Cont., 95, letter from B. Ziegenbalg, Madras, 17 January 1710.

bookbinders and typesetters as it did writers and bookkeepers. The setting up of a mission station not only involved considerations relating to mission strategy but the climatic, social, religious and cultural conditions in the mission region also had to be taken into account. The infrastructure of mission stations was integrated in different ways into its surroundings and there were many strands linking it to the local economy and society.

Intermediaries in the context of a mission also included people who could carry out the 'classical' functions of mediation with regard to the knowledge systems of a region and its languages: the language teachers of the missionaries and the interpreters. Since, as a rule, at least the pioneers among the missionaries could learn the local languages only after they arrived in the mission region, they had to find people who had the requisite knowledge and ability to help them communicate with the local population and who were also willing to place this knowledge at the disposal of Europeans. Interpreters and language teachers formed a bridge to local society and they were expected to enable the Europeans to have direct contact with the people in the future. Mission historians and biographers always strive to evoke images of the arrival of the first missionaries in Tranquebar and their inability to communicate with the local people. They then faithfully reproduce reports of the missionaries' chance encounter with the first interpreter and the first Tamil teacher.

> When we stepped onto land as healthy and cheerful as when we had boarded the ship, and when the Malabarian heathens here saw us, everyone began asking the other who we were and why we had come here. [...] In the beginning we couldn't speak with them at all, since we only knew Danish, but neither Portuguese nor Malabarian. Our first concern was, therefore, to learn Portuguese. I have a Malabarian as attendant, who is of high birth and who speaks good Portuguese. [...] Although this language is enough for our work, since my attendant is a good interpreter who can explain everything in their language to those Malabarians who do not understand Portuguese, yet we have now also started learning Malabarian and, for this purpose, I keep a heathen schoolmaster in my house.[4]

[4] AB 39, letter from B. Ziegenbalg, 25 September 1706 (translated from German). The interpreter was Modaliappa (born around 1685), apparently the grandson of a former border guard of the Danish East India Company and whose

While reading this one is reminded of Stephen Greenblatt's picturesque description of Columbus' landing in Trinidad and is receptive to the conclusion he draws: 'The early discourse of the New World then is full of questions that cannot be asked or answers that cannot be understood.'[5] This lack of language that is described above by Ziegenbalg was soon overcome with the help of local language experts. While the importance of local language teachers and interpreters was reduced in course of time, since European missionaries increasingly came with a better knowledge of languages, the mission could never completely do without them.[6] Indian language experts were also hired as scribes (*kaṇakkappiḷḷai*). They were either personally assigned to a missionary and accompanied him on his daily work, or they worked for the mission station and copied all kinds of documents.[7]

In addition to these, local informants and advisors contributed to the effective organization of missionary work by providing information about the country, its climatic conditions, or its social structure. The importance of such informants should not be underestimated, especially with regard to the scientific ambitions of the missionaries who, more often than not, had a university education. Many missionaries of the Tranquebar Mission were in contact with European scholars and understood the need to spend

father also worked for the Company. Modaliappa had had a good school education; he began to work for the missionaries on their arrival and wanted to become a Christian. Ziegenbalg taught him German in order to use him as an interpreter. At the beginning of 1708, however, Modaliappa left the mission. The schoolmaster mentioned here is almost certainly the father of the Christian Tamil poet and mission employee Kanapati Vattiyar (Christian Friedrich), who became famous. Even though he was Ziegenbalg's language teacher, the schoolmaster never converted to Christianity and later vehemently opposed his son's intention of becoming a Christian.

[5] Greenblatt, Stephen, 1991, *Marvelous Possessions: The Wonder of the World*, The University of Chicago Press, Chicago, 92.

[6] Often, older missionaries took over the task of teaching the newly arrived young missionaries the language. In the 1750s and 1760s it was Johann Christian Wiedebrock who taught Tamil and also often functioned as an interpreter. HB 107. Cont., 1551-60, Wiedebrock's curriculum vitae.

[7] In November 1728 Schultze reported the death of 'his' Telugu writer. This man, who was a Brahmin and had not converted, had copied the Telugu translations of the New Testament for Schultze. HB 27. Cont., 267, Schultze's diary, entry for 2 November 1727.

time on learning and research. This often led to criticism from the Mission directors. The information that they sent to Europe was, to a great extent, based on the work of Indian informants. In general, the co-operation between the informants and the missionaries was for a limited period of time, being oriented towards a particular goal or a specific theme. The reports often create the impression that a close relationship developed between the missionaries and these local individuals, who were not directly part of the mission, but with whom the missionaries had open and objective discussions on various topics although, or perhaps because, they were not willing to convert.[8]

The core area of socio-religious mediation was constituted by the direct inclusion of representatives of the local population in missionary work and their incorporation into the hierarchy of the mission. Since only a small number of European missionaries could be sent out at a particular point of time, their numbers were not enough when mission stations expanded and new Christian congregations required pastoral care. At such times local co-workers had to be recruited. However, it was not only a question of numbers. Even an excellent knowledge of the country and its languages was not always enough for a European to gain unlimited access to sensitive spheres of local societies. Even after a long stay in the region European missionaries could not shed the aura of foreignness and were still perceived as outsiders by the people there. The local mission employee, on the contrary, who came from the same caste, village, or from the same area was often met with a mixture of curiosity, goodwill and admiration, but also with doubt, rejection and contempt.

The present study focuses mainly on those local individuals who were active participants in the actual process of missionary work. From the very beginning the Tranquebar Mission tried to include Tamils directly in missionary work. A diary entry of 28 May 1707 already notes the appointment of a Tamil catechist. His

[8] In 1796 August Friedrich Cämmerer described the relationship with his Sanskrit teacher, a Brahmin. He calls him 'my Brahmin' and writes of 'friendly conversations' with him. NHB 52. St., 351-64. Christoph Samuel John made similar observations in 1793. Some Brahmins, he said, including a doctor, were willing to have conversations 'about scientific matters and about the Christian religion'. One of them gave John lessons in Sanskrit. NHB 46. St., 865f.

duties consisted in teaching the catechumen and in talking to the non-Christians about Christianity. This catechist did not remain an exception; rather, he represents the beginning of efforts to systematically recruit South Indian co-workers. The missionaries asked the European institutions supporting the mission to bear the following in mind:

> Such catechists from among the Indians are very necessary for this work, partly to interact with the catechumen in the manner described, partly to go out among the heathens, partly also to visit people from the congregation from time to time and to pay a daily visit to the sick. Because neither the heathens nor the catechumen, nor the congregants venture to ask the European pastors everything or tell us what is on their minds. Therefore, it is very necessary to have loyal persons from among them who observe and tell us all that is going on among these people and what the pastors must take into account.[9]

Initially, the missionaries needed local co-workers who were well-versed in their own language, literature and culture, i.e. had the kind of knowledge that the missionaries could not have to the same degree, but which was important to gain the people's confidence. In the early period, grounding in theology and knowledge of the Bible languages, Greek, Hebrew and Latin, were not the main components of their education.

> As regards our school children and their education we feel that these first ones should not yet be burdened with a vast array of subjects (learning Greek, Hebrew etc.). Rather, efforts should be directed at ensuring that by learning the word of God, reading, writing, arithmetic, geography and history in their own language they are trained in such a manner that, in time, they can become our co-workers, namely good schoolmasters and catechists, since we have the greatest need for such people.[10]

Towards the end of the eighteenth century there was a marked change. Besides the Bible languages, Sanskrit, but mainly European

[9] HB 6. Cont., 229, (translated from German).

[10] Letter from J.E. Gründler to A.H. Francke, 22 December 1710, HB 5. Cont., 11, (translated from German).

languages (English, French) became important in the schools. The reasons for this lie in the mission itself, but also in the changed aspirations of the population.

Preparing local co-workers for their duties in the mission and supporting them as employees required both organizational decisions and financial deliberations. The missionaries could only clarify these questions in consultations with the European side and wished to have direct talks with the superiors in Europe so as to avoid a long and protracted correspondence. After Ziegenbalg's attempts to go to Europe had to be postponed several times, it was finally Plütschau who embarked on the journey back to Europe in September 1711 in order to support the missionary undertaking from there in future.[11] He was accompanied by Timotheus (around 1696–1726), a young Tamilian, who was supposed to study theology in Europe and then return to India as a missionary.[12] The high expectations placed in this young Tamilian (he was about 15 years old when he left for Europe) were only partially fulfilled. On the one hand, he was visible proof of the success of missionary work in India and his presence in Europe undoubtedly contributed to a greater interest in the mission and to a greater flow of donations. On the other hand, Timotheus could not begin his planned course of study for various reasons and he returned to India in 1720 not as a missionary, but as a bookbinder.

Peter Maleiappen (around 1700–30) was the second Tamilian sent to Europe on behalf of the Tranquebar Mission. He accompanied Bartholomäus Ziegenbalg, who could finally embark on his long-planned journey in October 1714.[13] Officially, Ziegenbalg took the boy along in order to be able to practise Tamil constantly during his stay in Europe. Maleiappen was a representative object as well as a legitimating figure for the mission. He accompanied Ziegenbalg to all official meetings and talks in Halle, London and Copenhagen; he made an impression on the king of Denmark with a speech on 26 July 1715 in Stralsund, and proved his capabilities during

[11] AB 184f. Letter from Ziegenbalg to J. Lütkens, Madras, 16 October 1711.

[12] For the life of Timotheus see: Liebau, 'Die ersten Tamilen aus der Dänisch-Halleschen Mission in Europa'. Cf. also AB 205f. Letter from Ziegenbalg to J. Lange, Madras, 9 December 1711.

[13] For the life of Maleiappen see Liebau, 'Die ersten Tamilen aus der Dänisch Halleschen Mission in Europa'.

several audiences with members of the royal family in London at the beginning of 1716. He took part in the annual meeting of the SPCK in London. In August 1716 Ziegenbalg and Maleiappen returned to India. On the whole, Ziegenbalg's journey helped in the furtherance of missionary work. Misunderstandings that had arisen were cleared up and the mission regained its legitimacy in the eyes of many influential supporters. Maleiappen's presence contributed to this positive outcome. As the companion of the missionary he was a showpiece for the success of the mission and, at the same time, proof of the need for further efforts.

Thus, the first Indians taken to Europe fulfilled a dual function, which was comparable to their role in the Indian mission context. They were helpers and informants of the missionaries, representatives of the mission to the outside world—in Europe to the friends of the mission and in India to the entire population. Stephen Greenblatt writes: 'The native is seized as a token and then displayed, sketched, painted, described, end embalmed is quite literally captured by and for European representation.'[14] Although this evaluation, which refers to the sixteenth century, cannot be applied in its entire brutality to the early Tranquebar Mission, it nonetheless need to be borne in mind in the context just described.

A few months after Ziegenbalg's return the missionaries in Tranquebar began a special course of training for Indian catechists by setting up a seminary for talented pupils of the higher school classes.[15] However, another 15 years went by before the first Tamilian co-worker was ordained. In an essay of 1728 on the problems of missionary work the missionaries once again strongly reiterated the necessity of ordaining Indian co-workers and justified their views, among others, on the grounds that the number of Europeans in missionary service in India could then be reduced.[16] Two years later, the lack of ordained Indians was listed as one of the greatest hindrances in the 'conversion of the Malabarian heathens to Christianity':

[14] Greenblatt, *Marvellous Possessions*, 119.

[15] HB 13. Cont., 22; AB 471, letter from B. Ziegenbalg and J.E. Gründler to A.H. Francke, Tranquebar, 7 January 1717.

[16] HB 27. Cont., 195f.

> Although it is obvious from what has already been said, the matter is important enough to be mentioned independently as one of the hindrances on the side of the mission itself, that till now the office of the missionary and the pastor has been managed only by Europeans, and no native Indian has been ordained to such an office.[17]

After Aaron's ordination in December 1733 and the positive effect of this event, a new development set in, which the missionaries registered with great satisfaction: 'The respect that he has gained through this has made it easier for others to convert to Christianity and to overcome the disgrace attached to this.'[18]

Besides the fact that European missionaries were regarded as outsiders and that South Indian co-workers had easier access to the people, financial arguments and personnel matters were often used to justify the need for a greater inclusion of local co-workers. Early on, some missionaries expressed the idea that local workers should be ordained and thus—in canonical terms—be formally equal to the ordained European missionaries. In September 1709 Ziegenbalg, who was planning to go to Europe to talk to the mission directors and friends of the mission, saw the purpose of his trip, among other things,

> To show a way by which, from now on, the people who are to be used as missionaries can be trained adequately so that, in future, His Royal Majesty only need send out students who, once they have learned the languages, could be ordained by us here. For this, however, one of us here must be given the authority to ordain such people and, if necessary, also to ordain some persons from among the Blacks (Indians) [...][19]

While writing about the general demand to be allowed to carry out the process of ordination in Tranquebar after the newly-arrived

[17] HB 27. Cont., 195, (translated from German).

[18] HB 42. Cont., 799. Cf. also: HB 42. Cont., 798, letter to the court chaplain Ziegenhagen in London, 2 December 1735, (translated from German).

[19] Cf. AB 102–106, letter from B. Ziegenbalg, 27 September 1709, (translation from German). For Aaron's life and for the significance of ordination from the perspective of church history see Jeyaraj, 'Ordination of the First Protestant Pastor Aaron', 5; Jeyaraj, 'Die Ordination des ersten protestantischen Pfarrers Aaron in Südindien'.

missionaries had been adequately trained. Ziegenbalg, in the same breath, expresses the wish to also ordain representatives of the local population. From 1733 the missionaries ordained local co-workers in South India, but the European missionaries continued to be ordained in Europe. Missionaries, who were not ordained pastors, were rarely sent out.[20]

Even after the ordination of South Indian co-workers, however, neither the German missionaries, nor the Mission Board in Denmark mentioned the idea of an indigenous Church led by local workers. The Europeans were categorical about the need for a European presence, even though they repeatedly emphasized their willingness to include Tamilians in the work and to hand over responsibility to them. With the passage of time, however, there were visible shifts in the division of duties. In 1784 Christoph Samuel John summarized the advantages of local co-workers in the following manner:

> We differ greatly from those who come to listen to us in the colour of our skin, our clothes and other superficial things. This difference often arouses mere curiosity and draws a crowd. For this reason I have often wished to have the Malabarian skin colour and wear their kind of clothes so that I may encounter less curiosity and more trust. [...] So, although I am not of the opinion that the conversations of missionaries with heathens are unimportant, one does notice that the manner in which the national workers associate with the heathens yields better results. As a rule, the heathens are also friendlier towards them, who are their countrymen, and tell them more than they do us. Many things, which are impediments for us, are not difficult for the national workers. [...] The heat affects them less. While conversing in public places they cannot be distinguished by the colour of their skin or their clothes and

[20] The group sent to India in 1719 was an exception. The three missionaries—Nikolaus Dal, Johann Heinrich Kistemacher and Benjamin Schultze—had not been ordained before their departure. Schultze was ordained by Gründler shortly before the latter's death in 1720, Dal was also ordained in Tranquebar in 1730. Christoph Heinrich Horst had a very unusual biography. He came to India as an officer in one of the Hanoverian regiments and got to know the mission there. After leaving military service he was employed by the mission in various capacities and was ordained in 1806 in Tranquebar by Christian Pohle. NHB 64. St., VII-XI. Daniel Schreyvogel, sent out in 1803, was a catechist with the mission before he was ordained in 1813 in Tranquebar.

> thus do not create a sensation. They have free access to the houses of the heathens, they can talk to them more often and more extensively than we can. They can be more familiar with them, they express themselves with greater ease in their mother tongue and, depending on their audience, they can talk in a more common or a more learned language. They can also sing something to the heathens from their poetic books to prove a point, which is greatly appreciated here, whereas our European tongue and hearing cannot get accustomed to this rattling. If the national workers are really talented the heathens here consider them to be Njanigöl or wise men, who are greatly revered here and who they listen to with pleasure.[21]

After more than seven decades of missionary work in India Christoph Samuel John clearly determined the boundaries of the European missionaries and the possibilities open to South Indian employees. However, his conclusion was, by no means, to ask for a transfer of responsibility to the South Indian workers, or for a stop to European missionaries altogether. John argued for a clear shift in the work of the missionaries and stated that in future they would have to concentrate on training the local co-workers rather than work among the local population.

> The result of all this is, as I find it necessary to repeat, not in the least that the missionaries could be dispensed with or that they should not engage with the heathens, [...] but that a lot depends on the national workers, on their loyalty and their skill, and that it should be one of the main concerns of the missionaries to train them properly for this important work.[22]

INTERMEDIARY GROUPS IN MISSION REPORTS

The cooperation between missionaries and South Indian employees was particularly intensive in the early years of the mission. This cooperation was linked with permanent control, which included

[21] NHB 30. St., 700–709, 'Einige Vorschläge des Herrn Missionari Johns die Mission betreffend', here 701f., (translated from German).

[22] NHB 30. St., 702f., (translated from German).

weekly instructions and accounts of work.[23] With the territorial expansion of the mission, the responsibilities of many South Indian co-workers also increased. Often, there was a fairly great distance between the headquarters of the missionaries in Tranquebar and the actual place of work of a catechist or an assistant, which allowed only for monthly reporting. The report, however, was to be given in a written form, and this meant that if one was not in a position to go to Tranquebar it could be sent with another person.[24] In the annual collective diaries of the Tranquebar Mission the monthly reports from the country pastors, catechists and assistants are always mentioned against the dates on which these reports were presented in Tranquebar. Either entire reports were reproduced in a translation done by a missionary or excerpts were chosen that were deemed to be important.[25] The reports were reproduced in a third-person narrative, but sometimes also in the first person in a direct translation from the Tamil.[26] When a particular activity of one or the other missionary was recorded in the collective diary, it said 'one of us', 'another of us'; the local mission employees were mentioned by

[23] The first catechists and teachers, who were under Gründler's supervision, came to him every evening to report on the events and the results of the day. HB 17. Cont., Vorrede, 13 (refers to the year 1718). Such a close cooperation was later only seen with Christian Friedrich Schwartz in Tiruchirappalli when he was the only missionary of the DEHM there from 1762 to 1768 and, therefore, very dependent on the contact with local employees.

[24] Some of the early reports of individual catechists and assistants written on palm leaves are preserved in the Royal Library in Copenhagen. Cf. Jeyaraj, *Inkulturation in Tranquebar*, 330–34.

[25] In the archives of the Francke Foundations diaries of the national workers have been preserved under different catalogue numbers (AFSt/M 1 B 71 : 35, diary Sattianaden, December 1779, extracts published in NHB 24. St., 1417–21; AFSt/M 1 B 71 : 36, diary Schawrimuttu 1780, extracts published in NHB 24. St., 1421-23; AFSt/M 1 B 75 : 26, travel diary of the catechist Njanapiragaham of journeys to Ramanathapuram and Palayankottai, 2 February 1785, extracts published in NHB 31. St., 762–73; AFSt/M 2 E 37 : 2a, diary Philipp of 19 December 1775 to 5 March 1776; as also AFSt/M 2 F 1; AFSt/M 2 F 2; AFSt/M 2 F 3).

[26] Cf., among others, HB 37. Cont., 21-24. Monthly report of the catechist Aaron reproduced in excerpts in direct speech in the framework of the collective diary of the missionaries Dal, Bosse, Pressier, Walther, Worm and Richtsteig on 24 February 1733. HB 107. Cont., 1490–94, travel diary of the country pastor Diogo reproduced in indirect form in the third person in the framework of the collective diary of the missionaries J.B. Kohlhoff, Zeglin, Maderup and J. Klein on 13 January 1767.

name and/or function. In this way the division was made very clear and the different hierarchical categories were drawn.

Numerous letters of the catechists and of the two country pastors, Aaron and Diogo (about 1704–81), written in the 1740s to the editors of the *Halle Reports*, to the Mission Board in Copenhagen and to other persons in Europe have been preserved.[27] Like their European colleagues, the South Indian catechists and country pastors maintained a diary, especially when they traveled to the villages to meet the Christians. In the first volume of the NHB the reports of the Indians were also arranged as an entry in the diaries of the missionaries under the date on which the local co-workers presented them in Tranquebar. Under the name, the function and the place of work of a mission employee his activities were reproduced fairly extensively. From the 1780s onwards excerpts from the diaries or reports of the Tamilians appeared as independent components; in extent and arrangement they now formally had the same worth as the reports and diaries of the missionaries,[28] a form that is not

[27] HB 57. Cont., 1409f. (1741/42), letter written by the two country preachers to the Mission Board, in Copenhagen; 1411, letter written by the two country preachers to the editor of HB; 1412, letter written by Aaron to the editor; 1413–14, letter written by Diogo to Ziegenhagen in London; 1415–16 letter written by Rajanaykkan to the editor; HB 60. Cont., 1897–1912, extracts from letters written by the missionaries and country pastors received 1744, contains: letter by the two country pastors to the Mission Board in Copenhagen, 26 November 1743; letter by Aaron to the Mission Board, 14 January 1744; letter by Diogo to the Mission Board, 20 January 1744; letter by Rajanayakkan to the editor, 3 January 1744; letter by Aaron to a pastor in Saxony, 4 January 1744; letter by Diogo to a sponsor in Saxony, 4 January 1744; letter by Aaron to the editor, 14 January 1744; letter by Diogo to the editor, 20 January 1744. All letters appeared in the mission reports in German translation, done by the missionaries. Tamil originals are kept in the Archive of the Francke Foundations and can be searched under: http://192.124.243.55/cgi-bin/dhmeng.pl.

[28] In the 20th *Stück* of the *New Halle Reports* (NHB) the communications sent by the country pastors, catechists and assistants for the year 1780 have been put together under the title 'Reports of the national workers'. NHB 20. St., 933–45. The 50th *Stück* of the NHB is divided into chapters I to VI. Two of the six chapters contain documents of the South Indian co-workers: Chapter II contains extracts from reports submitted by the country pastors in the year 1795 and chapter III extracts from a diary written by the 'city catechist' Schawrirajen in 1795. NHB, vol. 5, Contents, XX. The 52nd *Stück* in the same volume of the NHB is only divided into chapter I 'von der Trankenbarischen Mission' and chapter II 'von den Englischen Missionen'. In chapter I reports and letters of the missionaries, of the country pastor Rajappen (1742–96/7) and of some catechists are on equal footing. NHB Vol. 5, Contents, XXI.

found in other German Protestant mission societies of the nineteenth century.[29] The reports are written in the form of a first person narrative, i.e. the South Indian co-workers, who are identifiable as authors, present their experiences and successes. In the nineteenth century the quantitative factor suppressed descriptions of personal and content-based conflicts. The missionary as the superior and supervisor of the Tamilians again came into the foreground. Local co-workers are now seldom mentioned by name. Instead, the ability of the Tamilians to manage their own churches in the future is now again a matter of doubt. The missionaries did not see the reason for this, for example, in the (continued) lack of training, but in the 'nature' of the Tamilians, whose 'national character', they felt, was marked by 'timidity, inconsistency and volatility'. These 'national weaknesses' meant that even the coming generations would need constant supervision. Indeed, the missionaries went so far as to question the ordination of Indians because, according to them, the country pastors were not in a position to do justice to their role.[30]

Authentic and autobiographical portrayals of Tamilians in the context of the Tranquebar Mission contain mainly descriptions of their religious experience leading to conversion or expressions of gratitude towards the missionaries and the financial supporters of the mission. However, it should be pointed out that even the résumés written by European missionary candidates and sent to Halle focused on an extensive description of the religious experience and thus were more in the nature of edifying tracts. Information about the life of the person was communicated only sparingly.[31] In contrast to this

[29] Although excerpts from the reports of local co-workers were published in the annual reports of the Evangelical Mission Society at Basel, the importance given to these reports was not as great as in the framework of the Tranquebar Mission. Cf. for example, *Sixtieth Annual Report of the Evangelical Mission Establishments at Basel*, 1 July 1895, The Experiences of a Native Traveling Pastor, 38–42.

[30] NHB 58. St., 842, report from Tranquebar, 1 January 1807.

[31] This practice changed only in the middle of the nineteenth century. The résumés of some of the local teachers in the mission files of the London Mission Society (LMS) and the Church Mission Society (CMS) are a good example of this. Some of these people had emerged from the context of the Tranquebar Mission. The documents contain important dates in their lives and facts about the family, education and career of the person concerned. One of the résumés has the title: 'The History of George Davenport or Daniel Pilley' and begins with the words: 'I was born of Christian parents in the great and celebrated city of Tanjore. My father

there are regular assessments of the local co-workers in the sources. When a co-worker was appointed to a new job, or was ordained, or when he died, his work was honoured in the mission reports.[32] The most important factor in the assessment of the 'national workers' was their usefulness as co-workers and the advantages for the mission. These criteria, which dominated in the conceptual canon of Christian missions, were, however, not restricted to the 'national workers' alone; they were also applied to the assessment of European missionaries or mission employees.[33] If a missionary felt that the life of an Indian would be particularly interesting for a European reader, he would ask this person to write the story of his life or to narrate it so that the missionary could write it.[34] On the whole, when portrayals of cooperation with South Indian individuals were sent to Europe, the reasons for this portrayal determined whether the successes of the Tamil co-workers were recognized or whether doubts about the employment of South Indians in the mission were expressed.

Reports on the work of local mission employees were coloured, to a great extent, by the personal attitude of the missionary concerned towards the use of Tamilians in the mission. Differing powers of observation as well as varying descriptive skills were only two of the many reasons for differences in these reports. Although the mission could not have been run without the cooperation of local employees, not all missionaries ascribed the same importance to their work. The

---

and mother were in early life converted to Christianity and received Baptism from the Rev. Mr Schwarts.' The reader then learns that the candidate was born in 1811, was baptized by [J.C.] Kohlhoff, attended the mission school and, after a period of confusion, he became a mission school teacher in 1834 and a catechist in 1839. Cf. SOAS/CWM South Indian (Tamil) Incoming Correspondence 1816–1860, Box no. 9, 1844–1847, 'Short Account of all the Native Teachers here employed at the expense of kind friends in England'.

[32] Thus, for instance, the biography of Philipp (1731/43?–88) was published in 1772 after he was ordained (NHB 10. St., 1333–36), and the biography of Ambrosius (1713–77) appeared in 1777 after his death (NHB 19. St., 766).

[33] Schneiders, Werner (ed.), 2001, *Lexikon der Aufklärung. Deutschland und Europa*, C.H. Beck, München, 291f.

[34] John wrote, among others, the story of Ananda Rayer's life, a Brahmin who had been a catechist for the Catholic mission and who later worked for the Tranquebar Mission as an informant and translator. NHB 67. St., 621-27. John also wrote the life-story of the *dubash* Daniel Pullei (see the beginning of the introduction as well as chapter four of this book).

role of the local co-workers in a mission station also depended on the personal equation of the missionaries with 'their' Indian co-workers. What was also important was how the co-worker perceived the significance of his own role and responsibilities as the representative of a religion to which the Tamilians, according to the missionaries, (still) did not have adequate access. The missionary Benjamin Schultze, who directed mission matters in Tranquebar from 1720 to 1726, is said to have had a negative attitude towards the work of the local employees.[35] Even in Christoph Theodosius Walther's early attitude D. Jeyaraj doubted the ability of South Indians to carry out missionary work equal to that of the Europeans. Walther, however, changed his opinion on the basis of new experiences and insights.[36] During the period when Jacob Klein (1721-90) was mostly responsible for training the catechists, regularly updated lists with the names of the 'national workers' were sent to Halle, but were generally not published there.[37] Christian Friedrich Schwartz tended towards a paternally strict, but also a well-meaning manner in his dealings with the Indian co-workers. Especially between 1762 and 1768, when he was the only missionary working in Tiruchirappalli, the catechists, teachers and assistants under his supervision alleviated his loneliness. Co-operation could, however, also gain paternalistic features: 'The catechists have to be encouraged every day in a friendly manner, otherwise they become lazy and dishonest.'[38] On the one

[35] Jeyaraj, 'Ordination of the First Protestant Pastor Aaron', 12.

[36] Ibid.

[37] AFSt/M 2 A 2 : 7, list of names of the 'national workers' in the Portuguese congregation and the Tamil city and village congregations, ??.??.1746; AFSt/M 2 A 2 : 8, list of names of the 'national workers' in the Portuguese congregation and the Tamil city and village congregations, ??.??.1743; AFSt/M 2 A 2 : 9, list of names of all the 'national workers', ??.??.1749; AFSt/M 2 A 2 : 10, list of names of the 'national workers' in the Portuguese congregation and the Tamil city and village congregations, 1 August 1763; AFSt/M 2 A 2 : 11, Number of 'national workers' in Tranquebar in 1749, ??.??.1749; AFSt/M 2 A 2 : 12, list of names of the 'national workers' in the Portuguese congregations and the Tamil city and village congregations, ??.??.1749; AFSt/M 2 A 2 : 13, list of names of the 'national workers' in the Portuguese congregations and the Tamil city and village congregations, ??.??.1749; AFSt/M 2 B 3 : 21, index of the 'national workers' by Jacob Klein, ??. October 1776; AFSt/M 2 B 3 : 22a, Tamil assistants in February 1777 by [Jacob Klein], ??.??.1777.

[38] NHB 2. St., 256, letter from Ch. F. Schwartz to G.A. Francke, 6 October 1768, (translated from German).

hand, the missionaries wanted and had to maintain a distance in order to establish their position, on the other hand, a relationship of trust and confidence between the South Indian mission workers and the missionaries undeniably benefited the common endeavour.

In the reports, letters and treatises of the Tranquebar Mission the reader constantly encounters different terms for, and verbal descriptions of the group of the South Indian co-workers or of individual representatives of this group. In the case of the Tranquebar Mission the expression 'national workers' was the term most commonly used by the missionaries for the local co-workers of the mission.[39] There was no official regulation for naming the group. The terms used by the missionaries range from 'workers of the nation', 'national helpers', 'national workers' to 'native helpers'. Bartholomäus Ziegenbalg divided the 'national workers' from a functional perspective into two groups: the 'workers for the Word', who were the country pastors, catechists, assistants and teachers, and 'workers for the external institutions' such as bookbinders, printers, washer men, book-keepers, cooks and grave-diggers.[40] This division was, however, not retained in the later reports. In the regularly maintained detailed descriptions of the condition of the mission members of the entire group were named—however the lists were not always complete. The missionaries understood the concept of nation not only in the ethnic, linguistic and geographical sense, but also in the religious sense. They talked of 'Protestant nations', the 'Mohammedan nations', as well as of the 'Malabarian nation' and the 'European nations'.[41]

The European side essentially took over the same terms used by the missionaries in India. What is remarkable in this context is that the term 'assistant' and 'worker' could be applied to a European as well as to an Indian. When, for example, the editor of the NHB,

[39] This term does not appear to have been used by other missions, which, as a rule, spoke of evangelists, helpers or mission assistants.

[40] HB 33. Cont., 858–74 (1733). Cf. also: HB, Vorrede, 27. Cont., § XV. Others named here are: soldiers, spice-merchants, flower-sellers, potters, brick makers, stone masons, wool-beaters, farm-workers, daily-wagers, basket-weavers, mat-weavers, grass-cutters, wood-sellers, porters and thatchers.

[41] Cf. for example, HB 8. Cont., 95, or 195; HB 9. Cont., 684; HB 10. Cont., 815.

Georg Christian Knapp (1753–1825), spoke in the preface to the 56th *Stück* in 1800 of the 'new Tranquebar assistants' ('neue Trankenbarsche Gehülfen'), he meant primarily the newly arrived European missionaries.[42] Terms such as 'workers in the mission institutions', 'employees in the institutions of the Danish mission', 'national assistants', 'workers of the nation' or 'assistants of the nation' were interchangeable.[43] In the later period of the mission the term 'co-worker' also appeared; one which makes the stronger tie of the person to the structures of the mission more evident.[44] In the reports of the Tranquebar Mission one seldom finds terms or descriptions with regard to the Indian co-workers, which highlight external characteristics or contain racial prejudices.[45] Despite all these mixed terms it was, in the final analysis, made very clear that the superiority of the European missionaries was absolute and unassailable. This was evident in the fact that the ordained South Indians were, *de facto*, not considered equals of the European missionaries and were not included in the missionary conference, which constituted the local governing and decision making body. Even as country-pastors they remained 'local co-workers' or 'local helpers'; the term 'local missionaries' was never used.

In Tranquebar and the rural districts that belonged to it since the 1730s the ratio of European missionaries to local co-workers changed only minimally. On the whole, there were always four or five South Indian co-workers (pastors, catechists, teachers or

[42] NHB, Vorrede, 56. St.

[43] See the prefaces to the individual issues, which were generally written by the editors of the reports and which often contained indications of the role of the South Indian co-workers in the relevant period.

[44] In a joint letter of 20 December 1766 from Johann Philipp Fabricius and Johann Christian Breithaupt to the editor of the *Halle Reports* (HB) the term 'national co-workers' is used. HB 106. Cont., 1469. Georg Christian Knapp writes about an Indian mission employee 'who is a native of the country and our co-worker'. NHB, Vorrede, 60. St., VI.

[45] In the first decades a distinction was always made between 'Blancs', i.e. the Europeans, and 'Blacks', i.e. the South Indians. The so-called Portuguese were also called 'Catholic Blacks'. HB 2. Cont., 107. These terms, however, rarely implied an assessment of the capabilities and the worth of a person. Value judgments were distinctly linked to religious criteria. In the late phase of the mission there were far more deprecatory opinions and doubts about the capabilities of the local people.

assistants)—and not counting the technical personnel—to one missionary. The following table shows the development in the numbers of European missionaries and South Indian employees in the mission station Tranquebar (city and rural districts) from 1706 to 1845. The South Indian employees enumerated here only include those who were directly involved with missionary work, i.e. pastors, catechists, teachers and assistants.[46]

TABLE 2.1 Number of European missionaries and local employees in the mission station Tranquebar (city and ural districts) from 1706 to 1845

Year	European missionaries	local employees
1706	2	
1709	5 (of who two were not ordained)	
1712	4 (of who two were not ordained)	6
1734	6	24
1735	6	31
1737	7	
1743	7	27
1744	7	31
1759		30
1760	7	33
1762	6	31
1763	6	30
1769	4	18
1770	4	18
1775	6	24 (including prayer leaders)
1778	6	28 (including prayer leaders)

[46] This survey is based on the statistical information provided in the *Halle Reports* (HB) and the *New Halle Reports* (NHB). However, a comparison between the two is problematic on account of the changing criteria for recording statistical data.

The ratio of European missionaries to Indian co-workers only represents a fraction of the mission structure as a whole. In order to get an idea of the entire extent of a mission station, a detailed description of all the co-workers of the station in Tranquebar for the year 1712 is being reproduced here in its entirety.

> [...] 1.) two missionaries 2.) One co-worker. 3.) One European teacher in the Danish school who is also the organist and sacristan in the Jerusalem church. 4.) One teacher in the Portuguese school. 5.) One Malabarian teacher for the older Malabarian school boys. 6.) One teacher for the younger Malabarian school boys. 7.) One female supervisor in the Malabarian girls' school who is assisted by one of the older girls to assign lessons to the others and to hear them repeat the lessons. This supervisor also visits and teaches the women of the congregation. 8.) A Malabarian catechist whose duties have been mentioned earlier. 9.) A Portuguese catechist. 10.) A female cook and the girls who have been assigned to her to feed the Malabarian school children. 11.) A female cook with one girl as assistant to feed the Portuguese school children. 12.) A person to teach the girls sewing and other household tasks. 13.) A manager whose duties have been mentioned earlier. 14.) A doctor for the schools and congregations. 15.) A gardener with one assistant for the garden in Boreiar. 16.) Another gardener in the newly set up garden in Tiliali. 17.) A domestic servant who is also the grave-digger. 18.) Two female water carriers who have to provide water for drinking and cooking every day to the kitchen, the house and the schools, since the water has to be fetched in pots from far away. 19.) A washerman who does a weekly wash of the clothes of all those who live in the house, so that young and old can wear clean clothes every Saturday. 20.) A house maid. 21.) Two Malabarian writers who help us missionaries when we need to dictate something in the Malabarian language and who also make copies of those books that have been written in this language or have been translated into this language. These books are then used in the schools or are, from time to time, distributed among the heathens.[47]

The later descriptions of the number of co-workers were, as a rule, less detailed. At the end of the 1720s the mission began to expand to the region surrounding Tranquebar and the so-called rural districts

[47] HB 6. Cont., 330f., (translated from German).

were incorporated into the area of work. In the statistical description for the year 1732 following South Indian co-workers were listed for the Malabarian city congregation of Tranquebar: '11 men, namely 4 catechists, 1 assistant, 1 Kanakappel, 1 printer, 2 school teachers, 1 church attendant and 1 grave digger: also 10 women, namely 1 supervisor, 1 instructor, 1 nurse, 1 school teacher, 2 buyers and 4 cooks'. For the Malabarian rural congregation the total number of school teachers and assistant mentioned is seven.[48] In addition, there were stations in Madras, Cuddalore and Tiruchirappalli, which were supported by the SPCK, but run by missionaries who had been educated in Halle and some of who had also worked for some time in Tranquebar and its surrounding region. In the annual mission statistics the details for the individual places were, from then on, given separately.[49]

Although the conversions that took place in the history of the Tranquebar Mission were primarily individual acts of conversion, it would be wrong to view these developments only as inner processes of change in individuals. Every decision required external impulses and influences and can only be explained on the basis of the social position, the level of education and the social environment of the person concerned. If one takes the fact into account that in most of the academic research into social backgrounds and social effects of religious conversion cases of mass conversions are highlighted, the question arises as to the applicability of these findings to the example of the Tranquebar Mission. It, therefore, becomes necessary to summarize the basic arguments of the current academic debate on religious conversion arising out of modern Christian missionary activity from the point of view of its validity for the present study.

Taking the convert and his individual motives as a starting point some authors regard conversion primarily as the outcome of an inner decision and less as an effect of external influences. This category comprises mainly biographical works that seek to understand an inner process of change. Conversion here is preceded each time

[48] HB 34. Cont., 1008f., (5 October 1732), (translated from German).

[49] For 1769, for example, along with the reports and statistics for Tranquebar, there were descriptions of the growth of the congregations and schools in the mission stations Madras and Cuddalore. Cf. NHB 3. St., 267–334 (Tranquebar); 335–51 (Madras); 352–420 (Cuddalore).

by the independent thoughts and actions of an individual. From among several options the acting subject chooses that option, which offers him the possibility of understanding and explaining the world better. This means that a person takes a decision based on a conscious, systematic comparison of the principles and teachings of different religious systems and that he examines their religious and social content with regard to their compatibility with an individual life style.[50]

If, in contrast to this, the point of departure is located in the content of religions, the authors argue with the methods of religious studies. In the context of the change from traditional tribal religions to so-called world religions it is stated that world religions are organized more conceptually and more systematically and are, therefore, more in a position to provide answers to the challenges of global developments. Monotheistic religions, in particular, are linked with social change and the ability to mobilize people, while traditional systems of faith, according to this view, are a thing of the past. Robert W. Hefner proceeds from the stability of the large 'world religions', since people from tribal and officially not recognized religions are always converting to new faiths, whereas world religions have outlasted and continue to outlast empires, realms and political systems. Hefner, therefore, posits the 'world-building aspect of religious conversion'.[51] He states 'All the world faiths relativize received social ways by announcing a Truth without which, they claim, human existence has no real meaning.'[52]

Against the background of a concrete historical situation, however, processes of conversion can neither be explained on religious grounds alone, nor exclusively through the biography of the person concerned. Rather, the historian must unravel a complex interaction of different historical events, social factors, biographical circumstances and religious teachings. He can only approach the spanning arch between social processes of transformation and their individual biographical

[50] Cf., among others, Lewis, R. Rambo, 1993, *Understanding Religious Conversion*, Yale University Press, New Haven.

[51] Hefner, Robert William (ed.), 1993, *Conversion to Christianity: Historical and Anthropological Perspectives on a Great Transformation*, University of California Press, Berkeley, 3.

[52] Ibid., 34.

characteristics through an inductive method, i.e. by unlocking and analyzing numerous biographies. A conversion is not the outcome of religious reflections alone. Reflections on matters of faith are also influenced by external factors and experiences. In his study of conversion in different regions of Java Robert Hefner established that the degree of influx into Christianity varied greatly across regions. In his analysis he proceeds from the idea that the reasons for this variation can only be explained by combining socio-historical factors and individual life histories. He expresses some doubts about the proposition that a person has a choice between two systems and chooses one that would better enable him to understand and explain the world. As against this he states that 'social, political and moral influences often take precedence over intellectualist explanation and control in the process of conversion.'[53] 'Thus, an individual can be committed to a particular belief system without understanding its conceptual truth of social entailment.'[54] In the relevant literature on the history of Christian missionary efforts there is often agreement about the idea that conversion to Christianity is the result of a problematic situation or an identity crisis of the person or group of persons concerned. It is generally understood that if a person is not—in Weber's terms—driven by the search for a new faith as an instrument to solve every day contradictions, then, as a rule, their actions are determined by purely material reasons.

With regard to India Dick Kooiman argues on the basis of socio-economic aspects of conversion movements among the 'untouchables' in Travancore that conversion in India can never be viewed as a purely individual act, but that it is always linked with the social sentiments of the disadvantaged and oppressed groups of society. Proceeding from the understanding that religion influences all spheres of human life, Kooiman shows through the example of mass conversions of *dalits* in the nineteenth century in Travancore that for these groups the change of religion was linked with changes in the social self-image: conversion was perceived as an act of social mobility, as the possibility of social protest or as an escape from discrimination and oppression. In this concrete

[53] Hefner, Robert W., 'Of Faith and Commitment: Christian Conversion in Muslim Java', in Hefner, *Conversion to Christianity*, 99–128, here 102.

[54] Ibid., 122.

context it was the encounter with Western imperialism, which led the *dalits* to engage with Christianity: 'that Christianity is adopted by people as part of a process of adaption to a new situation created by western imperialism.'[55] Kooiman, therefore, focuses on the active input of the converts and understands conversion as a search for self-determination by some social groups. Gauri Vishvanathan puts forward a similar argument when she makes a strong plea not to view conversion as an externally controlled process but, instead, to always place the subject(s) in the focus of the argument. It is only then, she states, that the interaction between missionaries and converts can be understood. With the example of Henry Newman who converted to Catholicism in 1845 she shows conversion as an act whereby an individual critically examines his society.[56]

Scholars who work with the dichotomy of the microcosm and the macrocosm while studying the local religion or a world religion combine the methods of the social sciences with those of religious studies.[57] Terence Ranger examines the proposition of locally situated traditional religions as microcosms against the macrocosm of the globally oriented world religions.[58] In order to refute the idea that microcosmically oriented traditional religions do not have the wherewithal to meet the challenges of the global perspective of Christianity, Ranger tries to turn this proposition around. He attests to the far-sightedness of African religions and shows that Christianity had to be 'localized' in order to establish itself in the African context. The Africans were not immediately willing to abandon their world and rush into the adventure of a completely new and unknown religion: 'the impact of Christianity and Colonialism is different from the notion of a frontal smashing of secure corporate identity.'[59] These insights led missionaries to 'standardize' the local traditional religions by listening to their histories and their teachings, by writing them down and introducing written languages, which, in turn, opened

[55] Kooiman, *Conversion and Social Equality in India*, 8.

[56] Vishvanathan, Gauri, 1998, *Outside the Fold: Conversion, Modernity and Belief*, Princeton University Press, Princeton, 44–72.

[57] Cf. Horton, Robin, 1975, 'On the Rationality of Conversion', Part I, *Africa* 45 (3): 219–35.

[58] Ranger, Terence, 'The Local and the Global in Southern African Religious History', in Hefner, *Conversion to Christianity*, 65–98.

[59] Ibid., 75.

up the possibility of influencing local religious teachings. Ranger proceeds in his argument from an existing reciprocal relationship between missionary work and conversion and shows that missions reacted to a diverse interest in Christian teachings as well as to a varying willingness to convert through a change in their methods. Although this correlation appears to be obvious and necessary for understanding conversion processes in the context of mission history, it has not always been sufficiently considered in research on mission history.

For the present study, which is concerned with the motives, the sense of identity and the role of the staff of local co-workers in a mission society, it is important to give due consideration to this reciprocal relationship between mission and conversion. In order to achieve the conversion of the local population—the goal of Christian missionary activity—the missionaries looked for ways to reach the people. The local language played a decisive role in this, and the local co-workers of the mission were best equipped for this. The Tranquebar Mission was not one of those missions where written languages had to be developed as a medium for the dissemination of the Christian faith and as a wide base of communication between the mission and the local population. Nevertheless, language skills constituted a decisive pre-condition for missionary work and translations were an important means for transferring the idea of conversion. Language was not only a means for translating texts, but also for transferring certain norms of life and a specific understanding of society. The translation of religious contents and teachings was embedded in a comprehensive scenario of intercultural encounter in which all the participants—in the interest of understanding and being understood—strove to find social equivalences corresponding to the alien context. Knowledge of religion and language alone was not enough. The translations could be meaningful only if the missionaries knew and understood the cultural and social context of the mission region, and only then would the transmission of Christian teachings and its way of life be met with curiosity and acceptance. Conversion could only produce a sustainable change if the potential converts in the local population were willing to undergo a change of identity beyond the change of religion. In the case of some groups this would lead to a fresh determination of their place in society. It is important, however, not to look only at parallelisms and reciprocal relations between mission and conversion. There is, rather, an interweaving and a melting together of both into a single indivisible element in the framework of cultural translations. If one looks at conversion as the interweaving of social and religious change, one arrives at Županov's conclusion that religious conversion is strictly a rational decision, a process of cultural, social and economic exchange and differentiation, as well as the result of intercultural encounters. She compares the process of religious conversion with cultural or linguistic translation.[60]

If we look at the history of global Christian missionary activity we see that the methods used to convince the people of the region about the validity of Christian dogma were very different and extended from the slow work of individual persuasion to quick and forceful mass conversions. Accordingly, the degree of self-determination of the convert in this decision has to be judged differently. When the Jesuit Francisco de Xavier simultaneously baptized tens of thousands of fishermen on the east coast of India in the sixteenth century, one can hardly assume that the converts had taken an independent and conscious step.[61] But, even when conversion happened under threat and the use of force, it did not imply that the missionized sections of the population were only passive victims of this action. Even in these cases one perceives a 'strategic action' taken by the people

[60] Županov, Ines G., 1999, 'Religious Conversion, Cultural Translation in Early Modern South India', *IIAS Newsletter* (19): 51. For the question of 'cultural translation' see also: Bachmann-Medick, Doris, 2002, 'Übersetzung im Spannungsfeld von Dialog und Erschütterung. Ein Modell der Auseinandersetzung zwischen Kulturen und Disziplinen', in Joachim Renn et.al., *Übersetzung als Medium des Kulturverstehens und sozialer Integration*, 275–91, Campus, Frankfurt, New York; Fuchs, Martin, 'Soziale Pragmatik des Übersetzens. Strategien der Interkulturalität in Indien', in Joachim Renn et al., *Übersetzung als Medium des Kulturverstehens und sozialer Integration*, 292–323, Campus, Frankfurt am Main, New York; Liebau, 'Alle Dinge, die zu wissen nötig sind.'

[61] For the 'Letter from Xavier to the Fathers of the Society in Rome, Cochin, 27 January 1545' see Sonntag, Franz Peter and Siegfried Foelz (eds.), 1977, *Die Briefe des Francisco de Xavier 1542–1552*, selected and translated by Elisabeth Gräfin von Vitzthum, with an introduction by Franz Peter Sonntag, Suhrkamp, Frankfurt am Main, 82.

concerned. Rowena Robinson points out to this in the context of an analysis of the edict issued by the inquisition in Goa.[62]

The methods used by the Pietists in the eighteenth century were, admittedly, different to the ones used in Xavier's times; the number of conversions was far smaller and individual conversions led to changes in the life of a person. However, this statement does not say anything about the voluntary nature of this decision and also about the insights, aims, expectations, wishes and hopes linked with it. With the Christian dogma the missionaries initially made a religious offer, which, under certain historical conditions, could be understood as a social offer and which was also accepted as such by some social groups. The missions used this connection by linking the religious with the social and propagating the equality of all human beings in the institutions run by them. This was something that the local population did not associate with traditional systems of faith.

MOTIVES FOR CONVERSION

With only a few exceptions, the South Indian employees of the Tranquebar Mission were Christians. Some of them grew up in Christian households, received a Christian upbringing and were, therefore, not choosing an unusual career when they entered into the service of the mission. Others had had an individual conversion experience, which had brought about a fundamental change in their lives, as a result of which they developed a strong motivation for missionary work. While considering the motives for conversion the specific circumstances of life of each of the persons concerned, the social conditions, the social background and the status of the person has to be taken into account. The work of the Tranquebar Mission was characterized by individual conversions, entire families seldom converted together.[63] Mass conversions to Christianity did not take place in the context of the Tranquebar Mission, if one disregards

[62] Robinson, Rowena, 2000, 'Taboo or Veiled Consent? Goan Inquisitorial Edict of 1736', *EPW*, 35 (27): 2423–31.

[63] It was only in the nineteenth century that missionaries reported about large family conversions. Some cases in Palayankottai became well known. Several families here asked the mission to give them confirmation classes. NHB 72. St., 1271, report of the missionaries Rhenius and Schmid dated 1823.

conversions on a larger scale under the influence of Clarinda (1746–about 1793) and Christian David (1771–1852) at the end of the eighteenth and the beginning of the nineteenth century.[64]

Besides the many individual experiences, events and expectations, which made a person change his faith and work with the Europeans, more general factors such as religious background and caste, level of education, social and material conditions of life, experiences of Christianity or of Christians also played a role. The specific methods of proselytizing used by the mission society concerned should also be taken into account. In a pietistic influenced mission, like the Tranquebar Mission, a high degree of individuality and a personal relationship to the faith constituted the point of departure. In keeping with this, the missionaries ensured that the future Christian engaged with substantive questions of the new faith according to his possibilities and abilities. Just as the individual motives for an interest in Christianity and in missionary work could vary considerably, the degree of engagement in the process of conversion and the expectations linked with this decision were different.

In each case there was an entire complex of circumstances that made a person change his religion.[65] When we have more

[64] For Clarinda see NHB, vol. 2, Vorrede VI, 21. St., 1095; 22. St., 1195; 23. St., 1302; 24. St., 1432f.; 29. St., 592; 31. St., 756f., 761, 772, 779; 33. St., 1028f.; 45. St., 785, 839; 46. St., 927; Packiamuthu, David, 'Schwartz, Clarinda and Sathianathan', in Jeyaraj, *Christian Friedrich Schwartz*, 58–73; Kadambavanam, Paul S., 1960, *Tirunelveli attiyācatin ārampam* (in Tamil), the Foundation of the Diocese of Tirunelveli, Chennai; Caldwell, Robert A., 1989, *A political and general history of the District of Tinnevelly, in the Presidency of Madras, from the earliest period to its cession to the English Government in AD 1801*, (Government Press, Madras 1881) Reprint: *A History of Tinnevelly*, Asian Educational Services, New Delhi/Madras; Caldwell, Robert A., 1881, *Records of the Early History of the Tinnevelly Mission of the Society for Promoting Christian Knowledge and the Society for the Propagation of the Gospel in Foreign Parts*, Higginbotham and Co., Madras; Madhaviah, A., 1992, *Clarinda. A Historical Novel*, (first ed. 1915), Nanbar Vattam, Tirunelveli; for Christian David see NHB vol. 5, Vorrede VII; 59. St., 1012, 1083; 60. St., 1091f; 70. St., 988, 999; RA Miskolark 9i, report on the situation of the Royal Danish Mission in Trankenbar in the year 1803 from Ch. S. John, J.P. Rottler, A.F. Cämmerer (duplicate, page 15); Archives of the Gurukul Lutheran Theological College and Research Institute, Chennai Acc. No. 384, Autobiography of the late Rev. Christian David (1771-1852).

[65] Dick Kooiman speaks of a complicated process, 'in which social, economic, psychological and spiritual motives were blended together in one complex whole'. Kooiman, *Conversion and Social Equality in India*, 8.

biographical facts at our disposal, our analysis of the motives becomes more realistic. Since we are not dealing here with mass conversions as the outcome of a common problem, but with individual paths of development, the biographical data must be investigated with great care. For many members of the group of people being studied here there are biographical portraits in which the motives may not be described explicitly, but from which one can deduce with some degree of certainty that the change of faith was an attempt to overcome some sort of a crisis or a feeling of dissatisfaction. Despite the individual nature of the ultimate decision to convert, the concrete reasons and occasions for a Hindu to accept Christianity were paradigmatic for a particular social group. In some cases, the persons had had direct contact with European missionaries, or experiences with Christians, or, in some way, had gained knowledge of Christian teachings. In the search for motives for conversion we see, on the one hand, factors, which led a person to reflect for some time and then to convert. On the other hand, unforeseen events could accelerate this development, or could even be the cause for it. When all these factors are taken into consideration conversion could be a reflection of, the beginning or the (temporary) conclusion of personal processes of change. It is difficult to draw a clear distinction between religious and social considerations. In the consciousness of the Indians daily life and the practice of religiosity constituted a unity. For the mass of the population religiosity was not an escape from daily life; it was not primarily spirituality but, as a means to solve problems, it was a practical part of their daily lives. These factors must be taken into account while attempting to reconstruct and analyze the motives of the 'national workers' and other local Christians. It is only then that we can avoid viewing conversions and the decision to enter missionary service in a one-sided way as a form of 'rice Christianity', or as a search for personal benefits through the co-operation with Europeans.

CONVERSION AS AN EXPRESSION OF SOCIAL DISSATISFACTION

Although personal benefit as a motive for conversion to Christianity cannot be discounted, it cannot be generalized as the only and most decisive reason for this step. In any case, Boissevain's approach, whereby an intermediary (broker) must be regarded as an entrepreneur 'who tries to manipulate norms and relationships for his own social and psychological benefit'[66] is too sweeping a statement for the group being studied. The self-interest of the protagonists, which was, by all means, present, cannot be compared with a desire for profit and, in this group of persons, it also extended to the group or the caste that they represented. Large conversion movements of the nineteenth and twentieth centuries, in the course of which entire villages or caste communities converted to Christianity, often took place in the context of far-reaching processes of social and economic change.[67] For *dalits*, who were not allowed inside Hindu temples, conversion to Christianity was linked with the goal of equality, since Christian churches were open to them. The rejection of caste distinctions in Christianity, which many associated with social equality, could become both the reason for conversion as well as the reason against it. In the *Malabarian Correspondence* members of high castes replied to questions from the missionaries concerning this.[68] But even for a *pa aiy r* who, on the basis of his position in society, should have been interested in overcoming caste distinctions, becoming a Christian did not automatically lead to an improvement in his position. It was only the mass conversions of the nineteenth century that led, more or less successfully, to the desired changes. In the context of the work of the Tranquebar Mission, however, individual conversions remained the norm and these were not always linked to an increase in the person's social standing. The social position of widows in Hinduism often led women, whose husbands had died, to approach the mission with their children and ask for baptism. This happened for instance in

[66] Boissevain, *Friends of Friends*, 7.

[67] Luig, *Conversion as a Social Process*, 13.

[68] To the question: 'Why do the Malabars refuse to convert to the Christian religion?' the missionaries received the following reply: 'There are many families of human beings [a]/created by God. Because we see/that the Christians do not observe these distinctions between families/but make them all into one [b]/also, despite the fact that in the two genders/the male and the female [c]/there is a great difference/they gather all the people into one congregation without any distinctions [d]; therefore, we would not like to become part of such a religion.' (translated from German), Cf. HB 7. Cont., 342f.

the case of the widow of the Tamil city school teacher Rajappen (1743?–73).[69]

European institutions, including mission stations, employed many Indians. Every mission station had religious, social and economic establishments and represented a fairly extensive enterprise with churches, graveyards, gardens, workshops, clinics, schools, hostels and other establishments. A network of such stations along with smaller outposts comprised the structure of the mission society in the region of its activity. In order to maintain and run such a structure it not only required a continuous flow of finances and goods from Europe, such as medicines or school-material, but also a reliable staff of co-workers in the country itself. As an employer, the Tranquebar Mission gave many South Indians a stable material foundation to provide for their families. Whereas in the early period non-Christians were often given employment, especially in the economic sphere, this practice was later avoided by training, among others, pupils of the mission schools in specific professions.

European trading societies liked to employ local Christians in their establishments and willingly took on Tamilians educated in mission schools who came recommended with an evaluation and a testimonial and were often specially trained for a profession. Sometimes, one or the other individual was forced to ask the missionaries to baptize him in the hope of then getting a particular post: 'In the afternoon a young man came to one of us and asked for baptism and a Christian name because he had been promised a job as a drummer in the Company and could not get this job unless he became a Christian.'[70] In 1729 the missionaries in Tranquebar reported that a Muslim, in desperation born of poverty, agreed to becoming a Christian because he hoped that the mission would then support him and his family. His three children were admitted to the mission school but were made to leave almost immediately when it became clear to the missionaries that the man was not taking his preparation for baptism seriously.

[69] Rajappen came in 1751, at the age of eight, as a Hindu with his mother and other siblings to Tranquebar. NHB 12. St., 1571f.

[70] HB 78. Cont., 938., report from Cuddalore, 30 March 1752, (translated from German).

> Some time ago a Mohammedan man, a Padtâni or Tulukker, driven by extreme poverty, arrived at the decision to convert to the Christian religion along with his family. Since he put up a good show we admitted his three children to our charity school, which was a great help for him in these circumstances. In the meantime, however, he found another way to earn a livelihood, which he soon misused; he again fell into his earlier habit of drinking and did not come for instruction in the Christian faith. That is why we had to give him and his children up after two months.[71]

Existential and material conditions, however, could also constitute reasons against conversion, since not every convert could count on employment with the mission to provide for himself and his family. Conversion was, initially, more likely to lead to heavy losses. Valuable social connections, the right to inheritance, the respect and the support of the village community were lost. Knowing these consequences and considering all the risks, Hindus were not always willing to move into an unknown new (Christian) way of life.

> Two people who cremate the dead have often stated in the presence of many heathens that they would not want to die without baptism, but that they knew no better time for this than at the end of their lives. Otherwise, they would not only lose their earnings, they would also incur the constant displeasure of the people if they did not wish to marry Mariammei and perform other heathen ceremonies.[72]

The lives of some mission employees demonstrate a marked interest in religious matters. The search for religious truth for oneself and the desire to pass on this truth to the people of the region or to the members of one's own caste often led these employees to consciously renounce all earlier comforts and security in order to build a new Christian existence for themselves against the will of the family. They often also dealt with the teachings of Christianity critically and compared the religious principles of different Christian denominations. As a Catholic, *paṟaiyār* and army officer, the catechist Rajanayakkan had engaged with different forms of Christianity even

[71] HB 28. Cont., 349, (translated from German).

[72] HB 61. Cont., 43f., diary of the Tranquebar missionaries, entry for 20 January 1744, (translated from German).

before he was employed by the Tranquebar Mission. In the search for a faith acceptable to Tamilians he linked religious change with social change. This included mediating the new teachings in a manner that was comprehensible and taking the sensibilities of the Tamilians into account while explaining Christianity.[73] In his comparative analysis of religions he, as a *paṟaiyār*, confidently took the possibility of having a voice as his point of departure. Although the Tranquebar missionaries were his employers and superiors, he did not accept their teachings uncritically. Rajanayakkan viewed Christianity as an enrichment, but also as a challenge for Tamilians, which should not be accepted blindly. His attempt as a *dalit* to help build a Christian Church in South India from below made him an exception for his times and for his background. His attempts, however, also failed because of the inability of the missionaries to recognize this as opposed to the social realities. Had a 'casteless' priest been ordained, it would have set the standard for the Danish-English-Halle Mission early on.[74]

Persons with a higher caste background, especially Brahmins, subjected Christian teachings to a critical examination before they decided to change their religion. In the history of the Tranquebar Mission there were only a few Brahmins with close connections

[73] Rajanayakkan felt that instead of talking about the crucifixion of Christ to the Tamilians, one should talk about his deeds, which is what the Moravian missionaries in Tranquebar did. UH, R 15 Tb N° 1 b, Diaria Trankebar 1768–1782, entry for 1 March 1771. Even the idea of an eternal life after death, he felt, could be a strange concept for the Tamilians and would, therefore, have to be approached with care. HB 50. Cont., 273, entry for November 1739. Rajanayakkan's written texts represented a synthesis of Christian contents and forms of Tamil literature. His story of the Passion in the Tamil *ammāṉai*-verse form titled 'Jesu náderudeia nádupadudelin ammánei' 1732 [sic?], mentioned by Ch. T. Walther in his list of Tamil literature, has not yet been found. Cf. KB Ny kgl. S 589c, 4⁰ Bibliotheca Tamulica consistens in recensione librorum nostrorum, mscr.-torum ad cognoscendam et linguam & res Tamulicas inseruientium, by Ch. Th. Walther, 1731 [sic?], N⁰ 28. Jeyaraj, however suggests, that it is possible that the year 1731 as the date of compilation of the list is incorrect, since the list contains some titles that were written after 1731. Cf. Jeyaraj, *Inkulturation in Tranquebar*, 133f. Unfortunately, there are very few references to Rajanayakkan's work as a poet and translator. In 1744 Benjamin Schultze made a reference to a translation of Johann Arndt's 'Paradiesgärtlein' done by the Tamilian. AFSt/M 2 B 7 2 B 7 : 13 : 13, catalogue of books in Telugu and Tamil available in Madras, Tranquebar, Copenhagen and Halle, 12 December 1744. In this there is the remark: 'Arndt's Paradies Gärtlein, 4 parts in Tamil by the Thanjavur catechist Rajanaikken'.

[74] Liebau, 'Tamilische Christen im 18. Jahrhundert'.

to the mission. One of them was Tiruvengada Asarier, assistant in Kanchipuram. He translated texts into Sanskrit, talked to young Brahmins and received payment for this from the mission. Despite his close contacts with the mission he never converted to Christianity and continued to apply the holy signs on his forehead.[75] On the recommendation of Ch. S. John the Brahmin Ananda Rayer participated in the Telugu translation of the Bible in Vishakapatnam as an informant and translator. Originally a Hindu *samnyasin*, he allowed himself to be baptized by Catholic missionaries, was employed for some time by the Catholics in Polthutoor and then stayed with the Tranquebar Mission out of an interest in Christianity and in the search for interesting work to match his abilities. He ascribed his study of different religions mainly to inner motives.[76]

If positive events and developments in the family were, in some way or another, associated with the contact to Christianity, it often happened that a person converted to Christianity out of a sense of gratitude, or that a family decided to let one of the children become a Christian and be educated in the mission school. An example of this is the life of Philipp (1731/1743?-88) who later became a country pastor. All the members of his family were originally Hindus. After the death of his father Philipp, who was then 10 years old, was taken away by a slave-dealer and sold in Tranquebar. According to the sources, another slave, whose freedom had already been bought, helped the boy to inform his mother about his fate. She set off at once to free her son and was able to do this with the help of the missionaries in Tranquebar.[77] Out of gratitude she later sent Philipp and his sisters to the mission school. The children were baptized and Philipp was trained for a career in the mission, initially as a schoolteacher, then as a catechist. He was ordained at the age of 40 and appointed as a country pastor.[78]

[75] Cf. NHB 69. St., 910–911, letter from L.B.E. Schmid (1788–after 1845) to the editor (1818).

[76] NHB 67. St., 621f.

[77] Germann, *Johann Philipp Fabricius*, 102.

[78] AFSt/M 2 E 37: 1, report on the ordination of the new country pastor Philipp by Johann Balthasar Kohlhoff, Daniel Zeglin, Oluf Maderup, Jacob Klein, Johann Friedrich König, Friedrich Wilhelm Leidemann, Christoph Samuel John, 28 December 1772; cf. also: NHB 10. St., 1330–42, report of the ordination of the new country pastor Philipp 1772.

Even if one cannot speak of coercive methods of conversion in the case of the Tranquebar Mission and even if the missionaries wished to ensure that the local people had some knowledge of the Christian faith at the time of conversion, there are cases where, in varying degrees, pressure was exerted on persons to convert. First and foremost, this applied to slaves who were forced to become Christians, since the Europeans wanted Christians as domestic servants in their houses or even as employees in the European administration. One can also speak of a certain amount of pressure when, in situations of need, help was only provided if the person concerned demonstrated a willingness to convert to Christianity. This was also the case in the so-called private baptisms undertaken when a person was dying. In such cases there was no need for instruction and even catechists were entitled to carry out such private baptisms if the situation demanded it. The dying man/woman gained a measure of relief with the promise of paradise and freedom from all sins.[79]

In times of extreme need or danger the mission stations were often islands of prosperity. This meant that there was a significant growth in the number of converts when the population was suffering on account of war or natural calamities. This connection between social interests, religious ideas and needs of the protagonists that has been described in Weber's sociology of religion[80] implies that there are social reasons for conversion. For a study of missionary work this means that the activities of European missionaries can only be successful if the corresponding need for conversion is felt by the people concerned.[81] When wars devastated the country people thronged to the mission. In 1738 the mission registered an increase in the number of converts in the rural congregations 'which was

[79] Thus, the catechist Muttu, who had devoted himself to the care of the sick, baptized three children 'in an emergency' on 15 December 1768. NHB 2. St., 209, excerpt from the diary of the missionaries in Tranquebar. At the end of 1768 a sick, old man, whose entire family had converted to Christianity, was given a private baptism. NHB 3. St., 171, excerpt from the collective diary of the missionaries in Tranquebar, entry for 2 January 1769.

[80] Weber, Max, 1988, 'Die protestantische Ethik und der Geist des Kapitalismus', in M. Weber, *Gesammelte Aufsätze zur Religionssoziologie 1*, (first published 1922) Mohr/Siebeck, Tübingen.

[81] Hefner, *Conversion to Christianity*.

caused by the constant turbulences of war there'.[82] As a result of this the number of junior catechists in this region had to be increased. In times of political and military conflicts and the concomitant rise in prices even the mission schools registered an increase in the number of pupils. In 1773 the missionaries in Tranquebar reported that the city school had 'grown much larger during the period of war and inflation'.[83] Similarly, during Thanjavur's military conflicts with Ramnad, Sivaganga and the Nawab of Carnatic in the 1770s, a noticeably larger number of local people converted to Christianity.[84]

CRITERIA OF SELECTION

The South Indian co-workers of the mission were selected by the European missionaries. Whereas in the early years, when there was a great need for language teachers and interpreters, the missionaries were dependent on chance encounters with the local population, they later increasingly devised an active and systematic policy of selection. The creation of educational possibilities and the growth of local Protestant congregations allowed them to look for suitable persons from a Christian environment in the immediate vicinity. In order to be able to draw on local co-workers, the missionaries tried to win over Protestant Christians of the second, third and following generations for a career in the mission. They would be trained as catechists and the most suitable among them would be ordained. Often, this collaboration with the mission was continued over generations.[85] Depending on the position that had to be filled the selection was either the decision of a single missionary or the outcome of a joint discussion.

[82] HB 47. Cont., 1333, (translated from German), 5 October 1738.

[83] NHB 12. St., 1572.

[84] NHB, Preface, Vol. V.

[85] The descendants of the blind teacher Joao (Johann) d'Almeida (before 1679–1746), who was baptized in 1707 by Ziegenbalg, can be traced over three generation at least down to his grandson Daniel Pullei. In the case of the first country pastor Aaron, the genealogical line has been reconstructed down to the present. Cf. Jeyaraj, *Ordination of the First Indian Pastor Aaron*.

The selection and the systematic training of new co-workers were undertaken through a programme of special education. The missionaries could observe and influence the development of young Christians over a long period of time in the mission schools. After a decision was taken collectively to prepare one or the other child for a career in the mission, this decision was communicated to the superiors in Europe. The child then got additional supervision and training and was sometimes given additional aid from the donations sent from Europe. Individuals with this kind of a biography usually did not hesitate to agree when such an issue was placed before them. In some cases, they themselves expressed a desire to enter into the service of the mission.

The missionaries used various criteria while evaluating and selecting candidates, since the persons had to fulfill a number of other conditions besides professional aptitude. Future Tamil co-workers had to be Christians and could not have any doubts about the Christian faith for only then would they be convincing representatives of this faith. Since the methods of the Tranquebar Mission did not include mass baptisms, the missionaries assumed that the decisions of potential converts were, to a certain extent, voluntary. Travel, conversations, sermons and religious instruction, therefore constituted important aspects of the work of missionaries and mission employees. If a Tamilian expressed a desire to convert to Christianity, permission for this was generally given after a brief period of religious instruction/catechization and followed by an examination in the general principles of Christianity. The Christian congregations set up in this manner represented the most important base for recruiting loyal 'national workers' for the mission. Non-Christian mission co-workers were the exception among the local employees and were found, in the initial phase of the mission, mainly in the sphere of household and service establishments. Caneirum (died 1748), a writer with the manager of the mission from 1712, who was responsible under Benjamin Schultze, among others, for rice procurement, was apparently the last non-Christian mission worker.[86]

Knowledge of the country, of the culture, philosophy, literature and religion of the Tamilians, as well as the experience and ability to manage

[86] AB 218; HB 6. Cont., 276; 22. Cont., 869; 69. Cont., 1447.

finances were qualities that were welcomed in a 'national worker'. Knowledge of the local political and social, but also of climatic and natural conditions, were advantageous when working in the villages or when traveling, alone or when accompanying the missionaries. In keeping with the principle that one had to know the religion of the other in order to argue against it, some catechists and pastors used their knowledge of the local culture and literature in their daily conversations with the local population, so that they could be more convincing about Christian teachings. As representatives of a Christian mission the 'national workers' were constantly in touch with the people in the mission region. In order to communicate the principles of Christianity they not only needed communicative and rhetorical abilities; personal contacts, association with and access to certain sections of the population (caste, gender) were also important for the success of a mission co-worker. The greater a person's reputation, the greater was the willingness to listen to his explanations and sermons.

Knowledge of languages was one of the most important prerequisites for employment with the mission. In the initial phase, the local people who helped the European missionaries worked primarily as translators or language teachers. Thus, Aleppa (Arhagappan, [circa 1660–1730]) was appointed mainly because of his versatile linguistic abilities. Having come into contact early on with institutions and representatives of European colonial powers, he became the main interpreter of the Danish East India Company around the turn of the century and was the chief of the Tamilians in Tranquebar. His knowledge of German, Dutch, Portuguese, Danish and Tamil made him a suitable language teacher and interpreter for the first two missionaries. They, therefore, arranged for Aleppa's return to Tranquebar after he had been banished from Company territory for certain transgressions.[87]

Besides knowledge and individual capabilities, the social background, especially caste, was a decisive criterion of selection for missionary service. Thus, for example, the French mission of

[87] Aleppa had an eventful and turbulent life. Although he always worked with the Europeans, he also often had conflicts with them. Cf. HB 2. Cont., 82f.; 6. Cont., 223f.; 21. Cont., 755f., 761; 30. Cont., 527; AB 59, 77, 81, 106, 110f,; See also Liebau, Kurt, 1997, 'Die 'Malabarische Korrespondenz' von 1712/1713 und das Bild der Tamilen vom Europäer', *asien, afrika, lateinamerika* (25): 53–73.

the nineteenth century in South Arcot tried to recruit their local co-workers from the higher castes, since they wanted to proselytize among these castes.[88] The Danish Mission Society in southeast India took another path. Initially it recruited its catechists, especially members of lower castes, from other missions like the American Arcot Mission, the American Madurai Mission, the CMS, the LMS or the Basel Mission. After the mission society had established itself and the number of congregants had increased, the Danish mission began to train its local co-workers in its own institutions.[89]

Even for the Tranquebar Mission the caste affiliation of a candidate for missionary service was an important consideration. Even though there was a long and substantial debate about this problem—which was continued with greater intensity in the Leipzig mission—pragmatic views finally prevailed over missionary claims and ideals. In the beginning the Tranquebar Mission converted, almost exclusively, members of the *paṟaiyār*. It was only from the 1730s onwards that people from different *śūdra* groups were also converted. Later, one could observe a greater interest on the part of the higher castes, especially in the educational institutions of the mission, although conversion was not necessarily linked with this. In any case, it was necessary to organize the religious care and control of a church congregation in such a way that its members would be willing to communicate with 'their' mission employee and not reject him on grounds of religious purity. If close and frequent contacts were necessary between the two, the question of a certain degree of correspondence with regard to caste became even more important. This also applied to the sphere of education. The selection of local mission employees had to be done keeping in mind the composition of the converts or the pupils. The parents, especially the Hindus (children of non-Christians were also taught in the schools of the Tranquebar Mission), were very mindful about who taught their children. In the early period at least, the missionaries of the Danish-English-Halle Mission recruited their

[88] Accordingly, the sermons were in High Tamil and there was a strict separation of castes in the churches. Even after this procedure was questioned in 1844, the actual practice did not change. The 'untouchables' were not allowed to become priests. Bugge, *Mission and Tamil Society*, 82f.

[89] Ibid., 83f.

local assistants from among the lower castes and the casteless. Most of the members of the newly established Christian congregations belonged, in any case, to the *paraiyār*. This strategy increasingly changed when, from the 1730s more and more members of *śūdra* castes became members of the Christian congregations. With this development the missionaries felt the need to also train and appoint *śūdra* assistants and catechists. On the whole, however, the majority of 'national workers' belonged to the *paraiyār*. The *veḷḷāla* constituted another large group. The principle of equal social status or caste parity between lay Christians and the mission employees responsible for them was only breached in the selection of country pastors. Although the large majority of converts were 'untouchables' and their numbers also dominated in most of the congregations, schools and Christian villages, not a single *dalit* was ordained during the entire period of the Tranquebar Mission. In the communications concerning this between the missionaries in India and the mission superiors in Europe, this question was never discussed openly and extensively.

Another important criterion for selection was the health and physical fitness of a candidate, since the South Indian employees had to take over most of the work involving travel, both in unfavourable weather conditions and to far away places. Sometimes a person did not fulfill all the requirements and compromises had to be made. In December 1729 Pressier made it very clear in an assessment of Aaron, who would later become the first ordained Indian country pastor, that although his health was not good, the mission needed him since, as a *veḷḷāḷar*, he came from a caste 'which is one of those that are respected'. Besides this, he remarked, Aaron is 'intelligent and gifted' and can 'also be used for more important things, especially to be sent out into the rural districts'.[90] On the occasion of Aaron's ordination Sartorius remarked: 'He has a pleasant gravity and seriousness in his conduct and these natural gifts are seldom found among the Malabarians'.[91]

Considerations of this kind went into the long-term selection and systematic preparation of a local mission employee. The selection

[90] HB 28. Cont., 477, 12 December 1729.

[91] HB 38. Cont., 261, 28 December 1733, (translated from German).

of a local mission worker for ordination was particularly lengthy and complicated.[92] Whereas the decision to appoint a teacher or a catechist was taken by the missionaries in India; for the process of appointing a country pastor the opinion of the European side was important, because the missionaries needed the permission of the Mission Board in Copenhagen to ordain a new country pastor.[93] The Europeans knew most of the potential candidates for the post of country pastor, mainly from the descriptions of the missionaries, but also from their own letters and reports. A detailed description of the course of some ordinations is available. The first country pastor Aaron was ordained on 28 December 1733 according to the customary practice of the Evangelical Church 'except for the fact that his habit had to be white, because black clothes do not suit the brown colour of the Indians and is also not common among them.'[94] On 20 October 1729 the Mission Board in Copenhagen had, in the name of the Danish king, authorized the ordination of a local pastor, but had left the decision regarding the choice of a person to the missionaries. The only consideration was that the person should have been in the service of the mission for some years and should have previously

[92] Aaron (1698/9–1745) ordination: 28 December 1733; Diogo (1704?–81) ordination: 28 December 1741; Ambrosius (1713–77) ordination: 9 April 1749; Philipp/Pulleimuttu (1731/43?–88) ordination: 28 December 1772; Rajappen (1742–96/97) ordination: 7 May 1778; Sattianaden (1750–1815) (also: Karpagam Sathiyanathan) ordination: 26 December 1790; Abraham, ordination: 17 March 1811; Njanapiragasam (1758–?) ordination: 17 March 1811; Adeikalam (Adeikkalam) ordination: 17 March 1811; Wedanayagam (died around 1812) ordination: 17 March 1811; Schawrirajen (circa 1755–1817) ordination: 1811?; Pakkianaden, ordination: 1817; Wisuwasanaden/Wisuwasi, ordination: 1817; Nallatambi, ordination: 1817.

[93] When a new person had to be ordained after the death of Ambrosius in 1777, the missionaries referred to the consent given long before by the Mission Board to ordain an Indian selected by the missionaries in India. It was meant for Rajappen. AFSt/M 1 E 37 : 3, supplement to the diaries of 1777. About the country pastor Philipp´s intended stay in the countryside by Johann Balthasar Kohlhoff, Daniel Zeglin, Johann Friedrich König, Christoph Samuel John, Johann Wilhelm Gerlach, Johann Peter Rottler, ??. ??. 1777.

[94] HB 40. Cont., letter from the missionaries in Tranquebar to Princess Charlotta Amalia (1708–82) dated 8 November 1734, (translated from German). See also: 'Nachricht von der Bestellung des ersten National=Predigers bey der Evangelischen Mission unter den Malabaren in Ost=Indien', HB 37. Cont., 147–72, 31 December 1733; HB 37. Cont., 168ff. (contains Aaron's résumé 168–72); AFSt/M 1 K 5 : 10, biography of Aaron, June 1745.

held other posts in the mission.[95] Initially, the three city catechists Aaron, Diogo and Schawrimuttu (around 1682–1763) were potential candidates for the post. During Easter celebrations in 1733 the concerned congregation was informed about the forthcoming election and about the candidates and was asked to prepare its decision. In this time the three catechists were given additional lessons.[96] After Schawrimuttu withdrew his candidature Diogo and Aaron each preached a trial sermon to the congregation at Pentecost.[97] The result of a verbal vote by the congregation and a written vote by the missionaries was undecided. Finally, in a secret ballot, the missionaries voted for Aaron, since he had already been working in the rural areas and, therefore, had more experience of this region.[98] He was then given a list of the requirements of the post along with his duties and was asked to accept the post of a priest in the Tranquebar Mission. Information about Aaron's acceptance was displayed publicly.[99]

All the country pastors who were ordained in the Tranquebar mission had previously followed a similar path within the mission system. This included education in a mission school, work as a teacher in one of the schools followed by a long period of work as a catechist. Thus, for example, the life of Ambrosius (1713–77), ordained as a country pastor in 1749, can be reconstructed beginning with his schooling in a mission school.[100] In 1729 Walther mentioned him as a pupil who, at this point of time—having been in the care of the mission for about 12 years—was being considered for the job of a teacher and a catechist.[101] Philipp was 29 years old when he was ordained. He had also gone through the entire mission system; he had been educated in the mission school, had then worked as a teacher and a city catechist before he was ordained as a country pastor.[102]

[95] HB 37. Cont., 149.
[96] HB 37. Cont., 154f.
[97] HB 37. Cont., 158.
[98] HB 37. Cont., 162f.
[99] HB 37. Cont., 166.
[100] NHB 19. St., 787f.
[101] HB 69. Cont., Vorrede, 1748 ordination of Ambrosius; NHB 19. St. 766, 787, 788.
[102] NHB 10. St., 1290–95, 1305, 1308, 1314, 1330–36, 1342, 1347, 1350f., 1357f. 13. St., 29 Vorrede IV, 23–33, 73. For Philipp see also: Vormbaum, Reinhold, 1851, *Eingeborene Lehrer des Evangeliums in Ostindien*, Schaub, Düsseldorf,

For the mission the ordination of a South Indian co-worker was also an occasion to demonstrate its integration into local society. Not only catechists of the Christian congregations in the surrounding areas, but also local chiefs were sent a special *ōlai* and invited to attend the festive ceremony of Philipp's ordination in December 1772.[103] Philipp was given an examination on questions of 'dogmatic theology, polemic theology, ecclesiastic history' and 'theological exegesis'.[104] On 7 May 1778 Rajappen, the former *śūdra* catechist of the rural congregation, was ordained as country pastor. He was given accommodation in Thanjavur and a *śūdra* as well as a *paṟaiyār* catechist were assigned to help him. Rajappen, who was born in a Christian family in 1742, was brought up in a mission school from the time he was eight years old. His grandfather, a *veḷḷāḷa* coiner by profession, had converted to Christianity along with his entire family and had worked for some time as a catechist under his baptismal name Marcus. Since Rajappen's father, Andreas, was a seaman, Rajappen grew up with his grandfather. Before being ordained as country pastor Rajappen had worked as printer, schoolteacher and catechist. The preparations for his ordination lasted from October 1777 till April 1778.[105] The detailed description of the preparations for Sattianaden's ordination in 1792 contains the questions put to him by the missionaries Christian Friedrich Schwartz, Joseph Daniel Jänicke (1759–1800) and Johann Caspar Kohlhoff (1762–1844), to which Sattianaden had to give written replies. The questions touched upon themes regarding the Christian way of life, morals and, also, Bible-interpretation.[106]

NEED FOR LOCAL CO-WORKERS

No Christian mission society could do without local helpers in the region where they worked. The need for local co-workers arose, on

(=Evangelische Missionsgeschichte in Biographien, vol. II), 57f.; Germann, *Johann Philipp Fabricius*, 102.

[103] AFSt/M 2 E 37 : 1.

[104] Ibid.

[105] NHB 13. St., Vorrede IV, 2; 20. St., 933, 939; 21. St., 1050, 1057, 1073–1079, 1097, 1108, 1113, 1126.

[106] AFSt/M 1 C 32a : 35, minutes of Sattianaden's examination. [Place not mentioned] 1791.

the one hand, because foreign missionaries often found it difficult to gain access to the local people, either due to language problems or the inability to have a sympathetic understanding for the people. On the other hand, the dearth of European volunteers for missionary service meant that it was necessary to supplement and extend the number of personnel locally. The numbers of local helpers or employees, their duties, powers and their position depended both on the missionary methods of the mission society concerned as well as on the religious and social background of the local co-workers, on the structure of local society, on the gender relationships and, last but not least, on the target group of missionary activity.

THE BACKGROUND OF THE CONVERTS

Among the converts and, therefore, also among the South Indian co-workers of the Tranquebar Mission, there were people from different castes, different social backgrounds and different religious communities. Seen as a whole, their individual points of departure and motives for conversion found a concrete form in the relevant religious, social and political conditions in the mission region. Thus, individual conversions were an expression of more comprehensive processes in the framework of intercultural missionary encounters and were, partly, paradigmatic for a social group.

In a region with a predominantly Hindu population the Tranquebar Mission directed the focus of its activities to the conversion of Hindus who constituted the largest group among the converts. The people who came from Hindu families were, more or less, closely tied to local traditions and religious communities. For them, a change of religion was often synonymous with a loss of social prestige and a loss of direct associates in the form of the extended family, the village community and the caste group. They were also expected to give up many daily acts, customs and traditions. For many, conversion was linked with a change in name, with an end to participation in Hindu religious festivals and, sometimes also, with a change in food and dress habits. Those who had to propagate the Christian faith as priests, catechists, teachers or assistants, were generally brought up in mission schools from an early age, were selected by the missionaries and were specially prepared for missionary work. Some Hindus did not convert to Christianity despite many years of intensive cooperation with the missionaries. These included—especially in the early years of the mission—mainly the interpreters and language teachers, and later some Brahmins or members of local ruling families who, despite a marked interest in intellectual exchange with the Christians, did not wish to convert to their faith.

The annual statistics of the Tranquebar Mission show that—especially in the early decades—many of the baptized were Catholics.[107] There had been Catholic Christians in Tranquebar long before the Lutheran missionaries set foot on Indian soil.[108] Although it is difficult to get exact figures for the number of Catholics who went to the Tranquebar Mission and, therefore, converted to Protestant Christianity,[109] it can be assumed that local Catholics were interested in contacts with the newly arrived Christians in the region. As Catholics they already knew about Christianity and often did not have reservations against Europeans. The encounter with the missionaries of the Tranquebar Mission opened up a new perspective on Christianity for them, and this often led to contradictions and conflicts with their earlier ideas about the Christian faith. Although these persons did not change their religion but 'only' their denomination within Christianity, there were often far-reaching consequences. In the course of the existence of the Tranquebar Mission there were many Catholics who went over to Protestantism and, time and again, former Catholics were appointed in missionary service. With Rajanayakkan's appointment as a catechist in Thanjavur in 1728,[110] the systematic work of the Tranquebar Mission among the Catholic population of the region began. Coming from a Catholic family himself, Rajanayakkan

[107] In a letter of 1728 Christian Friedrich Pressier mentions only Catholics who had asked to be admitted to the congregation in Tranquebar. Neither Hindus nor Muslims are mentioned. HB 27. Cont., 220.

[108] Cf. Grafe, 'The Relations between the Tranquebar Lutherans and the Tanjore Catholics'.

[109] To some extent, the English congregation in Thanjavur is an exception. Here, regular information was provided about Catholic converts and this can be collated from the sources. 808 Christians in Thanjavur converted from Roman Catholicism to the Lutheran faith between 1773 and 1800. NHB 59. St., 944.

[110] HB 28. Cont., 316.

became a Protestant and worked as a catechist of the Tranquebar Mission especially among the Catholics in Thanjavur.[111] The strategy of systematic missionary work among Catholics was continued after Thanjavur was opened up to foreign missionaries in 1753.[112] This sometimes led to tensions in the relations between the Tranquebar Mission and the Catholic missions working in south India.

TABLE 2.2 Development of the 'Portuguese congregation' in Tranquebar[113]

Year	Growth Total	No. of children	No. of Hindus	No. of Catholics	No. of slaves	Source
1727	50	33	11	1		HB, vol.2, V preface
1734	52	26+1	10	15	8	HB 20. Cont., V; 39. Cont., 354
1735	22	13		9		HB 40. Cont., V
1735 (2.H)	25	14	8+2	1		HB 42. Cont., V
1738		25	11	2		HB 47. Cont., V
1738 (2.H)					8	HB 48. Cont., 1438
1739 (1.H)	20					HB 49. Cont., V
1743	21					HB 58. Cont., V
1745 (1.H)		22	3			HB 63. Cont., V
1747 (1.H)	30	26	4			HB 67. Cont., 1106
1748 (1.H)	14	13	1			HB 69. Cont., 1412
1756 (1.H)	27					HB 85. Cont. 2

(*Contd...*)

[111] HB 26. Cont., 810.

[112] In 1753 the missionary Johann Christian Wiedebrock (in Tranquebar from 1736–67) held the first public divine service in Thanjavur. HB 80. Cont., 1212.

[113] The annual statistical data does not follow a fixed pattern. Therefore, it is often not possible to collate comparative data for every year. The number of children includes the newborns in the congregation as well as the ones baptized; (H= half of the year).

Table 2.2 (contd.)

Year	Growth Total	No. of children	No. of Hindus	No. of Catholics	No. of slaves	Source
1759 (1.H)	19					HB 91. Cont., 724
1760						HB 94. Cont., 1049
1761					7	HB 95. Cont., 1128
1762					3	HB 98. Cont., 205
1766					5	HB 106. Cont., 1273
1768	19	11	7	1	3–4	NHB 1. St., 3–4, 32, 37
1769	12	6	4	2+2	4	NHB 3. St., 268; 4. St. 452
1770	9	4	4	1	4	NHB 5. St., 559f; 6.St., 710
1772					6	NHB 10. St., 1288
1773	18		8			NHB 11. St., 1407f.
1774	13				11	NHB 13. St., 38f., 47
1776	13					NHB 17. St., 523
1777	23	12	8	3		NHB 19. St., 767f.
1789	18					NHB 39. St., 225
1790	11					NHB 41. St., 406f.

Missionary activity among the Muslims in the region was not successful. Since the initial work among Muslims that was carried out mainly by Benjamin Schultze and Christoph Theodosius Walther did not, in any way, meet the expectations, Muslims were no longer the target of missionary activity after the 1740s.[114] Schultze, who left India in 1743, had learned to speak and write Hindustani from the Muslims in the Madras region and had tried to reach out to the Muslims of the region through schools and polemical

[114] Cf. Liebau, Heike, 'Der Islam in Südindien im Spiegel der dänisch-halleschen Missionsquellen', in Michael Bergunder (ed.), *Missionsberichte aus Indien im 18 Jahrhundert. Ihre Bedeutung für die europäische Geistesgeschichte und ihr wissenschaftlicher Quellenwert für die Indienkunde*, 153–74, Verlag der Franckeschen Stiftungen, Halle.

publications. Besides the translation of Christian texts[115] Schultze wrote a Hindustani grammar[116] and a polemic against the Koran.[117] Walther, who was interested in linguistic and religious studies, asked for special literature in Arabic from Europe in order to distribute it among the Muslims in South India. He soon realized, to his disappointment, that the Muslims here did not know Arabic. He also sent information about the specificities of Islam in South India to interested European scholars.[118] The conversion of Muslim slaves, however, was not influenced by this change in mission strategy. Among the slaves who worked for Europeans in the region, or who were brought there by slave traders, there were people of different religions, including Muslims. In end effect, therefore, most of the

[115] Schultze, Benjamin, 1758, *Novum Jesu Christi Testamentum/In linguam Indostanicum translatum*, Typographia Orientali Instituti Judaici, Halae; Schultze, B., 1778, *Pauli Apostoli Epistola Ad Hebræos, in Linguam Indostanicum Translata*. A Viro Plur. Reverendo Benj. Schultzio Evengelico in India Missionario. Edidit D.Jo. Henr. Callenbergius, Institutum Judaicum & Muhammedaicum, Halae; Schultze, B., 1747, *Psalmorum liber [...] in linguam Indostanicam*, translatus a Benj. Schulzio ... Edidit Jo. Henr. Callenbergius, Typographia orientali Instituti Judaici, Halae; Schultze, B., 1751, *Evangelium Matthaei in Linguam Indostanicam Translatum*. A Viro Plur. Reverendo Benj. Schultzio Evengelico in India Missionario. Edidit D.Jo. Henr. Callenbergius, Typographia orientali Instituti Judaici & Muhammedici, Halae.

[116] Schultze, Benjamin, 1745, [Grammatica Hindostanica] *Viri Plur. Reverendi Benjamini Schultzii Missionarii Evangelici Grammatica Hindostanica [...]*. Edit Jo. Henr. Callenberg, Typographia Instituti Judaici, Halae. [Reprint: 1986, *Grammatica hindostanica von Benjamin Schultze*, ed. by B. Brentjes and C. Gallus, Univ. Halle-Wittenberg, Halle, WB 1986/38 (I 38)]. An annotated Urdu translation of this grammar was published in 1977 in Pakistan: Schultze, Benjamin, 1977, *Hindūstānī grāmar az Bengamin Šulze, A Grammar of Hindustani Language* by Benjamin Schultze, edited and translated into Urdu with Notes and Annotations by Abulais Siddiqi, mağlis-e tariqī-e adab, Lahore. Cf. also: Pelikan (Liebau), Heike, 1987, *Die 'Grammatica Hindostanica' des Benjamin Schultze (Quelle zur Erforschung des Dakkhini des 18. Jahrhunderts)*, ed. by Burchard Brentjes, Univ. Halle-Wittenberg, Halle (=WB 35 [I 41] 1987).

[117] Schultze, Benjamin, 1744, *Compendiaria Alcorani Refutatio Indostanice*, Autore Viro plur. Reverendo Benj. Schulzio Evangelico in India Missionario, edidit Jo. Henr. Callenberg, Institutum Judaicum, Halae. A German translation, completed by Schultze himself on 31 October 1741, is in the archives of the Francke Foundations: AFSt/M 2 A 5 : 21, Compendiaria Alcorani Refutatio Indostanice, Madras, 31 October 1741.

[118] In a long letter dated 5 October 1727 to J.H. Callenberg in Halle he explained the 'teachings and customs of Mohammedans in Tranckenbar'. HB 25. Cont., 117–46. See also: AFSt/M 1 B 8 : 5, Essay by Ch. Th. Walther [Tranquebar], ??. ??. 1730.

Muslims baptized by the missionaries of the Tranquebar Mission were slaves who, as a rule, were forced to undergo baptism by their (Christian) masters.[119] If slaves did not get permission from their masters to attend religious instruction, a catechist visited them once or twice a week and taught them separately.[120]

Initial difficulties in converting local people to Christianity also gave rise to the idea of helping the mission to advance with the purchase of slaves (not by purchasing their freedom!).[121] In view of the fact that parents in financially difficult circumstances sold their children, some missionaries did not find it an un-Christian act to acquire these children and raise them in the Church.

> Since parents, as is the custom here, in any case, wish to sell their children as slaves, it would not be wrong to buy them oneself for a small amount of money so that they would belong to our Church. I remember that we have two such children in our school who are doing very well and through them we have also been able to win over their parents.[122]

At the same time, the development of trade and shipping brought slaves from different regions to the east coast of India. The majority of these slaves, mostly Muslims, were transported from Bengal to South India. From Achin, Pegu too it was predominantly Muslims who came. The missionaries called them the 'Maleyans'. Some slaves came from the west coast of India. As children they had been sold by their parents in times of trouble to ship owners and slave traders.[123]

[119] NHB 9. St., 1181, 1186 (1772, Madras); 11. St., 1473 (1773, Madras).

[120] NHB 10. St., 1354–56, letter from Johann Friedrich König to the editor, G.A. Freylinghausen, 10 February 1773. At the beginning of missionary work Ziegenbalg and Plütschau had insisted that the slaves should have two hours of religious instruction daily. AB 43.

[121] Ziegenbalg formulated this idea as early as in 1706 in a letter to Francke. Young slaves would be bought and trained for work in the mission in the schools that were to be set up. AB 41, Tranquebar, 25 September 1706.

[122] HB 5. Cont. 187, letter from B. Ziegenbalg to A.H. Francke, 23 December 1710, (translated from German).

[123] NHB 10. St., 1354–56, letter from J.F. König to the editor, G.A. Freylinghausen, dated 10 February 1773. Arasaratnam states that in the seventeenth and eighteenth centuries rich landlords in Jaffna purchased Indian slaves. Arasaratnam, Social History of a Dominant Caste Society, 387.

The missionaries of the Tranquebar Mission regularly baptized slaves even after they, according to Nørgaard, had, with a great deal of effort, apparently managed to have a ban imposed on the slave trade.[124] In April 1733 the missionaries in Madras reported the baptism of a slave.[125] In July 1734 and in August 1738 the missionaries in Tranquebar baptized eight so-called serfs on each occasion.[126] Since the congregations grew by a total of 52 members, this corresponds to a ratio of about 15 %. Some of the slaves came from the houses of Europeans[127] where they remained slaves even as baptized Christians. Initially, the missionaries asked the Danish authorities in Tranquebar to send the slaves regularly to them for instruction.[128] This suited the Europeans since they were, in any case, interested in slaves who could be integrated better in their households with the help of a Christian-European education. Children of slaves in Tranquebar were not automatically considered slaves: 'A child born of slaves, whether legitimate or illegitimate—the latter not being rare—is considered a free person in Trankenbar.'[129] In 1755 the missionaries in Cuddalore baptized two adult slaves belonging to the Dutch Resident in Devanapatnam.[130] Of the 13 people baptized in the 'Portuguese congregation' in Tranquebar in 1774 eleven were slaves.[131] Most of these baptized slaves became members of the local 'Portuguese' congregations and worked as servants in Portuguese-speaking households, since Portuguese was the 'language of household servants'[132] in many rich families in Southeast India. It was reported in 1748 that a large part of the 306 members of the 'Portuguese' congregation in Tranquebar were

[124] Nørgaard, *Mission und Obrigkeit*, 37.

[125] HB 37. Cont., 177, report from the mission at Madras about the baptism of a slave, 3 April 1733.

[126] HB 39. Cont., 354, baptism of 8 serfs, Tranquebar, July 1734; HB 48. Cont., 1438, baptism of 8 serfs, Tranquebar, August 1738.

[127] HB 59. Cont., 1608, 31 baptisms of which 21 were in the city congregation, two female slaves from European houses. Tranquebar, 24 February 1743.

[128] Nørgaard, *Mission und Obrigkeit*, 160.

[129] NHB 10. St., 1356, letter from J.F. König to the editor, G.A. Freylinghausen, 10 February 1773, (translated from German).

[130] HB 84. Cont., 1752, Cuddalore, 18 December 1755.

[131] NHB 13. St., 1774, 38f.

[132] NHB 10. St., 1354–56.

slaves.[133] As a rule, these people did not know enough Portuguese, let alone Tamil,[134] which, however, was a precondition for baptism. Thus, in February 1774 the baptism of an African slave and of two Malaysians had to be postponed due to an 'insufficient' knowledge of the language.[135] Among the slaves who were brought to India from Africa, mainly from Mozambique, there were many Catholics who, before being sold as slaves, had been baptized by the missionaries there. For the German Protestant missionaries in southeast India the slaves remained slaves even after baptism. On 17 October 1780 they remarked in a letter to Batavia: 'The slaves from various heathen nations, who receive holy baptism in the Portuguese congregation are not freed but are urged as Christians to serve their masters even more faithfully.'[136]

Although the mission did not participate in the organized slave trade and did not buy or sell slaves to make a profit, there were, nonetheless, cases when the missionaries, for various reasons, acquired slaves.[137] The missionaries did not actively oppose slavery. On the contrary, Johann Friedrich König (1741-95), for instance, stated in 1773 that the slaves in the region were comparatively well off: 'From this You, Reverend Sir, will see that the lot of the slaves here in East India, at least on our coast, is far more bearable than in

[133] HB 69. Cont., 1412 (1st half of 1748). For further references to the baptism of slaves in the 'Portuguese' congregation see HB 94. Cont., 1049, Tranquebar 17 September 1760; HB 95. Cont., 1128, seven baptisms (all slaves in the 'Portuguese' congregation) Tranquebar 11 March 1761; HB 98. Cont., 205, baptism of three slaves, 'Portuguese' congregation, Tranquebar1762; HB 106. Cont., 1273, five persons baptized (2 slave boys & 3 slave girls), Tranquebar 1766; NHB 1. St., 32f., 37, Tranquebar, baptism of some slaves from European houses 1768; NHB 4. St., 452, four 'heathen' slave children baptized; NHB 10. St., 1287f, Tranquebar 1772, baptisms in the 'Portuguese' congregation, six 'somewhat grown up heathen slaves'.

[134] NHB 6. St., 710, four slave children were baptized in the 'Portuguese' congregation in Tranquebar, of whom one was born in Mozambique, one in 'Arabia' (1770); NHB 13. St., 38f. On 20 February 1774 thirteen persons were baptized in the 'Portuguese' congregation, 'among them 11 slaves from different countries, 4 from Bengal, two from Siam, two Maleyans, the other three from different regions of this coast', (translated from German).

[135] NHB 13. St., 1774, 38f.

[136] NHB 25. St., 7, (translated from German).

[137] For example: NHB 44. St., 710. A widow from Chidambaram '[...] sold her two sons to Mr John in the recent period of inflation.'

West India where slavery continues over generations and where they have the heavy work in the plantations, which is not the case here.'[138] According to missionary König, before the Europeans returned home they often freed their slaves and gave them a starting capital. The Danish governor, Hans Ernst Bonsack (1746–53), not only left a house and a sum of money for his slaves—a married couple—but he also laid down what they should do with this gift. Bonsack asked the mission to ensure that his instructions were followed.[139] In 1771 Ch. S. John met an old freed slave at the Cape of Good Hope who had been baptized by the missionaries in Tranquebar and had then been sold again.[140] When, on 21 June 1783, the Danish governor in Tranquebar prohibited slave trade in his territory and issued a decree whereby 'punishment would be meted out to those who took slaves out by sea or by land', Christian Pohle (1744–1818) expressed the desire for a similar decree in Tiruchirappalli where he was working for the SPCK.[141] However, reports about the sale of slaves continued even after this date: when the six year old child of a widow in the village of Wölipaleiam[142] disappeared in 1784, it was assumed that it had been sold as a slave and was bound for Mauritius.[143] When the Dutch were no longer an important trading and colonial power in Southeast India and many Dutch families returned to Europe, especially in the 1790s, their freed slaves turned to the missionaries.[144] Organized measures against slavery by Christian missions began only in the 1840s when the London Missionary Society and the Church Missionary Society started a campaign in Travancore to abolish slavery and used the abolition of slavery in the territories of the East India Company in India to bolster their argument. In the nineteenth century slaves in Travancore were punished if they had

[138] NHB 10. St., 1356, (translated from German).

[139] NHB 10. St., 1356.

[140] NHB 6. St., 855 (5 March 1771).

[141] NHB 29. St., 531.

[142] Velippalaiyam, on the outskirts of Tranquebar.

[143] NHB 31. St., 737f.

[144] In 1790 two adult female slaves, among others, who had worked for Dutch families, were baptized in Nagapattinam and Cuddalore. NHB 39. St., 296. In 1791 the missionaries baptized the widow of a freed slave, NHB 41. St., 440. Among the nine baptized Indians in 1792 in Tranquebar there were some Bengalis, freed 'Malayans or Mohammedans from Malacca and Batavia', NHB 44. St., 699.

contacts with the mission and slavery was officially prohibited there only in 1855.[145]

The main focus of the DEHM missionaries in their efforts to recruit Christians for missionary service was soon directed, however, to the Protestants of the second and further generations who, as a rule, had already been given special training in the mission for this work. Their importance grew with the passage of time. The missionaries also took care to see that mainly members of Protestant families were appointed, because they considered them to be more loyal towards the mission.[146] Parents who had once worked for the mission often wanted the same career for their children and, therefore, made them participate in the life of the mission from their early years. In 1748 Curupadam, the son of the first country pastor Aaron, became a city catechist in Tranquebar.[147] Two sons of the catechist Matthäus (1732–around 1805), Arulappen (around 1752–1805) and Christian, also became catechists.[148] In some cases, the family tradition can be traced back in this manner over several generations.

THE COMPOSITION OF LOCAL CO-WORKERS

The composition of the group of South Indian co-workers was primarily an outcome of the organizational perspective of missionary work. The general division made by Ziegenbalg into 'workers for the word' and 'workers for external institutions' reflected the relationship between direct missionary work and the maintenance of the general framework and conditions for the functioning of the mission. In 1731 the two city congregations and the four rural congregations, which belonged directly to the mission station in Tranquebar, employed the following co-workers: Six European missionaries and one European assistant, six local catechists, nine local assistants for the catechists, four local teachers and two local women who worked in the schools. In addition, there was a European type-founder who worked together with his son, two local bookbinders and two

145 Cf. Kooiman, *Conversion and Social Equality in India*, 78f.
146 HB 33. Cont., 881.
147 HB 69. Cont., Vorrede.
148 NHB 58. St., 852–57.

local assistants in the printing press, a local church warden, three local non-Christian book-keepers (*kaṇakkappiḷḷai*), one local non-Christian washerman, one local house servant (who also worked as the grave digger), a local female attendant in the women's house, two local women who made the purchases for the schools, a local woman for handicrafts, a local nurse and some water carriers.[149] In the statistics for the later years of the mission the co-workers in the different institutions linked with the mission were not listed in the same detail as in the early years, sometimes not at all. The 'Index of National Workers', compiled in 1766 by Jacob Klein, lists three country pastors, two catechists, four junior catechists, ten assistants, one prayer leader (male), one prayer leader (female), seven male teachers and one female teacher.[150]

A second level of composition was caste. The hierarchy among the local mission employees was determined by their caste affiliation. Usually, catechists were appointed to work in the villages they came from. Although accusations and persecution were particularly rampant there, it was, on the other hand, often also the place where the greatest intimacy with the people and the highest degree of acceptance could be achieved. Whereas the correspondence between caste and place of appointment was mentioned in the mission reports, a possible connection between caste affiliation and function in the mission was never spoken of. Here, however, conclusions can be drawn on the basis of the practice of ordination.[151]

A third factor in the composition of local mission employees that has hitherto been grossly neglected in research is gender. It was neither possible nor advantageous to appoint men everywhere. Women were needed in the schools to supervise and take care of the girls; they also cared for the sick in the mission station. In the work with the local population women were allowed access to female members of the family. Often, male and female employees travelled together and catechists were sometimes accompanied by their wives. In the framework of the Tranquebar Mission women were integrated into direct missionary work primarily as teachers or prayer leaders. The total number of female mission employees in these professions

[149] HB 33. Cont., 870–916, report from Tranquebar, 1732.

[150] AFSt/M 2 B 3 : 21.

[151] See the development of the catechist Rajanayakkan, pp. 208f and 227–31.

would have been between 30 and 40 (not counting the women in the technical sphere).

The number of South Indian mission co-workers grew irregularly. During phases of growth of the mission—not only as regards personnel, but also geographic expansion—the numbers increased; in times of economic difficulties and low success-rates of missionary work fewer local co-workers were employed. Whereas the main mission work in the central places could be carried out by one of the European missionaries living there, in the rural areas the local co-workers were often the only persons to whom the local Christians, or those interested in Christianity, could turn. Normally, a missionary initially visited different places together with an assistant or a catechist. The local co-workers received instructions regarding their duties in the villages. They usually lived in one of the villages of the district they worked in and constantly preached the Christian faith to the local population. If anyone showed an interest in the religion, this person was sent to the central mission station to be instructed in the Christian faith and to be prepared for baptism.[152]

Within the group of 'national workers' the country pastors[153] had the highest status. Subjected to a comprehensive examination by the missionaries and confirmed through an election in the congregation, they were, after being ordained, formally equal to the missionaries but, in reality, they did not have the same rights and decision-making powers as the latter. Like the other 'national workers' they were, in the final instance, subject to the orders of the European missionaries and were under their control. However, they were, in their turn, teachers, role models, contact persons and—to a limited extent—also supervisors of the catechists, teachers and assistants. The country pastors were specially trained to conduct divine services and carry out different religious ministrations. They

[152] In May 1770 the country pastor Rajappen brought a Roman Catholic family wanting to convert from Thanjavur to Tranquebar. NHB 5. St., 609.

[153] Rayariah D. Paul defines the term country pastor as a literal translation of the Tamil term *nāṭṭaiyar*, which was used very early on in Tamil churches. As against this, the European missionaries were called *aiyar*. The terms *aiyar* or *iyer* are also used by Hindus for the Brahmin priests. Cf. Rayariah D. Paul, 1961, *Chosen Vessels. Lifes often Indian Christian Pastors of the eighteenth and nineteenth Centuries*, published for the Senate of Serampore College by the Christian Literature Society, Madras, 12, footnote 1.

1717	Eilert (1718)	Schawrimuttu (1717-ca. 1720)
	Johann Beck (1718-1733)	David (1718-ca. 1754)
1730	Johann Anton Sartorius (1737-1738)	Arulappen (um 1739)
	Johann Ernst Geister (1737-1743)	
	Cäsar Pillow (1738-1754)	
1740		Ambrosius (1740-1748)
	Johann Zacharias Kiernander (1740-1758)	Muttu (1742-1743)
	Johann Christian Breithaupt (1747-1749)	Isaac (1746-1778/80)
		Andreas (1747-ca. 1749)
	Jens Johann (1749-ca. 1758)	Dewanesen (?-ca. 1748)
		Habacuc (1748-1795)
1750	Georg Heinrich Conrad Hüttemann (1750-1758)	Curupadam (1749-1751)
		Rajappen (ca. 1753-1785)
	Lewis Maede (1754)	Christoph Rodriguez (1756)
	John Kare (1754-1758)	
1760	Johann Christian Obeck (1762-1771)	Christian (ca. 1765-?)
		Sinappen (1769-1771)
	Christian Wilhelm Gericke (1767-1782)	
		Gabriel (ca. 1770-1779)
1770	William Powers (um 1770)	Manoel (ca. 1771-1800)
		Jesadian (ca. 1773-1778)
		Samuel (1775-1785)
	Christoph Heinrich Horst (1792-1803)	Tirusiluwei (?-1781)
		Dewasagayam (1794-1805)
1800	Immanuel Gottfried Holzberg (1803-1824)	Njana Ajudam (1805-?)
1820	David Rosen (1824-1829)	Schawrimuttu (1812-?)

ILLUSTRATION 2.1 Co-workers in Cuddalore (1717–1820)

1762	Christian Friedrich Schwartz (1762-1778)	Soedtinaicken (ca. 1762-1780)
		Dewanesen (1768-1788)
		Rajappen (1769-1785)
1770		Sattianaden (ca. 1770-1784)
		Ignasimuttu (ca. 1771-1792)
		Njanapiragasam (1771-1784)
		Abiseganaden (1772-1805)
		Wisuwasi (um 1772)
		Dewasagayam (1772-1794)
		Santappen (1775-?, 1794-?)
		Samuel (ca. 1775-1782)
		Wedamuttu (ca. 1776-1784)
	Christian Pohle (1778-1818)	Abraham (1777-ca. 1805)
1780	William Wheatley (um 1780)	Simeon (ca. 1785-ca. 1790)
	Johann Caspar Kohlhoff (um 1780) Christian Daniel Klein (um 1785)	Njanapiragasam (1786-ca. 1805)
1790		Peter de Silva (1790-ca. 1805)
		Christian (1791-1792)
		Johann Ariamuttu (1793)
		Njanajudam (1794-1805)
		Dewasagayam (1796-ca. 1805)
		Rasappen (ca. 1798-ca. 1800)
		Pirasagam (um 1798)
1800		Kurupadam (1805-1811) Jesadian (1805-?) Tajirian (1805-?)
1820	David Rosen (1819-1823)	

ILLUSTRATION 2.2 Co-workers in Tiruchirappalli (1762–1820)

were entirely responsible for the religious life of the congregations entrusted to them. This included preaching in the church as well as administering the sacrament. Country pastors were also allowed to prepare interested persons for conversion and to baptize them after instruction and examination. In the *instructio pastoralis* the missionaries formulated the concrete tasks for the office of the pastor in the Mayavaram district. According to this, the following activities were part of the duties of a country pastor: he is to look after the Christians in the district, if necessary, beyond the call of duty. His permanent residence should, therefore, also be in this district. He must preach publicly in the streets and in the church, administer the holy sacrament, ensure 'Christian decorum and order', supervise the catechists, educate the youth in the region, officiate at marriages and funerals and organize relief for the poor.[154] It was the duty of country pastors to supervise and take care of a territorial congregation. Besides ensuring a 'Christian way of life' among the members of the congregation, his official duties included teaching the catechumen, holding divine services, celebrating Holy Communion, officiating at baptisms, marriages and funerals. Country pastors regularly visited the places assigned to them, which were generally looked after by catechists and assistants, and carried out official ministrations that the latter were not allowed to do.[155] The country pastors were allowed to call meetings of the South Indian co-workers to clarify relevant questions and problems, and the presence of a missionary was not required at such meetings. In March 1737 the country pastor Aaron called a meeting with the catechists and assistants Rajanayakkan, Arhagappen, Muttu (in office from around 1730 till after 1779) and Sinappen, in which methods for mediating religious knowledge and questions regarding the manner of dealing with some members of the congregation were discussed.[156] Under instructions from Christian Friedrich Schwartz the country pastor Sattianaden helped the converted

[154] HB 37. Cont., 164f., report on the ordination of the first local country pastor, Tranquebar, 31 December 1733.

[155] The country pastor Philipp travelled to Thanjavur in July 1774 in order to carry out baptisms there along with the catechist Rajappen (1742–96/7). NHB 14. St., 150–52.

[156] HB 45. Cont., 1109.

Brahmin Clarinda to establish a Christian congregation.[157] The authority of the country pastor was also used to mediate in disputes or disagreements between mission co-workers and the congregation concerned. Thus, in 1781, the country pastor Rajappen was told to settle a dispute in Kawastalam (Kapistalam) between Jesadian and members of the congregation.[158] Country pastors were often given the task of initiating new assistants or catechists in their work, of introducing them to the local congregations during divine services and assisting them in the first few days of work.[159] Under the influence of enlightenment and rationalism the authority of the Tamil country pastors was jeopardized at the end of the eighteenth century. To some extent, even their position within the Tranquebar mission was questioned. In the 'General news about the condition of the mission in Trankenbar' of 1801 the idea of doing away with the post of country pastor is expressed. Instead, the role of the European missionaries would be strengthened and each would be given a larger group of local catechists and assistants.[160] In 1801 Ch. S. John asked different mission societies to send their missionaries to Tranquebar where they could be trained for their work by the experienced Halle missionaries.[161]

The main duties of the numerous catechists consisted in propagating the Christian faith to the baptized and others, as well as teaching the catechumen. The first Tamilian catechist was appointed on 28 May 1707. His duties included helping in the religious instruction for catechumen, visiting them regularly and taking every opportunity to talk to the non-Christians.[162] In 1733 the duties of the catechists were described extensively: they were to visit houses of Christians daily and also European houses with Christian slaves. During these meetings they would conduct short

[157] Frykenberg, Robert Eric, 1999, 'The Legacy of Christian Friedrich Schwartz', *International Bulletin of Missionary Research*, 23 (3): 130–35, here 131. Frykenberg calls Sattianaden, who was ordained in 1790, the first Indian missionary.

[158] NHB 27. St., 273.

[159] Philipp travelled in 1775 to Ramanathapuram in order to introduce the assistant Wisuwasi to his new rural congregation. NHB 14. St., 150–52; 167; 173; 15. St., 275, 278.

[160] NHB 58. St., 842.

[161] NHB 58. St., 895.

[162] HB 6. Cont., 229.

lessons with catechumen, which would serve to recapitulate and consolidate what the latter had learned in the classes conducted by the missionaries. The 'Order of Salvation', a handbook written in the form of questions and answers specially for this purpose, constituted an important tool for the work of the catechists. This text was based on teaching material for the Small Catechism developed by the American pastor Cotton Mather (1663–1728) and was specially adapted to South Indian conditions by Dal, Pressier, Walther and Martin Bosse (1724–49 in India). It was completed in 1727 and copied onto palm leaves before it was printed in Tranquebar in June 1731.[163] The catechists had to pay special attention to the conduct of unmarried young people. They had to visit the sick, organize and carry out funerals, manage a part of the alms and ensure, during marriages and other Christian festivals, that no 'heathen' customs crept in. Their most important duty, however, consisted in caring for the congregations assigned to them, i.e. in helping them to remember and consolidate what they had learned or in carrying out the occasional private baptisms on someone's deathbed. As many Christians as possible were expected to come to church on Sundays and listen to the missionary's sermon. The catechist supervised the divine service, preached the sermon himself sometimes or repeated the one preached by the missionary. The catechist had to regularly give an account of all his activities to the missionary.[164] Depending on the region in which they worked the large group of catechists was divided into rural or city catechists, and depending on the powers given to them, into catechists or junior catechists. When the question of Rajanayakkan's ordination came up in 1740 and when he was denied ordination on account of his caste background as a *paraiyār* (Diogo was ordained instead),[165] the missionaries quickly gave him the title of a senior catechist in order to highlight his individual importance and to avoid unpleasant justifications for not ordaining him.[166] On occasion, the care of a congregation included

[163] HB 25. Cont., 155. HB 32. Cont., 821, diary 1731, entry 20 June. HB 33. Cont., 883.

[164] Cf. HB 33. Cont., 883–85.

[165] Diogo, who was ordained on 28 December 1741, was responsible for the more distant districts of the rural congregation. HB 53. Cont., 491.

[166] HB 52, Cont., 701, letter from the missionaries to the editor, 30 December 1740.

punishing Christians, smoothening out disagreements and resolving conflicts between members of the congregation. The responsibility of a catechist for 'his' congregation also extended to the social and religious practices of the local Christians. He had to ensure that they did not take part in 'heathen' religious ceremonies and customs. Even when Christians took part in social protests such as leaving the village as a sign of dissatisfaction with the tax policies of the local landlord, the catechists were supposed to intervene and make the Christians return to the village.

> A catechist is, so to say, praecursor Missionariorum and a mediator between the missionaries and the Malabarians who run away from Europeans. Along with a thorough knowledge of catechism he must also have the ability to speak well and to hold a discourse; he must also possess the skill to deal with people and win them over, to supervise the congregation and other such things.[167]

Some of the duties that were laid down in the contract between the catechists and the mission resulted from the concrete working conditions of the catechist. Sattianaden, for example, had to take the following into consideration: if someone expressed a desire to convert, he was not authorized to make any kind of promises and had to inform the missionaries about this person. He was expected to preach the 'divine truth' to Catholics, but not attempt to convince these persons at all costs.[168] A few years later, the catechist Rajanayakkan received instructions for the work in Thanjavur. If a Catholic expressed a desire to convert to Lutheranism, Rajanayakkan was to first give him time for reflection. He then had to write down information about this person and the stated reasons for conversion on a palm leaf and send it to the missionaries in Tranquebar for their scrutiny. The same procedure applied if Rajanayakkan considered someone particularly suitable for the job of a catechist. The decisions were taken by the missionaries.[169] In October 1743 the missionary Kiernander in Cuddalore gave the following work description for a catechist:

[167] HB 29. Cont., 477, (translated from German).
[168] HB 26. Cont.1–3.
[169] HB 26. Cont., 15.

> I have also arranged for the catechist to go to the villages on the outskirts of the city twice a week in the afternoons. He will not only visit the new Christians there but will also make every possible effort to propagate the path of salvation to the heathens. He will devote one whole day in a week to go to the outlying cities and villages for this purpose: [...] The rest of the time, when he is free from the work of the school, he is expected to copy Malabarian books. Besides this, he has to help me teach the catechumen who are being prepared for Holy Baptism. And, because a few weeks of preparation is always necessary for those who will partake of Holy Communion for the first time as well as for others, he will also help me in teaching these classes.[170]

The importance given to education in the framework of the Tranquebar Mission resulted in a special status for the teachers and educators. While, in the early period, non-Christian teachers worked on behalf of the mission in local schools and were paid by the mission, with the development of their own network of schools the missionaries paid greater attention to the selection of professional personnel. Knowledge of religion and language as well as knowledge of other subjects were as important as the pedagogic abilities of the persons concerned. The teachers enjoyed the confidence of the missionaries and were also expected to gain the respect of the community, since the mission schools were open to all social and religious strata and they tried to reach as many non-Christians as possible. In the hierarchy of South Indian mission employees the teachers, the so-called schoolmasters, were formally ranked below the country pastors and the catechists. In their daily work, however, they also carried out the duties of the catechists. Responsible as he was for the care and education of the (Christian and non-Christian) school children, the teacher was often one of the most respected persons of a village community and he, therefore, often had the function of a bridge between the mission and the people of the village. Using the high esteem that teachers traditionally enjoyed in the local society, the Tranquebar missionaries of the early phase tried to recruit local

[170] HB 59. Cont., 1747f., supplement from the English Mission in Cuddalore. Diary of the missionaries Geister and Kiernander, entry 6 October 1743, (translated from German).

(Hindu) teachers, but they soon gave up this practice in favour of training their own teachers.[171] Compared to the country pastors and the catechists, the teachers' salaries were low. From time to time the missionaries tried to even out this imbalance by giving the teachers special gifts. In a letter of 1739 to the editor of the Halle Reports the missionaries informed him how they had given teachers gifts received from the sponsors:

> It is true that the schoolmasters have not been expressly mentioned: however, since various sponsors and benefactors sent donations for the workers in general, and since the schoolmasters have not received anything for some years; also since their work is often more difficult than that of the catechists—they work in the schools and also help out in the preparation of the catechumen—we felt we must give them, like the others, some material comfort.[172]

In some cases it was advantageous for the mission to appoint women. This applied to the sphere of actual missionary work among the non-Christian population where men did not have access, but also to the sphere of education where women were required for supervising and teaching the girls. For women there were hardly any possibilities of climbing the career ladder in the mission. Mostly, they helped out as Bible-women or prayer leaders and took care of the women members of the congregation or the women in the region. A few were directly trained as teachers. Maria (around 1705–28) was one of the pupils of the first girls' school set up by the Mission. After a few years she taught younger girls there and was later officially appointed a schoolmistress in the girls' school.[173] In the course of the work of the Tranquebar Mission only two female catechists were mentioned by name: the catechists Maria and Regina in Tranquebar.[174] Besides them there were two more female catechists in the 1780s in the 'Portuguese' congregation in Tranquebar whose names we do not know.[175] As a rule, women worked together with

[171] See also chapter five of this study.

[172] HB 52. Cont., 677, letter from the missionaries in Tranquebar to the editor, dated 19 December 1739, (translated from German).

[173] HB 6. Cont., 331; HB 26. Cont., 82; AB 263.

[174] NHB 51. St., 231.

[175] NHB 25. St., 72, 1780, letter from the missionaries to the Society of Scholars in Batavia, Tranquebar, 14 October 1789.

a male colleague and took on the missionary work with regard to women. Thus, for example, Rahel (1730–1801), a prayer leader, was assigned to the *paraiyār*-catechist Dewasagajam.[176] Wives sometimes accompanied a male mission employee on his work and, on his death, were often appointed in his place like Rahel, the widow of the catechist Ignasi (died 1770), who, after the death of her husband, became a schoolteacher in his former place of work.[177]

Both men and women carried out the work of a prayer leader. A prayer leader was appointed for a particular region and—like the other co-workers—had to maintain a diary, had to travel and organize divine services and Bible hours. In exceptional cases it could also happen that a prayer leader undertook an emergency baptism. Prayer leaders recapitulated the sermons of the missionaries and the country pastors. Female prayer leaders had to pay special attention to the women of the area. Often, a prayer house was adjoined to their house and people who were interested came to them to read the Bible and to pray. It is said about the prayer leader of the *paraiyār* in Tranquebar, Schinna Schawriammal: 'A small prayer house was built adjoining her house, in which she held a prayer hour and a small catechization mornings and evenings with the Christians who gathered there, and she exhorted them to lead an honest life.'[178] The women among the prayer leaders were often the widows of former mission employees. When Schinna Schawriammal died as a widow at the beginning of 1794, her successor was again a Christian widow, Annamei (born around 1770). Also Rajanayakkan's widow was appointed as a prayer leader.[179]

It was the task of the assistants to help an employee in a higher post. This could mean helping a missionary, a country pastor, or even a catechist during their travels by noting down, for example, the contents of the conversations with the local people, so that the person concerned could include all the details in the reports.[180] Writers, copyists and bookkeepers were indispensable co-workers of the mission. While listing the monthly costs of running the

[176] NHB 37. St., 13.

[177] NHB 59. St., 995–98.

[178] NHB 46. St., 915 (translated from German).

[179] NHB 10. St., 1347. NHB 46. St., 915, 927.

[180] HB 17. Cont., Vorrede, 14.

mission Ziegenbalg mentions, among other things, the 'frequent copying of Malabarian books'. In 1710 the mission engaged 12 Tamil writers for this work, 'so that one would have some books in reserve'.[181] To a great extent, the large group of technical employees remains anonymous in the mission reports. The fact of their existence is based on some statistical lists, but, even here, they are not included every year. It is only the mission accounts, which give us an approximate overview of this group of people. Here, rather than in the group directly concerned with missionary work, non-Christians were also employed.

TRAINING OF LOCAL CO-WORKERS

For each mission society the training of 'one's own' local co-workers assumed a different significance depending on mission methods, strategies and the educational background of the European missionaries. The first local helpers were usually not Christians and were recruited by the Mission—often by chance—on the basis of their knowledge and their capabilities. They were not specially trained for work in the Mission. When the missions were more established, they depended more on the converts and their descendants. Children who had been taught and raised in mission schools and whose parents had worked for the mission got preferential employment. One expected them to be more obedient, reliable and loyal, both to the Mission as well as to the missionaries as their superiors.

Within the Tranquebar Mission the missionaries realized early on that a practical method of education alone, which was limited to accompanying a missionary or receiving instructions from persons in higher functions, would not, in the long run, be sufficient for the growing requirements of missionary work. What was also necessary was systematic, content-based, theological training of the local co-workers. This requirement was addressed in 1716 by setting up a seminary to train local teachers and catechists. Originally, Ziegenbalg and Gründler had even thought of establishing a

[181] HB 5. Cont., 187, letter from B. Ziegenbalg to A.H. Francke, 23 December 1710.

seminary in Tranquebar where European missionaries could be prepared for their work in a particular region—through special language training, among other things. They described the seminary as one 'in which, on the basis of our experiences, the future workers would be prepared by learning East Indian languages and other good qualities and who, after this preparation, could be sent out among those heathens whose language they have learned here.'[182] However, they did not get a positive response to this idea from Europe. The aim of the seminary that was finally established to train local mission employees consisted in preparing selected pupils of higher classes for future work in the mission by imparting relevant educational content and paying attention to their upbringing. They would be 'taught dogmatic theology, study and exegesis of the Bible as well as other subjects to prepare them for service in the mission.'[183] Those who passed out of this seminary were appointed as writers, teachers, assistants and catechists in direct missionary work.[184]

The need for local co-workers who could be given greater responsibility and would, therefore, have to have a corresponding level of knowledge and education quickly grew and, in the early years, the best pupils of the seminary were often given work in the schools and congregations even before they had completed their education. Besides teaching the catechumen, their duties included looking after the congregations through contacts and conversations with the people.

[182] HB 8. Cont., 608, letter from J.E. Gründler and B. Ziegenbalg, 16 September 1712, (translated from German); HB 8. Cont., 614, letter from J.E. Gründler and B. Ziegenbalg. After Ziegenbalg had already proposed in 1709 that future European missionaries be sent out prior to their ordination, for which they could be prepared in India (Cf. AB 102–106, Letter from Ziegenbalg, 27 September 1709), this later proposal can be seen as a further attempt to influence, to some extent, the training of the mission co-workers, if not their selection. This kind of a special mission seminary was not established. The new missionaries learned the languages of the region individually, either with the help of older missionaries or under the guidance of an Indian language teacher.

[183] AB 471, letter from Ziegenbalg to A.H. Francke, Tranquebar, 7 January 1717, (translated from German). A few years before this the missionaries had already written to Francke and pointed out the necessity of such an institution. Cf. AB 226, Letter from B. Ziegenbalg, J.E. Gründler and Polycarp Jordan to A.H. Francke, Tranquebar, 10 September 1712.

[184] HB 33. Cont., 893f.

> One of the catechists has been sent as the Senior to Boreiar to look after the school and the congregation there. He must teach them God's word daily and supervise them well. He must also go among the heathens and propagate the will of God to them. Another one has been appointed hortatory in the Tranquebar congregation. His work is not to initiate people into the teachings of Christianity but, rather, to go around to all the houses, to observe the life of the Christians, to exhort them to led a pious life, to pray with them and to lead them by the hand and practise prayers with them. Yet another has been appointed to the congregation and it is his task to initiate them into the teachings of Christianity, to continuously improve their knowledge of these teachings and, from time to time, to read them chapters from the New Testament. Others have been appointed to teach the catechumen and to prepare those who wish to partake of Holy Communion one week in advance.[185]

This separate institution for training local employees existed till the beginning of the 1730s. Fifteen persons were being trained in this seminary in 1731. The costs for the seminary amounted to roughly 620 Reichstaler—an expense that could be defrayed from donations given by European Christian benefactors for the express purpose of maintaining and developing this educational institution.[186] After 15 years of the existence of this seminary most of the catechists had passed out of this institution.

> The catechists are taken from among those who have been educated in the seminary and who have worked for some time in the school. At the beginning of this work adults who came from the Roman Church or from heathenism to us also had to be taken and given adequate preparation: this sometimes still happens in an emergency. None of the former, however, are appointed catechists unless they have first worked as schoolmasters for some years and have then served as assistants, by which time they are of the right age and have the necessary experience. If a new catechist is required, he is publicly introduced to the congregation with prayers and God's word from the altar, alongside which the other catechists are gathered [...].[187]

[185] HB 17. Cont., Vorrede, 12f., (translated from German).
[186] HB 33. Cont., Vorrede, §IV.
[187] HB 33. Cont., 881, (translated from German).

The subsequent development of this seminary for training catechists in the framework of the mission is unclear. While this institution is mentioned in the extensive report of 1732 as a part of the mission complex,[188] this is no longer the case in the following years. Rather, so-called seminarists were selected in the boys' schools, who sometimes had additional classes. These pupils stood out not only because of their good academic performance, but also because of their conduct, which corresponded to the ideas of the missionaries. However, they were not taught completely separately from the others, but were part of the highest class in every subject and, therefore, had exacting and special lessons. Thus, reading as a subject in the Tamil boys' school in Tranquebar, for example, was divided into six classes to which the pupils were assigned according to their proficiency. 'The seminarists and those who can read printed books sit in the first class.'[189] On Tuesdays and Thursdays the reading classes included texts from Tamil philosophical and moral works. On the other days Christian texts were read. The pupils of the first class had special lessons in theology taught by one of the missionaries, which the assistants and teachers of the Tranquebar city congregation also attended. A missionary also taught geography and church history in the first class.[190] In 1751 the missionaries resolved to appoint Jacob Klein to give the seminarists special classes in exegesis and rhetoric.[191]

In the course of time it became common practice to have joint classes for seminarists, who had been selected for missionary service, and other talented pupils who were generally employed by a European establishment when they finished their schooling. With the growing number of pupils the missionaries also had to teach in the schools. The number of Indian co-workers required also rose, and one person alone could not take over the entire training. The integration of special help for future mission employees into the framework of mission schools initially took place for pragmatic reasons, on grounds of personnel and organizational principles. Later, however, this also

188 HB 33. Cont., 870.

189 HB 58. Cont., 1535, (translated from German).

190 Ibid.

191 HB 56. Cont., 566f., letter from J. Klein to G.A. Francke, 28 September 1751.

conformed to the changing political demands to which the mission had to react. On the one hand, interest in the mission began to wane in Europe towards the end of the eighteenth century, and there was a marked decline in willingness to support the mission financially as well as with regard to personnel. Since fewer missionaries were being sent out from Europe, the training of local co-workers assumed even greater importance. On the other hand, the changed social conditions in the mission region threw up new challenges for the educational establishments in India, which the mission could not ignore.[192] The integration led to a closer link between the general education offered and financed by the mission and practical mission training in the narrower sense.[193]

These changes became particularly evident in the comprehensive plans and practical measures introduced in the 1780s by Ch. S. John in the sphere of educational policies. Talented boys, the so-called selectans, were taught separately by the missionaries and 'prepared for the service of the Church and the common good'.[194] Along with their general education in religion, reading, arithmetic and writing, they were also given lessons in theology, history, geography, Portuguese and German.[195] This form of support for talented pupils was linked with their selection for various educational or professional avenues for further learning. The selectans were taught exclusively by the missionaries. The Tamil pupils who were selected were predominantly children of the 'casteless'.[196] In October 1780 Missionary Klein referred to a special attempt to teach some *paṟaiyār* separately as 'selectans' in order to make them fit for missionary service or for the 'common good'. The intellectual abilities of these

[192] As a result of the increasing activities of the British colonial administration the need for English-language education grew among many social groups. The development of a comprehensive colonial education network began, however, only in the middle of the nineteenth century. Till then, a considerable part of this requirement was covered by mission schools. For the role of the Danish-English-Halle Mission in this context see: Frykenberg, 'The Halle Legacy in Modern India'.

[193] Under the Leipzig Mission there was a marked return to specialization in the nineteenth century. The mission maintained a teacher's seminary in Tranquebar and a seminary for priests in Porayar. ELMB, 21, 1895, 385–89.

[194] NHB 25. St., 8.

[195] Ibid.

[196] NHB 26. St., 134.

boys were tested on the basis of a recapitulation of the Sunday sermons. They had classes in church history, geography, cosmography, Portuguese, German and arithmetic and they had to teach pupils of lower classes under supervision.[197] However, the 'selectans' were not only trained for missionary service, but also for work as merchants, bookkeepers and other employees of Europeans.[198] Those who were to be taken into missionary service later went through additional practical training with one of the European missionaries, i.e. they accompanied him on his walks and listened to his conversations with non-Christians. Thus, they gathered their first experiences through observation and participation.

The training of a co-worker did not come to an end when he assumed the post of a teacher or a catechist in the mission. At varying intervals events—sometimes lasting several days—were organized for an exchange of experiences and for further education.[199] Occasions for such seminars for advanced training were events for which all country pastors and catechists were present in Tranquebar, such as the death or the ordination of a co-worker, salary days, or when they had to present their reports. The contents of these seminars were not decided only on the basis of topical events. Lessons in church history, for example, were conducted systematically for the catechists.[200] The so-called 'parenetic hour' took place regularly, during which all Tamil co-workers were 'exhorted' with the help of literature.[201]

The missionary Ludwig Bernhard Ehregott Schmid (1787–after 1846) who worked for the CMS introduced a three-tiered training of local employees in the 1820s in Palayankottai. In the first course the subjects Tamil, English, arithmetic, geometry, history and geography had to be completed. This was, at the same time, the basic training

[197] Ibid.

[198] NHB 30. St., 672.

[199] Thus, in August 1731 the rural catechists stayed in Tranquebar and gathered every day in the mission house for lessons in theology. At the same time, they were expected to work on improving their skills in catechization. HB 32. Cont., 829. In October 1732 the rural catechists again spent a week in Tranquebar for their further education. HB 36. Cont., 1248.

[200] On the occasion of the death of Johann Anton Sartorius the rural catechists were given lessons on 28 June 1738. HB 47. Cont., 1392.

[201] NHB 1. St., 49.

for school teachers. In the second course, talented pupils studied, in addition, Sanskrit, general doctrine and Indian religions. On the completion of this course they could become catechists. The most talented pupils were delegated to the third, the preacher's course, in which the Bible languages were also taught.[202]

In all the educational measures for Tamil co-workers that have been described here only male co-workers are mentioned. Girls who were meant to work later as Bible women, prayer leaders or educators for the mission were obviously not given a comparable form of additional special education. Since women were appointed catechists only in exceptional cases, the missionaries probably found it more important to give the girls lessons in handicrafts and in household management rather than in theology and languages.

The character and contents of the education of local co-workers were closely tied with the goals and the methods of the mission and with the strata of people among whom missionary work was carried out. In her comparison of the educational methods of the French mission (*Société des Missions Étrangères de Paris/Pondicherry Mission*) and those of the Danish Mission Society in the second half of the nineteenth century in South Arcot Henriette Bugge states that the Danes did not want to organize comprehensive theological training for their Indian catechists. The missionaries themselves had been peasants and craftsmen, not theologians or students of other disciplines. This affected the methods of the mission. In addition, the missionaries of the Danish Mission Society were hardly interested in secular studies on different aspects of Indian society.[203] The French approached their work differently. They did not regard Christianity as a religion of the oppressed and of the lower sections of society. In order, therefore, to reach the Brahmins and members of higher castes, they had to organize the training of the catechists at a high level. They tried to recruit candidates for the post of catechist from the higher castes and taught the standard High Tamil, so that the future catechists could, on their part, speak to members of the upper classes.[204]

[202] NHB 83. St., 972.
[203] Bugge, *Mission and Tamil Society*, 94f.
[204] Ibid., 82.

In the Tranquebar Mission training was organized in accordance with mission strategy, on the one hand, and the local specificities and requirements, on the other. Learning by observation in actual practice constituted an important method. Assistants accompanied the missionaries, catechists or country pastors on their travels, when they spoke to the people and during other work. This method was always used and, especially in the early phase of the Mission, it was the only way to combine training with missionary work. Later, this method represented a kind of practical training for prospective catechists and, at the same time, it eased the burden of work for the higher placed employees of the Mission. Schoolmasters sat in on the theology lessons that were taught by a missionary, a catechist or a country pastor.[205]

At the very latest since 1716, when a seminary for catechists was established for a systematic, goal-oriented and need-oriented training of South Indian mission employees, lessons in theological subjects and in languages relevant to the Bible became important. Rhetoric and extempore speech in front of a school class or the congregation was already practiced under Gründler's direction in the first years of existence of the seminary. Bible exegesis played an important role from the beginning, because future employees would have to be able to argue convincingly.[206] Knowledge of languages was a basic precondition. Some local persons, who would later work as interpreters, were taught European languages. The first missionaries were very interested in and had a great respect for local languages. It was only in the later phase that some missionaries expounded the cultural superiority of European languages vis-à-vis the South Indian languages, concretely Tamil, and demanded a transformation of the educational system. Learning European languages, they felt, was a necessary basis for studying the natural sciences. At the same time, they also reiterated the need for both the Indian and the European co-workers to learn standard Tamil and Sanskrit.

> Without a European language—in the present situation the choice would be for German—their intellect can never be properly

[205] HB 59. Cont., 1747, supplement from the English Mission in Cuddalore. Diary of the missionaries Geister and Kiernander, entry for 6 October 1743.

[206] HB 17. Cont., Vorrede, 14.

> enlightened and enriched by a thorough grounding in the necessary fields. [...] Another valuable means for converting and winning over the heathens would be if at least some of the missionaries and workers of the nation were to learn the higher Malabarian language as well as Kirendum or the Sanscrut in which their oldest texts are written [...].[207]

While school children who received extensive training in European languages were the exception in the early years,[208] in the second half of the eighteenth century it was English rather than German, which was obligatory in many schools of the Tranquebar Mission.

Along with the mediation of knowledge and capabilities in different spheres, it was also important to bring up future representatives of the mission to be pious, obedient, god-fearing, honest, punctual and reliable human beings whose conduct would be emulated by others. The criterion for assessment was the use and the usefulness of the work of a catechist. The candidates were taught to strictly apportion their time; time and means were not to be wasted on unnecessary things. The seminary also trained the communicative abilities of future catechists and developed their ability to resolve conflicts.[209]

[207] NHB 30. St., 700–709, (translated from German).

[208] During his schooling in the mission the country pastor Ambrosius had first learned Portuguese and then also German. HB 27. Cont., 225f. Letter from Ch. Th. Walther, 10 January 1729.

[209] For the characteristics of a catechist cf. HB 26. Cont.,1–3.

CHAPTER THREE

The Hierarchical Structure of the Mission Organization

> [...] the overseas imperialist expansion was, as we have seen, not a linear process determined exclusively by the centres of power, but rather the result of constant interactions between colonial powers, or their local representatives, on the one hand, and the indigenous elites on the other. The interactions, however, were of a marked asymmetrical nature.[1]

LOCAL EMPLOYEES AND EUROPEAN MISSIONARIES

Modern Christian missionary work in non-European regions was characterized by various processes of communication and interaction in which two groups of actors, the European missionaries and the local workers, each with their own social, religious and ethnic backgrounds, were linked in their daily work and dependent on one another. The manner in which the contents, the execution and the results of this co-operation took concrete shape was influenced not only by the religious background and the mutual perceptions of the members of the two groups, but also by the reactions of the people in the mission region and by the sponsors of the mission in Europe. The first impression, underscored by the political and economic conditions, that the local co-workers were, both spiritually and materially, dependent on 'their' European missionaries is relativized when the relations between the two groups is viewed critically. It is true that the European missionaries were the more

[1] Mommsen, Wolfgang, 1994, 'Europa und die außereuropäische Welt', *Historische Zeitschrift*, (258, June 3): 661–95, here 663, (translated from German).

influential group in the daily life of the mission since they created the structures, determined the course of action and made every effort to ensure adherence to their plans through a strictly regulated system of functions and duties, control and punishment. Despite this there is clear evidence of processes of dialogue and negotiation within the mission, in which the local employees had an independent framework of action.

MISSION STATION AS A NEGOTIATING SPACE

The fundamental goals and the methods of work of a mission society were generally laid down at its foundation in the form of statutes and regulations. Such documents, which constituted the operating base for all Protestant mission societies established in the nineteenth century, contained the strategy and the methods of the mission and, on this basis it outlined the duties, rights and the scope of work of the missionaries.[2] In some cases they also contained references to co-operation with local mission employees without, however, directly defining the powers and duties of the latter.

When the Tranquebar Mission began its work in Southeast India European Protestant missionary work in its comprehensively organized form had not yet begun. At the end of the seventeenth century Protestant circles in Europe started thinking about carrying out missionary work in the manner of the Catholics, especially the Jesuits. Beginning with the plans of the Austrian Lutheran baron, Justinian von Welz (1621–68), who proposed the setting up of a mission society based on the Augsburg Confession (1530), continuing with Gottfried Wilhelm Leibniz' (1646–1716) ideas about Protestant missionary work in Russia and China and up to the establishment of the Society for Promoting Christian Knowledge

[2] Johannes Evangelista Gossner (1773–1858), for example, after he had already sent out missionaries, submitted a five-point statute for the establishment of a 'Small Mission Society of the Bethlehem Congregation' in 1839. It was only after this that the 'Evangelical Missionary Society for the Propagation of Christianity among the Natives of Heathen Lands' was established on 28 June 1842. Cf. von Stieglitz, Klaus, 1969, *Der unvollendete Auftrag*, Evangelischer Missionsverlag, Stuttgart, 14f. For the statutes of the societies see also: Holsten, Walter, 1949, *Johannes Evangelista Gossner. Glaube und Gemeinde*, Vandenhoeck und Ruprecht, Göttingen, 386f.

(SPCK) in 1698 as well as the Society for Propagating the Gospel (SPG) in 1701 in England, ideas about Protestant missionary activity increasingly gained currency.[3]

In the case of the Tranquebar Mission the missionaries were sent out without a mission society being established. The first missionaries of the Tranquebar Mission did not set out for India on the basis of a document charting a mission strategy, but on the strength of a royal decree which enjoined them to work for the propagation of the Christian faith among the local population. The concrete means to achieve this goal were not spelled out. This royal decree remained the fundamental document determining the course of work for the missionaries. In addition, a 'Royal Act' of 11 September 1711 laid down that the mission would be continued by the successors of the then reigning king, Frederick IV.[4] An endowment was created for this purpose from which an annual sum of 2000 Reichstaler was to be paid towards salaries for four missionaries as well as for maintaining schools and employees of these schools. Till the establishment of the Mission Board in 1714 the Danish king laid down the mission regulations. The actual supervision of the mission lay in the hands of Franz Julius Lütkens and, after his death, briefly with Johannes Trellund (1669–1735) and Jacob Lodberg (1672–1731).[5] In 1714

[3] Cf., among others, Gensichen, Hans-Werner, 1993, *Invitatio ad Fraternitatem. 75 Jahre Deutsche Gesellschaft für Missionswissenschaft (1918–1993)*, Lit, Münster, Hamburg. The last decades of the eighteenth century witnessed the founding of a spate of new mission societies in England in the wake of Protestant revival movements and their influence on the policies of the East India Company: *Society for Mission by the Baptists* (1784); *London Missionary Society* (1795); *The Edinburgh Missionary Society* (1796), *Church Missionary Society* (1801). These societies initially gave financial support to mission societies of other countries in India and also supplied them with literature, or they employed missionaries of other societies till 1813 when the East India Company changed its charter, allowing these societies to establish their own mission stations in India.

[4] HB 7. Cont. (not paginated), 'Send=Schreiben von den Gnaden=Bezeugungen Sr. Königl. Maj. in Dennemarck gegen das Missions=Werck in Ost=Indien'.

[5] Cf. Fenger, *Geschichte der Tranquebarschen Mission*, 79. After studying theology in Germany and England and after a stay in Italy Johann Trellund became a professor of theology in Copenhagen in 1711. Jacob Lodberg was a pastor in Copenhagen since 1707. In 1714 he became a member of the Mission Board. Cf. *Dansk Biografisk Leksikon*, 1933–1944, Grundlagt af C.F. Bricka, Redigeret af Povl Engelstoft under Medvirkning af Svend Dahl, Schultz, København.

Frederick IV ordered the establishment of a Collegium de Cursu Evangelii promovendo[6], whose task it was to coordinate the activities in support of the mission in Denmark, Norway, Germany and England, to look after the correspondence with friends and patrons of the mission as well as to evaluate suggestions and instructions for missionary work.

The Mission Board was also responsible for maintaining the link with the missionaries who had been sent out and for their constant supervision and care. Initially, every missionary who was to be sent out received individual instructions in addition to the existing Royal Instruction that was valid for all. The first of such instructions were more in the nature of a series of phrases of encouragement and adjuration, of appeals to the conscience and the faith of the men. Apart from the relatively concrete demands regarding the study of languages—for the India-bound missionaries this meant learning Portuguese and Tamil—only a few tangible and concretely accounted duties were laid down. A possible co-operation with local co-workers was not mentioned. The people of Southeast India appeared as a large ignorant mass who urgently required the help and the self-sacrificial devotion of the missionaries. An open letter of 1727 from August Hermann Francke to the five missionaries in southeast India also reiterated this basic idea.[7]

The individual instructions of the Mission Board became more detailed when the ideas and information in Europe about the work of the mission became more concrete. Whereas the instructions of 1719 for Nikolaus Dal, Johann Heinrich Kistemacher (died 1722) and Benjamin Schultze was essentially similar to the model described first,[8] the Board issued detailed instructions on 16 November 1775 for Johann Wilhelm Gerlach and he was told to present these

[6] AFSt/M 1 C 6 : 103, Founding charter of the mission board by Friedrich IV, King of Denmark and Norway, 10 December 1714. HB, Preface to the 8th Cont., text of the founding charter. For short biographies of the secretaries of the Mission Board see Nørgaard, Anders, 2006, 'Secretaries of the Mission Board in Copenhagen 1714–1868', in Gross et al., *Halle and the Beginning of Protestant Christianity in India, Vol. III,* 1565–67.

[7] August Hermann Francke, 1725, *Send=Schreiben an die Fünf Königl. Dänische Evangelische Herren Missionarios zu Tranquebar in Ost=Indien [...],* Waisenhaus, Halle.

[8] HB 14. Cont., 169–83.

on his arrival to the missionaries in Tranquebar along with the letter of appointment and the Royal Instruction. These individual instructions laid down Gerlach's duties as the director of the school to be set up in Tranquebar primarily for European children of the Lutheran faith. This was followed by a reference to the importance of co-operating with the other missionaries with regard to the extra-curricular work with the children, 'so that good order may prevail through joint decisions'.[9] There was no reference to co-operation with Tamil co-workers. Special farewell ceremonies were organized for the departing missionaries by the Mission Board in Copenhagen or by the SPCK in London in order to underscore the importance of their missionary task and the need to lead an exemplary life as representatives of the concerned institution.[10]

The criteria and methods for the selection of new missionaries was the subject of heated, and sometimes, controversial discussions during the entire period of the mission. Time and again suggestions came from various quarters concerning the selection of new missionaries, their duties or their legal status. In 1784 Christoph Samuel John made new suggestions in this regard in a 'Pro Memoria for new missionaries', which was signed also by Johann Peter Rottler.[11] This document emphasized the need to ensure the unswerving loyalty of the men concerned and reiterated that no one should be allowed to enter missionary service for personal gains.[12] In 1797 Rottler, John and August Friedrich Cämmerer sent the completed draft of new instructions for missionaries to the Mission Board in Copenhagen. The most important thing, according to this draft, was the pledge to serve the mission selflessly for a minimum period of 12 years. For the first time a period of stay was laid down for missionaries and other European employees in the mission region. The unspoken rule till this point of time was that the missionaries would stay in India permanently and would not

[9] RA Miskolark 3, No. 33, 1765–89, instructions for the missionary Johan Wilhelm Gerlach.

[10] Cf., among others, NHB 36. St., 1410–21 (Bidding farewell to Joseph Daniel Jänicke); NHB 45. St., 818–33 (Bidding farewell to Carl Wilhelm Pätzold).

[11] RA Miskolark 9g, *Pro Memoria* for new missionaries from Ch. S. John and [J.P. Rottler], Tranquebar, 20 January 1784.

[12] Ibid.

visit Europe again during their lifetime. These draft instructions also contained suggestions for organizing the decision-making process among the missionaries. The highest body in Southeast India was the missionary conference.

> No missionary is self-dependent, but is governed by the joint resolution of the conference. Therefore, no one can travel as he pleases or remain absent for several days and nor can he undertake anything which is directly connected with the mission, or which would have an impact on it, without having previously discussed it with his colleagues in the conference and having received their approval.[13]

There were also important suggestions for conflict resolution in cases where a missionary had violated disciplinary regulations.

> Should the mission, God forbid, be so unlucky as to have a missionary or an assistant fall prey to drunkenness or any other public vice leading to scandal, or should he prove to be so lazy or obstinate that he does not bother about the resolutions arrived at in a conference, or should he be unwilling to carry out his duties in the congregation, it would be good if the other missionaries had the authority to initially suspend such an unworthy person on half-salary till such time as the verdict of the higher Board can be known. Otherwise, he would remain a useless boarder of the mission for years unless he chose to go back or could be sent back.[14]

These suggestions were revised and, a year later, they were incorporated into an instruction for prospective missionaries as well as for other European employees. General and universally valid instructions for South Indian co-workers were not formulated even in 1798. The original considerations regarding a 12–year period were abandoned and the lifetime pledge was retained. This went against the ideas of the missionaries who had always reiterated the importance of sojourns in Europe, both for the welfare of the person concerned as well as for the development of the mission. A return to Europe was

[13] RA Miskolark 9h, some preliminary thoughts for instructing new missionaries and assistants from Ch. S. John, J.P. Rottler, A.F. Cämmerer [1797], (translated from German).

[14] RA Miskolark 9h, some preliminary thoughts [...], (translated from German).

now only permitted for reasons of health and with the relevant medical testimonials, in the absence of which the missionary would have to bear the cost of travel himself.[15] Even the passage in the instruction for prospective missionaries concerning disciplinary violations was formulated in a differentiated manner in the final version of 1798. The Mission Board in Copenhagen would only be informed after the matter was comprehensively discussed in the local missionary conference and the person concerned had been admonished. The Mission Board could then be requested to arrive at a final decision. Even if the person were to be eventually asked to return, he would have to be supported by the mission till his departure.[16]

The revised version of 1798 contained for the first time separate instructions for the non-ordained European employees of the mission: 'Instruction for a German catechist or schoolmaster in Trankenbar'.[17] One of the main points was that these co-workers were also expected to learn the local languages. In addition, they were to serve the mission unconditionally, regard the missionaries as their superiors and follow their orders. The instructions did not contain any guidelines for the co-operation with South Indian colleagues and nor were there any suggestions and criteria for the selection of local co-workers. In their decision to employ a local individual in the service of the mission the missionaries in the region could only fall back on themselves. In the framework of the missionary conference, therefore, they laid down guidelines for the South Indian co-workers at the different levels of work and issued individual instructions.

The different strands of the work of religious conversion came together in the mission station. It was here that the European missionaries transmitted religious knowledge to the South Indian co-workers in meetings that took place regularly, where strategies were also discussed and concrete action outlined. While carrying out these instructions and tasks the local workers often had to fall back on themselves, take decisions in concrete situations and act accordingly. The group of European missionaries was

[15] RA Miskolark 9h, instruction for a future missionary in Tranquebar, 1798.
[16] Ibid.
[17] RA Miskolark 9h, instruction for a German catechist or teacher inTranquebar, 1798.

the direct point of reference for the local employees. It was not a homogeneous group since the missionaries differed from one another with respect to their social and regional background, their education, their abilities and their attitude towards India and its people. As a group they were subordinate to the mission administrators in Europe, who had decision-making powers in personnel, financial and strategic matters. The opinion-building and decision-making process in the stations was regulated jointly in the missionary conference. The Tranquebar Mission did not have any appointed heads of station, even though in practice individual missionaries took on a leading role. Along with the ordained missionaries there were non-ordained co-workers and European technical and medical personnel.

The Tranquebar Mission was organized according to a strict hierarchical principle. The European missionaries had the authority to supervise and check the 'national workers'. In the written and oral reports that had to be submitted every month in Tranquebar the local co-workers of the mission gave a detailed description of the events in their region. After receiving new instructions from the missionaries they left Tranquebar again. 'In the forenoon on Fridays we gather for the conference at nine o'clock, where we deliberate about the conditions, events and arrangements in the congregations and schools. The country preachers and catechists also give their reports here.'[18] The missionaries also organized special training programmes for the local employees in different spheres of work. In 1737, for example, such meetings were devoted explicitly to the mistakes of the Catholic Church as well as to the relationship between Lutheranism and the Catholic Church.[19] The strict mission rules and the incontestable hierarchy in the functional structure did not exclude admiration of and recognition for the achievements of individual local co-workers of the mission. In 1733 Johann Anton Sartorius attested to Aaron's 'pleasant gravity and seriousness' just after he had been ordained. However, to underscore the importance of this estimation, he added that these qualities were 'seldom found among the Malabars'.[20]

[18] NHB 25. St., 6, letters from the missionaries in Tranquebar, 14 October 1780, (translated from German).

[19] HB 45. Cont., 1113; 46. Cont., 1244.

[20] HB 38. Cont., 261, diary entry for 28 December 1733.

The early missionaries used religious arguments and linked their criticism of various aspects of life of the Tamilians to the absence of the 'true' faith which, if accepted, would also lead to a change in these aspects of life. Later, this tendency of a singular confidence in the long-term power of faith was relegated to the background in favour of a direct struggle against such norms, traditions and customs of the Tamilians, which contradicted the moral and aesthetic sensibilities of the missionaries. John, in particular, tended to constantly emphasize the superiority of the European-Christian way of life over that of the Tamilians. This expressed itself, among other ways, in his educational methods and goals as, for example, when Tamilian children would be taught European table manners including the use of crockery and cutlery.[21] The 'integrated school' that John ran for a brief period for children of European, Indian and mixed origin was not directed at learning from each other, but rather at the 'civic education of Indians' to help them adapt to European norms.[22] When the city catechist Schawrirajen (1755–1817) accompanied John on a journey to Tiruchirappalli in 1795, the missionary traveled in a *palanquin* while the South Indian mission co-worker had to walk with the servants of the missionary.[23]

Daily life in the mission was characterized by a strict system of discipline and obedience, which everyone had to adhere to, regardless of their formal status. Disobedience, or the exceeding of one's powers, could result in harsh punishment. A violation of discipline by a missionary was a more difficult matter. Since there was no authorized managing body locally, such matters were first discussed in the missionary conference. However, the Mission board in Copenhagen had to give its consent to any reprisals that would eventually apply. First, the missionary conference met and determined the initial measures to be taken. In the case of serious offenses an attempt was made to involve the Danish trading company,

[21] NHB 30. St., 707.

[22] Cf. John, Christoph Samuel, 1813, *On Indian Civilization, or, report of a successful experiment made, during two years, on that subject, in fifteen Tamul and five English Native Free-Schools; with proposals for establishing a separate, liberal Native School Society, etc.*, F.C. and J. Rivington, London. John sent this treatise written in English, which deals with the 'civic education of Indians through schools' also as a manuscript to Halle, AFSt/M 2 C 17 : 6; cf. also NHB 66. St., 485, 486, 839.

[23] NHB 50. St., 131, diary of Schawrirajen 1795.

or, later, even the royal government. Whereas the punishments that the missionaries meted out to each other generally did not go beyond admonitions and appeals, since they had to wait for the decision of the European bodies, a system of punishment for South Indian co-workers was evolved in the course of time. The kind of measures taken was governed by the seriousness of the violation, but it also depended on the individual views of the missionary in charge.

The lowest form of punishment was an admonition.[24] The person concerned was made aware of his offense and, with a simultaneous appeal to his duties and responsibilities as a Christian and as a member of the mission, he was admonished to refrain from such shortcomings in the future. When the *paṟaiyār* catechists from the Kumbakonam district—Jesadian (died 1778), stationed in Rarasalam[25] and Keilasam, working in Tererhendur[26]—read out their diaries to the missionaries, they were both 'admonished for their laziness and carelessness'. However, they could not be suspended due to the lack of 'useful assistants', otherwise it would have happened immediately.[27] The missionaries also gave 'admonitions' in the sense of advice and urgent directions if they had doubts about the moral conduct of an employee or a member of the congregation. This also included advice on marital affairs or the settling of marital disputes.[28] For certain offences the persons concerned were expected to make public declarations of their repentance and atonement. It was often not enough to apologize to the superior instance; one had to publicly confess one's sins before the entire congregation and make a solemn promise to improve. The Tranquebar missionaries demanded such a public confession on 30 November 1709 from the blind Joao d'Almeida (1679–1746) who had been a catechist and a language teacher with the mission since 28 May 1707. At the time when Ziegenbalg was in prison (November 1708 till March 1709), however, and influenced by the Danish

[24] The term 'admonition' (*Ermahnung*) was also used for the instruction given to catechists and teachers every month. HB 64. Cont., 636.

[25] Probably Darasuram, Kumbakonam *tālūk*.

[26] This refers to Terezhendur in the Mayiladuthurai *tālūk*.

[27] NHB 33. St., 993.

[28] AFSt/H D 16 a, diary written by Benjamin Schultze, from 1 January 1720 to 31 December 1721, entry 13 November 1720. The daughter of the catechist Joao and her husband were 'admonished to live in harmony'.

preacher Johann Hassel, d'Almeida abandoned the mission and his congregation and wanted to go back to the Catholic faith. When he returned with his family to Tranquebar on 30 November 1709 and asked to be admitted to the congregation again, he was charged with the grave sin of breaking off relations with the community of his faith, for which he was told to give a public justification to the congregation. 'Since he had caused immense and open annoyance for the entire congregation here through his reversion, his reasons had to be presented publicly to the congregation.'[29] D'Almeida acquiesced to this step only after having reflected on it for several days.[30] On 6 April 1760 a Christian in Thanjavur had to give a public apology for having temporarily converted to Catholicism several years earlier.[31] In the case of illnesses Tamilian Christians often took recourse to traditional rituals, ceremonies and incantations, which the missionaries did not tolerate. The concerned members of the congregations had to kneel 'before God' and the congregation and beg for forgiveness.[32]

Christians could be debarred from Holy Communion or, temporarily, from the congregation.[33] The threat of not receiving a Christian burial was a serious one. 'Those who live a depraved life are debarred from Holy Communion and, if they show no signs of repentance and improvement before they die, they do not receive a Christian burial.'[34] The highest form of punishment for a member of the congregation was public excommunication, which was meted out, for example, in 1781 to a 'Portuguese' woman and her daughter who were members of the Tamil congregation in Tranquebar. The reason for excommunication was the fact that the daughter was the concubine of a European and the mother had tolerated and profited from this liaison.[35]

[29] HB 2. Cont., 81, excerpt from a letter from J.E. Gründler, Tranquebar, 7 December 1709, (translated from German).

[30] Ibid.

[31] HB 93. Cont., 989.

[32] HB 87. Cont., 383 (Madras 1757).

[33] In 1768 three persons in Madras, who had been debarred a year earlier, were re-admitted to the congregation after a public apology and penitence. NHB 1. St., 88; Cf. also NHB 26. St., 158 (1780); 27. St., 319 (1781).

[34] NHB 25. St., 45, (translated from German).

[35] NHB 27. St., 308.

Corporal punishment as a method of disciplining local co-workers was controversial among the missionaries, but was still practiced. In a diary entry for 26 June 1720 Benjamin Schultze writes: 'Lazarus, who beat his mother, received corporal punishment.'[36] 'Apostates' who displayed a tendency to join the Catholic Church also received corporal punishment.[37] It is not possible to say in general that corporal punishment was a 'Protestant instrument of education'[38] in Southeast India. Even in the case of the Tranquebar Mission the missionaries had differing opinions and applied them in practice. Whereas Benjamin Schultze was convinced about the importance and efficacy of this kind of punishment, Christian Friedrich Schwartz questioned the justification of corporal punishment. For some time, the Tranquebar Mission had its own jail. Timotheus and his brother Titus were locked up for one night for being involved in a drunken brawl.[39] Two women were put in jail for one night because they had insulted another woman by calling her a whore.[40]

If a person was unreliable, if he overstepped his powers or violated any of the rules of employment, the missionary conference threatened to transfer him, cut his pay or, in the worst case, to dismiss him. On account of an alleged long-standing alcohol problem the most well known catechist of the Tranquebar Mission, Rajanayakkan, was transferred.[41] Expulsion from school was also possible. In the context of the death of 24 year old Curunadan, who had been handed over to the Mission in 1729 by his Hindu relatives and who attended the Tamil Mission School, the missionaries in Tranquebar recounted his 'offense' in their diary on 24 April 1744. In 1741 there had been a 'scandal' (which is not described further) in the school, whereupon he was expelled from the school for 'pious conduct'.[42] In March

[36] AFSt/H D 16 a, (translated from German).

[37] AFSt/H D 16 a, 25 May 1720.

[38] Gründer, Horst, 1982, *Christliche Mission und deutscher Imperialismus. Eine politische Geschichte ihrer Beziehungen während der deutschen Kolonialzeit (1884–1914) unter besonderer Berücksichtigung Afrikas und Chinas*, Ferdinand Schöningh, Paderborn, 340.

[39] AFSt/H D 16 a, 22 July 1720.

[40] Ibid., 2 and 3 September 1720.

[41] Richter, Julius, 1924, *Indische Missionsgeschichte*, C. Bertelsmann, Gütersloh (1906), 121.

[42] HB 61. Cont., 110f.

1781 the 'Portuguese school master' in Tranquebar was suspended because of alcohol problems.[43]

The mission made an effort to involve local Christians, i.e. the members of the Christian congregations under its care, in its system for the administration of justice, for which special regulations had to be agreed upon. Since not all Christians led their daily lives permanently in the domain of the mission, different systems of justice often clashed with one another. The Danish governor Peter Anker (1744–1832) expressly asked the missionaries for suggestions on the organization of this sphere. On 20 July 1789 Jacob Klein, Johann Friedrich König, Christoph Samuel John and Johann Peter Rottler sent a letter in this regard to the Royal Government in Tranquebar asking for the regulation of jurisdiction. It dealt primarily with the conduct of Indian Christians, but excluded the mission employees, and was meant to be a 'draft of the rules that would be applicable to the Royal Danish Mission'.[44] The earlier rule had been that a supervisor would be appointed from the congregation who, with the permission of the government, would resolve disputes among the Christians and report back to the missionaries. After the Danish government in Tranquebar was placed under the king in 1777, it became the sole arbiter of disputes, which was not always in the interests of the Mission. The regulation was often exploited to settle differences of opinion with the Mission. The missionaries, therefore, petitioned the Royal Government in Tranquebar that they also be informed about complaints and accusations, that, further, only Christian translators be appointed for the work of the court and that disputes among Christians not be dealt with in the local, the so-called 'Black Courts'. They also demanded a say in determining the amount and the nature of punishment meted out to Christians. 'The missionaries, and those they use to run the Mission, can best judge what constitutes depravity and how such people are to be punished or prevented, since they are the best-informed about the conditions, needs and necessary rules of a mission.'[45] In return for co-operation based on mutual respect the missionaries promised:

[43] NHB 31. St., 743.

[44] RA Miskolark 3b (1770–1810), *Pro Memoria* from J. Klein, J.F. König, Ch. S. John and J.P. Rottler, Tranquebar, 20 July 1789.

[45] Ibid., (translated from German).

> if the Respected Royal Government gives us the power to maintain Christian discipline and order in our congregation, we would also be in a better position to prevent our Christians from taking part in public riots and disturbances than has been possible so far with our many restrictions.[46]

MATERIAL DEPENDENCIES

A Mission society was not only a religious undertaking, but also an economic entity and, as such, it was compelled to work according to economic imperatives. In order to meet the constantly increasing expenditure with regard to personnel and travel costs, as well as the running of churches, schools and orphanages, new sources of income had to be accessed. The major portion of the expenditure was covered by funds from Europe. This included not only the funds sent from the Royal Danish side which paid for the salaries of the missionaries and the costs of basic activities, but also donations by friends of the Mission in various parts of the world. The latter were partially used for the benefit of a particular person or a concrete project. In addition, the missionaries looked for other local sources of income—even for their individual material needs—ranging from paid supervision of children or income from property[47] to private business ventures,[48] or even participation in the illegal alcohol business.[49]

The salaries of the missionaries and the other European co-workers were determined by the institutions responsible for the Mission and

[46] Ibid., (translated from German).

[47] NHB 72. St., 1142.

[48] In 1744 the setting up of a factory for knitted socks in Madras was discussed (HB 58. Cont., 1581). In 1762 a weaving unit was established in Madras which functioned till at least 1767 (HB 97. Cont., 154; 106. Cont., 1471). Christoph S. John set up a lime kiln in Tranquebar in the 1780s (NHB 30. St., 684). A coconut plantation in Vepery yielded a profit of roughly 100 Stern pagodas annually for the missionaries there at the beginning of the nineteenth century (NHB 72. St., 1140).

[49] Benjamin Schultze traded in beer and wine as well as in home-distilled brandy. Cf. particularly some entries in the manuscript of the diary for 1720: AFSt/H D 16a, entries for 20 May, 8 September, 15 and 31 December 1720. When he left Tranquebar in 1726 to work in Madras he handed over 6000 Reichstaler to the missionaries. AFSt/M 2 H 3 : 15, letter from Benjamin Schultze to [Gotthilf August Francke], ??. ??. 1728, containing accounts for the expenditure of the mission in Tranqebar; Cf. for this also Nørgaard, *Mission und Obrigkeit*, 139.

the corresponding amount was sent by ship to Tranquebar, where it went into the Mission account and was distributed from there. All expenditure was accounted for in detail and the accounts were sent to Europe regularly. A missionary received a pre-determined salary, initially from the Danish king and later from the Mission Board. At the start of the Mission a missionary's salary amounted to 200 *Reichstaler* annually.[50] The SPCK provided the salaries for the missionaries it employed and it also gave the necessary financial means to run the stations in Thanjavur, Tiruchirappalli, Cuddalore and Madras.[51]

Rising prices in South India constantly necessitated revision of the salaries paid to missionaries and their co-workers.[52] A comparison of the Mission expenditure in Tranquebar in the 1720s with the expenditure in 1780 shows the dramatic price rise. According to Schultze, who made some suggestions in the 1720s regarding the distribution of the annual costs of the mission in Tranquebar, these costs comprised the following: four missionaries at 200 *Reichstaler* each = 800 *Reichstaler*; Jens Sievertsen (around 1690–1741), the 'Portuguese' school teacher, = 110 Reichstaler; three other European co-workers at 88 *Reichstaler* each = 264 *Reichstaler*; all Indian Mission co-workers taken together—500 *Reichstaler*; clothing and food for the children of the poor in the care of the Mission—300 *Reichstaler*; expenditure on repairs and renovations—150 *Reichstaler*. Thus, total expenditure amounted to 2124 *Reichstaler*.[53] Around 1780 the funds provided annually by

[50] HB 1. Cont., 65.

[51] 'Everything that comes here from England and Germany is shared equally with Trankenbar. Thanjavur now has 4 mission stations, and everything that the Society in London sends is also distributed between these four stations.' (translated from German), NHB 55. St., 710, letter from I.G. Holzberg to Johann Christian Christoph Ubele (1767—after 1846) in London. Thanjavur, 11 October 1798.

[52] 'Houses in Madras are, therefore, rare to find and expensive. Not only houses, but also food. 3 chickens cost 1 Pagoda (2 Rhtlr.), 3 eggs cost 2 Fano (4 Ggr.). A quarter of the front of a sheep costs 8 Fano (16 Ggr.) and the back 12 Fano (1 Rthlr.). I cannot name any article of food, which has not doubled in price, indeed, some have become four times more expensive. For 1 Fan. one could get 3 allacks of rice and now rice is not sold in the open market any more.' (translated from German), NHB 25. St., 49, letter from Johann Christian Breithaupt, 13 September 1781.

[53] AFSt/M 2 H 3 : 15.

the Royal Danish side amounted to 3000 *Reichstaler*. The annual expenditure at this time was roughly to the tune of 9000 *Reichstaler*. This difference was sought to be bridged by donations from friends of the Mission in Europe and India. At this point of time the younger missionaries received an annual salary of 200 *Reichstaler*, the older ones got 400 *Reichstaler*, while those in the service of the English society received £50 sterling.[54]

In a memo of 1784 John and Rottler pointed out that unmarried missionaries received 350 Tranquebar Courant annually, while married missionaries were paid a salary of 400 Tranquebar Courant. The unmarried ones paid a small sum for board in a missionary family. They were also given a house or a place to stay, a pre-determined ration of wine and a servant who had to be paid a small monthly salary of 2.5 (Tranquebar Courant? H.L.)[55] In their suggestions of 1797 for improving the salary structure John, Cämmerer and Rottler pointed out the possibility of a legal source of income by taking Tamilian children into missionary households and educating them.[56]

The revised version of these suggestions also contains a reference to possible allowances in addition to the salary as well as further privileges such as a larger house or a paid trip to Europe for missionaries who did good work. Such gifts could, however, only be given with the unanimous consent of all the missionaries.[57] For European co-workers who were not ordained the following scheme of reimbursement was envisaged:

> Apart from free accommodation his salary in the beginning will be 200 rp [rupees, H.L.] Tranquebar Courant. His voyage by ship is free and, as a passenger, he would have a place at the second table.

[54] NHB 25. St., 5, letter from the missionaries in Tranquebar, 14 October 1780.

[55] 'The salary was earlier 200 Danish Crowns, but since the Tranquebar Courant is roughly 30 percent less than the Danish Crown, and since provisions have become much costlier, the praiseworthy Mission Board has had the goodness to raise the salary gradually to 350 Tranquebar Courant. Each one of us has his own house, but some of the houses have an annexe, for example, a school, the library, etc., which the concerned person has to supervise.' (translated from German), RA Miskolark 9g, *Pro Memoria* for new missionaries [...], Tranquebar, 20 January 1784.

[56] RA Miskolark 9h, some preliminary thoughts [...], [1797].

[57] RA Miskolark 9h, instruction for a future missionary in Tranquebar, 1798.

> [...] he can also expect an increase in salary, to which the worthy Mission Board would gladly give its consent on the recommendation of the missionaries, who would have to send a credible testimonial about his zeal and his loyalty.[58]

A comparison of the salaries of the European and the South Indian co-workers reveals that even where the duties were similar the salaries of the Europeans were significantly higher than those of the Tamils. While determining the salaries it was generally assumed that the European co-workers had a higher standard of living. Because of their living, clothing and eating habits they apparently required more than the Indians who were familiar with the climate and local food.[59] This, however, could not mask the fact that even the missionaries knew how low the salaries of the local co-workers were in real terms and how difficult it must have been to live on these salaries especially when, as was often the case, entire families had to be supported. In 1780 Schwartz remarked about the then catechist and later country-preacher Sattianaden: 'I cannot understand how he manages with his salary. Besides his wife and two children he also has his mother, his mother-in-law and his mother's sister living with him. While it is true that they also do spinning, it is not enough to feed or clothe them.'[60] These differences in the salary structures between European and South Indian co-workers led to Ch. S. John's suggestion in 1785 to further cut down the number of Europeans in the mission and to increase the number of local workers, 'so that the money thus saved could be distributed among the other missionaries.'[61]

[58] Ibid., (translated from German).

[59] Thus, around 1709 Ziegenbalg calculated the monthly cost of living of a soldier to be two or, at the most, three *Reichstaler*. A 'normal' Tamilian used to be able to manage on 12–16 *Groschen* but now, on account of the rise in prices, he too required more than one *Reichstaler* (cf. HB 3. Cont., 120). Compared to Europeans in India the Tamilians, it is claimed, are accustomed to a diet-like fare consisting of 'only simple food and drink' (HB 3. Cont., 126), primarily rice, to which they added 'fish or green vegetables for half a penny as an accompaniment' (HB 4. Cont. 181, letter from P. Jordan of 4 October 1710).

[60] NHB 35. St., 148, letter from Ch. F. Schwartz to Friedrich Wilhelm Pasche (1728–1792) in London, Thanjavur, 10 October 1780, (translated from German).

[61] RA Miskolark 4 (1765–89), letter from Ch. S. John, 7 December 1785, (translated from German).

The amount and the nature of remuneration received by South Indian mission employees was not explicitly set down—least of all by the European mission institutions. The missionaries in India, however, introduced a system of regular payment very early on. A letter dated 10 September 1712 from Bartholomäus Ziegenbalg, Johann Ernst Gründler and Polycarp Jordan (1677–1728) to August Hermann Francke states that all employees received a monthly salary.[62] In 1713 the European employees received 49 *Reichstaler* each as a monthly salary, while the local co-workers got 20 *Reichstaler* each.[63] The language teacher and interpreter, Aleppa, was given an annual sum of 100 *Reichstaler* for his services.[64] Before Benjamin Schultze left Tranquebar for Madras he presented a detailed list in 1725 of salaries to be paid to all mission co-workers who would be appointed in Madras. According to this list a missionary was supposed to get 300 *Reichstaler*, an assistant 120, a catechist 36, a teacher 36, a writer 28, a 'Waruga' (Telugu) teacher 25 *Reichstaler*.[65]

TABLE 3.1 Expenditure on South Indian co-workers in Tranquebar around 1725[66]

Name	Function	Annual Salary in *Reichstaler*
Joao d'Alemeida	'Portuguese' catechist	44
Pedro da Costa	'Portuguese' school teacher	23
Diogo	'Portuguese' catechist	24
Barbara	'Portuguese' school teacher	22
Tschawerimuttu	'Malabarian' catechist	33

(contd...)

[62] AB 229. This system remained in force later also. In 1732 there were 11 payment days in Tranquebar. Cf. HB 36. Cont., 1229f.

[63] AB 294, letter from Ziegenbalg and Gründler to Georg Heinrich Neubauer in Halle, September 1713.

[64] AB 59, letter from Ziegenbalg, September 1706. Cf. also Liebau, Die 'Malabarische Korrespondenz' von 1712/1713, here especially 56–58.

[65] AFSt/M 2 H 3 : 15. Of the posts named here, that of the missionary was definitely to be filled by a European. The assistant would probably also be European. The other persons were, as a rule, Indians who, on an average, would receive 10% of the salary of their European superiors.

[66] Ibid.

Table 3.1 (contd...)

Name	Function	Annual Salary in *Reichstaler*
Aaron	'Malabarian' catechist	33
Maleiappen	Writer	33
Bendito	Book binder	33
Mapathi	'Malabarian' compositor	24
Johannes	Bearer ('Auftrager', someone who serves food)	17
David	School teacher	22
Christoph	School teacher	20
Petrus	School teacher	17
Enoch	School teacher	17
Christian	Assistant to the type-founder	12
Caneirum	Mission accountant	24
Friedrich	Guard	11
[unnamed]	Grave digger	11

In the list of expenditure for the mission in Tranquebar for the period from 5 October 1725 till 5 October 1726, the following salaries were disbursed:[67]

TABLE 3.2 Overview of salaries for the mission station in Tranquebar 1725/26

Function	Salary (*Taler, Fanam, Kas*)
5 missionaries	1000/0/0
5 Europeans (schoolmaster, printer, manager, type-founder, inspector)	389/0/0
Book binder ('9 Quarter')	36/0/0
3 free assistants (daily wagers)	16/5[?]/0
Two 'Malabarian' printers	42/1/0

(contd...)

[67] AFSt/M 3 I 3, accounts from Tranquebar 1725–64.

Table 3.2 (contd...)

Function	Salary (*Taler, Fanam, Kas*)
Assistants of the type-founder	11/0/0
12 Indian co-workers (catechists, 'Malabarian' and 'Portuguese' school teachers, writers	315/4/0
Seven 'heathen' school teachers	90/11/0
'Malabarian' and 'Portuguese' school teachers and Seminarians	8/3/5
Two *kaṇakkappiḷḷai*	33/10/0
A domestic servant and grave-digger	11/0/0
A washerman	6/5/0
Several water carriers	7/7/38
'Malabaria' and 'Portuguese' cooks	10/6/60

In 1728 there were four additional catechists with an annual salary of 22 *Reichstaler* each.[68] In 1732 Diogo, as one of the youngest catechists, received an annual salary of 33 *Reichstaler*. Around 1733 the annual salary of a catechist was about 36 Taler, while that of an assistant was about 24 *Taler*.[69]

The South Indian co-workers were financed from special funds donated by friends of the mission in Europe for this specific purpose. Partly, the missionaries also paid their employees from their own salaries. Donations were often earmarked for a particular person. The sponsors had the right to special individual reports about the life, the difficulties and the successes of the person they were sponsoring. The following letter of 23 July 1745 from a pastor near Bayreuth to the catechist Josua (died 1763) and his wife, accompanied by a donation of two *Reichstaler*, shows that sometimes a personal link developed between a donor and a Tamil mission worker:

> Deeply esteemed Brother in Jesus Christ! The afflictions, the toil, the steadfastness that I have observed in him have bound me dearly to him in the Lord. Praise be to the offering of the lamb that you

[68] AFSt/M 2 H 3 : 15.
[69] HB 36. Cont., 1229f.; HB 33. Cont., 885.

have offered up your life several times already for the glory of Christ. Continue to do so with good cheer, my dear couple! Even if your Marrawer are only a few today, tomorrow they will come in large numbers: the Lord has prophesized this. Continue sowing, and in the end the harvest will certainly be good. Let the winter pass. Please accept this paltry offering in love. May it be blessed by Jesus Christ, small though it is. Please give my greetings to all the missionaries, especially to the translator of this letter. If it is permitted, I would like to ask for a small *oles* of three words with a German or Latin translation. My soul is with him in Christ while I live: and I commend him also to His mercy. Near Bayreuth, July 23, 1735.[70]

This was followed by a poem. The letter was addressed to 'Josua, the faithful servant and co-worker in Jesus Christ, junior catechist in the congregation of the Lord in the Marrawar country [...]'[71] In a palm-leaf letter of 1733 the city catechist in Tranquebar, Schawrimuttu, personally thanked a mission donor for the 60 Taler that she had donated for him.[72] Since no rules and criteria had been laid down in the Tranquebar Mission for the payment of local co-workers, the salaries differed depending on the place, the time and the local conditions.[73] The salaries for the South Indian co-workers were paid either in cash or in kind depending on the situation of the mission and the needs of the person receiving the salary. In their monthly reports to the missionaries in Tranquebar the local mission co-workers who worked in the districts also presented their bills for expenditure linked with their work, and they received their wages as well as compensation for expenditure in cash or kind.[74] In 1765 the catechist Habacuc (died 1795) in Cuddalore received a monthly wage of nine *pagoda* and 10 *fanam*

[70] HB 64. Cont., supplement to the preface, (112), (translated from German).

[71] Ibid. Personal letters of this kind are seldom found in the sources and were probably not customary in the dealings of the sponsors with the South Indian co-workers of the mission. In most cases there was only a mention of the person for whom the donation was meant, or, without names being mentioned, the function or the aspect of the mission for which the donation was to be used was laid down.

[72] HB 38. Cont., 246–48.

[73] In 1732 the South Indian co-workers were divided into seven wage-classes. HB 36. Cont., 1232f.

[74] HB 36. Cont., 1233. With this, the monthly wage of an Indian co-worker could sometimes go up to four *Reichstaler*.

in cash along with 120 *marakkāl* of rice.[75] After a bad harvest in 1767 the local workers could only be paid in cash.[76] In addition, country-preachers, catechists and other mission co-workers were sometimes given their own piece of agricultural land.[77] In 1771 the cost of the standard of living of country preachers, catechists and teachers employed with the mission was more than 1000 Reichstaler, 'although they all receive only a paltry wage' as those responsible for the mission had to admit.[78]

TABLE 3.3 Comparison of monthly wages in Madras in 1751 and 1756[79]

Person	Salary (1751) (*Pagoda, Fanam*)	Person	Salary (1756 (*Pagoda, Fanam*)
Tamilian catechist Schawrimuttu	1/27	Schawrimuttu	1.75/0
'Portuguese' catechist Paul	1/18	Paul	1.5/0
'Portuguese' school-master Derk Steenhoven	2,1/0	Steenhoven	(till May) 3.5/0
Kaṇakkappiḷḷai Njanappen	1/9		
Tamil school teacher Enoch	1/6	Enoch	1/6
Two additional Tamil school teachers, Alexander and Nalappen	Each 1/0	Village school teachers Alexander Boas, Nalappen	Each 1/0
Two additional copyists Boas and Wedamuttu	Jan.-June together1/33; from July each 1/0		

(contd...)

[75] AFSt/M 3 I 3.

[76] NHB, 1. St., 153, letter from Ch. W. Gericke and G.H.C. Hüttemann to G.A. Francke, 23 January 1769.

[77] As was the case with the catechist Arulananden who cultivated a plot of land after leaving the service of the mission. NHB 28. St., 427.

[78] NHB 15. St., 142, speech given by G.A. Freylinghausen.

[79] AFSt/M 3 I 13, accounts, 1715–20; 1748–1828.

Table 3.3 (contd...)

Person	Salary (1751) (*Pagoda, Fanam*)	Person	Salary (1756 (*Pagoda, Fanam*)
		Two assistants for Enoch	Each 1/6
		'Portuguese' school teacher Leander from September	1/6
Manager of the establishments In the outlying villages Maleappen	0/15		0/15
Washerman Adinaden	1/0	Washerman	1/0

These wages were also paid in 1764 and 1765 for the corresponding functions.[80]

Although there are detailed accounts with particulars about the salaries for the different professional groups, diachronic and synchronic comparisons sometimes require extensive calculations. The currency system in South India in the eighteenth century was prone to frequent changes on account of political and economic developments. On the one hand, local rulers minted their own coins; on the other, the invading European powers tried to document and establish their position in the country by minting special coins or by introducing European currency. With the permission of the Nayak of Thanjavur even the Danes minted their own coins in the region they administered around Tranquebar. The treaty between the Danes and the Nayak laid down that Danish crowns could be used for trade in the Thanjavur region, but this was evidently valid only for a limited period. Like the English and the French the Danes also minted rupees. Accordingly, the missionaries gave details of salaries in European currencies (*Reichstaler*) or in regional Indian currencies (*Pagoda, Fanam, Kas,* and Rupee). Since it is difficult to ascertain the actual purchasing power and the actual costs of living, it is only possible to draw useful conclusion from comparisons

[80] AFSt/M 3 J 13.

between the different categories of mission co-workers. Keeping all these facts in mind it can be said that these wages allowed the local workers to live modestly. The real advantage of being employed by the mission lay in the regular payment of wages in whichever form this happened.

TABLE 3.4 The amount of rice that could be purchased for one *Fanam* (in *medides*)[81]

Year	Rice per *Fanam* (in *medides*)
1742/43	6 ½ to 6.75
1743/44	6 5/8 to 6.75
1744/45	8 to 8.25
1745/46	12.5
1746/47	6.75
1747/48	6.5
1748/49	8
1749/50	6.5
1750/51	4.5 to 4.75
1751/52	5 to 5 1/8
1752/53	6.75 to 7
1753/54	7.5 to 8
1754/55	4 3/8 to 4.75 (rice from Bengal 2.5 to 2 5/8
1755/56	3 4/8 to 5
1756/57	4.5 to 4 3/16 (rice from Bengal 3)
1757/58	9.5 to 12 1/8 (rice from Bengal 4)
1758/59	11 to 15
1760/61	6 7/8
1761/62	7 1/8 to 7 3/8
1762/63	9 ¼ to 5.5
1763/64	6 to 7 ¾

[81] Details from AFSt/M 3 I 3.

Sometimes schoolteachers employed by the mission resigned their jobs in order to become soldiers, since the pay was higher. Facts such as these allow us to derive some conclusions about the actual worth of the salary.[82] Ch. F. Schwartz in Tiruchirappalli had appointed catechists, assistants and teachers to work with him, and these received their salaries from the English East India Company. Some of them were soldiers on a leave of absence who had to report immediately for military duty if war broke out or there was an enemy attack. They received their soldier's pay as well as additional voluntary fees paid by the parents of the school children.[83] Schwartz partly paid his co-workers out of the money he received from the East India Company for tending to the spiritual needs of the soldiers in the English garrison.[84] In 1777 the missionary reported that he was paying eight local assistants out of his monthly salary of 20 *pagoda*s from the East India Company.[85] In 1783 Johann Zacharias Kiernander informed his superiors in Europe that the mission in Calcutta was not in a position to pay the schoolteachers there a salary of 100 *Sicca-Rupees* and, therefore, the teachers would henceforth be recruited from among former pupils of the mission who felt

[82] NHB 24. St., 1379, report about the death of Phanuel (1779), who had been a junior catechist in the Kumbakonam district. He had attended the city school and became a teacher in Thanjavur in 1766. However, he gave up this job and became a soldier for the higher salary, only to return to the mission later. NHB 20. St., 968: the youngest teacher in Tiruchirappalli requested to be discharged since he had found a job which paid him more (1777).

[83] 'Till now I received my salary from Tranquebar. However, because this year the esteemed Society sent the annual salary for my workers in Tiruchinapally, regardless of who they are, my brothers in Tranquebar have retained the money meant for me since this August. Whatever the esteemed Company here gave me of their own accord has been used entirely to build the church and the mission houses.' (translated from German), RA Miskolark 9f, *Pro Memoria* for new missionaries from Ch. F. Schwartz, Tiruchirappalli, 12 October 1771. Cf. also NHB 21. St., 1087 (1778).

[84] 'The catechists, whose numbers have now increased to six, have willingly helped me in the work of God. Their pay, which consists of 2 pagodas a month, comes from the money that the Company gives me for my services to the garrison.' (translated from German), RA Miskolark 9 f, letter from Ch. F. Schwartz to the Mission Board, Tiruchirappalli, 12 October 1771.

[85] NHB 20. St., 363, letter from Schwartz to G.A. Freylinghausen, 25 September 1777.

obliged to work for the mission, even if the salary was meager. These people, however, would leave the mission schools as soon as they got better jobs.[86]

There were no limits to the wealth of ideas that the missionaries developed in order to deal with the financial bottlenecks that kept increasing. In the 1820s the missionaries Gottlieb Ewald Rhenius (1790–1838) and Ludwig Bernhard Ehrengott Schmid at the mission station in Palayankottai asked the members of the congregation for a monthly contribution and set up a parish account.[87] In the 1830s Daniel Schreyvogel introduced a special form of incentives: the teachers working under his supervision received Rupees 2.5. They would receive half a Rupee more each month for five new school children. On the other hand, for the days that they were absent, except in the case of illness, a part of their salary would be deducted.[88]

Although there were large differences in the salaries paid to the European and the South Indian co-workers, the local employees and their family members were integrated in the social welfare system of the Tranquebar Mission like their European colleagues. If they were ill they received regular visits from the missionaries. A special fund called 'Institute for the Poor' or 'Alms Institute' was set up for the poor and for the families of deceased mission employees. Alms were regularly distributed to widows, orphans, the old and the infirm.[89] Widows of former local mission employees received regular 'widow's alms', which was higher than the alms given out to the families of Christians who had not been working for the mission.[90] Around 1730 the widows of parish members received between one and two *Fanam* a month or its corresponding worth in rice.[91] In their letter of 20 December 1766 Johann Philipp Fabricius and Johann Christian Breithaupt (1719–82) described the assistance rendered by the mission to the families of parish members. Every year there were financial requests for 'maintenance, clothing, repairs of huts

[86] NHB 33. St., 1098, Kiernander's letter of 31 December 1783.

[87] NHB 72. St., 1275, report of the missionaries Rhenius and Schmid from Palayamcottah 1823.

[88] NHB 84. St., 1248.

[89] Cf. HB 32. Cont., 829; HB 33. Cont., 885; HB 64. Cont., 610.

[90] HB 33. Cont., 885, report of the missionaries from Tranquebar 1732.

[91] HB 32. Cont., 829.

and assistance in the case of illness'.[92] One of the missionaries regularly visited the catechist Philipp (country-preacher from 1772) during his illness in 1769.[93] In the initial years of the mission, till Benjamin Schultze stopped this practice for financial reasons in 1720, newly-married couples of the congregation received a gift from the mission.[94]

TRAVELS BY MISSIONARIES AND LOCAL WORKERS

The co-operation between the missionaries and the South Indian co-workers was most direct and intensive during the journeys undertaken together. During this time they found themselves, in a manner of speaking, in neutral territory and were particularly dependent on each other. The shared work demanded a high degree of mutual trust—not only because the success of their daily work could only be achieved if both sides acted in unison—but also because they had to be able to depend on each other in situations that could be dangerous. In the context of mission travels hierarchies and dependencies could temporarily shift if the position and knowledge of the local co-worker led him to take a decision that the missionary had to accept.

As a means for encounters, contacts and conversations with the villagers, regular trips and travels constituted a necessary and essential basis of missionary work. From the beginning the missionaries, catechists and assistants from Tranquebar jointly visited places in the vicinity, and it was the duty of the Tamil workers accompanying the missionaries to establish contact with the local people. The Tamil co-workers were not only indispensable because of their knowledge and their abilities, but they also constituted an invaluable form of representation and legitimacy for the Europeans. Local co-workers were appointed permanently in many places to look after the Christians in the region assigned to them. After some Tamilians had been ordained, the missionaries and the country

[92] HB 106. Cont., 1469.

[93] NHB 4. St., 427 (15 July 1769); 452 (24 September 1769); 454 (29 September 1769).

[94] AFSt/H D 16a, 27 May 1720.

preachers traveled together, and here too the South Indian preachers were responsible for establishing contact with the local population. When Christian Friedrich Schwartz and Daniel Zeglin (1716–80) visited the Raja of Thanjavur in 1759 they were accompanied by the country preacher Diogo, who was meant to establish contact with the people and who organized accommodation for the missionaries in the house of a local weaver.[95] John traveled in 1791 and 1792 along with the catechist Schawrirajen to the rural congregations in Tiruppalatturai, Rarasalam, Kanjanur and Tererhendur.[96]

In the course of time it became common for the ordained local preachers, the catechists and assistants to travel without a European and tend to the often widely dispersed Christian congregations. This practice not only arose due to the lack of European co-workers, but also because of the increased willingness of the local Christians to accept their countrymen. Indian country preachers or catechists now had their own servants and assistants to deal with the training of their successors or with the work connected with travel. Travel became the predominant duty of the South Indian country preachers. With this they took over an aspect of the work that was particularly taxing for the European missionaries because of the weather conditions in summer and during the monsoons, but also because they had to forgo the comforts of daily life while traveling. The missionaries were thus able to concentrate on their place of work and could avoid long absences, since the journeys often lasted for several months. With no one to depend upon, the Tamil mission co-workers took independent decisions on these journeys, about which the missionaries were only informed subsequently in the travel reports. During their visits to different places the duties of the country preachers involved: teaching and baptizing the catechumen, performing special divine services, giving Holy Communion, visiting army camps, military hospitals or prisons, looking after Christians, working among and convincing people who had turned away from the Christian faith. On these journeys they were not only accompanied by the usual posse of servants such as cooks and porters, but also by assistants or catechists.[97] The

[95] HB 91. Cont., 790–808, diary of the journey to Thanjavur 1759.

[96] NHB 43. St., 584; 44. St., 702–04.

[97] HB 59. Cont., 1637, diary of the missionaries in Tranquebar, 15 March 1743.

importance of the travels undertaken by the country preachers in the framework of the mission became evident in the 1770s when the two long-serving country preachers Diogo and Ambrosius were no longer in a position to travel because of their advanced age and deteriorating health. In a letter dated 13 January 1775 the missionaries urgently requested the Mission Board in Copenhagen for permission to ordain a fourth country preacher, 'because Diogo, who appears to be still able to walk a little, refuses to undertake a journey of several days. We cannot expect Ambros to undertake a journey, partly because of his poor eyesight [approaching blindness, H.L.] and partly because of his real physical weakness.'[98] Only Philipp could still carry out his duties.

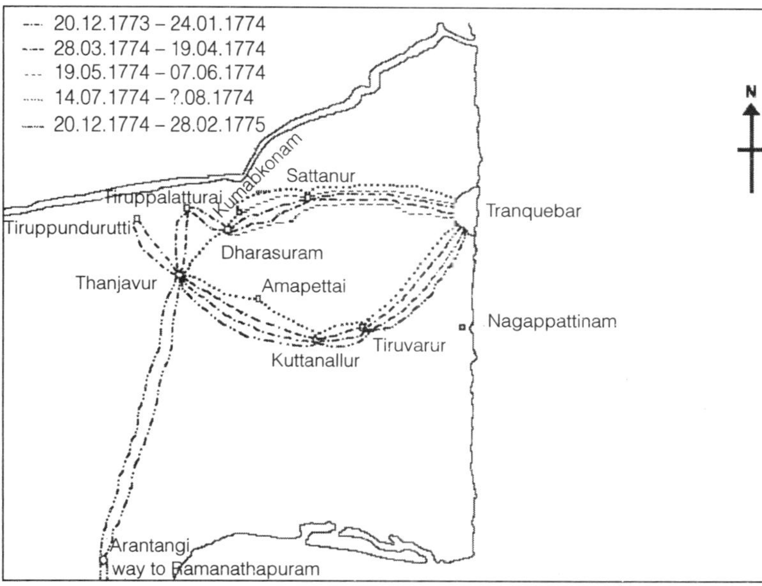

MAP 3.1 Mission journeys carried out by the country preacher Philipp 1773–75 (copyright: Kurt Liebau)

[98] Ambrosius died in 1777. Diogo finally left the mission in 1779. Philipp died in 1788. Rajappen and Sattianaden were ordained as new country preachers in 1778 and 1790 respectively. Cf. NHB 14. St., 175, (translated from German); 19. St., 766; 21. St., 1050; 23. St., 1276; 37. St., 95, 97, 104; 40. St., 385.

Catechists, too, travelled alone or accompanied by an assistant. In August 1768 the catechist Dewanesen and the assistant Muttu Schawri travelled from Tiruchirappalli to Thanjavur, Arantangi, Mahadevpattanam (Madewipadtnam) and several other places. Besides the usual conversations with people of other faiths they had been told to convince 'apostate' Christians to return to the fold.[99] When deaths were reported catechists or junior catechists went to these places to look after the families or to organize the funeral ceremonies.[100] Assistants were sent to care for the Christians in the camps of the local armies if these were located nearby.[101] Catechists and assistants were told to visit Christians in far-flung places so that the latter felt they were being looked after and the religious link was maintained.[102] Through these travels, by stationing individual co-workers in the villages, by maintaining a regular and well-organized contact among one another and with the relevant mission station, an extensive mission network was established. In this way the local Christians could be looked after constantly and a permanent and quick flow of information was possible. When the missionaries wrote a palm-leaf letter on the death of Obuch in 1745, which was passed on to all the co-workers with instructions to read out the contents to all the Christians in their area, even those, who had

[99] These kinds of tasks were generally given to Indians (NHB 2. St., 173–75). In 1777 the assistant Michael (died 1781) travelled to Tirumangalakodtei (Tirumakkotai, Mannarkudi *tālūk*) to talk to 'apostate' Christians. In 1779 the assistant Matthaeus travelled to Kadtanawadi (Kattumavadi) to speak with the inhabitants who had renounced the Christian faith. NHB 19. St., 782f; 23. St., 1388.

[100] The junior catechist Schinappen traveled in the Mahadevpattanam district to Thanjavur and Anitschiaburam (probably Arichchapuram, Mannarkudi *tālūk*), Mannarkudi, Rarasalam when deaths were reported from there. NHB 3. St., 300.

[101] In 1771 the *śūdra*-assistant Rajappen went to the military camp at Ramanathapuram, but he was not allowed to enter the fort. In Arantangi he took care of the Christian soldiers in the garrison. NHB 7. St., 905f.

[102] From December 1777 till January 1778 the two catechists traveled from Vallam to the south to give succor to the Christians dispersed in the villages (NHB 20. St., 980–987). In March 1790 the catechist Njanapiragasam undertook a journey to some villages; in April 1791 he traveled from Tranquebar to Thanjavur and, on the way there and back, he visited many places where Christians lived; from 17 August till 20 September 1791 he undertook another journey to various villages (NHB 41. St., 411f, 418f; 42. St., 519–22).

probably never met the missionary personally, learned about his merits and his death.[103]

HIERARCHIES AMONG LOCAL MISSION EMPLOYEES

Most of the South Indian co-workers did not always have a missionary they could turn to in their daily work. They worked in the villages or regions assigned to them and went to the mission station once a month to present their monthly report. In the interim period the employees who worked in places close to one another maintained contact with each other. Relations among the local workers as well as the form and nature of their mutual dealings were influenced mainly by three factors. The decisive factors were their function within the mission and their caste background, with the latter determining the possibilities and limits of communication even in the framework of the mission. Both these aspects were breached by the kinship relations among the workers.

CAREER PATH OF LOCAL MISSION EMPLOYEES

Once a person had decided to enter into the service of the mission they generally left the job only when they died. A Tamilian was normally at first appointed as an assistant or as a schoolteacher. If his work met with the approval of the missionaries he could, in the course of time, be appointed in higher positions—the highest being that of the country preacher. The daily work of the mission was organized in such a way that the assistants assisted co-workers in higher functions and could thus gather experience as well as prove their capabilities. The catechists and country preachers who were assigned assistants to help them in their work were also entrusted with pedagogical tasks, since the work of the young assistants was part of their practical training and the evaluation of this work by the higher functionary was decisive for the further career of the assistants. There were no norms laid down for the length of time of this form of practical training. Generally, a co-worker remained an assistant for a few years before

[103] HB 64. Cont., 640.

he became a teacher or a catechist. The country preacher Aaron, for example, supervised the junior catechist Schawri and the assistant Njanajudam in the 1730s.[104] In the forties Saruweien and Christian were, among others, Aaron's assistants.[105]

This method of having the assistants accompany and assist co-workers in higher positions not only helped in the practical training, but also in selecting suitable candidates for higher posts in the mission. David (1699–1762), for example, who attended the mission school in Tranquebar for four years and subsequently gained his first practical experiences in the service of the mission by accompanying Bartholomäus Ziegenbalg on his travels, became a teacher under Schultze and Walther and simultaneously underwent training in the mission seminary to become a catechist. In his old age he worked as a writer with the mission.[106] Others, on the contrary, like Wisuwasi[107] or Jesadian[108] remained assistants their entire lives. However, they were not kept as permanent assistants of a higher functionary but had scope for independent action which, in the case of Jesadian, equaled that of a catechist.

There was a constant exchange of information, reports and instructions between the missionaries and the other workers of a mission station. Depending on the distance of their place of work from the mission station the Tamilians had to give an account of their work either once a week or once a month. Those local co-workers who worked far from the mission station or in regions that were not easily accessible for Europeans, either for political or for other reasons, had the greatest scope for independent decisions. Thus, the catechist Rajanayakkan worked for over 20 years in Thanjavur without a European missionary, and he used this latitude to develop his own ideas about missionary work.[109] As an officer of

[104] HB 39. Cont., 304, diary February 1734.

[105] HB 61. Cont., 102, Saruweien and Christian are mentioned as Aaron's assistants (1744).

[106] HB 16. Cont., preface; 29. Cont., 478; 97. Cont., 51.

[107] HB 64. Cont., 178f; NHB 14. St., 167.

[108] Jesadian was an assistant and a teacher in Rarasalam and in Kanschenur (Kanjanur). He died in May 1778. About his person see NHB 10. St., 1310; 13. St., 50–57, 72f; 15. St., 285; 16. St., 397, 447; 17. St., 540, 589; 18. St., 678; 19. St., 794, 811, 819; 21. St., 1127.

[109] Liebau, 'Tamilische Christen im 18. Jahrhundert'.

the Thanjavur army he had come into contact with the missionaries in Tranquebar in 1726 while stationed in Porayar[110] and had declared his interest in missionary work. After a thorough examination in 1727 the missionaries entrusted him with the propagation of the Christian faith in Thanjavur—a region that European missionaries were not allowed to enter till the 1750s.[111] In 1742 Rajanayakkan set up a school in Thanjavur,[112] which was also open to Hindus and Muslims. Apparently, large sections of the population held Rajanayakkan in high esteem and, in many respects, he was a model for the *paṟaiyār*. Even before he was appointed as a catechist of the Tranquebar Mission, members of the *paṟaiyār* followed his example and joined the Protestant faith. Among his first converts was Sattianaden, who later became a catechist of the Tranquebar Mission in the Mayavaram district.[113] There are also some cases that bear witness to Rajanayakkan's reputation among the local population: despite his religion and despite his contacts with the European missionaries local village elders of *paṟaiyār* communities in Thanjavur, among them also Catholics, asked him to mediate in disputes.[114] However, after more than 30 years of successful work for the mission, in the 1760s discord between Rajanayakkan and the Halle missionaries increased to such an extent that he was transferred shortly before his death.[115]

Christian David was educated in mission schools and he trained under John, Schwartz, Jänicke and Kohlhoff as a teacher and a catechist. From 1800 till his death in 1852 he worked for the British in Jaffna and Colombo. As a catechist under the supervision of the Scottish preacher James Cordiner (1775–1836) he was allowed to preach and baptize and also to conduct marriage and funeral ceremonies.[116] In addition, he carried out the task of an inspector of schools; he was responsible for the supervision and control of local

[110] HB 25. Cont., 10, 17, 21f., 27f.

[111] HB 25. Cont., 36, Tranquebar diary, July 24, 1727.

[112] HB 58. Cont., 1494, report 1743; cf. also Lehmann, *Es begann in Tranquebar*, 241.

[113] Sattianaden converted to Protestantism in September 1727 (HB 29. Cont., 478).

[114] HB 74. Cont., 181 (1750); HB 50. Cont., 287 (1739).

[115] HB 106. Cont., 1230. Alcohol problems were cited as the reason for his transfer. NHB 4. St., 422, 482; 8. St., 993.

[116] NHB 59. St., 1012.

teachers, catechists and assistants as well as for the collection of statistical data. He had to visit every school in the district at least three times in a year. Christian David was also given independent charge of selecting catechists for the guidance and supervision of teachers in the network of schools[117] and they were expected to maintain a diary and report regularly to him about their work.[118]

The formal request from the catechist Schawrirajen was also an indication of a certain degree of independence that the local co-workers had. Schawrirajen had been appointed as the Tamil teacher for the newly-arrived missionary Lambert Christian Früchtenicht. Shortly after taking up this job he refused to teach Früchtenicht and submitted a written complaint on 1 May 1800 to Cämmerer, John and Rottler, in which he clearly described the missionary's alcohol problems and his unreliability. He stated: 'For these reasons I would not like to go and teach such a person and request that I be allowed to assume my former responsibilities in the congregation again.'[119]

The differences in the clothes worn were a visible expression of one's position within the local society and, in end effect, even within the mission. Differences in this regard partly arose from former caste affiliations. They had to do with the quality of material, the length of the clothes and the manner in which women covered their upper bodies.[120] In principle, within the Tranquebar Mission, local Christians were not asked, or forced, to wear European clothes. With the exception of the ordained country preachers, even Christians in a missionary post wore their traditional South Indian clothes. Male assistants, catechists and teachers wore a cloth wrapped around the hips, either hanging down or pulled between the legs and fastened in front (*lungi*). To cover their upper body they draped a cloth

[117] NHB V. vol., preface VII. 60. St., 1085.

[118] NHB 60. St., 1087.

[119] Cf. RA Miskolark 9i, letter from Ch. S. John, J.P. Rottler and A.F. Cämmerer to the Mission Board 6 August 1800 with the enclosed copy of a letter from the catechist Schawrirajen to the missionaries, 1 May 1800, (translated from German). Früchtenicht was suspended and he returned to Europe in 1802. The missionaries forwarded this information to the Mission Board in Copenhagen to justify their demand for the suspension of the missionary in question.

[120] For the connection between attire and identity in India see Tarlo, Emma, 1996, *Clothing Matters: Dress and Identity in India*, C. Hurst & Co. Publishers, London.

around their shoulders.[121] Women wore a garment resembling a sari without the blouse. The cost of clothes for children amounted to not more than half a *Reichstaler* annually since they were given clothes, at the most, three times a year, which were often made of poor quality material.[122]

The South Indian workers thus retained their traditional attire. The only exceptions were the ordained country preachers who were special representatives of the Mission. They wore the priestly robes, which, however, were of a different colour from those of the European missionaries. While the Europeans wore a black robe, the Indians wore a light-coloured one.[123] Country preachers did not wear a wig as was customary for the missionaries till the middle of the eighteenth century, but they did put on a turban as a sign of their social prestige.[124] The above mentioned Christian David, who from 1800 onwards worked as a catechist in Ceylon, was given instructions by his superiors 'to ensure that your outward appearance is always presentable and, till you receive further instructions or special permission, to wear clothes made of white muslin as is customary in the nation.'[125]

Although the missionaries were not supposed to wear South Indian clothes, but often did so in their homes for reasons of comfort, a compromise was reached in the selection of material.

[121] In 1729 Ch. F. Pressier described the clothes worn by the Indian co-workers of the Catholic mission in Madurai: They wore a short camisole (shirt) with sleeves and, for church, they put on a long full-length upper garment with sleeves. The colour of the clothes was generally yellow. HB 29. Cont., 417f.

[122] HB 33. Cont., 997, letter from Sartorius to a relative dated 8 February 1732; HB 4. Cont., 181, Letter from Jordan, 4 October 1710.

[123] Daniel Jeyaraj ascribes this difference to the fact that the Tamilians associate the colour black with death and mourning, while for the Europeans the colour black in this context is meant to denote learning and piety. Cf. Jeyaraj, Daniel, 1998, 'Ordination of the First Protestant Pastor Aaron—28.12.1733 and its Significance. A Contribution to Church History', in Daniel Jeyaraj (ed.), *Ordination of the First Indian Pastor Aaron*, 1–79, Lutheran Heritage Archives, Chennai, here 24f.

[124] Cf. the portrait of the first Indian pastor of the Tranquebar Mission, Aaron. Copperplate by Gottfried August Gründler, first half of the eighteenth century, in: Liebau, Heike (ed.), 2006, *Geliebtes Europa, Ostindische Welt 300 Jahre interkultureller Dialog im Spiegel der Dänisch-Halleschen Mission, Jahresausstellung der Franckeschen Stiftungen zu Halle*, Verlag der Franckeschen Stiftungen, Halle, 89.

[125] NHB 6. St., 1085, instructions for Christian David, (translated from German).

Both symbolic and pragmatic aspects dictated the choice of attire. In 1710 Ziegenbalg's reply to a question concerning the dress of Europeans in Tranquebar was the following:

> As far as dress is concerned, the Europeans dress here just as they do in Europe, each according to the custom of his country, only that one has to wear light silk East-Indian clothes in summer. In the rainy season, however, it is possible to wear a coat made of European material. I, myself, have till now always worn a coat and a jacket made of European material, which have served me well both against the heat as well as against the cold.[126]

While travelling Ziegenbalg sometimes exchanged his European clothes for light white clothes.[127] Pressier described his own dress as follows:

> As far as clothes are concerned: the lighter and thinner, the better. [...] A coat made of European material is unbearable here. At home it is safe to wear an unlined waistcoat made of material such as canisas. When we go out we are dressed in black coats made of a thin material, but in European style. We go to church dressed in priestly robes in Danish style as are still worn in Mecklenburg and Hamburg.[128]

CASTE AFFILIATIONS ON DAILY WORK

In daily work there was an overlap between the functional hierarchy within the group of 'national workers' and caste-hierarchy, since caste remained an essential factor of identity even after conversion to Christianity.[129] The manner of dealing with this phenomenon was the subject of heated discussions in many Christian mission societies. The caste structure of the local society, on the one hand, but also

[126] HB 3. Cont., 120, (translated from German).

[127] HB 4. Cont., 169, letter from B. Ziegenbalg, 11 September 1709.

[128] HB 24. Cont., 1046, (translated from German).

[129] In connection with the conversion practices of the Catholic missionaries in the sixteenth century Horst Gründer states: 'The paradoxical result of the conversion of the Paraver was that they did not break free of the caste system, but that their acceptance of Christianity led to much more strongly defined power-structures and a greater caste-consciousness.' (translated from German), Gründer, *Welteroberung und Christentum*, 285.

differing interpretations of the missionaries, on the other, influenced the practical dealings with the caste problem.[130]

Research on the relationship of the Tranquebar Mission to caste is, even today, limited to setting up an opposition between the early phase in which, under Ziegenbalg and Gründler, caste distinctions were apparently not permitted in the congregations, and the subsequent changes beginning with Walther who is said to have 'introduced' caste within the Mission again. Such observations generally lead to a condemnation of Walther and his colleagues for having succumbed to local pressure and established caste in the Christian congregations: 'By introducing caste into the Church the mission laid bare its own weakness.'[131] This interpretation, which divides missionary work into a 'casteless' phase in keeping with Christian claims and another phase that abandons these claims and permits caste differences, suggests that the decisions in this regard lay within the purview of the European missionaries alone. It does not take the attitudes and the reactions of the Tamilians adequately into consideration. At no point of time was there an official policy in the Tranquebar Mission with regard to the manner of dealing with the caste system in India. In fact it was in this sensitive area that the scientific knowledge, the general observations and the religious beliefs of the missionaries encountered traditionally established socio-cultural structures that could not be forcibly suppressed through the acceptance of a new faith. Although for most of the Tranquebar missionaries successful missionary work did not necessarily imply a Europeanization of society, they were subject to the pressure of legitimizing their work to European financial

[130] Lutheran and Roman Catholic missions had a more tolerant attitude towards the caste question than other Protestant missions. Cf. Forrester, 'Indian Christian's Attitude to Caste in the Nineteenth Century', 131. As a result of the long-standing caste dispute in the Leipzig Mission the missionaries arrived at a compromise advantageous to their mission strategy. In 1861 Karl Graul (1814–64) stated that although caste and Hinduism were inextricably linked with one another, for Christians caste remained an institution of civil society. Cf. Graul, Karl, 1861, *Die Stellung der Evangelisch-Lutherischen Mission in Leipzig zur Ostindischen Kastenfrage*, Verlag de Evang.—Luth. Mission, Leipzig, 3. For the 'caste conflict' in the Leipzig Mission see Nehring, Andreas, 2003, *Orientalismus und Mission. Die Repräsentation der tamilischen Gesellschaft und Religion durch Leipziger Missionare 1840–1940*, Harrassowitz, Wiesbaden, 114–24.

[131] Jeyaraj, *Inkulturation in Tranquebar*, 235, (translated from German).

sponsors and political decision-makers who saw civilizing and Christianizing as an indivisible entity. The decisions and actions of the missionaries in India were a result of concrete local facts and the tactical requirements of the Mission.

As a result of historical developments the South Indian caste system took on different local forms. For centuries many rulers in South India had used the Brahmins to legitimize their own rule and had, therefore, showered them with gifts and privileges which, in turn, consolidated the latter's position.[132] The dominant position of Brahmins in South Indian society led to a particularly dogmatic and rigid form of the caste system in which the *kṣatriya* and *vaiśya* had very little influence. The *śūdra*, on the other hand, whose social importance and prestige was higher than in other regions of the Indian sub-continent, had a correspondingly larger role to play. The *veḷḷāḷar* assumed a special significance in South India in the context of agriculture.[133]

At the lowest level of social acceptance—and they were also perceived in this manner by the missionaries—were the *paṟaiyār*, the 'untouchables'.

> The low castes of these heathens are the fishermen and the many kinds of Báreier, among whom some are cobblers, others are stocking-weavers, daily-wagers and people who cremate the dead; they also do all kinds of menial work and eat and drink all sorts of things. These low castes also include the basket-weavers, the Shánar, i.e. those who extract the juice from palm and coconut trees, from which the Indian arack is made [...].[134]

These people who were considered impure developed their own religious structures, maintained small temples and had their own *paṟaiyār* priests. The *paṟaiyār* worked predominantly in the agricultural sector where they were exploited to such an extent by the land-owning castes that the French missionary Jean Antoine

132 Cf. Subhramanian, N., *Social and Cultural History of Tamilnad*; also Subhramanian, N., 1989, *The Brahmin in the Tamil Country*, Ennes Publications, Madurai.

133 The leading families of the *veḷḷāḷar*, such as customs officials or district heads, were landowners on a large scale. They had the title of *mutaliyār*. Below them were the village officials with the titles of *talaiyāri*, *maṇiyakāraṉ*, *vitānai*, whose responsibilities were at the village level. Arasaratnam, 'Social History of a Dominant Caste Society', 378.

134 HB 6. Cont., 399, (translated from German).

Dubois (1766–1848), who came to India in 1792, viewed them as the slaves of the country. 'In fact, these Pariahs are the born slaves of India; and had I to choose between the two sad fates of being a slave in one of our colonies or a Pariah here, I would unhesitatingly prefer the former.'[135] This slave-like existence was not the fate of all 'untouchables'. By joining for instance the army, but also by working for the Europeans or for Christian missions, members of these groups had succeeded in attaining a social position that gave them material security as well as social prestige. Furthermore, the population structure in the cities differed from that of the countryside, and this also affected the conversion policies of the missions. 'In towns the majority of Christians was low caste, in the country-side the number of caste people was generally high.'[136]

The horizontal division of Indian society in *varṇas* (*varṇa*, Sanskrit: colour, race, gender) and castes and *jātis* (*jāti*, Sanskrit: birth, descent) was intersected in South India by a vertical differentiation that partly relativized the norms, alliances and constructs of the caste structure. The division in 'castes of the right hand' and 'castes of the left hand' was a phenomenon in Tamil society from the eleventh till the beginning of the nineteenth century. While Brahmins were generally excluded from this division, it applied to the *paṟaiyṉr* and *śūdra* groups. The left hand, which in the Tamilian understanding is generally identified with impurity, also symbolized the 'impure' communities in this system, while the 'castes of the right hand' were more powerful and had a positive connotation.[137] During the period of Vijaynagar rule the competition between 'castes of the right and of the left hand' had increased as a result of changes in the agrarian structure. The division between the two was sometimes so rigid that members of the 'left hand' and those of the 'right hand' were not allowed to work, live, eat or perform religious ceremonies together.[138] There were constant conflicts between the two groups.

[135] Dubois, Jean Antoine, 1978, *Hindu Manners, Customs and Ceremonies*, (Madras 1906) Reprint, Oxford University Press, New Delhi, 49.

[136] Hambye, *History of Christianity in India*, Vol. III, 128.

[137] Appadurai, Arjun, 1974, 'Right and left hand castes in South India', *IESHR*, 11 (2/3): 216–59; Brimnes, *Constructing the Colonial Encounter*; Stein, 'Integration of the Agrarian System'.

[138] Arasaratnam, Sinnappah, 'Pre-modern commerce and societies in Southern Asia. Inaugural lecture delivered at the University of Malaya, Kuala Lumpur on

In the eighteenth and nineteenth centuries conflicts between the caste groups of the right hand (*valaṅkai*), for example, mercantile *jāti* of the *kōmaṭṭi* and *balija*, and those of the left hand (*iṭaṅkai*), for example *perichetti*, were not unusual.[139] This vertical division into two caste alliances competing in the social and religious-ritual sphere went through all the caste groups, and, repositioned them in such a way that Brahmin castes of the groups of the 'right hand' were sometimes aligned with those of the *śudra* against groups of the 'left hand'.

This caste structure of local society was only partially reflected in the composition of the mission congregations. Since members of the Brahmin castes generally proved to be intractable with regard to conversion,[140] the missionaries focused their activities on members of the *śūdra* and *paṟaiyār* groups. Initially, the *paṟaiyār*, as the weakest section of the population, were the ones most open to the new faith, especially since it held out the promise of placing them on equal terms with other sections of society. For members of higher castes it was important to maintain their caste-status and the social position linked with this. This is one major reason why they could not accept Christianity with its claim of universal equality regardless of caste.[141] Dennis Hudson assumes that 90% of the congregations of the Tranquebar mission was made up of *paṟaiyār*-Christians,[142] but this obviously does not apply to the entire period of missionary

21 December 1971', in Sinnappah Arasaratnam, *Maritime Trade, Society and European Influence in Southern Asia 1600–1800*, I, 1–22, Aldershot, Brookfield, 10.

[139] Cf. Appadurai, 'Right and left hand castes in South India'. The attitude of British and Danish authorities in India towards these conflicts is the subject of the factual study of the Danish historian Brimnes, *Constructing the Colonial Encounter*. See also Ahuja, *Die Erzeugung kolonialer Staatlichkeit*, 36.

[140] In the preface to the first volume of the NHB in 1776 G.A. Freylinghausen stated that no Brahmin had converted till that point of time. NHB, Preface to the first volume, XXI.

[141] Cf. HB 7. Cont., 342, 'Die Malabarische Correspondentz [...] The third question: Why the Malabarians refuse to convert to Christianity?' 'For members of the higher castes conversion to Christianity meant a personal and social loss that could hardly be compensated, which is why there were practically no conversions from among these sections.' (translated from German), Gründer, *Welteroberung und Christentum*, 278.

[142] Hudson, *Protestant Origins in India*, 42–48, 160. The period between 1720–60 is, however, not really taken into consideration here.

activity. As *dalits* the *paraiyār* represented a large section of the marginalized and exploited in South Indian society. For many, the decision to convert was also linked with the hope of greater social recognition, i.e. being allowed to enter a church (*dalits* were not allowed to enter Hindu temples), and gaining access to education (the schools set up by the Danish-English-Halle Mission included children of Christian and non-Christian *paraiyār*).[143]

In the first decades of missionary work the congregations in and around Tranquebar as well as in the so-called English stations consisted predominantly of members of former *paraiyār* groups. At the beginning of the 1740s Johann Ernst Geister and Johann Philipp Fabricius stated that the majority of congregationists in the Company-ruled villages around Madras were *paraiyār*.[144] In order, however, to enhance the reputation of the mission both in India and in Europe members of higher social classes also had to be addressed by the mission. In 1777 the number of Christians in the congregations in and around Tranquebar was roughly 16,000, of whom only several hundred in Tranquebar came from the *śūdra*—castes, especially the *veḷḷāḷar*.[145] The annual reports from this period also show a marked increase in attention paid to the *sudra*. In the first half of 1773 thirteen *śūdra* and three *paraiyār* were baptized in Tranquebar; in the second half of the same year two members of *śūdra* castes and 22 *paraiyār* were prepared for baptism.[146] In 1774 there were 30 *śūdra* and 3 *paraiyār*.[147] It was not without a degree of satisfaction, therefore, that the missionaries commented in 1787,

> that, for some time now, our congregations have been growing with the addition of respected families from the higher caste and, in our schools too, there are far more children from this caste than

[143] About Dalit Christians in colonial South India, see: Mallampalli, Chandra, 2004, *Christians and Public Life in Colonial South India, 1863–1937*, Routledge Curzon, London, New York, 170–93.

[144] HB 61. Cont., 177, Madras 1744.

[145] This high percentage of 'untouchables' had been criticized by a professor in Göttingen. In his reply dated 4 January 1778, Ch. S. John justified the work of the mission by rejecting the characterization of the *paraiyār* as 'ignorant rabble'. NHB 20. St., 951–54.

[146] NHB 11. St., 1439–44; 12. St., 1579–84.

[147] NHB 14. St., 140f., report from Tranquebar, 16 October 1774.

> from the lower castes. Although we welcome everyone who shows a willingness to learn regardless of which caste they are from, this nation will respect Christianity more and the people can be more easily persuaded to accept it if they see that it is not only the lowest and most despised caste among them which has converted to Christianity [...].[148]

In the long-term perspective, therefore, the conversion of members of high castes appeared to be a far better basis for the development of Christianity in India. Caste affiliation thus became an essential instrument in the work of conversion. When the *Madras Courier* accused the mission on 24 May 1793 of only converting members of the lower castes, Ch. F. Schwartz was able to deflect this public criticism.[149] In a letter to the SPCK dated 13 February 1794 he stated that the ratio of *paṟaiyār* in the Christian congregations in Thanjavur, Tranquebar and Madras was less than one-third as against two-third members 'from higher classes'.[150]

Knowledge about caste in Indian society among the Tranquebar missionaries was based on the study of original Tamil literature, on the studies of European travelers to India, on information gained through correspondence with local scholars as also on their own observations and experiences of the structure of local society.[151] Like all Europeans working in South India the Christian missionaries came into contact with the caste system but, because of the claim of Christian missionary work that all Christians were equal, the missionaries were especially called upon to take a position on this. The strategies adopted by Christian missions in dealing with the caste system thus ranged from conscious tolerance or a calculated

[148] NHB 35. St., 1282, (translated from German).

[149] NHB 51. St., 276.

[150] NHB 51. St., 277f.

[151] Most of the Tranquebar missionaries did not use the term 'caste', even if the interlocutor used it. In keeping with their own ideas and experiences the missionaries spoke of 'estates' (*Stände*) and 'families' (*Geschlechter*), HB 9. Cont., 772, 'Das funfzehende Gespräch mit einigen Heyden'. Ch. T. Walther, who talks of 'castes and families' as parallels, is an exception. Cf. among others, HB 27. Cont., 172f, 177. The terms 'Hindu' and 'Hinduism' also do not appear in the mission reports. Fenger is wrong when he writes that the 'blackish-brown Malabars' are called 'Hindus' in the reports. Fenger, *Geschichte der Tranquebarschen Mission*, 22.

inclusion to an uncompromising struggle against this system.[152] For the missionaries of the Tranquebar Mission the assessment of the Indian caste system was a practical necessity. While the early missionaries were of the view that they could propagate a kind of European Christianity among the Indians and simply ignore caste differences after conversion, it soon became apparent that these differences continued to play a role among the Christians in the mission congregations. The caste question, with which some missionaries engaged intensively, also became a key factor[153] in mission strategy.

As the first missionary of the Tranquebar mission Bartholomäus Ziegenbalg took a position on this social phenomenon. His *Ausführliche Beschreibung des Malabarischen Heidenthums*[154] contains a five-page listing of the 'manifold families or guilds'. Proceeding from the four 'main castes', the Brahmins, the Kshatriyas, Vaishyas and Shudras, Ziegenbalg divided Indian society into 98 'families', 71 of which he associated with the *śūdra*. After naming the four 'main castes' he gives a detailed characterization of the *śūdra* caste, a method arising from Tamil social reality, since the castes of the *śūdra* represented a large majority of the population and were the dominant professional groups.[155] Ziegenbalg considered profession

[152] Cf. Gründer, *Welteroberung und Christentum*, 289.

[153] Nehring, *Orientalismus und Mission*. 114–24. Jürgen Stein's work presents a chronological account of Christianity with reference to the caste question. Compared to this long-term study the observation of attitudes within the Tranquebar Mission is only a snapshot. Stein, *Christentum und Kastenwesen*.

[154] The original title is: 'Ausführliche Beschreibung des Malabarischen Heidenthums, darinnen [...] ihre Principia und Lehr-Sätze sowohl in Theologicis als Philospohicis umständlich entdecket und zur dienlichen Unterricht dem geliebten Europa communicirt werden/.../'. The manuscript was written between 1711 and 1713 and sent to Halle, Cf. also Jeyaraj, *A German Exploration of Indian Society; Caland, Ziegenbalg's Malabarischen Heidentum*.

[155] Gita Dharampal-Frick explains Ziegenbalg's noticeable interest in the *śūdra* as the dominant group through his pietist background on the one hand and, on the other, through the perspective of mission strategy. In contrast to the Jesuits who directed their conversion attempts at Brahmins, the Tranquebar mission concentrated on the *śūdra*. Dharampal-Frick, Gita, *Indien im Spiegel deutschen Quellen der Frühen Neuzeit*, 230. While evaluating mission strategy, however, it is important to remember that the Tranquebar mission began its work among the *paṟaiyār*, and that the first *śūdra* was only converted after Ziegenbalg's death.

and an endogamous life style to be the most important characteristics of caste separation and differentiation.[156] Parallel to the 'families' were, according to him, persons of standing, namely the 'kings, priests, poets, schoolmasters, councilors, governors and other high ministers.'[157] It was possible to obtain such a position through one's work without losing one's 'caste'. At the end Ziegenbalg explained the position of the 'Gnanigöl', the learned men who rejected caste differences in their daily life and maintained contacts with representatives of all castes. He did not explain the different groups among the Brahmins, but limited his comments to their role as priests in the religious system of the Hindus. In the context of a description of agriculture in South India the focus was on the various sub-divisions of the *veḷḷāḷar*-caste.

In the *Malabarian Correspondence* conducted from 1714 to 1717[158] the structure of the four *varṇa* is also described: 'There are four main castes among us, namely the Brahmin caste, the Kshatriya caste, the Vaishya caste and the Sudra caste.'[159] In contrast to Ziegenbalg's noticeably detailed analysis of the *śūdra* castes, the *Malabarian Correspondence* focuses attention on the Brahmins and on their life rituals and norms. The *śūdra* in this framework would be those 'who, in light of the honour accorded to their caste, enjoy the greatest esteem after the Brahmins, and among who one still finds men of learning and science.'[160] *Brahmins*, however, did not only work in the religious sphere, there were also 'worldly' *Brahmins* who were mainly active in trade.[161]

The large mass of the *paṟaiyār* was the most visible social group in the local society. In the conversations with Hindus and Muslims published in 1718 it is stated:

> As regards the Bareier, this country can do without you Brahmins more easily than without them, because they are not ashamed

[156] Dharampal-Frick, *Indien im Spiegel deutscher Quellen der Frühen Neuzeit*, 195.

[157] Ibid., 198.

[158] See pp. 259f of this study for more details on the 'Malabarian Correspondence'.

[159] HB 7. Cont., 364.

[160] HB 7 Cont., 346, (translated from German).

[161] NHB 8. St., 1023.

> of doing any kind of work and carry out all the tasks that others refuse to do, either from a false sense of pride, or because it is against their caste, or because they think it would render them unclean.[162]

In the final analysis the observation of social reality also led to a description of the deviations from 'classical' caste structures. In 1717, when members of different castes fled a village in protest, the missionaries Ziegenbalg and Gründler described the system of caste alliances characteristic for South India:

> All 96 "families" can be divided mainly in two groups, namely the right and the left hand. The right hand had all kinds of demands from the left and vice versa. Finally, when the left hand saw that they would not be accommodated, they ran away from the city and Company territory. After this there was no blacksmith, no carpenter etc to be hand, and the Company as well as others could not do without them. Since the right hand felt that the Commandant would consent to some of the demands of the left hand in order to get them back, they too fled the city. Among the latter were the merchants, the shopkeepers, the sign-painters, the masons etc. They also stopped supplies coming in from the country-side, and we in the city could not get provisions, wooden articles or water.[163]

The interpretations of later missionaries were also based on a mix of a knowledge of literature, on the one hand, and daily observations, on the other. On 27 July 1727 Dal, Pressier, Bosse and Walther noted in their diary: 'that the Malabarians are commonly divided into the following three general kinds, namely 1) the Brahmins, 2) the Suttirer and 3) the Parreier.'[164] In 1728 the same missionaries explained the caste system of the Tamilians while describing the hindrances

[162] HB 9. Cont., 711, Fifth conversation, (translated from German).

[163] AB 507, Letter from B. Ziegenbalg and J.E. Gründler to A.H. Francke, Tranquebar, 22 December 1717, (translated from German). According to the observations of the missionaries the group of the 'left hand' contained blacksmiths, carpenters; the group of the 'right hand' merchants, shopkeepers, sign-painters, masons. On the practice of abandoning villages as a form of protest against social grievances see Ahuja, *Die Erzeugung kolonialer Staatlichkeit*, 162–74.

[164] HB 25. Cont., 38, diary of the missionaries Dal, Bosse, Pressier, Walther, 27 July 1727.

and difficulties in the work of conversion.[165] After listing the most important groups they described the characteristic features of the caste system. They first talked about endogamy and then about the hereditariness of professions. A further feature was the question of becoming unclean through contact with members of other castes (ritual purity). In conclusion, the social cohesion within the castes is emphasized.[166]

The missionaries increasingly adopted the view that caste was not to be viewed as a religious phenomenon, but primarily as a factor of civil society similar to the division into estates in Europe and, as such, it was incontestable. If, therefore, things were viewed in such a way that Christianity, in the process of inculturation, adapted itself to the outwardly manifest forms of Indian culture,[167] then this withdrawal from a religious interpretation of the caste system meant that its removal was no longer an important priority.[168] Although the missionaries were interested in raising the living and educational standards of 'their' converts, they were wary of changing centuries-old hierarchies, which, however, was necessary for the striving of the *paṟaiyār* for a higher social position. The missionaries thus unconsciously recognized the connection between the manifestation of religious forms in daily life and the cultural traditions of the region. The conclusion John drew from this was not to oppose and overcome caste differences, but to exclude the *paṟaiyār* from conversion efforts. 'Just as one has to be careful while accepting Roman Catholics, this same prudence is necessary with the Pareiers from among the heathens, since it is to be feared that they are most likely to become dissolute and drunkards [...].'[169]

[165] HB 27. Cont., 165–99, report of the missionaries Dal, Bosse, Pressier, Walther, 23 October 1728.

[166] HB 27. Cont., 173–76. See also AFSt/M 1 B 1 : 18, excerpt of a letter from Christoph Theodosius Walther to Johannes Schrodt, 11 November 1728.

[167] Gründer, *Welteroberung und Christentum*, 290.

[168] The analytical distinction between caste as a religious institution, on the one hand, and as an institution of civil society, on the other, increasingly shifted in favour of the latter. This view also dominated the work of the missions in the nineteenth century. Forrester, 'Indian Christian's Attitude to Caste in the Nineteenth Century', 138. See also Dirks, Nicholas B., 2001, *Castes of Mind: Colonialism and the Making of Modern India*, Princeton University Press, Princeton, 21–8.

[169] NHB 32. St., 891, excerpt of a letter from John to G.A. Freylinghausen, 10 September 1785, (translated from German).

According to Fenger, John identified with Ziegenbalg's method to the extent that he felt that by emulating his association with learned men and his efforts to learn High Tamil Christians from 'higher families' could be won over. Under John's management, however, a growing contempt for Tamilians is discernible. In a manner of speaking, caste prejudices thus expand into prejudices against the entire population. According to John, the importance of case distinctions would, in any case, be reduced under the conditions of English rule in India.[170] A.F. Cämmerer tried to understand the role of Brahmins in South Indian society on the basis of classical literature and he focused on their religious ideas. He wrote about the *samnyāsin* who had renounced the world, and he saw the respect accorded to them by the people of the country. In his explanations of the religious stages of life of a Brahmin and the reasons for their erudition, Cämmerer referred, among others, to Pierre Sonnerat's (1748–1814) *Reise nach Ostindien*.[171]

The early missionaries of the Danish-Halle Mission tried to establish Christian congregations in which caste differences would no longer be important, given the new religious community to which they all now belonged, since they viewed caste and Christianity as incompatible. Till the 1720s the caste problem does not seem to have been important in the understanding of missionary work. In the daily life of the mission this meant that Christians had to sit together without regard to their caste affiliations and drink from the same cup during communion. However, it soon became apparent that the missionaries experienced a conflict between their religious duties and the practical requirements of local social reality. Whereas the first and second generations of Royal Danish missionaries concentrated on the association with more highly-placed sections of society and began work among them, under Schultze there was initially a re-orientation towards the lower sections of the population.[172]

170 NHB 58. St., 896.

171 NHB 52.St., 351f; The complete title of Pierre Sonnerat's book is *Reise nach Ostindien und Sina auf Befehl des Königs in den Jahren 1774–1781 unternommen. Aus dem Original in einen feinen Auszug gebracht*, Schneider, Frankfurt, Leipzig 1784.

172 Fenger is ambivalent about this focus on the 'common man' since, on the one hand, it led to a greater number of conversions while, on the other, it opened the doors, in his opinion, to 'greater depravity in the congregations'. Fenger, *Geschichte der Tranquebarschen Mission*, 122.

In 1727 Dal, Bosse, Pressier and Walther described this conflict in their diary:

> Therefore, when such people (the *paraiyar*, H.L.) became Christians, our predecessors had no choice but to assign a separate place in the church for them, and they accepted this gladly. It cost great effort to remove this distinction in the church later. When we had just arrived from Europe, we too felt that this was correct and had to be done. See the diary of the previous year 1726 under 22 February. However, our catechists have been constantly dinning into our ears that the heathens are always reproaching them for it [...]. After several discussions we have come to the conclusion that order is in keeping with Christian humility and eternity and have decided that the Parreier will now sit one foot apart from the Suttirakköl in the church. However, there will be no distinction made when the sacrament is administered.[173]

From this point on the reports sent by the missionaries always cite 'caste differences' in order to justify particular measures and expenditure, or the goal of overcoming these differences is cited to legitimize intensive missionary activity. In a letter to Gottfried August Francke in 1732 J.A. Sartorius and B. Schultze justified the need for building a church in Madras by pointing out, among other things, that the lack of space in the prayer-hall did not allow for a separation of the *paṟaiyār* and the *śūdra*.[174] With the increasing number of *śūdra* converts since the 1730s the missionaries had to often make compromises in their dealings with caste questions, since *paṟaiyār* Christians were not accepted as catechists or assistants in *śūdra* areas, and Christian *śūdra* parents did not send their children to a school where there was either a large number of *paṟaiyār* children or there was an 'untouchable' as a teacher.

The caste problem became particularly explosive in connection with divine services. Whereas in the early years there was no fixed seating order in the churches, the South Indian catechists in the 1720s insisted on the observation of caste distinctions in the seating

[173] HB 25. Cont., 38f., diary of the missionaries in Tranquebar, 27 July 1727 (translated from German). The passage referred to in this quotation does not appear in print. Cf. HB 22 Cont., 861.

[174] HB 33. Cont., 990f., letter from B. Schultze and J.A. Sartorius to the editor of the Halle Reports, Madras, 26 January 1732.

order in church.[175] Later, this separation of castes was sometimes taken to such an extent that there were two separate congregations in one place for members of the different caste groups. This was the case in the 1780s in the English mission in Tiruppalatturai, where there was one *paṟaiyār* and one *śūdra* congregation. While the *paṟaiyār* congregation was under the care of the mission in Tranquebar and a local catechist, Christian Friedrich Schwartz looked after the *śūdra* congregation, since a suitable catechist was not available locally: 'There is another small Suttirer-congregation in Tirupalaturey, which does not bring us much joy. We sometimes send a catechist there, but till now we have not been able to find a capable person from the so-called higher caste.'[176]

The celebration of communion achieved a special symbolic significance. While the presence of people of different caste backgrounds in one room was already a problem, drinking from the same cup was a far greater test. The reports of the first missionaries hardly contain any detailed descriptions of the celebration of communion, but there are also no indications of a possible separation of castes.[177] As against this, the missionaries in the 1720s asserted that they allowed all members of the congregation to take part in a common celebration of communion and also that they succeeded in making them drink from the same cup.[178] When the decision was taken in 1727 to allow members of different castes to sit separately, there was apparently no such distinction made while administering the sacrament.[179] Members of the congregation who refused to take part in divine services or in Holy Communion with members of other castes were sometimes given severe punishments.[180] Fabricius and Breithaupt reported in 1779 about the English mission in Madras 'that the Madras mission had never kept two different cups for the Sutirer and Pareier while administering the sacrament, but that

[175] HB 25. Cont., 39, diary of the missionaries in Tranquebar, 27 July 1727.

[176] NHB 36. St., 1396, reports from the English missions in Thanjavur 1788, (translated from German).

[177] Lehmann, *Es begann in Tranquebar*, 98f.

[178] HB 27. Cont., 184, Dal, Bosse, Pressier and Walther on the hindrances for the mission, 23 October 1728.

[179] HB 25. Cont., 39, daily register of the missionaries in Tranquebar, 27 July 1727.

[180] HB 33. Cont., 879f., report from Tranquebar 1732.

only one cup was used for both castes.'[181] Daniel Schreyvogel, who came to Tranquebar in 1804, was ordained there in 1813, entered English mission service in 1826 and worked in Madurai. He debarred some members of the *śūdra*—castes from the congregation and forbade them from entering the church because they wanted to receive communion before the others.[182] As a result of Schreyvogel's uncompromising stance towards caste differences, the Christians of his congregation in Vepery (Madras) submitted a petition to the governor in 1834.[183]

As a mark of conversion many missions employed the practice of making catechists and people of different castes have a meal together. Generally, there was resistance to this practice. Henriette Bugge points out to cases in the nineteenth century, where a young man who was being ordained either had to eat something prepared by an 'untouchable' or eat with one of them.[184] Although the Tranquebar Mission also felt that the separation of castes at meals was a relict of 'heathenism' that had to be overcome, it did not try to force Indians to eat together. From time to time, and not without a certain amount of pride, the missionaries reported on apparent successes: 'On one of his journeys our country preacher Rajappen actually shared a meal with a distinguished European, which he could only do since his countrymen would not hear about it. However, even he would not be able to eat beef because of the fear of not being able to keep it down.'[185]

A person's caste background was a decisive criterion in the appointment of a mission worker and while choosing his place of work. On the one hand, the rigid structures of the South Indian caste system affected the work of the mission and, in case of doubt it was caste affiliation rather than capabilities that decided the career of a mission co-worker. On the other hand, catechists, teachers and assistants of different castes worked together in the mission without being in permanent conflict with one another. It was only in the matter of eating together that caste was often insurmountable. Sometimes,

[181] NHB 25. St., 45, excerpt of a letter from Fabricius and Breithaupt, October 11, 1779, (translated from German).

[182] NHB 84. St., 1247.

[183] Subramanian, 'Caste System in the Tamil Country in the 19th century', 43.

[184] Bugge, *Mission and Tamil Society*, 90–92.

[185] NHB 44. St., 709, (translated from German).

the group of Tamil mission co-workers had to separate if in a particular place the presence of an 'untouchable' was undesirable.[186] In various situations the local workers even had to maintain a distance from the missionaries because of their caste affiliations. In 1764 Zeglin reported on his journey to Madras accompanied part of the way by the country preacher Ambrosius: 'On 16 March, the country preacher sat down to eat a small distance away from me in order not to offend the Malabarians who would not understand.'[187]

Although till at least the last one-third of the eighteenth century most of the converts of the Tranquebar Mission belonged to the *paṟaiyār* groups, the compulsion to appoint *śūdra* workershad set in much earlier. According to the missionaries, a *śūdra* had to be appointed to look after the *śūdra* Christians in the district congregations aroundTranquebar.[188] After Schwartz had converted a number of people from the *śūdra*—community there, the congregations inThanjavur could no longer be looked after only by a *paṟaiyār*. The *paṟaiyār* Rajanayakkan, who had worked for almost 30 years for the Tranquebar Mission in Thanjavur, but who was not ordained because he came from the *paṟaiyār* caste, no longer vouchsafed the general acceptance of the mission by the people there. 'It can be noted here that for the Sutiers, i.e. the middle-class, and for the Bareier, i.e. the peasants, one must have, for each class, catechists of the same background, especially in the districts. At a pinch, a Sutirer catechist can be appointed for Bareier, but not the other way around.'[189] Rajanayakkan, whose eye-sight was by now weak and who the missionaries did not approve of any more on account of his undesirable contacts with the Moravian Brethren inTranquebar,[190] was to be transferred in 1769, on Schwartz's advice, fromThanjavur to Arantangi.[191] It is significant that his work inThanjavur was taken

[186] On one of his journeys Ambrosius, belonging to a higher caste, could not take his assistants, who belonged to the 'untouchables' with him through a 'Brahmin street'. NHB 1. St., 56f.

[187] HB 101 Cont., 600, Zeglin's travel diary, April 1764, (translated from German).

[188] HB 32. Cont., 821. Aaron was explicitly meant to visit Christians of the *śūdra*-castes.

[189] HB 33. Cont., 882. Cf. also NHB, 4. St., 422, 3 July 1768, (translated from German).

[190] NHB 4. St., 457, 4 October 1769.

[191] NHB 4. St., 422; NHB 8. St., 993.

over, again on Schwartz's recommendation, by a *śūdra*, the 'Suttirer catechist' Rajappen (1742–96/97).[192] When children were selected for a career in the mission, *śūdra* children were given preference over the *paṟaiyār* since, as John openly admitted in 1778, 'the mission had more use for them'.[193] Among the South Indian co-workers of the mission it could be seen that the higher the position in the functional hierarchy the greater was the proportion of *śūdra* members, especially representatives of the *veḷḷāḷar*-community.[194]

For the second half of the nineteenth century Duncan Forrester states that local co-workers had a more tolerant attitude towards caste than the European missionaries. Members of high castes were especially particular about observing caste rules, while members of the lower castes placed greater value on the social status acquired through conversion to Christianity than on their original caste affiliation.[195]

> Most high-caste converts had knowingly embraced a caste-free church, while the low-caste and untouchable converts were attracted to Christianity to a great extent because it represented a way of escape from the caste system into a broader community of shared opportunity and self-respect.[196]

We can see in the final analysis how the perpetuation of cast-identity became a foregone conclusion even for the missionaries through the introduction of terms like 'Paraiyar Christians'[197], which represented

[192] NHB 8. St., 1064. Rajappen was ordained in 1778 and went to Tranquebar as a country preacher. Cf. also NHB 4. St., 482, letter of the missionaries of 28 July 1769.

[193] NHB 35. St., 1313.

[194] Even in the missions of the nineteenth century in South India most of the ordained pastors were members of higher castes. According to Hudson all the influential co-workers of the Tranquebar mission had a similar background—*veḷḷāḷar*. Hudson, Protestant Origins in India, 42–48. This estimate, which is correct with regard to the ordained pastors, would have to be questioned where other groups of national workers are concerned. Among the catechists there were, by all means, members of the *paṟaiyār* and, within the groups of subordinate functionaries such as teachers and assistants, prayer-leaders and Bible women, their proportion corresponded to the composition of the concerned Christian congregations.

[195] Forrester, 'Indian Christian's Attitude to Caste in the Nineteenth Century', 132.

[196] Ibid., 147.

[197] This term appears for the first time in the diary of the Tranquebar missionaries in the report of 14 October 1752 about the journey undertaken by the ordained

the verbal acceptance of this fact. At the end of the nineteenth century the *Propaganda Fide*, and even the Jesuit order, changed caste politics in the sense 'that now ordination was also possible for Catholics from lower castes—however only to a limited extent.'[198] As long as the Tranquebar Mission worked in Southeast India, the 'casteless' were silently overlooked in suggestions for ordination.

In the educational system of the DEHM the caste structure primarily influenced the selection of teachers. In the initial years the missionaries tried to have common classes for children of different castes.[199] In 1726 a special school was set up in Porayar for *paṟaiyār* children, while the school in the mission house was attended mainly by *śūdra* children. Even in the other schools it became necessary to separate the *paṟaiyār* from the *śūdra* in order to ensure that the schools continued to function.[200] Rajanayakkan reported that his school in Thanjavur was attracting many *śūdra*, and he requested that a *śūdra* teacher be sent immediately since the parents did not want their children to be under the supervision of an 'untouchable'. On the basis of his experiences John came to the conclusion that appointing *śūdra* as catechists and teachers would be advantageous for the mission. 'The mixing of the Parreier with the Suttirer boys is difficult, especially in our houses. It is also desirable that most of our catechists and schoolmasters be of the Suttirer-caste.'[201]

The missionaries also took the caste structure of their surroundings into account, especially while organizing the vocational lessons. Problems always arose when particular kinds of work, which were associated with the work of a specific *jati*, were to be taught in a school. Thus, in 1728, in the context of vocational training in

---

pastor Ambrosius. 'In Tarmaburam one of our Parrier Christians took him [i.e. Ambrosius, H.L.] to a close relative of the Ramalinganaicker, for whom he works.' (translated from German), HB 78. Cont., 888–90, here 890. Similarly, the terms 'Suttirer-heathens' and 'Parreier-heathens' were in use: NHB 11. St., 1439–44 (1773).

[198] Stein, *Christentum und Kastenwesen*, 159.

[199] HB 11. Cont., 958.

[200] HB 22. Cont., 861, diary of Pressier and Walther 1726. Cf. also HB 33. Cont., 894f. § 7.

[201] NHB 30. St., 709, letter from John, October 18, 1784, (translated from German).

a school, it was said that a fabric painter and a tailor had been successfully trained and placed in jobs. Doubts were, however, expresses with regard to the *paraiyar*: 'The Barreier boys cannot be sent into any profession, but have to accustom themselves to manual work early on. Therefore, we should not keep them too long in the schools [...]'.[202] Similar considerations played a role when the mission in Tranquebar introduced 'all kinds of work with Malabar cane' and made the school children manufacture rice baskets, mats, chairs and beds from it. This work was introduced because 'the caste distinctions do not create such problems in this' as with other jobs and all the children can work at it. It was more difficult with crafts that were ascribed to certain castes, and some attempts of the mission to teach these in the schools failed.[203] Since the English preferred to employ Brahmins as accountants, Brahmin parents sent their children to the so-called English mission schools where the missionaries were prepared to make the necessary compromises.[204] '[...] they are all from the most respected families in the city and from the higher castes, and the main intention of the parents is to equip them for service with the Europeans. Even if we manage to achieve only this, the work with them will not have been in vain.'[205] This trend of high-caste Hindus allowing their children to be educated in the English mission schools continued till the middle of the nineteenth century. After that the competition from public schools became stronger and mission schools increasingly lost their leading position.[206]

[202] HB 26. Cont., 58, daily register of the missionaries in Tranquebar, 31 July 1728. Cf. also HB 2. Cont., 862, dairy of the missionaries Walther and Pressier 1726, (translated from German).

[203] NHB 35. St., 1263. In Kuttanallur, for example, there was a street of mat-weavers whose work was known far and wide. They planted a special kind of reed, some of which was dyed for use. The mats themselves were very popular because of the figures that had been weaved into them (elephants, flowers etc.) and because of their cooling qualities.

[204] NHB 2. St., 263.

[205] NHB 30. St., 708, (translated from German).

[206] In the 1820s the Anglican mission in Palayankottai also recorded numerous high-caste pupils in the seminary there. NHB 72. St., 1268. On the status of the mission educational system in India in the 19th century see Mathew, A., 1988, *Christian Missions, Education and Nationalism: From Dominance to Compromise, 1870–1930*, Anamika Prakashan, New Delhi.

KINSHIP RELATIONS OF SOUTH INDIAN WORKERS

Kinship relations influenced communication between the South Indian co-workers and are a factor that cannot be ignored. A distinction has to be made between the familial context at the time of conversion, which the convert sometimes lost through the change of faith, and the context that arose after the person had entered the service of the Mission.

The separation from the original familial context was often a long lasting, contradictory and, sometimes, painful process. The conversions in the Tranquebar Mission were mainly individual conversions. However, in many ways, the relatives of the person concerned played a significant role. In Hindu families, but also in Catholic ones, relatives normally rejected the conversion of the family member and often mounted massive attempts to convince the person that his action was wrong. Requests, threats and violence often led the person concerned to re-think his decision or to revoke it. Sometimes, however, the conversion of one family member led to the conversion of other members or of entire families.[207] When the former Catholic Rajanayakkan was taken into the service of the Mission, he brought his brothers Sinappen (died 1772) and Tairiappen with him. Sinappen was—initially on a trial basis—made his assistant, and probably remained with Rajanayakkan in Thanjavur as a junior catechist till 1746. Subsequently he worked in Kumbakonam where he died in 1772.[208] The younger brother, Tairiappen, helped Rajanayakkan periodically as an assistant.[209] Christian Wilhelm Gericke appointed another relative of Rajanayakkan, Gabriel, as a catechist in 1775 in Cuddalore.[210] The relationship between employees of the Mission and their Hindu/Catholic relatives differed from case to case, and difficulties did not necessarily arise. Even after conversion Aaron,

[207] As was the case of Ignasimuttunaicken (died around 1745) who converted from the Roman Catholic to the Lutheran faith with his entire family. In the 1730s Ignasimuttunaicken was an assistant in Tattenur, after which he spent 12 years in Madurai, returning to Tranquebar in 1744. HB 61. Cont., 96.

[208] HB 26. Cont., 12–16. In the annual statistical reports Sinappen appears in 1746 under Thanjavur (AFSt/M 2 A 2 : 7). For Sinappen see also HB 29. Cont., 478; NHB 10. St., 1347.

[209] HB 29. Cont., 478, report of 12 December 1729.

[210] NHB 15. St., 338, report from Cuddalore 1775.

according to the reports, enjoyed good relations with the Hindu members of his family. His father remained a Hindu and died in 1732 shortly before his son was ordained. However, after his father's death Aaron's mother and sister converted to Christianity.[211]

The local workers of the Tranquebar Mission constituted a professional group whose members had a varied social standing. The fact that this group consisted of members of different castes, whose daily work brought them together, was a huge challenge for developing private contacts and familial relations. Teachers, assistants, catechists and ordained pastors employed by the mission preferred their children to intermarry within the group. Since the possibilities of finding a marriage partner had, in any case, become limited through conversion, members of the Mission first tried to get their children married within their own congregation. While doing this they also looked at the caste background and the function that the family of the chosen partner had in the Mission. Aaron's first wife Rahel (died 1731) was a Christian in the Tranquebar congregation, daughter of a teacher who had also converted from Hinduism. When he got married Aaron was also a teacher.[212] Diogo also initially married a woman from the congregation.[213] As ordained pastors they looked for marriage alliances for their children within their own group. On June 23, 1745 Porumei, a daughter of the first ordained pastor Aaron, married the teacher Thomas, a son of the other ordained pastor Diogo, in the church in Tranquebar.[214] The ordained pastor Rajappen married off one of his daughters to the catechist of Thanjavur and later ordained pastor, Njanapiragasam, with whom he also worked.[215]

Children born in Christian families were considered Christians; they were baptized and generally received religious instruction. Christians who were part of a mission congregation could send their children to one of the mission schools. Children of mission employees who attended mission schools remained under the special

[211] HB 63. Cont., 549.

[212] HB 63. Cont., 551f.

[213] RA Miskolark 9b, translation of a letter from Diogo to the Mission Board, 28 September 1748.

[214] HB 63. Cont., 513.

[215] NHB 30. St., 774, report of the ordained pastor Rajappen about his journey to Palayamkottah. Njanapiragasam was ordained in 1811.

supervision of the missionaries. As assistants, they already began to accompany their fathers or brothers on their journeys, or in the undertaking of a mission task. Two sons of the ordained pastor Diogo entered missionary service. Thomas was sent to Kiernander in Cuddalore in 1743 as a teacher in the Tamil school to replace the local Hindu teacher,[216] and another son, Nianapirasadam, was the second city catechist in Tranquebar.[217] In certain regards this was an economy measure and a safety net for the Mission since it could expect a high degree of loyalty from relatives of a faithful and conscientious mission employee. As a child, Arulappen (1729 or 1735–95) attended the mission school in Tranquebar along with his brother Rajappen (1743–73) and his nephew Schawrirajen (1755–1817).[218] As adults, all of them became employees of the mission: Arulappen became a catechist in Tranquebar, Rajappen became the (Tamil) schoolteacher in Tranquebar and Schawrirajen was a catechist in Tranquebar before being ordained as a pastor. Children of mission employees often took over functions similar to those of their fathers: Samuel, the son of the city assistant Rasappen (died 1763), first worked in the school in Porayar and them became a prayer-leader in Tranquebar in 1773.[219] Jesadian, the assistant in the Mahadevpattanam district, was the son of the prayer-leader in Anitschiaburam, Pallarajen (died 1769).[220] Some worked as children with their fathers and took over the function after the father died. Thus, two years after the death of the catechist Sattianaden in 1791 his son Dewasagayam (died after 1805) took his place. He had worked earlier as his father's assistant.[221]

Sometimes, the history of a family as a history of mission co-workers can be traced over several generations. Daniel Pullei, for example, was born in 1740 as the son of poor Christian parents who were members of the mission congregation in Tranquebar. His grandfather, the blind Johann d'Almeida, had converted from Catholicism to Protestantism and had worked as a catechist of the

[216] HB 59. Cont., 1729, entry for 18 May 1743.
[217] NHB 10. St., 1330.
[218] NHB 50. St., 140.
[219] NHB 12. St., 1591.
[220] NHB 3. St., 274, 285.
[221] HB 101. Cont., 520, NHB 42. St., 507f.

Tranquebar Mission from 1707 to 1744.[222] D'Almeida's youngest daughter, Dawaschiai, married the Tamil schoolteacher Petrus on 7 May 1720.[223] It cannot be clearly established whether Daniel Pullei was the child of this daughter or of another child of d'Almeida. Daniel Pullei himself had six children: two sons and four daughters. He too saw a future for them in the Mission, but he did not have any lasting success in his endeavours in this regard. His oldest son was sent in 1787 to Christian Pohle in Tiruchirappalli to be trained for missionary service, but he did not last out.[224] The second son died young as an alcoholic. One daughter was mentally challenged.[225] With John's help Daniel Pullei tried to send one of his sons to Europe for his education, but their attempts were unsuccessful.[226]

One of the most successful catechists of the Tranquebar Mission, Sattianaden, was the son of a Catholic catechist in Kumaramangalam who had often sent his son to the missionaries in Tranquebar in order to establish contact with them.[227] Sattianaden belonged to the early generation of Tamil workers when, due to a lack of trained workers for the different posts Catholics were often appointed, since they knew the Bible and the Christian articles of faith and could, therefore, be used almost immediately. Sattianaden, who could read and write, had, on several occasions, offered to help the missionaries and had expressed his intention of entering the service of the mission.[228] This decision would also have been influenced by the fact that his father, on account of his tolerant attitude and his interest in co-operation with the Tranquebar missionaries, had aroused the ire of his Catholic employers and had received threats.[229] When

[222] AB 63; HB 59. Cont., 1517, 14 January 1744.

[223] HB 20. Cont., 443, dairy 1720.

[224] NHB 36. St., 1369, Pohle's daily register, 8 February 1787.

[225] AFSt/M 1 K 5 : 16.

[226] RA Miskolark 9g, *Pro Memoria* from Christoph Samuel John, 12 December 1784.

[227] HB 25. Cont., 59, diary of the missionaries in Tranquebar, 29 September 1727: Sattianaden brought a letter from his father to the missionaries in Tranquebar. HB 25. Cont., 62, diary, 6 November 1727: As the son of a Catholic catechist Sattianaden brought a Hindu to Tranquebar for baptismal preparation.

[228] HB 25. Cont., 70, December 1727.

[229] HB 25. Cont., 64f., diary of the missionaries in Tranquebar, entry for 6 November 1727.

Sattianaden asked the missionaries in Tranquebar in December 1727 to baptize and employ him, they were immediately willing to appoint him as a catechist in the rural districts, since none of the existing local mission workers at that time appeared suitable for this work.[230]

The marriage practices and the passing on of the profession to the next generation suggest that, in the course of time, a special feeling of identity developed among the South Indian co-workers of the DEHM, both on the basis of the common religion as well as on the basis of caste affiliation and status. Besides the professional ties, the familial networks represented structures that were consciously established and used by the mission employees as part of their life-strategy.

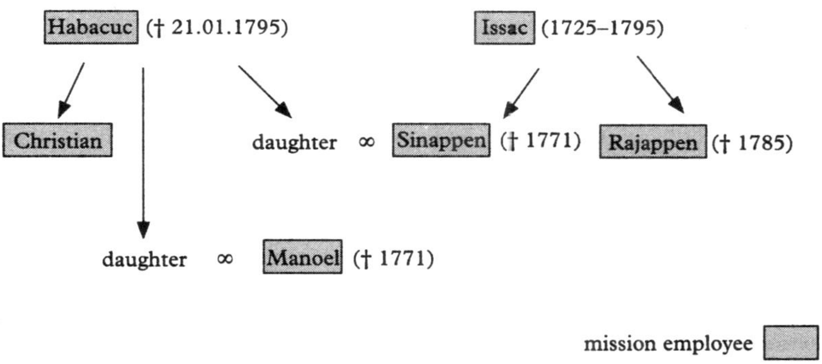

ILLUSTRATION 3.1 Familial connections of the South Indian mission employees in Cuddalore

The organized mediation of religious teachings through Christian mission societies was accompanied by a multi-layered process of appropriation, systematization, assimilation and spread of knowledge in the most varied fields. Like mission activity in the narrower sense these processes of knowledge transfer and knowledge production depended on the co-operation between the Europeans and the local people. Although in the framework of research on the

[230] HB 25. Cont., 70, 71, diary of the missionaries in Tranquebar, December 1727.

employees in Tiruchirappalli

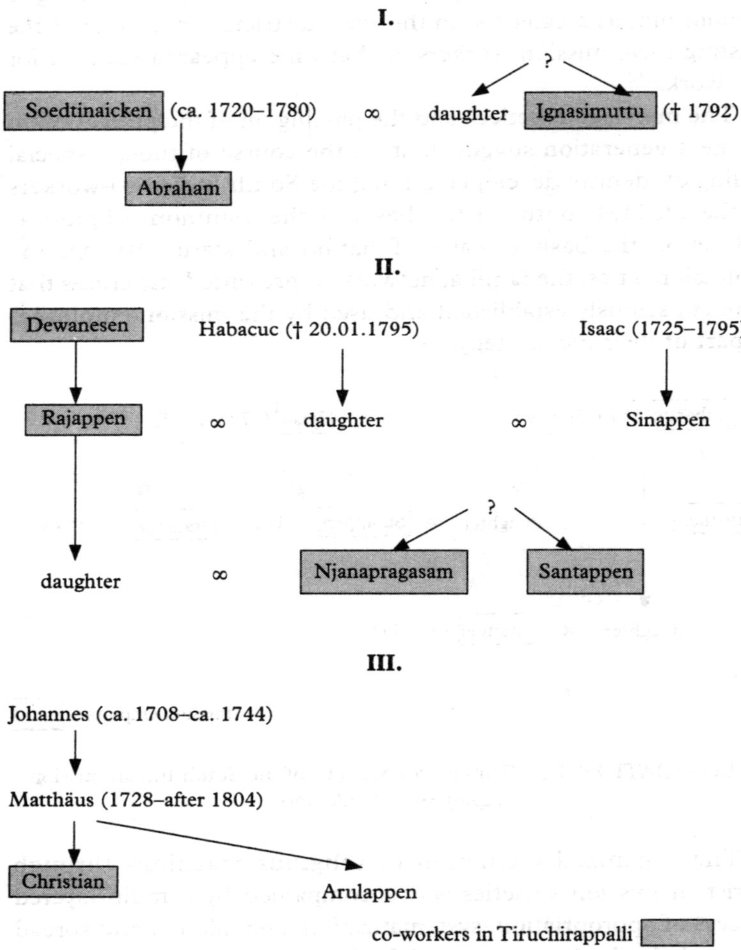

ILLUSTRATION 3.2 Familial connections of the South Indian mission employees in Tiruchirappalli

Tranquebar Mission the scientific achievements of the missionaries have been the object of numerous studies, the contribution of local informants and mission co-workers to these achievements has hardly been mentioned in the existing research on mission history. At most, the missionary is regarded as a scholar, and his scientific achievements are, therefore, the focus of interest. In some cases, the participation of local informants or assistants of missionaries is referred to as a conjecture rather than as a reliable fact. It is also because of the missionaries that there is no precise information about these persons, since the former, as a rule, wrote very little about those who helped them and, generally, were completely silent about them. By looking behind the scenes of missionary research, however, we might be able to get some answers with regard to the local informants.

MISSIONARY RESEARCH ACTIVITIES

The efforts made by the early missionaries to gain knowledge about the mission region and its people were, in their opinion, not only consistent with the mission mandate and with the idea of the superiority and universality of Christianity, but were, in fact, a precondition for carrying out the task of the Mission.[231] Knowledge about the thoughts and actions of the people to be converted was considered an important basis for the successful propagation and the credible mediation of the Christian faith.

> The Royal Danish missionaries in Tranquebar particularly required two external resources for carrying out their work among the heathens successfully: firstly, a knowledge of the language of the country, without which it was impossible to convince the heathens about their mistaken beliefs and to propagate the gospel of Christ. Secondly, a knowledge of the heathenism of these people to whom they have been sent by God. Using the heathen's own teachings they have been able to demonstrate the falsity of their idolatry to them: [...].[232]

[231] As demonstrated in the collection of articles in: Liebau, et al., *Mission und Forschung.*
[232] HB 7. Cont., preface, (translated from German).

The institutions supporting the mission and the donors in Europe also expected the missionaries to report about their 'secular' observations and experiences in the mission region.

South Indian informants significantly influenced the manner in which the European missionaries perceived local society. As travel companions, interpreters, language teachers or expert interview partners they sketched the outlines of the images that the missionaries absorbed and passed on to their European correspondents. They filtered local knowledge by deciding what information the Europeans should get and what should be kept from them. Some of the informants had many years of experience in dealing with Europeans before they came into contact with the Danish-English-Halle missionaries. These informants knew European languages, were acquainted with the European way of life and could thus deal with the missionaries capably. Others were, on account of their specialized knowledge in religion, literature, botany or medicine, of special interest for the scientific ambitions of the Europeans. This co-operation resulted in numerous reports, tracts, thematic treatises and systematic studies, of which the European missionaries are hitherto considered the sole authors. One does not always find references in the sources to the local informants who were involved in the work or to the manner in which this co-operation took place.

Research on religion was the most obvious in the list of scientific interests of Christian missionaries since knowledge of the religious beliefs of the Tamils provided important arguments in religious debates and in daily missionary propaganda. With regard to 'knowledge about the heathenism of the people' Dal, Pressier, Bosse and Walther reiterated in a letter to G.A. Francke dated 10 July 1737 that this 'is necessary as an external resource and serves to demonstrate to the heathens the falsity of their idolatry on the basis of their own teachings [...]'.[233] The studies of religion undertaken by the Tranquebar missionaries were directed both at the teachings and contents of Brahmanical Hinduism as well as at elements of folk-religion.[234] The former was based on a study of literature and

[233] HB 45. Cont., 1182, (translated from German).

[234] For the different religious traditions in colonial Tamilnadu which form what was later identified as 'formal Hinduism' see: Bayly, Susan, 1989, *Saints, Goddesses*

regular contacts with learned Brahmins, while the latter resulted mainly from the missionaries' own observations supplemented by the explanation of local attendants.

The informants for religious studies often were Brahmins, since they knew the holy texts. Brahmins, however, were not converts, let alone mission co-workers. In order to collaborate with them, therefore, a suitable basis of communication acceptable to both sides had to be found. This could consist in payment of a sum of money to a person for the information provided or for his work while maintaining confidentiality about the contact. It was also possible, however, for the co-operation to be based on mutual scientific interests.

Among the most comprehensive studies on religion were Ziegenbalg's efforts to understand Hinduism, which are documented in his works Genealogie der malabarischen Götter and Malabarisches Heidentum.[235] Pressier, who had been an eye-witness to the ritual bathing ceremonies of Hindus at the mouth of the Kaveri river while on a journey accompanied by a catechist in 1728 to Kaverippattanam, received permission to attend a sacrificial ritual conducted by a Brahmin. The missionary then gave an extensive description of this ceremony in his travel-report.[236] Ch. T. Walther used information given by Muslim and Hindu priests in his 'Anmerkungen über etliche Schriftverkehr, bei Gelegenheit einiger Lehrsätze oder Gebräuche der hiesigen Heiden, teils auch der Muhammedaner'.[237] In 1735 J.A. Sartorius sent a folding altar for

---

and Kings. Muslims and Christians in South Indian Society 1700–1900, Cambridge University Press, Cambridge, 40, 70.

[235] The studies by Bartholomäus Ziegenbalg mentioned here were not published by Halle. *Malabarisches Heidentum* was edited in 1926 by Willem Caland in Amsterdam. *Genealogie der malabarischen Götter* was edited by Wilhelm Germann and published in 1867 in Madras and Erlangen. Ch. S. John, who wrote in 1784 that a manuscript of the *Genealogie der malabarischen Götter* was available in the mission library in Tranquebar, regretted that Ziegenbalg's works had not been published since they would have been very important for the understanding of classical Tamilian thought. RA Miskolark 9g, Some suggestions regarding the Mission by Ch. S. John, Tranquebar, 20 February 1784. Both works have recently been edited and commented by Jeyaraj, *Bartholomäus Ziegenbalgs Genealogie der malabarischen Götter*; Jeyaraj, *Genealogy of the South Indian Deities;* Jeyaraj, *A German Exploration of Indian Society*.

[236] HB 26. Cont., 109–16.

[237] ['Notes on some correspondence regarding some teachings or customs of the heathens here, including Muslims']. This work was written around 1730; AFSt/M

the worship of the god Viṣṇu to Halle, which he had obtained from a Brahmin. He probably also got the explanations for the individual figures, which he sent with the altar, from this Brahmin who went from village to village with his 'box of idols' and told stories about Viṣṇu on the basis of these figures.[238]

At the request of European scholars Dal, Bosse, Walther and Pressier attempted to obtain a translation of the *āyurveda*, one of the holy texts of the Hindus. The *āyurveda* contains chants that the priests used for sacrificial ceremonies.[239] With the help of the Brahmin Krishna (Crüschtna), who the missionaries had known for a long time and to whom they offered a 'reasonable payment', they were able to prepare a summary of the most important teachings in each chapter. The missionaries had to promise the Brahmin that they would not disclose his name.[240] In 1777 Klein sent two so-called *Sastiram*, or interpretations of signs, to Halle, which could only have been undertaken by a Brahmin. In this case, the informant is also named: 'Both are translated narratives of the Brahmin Woengitta Suba-Rajer Aien in Nagapatnam, 9 January 1777.'[241]

In particular, the missionaries were interested in the hook-swinging festival of the fishermen, which some of them personally went to see.[242] In the commentaries to the *Malabarische Korrespondenz*

---

1 B 8 : 5. It contains customs, usages and teachings of Muslims. See also HB 25. Cont., 117–46, Walther's letter to J.H. Callenberg in Halle 'Von den Lehrsätzen und Gebräuchen der Muhammedaner zu Tranckenbar'.

238 HB 40. Cont., 539–58. Leipold, Aletta (ed.), 2007, *Vishnus Weltentraum. Geheimnisse des Indienschrankes in der Kunst—und Natralienkammer der Franckeschen Stiftungen*, Verlag der Franckeschen Stiftungen, Halle.

239 Cf. von Glasenapp, Helmut, 1986, *Indische Geisteswelt. Vol. I Glaube und Weisheit der Hindus*, Dausien, Hanau, 15–28; Mehlig, Johannes (ed.), 1987, *Weisheit des alten Indien. Vol. I. Vorbuddhistische und nicht-buddhistische Texte*, Kiepenheuer, Leipzig, Weimar, 9–20.

240 HB 45. Cont., 1182, letter from Dal, Pressier, Bosse and Walther to G.A. Francke, 10 July 1737; see also HB 36. Cont., 1251–94, 'Haupt=Inhalt des Iasdurvedam, eines von den vier Gesetz=Büchern der Brahmaner'.

241 NHB 18. St., 675–78, here 678.

242 HB 7. Cont., 380; 20. Cont., 457; 21. Cont., 747; 48. Cont., 1457; 64. Cont., 642; 65. Cont., 831; 98. Cont., 198; 102. Cont., Preface, (155), 649; AFSt/M 2 B 1 : 8 desription of the swingle festival of the fishermen by Johann Gerhard König, [Tranquebar] 1768. *Hook-swinging* was a popular ritual in Bengal and in central and South India till the end of the nineteenth century. After 1857 the colonial government

it is mentioned as a brutal ritual.[243] In 1721 Schultze gave a detailed description of this festival based on his own observations:

> On October 3 the fishermen celebrated their festival, which I went to see, not because I wanted to, but in order to be able to convince them of their blindness afterwards. In the village closest to the city they had fixed a lever shaped like a gallows in a tall tree in such a manner that the apparatus could rotate. One person after another allowed himself to be hung there. This was done in the following manner: there were two strong hinge-hooks which they inserted into the back of the fisherman's bare upper body in such a way that it caught a large piece of his flesh, from which the end of the hook emerged. There was a rope on the hook, which they tied to the lever of the gallows and then pulled the miserable man hanging by it to the top. They let him dangle there for a quarter of an hour or more till he was on the verge of unconsciousness. Then they wound him down again, tore out the hook from his body, bandaged him and let him go. When I saw this cruel spectacle and saw the cheerfulness of this man, how he came almost dancing for this torture, and how he was bent by the hook when he was pulled up, I was overcome with such horror that I thought I would faint. Therefore, I turned away and hurried home in deep shock with the co-worker who was with me at the time. Oh, what a strong argument I have gained to try with all my strength to help these poor heathens escape the devil's tyranny![244]

In 1727 Dal, Bosse, Pressier and Walther observed various rain ceremonies performed by Tamil adults and children. Since it had not rained for a whole month, the ceremonies were very intense and each lasted several days.[245] Sartorius collected facts for his treatise Abgötterey. Ceremonien und Gebräuche from 'his

---

in Bengal and in the Madras Presidency undertook measures to combat it. See Oddie, Geoffrey A., 1995, *Popular Religion, Elites and Reform: Hook-Swinging and its Prohibition in Colonial India, 1800–1894*, Manohar, New Delhi.

[243] HB 7. Cont., 380.

[244] HB 20. Cont., 457; see also 21. Cont., 747, (translated from German).

[245] The missionaries described how, at one time, the figure of a man, who appeared to be dead, was drawn with sand and mourned. Similarly, how another time a wooden figure was made symbolizing a dead man, which was carried through the city to the accompaniment of drum beats and was finally burnt by a gravedigger. HB 25. Cont., 69f., diary entries for 22 and 28 November 1727.

association with the people of the country' and compiled them according to the model of Johann Spencer's (1630–93) treatise *De legibus Hebræorum ritualibus*.[246]

Although, from the point of view of the mission strategy, the interest of the missionaries in Islam in South India was not as pronounced as the need to understand the religious views of the Hindus, there were still some missionaries who devoted extensive studies to the Muslims and their teachings.[247] Growing European interest in Islam[248] and the scientific developments in Halle[249] had

[246] HB 46. Cont., 1322f. Spencer, Johann, 1732, [...] *De Legibus Hebræorum Ritualibus Earumque Rationibus, Libri Quator: Ad Nuperam Cantabrigiensem. In Qua Liber Quartus. Varia Capita & Dissertationes Aliaque Autoris Supplementa, Accesserre, Accurata, Efformata; Præmittitur Christoph Matthæi Pfaffi [...] Dissertation Præliminaris, Qua De Vita Spenceri, De Libri Pretio & Erroribus Quoque Disseritur, Autoresque, qui contra Spencerum scripsere, Enarrantur.* Tubingæ Sumtibus Johannis Georgi Cottæ.

[247] For the role of Islam in the work of the mission see Liebau, Heike, 1999, 'Der Islam in Südindien im Spiegel der dänisch-halleschen Missionsquellen'; Frenz, Matthias and Hansjürg Descher, 2006, "Das Werk der Bekehrung'—Überlegungen zum Verhältnis von Pietismus, Aufklärung und Mission im frühen 18. Jahrhundert', in Michael Mann (ed.), *Europäische Aufklärung und protestantische Mission in Indien,* 33–56, Draupadi Verlag, Heidelberg.

[248] From the sixteenth century onwards in Europe knowledge about Islam increased and a systematic study of Islam began. Chairs for Arabic were set up in several European universities. In 1705 the Dutch professor for oriental languages in Utrecht, Hadrianus Relandus (1676–1718) published his two-volume work 'De religione Mohammedanica libri duo', which contained a scholarly portrayal of Islam. There was interest both in Islam as a religious dogma (Koran) as well as—in the interests of practical mission—in the manner in which the adherents of the faith conducted their lives. From the point of view of the Europeans this was directed mainly at the Turks and Arabs rather than at the Muslims in India. Cf. for this Hourani, Albert, 1994, *Der Islam im europäischen Denken*, Fischer (S.), Frankfurt am Main.

[249] In 1728 Johann Heinrich Callenberg established the Institutum Judaicum et Muhammedicum in Halle, an 'organized institution for the Jewish mission', which was closely linked with the Mohammedan mission. Callenberg's interest in the Orient was strongly influenced by Salomo Negri who was then teaching in Halle and from whom Callenberg learnt Arabic. Like August Hermann Francke, professor for oriental languages, Callenberg did translations into Arabic and Turkish and wrote polemical texts against Mohammed and the Koran, which were then sent out as propaganda material. Callenberg had direct contact with Christoph Theodosius Walther and with the SPCK. The Institutum Judaicum et Muhammedicum had its own printing press, which was periodically used to its maximum capacity with the production and distribution of Arabic texts. Even after Callenberg's death in July 1760 the work of the institute was carried on by Stephanus Schultz (1714–76), who had worked for Callenberg since 1739. After Schultz's death the importance of the Institutum

made it possible for the missionaries to engage with Islamic tenets and with the Arabic language before their departure for South India.[250] The knowledge they gained through this undoubtedly sharpened their understanding for the problem of Islam, but it was not sufficient for intensive dealings with South Indian Muslims. The missionaries realized that they had to add to this knowledge both in terms of religious ideas as well as with regard to language. The knowledge acquired in Europe about Islam as a faith and the mode of life associated with its adherents could not be applied directly to Indian conditions.[251] Christoph Theodosius Walther engaged intensively with the 'Muslim-Malabarian' language, with which he meant a special form of Tamil that was written in the Arabic script and was mixed with a large percentage of Arabic vocabulary.[252] Benjamin Schultze, Christoph Theodosius Walther and Christian Friedrich Schwartz were those who, with other means and methods, would continue Ziegenbalg's theological-philosophical dealings with South Indian Islam that had been based on direct and close contacts. Benjamin Schultze learnt Hindustani in order to communicate with the local Muslims. His polemical text Refutatio Alcorani, published by the Institutum Judaicum in 1744 with a foreword by Johann Heinrich Callenberg, consists of four sections: about god, about men, about the Prophet and about the differences between Jesus and Mohammed.[253] Walther knew Arabic, and he was sent

---

Judaicum gradually diminished till it was finally closed down in 1792. For the history of the Institutum Judaicum see Aring, *Christen und Juden heute*, 139–54.

[250] HB 8. Cont., 515, Conversation between a Muslim inspector and supervisor of different Muslim priests and B. Ziegenbalg, 1707. For the attitude of the first missionary of the Danish-Halle mission see also Gensichen, Hans-Werner, 1959, 'Bartholomäus Ziegenbalg und der Islam', in Georg Hoffmann and Karl Heinrich Rengstorf (eds.), *Stat crux dum volvitur orbis. Eine Festschrift für Landesbischof D. Hanns Lilje, Abt zu Loccum, zum sechzigsten Geburtstag am 20. August 1959*, 140–46, Lutherisches Verlagshaus, Berlin.

[251] For the development of Muslim religious traditions and communities in colonial South India see for instance: Bayly, *Saints, Goddesses and Kings*, 104–50.

[252] HB 25. Cont., 117, letter from Ch. T. Walther to J.H. Callenberg.

[253] Schultze, *Compendiaria Alcorani Refutatio Indostanice*. The German translation of this work, done by Schultze himself, is in the archives of the Francke Foundations AFSt/M 2 A 5: 21. Schultze based his work on: Maracci, Lodovico, 1698, *Alcorani textus universus: Ex correctionibus Arabum exemplaribus summa fide, atque pulcherrimis characteribus descriptus. Eademque fide, ac pari diligentia ex Arabico idiomate in Latinum*

literature in Arabic and Persian from Germany, which he tried to distribute to the Muslims, but they could not read them. Walther himself wrote polemical tracts against Islam, such as his 'Gespräch eines Muhammedaners mit einem Christen' (Conversation between a Muslim and a Christian),[254] which was written in Tamil in 1727 and published in a German translation in 1732. In 1731 a Muslim merchant wrote a reply to this 'Conversation' after reading and discussing it with the missionaries.[255] The German translation of this reply was published in the Halle Reports in 1736.[256] The low rate of conversion among Muslims, the decline of Islam as a political factor in South India and reduced European interest in Islam led to the fact that the engagement with Islam of the Danish-English-Halle missionaries had diminished by the end of the eighteenth century.

Besides studying local religious beliefs, the missionaries of the Tranquebar Mission considered language-acquisition as a necessary pre-condition for missionary work. The significance of language learning, on the one hand, and the high level of theoretical knowledge of the missionaries in this field, on the other, meant that from the beginning research on language was an important component of their research activities.[257] Although the grammars

---

translatus; Appositis unicuique capiti notis, atque refutatione: His omnibus praemissus est Prodromus Totum priorum Tomum implens, in quo contenta indicantur pagina sequenti, auctore Ludovico Marraccio, Patavii.

[254] HB 29. Cont., 501–24. Arno Lehmann sees this as 'an early sign that the Lutheran missionaries did not overlook the followers of Islam and studied their religion and their books,...', (translated from German). Cf. Lehmann, *Es began in Tranquebar*, 209.

[255] HB 33. Cont., 824.

[256] HB 40. Cont., 531–34. In Walther's 'Conversation...' a Muslim asks a Christian questions and expects a comparison between the principles of both religions. The debate ends with the words of the Muslim: '[...] therefore, I am resolved, in God's name, to give up my superstitions and follow your good teachings, for which I thank you from my heart.'; HB 29. Cont., 524. In the Reply, the Muslim merchant shows that Islam is a 'good and the true religion'; HB 40. Cont., 531. After presenting his point of view on some of the points brought up by Walther (polygamy, five-fold prayer, fasting) he formulated a provocative conclusion stating that the German missionaries probably had doubts about their own religion and were, therefore, in search of the true faith. Why, he asks, would they otherwise be so restless, accept the hardships of mission life and search for religious truth all over the world in books and in many languages? HB 40. Cont., 542f.

[257] For the role of language research done by the missionaries see, among others: Lehmann, 'Halle und die südindische Sprach-und Religionswissenschaft';

and dictionaries written by the missionaries do not always conform to high scientific standards, they contributed to the transmission of knowledge about languages. They also enabled language acquisition by Europeans and contained the first attempts at systematizing and comparing languages.

Bartholomäus Ziegenbalg began with an 'Anweisung zur Erlernung des Tamilischen—in Deutsch' which later became part of his Grammatica Damulica published in 1716. In 1712 Ziegenbalg compiled a dictionary on palm-leaves, which was transferred to paper in 1726. From 1735 onwards it served Sartorius in Madras as a basis for further work, which, in turn, was continued by Geister in Cuddalore. This work was completed in Madras from 1744 onwards by Fabricius. His Tamil-English dictionary was published in 1779; in 1786 an English-Tamil dictionary came out, and in 1787 a bi-lingual grammar in English and Tamil appeared. In addition, Fabricius compiled a Tamil-Latin and a Latin-Tamil dictionary. During his 50–year stay in India he translated a series of Christian texts and hymns into Tamil and continued work on the Bible-translation into Tamil begun by Ziegenbalg and Schultze.[258] The fate of the Tamil-English-Lexicon by Fabricius, published in 1779, can be traced up to the present. After the missionary's death a new edition was brought out in 1809 under the title A Malabar and English Dictionary. A further expansion of this was M. Winslow's A comprehensive Tamil and English dictionary of High and Low Tamil *[...]*, published in 1862. E. Männing's *A dictionary of Tamil and English [...]* published in 1897 was also based on the original Fabricius-dictionary. In 1989 a *Tamil-English dictionary, based on 'Malabar-English dictionary'* (2nd edition, revised and enlarged (Tranquebar), 1910) appeared as a reprint. Even today Winslow's dictionary is considered a standard work.[259]

Lehmann, 'German Tamil Studies'. Lehmann, 1961, 'The German Contribution to Tamil Studies', *Tamil Culture*, Vol. IX (2, Apr.-June): 109–116. A critical overview can be found in Jürgens, Hanco, 2006, 'German Indologists *Avant la Lettre*: Changing Horizons of the Halle Missionaries in Southern India', in Gross et al., *Halle and the Beginning of Protestant Christianity in India*, Vol. III, 1047–89.

[258] For the language research done by Fabricius see, esp. Rajan, Rekha Kamath, 2006, 'Johann Philipp Fabricius and the History of the Tamil Bible', in Gross et al., *Halle and the Beginning of Protestant Christianity in India*, Vol. III, 1299–1308.

[259] Winslow, M., 1996, *Winslow's A Comprehensive Tamil and English Dictionary*, Asian Educational Services, Madras, New Delhi.

The practice of dealing with literary Tamil, begun by Ziegenbalg and continued by Walther and Fabricius, was taken up again in the last phase of the Tranquebar Mission by Cämmerer, but it no longer had the importance that classical language studies had in the first few decades.[260]

Even John, whose name is mainly linked with studies in the natural sciences, was interested in Indian scholarship and its propagation in Germany and Europe. After John's death Johann Christian Christoph Rüdiger (1751–1822), professor at the university in Halle, reported about the usefulness of his correspondence with John in India, which had lasted 36 years. John had sent the scholar Indian books and manuscripts, works of classical Tamil and Sanskrit literature.[261] The missionary also translated works of classical Tamil literature into German[262] and engaged with questions of language development in numerous articles.[263]

The studies by Benjamin Schultze, in particular, contributed to the development of general linguistics in Europe.[264] In contrast to

260 Cämmerer learnt Sanskrit. He translated works of the *tiruvaḷḷuvar* from Tamil. See NHB, preface to 42. St., V; 66. St., 527; Tiruwalluwer, 1803, *Gedichte und Gedenksprüche* (aus der Tamulischen Sprache übers. von August Friedrich Cämmerer), Raw, Nürnberg.

261 NHB 66. St., 525–29.

262 AFSt/M 2 B 7 : 5, translation of the Malabarian book of the morals Atusudi [Atticûti] written by Aweiar [Auvaiyâr] by Christoph samual John, ??. ??. 1789, (cf. NHB 39. St., 263–65); AFSt/M 2 B 7 : 6, translation of the Malabarian book of Morals Mūdurai [Mūturai] written by the famous philosopher Aweiar [Auvaiyār] by Christoph Samuel John, ??. ??. 1789, (cf. NHB 39. St., 267–69); AFSt/M 2 B 7 : 7, translation of the Tamil book Ulagag a Nidi [Ulakanīti] by Ulakanatan by Christoph Samuel John, ??. ??. 1789; AFSt/M 2 B 7 : 8, translation [by Christoph Samuel John] of a small Tamil book of morals called Pottia mālei by Muttu-t Tāntavar, ??. ??. 1789; AFSt/M 2 A 5 : 3, translation of the Malabar book of edification for simple Christians, specially done in three volumes (till p. 20?) by Christoph Samuel John, (cf., NHB 44. St., 741).

263 AFSt/M 2 B 7 : 2, some remarks for correction of spelling and pronunciation of Tamil words in the Mission Reports and in other historical and geographical texts, ??. ??. 1789, (cf. NHB 44. St., 725–33); AFSt/M 2 B 7 : 3a, names commonly used by Tamil Christians and their meaning, by Christoph Samuel John, ??. ??. 1789, (cf. NHB 38. St., 205–10); AFSt/M 2 B 7 : 3b, names that are common among the heathen Tamilians, by Christoph Samuel John, ??. ??. 1789, (cf. NHB 44. St., 733–35).

264 For more details see Liebau, Heike und Kurt Liebau, 2003, 'Der Missionar Benjamin Schultze: Eine Notiz zu seiner Korrespondenz und sein Beitrag zur

his predecessor Ziegenbalg, who studied the literary form of Tamil, Schultze focused on the colloquial language, a method that had consequences for his language studies. Schultze, who had studied European and classical Bible languages before coming to India,[265] learned several Indian languages as a missionary, and this inspired him to compare languages. In the initial years of his work as a translator Schultze completed the translation of the Bible into Tamil, which Ziegenbalg had begun; he wrote numerous Tamil hymns and translated edifying works from German into Tamil. After Schultze shifted to Madras in September 1726, he began to translate a number of Christian texts, including the New Testament and Luther's Small Catechism, into Telugu.[266] In conjunction with these translations Schultze also compiled an English-Telugu-Tamil-Latin dictionary, which was, however, never published.[267] The Grammatica Telugica in Latin, which Benjamin Schultze completed in 1728, also remained unpublished.[268] A work conceived as a bi-lingual Telugu-English textbook[269] appeared in the form of a conversation-book in German and English. It is not merely a language textbook, but it also offers insights into contemporary life

---

Herausbildung der vergleichenden Sprachwissenschaft', in Heike Link and Thomas Müller-Bahlke, *Zeichen und Wunder. Geheimnisse des Schriftenschranks in der Kunst—und Naturalienkammer der Franckeschen Stiftungen*, 94–110, Verlag der Franckeschen Stiftungen, Halle.

[265] At the university in Frankfurt/Oder, where Schultze studied from January 1716 till March 1718, he enrolled for courses in Hebrew, Italian, Spanish, Dutch and English. Syrian was added later. Cf. Liebau, Kurt, 2006, 'Benjamin Schultze—Childhood and Youth' in Gross et al., *Halle and the Beginning of Protestant Christianity in India*, Vol. II, 567–94, here 588.

[266] On Schultze's Telugu-works see Liebau, Heike, 1995, 'German Missionaries as Research Workers in India: Their Diaries as Historical Sources. Benjamin Schultze (1689–1760)—Exception or Norm?' *Studies in History*, 11 (1): 101–118; Satyanarayana, Adapa, 2006, 'The Contribution of Benjamin Schultze to Telugu Language and Learning', in Gross et al., *Halle and the Beginning of Protestant Christianity in India*, Vol. III, 1163–80.

[267] AFSt/H J 66 : 2, Benjamin Schultze: Vocabularium Telugo-Tamulo-Biblicum Novi Testamenti, 1728.

[268] AFSt/H J 66a, Benjamin Schultze: Grammatica Telugica, Madras 1728.

[269] AFSt/H J 69, Benjamin Schultze: Multilingual Conversation Book. 30 dialogues on everyday themes in Madras, Telugu-English. Manuscript, around 1730.

in the city of Madras.[270] Against the wishes of the SPCK, in whose services he was in Madras and who were afraid that he would neglect his missionary duties,[271] Schultze also learnt Hindustani in its South Indian version, the so-called *dakhinī*. His Grammatica Hindostanica, written in 1741 in Madras and published in 1745 in Halle, reflects the Hindustani spoken in the Madras region in the middle of the eighteenth century.[272] Schultze's Hindustani grammar was used in Bengal in the 1760s as a basis for a more developed Hindustani grammar.[273] After returning to Europe in 1743 for reasons of health, Schultze continued his linguistic research and his editorial work in Halle at the Francke Foundations. He devoted himself especially to the publication of his works in Tamil, Hindustani, Telugu, Syrian and English, since his works in Portuguese and Danish had already been published during his initial years as a missionary. For the Telugu publications the Telugu letters for the printing press were made in Halle according to prototypes provided by him.[274] Towards the end of his life Schultze also began to translate the Koran from

[270] Schultze, Benjamin, 1750, *The Large and Renowned Town of the English Nation in the East Indies upon the coast of Coromandel, Madras or Fort St. George, representing the Genius, the Manners, the Carriage, the Behaviour and the very Character of the natives: likewise their trade and house-Keeping, the Product of the country and usefullness of the Gardens, by way of thirty familiar Dialogues, written originally in the Waruga or Gentou Language; but afterwards translated into the English Tongue, for the benefit of some curious readers*, Waisenhaus, Halle; Schultze, Benjamin, 1750, *Die auf der Küste Coromandel in Ost-Indien befindliche große und berühmte Stadt der Englischen Nation Madras oder Fort St. George [...]*, Waisenhaus, Halle. For more details on this work see: Satyanarayana, Adapa, 2010, 'Benjamin Schultze (1689–1760): The Foremost Telugu Linguist', in Liebau et al., *Mission und Forschung*, 239–55; Liebau, 'Alle Dinge, die zu wissen nötig sind.'

[271] SPCK, ME/Cs 3, letter from H. Newman (1670–1743), secretary of the SPCK, to B. Schultze, London, 26 January 1742.

[272] Schultze's grammar is considered the second European grammar of this language after the one written by John Joshua Ketelear (born 1672). See Kelelear, John Joshua, 1743, 'De Lingua Hindustanica', in David Mill (ed.), *Dissertationes selectae: variae S. literarum capita exponentes et illustrantes. 455–88*, Lugduni Batavorum, Wishoff.

[273] The manuscript of this extended work was edited and published in Lahore in 1977 by the Pakistani scholar Abulais Siddiqi under the title 'Hindūstānī grāmar az Benǧamin Šulze' (Urdu).

[274] AFSt/M 3 J 11, accounts from the Cansteinschen Bibelanstalt related to the Mission in India, 1746–1758.

Arabic into Hindustani.[275] Schultze's efforts at comparing languages should be viewed with reference to his role in the early stages of the development of comparative linguistics. Like in other areas of knowledge encyclopedic works were also written in the field of languages, in which material was gathered on many languages of the world. Schultze's collection of translations of the Lord's Prayer and the alphabets of Asian languages,[276] begun in Tranquebar, later became part of the Orientalischer und Occidentalischcer Sprachmeister by Johann Friedrich Fritz (Leipzig 1748).[277] The Sprachmeister later played a significant role in the compilation of the Mithridates by Johann Christoph Adelung,[278] in which information was collated on more than 500 languages. Schultze's comparison of the numerals in Sanskrit and Latin is interesting. It led him to the question about the relationship between the two languages and their connection in terms of the history of languages:

> When, shortly thereafter, I began to learn Kirendum [Sanskrit, H.L.], I found that they had almost pure Latin words in their numerals. The question here is how the Brahmins got these words. Whether they borrowed them from the Portuguese language, which has been around in India for 200 years now, or whether they got them many years ago from the old Romans and from Latin? I cannot come to any conclusion in this matter. But I doubt that the Brahmin language came into being only some 200 years ago and that they only then started counting with foreign words.[279]

[275] RA Miskolark 9d, letter from B. Schultze to a Counsellor of Justice, 23 March, 1759.

[276] AFSt/M 2 B 8, the Lord´s Prayer in different Indian languages, ??. ??. 1730.

[277] Fritz, Johann Friedrich, 1748, *Orientalisch—und Occidentalischer Sprachmeister*, Gessner, Leipzig.

[278] Adelung, Johann Christoph, 1806, *Mithridates oder allgemeine Sprachenkunde mit dem Vater Unser als Sprachprobe in bey nahe fünfhundert Sprachen und Mundarten*, Part I, Vossische Buchhandlung, Berlin. On p. 659f., the author refers to the work done by Benjamin Schultze: 'This man [Benjamin Schultze, H.L.] who knew nothing about the philosophy of language and language criticism, but who possessed a great deal of information about languages, enlarged and improved our knowledge about scripts, arranged the L.P. [Lord's Prayer, H.L.] according to geographical regions, replaced many formulae with better ones and enriched older collections [...]' (translated from German).

[279] HB 21. Cont., 708, (translated from German).

Healing methods and medicines used by Tamilians constantly attracted the attention of the missionaries interested in the natural sciences and medicine. Some missionaries, especially those of the later generation, had a basic knowledge of medical science. Christoph Heinrich Horst had even studied medicine. Apart from missionaries, mission doctors were also sent to India periodically, and they took with them the high standards of Halle medicine and pharmacy in the context of prevailing European standards.[280] The sources provide little information about the dealings of the mission doctors with their Tamilian colleagues. The doctors themselves are scarcely heard in the mission reports. It was rather the missionaries themselves who were interested in local healing methods and who recognized the importance of their local experiences for European medicine. The trained doctors, on the other hand, considered European medicine to be superior and they appeared to reject the idea of learning from their Tamil colleagues. Among the early missionaries it was mainly Gründler who was interested in medical issues. Having arrived in Tranquebar on 20 July 1709, he began to study medical literature in Tamil in February 1712 in order to transfer Tamil knowledge to European doctors.[281] At his request a Brahmin compiled a description of Tamil medical knowledge, in which the foundations and methods of Tamil medical study were also presented. Gründler included this Sciagraphia medica in the Malabarischer Medicus that he compiled.[282] He sent the manuscript in 1712 to Halle, but it was never published.[283]

280 The mission doctors were: Caspar Gottlieb Schlegelmilch (died 1730), Samuel Benjamin Cnoll (1705–67), Johann Gerhard König (1728–85), Johann David Martini (1751–91), Johann Gottfried Klein (1766–1821). See also: Lehmann, 'Hallesche Mediziner und Medizinen am Anfang deutsch-indischer Beziehungen'; Neumann, Josef N., 2006, 'Tamil Medical Science as perceived by the Missionaries of the Danish-Halle Mission in Tranquebar', in Gross et al., *Halle and the beginning of Protestant Christianity in India*, Vol. III, 1135–54; Neumann, 2006, 'Medizinische Forschungen', in Liebau, *Geliebtes Europa//Ostindische Welt*, 180–93.

281 HB 6. Cont., 286.

282 HB 7. Cont., 392, the fifth letter of the *Malabarian Correspondence*. See also Gründler, *Die Malabarische Korrespondenz*, 114.

283 AFSt/M 2 B 11, 'The Malabar Doctor', which gives a brief account of the heathen principles of medicine; of the manner in which they cure the sick and the medicines they use. Collected and translated for the information of doctors in Europe from the medical books of the Malabarians by J[ohann]. E[rnst]. G[ründler].

Whenever local healing methods or the composition of medicines was explained to the missionaries they noted it down and sent the information to Europe. In 1730, for example, they observed a Tamil doctor treating an eye-problem, and he evidently explained the exact formula of his eye-ointment.[284] Generally, the Indians, who often passed on family knowledge to the next generation, did not give out their formulae in order to maintain their monopoly on this knowledge. Europeans could only buy this knowledge, which was often imperative for survival under Indian conditions.

> Samuel, the former servant of Missionary Schwartz, has a prescription against the bite of a cobra and against the bite of rabid dogs etc. with which he had cured many people in the presence of Mr Schwartz. Some of these cures caused quite a sensation and brought him great fame. [...] He maintained a great deal of secrecy about the prescriptions till the Madras government requested Mr Schwartz to send this man to Madras in order to discover this secret so necessary for the public good, and for which he would be suitably rewarded. This happened, and I met him three years ago on the way back from Madras, where he was going, and where he received 200 star-pagodas for disclosing his formula.[285]

Local doctors were employed as teachers to teach the children about hygiene and to look after their medical problems. Catechists and assistants with medical knowledge and expertise were particularly valued and made a good impression on the people. The junior catechist in Tiruppalatturai, Muttu, was invaluable to the mission because of his knowledge of medicine. The combination of missionary work and the cure of the sick brought the mission high repute and this, in turn, meant that the missionaries held Muttu in high esteem.[286]

[ ], Porayar 1712. For more details see: Neumann, Josef N., 2010, '*Malabarischer Medicus*—eine ethnomedizinisch-historische Quelle des frühen 18. Jahrhunderts', in Liebau et al., *Mission und Forschung,* 195–203.

[284] AFSt/M 1 B 20 : 7, letter from Martin Bosse to Gotthilf August Francke, 24 January 1735. Cf. also HB 30. Cont., 529, diary of the Tranquebar missionaries, 20 February 1730.

[285] NHB 43. St., 649f., letter from Ch. S. John to J.R. Forster, 20 January 1792, (translated from German).

[286] NHB 16. St., 397; 18. St., 675.

The extensive observations of nature by the missionaries were not only a consequence of their personal interest in the flora and fauna of India, but were often a result of communications with European scholars. The latter constantly provided the missionaries with the latest literature in different fields of knowledge and asked concrete questions aimed at improving and developing scholarly knowledge. Ch. T. Walther, for instance, combined his observations of nature in a fascinating way with reflections on language. In a letter dated 22 October 1733 he described the birds of South India, knowing that such descriptions would be interesting for scholars in Europe. Walther not only gave the German and the Tamil name for a bird, he also indicated derivations from and possible similarities with Hebrew, Arabic, Persian and Sanskrit. In addition, he mentioned further literature and earlier mentions of these birds in the mission reports.[287] The number of scientific studies carried out within the mission context increased in the second half of the eighteenth century. The growing trend of collection, systematization and encyclopedic processing of knowledge in the age of Enlightenment was increasingly reflected in the scientific work done by the missionaries and their scientific correspondence. The role of the natural sciences in the Tranquebar Mission could be seen also in the selection of missionaries, among whom there were some who had studied natural sciences. The missionaries Johann Peter Rottler and Christoph Samuel John, who were members, or honorary members, of various European scholarly societies,[288] maintained an intensive scientific

[287] HB 38. Cont., 221–31.

[288] Christoph Samuel John was a member of the following societies: Sacri Romani Imperii Academia Caesareo-Leopoldina Naturae Corisorum (today: Deutsche Akademie der Naturforscher Leopoldina); honorary doctorate on 30 April 1795; Gesellschaft Naturforschender Freunde Berlin; Regensburgische Botanische Gesellschaft; Naturforschende Gesellschaft Jena; Freie Ökonomische Gesellschaft St. Petersburg; Asiatic Society Calcutta; Gesellschaft zur Beförderung Indianischer Kenntnisse und Industrie; Gelehrte Gesellschaft Tranquebar; The United Brothers (an association for the promotion of the study of botany in South India). Johann Peter Rottler was a member of following societies: Sacri Romani Imperii Academia Caesareo-Leopoldina Naturae Corisorum; honorary doctorate on 30 April 1795; Gesellschaft Naturforschender Freunde Berlin; Regensburgische Botanische Gesellschaft; The United Brothers. August Friedrich Cämmerer was a member of the Sacri Romani Imperii Academia Caesareo-Leopoldina Naturae Corisorum, honorary doctorate on 12 February 1803. For more details on the studies of the missionaries

contact with European scholars for many decades. Their collections of the Indian animal and plant world[289] came about with the help, among others, of Johann Reinhold Forster (1729–98), to whom they wrote on 12 January 1792:

> It would be excellent if a scholar or a society were to compile the knowledge gathered so far about East India [...]. Please continue to grant us your valuable written lessons, support us with books on India, with the necessary equipment for preserving and transporting natural history specimens, and you can be assured of our active gratitude.[290]

In a letter to Forster dated 20 January 1792 John gave detailed answers to 18 questions,[291] among others, about characteristics of the behaviour of snakes and the preparation of anti-venoms for snake bites. John did not consider himself to be a natural scientist, but rather as a 'helper of natural scientists', a description that could easily be combined with his job as a missionary.[292] John received a

---

in the natural sciences see Hommel, Karsten, 2006, 'Naturwissenschaftliche Forschungen', in Liebau, *Geliebtes Europa//Ostindische Welt*, 163–179; Hommel, Karsten, 2006, 'Physico-Theology as Mission Strategy: Missionary Christoph Samuel John's (1746–1813) Understanding of Nature', in Gross et al., *Halle and the Beginning of Protestant Christianity in India*, Vol. III, 1115–35; Hommel, Karsten, 2010, "Für solche [Theologen] wolle Gott seine Ost-indische Kirche in Gnaden bewahren!' Physikotheologie und Dänisch-Englisch-Hallesche Mission', in Liebau et al. *Mission und Forschung, 1*81–94.

[289] Research on the scientific collections of the missionaries is still at a nascent stage. Since the scientific correspondence usually took place directly with the scholars, it is not easy to locate. Two well-known collections can be mentioned here: Johann Peter Rottler's collection of herbal plants is in the Haussknecht herbarium of the Friedrich Schiller University in Jena. Fish dissections by Christoph Samuel John are in the collection of the famous ichthyologist Marcus Eliser Bloch (1723–99) and, as part of this collection, they are now in the Berlin Museum for the Natural Sciences. For more information on these collections see: Hoppe, Brigitte, 2010, 'Von der Naturgeschichte zu den Naturwissenschaften—die Dänisch-Halleschen Missionare als Naturforscher in Indien vom 18. bis 19. Jahrhundert', in Liebau, et al., *Mission und Forschung,* 141–66; Landsberg, Hannelore, 2010, 'Eine Fischsammlung aus Tranquebar, die Berliner Gesellschaft Naturforschender Freunde und deren Mitglied Marcus Eliser Bloch', in Liebau et al., *Mission und Forschung,* 167–80; Liebau, *Geliebtes Europa//Ostindische Welt,* 235f.

[290] NHB 43. St., 675, (translated from German).

[291] NHB 43. St., 648–64.

[292] NHB 48. St., 1093.

lot of information and material from South Indians, but there are very few references to these people in the sources, and the references are generally limited to anonymous statements such as: 'according to the information received from Malabarians'. At one place John mentions a 'drawing teacher' who did the drawings of animals and plants, which the missionary sent to Halle along with his own descriptions.[293] Studies by Tamilians were simply translated and found their way into the mission reports, as was the case with the description of the different kinds of cobras. The author of the study, however, was not mentioned by name.[294]

On their journeys into the interior districts the missionaries and South Indian co-workers noted the names of the places that they travelled through. Along with a description of the route and the location, the geographical information also contains references to the size, the social structure, places of interest and other details of each place. In a diary entry for 3 April 1726 Benjamin Schultze described the city of Porto Novo:

> It does not have any walls, but is situated in the middle of many palm-trees. It has a fairly wide radius, making it larger than Cudulur. Cudulur, however, is much larger than Tranquebar. In Porto novo there are six streets going north from the centre and nine from east to west. Half of the inhabitants are Moors and half are heathens. The sovereign, or commandant, is a Brahmin named Wengittareier. He not only rules over Port novo, but his influence also extends to other cities and places.[295]

Benjamin Schultze wrote an extensive geographical-cultural study of Madras,[296] and Johann Zacharias Kiernander penned a description of Madagascar.[297] In the early years of the Tranquebar Mission, in particular, the missionaries drew maps of the mission

293 NHB 43. St., 655.

294 NHB 32. St., 869–873, 36. St., 1368.

295 HB 22. Cont., 798. Diary of B. Schultze under 3 April 1726, (translated from German).

296 Schultze, *The Large and Renowned Town*; Schultze, *Die auf der Küste Coromandel in Ost-Indien befindliche große und berühmte Stadt*.

297 AFSt/M 2 D 35 : 7, report by Johann Zacharias Kiernander about the people of Madgascar and their language, Cuddalore, 31 January 1758.

region[298] or provided outlines for maps, which were prepared in Europe on this basis.[299]

Whereas geographical observations were, in a certain sense, part of the missionary routine, there are hardly any reflections on the history of the mission region in the sources. The one exception is the survey of rulers of the Mughal empire 'Von der Succession in dem großen Mogulschen Reiche [...]', written by Benjamin Schultze and revised by Christoph Theodosius Walther.[300] Apart from this, the reports, letters and diary entries contain a wealth of facts about historical events and developments, which served contemporary scholars as historical sources.[301]

In addition to observations of the natural world there are also detailed notes on the weather, maintained over long periods of time, in which daily temperatures, wind directions and wind velocity as well as barometric levels are recorded. Detailed weather observations by Johann Ernst Geister are available for the year 1732.[302] The

[298] AFSt/A 45/02/06 (anon.), probably Christian Friedrich Pressier: Plan of the city of Tranquebar, 1729, coloured drawing.

[299] AFSt/M 1 B 13 : 29. This Letter written 24 January 1733 by G.A. Francke to several missionaries contains a reference to a guide for preparing a map with Tamil inscriptions; BFSt: Kt: 256, Plan and View of the Royal Danish Fort and City, Dansburg and Trankenbar, on the Coromandel Coast in East India according to the geometrical draft [...] Coloured engraving by Matthäus Seutter on the basis of the sketch provided by a missionary in Tranquebar. Augsburg, around 1745; BFSt: Kt: 247, Accurate geographical plan of the Royal Danish city and fort Trankenbar or Tarangambadi and Dansburg on the Coromandel Coast in East India along with the places and villages belonging to it [...] Coloured engraving by Matthäus Seutter on the basis of the sketch provided by a missionary in Tranquebar. Augsburg, around 1745.

[300] AFSt/M 2 H 2 : 21, account of the Mughals from "Aureng-Sib", ??. ??. 1727 [Benjamin Schultze]; AFSt/M 2 H 3 : 11, information about the Mughals from "Aurang-Sib" onwards, ??. ??. 1727 [Benjamin Schultze]; HB 27. Cont., 269–73; AFSt/M 1 B 1 : 9, letter from Christoph Theodosius Walther to Johann Heinrich Callenberg, Tranquebar, 30 January 1728, containing a reference to the above texts of Benjamin Schultze.

[301] For instance, Georg Christian Knapp, editor of the NHB, requested Matthias Christian Sprengel to publish a description of the conquest of Seringapatnam in 1799 on the basis of information culled from the mission reports. Cf. NHB, 56. St., appendix to the preface, VII-XII.

[302] AFSt/M 2 B 2 : 2, 'Wind—and weather observations 1732–1737', Madras, 20 October 1732 [sic?]. For the scientific importance of these meteorological observations see: Brentjes, Burchard, 1987, 'Meteorologische Beobachtungen

missionaries in Tranquebar noted their weather observations for the entire month of December 1776.[303] Over a period of almost three years (1789–91) one of the missionaries (name unknown) noted the temperature, the barometric reading and wind direction three times a day.[304] In addition, some missionaries provided a general description of the climatic characteristics of south India in comparison with the climate of Europe and also described storms and natural catastrophes.[305] Astronomical observations and reflections on the Tamil calendar played an important role.[306] The descriptions by Ch. Th. Walther in this area are especially well known.[307]

The secondary use of missionary sources and material collections, or the direct use and application of studies by the missionaries (for example, grammars and dictionaries) often depended on chance. An interesting case is the history of the studies by the missionary Ch. T. Walther on the Tamil calendar, which was based on interviews with two Brahmins who had copied parts of the calendar for him and given their explanations.[308] His treatise on the Indian calendar was published in 1738 in an edition of the works of the Theophil Siegfried Bayer, a member of the St Petersburg Academy of the Sciences.[309]

---

des 18. Jahrhunderts in Madras', in *Burchard Brentjes* and *Hans-Joachim Peuke*, *Wissenschaftsbeziehungen zwischen Halle und Indien in Tradition und Gegenwart*, 27–38, Martin-Luther-Universität Halle-Wittenberg, Halle (Saale) (=WB 1987/44 (I 42).

303 NHB 18. St., 668–70.

304 AFSt/M 2 B 2 : 17, meteorological observations in the year 1791, place not mentioned.

305 AFSt/M 2 E 27 : 8, news about the weather and the storm during the monsoon period 1794, by Christoph Samuel John, Tranquebar, 18 January 1795; Cf. also NHB 48. St., 1089–99.

306 AFSt/M 2 B 2 : 19 (anon.), some remarks and reflections on the Malabarian calendar, 30 December 1727; AFSt/P TAM 79 (anon.): 'Der Malabaren Sternkundigkeit und 12 Himmelszeichen'. Tranquebar 1719–28 (Palm leaf manuscript). The astronomy consists of nine planets, twelve zodiacs and twenty-seven constellations, probably sent to Halle in 1727 by the Tranquebar missionaries.

307 AFSt/M 1 B 3 : 21, letter from Christoph Theodosius Walther, Christian Friedrich Lange and Martin Bosse to Johann Joachim Lange, 8 October 1726.

308 HB 25. Cont., 113, letter from Walther to Prof. Lange in Halle.

309 Bayer, *Historia regni graecorum bactriani*. Bayer's unpublished papers contain letters from other missionaries of the Tranquebar mission. Cf. Glasgow University Library Special Collection, Manuscript Documents, Reference Code: GB 247.

FORMS AND METHODS OF INTERCULTURAL KNOWLEDGE

As a result of the daily communication between missionaries and South Indian co-workers and informants and of the continuous intellectual exchange various practices of knowledge-transfer were institutionalized.[310] For the Tranquebar missionaries, almost all of who had completed their university studies, the study of literature as a means to gain knowledge was an obvious tool. In order to study, translate and evaluate religious and philosophical literature they not only required an excellent knowledge of language, but also an extensive knowledge of the country. The missionaries carefully registered and evaluated the scientific literature on India that was available in Europe in the eighteenth century. Among other books, the mission library in Tranquebar contained 'a scientifically reliable history of Christianity in India' written by Mathurin Veyssière la Croze (1661–1739), the court librarian in Berlin.[311] In 1710 the missionaries asked for a copy of the Asia-volume from the four-volume geography of the earth by the Frenchman Jean Baptiste Tavernier (1605–1689).[312]The missionaries derived their knowledge of Tamil philosophy and Hindu teachings from a study of classical literature, especially in Tamil, but also in Sanskrit. Learned local individuals usually assisted the missionaries in their study of Tamil literature. Ziegenbalg appointed a poet and several writers to help him in the reading of classical Tamil literature. The poet introduced him to the relevant background of the literary material and familiarized him with the author. A *kaṇakkappiṭṭai* had to note down new words and phrases, and the poet explained these to the missionary. In 1708 Ziegenbalg began to translate the Tamil book of morals, *ulakaniti*

[310] While talking about the manner in which Ziegenbalg propagated Christianity to Hindus and Muslims in his dealings with them, Fenger mentions travel, correspondence and conversations as the most important forms. Fenger, *Geschichte der Tranquebarschen Mission*, 46, 65.

[311] La Croze, M.V. 1727, *Abbildung der Indianischen Christen-Staats.* [...] Translated and with comments by M. Georg Christian Bohnstedt. Spörl, Halle. Cf. Gensichen: *Invitatio ad Fraternitatem* 7, 28. Gensichen refers to AB 289, letter from Ziegenbalg and Gründler to Francke, 9 September 1713.

[312] HB 2. Cont., 91, excerpt of a letter from Gründler, Tranquebar, 6 January 1710.

into German with the help of the young poet Christian Friedrich (ca.1685–after 1740.)[313] In the foreword Ziegenbalg describes the services rendered by the Tamilian: 'To the best of my knowledge I have translated all the Malabarian words very accurately into my mother-tongue, and for almost each rule I have written a short explanation that was given to me by the young Malabar poet who was working for me then.'[314]

In the eighteenth century, which is considered the epistolary century, correspondence, both in the private as well as in the professional sphere, was the most important means of communication and information for the Protestant missionaries. It also represented an important instrument for their personal edification and self-reflection. Besides their private and their official correspondence, many missionaries maintained a scientific correspondence with European and Indian scholars. In the 1730s there was a lively, hitherto unexamined, correspondence between the missionaries in Tranquebar, especially Ch. T. Walther, and the professor of the Petersburg Academy, Theophil Bayer. Bayer sent them numerous scientific questions to which the missionaries replied as extensively as possible. These concerned problems from varying fields, such as botany, zoology, geography or music.[315] For his part, Bayer offered the missionaries help in preparing maps.[316] The missionaries with the most extensive contacts were those interested in the natural sciences, John and Rottler. John carried on a correspondence with scholars like Johann Reinhold Forster, Matthias Christian Sprengel (1746–1803), Johann Christian Daniel von Schreber (1739–1810) and Johann Christian Christoph Rüdiger.[317] Through their extensive correspondence with European scientists, clergymen and travelers in India the missionaries systematically gathered

[313] For Christian Friedrich (or Kanapati Vattiyar) see: Young, Richard Fox and Daniel Jeyaraj, 2006, 'Singer of the 'Souvereign Lord': Hindu Pietism and Christian Bhakti in the conversion of Kanapati Vattiyar, a Tamil 'Poet'', in Gross et al., *Halle and the Beginning of Protestant Christianity in India*, Vol. II, 951–72.

[314] KB Oriental Department. Cod Tamul 5 'Ulaga Nidi oder weltliche Gerechtigkeit'. Ziegenbalg's translation of 3 September 1708, (translated from German).

[315] HB 31. Cont., 731–75, letter from the missionaries to Th. Bayer, 15 October 1730.

[316] HB 42. Cont., 799–804, letter from the missionaries, 30 December 1735.

[317] NHB 66. St., 525. For Ch. S. John's correspondence see also: Hommel, Karsten, 'Wissenschaftliche Forschungen', 168.

knowledge, remained in touch with scientific developments in Europe and could request their correspondents in Europe to send them new materials, instruments and literature. In order to carry out his scientific dissections and for teaching science John asked for the following equipment from Europe in 1784: a large globe, a telescope, a hand-held microscope, an air-pump, an 'electrical machine' and a thermometer.[318]

The Tranquebar missionaries maintained contact with different scholarly societies in Europe and in the European colonies. Thus, in 1778, they were asked to become members of the scholarly society established in Batavia and to participate in the scientific competitions initiated by the society. From this point of time onwards an exchange of information and literature took place. The society even gave financial support for the research undertaken by the mission.[319] The missionaries were also in contact with the Asiatic Society of Bengal, established in 1784 in Calcutta by William Jones (1746–94), which promoted the development of Indian studies. The missionaries regularly received the journal, *Asiatick Researches*, published by this society in Calcutta.[320]

Correspondence between the missionaries and Indian scholars, practiced especially in the early years of the Tranquebar Mission, was a method of gaining or exchanging information. In a letter written in Tamil on August 1, 1712 the missionaries turned to some Brahmins who had extensive knowledge of the religious texts, laws and traditions of the Hindus. By sending these Hindu scholars a list of questions they invited them to an exchange of ideas. The missionaries also announced that they would send the contents of this correspondence to their superiors in Europe.[321] The most well known correspondence, unique with respect to its contents and extent, is the exchange of letters that took place under the name *Malabarische Korrespondenz* from 1714 to 1717 between Johann Ernst Gründler and Bartholomäus Ziegenbalg, on the one hand, and Aleppa, the former chief interpreter of the Danish East India

[318] RA Miskolark 9g, *Pro Memoria* for new missionaries by Ch. S. John and [J.P. Rottler], Tranquebar, 20 January 1784.

[319] NHB 26. St., 131, 13 October 1780.

[320] NHB 43. St., 652, letter from John to Forster, 27 December 1794.

[321] HB 6. Cont., 315.

Company, on the other.[322] Aleppa, who compiled the 99 replies from South Indian interlocutors, used his contacts and association with Brahmins and then processed their opinions and information.[323] The later missionaries did not continue this kind of correspondence. In 1732 already, the missionaries explained how their interests and methods had changed. The correspondence with the 'heathens', which meanwhile only concerned non-essential matters, had been important in the early phase of the mission, they said, because the first missionaries had to understand the nature of 'heathenism' in order to carry out their work. The time had come, they felt, where it was more useful to correspond with Christian churches in the English and Dutch colonies. This correspondence, however, essentially served as an exchange of experiences and a sharing of literature.[324] At various times correspondence with members of the local population was taken up again, but these letters were generally not translated and published, or they were never sent to Europe in the first place. In 1738 Sartorius reported that he had initiated a correspondence with a Brahmin, which, however, broke off, since the mediator, who had established the connection, landed in legal difficulties.[325] In the second half of the eighteenth century the correspondence with Indians was increasingly replaced by the scientific exchange with European scholars.

Besides correspondence, debates represented an important means of gaining and exchanging knowledge. The contents of these (often) public debates concerned religious issues as well as moral or philosophical questions. Such debates sometimes came about by chance in missionary interactions with the local population. At other times they were prepared in advance and carried out in a public place in front of the townspeople. Members of the

[322] On the Malabarian Correspondence see: Duverdier, Gerald, 1977, 'Die 'Malabarische Correspondentz' und A.H. Francke', in Rosemarie Ahrbeck und Burchard Thaler (eds.), *August Hermann Francke 1663–1727*, 108–21, Halle (=WB 1977/37 (A 39); Gründler, *Die Malabarische Korrespondenz*.

[323] G. Duverdier calls this work a unique source on South India and regrets that correspondence of this kind was later neglected in favour of journeys by the missionaries into the interior districts of the country. Duverdier, 'Die 'Malabarische Correspondentz'', 109f.

[324] HB 33. Cont., 912f.

[325] HB 46. Cont., 1323, letter from Sartorius to G.A. Francke, 3 February 1738.

Tranquebar Mission, both Europeans and Tamils, engaged in verbal duels with scholarly Hindus, Muslims, or even employees of Catholic missions. The missionaries instructed their writers to record the conversations with the local population or with visitors to the mission institutions in the form of dialogues. Thus, there arose, among others, the eighteen conversations that Ziegenbalg sent to the Danish royal family during his trip to Europe. The themes of these conversations and debates were: causes of poverty among the people; the concept of god in the different religions; the role of women in Islam, Hinduism and Christianity; Tamil literature; religious customs; the role of caste in Indian society.[326] There are detailed reports about regular conversations between the catechist Rajanayakkan and Muslim spiritual leaders. 'In the presence of many Muslims'[327] public debates were held about the Koran and the New Testament. In their discussions with Muslims and others the catechists also used the earlier mentioned 'Gespräch zwischen einem Muhammedaner und einem Christen' by Walther, or they distributed copies of the same.[328] The replies given by the local people do not always reflect the desired curiosity and gratitude for the information given. On the contrary, they often countered the statements of the Europeans regarding the truth and the superiority of Christianity with critical remarks, and often accused the Europeans of trying to impose a foreign religion on them. In some cases, a debate led to a kind of public competition in which, according to the course of the debate, one or the other side declared themselves victorious.[329] On such occasions the missionaries and their Tamil employees profited from the rhetorical training they had undergone during their university studies, or, in the case of the latter group, while studying to become catechists in India. The portrayal of knowledge in the form of arguments and counter-arguments, partly in a bombastic, ornamental Baroque-style, was very popular with the European reading public till late in the eighteenth century, but in the context of the Tranquebar Mission it was more characteristic for the first decades.

[326] HB 9. Cont., 662–808.

[327] HB 52. Cont., 628, report of October 1740.

[328] HB 74. Cont., 222f.; 78. Cont., 914; 79. Cont., 1064.

[329] HB 64. Cont., 636.

Sometimes the missionaries required specialized knowledge, often available to people who were not Christians, or who did not want to work in the context of the mission. In such cases the missionaries looked for people willing to carry out a commission against payment, or someone who could be employed for the limited period of the project. When Ziegenbalg needed someone to make drawings of the gods for his book Genealogie der malabarischen Götter, there was a long drawn-out search and protracted negotiations till someone was found who was willing to do this work anonymously.[330] When European correspondents asked for a description of the geographical, economic and social conditions of the Thanjavur kingdom, which European missionaries were not allowed to enter, they sent two non-Christian employees of the mission, Canneiro and Tschareiappen, into this region in 1712 with detailed instructions. On the basis of the questions and criteria laid down in these instructions the two men were asked to provide a written account of their observations.[331] On the basis of the 26 letters that Ziegenbalg and Gründler received from their two co-workers they compiled the Kurtze Nachricht von dem Tanjourischen Lande auff der Küste Coromandel in Ostindien.[332] Benjamin Schultze employed a Muslim on a part-time basis in order to carry out translations into *hindustānī/dakhinī*.[333] The Muslims were more than willing to teach the Christian missionaries the basics of their language, but it was far more difficult to find a Muslim who was willing to help in writing a critique of the Koran. This is what Benjamin Schultze discovered in 1740 while writing his book Refutation Alcorani[334] in Hindustani. While the assistant willingly wrote the first chapters of the book containing a description of the Christian faith, the following occurred during the writing of the fourth chapter:

> [...] however, when I reached the fourth chapter and he had to write this and that about Mohamed, he became so subdued, dismayed and

[330] Cf. Jeyaraj, *Inkulturation in Tranquebar*, 121, footnote 432.

[331] AB 262, letter from Ziegenbalg, Gründler and Jordan, 22 October 1712.

[332] AFSt/M 1 C 4 : 11, letter from Bartholomäus Ziegenbalg and Johann Ernst Gründler to [unknown], Tranquebar, 17 September 1712.

[333] HB 28. Cont., 398f., diary of Benjamin Schultze, 3 October 1729.

[334] Schultze, *Compendiaria Alcorani Refutatio Indostanice*.

> dejected that he could hardly speak, and he broke out in a cold sweat. I urged him not to lose courage since I was not rebuking Mohamed but only dictating the absolute truth, which comes from God and is universally valid.[335]

In the 1730s the missionaries Bosse, Walther, Sartorius and Pressier found a Brahmin named Krishna to translate the *āyurveda*. However, he maintained his traditional obligations and was only willing to do an oral translation with detailed explanations of difficult concepts and refused to be part of any written exposition.[336]

Some missionaries worked with local people on a regular basis in order to pursue their scientific interests alongside their missionary work. Ziegenbalg generally had several Tamilians around him who assisted him as interpreters, translators, language experts, or also as experts for the customs and manners of the country, for Tamil literature, philosophy and religion. Writers recorded the conversations, made lists of new words and phrases or wrote books and treatises that Ziegenbalg dictated to them.[337] In this way Ziegenbalg was able to carry out his methodically exacting and effective study of language and literature and also combine this with observations on the country and its culture.

In his initial years in Tranquebar Schultze worked with the teacher Peter Maleiappen (ca. 1700–30) who had also been a pupil of the Mission.[338] During his time in Tranquebar Schultze had also taken up a study of Sanskrit with the help of an unnamed Brahmin, but he discontinued this study after the death of his teacher in

[335] AFSt/M 2 A 5 : 21, (translated from German).

[336] The Brahmins committed the *veda* to memory and recited them. The Brahmin offered his translation in this form. HB 45. Cont., 1182–1286. Cf. also Jeyaraj, *Inkulturation in Tranquebar*, 127f.

[337] Ziegenbalg had Catholic books in Tamil read out to him and dictated the changes and revisions he wanted (cf. AB 171). When W. Caland published the *Malabarisches Heidentum*, he was astonished to see that the German manuscript had an inordinate number of grammatical mistakes and he came to the following conclusion: 'The whole thing gives the impression of having been written by someone who was not a German.' This unknown writer was probably Aleppa. See: preface to Caland, *Ziegenbalgs Malabarisches Heidenthum*; See also Jeyaraj, *A German Exploration of Indian Society.*

[338] For more on Peter Maleiappen and his importance for the Danish-Halle Mission see: Liebau, 'Die ersten Tamilen aus Tranquebar in Europa'.

1725.[339] Similarly, a Brahmin taught Schultze Telugu after the missionary settled in Madras in September 1726.[340] With his help Schultze translated a number of Christian texts till 1732 including the New Testament and Luther's Small Catechism.[341] The last missionary, August Friedrich Cämmerer, learnt Sanskrit for many years with the help of a Brahmin. A relationship of trust had developed between Cämmerer and this Brahmin, and the latter was thus willing to have long discussions with the missionary on local customs and traditions.[342] The research undertaken by the missionaries not only took up a lot of time, but it was also expensive. In the 1780s Christoph Samuel John asked for large amounts of money several times in order to carry out his research alongside his missionary work.[343] As a rule, such requests were granted since European interest in the authentic knowledge provided by the missionaries was constantly on the increase, and this also led to a greater tolerance towards the non-religious 'digressions' of the missionaries.

In their search for suitable informants the missionaries often encountered educated South Indian individuals who were also interested in a scientific exchange with Europeans. Ziegenbalg's first Tamil teacher, who was poor 'but came from a princely family', learnt

[339] This Brahmin translated the Small Catechism from Tamil into Sanskrit. Cf. AFSt/M 1 B 2 : 7, Diary and account of the taking over of the paper mill by the mission, written by Benjamin Schultze, 1 January 1725 (to 30 June 1725), here diary entry for 13 February 1725. I am grateful to Heike Link for the reference that Catalogue B (1741) of the Art and Natural History Cabinet of the Francke Foundations contains a remark about a later Sanskrit-text by Schultze that has not been handed down: 'Ein auf Palm=Blätter geschriebenes Buch, so von H. Missionario Schultzen zu Madras in Indien anno 1737 geschrieben worden. Es ist ein Lehrbuch der Granthamischen Sprache.' This is probably a copy of the Sanskrit text-book, which Gottlieb Siegfried Bayer (1694–1738) sent to Schultze for his Sanskrit studies from St. Petersburg. Cf. HB 48. Cont., 1628f.

[340] HB 25. Cont., 77, diary of B. Schultze, entry for 2 January 1727.

[341] The joint diary of the Madras station notes for 25 March 1733 that the Brahmin who 'wrote the Warduga [Telugu, H.L.] Bible translation' had been re-employed to revise this work. HB 37. Cont., 177. The work of the Brahmin, Ananda Rayer, who was also involved in a later translation of the Bible into Telugu, was appreciated even beyond Tranquebar. NHB 67. St., 621f.

[342] NHB 52. St., 353.

[343] RA Miskolark 9g, some suggestions regarding the Mission by Ch. S. John, Tranquebar, 20 February 1784; RA Miskolark 9g, *Pro Memoria* for new missionaries by Ch. S. John, Tranquebar, 27 October 1794.

German from the missionary.[344] In the *Malabarische Korrespondenz* a Brahmin offered to explain the 'Takkacastiram' orally and to discuss its contents. It would be very difficult to translate into Tamil, he stated, and, therefore, it could not be sent in a written form as desired by the missionaries.[345] Sartorius, who enthusiastically noted the interest of educated Indians in scientific exchange, regretted that he could not offer the Brahmin the desired setting for such discussions:

> [...] if my financial means had allowed it, I would have built a small hall or a shed in a garden outside the city where I could sometimes go in the evenings, so that the heathens, who lay a lot of store by ceremonial purity and [...] do not like to enter European houses, would have less inhibitions about coming to me for discussions, which several of them want to do.[346]

Some Tamils, educated and brought up by the mission, devoted their adult lives to spreading European knowledge in South India, or to the synthesis of European and South Indian elements in the arts and sciences. Serfoji II developed a marked interest in European literature, art and the natural sciences. European subjects and methods of teaching were included in the curriculum of the public schools that he set up and funded. Especially in the area of medicine Serfoji tried to combine European and Indian teaching methods. Vedanayakam Sastri (1774–1864), who, like Serfoji, was brought up and educated by Christian Friedrich Schwartz, was the first well-known Protestant poet in Tamil. He taught astronomy and mathematics in the mission school in Thanjavur. In addition to this, he processed information about the natural sciences in a typical Tamil poetic form.[347]

The missionaries used every opportunity they had to observe their surroundings and to talk to interesting and extraordinary

[344] AB 34, letter from B. Ziegenbalg, 5 September 1706.

[345] HB 7. Cont., 392. The Malabarian Correspondence, Fifth letter. See also: Gründler, *Die Malabarische Korrespondenz*, 114.

[346] HB 46. Cont., 1323, letter from Sartorius to G.A. Francke, 3 February 1738, (translated from German).

[347] Indira Peterson has made a significant contribution to the study of the effects of missionary learning on Indian society through her research on the work of Serfoji and Vedanayakam Sastriyar. Cf. Peterson, 'Science in the Tranquebar Mission Curriculum'; Peterson, 'Tanjore, Tranquebar and Halle'.

persons. A Tamilian, who had returned to India after learning the art of paper-making in China and who lived near Tranquebar, allowed the missionaries to observe his work.[348] They attached special importance to information provided by travelers and to eyewitness accounts about conditions in other parts of the country or elsewhere. To this end they established contact with the crews of ships that docked and asked them questions about conditions in their port of origin.[349] Christoph Samuel John observed a Malaysian who distracted a snake with some garlic.[350] Jacob Klein was allowed to watch a priest interpreting signs during the *Pongal* festival.[351] This festival was celebrated for three days during the solstice, when the sun returns to its northern orbit. In Hindu belief this moment is preceded by an unlucky month and followed by a lucky one.[352] In his extensive descriptions of exotic plants, which he studied at the request of a European professor of medicine, Walther referred to his own observations as well as to what others told him.[353]

In their efforts to provide the missionaries with information that the latter required for their research, analyses and reports the South Indian assistants could fall back on existing contacts and networks. When, for instance, Bartholomäus Ziegenbalg sent some writers to buy literature from Brahmin widows, he remarked: 'However, to get these [the books, H.L.] I had to send my Malabarian writers on long journeys into the interior. They located such books in the possession of Brahmin widows and bought these from them for a small sum of money.'[354]

The Mission also began to establish an information network of its own. Catechists and teachers living in the villages were expected to give regular reports about the situation of the local Christians and other events of village life. These reports were usually written on palm leaves, excerpts of which were translated by the missionaries

[348] AFSt/M 1 C 4 : 13, letter from Bartholomäus Ziegenbalg, Johann Ernst Gründler and Polycarp Jordan to Anton Wilhelm Boehme, Tranquebar, 20 September 1712.

[349] HB 25. Cont., 23f., news about Aceh ('Adschin') from the crew of the ship 'Gülden=Löwe', diary entry for 29 March 1727.

[350] NHB 43. St., 649.

[351] NHB 18. St., 675–78.

[352] Dubois, *Hindu manners, customs and ceremonies*, 572.

[353] HB 29. Cont., 444–54.

[354] AB 77, letter from Ziegenbalg to J.F. Lütkens in Copenhagen, 22 August 1708, (translated from German).

and published in the mission reports as proof of successful co-operation and of the abilities of the South Indian co-workers. On 25 July 1728 the newly baptized Rajappen sent a report about Hindu rituals.[355] On a journey with Walther Peter Maleiappen reported on conversations between local people.[356] Rajanayakkan sent information about various practices in the Catholic mission.[357] How well the contacts of the Mission functioned became evident when the missionaries in Tranquebar asked Schultze in Madras to write a 'history of the Moghuls'. Schultze asked an Armenian for help, who, in turn, mobilized a correspondent in Arcot (Arkaru). The correspondent wrote the required report in Persian, the Armenian translated it into Portuguese, and Schultze translated the Portuguese report into German.[358] Through their work in the field of education the missionaries came into contact with people of diverse regional, social, religious and professional backgrounds who were often asked by the missionaries for their help. John, who also had children of seamen in his school, constantly asked the latter for reports about and objects from the places they travelled to. He also had several 'collectors' on the coast and in the interior who gathered natural specimens for him, which John then wrote an explanation for and prepared for transport to Europe.[359]

As a rule, the informants and language teachers of the missionaries did not process their own scientific ideas. Apart from a few exceptions, independent translations, creative works or theological treatises by them are not known to exist. However, their contribution in assisting Europeans is greater that had been assumed so far, if, in fact, it has been assumed at all that the Europeans received help from local learned men.

On the one hand, the missionaries themselves found it important to be considered the authors of the works and, on the other hand, reports about active co-operation with the Indians and their contribution to a translation were often not found worthy of mention

355 HB 26. Cont., 55–57.

356 HB 26. Cont., 91.

357 HB 26. Cont., 146.

358 HB 27. Cont., 261, 269–73.

359 NHB 48. St., 1093. In this letter John mentioned correspondence with parents of the mission pupils in Madras, Coringa, Bengal, Sumatra, Malacca, Batavia, Ceylon, Cochin and Tuticorin.

when the work was being published. Thus, the entry in Schultze's diary that Peter Maleiappen had completed the translation of the Book of Communion[360] did not appear in the published version of this diary, which does not contain any entry for this date.[361] Malaiappen's share in Schultze's translations, which he corrected, was very high. This fact emerges from some statements concerning the method of co-operation: 'I sat down with a kanakappel, or a writer, placed the original Hebrew version in front of me and also took the help of all available versions along with other useful resources and began to translate the Book of Ruth in God's name.'[362] The description of the manner in which they co-operated shows that Malaiappen must have had an excellent knowledge of German and of the Bible.[363] He would have been able to consolidate his knowledge of German when, in his function as Ziegenbalg's Tamil teacher, he accompanied the latter on his journey to Denmark, Germany and England from October 1714 till September 1716.[364] Maleiappen worked for several years with Schultze and, apart from Bible texts, he also translated Christopher Wilken's Communion-Book.[365]

The efforts of many missionaries of the Danish-English-Halle Mission to gain knowledge of the country and their scientific research in diverse fields presupposed an intensive engagement with the local society. In many cases this also led—beyond recognition of the local achievements—to a critical view of their own civilization. The ambivalent attitude of Europeans to Asia, remarked on by Reinhard Wendt, which oscillated between contempt, on the one hand, and the notion of Asia's equality, or even superiority, on the other, is clearly valid for the Christian missionaries.[366]

360 AFSt/H D 16 a, entry for 14 July 1720.

361 HB 20. Cont. In Schultze's published diary of 1720 the entry for 14 August is missing.

362 HB 20. Cont., 479, 18 March 1723, (translated from German).

363 Liebau, 'Die ersten Tamilen aus der Dänisch-Halleschen Mission in Europa'.

364 Ibid.

365 AFSt/H D 16 a, 1 January 1720–31 December 1721, entry for 14 July 1720. Wilken, Christopher, 1722, *Voerdige Comminicant. Translation from German into Danish by Benjamin Schultze*, Mission Printing Press, Tranquebar; Wilken, Christopher, 1721, *Venerable Communicant (Tamil). Translated by Peter Maleiappen, ed. by Benjamin Schultze*, Mission Printing Press, Tranquebar.

366 Cf. Wendt, 'Allgemeine historische Perspektiven: Grundstrukturen des europäischen Interesses in Asien', 264.

CHAPTER FOUR

Dialogue and Conflict

> It is not possible for a religion with a missionary purpose to remain a corpus alienum, residing in a splendid isolation ... It has to be confronted with the life of the people among whom it is working.[1]

The historical conditions for the rise, the existence and the growth of Christian mission societies were characterized by complex political, economic, social and religious factors in the countries that sent out missionaries as well as in the mission region. On the one hand, the rise of missionary movements in Europe was stimulated by geographical explorations and commercial aspirations as also by a new perspective on hitherto alien parts of the world. On the other hand, political alignments and cultural specificities of the mission region created the decisive conditions for the manner in which Christian missionary activity was received. As actively functioning and negotiating institutions interested in creating favourable conditions for the realization of their plans, the mission societies made every effort to establish and maintain good contacts with the economic, political and religious powers in their region. Their contacts with economic and political institutions determined the legal and material support available to them as well as access to technology and networks. In addition to this, the mission also actively looked for religious and intellectual interactions with other Christian missions, with scientists and scientific societies.

If European Christian missions in India had to deal with different kinds of power structures and come to an arrangement with them,

[1] Tiliander, Bror, 1974, *Christian and Hindu Terminology: A Study in their Mutual Relations with Special Reference to the Tamil Area*, Almquist & Wiksell, Uppsala, 16.

then this also holds particularly true for the local co-workers who found themselves equally obligated to their own cultural background and their new European-influenced Christian identity. Their self-definition as an intermeshing of local and alien religious and social elements determined their actions in the framework of the mission.

A MARGINALIZED SOCIAL GROUP OR A NEW ELITE?

Differing motives and interests among the local population in Southeast India (and, therefore, among the converts and the co-workers of the Mission) led to a differentiated perception of the Tranquebar Mission. The life of the converts was impacted by the competing pulls of family, village community and caste, on the one hand, and the new religious affiliation on the other. Although the converts continued to be integrated in local structures, their link with the Europeans had made them strangers in the eyes of their fellow creatures. At first, the Tranquebar Mission viewed the entire population of a mission region as potential converts but, on the basis of practical experience and an analysis of the social structures, it distinguished between religious and social groups with a high degree of willingness to convert and those that were not open to the new faith. As a result, their religious activities were focused on particular groups of the local society.

EXCLUSION AND ISOLATION

The work of a Christian mission was visible to the local population firstly in the form of direct missionary activity such as divine services, sermons, conversations and interactions in public places and, secondly, through social work in the health and education sectors. In all this it was not the mission society as an official institution, which was perceived as the active agent, but its European and local representatives who were in direct contact with the people. Both in their actual religious work as well as in their social endeavours the mission co-workers were dependent on the interest and participation of the people, and they counted on the curiosity, tolerance and religious interest of their listeners. However, they also took certain material interests and practical needs of the people into account.

In the final analysis every convert had to find his individual method to reconcile Christian teachings with this cultural and social background. Often, a convert confronted this inner conflict through an open and demonstrative public rejection of hitherto accepted religious symbolism, while continuing to maintain elements of his culture and lifestyle privately. By converting he gave up familiar safeguards and ventured into unfamiliar structures, albeit in the hope of a new and, in his concrete situation, more important affiliation. Conversion dislodged hitherto clearly defined religious and social relations, since the original Tamil community of the convert did not offer much space for the new religious identity of one of its members. Many converts linked the change of religion with the hope of a better social position than that of their Hindu family, caste and community members and often developed an attitude of superiority towards those who had remained 'heathens'.[2]

Many South Indians were discouraged from converting by the view commonly held among the people that converts to Christianity broke with social norms and traditions and harmed not only themselves but also their entire family. In the thirteenth letter of the *Malabarische Korrespondenz* the missionaries ask why the local people refuse to convert to Christianity. The reply names, among other things, the cohesiveness of the family and the importance of friends:

> The reasons, however/which stop us/from going over to your Church/ are the following: 1) because we have many friends/who are not inclined to do the same. If we were to take this step alone/we would face life-long persecution/and would not find safety or protection anywhere. 2) Because all of us find it very difficult to abandon/what our parents and forefathers believed in. Everyone would like to respect his parents and forefathers/and tread the same path/that his nation has gone along and still does. 3) Because we have to carry on our trade and earn a living in our nation. 4) Because we are married/ and have a wife and children/who would give us a lot of grief.[3]

[2] The converts often called those who did not convert to Christianity *akkiyāṉi*, the ignorant. HB 106. Cont., 1449.

[3] HB 7. Cont., 415, (translated from German).

If a person decided to convert, he was often tormented by his family and excluded from his profession, so that he was forced to leave his house or his village.[4] Pressure was not only brought to bear on the convert himself, but the measures taken by the families and members of the caste group were often also directed against the missionaries who were considered to be 'equally guilty'. The higher the social standing of the family and caste of the convert, the public protests were greater and more protracted.

In 1762 the missionaries in Tranquebar reported several incidents with members of high castes. When a 'somewhat respectable inhabitant of Tilleiali' came to Tranquebar for baptismal preparation, numerous relatives appeared in the days after his arrival in order to prevail upon the missionaries to convince the perspon to remain a 'heathen'.[5] When a boy from the *kōmaṭṭi* caste wanted to be baptized against his parents' will, his father and other relatives came to lodge an official protest with the mission. They felt that the son's decision was a loss for the family, and they demonstrated great sorrow about a decision they failed to understand.[6]

Isaac's (around 1725–95) relatives carried out a long, consistent and organized struggle for his reconversion. In 1745, at the age of 20, the Tamilian allowed Johann Ernst Geister to prepare him for baptism, and in August of the same year he was baptized by Johann Zacharias Kiernander. From then on he earned his living from this missionary by working as his writer for a monthly wage of 12 *Fanam*. Later, on Kiernander's recommendation, Isaac went to Tranquebar to work as a teacher. His brother, Rangen, with whom Isaac had lived in Cuddalore, then mobilized the relatives and organized an extensive campaign against the missionaries. On

[4] The Christian couple Christian and Teiwaj left their farm in Tennenkudi (probably Tennangudi in the Thanjavur *tālūk*) for some time. Even after influential members of the village had made it feasible for them to return to their farm, they continued to live in uncertainty. As a Christian, and as a worker in the local rest house, Christian remained constantly exposed to hostility. Some members of the village community denied him the share of rice he was entitled to for his work, and guests in the rest house refused to accept water or food from his hands. HB 96. Cont., (238), 1297f.; 97. Cont., (5), 40, 54, 130. Their story was described at length in the mission reports, after which friends of the mission sent donations expressly for the couple. HB 100. Cont., (97).

[5] HB 97. Cont., 45.

[6] Ibid., 55.

30 August 1745 around 300 Hindus gathered in front of the mission house in Cuddalore and demanded that Isaac be given to them. Such demonstrations occurred repeatedly in the following weeks. The action was accompanied by the threat of a public hunger strike in front of the mission building and the announcement that there would be a mass exodus of the community from Cuddalore. When 50 persons demonstrated again on 7 September the pressure on the mission was so great that the governors intervened. In a discussion with the Danish governor in Tranquebar Isaac assured him that his decision to be baptized had been a personal one free of any coercion. Upon hearing this, the English governor in Cuddalore initiated steps against the rebels.[7]

If a relative joined the new faith, the family's displeasure was often expressed through radical measures. The exclusion of a person from a family unit was documented by disinheriting him. Families were, at least temporarily, torn apart by conversion, if the partner was not (immediately) willing to take the same step. Women did not necessarily follow their husbands into the new religion; in fact they often tried to prevent baptism of their children.[8] Sometimes, the displeasure of the relatives or of the village community turned into open aggression. In times of crises, particularly, the anger against Christians was instrumentalized and consciously fanned. Christians were deemed to be the cause of inexplicable natural catastrophes, diseases or epidemics. When an infectious fever claimed many lives in Tranquebar, the people also turned a superstitious eye towards the Christians and declared them to be the cause of the disease.[9] Since the local mission co-workers, especially, were constantly on the move between different places, the local people accused them of spreading diseases in this way.

The local workers of the Tranquebar Mission were often especially exposed to problems when they were appointed in the villages that they came from in the hope that they would be viewed as role

[7] HB 64. Cont., 720–37.

[8] The wife of the *śūdra*, David, refused to become a Christian after he was baptized and, only later, allowed the children to be baptized. HB 90. Cont., 691f; 91. Cont., 770. The wife of the junior catechist Njanapragasam (died 1735) lived apart from her husband for some time after his baptism, and it was only six months later that she also agreed to be baptized. HB 41. Cont., 552f.

[9] HB 61. Cont., 81.

models. In many cases, their relatives had not accepted their decision to convert and, in order to save the family honour, they opposed it in every possible way. Mission employees and their families were thrown out by the people of they village, they were punished with restrictions, threatened and subjected to violent attacks.[10] In June 1739 Aaron reported angrily that on his journey the people had 'contradicted him defiantly with blasphemous talk'.[11] A few years later, in April 1743, when he had been sent to the Mayavaram district, a *maṇiyakāraṉ*, some *kaṇakkappiḷḷai* and *talaiyāri* of the king insulted him and took him prisoner, and he was freed only after local Christians intervened.[12] In 1750 the missionaries reported an incident in which Arulappen (died 1769) helped Parensimuttu's wife during an attack by Hindus.[13]

In order to apply pressure on the mission co-workers, the entire village community sometimes threatened to boycott all professional services and to exclude them from the community. The concerned co-worker was no longer allowed to participate in village ceremonies. In times of trouble he could not expect any help, and he was even denied access to the necessities of life. In end effect this meant that the person was banished from the village, since it was not possible to live there under these conditions. In 1762 the assistant Matthaeus in the Mayavaram district was excluded in this manner from village life: 'They then publicly excluded him from the support of the community in times of joy and sorrow, they did not allow him fire and water, denied him the services of a washer man as well as all neighbourly help, [...]'.[14] Matthaeus approached the members of the village council[15] and suggested that, since a solution did not

[10] When Ziegenbalg was in prison (November 1708–March 1709) Aleppa and his family members were locked up and then driven out of Tranquebar. Cf. Liebau, Kurt, 'Die 'Malabarische Korrespondenz'. Sumitasen, an assistant in Tattenur, was driven from his house and had to temporarily stay in another place. The missionaries intervened in the conflict with the local headman and thus made it possible for the assistant to return. HB 64. Cont., 636–38. A village headman in the Mayavaram district prohibited the assistant from using the village well. HB 64. Cont., 600, 611, 664.

[11] HB 50. Cont., 183.

[12] HB 59. Cont., 1673.

[13] HB 74. Cont., 183.

[14] HB 97. Cont., 38, (translated from German).

[15] The village council consisted of 'some reputable persons of the place from the Suttirer caste'. HB 97. Cont., 40.

seem possible, the Christians of the village could be given a separate place in the village to build their houses and live. Although this was not granted, the protest led to the revocation of reprisals against him.[16] Some people of the village also captured the assistants Ignasi and Canagappen when they wanted to take a group of Hindus to Tranquebar for baptismal preparation.[17]

Mass protests against new converts took place in the first years of the nineteenth century in the Tirunelveli/Palayankottai region. In this case, the Hindus not only resorted to physical violence, they also began a widespread campaign against Christians of various professional groups, and the latter found it difficult to defend themselves against the accusations.[18]

The local authorities, village headmen, Hindu priests and other influential persons regularly asked Christian converts and local mission co-workers to participate in traditional religious ceremonies despite their new faith and their position. Christians who were daily-wagers were ordered by their masters to pull the chariots in processions to mark Hindu ceremonies.[19] The missionaries and local mission workers were displeased about the fact that Christians from the various congregations were often not given a day off from work on Sundays and Christian holidays by their employers to attend divine services.[20]

Hindus in important positions expected gifts as a mark of respect from the district catechists, when they took up their jobs in the district. Thus, Sinappen was punished in December 1763 because he refused to give the local *Nayak* a present.[21] Local authorities had decision-making powers with regard to the purchase of land and the construction of houses, both private houses for the mission employees

[16] HB 97. Cont., 40.

[17] HB 67. Cont.,1142.

[18] NHB 61. St., 46, diary of Ch. W. Gericke, 1801.

[19] HB 97. Cont., 9f.

[20] On a journey in the Mayavaram district during the Easter festival in 1766 the Tamil pastor complained 'that this time very few people had gathered in all the places, and he mentioned the reasons for this that he heard from the Christians: that the pandaram in Pulliruckumwelur, to whom the king had leased out this entire district, drives his people to hard work and does not even let them sleep in their own houses.' (translated from German), HB 105. Cont., 1034f.

[21] HB 100. Cont., 427.

as well as of churches and prayer-houses. Dewasagajam, assistant in Tiruppalatturai, encountered many difficulties while building a new prayer house that was to be built as an extension to his own house. He was able to get the relevant permission only after repeated interventions with the local and the district authorities.[22]

When the Tamil pastor Philipp (ordained in 1772) wanted to settle down in his place of work after the death of his colleague Ambrosius, unforeseen problems arose in the search for a suitable place to build a house. Initially, the choice fell on the village of Tirukkalacheri, since it provided easy access to all the places in the Mayavaram district. Since Tirukkalacheri belonged to the region under the Danish Company, the governor was approached for permission to build a house. He tried to take the reaction of the villagers to this proposed step into account, and the majority was against the presence of a Tamil pastor. Therefore, the search for another place began. The mission entered into a compromise with the catechist Arulananden, who was willing to arrange land for Philipp in Nallattukudi if he would also be allowed to live there, and if the mission advanced him money to build his own house. 'Although we would be sorry to see him go, since he carries out his duties as inspector of the external matters of the school very faithfully, we had to agree to his proposal to carry out our plan, since the Indian pastor would encounter numerous difficulties if he were not there.'[23] Here too, the people were hostile; there were violent protests, and the house was built only after a payment of five Reichstaler.[24]

For Brahmins and *paṇṭāram*, the non-Brahmin priests, Christian missionaries were adherents of an alien faith and, since they wanted to convert people to this faith, they were, *a priori*, religious opponents. In many cases, however, there was communication between Hindu and Christian priests. This is because individual social positions were clearly marked, because both sides viewed public religious debates as a challenge and because knowledge about the 'Other' could be

[22] NHB 32. St., 861ff., report from J. Klein 1785.

[23] AFSt/M 2 E 37 : 3, Supplement to the diaries of 1777. About the country pastor Philipp's intended stay in the countryside by Johann Balthasar Kohlhoff, Daniel Zeglin, Johann Friedrich König, Christoph Samuel John, Johann Wilhelm Gerlach, Johann Peter Rottler, ??. ??. 1777.

[24] Ibid.

used as an argument against the 'Other' in daily encounters. Local mission employees, Indian pastors and catechists actively sought out discussions with Brahmins and *paṇṭāram* in order to demonstrate and prove their own rhetorical abilities to the missionaries. The numerous descriptions of such encounters show that they focused mainly on questions of faith, on moral problems and norms of life or traditions. Although the beliefs of the opposing side were questioned in such conversations, the 'opponent' was important in the attempt to prove one's own worth. Hindu priests considered public religious disputes with Christians legitimate, but the Brahmins and *paṇṭāram* of a region kept a close watch on each other to make sure that none of their own kind converted to Christianity.[25]

TOLERANCE AND INSTRUMENTALIZATION—LOCAL CO-WORKERS AS THE LOCAL AUTHORITY

Despite a certain mutual moral condemnation, the daily social intercourse between Hindus and their Christian relatives, or the inhabitants of the village, was not only marked by rejection and exclusion. Many converts continued to be held in high esteem by the Hindus. Sometimes, Hindus gave a member of the family into the care of the missionaries out of a feeling of gratitude or because of the chances of a good education.[26] Others supported the conversion of a family member to Christianity, or accepted his decision and continued to have dealings with him. Differing religious affiliations did not destroy the unity of these families. During a stay with the missionaries in Cuddalore Aaron visited his Hindu relatives there, who he had not seen for more than 20 years, and he also introduced them to the Christian missionaries.[27] Even as Christian mission workers converts were included in family decisions, they took part in important events and regularly visited their relatives when working in the districts. Hindus who had Christian relatives were often

[25] As a reaction to his conversion, the former *paṇṭāram* Arunasalam (1735–99) received a warning from the collegiums of *paṇṭāram* together with an appeal to find his way back. He was told that through his decision he had exchanged a 'princely life' for that of a *paṟaiyār*. HB 98. Cont., 288f., 297f.

[26] Cf. the example of the Indian pastor Philipp pp. 137, 467f of this study.

[27] HB 57. Cont., 1437.

particularly helpful towards the missionaries or the Tamil members of the mission. During a journey in 1776 the catechists Soedtinaiken (around 1720–80) and Abiseganaden from Tiruchirappalli found a place to stay with the Hindu relatives of a Christian from the local congregation.[28] A Hindu weaver in Manschelpadtei temporarily gave shelter to the assistant Muttu Schawri and a group of Christians who had to leave Thanjavur in 1758 during the French siege of the city.[29] The teacher and catechist in Thanjavur and Tiruchirappalli, the *śūdra* Dewanesen, got help from the Hindu village headman after his wife and children had been attacked by Hindu relatives.[30] Muttai, a Christian woman from a *śūdra* background, was accepted by the local people in Tenkobenur,[31] who also held her in high esteem.[32]

The respect enjoyed by members of the mission, which was, for obvious reasons, often highlighted in the mission reports, was also based, on the one hand, on their influence and contacts. The local mission co-workers demonstrated the authority linked with their positions to their relatives and to the local people, but they also strove to establish a certain intimacy in order to win the trust of the people. For members of the Christian community and for those who wanted to become Christians the South Indian mission employees were people who were in constant touch with the European missionaries. On the other hand, the mission took care of provisions in times of scarcity on account of droughts and wars. In March 1790, Jacob Klein travelled from Tranquebar to Lalgudi with the catechist Njanapiragasam and the inspector of the charity school, Schinappen. Aside from the propagation of the gospel, the purpose of the journey was to acquire *nellu*, in case, as was feared, a war broke out.[33]

Another reason why mission employees were accepted and respected was because they were well educated. Sometimes, the people used the term *nāṭṭaiyar* for the Indian Christian pastors as they did for the Brahmin priests[34] and many local mission workers

[28] NHB 18. St., 683–86.
[29] HB 90. Cont., 686.
[30] HB 101. Cont., 504, report from Rajanayakkan and Dewanesen 1764.
[31] This probably refers to Tenkovanur in the Mannarkudi *tālūk*.
[32] HB 97. Cont., preface, (7); 69, report from Tranquebar 1762.
[33] NHB 41. St., 413–16.
[34] Cf. Paul, *Chosen Vessels*, 12.

were called 'Ñanikal' by the people on the basis of their education, as Christoph Samuel John proudly mentioned in his suggestions for the improvement of the mission.[35]

Indian pastors, catechists, teachers in mission schools and assistants constituted the connection between the missionaries as representatives of European religious communities and the local population. Local mission co-workers not only contributed to the spread of Christian teachings among the 'heathens', but they also looked after the local Christian congregations. Catechists were allowed to punish Christians for disobedience, for moral lapses or for practicing Hindu traditions.[36] The duties of the local mission employees included supervising and, if necessary, bringing back Christians who had left the village as a form of protest, or because of economic necessity, because of the danger of war or for other reasons. The local employees apparently had greater persuasive powers that the European missionaries for this task. Josua, the *śūdra* assistant and junior catechist in the Mahadevpattanam district, travelled with Muttiappen into the Maravar region to look for the Christians who had fled there because of a drastic rise in prices.[37]

If Protestant Christians returned to the Hindu fold or converted to the Catholic faith, it was the duty of the local co-workers to persuade them to re-convert.[38] While this was treated primarily as a religious matter, in which the Protestant missionaries had to negotiate with representatives of the Catholic missions or with Hindu priests, cases of fleeing the village involved the economic and political interests of the local and the colonial authorities. If there was no agricultural and handicraft production in empty villages, it became an existential problem even for the village elders and for the mission stations there. During the social unrest from August to December 1787 Daniel Pullei was the interpreter and mediator between the missionaries and the rebellious inhabitants. The Tranquebar Mission was involved in this unrest because many of the rebels

[35] NHB 30. St., 702.

[36] NHB 53. St., 408.

[37] HB 84. Cont., (302).

[38] NHB 11. St., 1423–28. In 1773 the Tamil pastor Philipp and the catechist Rajappen travelled to many places to win back Christians who had become Hindus again, or who had gone over to the Catholic Church.

belonged to the Christian population of Tranquebar. When they left their homes and went to the territory of the king of Thanjavur, the missionaries had a very pragmatic interest in their return, since most of the Christians were agricultural labourers, without whom it would not have been possible to bring in the harvest.[39]

The local co-workers constantly sought contact with non-Christians, while most of the latter had very little reason to be in touch with the local mission representatives. Exceptions to this were in situations when they looked for help in material difficulties, in cases of illness, in legal matters, or when a family member converted to Christianity. Encounters came about if there were Christian congregations nearby, or if there were Christian schools or hospitals in the vicinity. Interest in Christianity depended on each person's individual situation and personal experiences.[40] The assistants in rural areas, especially, lived at close quarters with the villagers and without the constant presence of a missionary. Although the missionaries regularly visited Christian congregations outside the main stations, the South Indian pastors and co-workers were the actual points of reference for the villagers, especially in remote places. The most impressive example for this is Christian David who, after being educated and trained by the DEHM, worked alone for many years among the people of Jaffna as a representative of an Anglican mission society. He was responsible for recruiting, guiding and supervising local co-workers and teachers. The extent of his responsibility becomes evident when one hears that he had to visit the 47 churches and schools in the districts of Jaffna and Mannar thrice a year.[41]

Tamil mission co-workers were often appointed in their native villages, since the catechists and priests—despite all condemnation and animosity—had easier access to members of their own caste

[39] Liebau, 'Indische Angestellte in der dänischen Kolonialadministration'.

[40] On 8 September 1769 the junior catechist of the Kumbakonam district, Sinappen, a brother of Rajanayakkan, received a request from the village headman, Padtisuram (Pattisvaram) to give medical help to a sick Hindu. NHB 4. St., 446, Tranquebar diary. On 11 October 1769 Sinappen was asked to deliver the eulogy at the funeral ceremony of a *cheṭṭi*. NHB 4. St., 459.

[41] UTC Bangalore, Microfilm collection, SPCK reel 5, letter of 20 March 1802.

and their village community. The pastors Rajappen and Sattianaden recorded a large number of conversions in their native places. This led to the formation of Christian groups, in which earlier shared interests established a strong link between the members.[42]

In the eyes of the members of Christian congregations and for individuals intending to convert, the Indian catechists and pastors represented a new religious authority. The 'national workers' were in regular contact with the mission stations, on whose behalf each one of them worked in a particular position according to the instructions they had received. In the perception of the people around them the local mission co-workers were a quantitatively small elite who had close ties with the local population, but who commanded a much larger action radius through their contacts with Europeans. Although they were closely associated with the European missionaries, the South Indian workers of the Tranquebar Mission continued to be strongly influenced by their regional and social background and carried over a part of their 'Indian' life into their Christian identity. There were no fixed boundaries between contempt for and acceptance of the local mission employees.

As a result of the structures of the Mission Tamil mission employees often performed dual functions in a village congregation. Besides their work within the mission, they were also involved in the work of the local schools, in local courts of law or, if they had knowledge of medicine, they worked as doctors. The existence of schools, hospitals and handicraft workshops run by the mission led not only to an improvement of the social conditions of a place, but also brought the people in constant touch with Christian teachings. Mission schools had the reputation of being good educational institutions and because of this, influential Hindu families also sent their children to these schools and were willing to put up with the intensive propagation of the Christian faith.

As teachers in the mission schools South Indian mission employees influenced events in the place even though they did not receive a collective remuneration from the village community, as was traditionally the case. The local mission schoolteachers received a small salary from the Mission since the majority of the pupils

[42] For group conversions see Grafe, *History of Christianity in India, Vol. IV, Part 2*, 92.

could not pay the fees, but, instead, received provisions, clothing and schoolbooks from the Mission. The mission schools were open to members of different social and religious groups. This often led to conflicts and aggression, which sometimes forced the mission to make compromises. Often, additional teachers had to be appointed in order to conform to certain caste constellations. The Mission was also forced to resort to differentiated offers for vocational training. If a pupil received training in a profession that was pre-determined by his caste affiliation and corresponded to his social position, he had a good foundation for becoming economically independent. The breadth of subjects taught but also the teaching methods, ensured that the schools were widely praised, not only in Christian circles. Especially in the later decades of the eighteenth century, and mainly in the English mission stations, there was an increased interest in these schools among influential Hindus, who hoped that their children would have better prospects if they were educated in a European school.

The reputation that Tamil mission co-workers enjoyed in their local social environment was reason enough for the local authorities to use them for self-seeking considerations. While selecting a supervisor from the group of *dalit*-Christians in Tiruppalatturai in 1744, the mission negotiated with the head of all the 'untouchables' of the place, a Hindu, to come out publicly in support of the selected Christian supervisor in order to strengthen the latter's authority. The Christian, Muttu, who was already a *cērvaikkāraṉ*, a border-guard, was elected by about 40 *paṟaiyār*-families, of whom half were Christians and the other half Hindus.[43] The report about this says:

> It was the same person who, after our advice had been sought, was now chosen by all the people under him. In order to give the matter greater weight, one of the most important heathens of this town, who is the chief of all the Parreier, and who appoints their heads, was asked to confer the requisite authority on this man who had been chosen as the supervisor of our Christians by this caste. He did this in the presence of the other heathen supervisors of such villages, and they too consented to this.[44]

[43] HB 61. Cont., 44.

[44] HB 61. Cont., 177, (translated from German).

In 1767 the *Raja* of Thanjavur appointed Rajanayakkan as the 'head of the untouchables' and hoped that this would put a stop to the constant conflicts between the *paṟaiyār* of the 'right hand' and those of the 'left hand'.[45] Rajanayakkan, however, viewed this appointment as an instrumentalization of his person and shortly thereafter—officially for reasons of security—he left Thanjavur and went to Tranquebar.[46]

When problems arose between the people and the local Hindu authorities, the well-known mediating skills of some mission co-workers were in demand. Sattiananden, an assistant in the Mayavaram district, mediated between a border-guard and the inhabitants of a village who had revolted against their local authorities. The border-guard, who had already issued orders for measures to be taken against the rebels, was willing to accept Sattiananden as a mediator and spokesperson.[47] On the other hand, the mission employees used the influence of the non-Christian caste leader, or *maṇiyakāraṉ*, by negotiating with them, or, in some cases, co-operating with them. Thus, they demonstratively strengthened the latter's authority. By doing this they hoped to secure the loyalty, or at least the tolerance, of these influential people.

Even where moral questions were concerned, the people called on the authority of South Indian mission co-workers or of local Christians as 'neutral' figures of respect. There are some cases that bear witness to the respect accorded to a mission co-worker by the people: the *maṇiyakāraṉ* of *paṟaiyār* villages, also of Catholics, on the outskirts of Thanjavur would ask the catechist Rajanayakkan to resolve disputes despite his religious affiliation and his contacts with the European missionaries.[48] The elders of a village, who, for a while, had judicial powers within the village, played an extraordinary role. They often asked mission assistants to mediate in disputes between different groups of people. When a toddy-tapper was to have his hand cut off for indulging in sexual relations with his sister-in-law the first assistant of the *paṇṭārattar*

[45] For more details on the caste question see pp. also pp. 36–38, 131–33, 141–43.
[46] HB 108. Cont., 1681f.
[47] NHB 1. St., 29, 63.
[48] HB 50. Cont., 287; 74. Cont., 181.

(local judge) asked a mission assistant to mediate. The punishment was reduced to a fine.[49]

Sometimes members of local Christian congregations carried out important administrative functions at the local level. Njanamuttu, for example, was a *cērvaikkāraṉ* in Claruwayel (Kilarvayal?)[50] As loyal persons with an authoritative and representative function these Christians were important for the mission because of their elevated status; special care was taken of them, and they were constantly reminded of their Christian responsibilities and their function as role models. In addition, South Indian employees could attain important positions at the local level, particularly in bodies that administrated justice. Since the mission constantly insisted on its own jurisdiction vis-à-vis the colonial authorities, there was always a demand for local individuals who were in a position to resolve civil disputes among mission Christians. Many places also had a so-called 'Black Court' where legal disputes in the local population were settled by Indians, but under European supervision. Mission employees often worked in these courts as representatives of the local population. Aaron (died 1804) and Dewaprien (died 1804), who were elders of the congregation in Tranquebar, also had a seat in the Tamil ('black') court at the end of the eighteenth century.[51] Particularly in times of legal uncertainty mission Christians in this function were very important for the missionaries, since the former could represent their interests in the settlement of disputes. The oldest son-in-law of the *dubash* Daniel Pullei was the defense judge for the Christians in Porayar.[52] Daniel Pullei himself worked in the 'Black Court' in Tranquebar.[53] The missionaries often took recourse to 'their' Christian *dubash* as mediators in legal matters. In a memo sent to the Danish authorities in Tranquebar in November

[49] NHB 34. St., 1131.

[50] HB 61. Cont., 73, diary of the missionaries in Tranquebar, 8 March 1744.

[51] NHB 62. St., 191.

[52] NHB 52. St., 338, excerpt from the diary of the city catechist Schawrirajen, 1796.

[53] AFSt/M 1 K 5 : 16; HB 102. Cont., 672, footnote (**) The explanation given there is: 'The Black Court consists only of Malabarians, or black court members, namely two of our Christians, two papists, two heathens, two Mohammedans and the President, who is a Providiteur or Padtna-Sami (mayor), and where the affairs of the Blacks are decided.' (transated from German); cf. also Ahuja, *Die Erzeugung kolonialer Staatlichkeit*, 58.

1794 the missionaries demanded that in the case of disputes among Christians there should either be a return to the earlier practiced internal jurisdiction of the mission, or that 'an order be given that the investigations and arbitrations be done not by the heathens and dubashes, but by the royal interpreters Daniel Pullei and Pragasa Pillei, who were already confirmed as members of the court, or by the assistant judge, Dewapria Pullei, along with some leaders of the congregation.'[54] Officially, this demand was not acceded to, but, unofficially, many cases were dealt with internally by the mission despite this not being allowed.[55]

DANIEL PULLEI: THE FIRST INTERPRETER OF THE ROYAL GOVERNMENT

Daniel Pullei, who Christoph Samuel John described as one of the 'most capable and successful Tamilians in royal service',[56] was one of those mission pupils who began his life in the framework of the mission and then went on to work for the European trading and colonial powers in India. He was born in 1740 into a poor Christian family that originally belonged to the *vellāla*-castes. Daniel Pullei's grandfather, the blind Johann d'Almeida, had converted from Catholicism to Protestantism and had worked as a catechist in the Tranquebar Mission. After his father's early death his mother handed him over to his grandfather.[57] The missionary Gottfried Wilhelm Obuch urged d'Almeida to send the boy to the Tamil mission school in Tranquebar, where he remained even after his grandfather's death in 1746. Mainly because of his interest in languages Daniel Pullei became the personal attendant to the missionaries and could thus improve his knowledge of German and Danish.[58] In 1760 the Danish governor Hermann Jacob Forck (in office from 1760–61) offered the mission employee the job of the second interpreter in the Company. Daniel Pullei accepted this position against the wishes

[54] RA Miskolark 9h, *Pro Memoria* from the Tranquebar missionaries to the government, 24 November 1794, (translated from German).

[55] Nørgaard, *Mission und Obrigkeit*, 212.

[56] AFSt/M 1 K 5 : 16, 2nd page.

[57] AFSt/M 1 K 5 : 16; HB 66. Cont., 1041.

[58] AFSt/M 1 K 5 : 16.

of the missionaries who would have preferred to keep him in the service of the mission as a catechist and then pastor. Under Peter Hermann Abbestée (governor from 1761–75; 1779–88) Daniel Pullei became the 'First Interpreter of the Royal Government'[59] and remained in this position till the end of his life.[60]

As an interpreter, mediator and advisor in political matters Daniel Pullei worked very closely with his employers and, among other things, he accompanied Danish delegations to the Indian princely courts. Daniel Pullei was equipped with certain rights, which, if the need arose, he could also use against his own people. As a *dubash* he had to carry out both political and commercial business for his superiors.[61] In 1764 he was a member of the Danish delegation in Thanjavur when Tuljaji II ascended the throne.[62] Since he also spoke Hindustani—besides his native Tamil—he accompanied delegations to the military camps of the ruler of Mysore, Haider Ali (ruled 1760–82), one of these delegations being that of the secretary of the Danish Asiatic Company to a general of Haidar Ali's troops in 1780.[63] On 18 February 1781 and in April 1782

[59] In 1764 Selaselli Setty was the Company-*dubash*. Cf. : Larsen, *Guvernører, Residenter, Kommandanter*, 92. When Tuljaji II was crowned *Raja* of Thanjavur in 1764, both Selaselli Setty as well as Daniel Pullei appear to have been present at the coronation.

[60] For some time Peter Anker (Danish governor in Tranquebar from 1788–1806) favoured the *dubash* Pirakaca Pillei (in office 1780–94), but he then distanced himself from the latter. Cf. : Rasch, Aage, 1967, *Dansk Ostindien 1777–1845. Vore gamle Tropekolonier VII*, Fremad, Copenhagen, 137.

[61] The range of duties of a *dubash* are also described by Arasaratnam, Sinnappah, 1995, 'Society, power, factionalism and corruption in early Madras 1640–1746', in S. Arasaratnam (ed.), *Maritime Trade, Society and European Influence in Southern Asia 1600–1800*, 113–34, Aldershot, Brookfield, 128. Many *dubashes* were from the *mutaliyār*-caste; Brahmins also took on this function. They occasionally also took on the role of financiers for English businessmen. Cf.: Arasaratnam, 'Indian intermediaries in the trade and administration', 138.

[62] AFSt/M 1 K 5 : 16. Susan Neild-Basu states with regard to the *dubashes* of the Madras region: '[…] these groups inevitably had a tremendous influence on the development and environment of these colonial urban centers.' Neild-Basu, 'The Dubashes of Madras', 1. Thus, Ananda Ranga Pillai, for example, as the *dubash* of the French governor Joseph François Dupleix (1697–1764), had enormous power, was affluent and well-respected, and enjoyed ritual and symbolic rights. Pillai, *The Personal Diary of Ananda Ranga Pillai from 1736 to 1761*, Vol. 1, 142.

[63] AFSt/M 1 K 5 : 16. The secretary was supposed to hand over a large sum of money, and Haidar Ali threatened that the *dubash* would be taken hostage if his

Daniel Pullei was taken hostage by a division of Haidar Ali's army and was kept prisoner.[64] In the intervening period he took part in negotiations with representatives of the Mysore camp as a mediator and interpreter.[65] His stay in the military camp of Haidar Ali's troops in 1782 lasted for several months. His status as a hostage ended after the death of the official Danish representative, the 'resident' Surstädt, in June 1782, and, in his place, Daniel Pullei was then brought in for audiences with the Muslim army commanders.[66] It was only after peace talks began in August 1782 and—also at Daniel Pullei's urging—the new Danish 'resident' Olearius was sent to the camp that he could return to Tranquebar.[67] In a later report about this period Missionary John stated: 'He confessed that he had to say what the Sultan wanted to hear and invented many things that he knew would please the Sultan.'[68]

Daniel Pullei did not mediate only in military politics. From 1782 till 1785 the 'Royal Government Interpreter' represented the Danish colonial government several times in Thanjavur in matters of land tenure.[69] The *Raja* of Thanjavur had granted the Danes lease rights over some villages in the Tirukkalacheri district for 90 years in return for credits with a favourable rate of interest. These agreements had to be re-negotiated during the course of the war. On 26 October 1784 Daniel Pullei went on an official mission to Thanjavur for important talks in this regard.[70] At such negotiations the *dubashes* of the concerned rulers, who were given extensive

demands weren't met. UH, R 15 T, N⁰ 35, 129. St., letter from Gottfried Raabs, Tranquebar, 27 August 1781. The Moravian missionaries reported that in 1781 the demand was for a sum of 1,00,000 rupees. Cf. also: Diller, *Die Dänen in Indien, Südostasien und China*, 187.

[64] NHB 28. St., 385, 430–46, extracts from letters written by Daniel Pullei, translated by J. Klein.

[65] NHB 28. St., 399, 26 February 1781.

[66] NHB 28. St., 430–46, here 438f.

[67] NHB 28. St., 445. Cf. also RA AsK, N° 2183 c, Breve fra Tolken Daniel I Tanjore ang indløsning af pantsatte landsbyer 1783–1784 (Tamil), No. 11, letter from Daniel Pullei of 31. Avani (tam. *āvaṇi*) 1782.

[68] AFSt/M 1 K 5 : 16, 23rd page, (translated from German).

[69] The major part of an extensive collection of letters in the Rigsarkivet in Copenhagen that have not yet been studied is from this period. RA AsK, N° 2183c, Breve fra Tolken Daniel [...] 1783–1784 (Tamil).

[70] UH R 15 Tb, N° 1c, Diaria Trankebar 1783–1799, entry for 26 October 1784.

powers, generally met with one another directly. Daniel Pullei's partner in these negotiations was the Raja's *dubash*, Panchaiyappa Mudaliyar (in office from 1780–94).[71] Daniel Pullei reported regularly about the course of these talks to the second government interpreter in Tranquebar, Pirakaca Pillai.[72] When the negotiations were completed after a month, the *raja* of Thanjavur wrote a letter in appreciation of Daniel Pullei's work.[73] In October 1785 Daniel Pullei again stayed in Thanjavur on an unofficial mission for complicated and long-drawn out negotiations about territorial matters. On 10 October 1785 he wrote to the missionary Jacob Klein that he did not know when 'the matter for which he had come would be resolved'.[74] In 1786 Denmark was given lease rights over the entire region of Tiruwidakarhi for 35,000 pagodas.[75]

His work and his efforts in various important political events, in which he always displayed diplomatic skills, brought Daniel Pullei the respect of Europeans and Indians alike. This could be seen in his role as mediator during caste disturbances in August 1787 in Tranquebar, when people protested against the manner of functioning of the King's Counsel and some caste groups moved out to the territory of the King of Thanjavur.[76]

For Daniel Pullei Christianity and close ties with the mission always remained an important part of his identity. He received boundless encouragement from the mission and remained loyal to it. Despite the move from the mission context to the political arena Daniel Pullei maintained personal contact with some missionaries. In

[71] RA AsK, N° 2183c, Breve fra Tolken Daniel [...] 1783–1784. Cf. also: Neild-Basu, 'The Dubashes of Madras', 15f.

[72] RA AsK, N° 2183c, Breve fra Tolken Daniel [...] 1783–1784.

[73] Strandberg, Elisabeth, 1983, *The Modi Documents from Tanjore in Danish Collections*, Franz Steiner, Wiesbaden, 307. In 1785 lease rights for 14 villages were handed over to the Danes.

[74] NHB 32. St., 884, letter from Klein to G.A. Freylinghausen, 23 October 1785.

[75] NHB 33. St., 1023, letter from Klein to the editor of the mission reports, 27 January 1786.

[76] UH R 15 Tb, N° 1c, Diaria Trankebar 1783–1799, entry for 23 and 24 September 1787. Through this action the rebels expressed their displeasure about social abuses, especially about the privileges and powers of some *dubashes* of the *saluppaṉ cheṭṭi* (linen producers/tradesmen) caste who worked for European powers. See for this: Liebau, 'Indische Angestellte'; Brimnes, *Constructing the Colonial Encounter*, 103; Nørgaard, *Mission und Obrigkeit*, 194.

addition, his position as a *dubash* gave him social prominence, which made him an important and interesting partner for the mission. His work as the head of the Tamil congregation in Tranquebar, the close ties to the missionaries there and his interest in translation represented ways of dealing with principles of religion and also offered him the possibility of compensating for 'un-Christian' actions, for which he was often criticized. As a moneylender he had—like many *dubashes*—lent out large sums at a high rate of interest.[77] However, as a wealthy Indian, he had also bestowed generous amounts of money and gifts upon the Tranquebar Mission in the 1780s.[78]

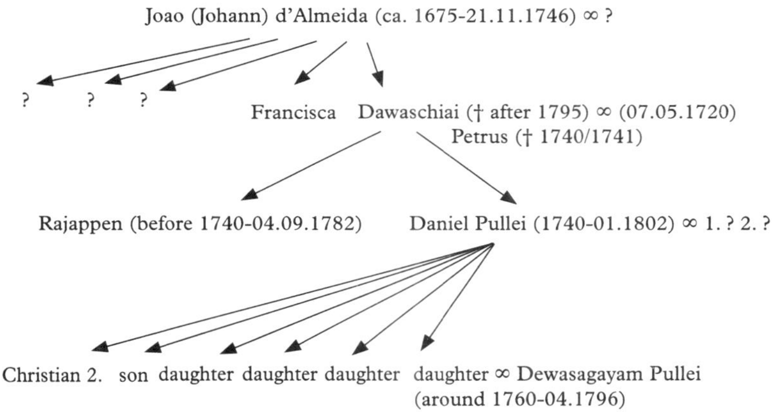

ILLUSTRATION 4.1 Genealogy of the *dubash* Daniel Pullei

AUTHORITIES AND LOCAL MISSION EMPLOYEES

On account of its territorial expansion and its long history of almost 150 years, the DEHM was confronted with different social structures, historical events and changing political constellations, all of which

[77] The interest rate was 8–12%. AFSt/M 1 K 5 : 16. Cf. also Neild-Basu, 'The Dubashes of Madras', 22.

[78] 'He has had a nice wall and fence built around the churchyard of the Bethlehem church at his own cost and, only recently, he has ordered an organ from Copenhagen for 300 Rthlr. for our city church', (translated from German). NHB 30. St., 674, diary of the missionaries, Tranquebar 1783.

forced it to enter into compromises with different political powers. Despite the understanding of the individual missionary, who might have seen himself as a neutral entity responsible only for his religious duties, the Danish-English-Halle Mission as a whole could not remain a politically neutral institution. Missionary work was linked to negotiations and deals with the Danish colonial authorities, the local rulers in Thanjavur and with representatives of the English colonial power that was becoming increasingly stronger. Each of these powers developed their own position with regard to Christian missionary work depending on their interests, and this resulted in special forms of (mutual) co-operation and concessions.

Besides the specificities arising out of the time and place of missionary work in India, the European balance of power played an important role for the religious and secular decision-makers in India. The missionaries in the region were both participants in and victims of political developments in South India, which witnessed constant conflicts between European and local powers involving political intrigues, military conflicts and changing power constellations. However, the social commitment that the missionaries viewed as an essential part of their strategy did not allow them to seal themselves off from political and social developments. Although the mission made an effort to appear impartial, it was this demonstrative political neutrality itself, which often resulted in individual missionaries or South Indian employees being placed in a position of trust by different social forces.

THE DANISH AUTHORITIES

From 1620 onwards various Danish trading companies were the supreme authority in Tranquebar, on whose orders a commander or governor was appointed along with a privy council consisting of three to five members.[79] In 1704 the Danish king, Frederick IV, called for the establishment of a Lutheran overseas mission in this colony and thus provided the impetus for the first organized Protestant mission in India. The appointment of the Mission was done on the

[79] Nørgaard, *Mission und Obrigkeit*, 12. For the trading companies see: Krieger, *Kaufleute, Seeräuber und Diplomaten*, 12.

instructions of the king, but the trading companies were not under him. This meant that the government of the trading company and the mission authorities associated with the monarchy had to come to a mutual understanding about the norms of their parallel existence in the overseas colony.

The basic conflict of interest between the commerce and profit-oriented representatives of the trading companies on the one hand, and the missionaries, on the other, who were equipped with royal instructions for conversion, was the backdrop for a constant struggle between the two regarding spheres of influence and authority. The actual power equations became evident at the beginning of missionary work already, when the Danish commandant Hassius had Ziegenbalg imprisoned in November 1708 for several months. Shortly before Ziegenbalg's trip to Europe in 1711 'amnesty' was declared 'between the Royal Commandant of Dansburg in Tranquebar and the Privy Councillors, on the one hand, and the Royal Missionaries, on the other hand', giving a public signal for reconciliation.[80] However, conflicts kept arising and constant talks were required to resolve them in such a way that neither side suffered too much damage.

The realization of the mutual dependency of mission and trade also led to the willingness towards mutual support. As a result of Ziegenbalg's negotiations during his trip to Europe and of Gründler's skillful diplomacy in Tranquebar it was agreed that the Mission would receive various privileges.[81] In 1714 the Mission Board was also established in Copenhagen to channelize future conflicts. From what was initially a private undertaking of the king, the Mission became an 'official state mission'. Since the Mission Board had direct access to the king, the status of the mission was further strengthened in the eyes of the Danish public.[82] The tensions between the trading companies and the missionaries, however, remained, and the views of the first missionaries about the reasons for this tension were valid even in later years.

> [...] because they see that we correspond with many and with highly-placed people in Europe [...], because the gentlemen here

[80] HB 9. Cont., 647–49.

[81] Nørgaard, *Mission und Obrigkeit*, 72f.

[82] Ibid. 68.

> have a large amount of private trade-dealings with the leaders of the heathens and with the Papist priest, [...] because they correspond and deal with the elite of the Roman Church and allow themselves to be carried away by the latter, [...] because, from the beginning, we spoke against the vexatious lifestyle of the European Christians in East India and have insisted upon a life that is in accordance with the gospel and one that can inspire the heathens to convert; [...] because they have already decided in their minds that our work should not be continued, [...] because they have attacked us through imprisonment and other forceful means and we had to report these matters to Denmark.[83]

During a period of economic difficulties in the 1720s the Danish trading company tried to save their undertaking by issuing a call for financial participation by interested people in the shareholding company.[84] However, the downward trend could not be stopped. Since it was difficult to maintain the company, it was disbanded in 1729 and re-established as the *Asiatisk Kompagni*. This company continued to use the colony in Tranquebar and managed the Danish Asia-trade with brief interruptions till 1843, whereby the 1750s are considered to be its golden age.[85] Particularly during these years the Company tried to instumentalize the mission and its co-workers for colonial aims, for example, when they planned to annex territory in the Nicobar islands, which, as the missionary Peter Dame stated, required 'a great deal of attention' from the missionaries.[86] For the Danish settlement that was to come up on the Nicobar Islands it was planned that 'various members of our Portuguese congregation would initially have to stay there for some time.'[87] Even when the Danes received permission from the 'Grand Mughal' in 1755 to establish three lodges and a fort in Bengal for the Danish company, they requested that a missionary help them.[88]

[83] AB 39, letter from B. Ziegenbalg and J.E. Gründler to J. Trellund and J. Lodberg, Tranquebar, 3 September 1714, (translated from German).

[84] *The Directors of the Royal Danish East India Company, Pvt. Ltd. hereby announce/...* J. Holmste, 16 December 1727.

[85] Cf. Nielsen, Axel, *Dänische Wirtschaftsgeschichte*, G. Fischer, Jena, 291; Krieger, *Kaufleute, Seeräuber und Diplomaten*, 14.

[86] HB 84. Cont., 1707, letter from P. Dame, 9 February 1756.

[87] HB 84. Cont., 1699, letter from J. Klein, 11 October 1755.

[88] Ibid.

In 1772 the monopoly of the Asiatic Company in the Danish Asia-trade came to an end. From this point of time on private persons in Denmark were also allowed to have trade with India. With this, the supreme command of the trading company over the colony Tranquebar was also affected. In 1777 the colony was officially placed under the administration of the royal government. The secular Danish government in Tranquebar was now placed under a Commerce Board, and this meant that the relations between the mission and the colonial authorities had to be redefined. The growing strength of the English in southeast India and the weakening of Danish foreign trade at the time of the Napoleonic wars led to a decrease of Danish positions in India.[89] As a result of the decline in Tranquebar's economic significance for the Danes, they disbanded their trading society in 1843 and began negotiations with England for the sale of their trading posts Tranquebar in Southeast India and Serampore in Bengal.[90]

The Tamil co-workers of the mission in Tranquebar and the surrounding districts dealt with the authorities only indirectly. They were placed directly under the European missionaries who, when the need arose, mediated between the South Indian employees and the Danish authorities in Tranquebar, as well as with the guiding institutions of the mission in Halle and Copenhagen. This also applied to the local pastors whose ordination formally made them equals of the missionaries, but who could not contact the authorities without first discussing it with the missionaries or without their permission. Language was also an impediment to direct contact, and the missionaries had to be used as mediators. The Tamil original of every letter written by a pastor or a catechist to the authorities was sent to Europe along with a translation done by a missionary, who sometimes also added his comments. The same was true of the work-related reports of the assistants, catechists and pastors, which were included in the mission reports only after they had been revised by a missionary. The language-barrier that every missionary encountered

[89] The Danish territories around Tranquebar were occupied by British troops in 1801/02 and between 1808 and 1815. This meant that the maritime link between Tranquebar and Denmark was interrupted. Cf.: Krieger, *Kaufleute, Seeräuber und Diplomaten*, 200.

[90] Nørgaard, *Mission und Obrigkeit*, 189f.

on his arrival in the mission region was reversed in this context. Ways and forms had to be found to allow South Indian mission employees to speak for themselves while presenting matters to the European mission superiors and to people interested in the mission.

The missionaries were, however, not concerned about making it possible for the local workers to have their say. Rather, they were interested only in documenting the active co-operation of local Christians in the work of conversion. Tamils working for the mission were thus also instrumentalized for purposes for representation and legitimization. This practice became particularly clear during the visits of Peter Maleiappen and Timotheus in Europe. The two young mission pupils went to Europe with Ziegenbalg and Plütschau respectively and were introduced in mission circles there. Their presence in Europe had also helped to counter criticism of Protestant missionary activity in India.[91] Many decades later, when John urged that young Indians should be sent to Europe to study, it was not only for economic reasons, but also for representational purposes.[92]

Although personal contacts and a regular independent correspondence between the converted Indians and the European financial bodies and decision-makers were neither desired nor possible, there were situations in which the local employees turned directly to the Mission management and vice versa. One such situation was the ordaining of an Indian pastor who, after this event, generally introduced himself in a letter to the management and expressed his thanks. In the 1740s and 1750s the country pastor Diogo carried on a regular correspondence with the Mission Board in Copenhagen and with Gotthilf August Francke in Halle, whereby it was often a case of joint letters that he wrote together with his fellow-pastors Aaron or Ambrosius. From 1743 till 1754 the South Indian pastors sent a personal letter once a year to their superiors in Europe about the progress of their work, their willingness to continue their work in the service of the mission with dedication and loyalty and pledging unconditional obedience to the missionaries. The missionaries

[91] These events are dealt with in greater detail pp. 110f of this study.

[92] NHB 32. St., 896, Ch. S. John to G.A. Freylinghausen, 10 September 1787.

translated the replies from Europe for their South Indian pastors.[93] They also used these replies from the mission authorities as an opportunity to give instructions to the local workers and commented and interpreted these letters separately in the monthly classes.[94] The Tamil mission employees took these letters while traveling and read them to their congregations.[95]

The letters from the South Indian co-workers did not contain only edifying reflections and declarations of loyalty. Assessments of the political situation in the mission region, or reports of the persecution of Christians were also communicated. Diogo's opinion regarding the possibility of regular missionary work in Thanjavur was significant. On the basis of his own observations Diogo informed the editor of the mission reports in Halle on 24 January 1747 that he did not think the time was ripe for this.[96] This was not the only critical situation in which it benefited the missionaries to let a Tamil colleague speak and thus have their own opinions communicated to the Mission

[93] HB 57. Cont., 1413f, letter from Diogo to Friedrich Michael Ziegenhagen, 5 January 1743; HB 57. Cont., 1411, letter from Diogo and Aaron to G.A. Francke, 26 January 1743; HB 57. Cont., 1409f., letter from Diogo and Aaron to the Mission Board, 26 January 1743; AFSt/M 1 B 32 : 17, letter from Diogo to Gotthilf August Francke, 20 January 1744; AFSt/M 1 B 32 : 40, letter from Gotthilf August Francke to Aaron, 7 January 1745; AFSt/M 1 B 32 : 41, letter from Gotthilf August Francke to Diogo, 7 January 1745; AFSt/M 1 B 33 : 2, letter from Aaron and Diogo to the Mission Board in Copenhagen, 24 January 1745; AFSt/M 1 B 33 : 36, letter from Gotthilf August Francke to Aaron and Diogo, 5 November 1745; HB 66. Cont., 1071f., letter from Diogo to the Mission Board, 24 January 1747; HB 66. Cont., 1072f., letter from Diogo to G.A. Francke, 24 January 1747; RA Miskolark 9b, letter from Diogo to the Mission Board, 28 September 1748; RA Miskolark 9b, letter from Diogo to the Mission Board, 16 October 1749; RA Miskolark 9b, letter from Diogo to the Mission Board, 8 December 1750; RA Miskolark 9c, letter from Diogo and Ambrosius to the Mission Board, 20 October 1752; RA Miskolark 9c, letter from Diogo and Ambrosius to the Mission Board, 2 October 1753; AFSt/M 1 B 44 : 22, letter from Diogo and Ambros to Gotthilf August Francke, 1 February 1755; RA Miskolark 9c, letter from Diogo and Ambrosius to the Mission Board, 10 October 1755; AFSt/M 1 B 47 : 27, letter from Diogo to Gotthilf August Francke, 11 October 1756.

[94] HB 82. Cont., 1426, diary of the missionaries in Tranquebar, 10 October 1754.

[95] HB 78. Cont., 876; 81. Cont., 1332.

[96] HB 66. Cont., 1072, Diogo to G.A. Francke, 24 January 1747.

Board or to Halle without having to express their own reservations or their criticism. Jacob Klein thus quoted Rajappen in his critical assessment of the change of government in Tranquebar after the new governor, Peter Anker, had taken charge, and who feared that this would lead to a decline in the reputation of the Mission.[97]

Viewed in its entirety the volume of direct correspondence between South Indian co-workers and European mission bodies was very small. The European missionaries were still the main people who described their experiences in India to a European readership, and for the latter it was probably more important to know what the missionaries thought of a local co-worker rather than to actually read his thoughts. Generally, the reports, ideas and views of the co-workers were communicated through indirect reporting to the mission authorities in Europe. In Tranquebar, the local employees informed the missionaries about conditions and developments in mission congregations during the regular Friday-meetings of the co-workers. They were also expected to read out their reports and talk about the problems and achievements of every member of the congregation on the basis of the church-books.[98]

The Danish colonial authorities in Tranquebar also included the priests who were responsible for the pastoral care of European civil and military personnel. The relationship between the mission employees and these priests was initially characterized by mistrust, mutual scrutiny and careful consideration. After a few years, however, the areas of responsibility were clearly demarcated and compromises reached. This was expressed, not least, in the formal diplomatic actions and gestures of mutual respect: when the Zion church in Tranquebar was under repair from June to December 1729, the Danish congregation used the New Jerusalem church for divine services.[99] In 1731 the ceremonies for the 25th anniversary of the mission took place in the Danish Zion church in Tranquebar as a sign of mutual understanding.[100] The song written for this occasion—*Compagnie und Mission*—sealed the harmony between

[97] AFSt/M 1 C 31a : 30, letter from Jacob Klein to Johann Ludwig Schulze, Tranquebar, 20 January 1790. Cf. also Nørgaard, *Mission und Obrigkeit*, 195.

[98] HB 73. Cont., 121.

[99] HB 28. Cont., 384.

[100] Nørgaard, *Mission und Obrigkeit*, 175.

representatives of the mission and those of the Company. The text of the song stated that 'they are not opposed to each other' and that 'they stand together'.[101] At the ceremony for the ordination of the first Indian pastor of the Tranquebar Mission there were 11 priests present. Besides the six 'Royal Danish' missionaries and a missionary in English service there were two Danish priests of the local Zion church as well as two naval chaplains.[102] There was mutual co-operation and each had access to the other church. Since their duties sometimes intersected and a clear division was not always possible, the management of the Asiatic Trading Society even suggested in 1740 that the missionaries take on the duties of the colony priests as well, a suggestion that the missionaries, however, did not accept.[103] At the beginning of the 1750s the missionaries, in fact, continued to request that the rules of the Danish Church be applied to them in a modified manner since the mission had always handled matters in a certain way.[104]

The mission had to make compromises and adjustments in the pastoral care of the German-speaking population in Tranquebar. Since the majority of the Danish-Halle missionaries were Germans, it was natural to hand over the spiritual care of the Germans living in the mission region to them. The Germans were primarily soldiers and officers of Danish regiments. Till the arrival of the first missionaries in 1706 Danish clergymen had conducted divine

[101] AFSt/M 1 B 12 : 7, song: 'The established harmony between Zion and Jerusalem', ??.??. Tranquebar 1729 ['Die wohlgegründete Harmonie zwischen Zion und Jerusalem'].

[102] HB 37. Cont., 171.

[103] Nørgaard, *Mission und Obrigkeit*, 185. During A.F. Cämmerer's time, however, this could no longer be avoided.

[104] RA Miskolark 9c, letter from Klein, Poltzenhagen and Schwartz to the Mission Board, 27 October 1751. 'In the rituals of the above-mentioned Royal Danish Church, for example, an exorcism is conducted during holy Baptism, which the mission here has not done since the beginning. In addition, the rules lay down the unconditional granting of absolution after confession, which had hitherto not been the norm. Rather, without giving offense to anyone, absolution is only granted with conditions, or on request, [...] Our humble and dutiful request is that Your Excellency and our Revered Gentlemen give us dispensation from the strict observance of Royal Danish rituals and, if it may please you, to graciously license the hitherto introduced custom, since it has not been used either in our congregation or outside of it.' (translated from German).

services for them. Now, the German soldiers and officers themselves established contact with their countrymen.[105] However, the pastoral care of military personnel was not an official responsibility of a mission, which, according to the Royal Instruction, had to devote itself exclusively to the local population. Nevertheless, the missionaries conducted divine services in German for the Germans and other Europeans in Tranquebar and, in the final years of the mission, they also temporarily took over parish duties for the Danes.[106] The question of a suitable place for these services led to conflicts. Should these be held in the Danish church, or in the house of a missionary? The Danes feared a loss of authority[107] because this pastoral care made some Europeans give the mission financial and moral support.[108] When the missionaries wanted to conduct the prayer-hours with German soldiers in their houses instead of in the Danish church, this aroused the displeasure of the Danish authorities.[109]

The mutual dependency of the Danish-Halle Mission and the Danish colonial authorities was particularly evident when young Tamilians educated in the mission schools sought employment with the Company. Till the arrival of the first Protestant missionaries the Company had met its requirements for Indian Christians from the ranks of the local Catholics. The Tranquebar Mission, therefore, initially had trouble while trying to place members of their congregations in Company service. Official agreements had to be drawn up to ensure that preference was given to mission Christians.[110] Indians educated in mission schools were sent to European institutions for jobs as accountants, interpreters, soldiers, teachers, domestic

105 AB 43.

106 HB 77. Cont. 785; 78. Cont., 856; see also Nørgaard, *Mission und Obrigkeit*, 15f., 28–30.

107 AB 60.

108 Christoph Wilhelm von Schlegel, brother of the more well-known August Wilhelm von Schlegel (1767–1845) and Karl Wilhelm Friedrich von Schlegel (1772–1829), was in South India as a Royal Danish Chamberlain and Chief Steward. He laid down in his will that 200 *Reichstaler* should be used for the care of indigent and sick Christians. HB 92. Cont., (182).

109 Lehmann, *Es begann in Tranquebar*, 67.

110 Such agreements did not always last. A first agreement reached under Gründler was nullified after his death and renewed only in 1730. Nørgaard, *Mission und Obrigkeit*, 52, 127, 147. See also Jeyaraj, *Inkulturation in Tranquebar*, 176, 189.

employees, or even artisans,[111] especially after the responsibility for the colony of Tranquebar was transferred from the trading society to the Danish state in 1777. The number of mission Christians in the service of the Danish Company increased from an average of 20 to 25 in the 1730s to 50 or 60 in the 1760s, and to about 80 in the seventies. Most of them were appointed as soldiers (*talaiyāri*), some as toll officers or as sextants in the Danish Zion church.

TABLE 4.1 Mission Christians from the 'Portuguese' and Tamil city congregations in Tranquebar in the service of the Danish trading company[112]

Year	Mission Christians in Tranquebar in the service of the Danish Company
1735 (1st half)	from the 'Portuguese' congregation: 17 persons from the Tamil congregation: 22 soldiers, workers, sextants
1735 (2nd half)	from the 'Portuguese' congregation: 1 toll-collector, 15 soldiers from the Tamil congregation: 6 soldiers, 12 *talaiyāri*, 4 workers, 2 sextants
1738	20 'Portuguese', 7 Tamil soldiers, 2 sailors, 4 workers, 2 sextants in the Danish Zion church, 1 toll-collector
1739	19 'Portuguese', 8 Tamil soldiers, 16 *talaiyāri*, 2 sailors, 2 sextants, 1 writer
1763	from the 'Portuguese' congregation: 1 sub-collector, 1 sub-constable, 13 soldiers from the Tamil congregation: 32 soldiers, 10 *talaiyāri*, 2 sextants
1764	from the 'Portuguese' congregation: 1 junior officer, 15 soldiers from the Tamil congregation: 32 soldiers, 10 *talaiyāri*, 2 sextants
1766	from the 'Portuguese' congregation: 1 sub-collector, 11 soldiers, some seamen from the Tamil congregation: 41 soldiers, 11 *talaiyāri*, 2 sextants

(contd...)

[111] Nørgaard, *Mission und Obrigkeit*, 200.

[112] HB 40. Cont., preface; 42. Cont., preface § VIII; 47. Cont., 1333; 49. Cont., 4; 99. Cont., 303; 101. Cont., 499; 105. Cont., 997; 106. Cont., 1485; NHB 1. St., 3–4; 17. St., 523; 19. St., 767f.

Table 4.1 (contd.)

Year	Mission Christians in Tranquebar in the service of the Danish Company
1767	from the 'Portuguese' congregation: 1 sub-collector, soldiers from the Tamil city congregation: 38 soldiers, 18 *talaiyāri*, 2 sextants
1768	from the 'Portuguese' congregation: sub-collectors, 8 soldiers, 3 pipers, sailors from the Tamil congregation: 26 soldiers in 'Portuguese' uniform, 10 *sipāhī*, 13 *talaiyāri*, 2 sextants
1776	Some from the 'Portuguese' congregation. 13 *sipāhī*, 28 soldiers in 'Portuguese' uniform, 21 *talaiyāri* including 3 postmen for the newly-established postal service to Madras and Nagapattinam
1777	15 *sipāhī*, 11 *talaiyāri*, 13 persons from the 'Portuguese' and 31 persons from the Tamil congregation.

Depending on the economic situation the mission had to either request the Company to employ 'their' Christians, or it had to train the Indians in special professions according to the stated requirements of the Company and the administrative authorities. As a rule, some children were always directly prepared for employment with the Company, and they were sometimes introduced to the Company at an early stage. Along with those who worked for and were paid by the Mission, it was these people in secular jobs who contributed in a major way to the manner in which the Mission was perceived by the world around it.

The agreements and the co-operation between the Mission and the trading society did not only concern personnel, but also the institutional sphere. With the construction of a paper-mill in Porayar in 1715 the Mission and the colonial authorities were both pursuing common economic interests. This undertaking was financed by joint capital investments of the Mission and the commandant, but it had to be abandoned in 1720 due to its inefficiency.[113] When the need arose, the Mission printing press in Tranquebar printed

[113] Nørgaard, *Mission und Obrigkeit*, 83. Liebau, 'Buchdruck und Missionsbibliothek'.

documents for the Danish administration. For example, in 1785 the press printed the regulations for the right of Indians in European service to give notice, and the regulations for the cleaning of the city.[114] The missionaries often perceived their willingness to oblige the colonial authorities as one-sided. In a memo of 1800, however, the missionaries emphasized that although private contacts with the authorities were good,

> [...] if we ask for something on behalf of the mission we encounter a lot of problems [...] Is there any reason for wishing away the mission from Tranquebar? Isn't it true that large sums of money come into Tranquebar every year through the mission and through its foreign pupils, helping to maintain a large part of the colony? [...] Where would parents send their children to be taught in European languages before a Danish school is established? From where do they get their best interpreters, writers and domestic help? Even most of the heathen dubashes were trained by the missionaries before they could get work.[115]

The relations between the colonial administration and the South Indian mission employees were constantly tested in the sensitive matter of legal jurisdiction. Initially, the Company did not allow the mission its own jurisdiction.[116] In practice, however, the proposed court of the Church Council to deal with marital disputes, which would consist of members of the Danish church, the secular authorities and of the Mission, developed into a mission court with representatives of the authorities present during the proceedings.[117] The setting up of this court was a result of the negotiations carried out by Ziegenbalg during his trip to Europe. Besides the court, the elders of the congregations also played an important role. They were given judicial powers to resolve ordinary disputes and could impose punishments.[118] The missionaries Christoph Theodosius Walther, Christian Friedrich Pressier and Martin Bosse were of the opinion that legal jurisdiction

[114] NHB 33. St., 1006.

[115] RA Miskolark, 9i, *Pro Memoria*, 1800 [no date or signature], translated from German).

[116] Nørgaard, *Mission und Obrigkeit*, 52.

[117] Ibid., 89, 109, 164.

[118] Ibid., 89.

was a matter for the secular colonial authorities.[119] Under their influence the work of the court that had begun under Gründler was again restricted in 1729. The Mission would now deal independently only in cases of marital disputes among its congregants. A supervisor in the Christian congregation would only settle minor disputes independently. In 1732 the newly established Asiatic Company laid down rules for ecclesiastic courts in which missionaries would also function as judges.[120] After the state took over the Asia trade in 1777, the independent mission jurisdiction was again called into question. A Tamil plaintiff now had to turn to the *dubash* who forwarded his complaint to the relevant European authority.[121] The missionaries did not agree with this changed practice and requested that the old mission jurisdiction be re-introduced, especially since Governor Anker himself had confirmed this when assuming office. There were considerable disputes about this, particularly in the 1790s.[122] From 1823 onwards the mission in Tranquebar was placed under the jurisdiction of the Danish authorities, even in legal matters.[123]

THE RULERS OF THANJAVUR

European presence in Thanjavur went back at least as far as the rule of Raghunatha Nayak who allowed the Dutch and the Danes, besides the Portuguese, to set up trading posts, settlements, factories and forts.[124] Although some tolerant and educated members of the ruling dynasties in Thanjavur were also open to a religious and intellectual exchange with Christian missionaries, they did not allow extensive missionary work among the people. The Tranquebar Mission began its work in the south-east Indian Danish colony at a point of time when the colony had existed as a trading post for almost one hundred years.[125]

119 Ibid., 145.

120 Ibid., 154.

121 RA Miskolark, 9h, *Pro Memoria* from the Tranquebar missionaries to the government, 24 November 1794.

122 Nørgaard, *Mission und Obrigkeit*, 164f.

123 Ibid., 191f.

124 Arasaratnam, 'Mare Clausum, the Dutch and Regional Trade in the Indian Ocean', 73.

125 For the beginnings of the Danish trading colony Tranquebar see pp. 62–74 of this study.

Besides the district Thanjavur, the kingdom of Thanjavur contained six other districts (Mayavaram, Kumbakonam, Tiruvadi, Vallam, Mannarkudi, Pattukottai) that were ruled by local administrators on behalf of the Raja of Thanjavur.[126] Ziegenbalg and Gründler had already made the first attempts to get permission for missionary work outside the Danish sphere of influence, but they abandoned this idea because they apparently could not finance the customary gifts required for this.[127]

When mission employees travelled to Christians in the surrounding districts the toll-taxes always proved to be a major impediment to unrestricted missionary work.[128] Because it was difficult for Europeans to travel to the interior of the country, in 1712 the missionaries asked the two mission co-workers, Canerum (died 1748) and Tschareiappen, to ascertain the possibilities for missionary work in Thanjavur.[129] Contacts to the *subahdar* (administrator), who was appointed by the Raja and was responsible for the Tranquebar region, proved helpful. In 1717 Ziegenbalg and Gründler reported that the *subahdar* for their district had been changed. The Brahmin who had formerly held this post had been sent a gift and a book, they stated, and, when the opportunity arose, they would also introduce themselves to the new administrator with a gift.[130]

Although the first steps had been taken towards Thanjavur, none of the missionaries could establish themselves in this region. They did not have either permission from the raja or consent from Denmark. Benjamin Schultze intensified the efforts of the mission to establish contact with the Royal House in Thanjavur. Already during his time in Tranquebar he had corresponded with a relative

[126] Habib, *An Atlas of the Mughal Empire*, 65.

[127] HB 2. Cont., 84, 90, letter from Gründler, January 6, 1710; 2. Cont., 93f., letter from Gründler and Ziegenbalg, 16 January 1710; cf. also 2. Cont., 105; 3. Cont., 138; 4. Cont., 181; Lehmann, *Es begann in Tranquebar*, 214.

[128] In 1716 Christians in Mayavaran, Thanjavur, Mahadevpattanam and the Maravar district had to be taken care of. HB 33. Cont., 870; AFSt/M 2 A 2 : 7. For ten years the missionaries placed the number of Christians in the Thanjavur region at 143 ('Malabarische Landgemeine im Königreich Tanschaur'). The centres were in Mayavaram, Mahadevpattanam and Thanjavur. HB, preface to 26. Cont.; cf. also HB, preface to 27. Cont.

[129] AB 218, Ziegenbalg to Gründler in Madras, Tranquebar, 13 August 1712. AB 236, Ziegenbalg and Gründler to Böhme in London, Tranquebar, 16 September 1712.

[130] AB 496, letter from Ziegenbalg and Gründler, 20 November 1717.

of the ruler of Thanjavur, Telungarasa.[131] This correspondence began in 1722. Schultze introduced himself clearly as a missionary, offered his services openly and sent edifying Christian tracts. There was a mutual exchange of pleasantries and small gifts.[132] In one of the letters Prince 'Rutturosiraja', after confirming the receipt of three books, a pistol, a dog and a bottle 'with all kinds of rare things', emphasized the importance of mutual contacts: 'It is not necessary to write a lot, friendship is the best and it is enough. [...] For us, friendship is the most important thing.'[133] Schultze also tried to negotiate with the authorities in Thanjavur on legal matters concerning the Christians there.[134]

In Madras Schultze tried to extend his contacts with the local authorities to the region of the Nawab of Arcot,[135] while the missionaries in Tranquebar continued their efforts to win over the rulers of Thanjavur for the mission. They regularly undertook attempts to enter the territory of Thanjavur with their work. The missionaries were finally able to establish permanent, albeit indirect, contacts with the court of the raja during the rule of Tuljaji I. An unexpected opportunity presented itself when a Catholic officer of the army of Thanjavur, Rajanayakkan, was stationed in Porayar and displayed an interest in Evangelical dogma.[136] His family, which originally came from the *paṟaiyār* caste, had been Catholic for three generations.[137] As a young man Rajanayakkan had learnt to read and write[138] and had, like many Catholics, entered military service in the army of Serfoji I, where he had the post of a junior officer

[131] Cf. HB 20. Cont., 458, 474f.; 21. Cont., 647–51; 44. Cont., 921.

[132] B. Schultze sent three of these letters from the king, written on palm-leaves, in a box, along with other things, to Halle. AFSt/M 1 B 2 : 13, [Benjamin Schultze's] correspondence with Prince Rutturosirāsha, 21 January 1722; cf. also HB 21. Cont., 646f., 650f.

[133] AFSt/M 1 B 2 : 13; cf. HB 21. Cont., 651f, Thanjavur, May 1725, (translated from German).

[134] HB 21. Cont., 652f., 23 July 1723.

[135] HB 56. Cont., 1359, 1361, 1367.

[136] For more details on Rajanayakkan see: Liebau, 'Tamilische Christen im 18. Jahrhundert'; Jeyaraj, *Ordination of the First Protestant Indian Pastor Aaron*, cf. here the preface by K. Rajaratnam, V-VII.

[137] HB 34. Cont., 1080.

[138] HB 25. Cont., 18; 34. Cont., 1080.

(*cērvaikkāraṉ*).[139] Later, in Thanjavur, he also learnt German.[140] He heard about the new Christian teachings from the mission bookbinder in Porayar in 1726/27, visited the mission school there and then turned to the missionaries with a written request for literature.[141] In the course of a correspondence lasting more than a year between Rajanayakkan and the Lutheran missionaries in Tranquebar the latter explained the Christian dogma to him in written form.[142] Rajanayakkan came to Tranquebar at irregular intervals, often accompanied by others who wanted to convert, and had conversations with the missionaries about the differences between Catholic and Protestant tenets.[143] At the end of July 1727, when Rajanayakkan was to leave Porayar with his soldiers and return to Thanjavur, the missionaries asked him to send them regular reports about the situation of Christians in Thanjavur.[144] Knowing that the missionaries were interested in him and believing in his own abilities, Rajanayakkan demanded that they send him literature regularly and insisted that they help 'his' converts find employment with the Europeans.[145] Finally, he also requested

[139] In the military context *cērvaikkāraṉ* refers to a captain commanding a unit. Lehmann interprets the term also as referring to a caste (*cērvaikkāraṉ*), 'junior officer Rajanaikkan from the Serwei-caste'. Lehmann, *Es begann in Tranquebar*, 240.

[140] HB 29. Cont., 478, report, 12 December 1729. There were some Germans working in the military sphere at the court of the *Raja* of Thanjavur. Among them was Johann Wilhelm Berg from Hamburg who was often mentioned in the reports and was probably Rajanayakkan's German teacher. Cf. also AFSt/M 2 A 2: 5a, Information about Germans in the service of the king of Tanjore, ??. ??. 1750.

[141] HB 25. Cont., 10, diary of the missionaries in Tranquebar, 3 February 1727. Before this, Rajanayakkan had dealt with Catholic dogma extensively and had also developed an interest in religious history. He, therefore, used every possible opportunity to acquire Christian literature. A Catholic mendicant friar had given him publications of the Tranquebar Mission. Cf., among others, HB 34. Cont., 1079–83.

[142] HB 25. Cont., 11, 16, 20f., diary of the missionaries in Tranquebar, February 8, February 18 and March 24, 1727.

[143] HB 25. Cont., 17, 21f., 27f., 32, diary of the missionaries in Tranquebar, entries for 22 February, 24 March, 13 May, 10 July 1727. Rajanayakkan commanded a unit of 50 soldiers, 20 being stationed in Porayar, while the remaining 30 stayed back in Thanjavur. HB 25. Cont., 36, 24 July 1727.

[144] HB 25. Cont., 36, diary of the missionaries in Tranquebar, 24 July 1727.

[145] HB 25. Cont., 39/40, diary of the missionaries in Tranquebar, 29 July 1727.

employment with the mission.[146] In order to be certain in their assessment of Rajanayakkan the missionaries sent out their catechist and confidante, Aaron, to Thanjavur 'mainly also to get information about Rajanayakkan's circumstances...'[147] It was only after Aaron had reported back to them that they consented to Rajanayakkan's appointment.

Rajanayakkan reacted immediately with far-reaching ideas about the work he wanted to do, asked for additional co-workers as well as for money to build a church.[148] At the Easter celebrations of 1729 Rajanayakkan was introduced to the congregation in Tranquebar as the new catechist for the Mahadevpattanam district.[149] At that point of time, the congregation of this district already had about 200 members.[150] Rajanayakkan's brothers Sinappen and Tairappen helped him for a while as assistant and junior catechist.[151]

Till the beginning of the 1750s the European missionaries did not have permission to stay in the territory of the ruler of Thanjavur and—with the exception of some episodes—they did not travel in the Thanjavur region or to the city. In 1728 Christian Friedrich Pressier undertook one of the few steps in this direction. Accompanied by a catechist and a *kaṇakkappiḷḷai* he set off for Thanjavur at the invitation of Prince Telungarasa with whom he too, like Schultze, had maintained a personal contact for some time. Although he was equipped with this invitation, the security police in Thanjavur made very sure that the guest did not carry out missionary activity on his way to the city. Even though those accompanying him were allowed to talk to the people, Pressier was prevented from doing the same. Telungarasa's interest in meeting the European missionary was motivated less by religious reasons, but rather by the desire of this educated prince to extend his knowledge in

[146] HB 25. Cont., 41/42, diary of the missionaries in Tranquebar, 5 August 1727. This happened on 4 August 1727; Rajanayakkan became a member of the Lutheran Church on 1 February 1728, HB 33. Cont., 898.

[147] HB 26. Cont., 15, diary of the missionaries in Tranquebar, 25 January 1728.

[148] HB 26. Cont. 12, diary of the missionaries in Tranquebar, 17 January 1728.

[149] HB 28. Cont., 316, diary of the missionaries in Tranquebar, 16 April 1729; HB 30. Cont., 899. The mission had, in the meantime, divided its area of work into four districts.

[150] HB 27. Cont., preface § XV.

[151] HB 26. Cont., 12–16; 29. Cont., 478.

different areas, especially in geography. The two (unnamed) Indians, who accompanied the missionary, mainly worked as (Marathi) interpreters. During their last days in Thanjavur the small delegation was allowed to go around the city. The missionary, however, was asked to restrict his conversations to people of the royal court, since the European's safety could not be guaranteed in areas ruled by local administrators.[152]

Since Pressier's journey had not brought about the desired permission for regular missionary work in Thanjavur, the self-styled catechist Rajanayakkan remained the sole representative of the mission there. The constant wars between Thanjavur and the kingdom of Madurai in the 1730s and 40s also made it difficult to establish a mission station there. Rajanayakkan used the 25 years in which he represented the Mission in the Thanjavur region to mark out his personal sphere and to put his ideas of missionary work into practice. By 1732 he already had three assistants.[153] In 1742 he set up a school[154] that was also open to Hindus and Muslims. Despite all his missionary successes his caste background often represented a hindrance. For the school that Rajanayakkan had established, and which was in an area dominated by *śūdras*, the parents insisted that a *śydra* teacher be found for their children. The choice fell on Gurupadam, a son of the *śūdra* assistant Arhagappan.[155]

Whereas the former language teacher and interpreter for the Mission, Aleppa, having been banished from Tranquebar by the Danish commandant, Hassius, in 1711, was arrested in Thanjavur for his contacts with the Tranquebar missionaries and imprisoned for a few months on the orders of the king,[156] Rajanayakkan did not face any harassment from the local authorities. However, the raja did try to make the Indian mission employees take active part in Hindu religious processions. When Rajanayakkan supervised a Hindu cremation on the orders of the raja, the missionaries in

152 HB 26. Cont., preface, § VIII, 129–52.

153 HB 33. Cont., 899.

154 HB 58. Cont., 1494, report 1743. Cf. also Lehmann, *Es begann in Tranquebar*, 241.

155 HB 58. Cont., 1520, 1602f.

156 AB 191. Aleppa had been banished from Tranquebar once before, in 1709, on the orders of the commandant, AB 95, 109. Cf. also Jeyaraj, *Inkulturation in Tranquebar*, 191.

Tranquebar were horrified and immediately initiated measures for punishment. 'We have withheld an entire month's salary from the catechist Rajanayakkan so that he may free himself entirely from the job given to him by the king.'[157] In 1769, when alcohol problems and contacts with the Moravian Brethren were added to the list of his wrongdoings, Rajanayakkan was transferred to Arantangi.[158]

In view of the fact that it was difficult for Europeans to travel freely in Thanjavur the missionaries sent Tamil co-workers there from time to time whose job was to get information about conditions for missionary work. For Christmas celebrations in 1746 Diogo was meant to visit the Christians in Thanjavur, but the Catholics and Hindus prevented his visit. As a result, Diogo came to the conclusion that the time was not yet ripe for establishing a permanent mission base in Thanjavur.[159] Despite this, the pastor began to travel to Thanjavur regularly. By the beginning of the seventies he made two or three trips every year to the region—at Christmas, Easter and Whitsuntide.[160] From 1772 Philipp took over most of this work.[161]

From the beginning of the 1750s some missionaries also traveled at irregular intervals to Thanjavur where, in the meantime, political developments were marked by the rivalries between the English, the French and the Muslim rulers of South India. In 1753 Petrus Dame and Johann Christian Wiedebrock traveled to Thanjavur. In July and August 1753 Wiedebrock preached publicly for the first time in the city.[162] During this time tensions developed between the Raja of Thanjavur and the Danes in Tranquebar, since the Danes were also trying to extend their territory in view of the

[157] AFSt/M 1 B 43 : 13, letter from Jacob Klein to Gotthilf August Francke, Tranquebar, 8 October 1753, (translated from German). Cf. also Germann, *Missionar Christian Friedrich Schwartz*, 56.

[158] 'Rajanaicken is still deep in debt and, unfortunately, most of his debts, as we hear, are on account of his drinking. He cannot give it up....' (translated from German), AFSt/M 1 B 48 : 11, letter from J. Klein to G.A. Francke, Tranquebar, 16 October 1758. See also NHB 4. St., 422, 482; 8. St., 993.

[159] HB 66. Cont., 1072, letter from Diogo to G.A. Francke, 24 January 1747.

[160] For the years 1768–1772 see NHB 1. St., 8f., 52f.; 3. St., 272f; 5. St., 875f., 913f.; 9. St., 1137, 1178f.

[161] For the year 1772 see NHB 10. St., 1291–5, 1350–53; 11. St., 1423–28, 1444–48, 1459–64.

[162] HB 80. Cont., 1195–1208, Wiedebrock's travel diary 1753.

growing presence of the English and the French. In 1756 the Danes occupied a village in the territory of the Raja of Thanjavur and set up defensive positions there, but they were driven back by the Raja's troops who started a counter-attack on Danish settlements.[163] In 1762 Christian Friedrich Schwartz made a journey to Thanjavur with Jacob Klein. Daniel Zeglin, who had accompanied Schwartz to Thanjavur in April 1759, stayed there for two months in 1765, partly at the request of the German captain Berg, who was in the service of the king of Thanjavur, to provide pastoral care to the Europeans, including Germans, there, and partly to visit the Christians in the villages along with Rajanayakkan.[164] A year later Peter Dame was supposed to take over these duties, but he died during his stay in Thanjavur.[165]

In the final analysis it was Christian Friedrich Schwartz who established missionary work in Thanjavur. During a journey permitted by the Raja in April and May 1769 he had talks with the king who, in the end, requested him to settle down there. After consulting his colleagues in Tranquebar, the missionary acceded to the raja's request in the interest of the mission and the prestige it would gain from this.[166] In 1773 the Nawab of Carnatic allied with the English against the Raja and invaded Thanjavur in August of the same year. With the capture of the Raja and the appointment of an English Resident in Thanjavur the conditions for missionary work also changed.[167] Schwartz, whose contacts with the royal family were good and who was also respected by a large section of the population as a 'German swami', was asked by Tuljaji II to conduct negotiations on his behalf with the English in Madras. Initially, Schwartz refused, since he felt that the task would contradict his position as a missionary. In 1776 the deposed raja, Tuljaji II, was nominally reinstated—partly also through Schwartz's mediation—but the English remained the de facto administrators of the country.[168]

[163] Krieger, *Kaufleute, Seeräuber und Diplomaten*, 133.
[164] HB 103. Cont., 784–812.
[165] HB 105. Cont., 984; 106. Cont., 1369, 1377.
[166] HB 108. Cont., (330f.) 1731f.
[167] Rajayyan, *History of Madurai*, 262f.
[168] Ibid., 271.

In the seventies and eighties Ch. F. Schwartz, who, in the meantime, spoke Persian, Hindustani and Marathi, apart from English and Tamil, carried out negotiations on behalf of the English with the ruler of Mysore, Haidar Ali, and, after the latter's death, with his son, Tipu Sultan. In 1778 the missionary finally settled down in Thanjavur to establish a mission station there on behalf of the SPCK and with the permission of the English administration,[169] which often asked him to mediate in political and social conflicts. When Schwartz was asked to go to Haidar Ali's residence in Seringapatnam in 1779 he justified his acceptance with the belief that he would be able to help the people in their turmoil. However, he was careful about emphasizing his outward distance in these matters. He justified his work for the English with the idea that successful negotiations would ultimately benefit the people. The gifts he received from the English for his political work went to the mission.[170] When a large number of Christians left Thanjavur in 1786 due to increasing exploitation and persecution by the Raja, the governor appointed a commission of which Schwartz was also a member. The raja was then forced to give up certain practices and decrease many taxes.[171]

THE ENGLISH IN SOUTH INDIA

The English East India Company was against Christian missionary activity in regions under their control since they did not want trade to be hindered in any way. Only pastoral care of their own employees was permitted. As a result, the two most important Anglican mission organizations, the Society for Promoting Christian Knowledge (SPCK), founded in 1698, and the Society for Propagating the Gospel (SPG), founded in 1701, supported Protestant missions of different derivations with funds or with literature. In the eighteenth century the SPG had established its sphere of work among the Christians in North America, while the SPCK concentrated on East India. Wherever missions were established in the names of these

[169] NHB 55. St., 637–45, biography of Ch. F. Schwartz.
[170] NHB 24. St., 1410.
[171] NHB 34. St., 1154, 1157, letter from Ch. F. Schwartz, 17 July 1786.

organizations, it was with the help of or through the recruitment of workers of other mission societies.[172]

The co-operation between the SPCK and the Tranquebar Mission began in 1709 in Europe. After the mission reports from South India had received an enthusiastic response in Germany, Anton Wilhelm Böhme (1673–1722) in London, chaplain of the prince-consort, Georg of Denmark (1651–1708), translated some of the mission documents into English and thus promoted interest in evangelical missionary work in England.[173] It was Böhme who established the contact between the SPCK and the missionaries. Ziegenbalg and Plütschau became corresponding members of the society, which also set up a special Malabar Committee to co-ordinate its work in India.[174] At the same time, the directors of the Francke Foundations, beginning with August Hermann Francke (since 1699), were, as a rule, also corresponding members of the SPCK.[175]

When Bartholomäus Ziegenbalg stayed in London in 1714 during his trip to Europe, he was received not only by representatives of the Society for Promoting Christian Knowledge. From London Ziegenbalg reported to Halle that he had spoken with the Archbishop of Canterbury and the Bishop of London, had handed over a complete bound edition of the East India reports at the royal court and had visited the king as well as the Prince and Princess of Wales.[176] George I (1660–1727), king of England and head of the Anglican Church, manifested interest in the missionary and, in a letter that

[172] For the history of the SPCK see, among others, Brunner, *Halle Pietists in England*.

[173] Böhme, a pupil of August Hermann Francke, first translated the latter's *Segensvolle Fußstapfen* into English. The work appeared in 1705 under the title *Pietas Halensis*. After that he translated the *Merkwürdige Nachricht aus Ostindien* that had been brought out by Joachim Lange in 1708, and published the translation under the title *Propagation of the Gospel in the East*. See: Sames, Arno, 2006, 'Beziehungen zwischen Kopenhagen, Halle und London', in Liebau, *Geliebtes Europa//Ostindische Welt*, 29–34.

[174] A letter to this effect was sent to the missionaries on 7 September 1710. HB 6. Cont., preface, 11. Koilpillai, Victor J., 1985, *The SPCK in India 1710–1985. An Account of the Work of the Society for Promoting Christian Knowledge*, ISPCK, London, Delhi. Cf. also Brunner, *Halle Pietists in England*.

[175] Thus, for example, Johann Georg Knapp was appointed corresponding member of the SPCK in 1770. NHB 1. St., Vorrede; (5). St., preface (113).

[176] MNOIM, 32, 1/2, 1880, 119f., letter from Ziegenbalg to A.H. Francke, 14 February 1716.

followed, he assured the missionaries in Tranquebar of his goodwill and his willingness to support the missionary endeavour.[177]

After his arrest in Tranquebar in 1708/09 and after the differences in the matter of Johann Georg Bövingh (1676–1723), Bartholomäus Ziegenbalg had already established contact with representatives of the SPCK and had even considered a new beginning for the mission under the direction of the SPCK.[178] The contacts between the German missionaries and representatives of the SPCK, or of the English East India Company, were, however, initially limited to concrete projects. Thus, in 1711, the SPCK sent not only money and books to support the schools in Tranquebar, but also the technical equipment for a printing-press along with a trained co-worker for the press—the former teacher of a London school, Jonas Finck (died 1711).[179]

What began as an informal co-operation between the Tranquebar Mission and the SPCK developed, under the growing strength of the English colonial power in South India, into a network of missionary institutions financed and equipped by the English partners, but run by German missionaries and Indians trained in the Danish-English-Halle Mission. The SPCK, for its part, requested officials of the Company to support the missionaries who wanted to establish themselves in the territory of the English East India Company, which was the basic precondition for the beginning of the English missions under the direction of the SPCK.[180] Spurred on by the growing interest in missionary work in England, Englishmen working in India helped mission projects with donations of money.[181]

[177] HB 14. Cont., 166f., letter from George I., August 23 (September 3), 1717; AB 515. Cf. also Pascoe, Charles Frederick, 1901, *Two Hundred Years of the S.P.G. An Historical Account of the Society of the Propagation of the Gospel in Foreign Parts 1701–1900*, S.P.G., London, 501.

[178] Cf. Nørgaard, *Mission und Obrigkeit*, 49, 54.

[179] Finck died on the voyage to India. The English fleet entered into an encounter with French ships resulting also in the loss of a part of the printing press.

[180] Koilpillai, *The SPCK in India*, 10.

[181] An English chaplain in Madras volunteered to advance 600 *Reichstaler* from charity funds to the missionaries in 1714, since the arrival of ships with the funds from Europe had been delayed. HB 8. Cont., 630, letter from Ziegenbalg and Gründler, 9 October 1713.

After Ziegenbalg's return from Europe the co-operation between the Danish-Halle missionaries and English officials, which was initially based on personal contacts and mutual sympathies, became more intensive and was increasingly institutionalized. In order to make the co-operation more official the missionaries sought direct access to the English governors and residents. Thus, Ziegenbalg and Gründler sent the new governor of Madras, Joseph Collet, a brief description of the work of the mission when he arrived in July 1717. The tract contained an exhaustive description of the goals, the methods and the institutions of the mission, named all the co-workers and expressed appreciation for help that had hitherto been received from English sources.[182]

In the course of time English mission stations were set up in Cuddalore, Tiruchirappalli, Thanjavur, Calcutta and Madras on the initiative of the SPCK and run by Danish-Halle missionaries together with their local co-workers. The stations were financed by the SPCK in London. The mission stations were on English colonial territory with the approval of the English East India Company. This process began in 1717 when the SPCK planned to set up schools in Madras and Cuddalore with personnel and organizational support from the missionaries in Tranquebar. They first requested Ziegenbalg to send suitable South Indian teachers for the new schools.[183] William Stevenson, chaplain in the English East India Company, also participated in the project.[184]

In 1728 the SPCK received land from the East India Company to set up a mission station in Madras with the Lutheran missionary

[182] Ziegenbalg, Bartholomäus and Johann Ernst Gründler, 2002, 'Kurze Beschreibung der Tätigkeit der Mission [...]', in Niels-Peter Moritzen (ed.), *Von den Anfängen evangelischer Mission: zwei unbekannte Missionsschriften von 1713 und 1717*, 10–49, Verlag für Kultur und Wissenschaft, Bonn. The earlier governor in Madras, Edward Harrison, had left for England on 8 January 1717. Collet arrived in March of the same year. Cf. also AB 478, letter from Ziegenbalg and Gründler to Christian Benedikt Michaelis, January 1717. AB 493, letter from Ziegenbalg and Gründler to the Mission Board, 20 November 1717.

[183] HB 14. Cont., 156, B. Ziegenbalg and J.E. Gründler to A.H. Francke, 22 February 1718; 14. Cont., 164, letter from Ziegenbalg and Gründler, 5 December 1718; AB 493, Ziegenbalg and Gründler to the Mission Board, 20 November 1717.

[184] Pascoe, *Two Hundred Years of the S.P.G.*, 505.

Benjamin Schultze.[185] He was the first missionary of the Danish-Halle Mission to enter into the services of the SPCK. Others followed. Despite the formal transfer to another mission society these missionaries maintained contact with the Tranquebar Mission and the Francke Foundations in Halle. As employees of the SPCK the missionaries, who were earlier under the Danish crown, were now associated with the English colonial power in South India, and this sometimes had serious consequences in times of military and political conflicts. During the siege of Madras by the French the German missionaries working there had to leave the city along with the English inhabitants. On 21 September 1746 Madras was occupied by French troops. The co-workers of the mission station—teachers, school children and domestic help—left the city and went to Pulicat under Dutch protection. The mission buildings were destroyed, the mission garden was laid waste. When the city was returned to the English on 1 September 1749 the mission co-workers also returned, and the station was re-built with the help of the English authorities.[186] Viewed by the French as English allies, the mission station in Vepery near Madras was attacked by French troops in December 1758. Johann Philipp Fabricius went to the French camp and tried to mediate on behalf of the Mission.[187] From 1758–60 Cuddalore was in French hands, which also meant that the Danish-English-Halle missionaries had to leave the place during this period.[188]

In 1784 the missionaries in Tranquebar felt that the co-operation with their English colleagues was an important component of their missionary existence in India: 'Our association with the English missionaries is and remains very close, and we regard the mission as one, with different accounts, but with the same ardent interest [...].'[189] Even when the English, having defeated Tipu Sultan in 1799, established their rule over large parts of South India, the East

[185] Koilpillai, *The SPCK in India*, 11.

[186] HB 77. Cont., 833–46, speech by Friedrich Michael Ziegenhagen to the congregation of the German court-chapel, London, 14 October 1753.

[187] HB 91. Cont., 734f.

[188] Packiamuthu, David, 2000, 'The Beginnings of Protestant Mission in Madras', *ICHR*, XXXIV (2): 93–116.

[189] RA Miskolark 9g, *Pro Memoria* for new missionaries, from Ch. S. John and [J.P. Rottler] Tranquebar, 20 January 1784, (translated from German).

India Company did not officially allow missionary work, but the general climate towards missions had become much more favourable under the growing influence of Anglican revival movements and newly-established mission organizations in England. Despite the indifference to religion that marked the attitude of the East India Company as an economic and political body, some of its officials gave moral and financial support to certain mission activities. For many Englishmen there were sufficient reasons for promoting the work of the mission, especially the mission schools. Englishmen, living and working in India, particularly supported missionary work by, for example, financing the education of some children,[190] or by donating money for building churches or schools. Highly placed officials of the Company were also among the donors.[191] Some officials regarded it as their religious duty to remember the Mission in their will.[192] Even English organizations donated money for the Mission, among others in the 1750s, the Society of Young Christian Artisans in London.[193]

What was decisive in the relationship between the Mission and the colonial rulers—at least from the point of view of the missionaries—was the attitude of the Company to the local Christians in their territory. This included the creation of a legal foundation for the life of the Christian community in general and the willingness to employ Christian Indians in particular. In the interest of political stability in their territories highly placed English officials made various efforts through the promulgation of laws and decrees to create a favourable climate for the Christian population and to prevent religious conflicts. This development became very apparent after English rule was

[190] The Englishman Bohle, Resident in Nagapattinam, sent 12 pagodas in 1760 for the education of two children in Tranquebar. HB 94. Cont., 1045.

[191] Englishmen donated money to Ch. F. Schwartz for maintaining the English school in Tiruchirappalli and organized collections for building a church. HB 103. Cont., preface (181f.). Andrew Newton, commissioner of the English troops in Tiruchirappalli, donated 10 pagodas to the mission and had a house built for conducting divine services. HB 95. Cont., 1115, 97. Cont., 27, 119f.

[192] James Hunter, former teacher in the English congregation at Cuddalore, asked for a part of his legacy to be paid out to the mission. HB 89. Cont., 632. The Englishman Clarenbault in Dacca bequeathed 500 rupees to the mission in Tranquebar in his will. HB 93. Cont., 933f.

[193] HB 85. Cont., (30f.)

established in Thanjavur where the Christians had earlier been exposed to severe persecution. The Christians living there were now given legal rights. The administrator of the English territories passed a decree in 1800 according to which Christians would not be forced to work in the fields on Sundays, and would use this day instead to rest and to attend divine services. In addition, Christians would no longer be required to take part in local Hindu ceremonies and processions or to draw the chariots for the processions.[194] The decree also stated that every catechist would be given a piece of land to build a house, a prayer house and a school.[195]

Against its propagated principle of religious neutrality highly placed officials of the English East India Company interfered in mission matters when they saw their commercial interests being harmed by the work of the mission. In 1750 the governor of Madras accused the missionaries of forcibly converting Hindus to Christianity and he, for his part, therefore forcibly kept Indians away from religious instruction. Fabricius then sent his catechist Schawrimuttu (died 1773) along with the mission scribe to the governor with a sharply-formulated 'petition' in which he wrote:

> You would also be aware of the fact that we were sent for this work to Madras by the Highly Esteemed Society in England and with the consent of the Highly Esteemed directors of the East India Company. Forgive us when we say that it appears to us that You, instead of assisting such a divine venture, as should be done, seem to be more inclined to preventing us from doing what Christ commanded.[196]

This aggressive reaction from the mission to the demonstration of power by the governor caused the latter to invite Fabricius for talks in which the governor explained his reservations against Christian missionary activity. Among other things, the governor considered it harmful to convert people of higher castes, since this could possibly make others leave Company territory.[197]

[194] NHB 58. St., 841, Tranquebar 1800.

[195] Till then the mission had to lease land from the local landowners when an employee had to be established in a place. Ibid.

[196] HB 73. Cont., 137, diary of Fabricius, 25 May 1750, (translated from German).

[197] HB 73. Cont., 139.

The officially reiterated religious neutrality of the East India Company meant that the Company did not feel obliged to employ Indian Christians. On the contrary, Sinappah Arasaratnam has stated that while the Danes, and even the French, preferred to employ Christians in their administrations, the English in Madras initially preferred Hindus.[198] From the middle of the eighteenth century onwards there was a growing demand in the Company for well-educated Indians with knowledge of English, of European accounting, of the natural sciences and of the European way of life and conduct. At the same time, Indians of different religious backgrounds also became more interested in this kind of education. The missionaries made every effort to adapt their educational methods to these conditions. In the so-called English schools in different places they educated local people in such a way that the latter fulfilled conditions for employment with the Company. At times, Englishmen stated the specific requirements for the education of young Indians and then supported this education. In 1803 two young Tamilians in Tranquebar received a supplementary training in mechanical drawing at the request and with the funds of an English engineer, since these boys were to be later employed as draughtsmen and scribes.[199] From the second half of the eighteenth century onwards Hindus also attended the English schools in Cuddalore, Thanjavur, Tiruchirappalli or Madras, since they too wanted an English education like the mission Christians. Time and again the missionaries had to expressly request the Company to employ Christians. In 1751 the governor in Cuddalore promised to give preference in future to the Christians of the mission congregation over others. He also allowed the Christians working for the Company to attend classes in the Mission for some time to refresh their knowledge.[200]

On the other hand, former members of the English army or of the Company worked for different reasons for the Mission. English soldiers taught temporarily in the schools set up by Schwartz and continued to receive their pay during this time from the English

[198] Arasaratnam, 'Indian intermediaries', 140.

[199] RA Miskolark 9i, report on the situation of the Royal Danish Mission in Tranquebar in the year 1803 by Ch. S. John, J.P. Rottler, A.F. Cämmerer (duplicate), page-leaf 5.

[200] HB 76. Cont., 578.

colonial administration. Schwartz was very aware of his involvement with emerging colonial structures. This process, whereby missionary work was increasingly attuned to the requirements of the English colonial authorities, became particularly apparent in the educational system in the last decades of the eighteenth century through the model of the so-called provincial schools, which catered mainly to non-Christian sections of the population interested in an English education.[201] The pressure applied by the English colonial power on the missionaries became increasingly evident. In a letter of 1785 to Gottlieb Anastasius Freylinghausen John emphasized that the mission would have to become 'more valuable and necessary to the Europeans' without neglecting its actual aim of conversion. John was thinking mainly about setting up schools to educate children for English and Dutch employment.[202]

Despite the separation of the commercial interests of the East India Company and the various missionary activities in their territories, which the Company accepted, but did not officially promote, officials of the East India Company often took the help of mission employees. This sometimes took the form of translation work or political mediation. On account of his knowledge of languages and his political reputation Christian Friedrich Schwartz worked as an interpreter and mediator for the English in negotiations with local rulers. In return, the English supported him. The personal relationship between the missionary and representatives of the English army such as the chief engineer of their troops in Madras, Major William Stevens (died 1778), and General Hector Munro (1726–1805), proved to be advantageous for the mission in Thanjavur.[203] On 10 March 1779 Munro personally laid the foundation stone for an English church, which had been built largely with donations from Englishmen and was primarily meant for members of the English garrison.[204] Besides Schwartz, Christian Wilhelm Gericke also took on the role of mediator in conflicts

[201] For the provincial schools see pp. 360–72 of this study.

[202] NHB 32. St., 897f. Ch. S. John to G.A. Freylinghausen, 10 September 1785.

[203] NHB 24. St., 1409.

[204] NHB 23. St., 1320; Neill, Stephen, 1985, *A History of Christianity in India 1707–1858*, Cambridge University Press, Cambridge, 105.

between the English, the French and Haidar Ali.[205] On the basis of their long experience and their often excellent knowledge of the country and its languages, the English were also interested in mission employees for their new academic institutions. Carl Wilhelm Pätzold, who had first worked with Gericke, was asked to teach in the Fort William College in Calcutta, but he did not stay there for long and returned to Vepery after a short time.[206]

Mission employees often took on the pastoral care of the English, of military personnel and of prisoners, since the English colonial clergymen responsible for this were often overwhelmed with pastoral services in the civil and military spheres. In many cases, German missionaries took on these duties for members of the English army. Missionaries in Cuddalore helped with the English army there when the army chaplain fell ill.[207] After New Year in 1762 Georg Heinrich Conrad Hüttemann was requested to hold a thanksgiving service on one of the English battleships, since it had survived the storm on the night of the New Year without any damage. Other ships like the *Aquitaine* and *Sunderland*, each with its 70 cannons and crew, had been completely destroyed.[208] In 1794 Johann Caspar Kohlhoff tended to the English soldiers of the 74th Royal Regiment in Thanjavur.[209] While the efforts of the German missionaries presumably contributed to raising the soldiers' morale, Indian mission co-workers also went into army camps to tend to the local Christians. Members of the mission were, however, also approached for official religious functions in the civil sphere. In October 1759 Georg Heinrich Conrad Hüttemann officiated at the wedding of the English resident, Bohle, in Nagapattinam,[210] while Fabricius did the same for Robert Clive (1725–74) in Madras.[211]

The co-operation between officials of the English East India Company, representatives of the SPCK and employees of the Danish-

[205] Koilpillai, *The SPCK in India*, 17f.

[206] Ibid.

[207] HB 82. Cont., 1488, report, October 1754.

[208] HB 96. Cont., 1340f. report from G.H.C. Hüttemann. Cuddalore 1761.

[209] NHB 41. St., 479; 44. St., 753; 45. St., 849f; 48. St., 1120.

[210] HB 92. Cont., 848.

[211] Dodwell, Henry, 1986, *The Nabobs of Madras*, Asian Educational Services, New Delhi, 94.

English-Halle Mission encouraged new Anglican mission societies to try and establish themselves in South India at the beginning of the nineteenth century. In the middle of the eighteenth century a broad revivalist movement developed within the Anglican Church, which was significantly inspired by John Wesley (1703–91). Under the influence of Charles Grant (1746–1823), member of the Court of Directors of the East India Company, a demand was raised in England in 1793 to include a paragraph in the charter of the Company allowing missionary work in British territories in India. Although this finally happened only in 1813 when the charter was revised, the work of Protestant revival movements continued to become more apparent in England. As a result of these developments the Baptist Missionary Society was established in 1792, the London Missionary Society in 1795 and the Church Mission Society in 1799.[212] The Scottish Church set up the Scottish Missionary Society in 1796. The new charter of the East India Company envisaged the appointment of a bishop in Calcutta and an archdeacon each in Calcutta, Madras and Bombay. With this, the British parliament opened the doors for widespread missionary work in India.[213]

In the first decades of the nineteenth century Anglican mission societies gradually took over the care of the congregations in the stations set up by the Halle missionaries. In 1814/1815, at the request of Christoph Samuel John, the Church Missionary Society sent five missionaries trained in the Berlin missionary seminary to the station in Tranquebar where August Friedrich Cämmerer supervised them.[214] Hardly any new missionaries had been sent out since the beginning of the nineteenth century by the Danish and Halle authorities and it became difficult to guarantee the continuous work of the various mission stations.[215]

[212] Cf. Ward, *The Church Mission Society*, Introduction.

[213] Koilpillai, *The SPCK in India*.

[214] NHB 66. St., 559.

[215] After Gericke left Cuddalore in 1782, the teacher Manoel (died 1805) had looked after mission matters on his own for almost ten years. Christoph Heinrich Horst came to Cuddalore only in 1792, followed in 1803 by Immanuel Gottfried Holzberg (till 1824) and, at the end of the 1820s Daniel Schreyvogel was there for a brief period. Although, after the death of Ch. F. Schwartz in 1798 missionaries like Horst (till 1810), Christlieb Augustin Jacobi (till 1814) and, mainly, Johann Caspar Kohlhoff worked in Thanjavur, they could not cope with all the pastoral work that

The decrease in support from Copenhagen and Germany was inevitable since both the countries were involved in different wars. For the missionaries in Tranquebar, therefore, the monthly gift of 100 pagodas from the Madras station (that was briefly raised to 300 pagodas) was very welcome.[216] The Mission Board in Copenhagen had, in fact, ended all support. In 1820 the SPCK took over 11 district congregations of the Tranquebar Mission.[217] At this point of time the Danes were also considering a sale of their territories around Tranquebar.[218] In 1825 the responsibility for most of the stations and for the German missionaries working there was handed over to the SPG. In 1825 a Royal Resolution was passed in which the original task of conversion was withdrawn and the Mission was—as far as the content of work and finances were concerned—placed under the jurisdiction of the government.[219] In 1825 the SPCK also handed over the responsibility for the Mission in South India to the SPG.[220]

THE CONTENTIOUS FIELD OF CHRISTIAN MISSIONARY EFFORTS

In their daily work missionaries and local employees of the Tranquebar Mission constantly came into contact with representatives of other Christian missions or with priests of other denominations. Catholic orders, for example, had an organized network of mission stations in European trade-settlements. Direct and indirect contacts between their representatives and members of the Tranquebar

---

was required. With the death of Christian Pohle in 1818 the station in Tiruchirappalli appeared deserted. In the English station in Madras a certain amount of continuity was guaranteed by the work of Ernst August Georg Falcke (1784 till 1824), Lauritz Peter Haubroe (1822 till 1824) and Johann Peter Rottler (till 1836). August Friedrich Cämmerer worked in Tranquebar till 1837

[216] John, *On Indian Civilization*, 3. John, who perceived personnel problems as the main difficulty of the mission, would have, mainly for health reasons, liked to return to Europe in order to select and prepare missionaries for the work in India. John, *On Indian Civilization*, 8, 11.

[217] Nørgaard, *Mission und Obrigkeit*, 228.

[218] Ibid., 229.

[219] Ibid., 234.

[220] Koilpillai, *The SPCK in India*, 19f.

Mission often led to conflicts and rivalries, but sometimes also to co-operation. The relations between the Tranquebar Mission and members of Dutch settlements on the south east coast of India and Ceylon was less prone to conflict. Halle missionaries, or Indians trained by them, were given refuge in times of political crises; they looked after the congregations there and also co-operated with the Dutch on different matters. The presence of the Moravian Brethren in Tranquebar between 1760 and 1802 was, however, a chapter filled with conflict. Since they were located in the immediate vicinity of the Danish-Halle Mission, many South Indian employees were also affected by this conflict. I have refrained from adding a special section on the development of relations with the SPCK and other Anglican organizations. They are, rather, an integral component of this study since I view the Mission as a Danish-English-Halle venture.[221]

COMPETITION AND SOLICITATION OF EMPLOYEES

Catholic congregations had existed on the south east coast of India long before the arrival of the first Protestant missionaries. These congregations came into existence due to the presence of the Portuguese in India. Franciscan monks who were responsible for the pastoral care of the crews of the Portuguese ships extended their activities to the local population after their arrival in India. Once the *padroado* was officially introduced mission stations were established in the Portuguese settlements on the Indian coast, as also in Ceylon and Burma.[222] Besides the Franciscans it was mainly the Jesuits who

[221] See footnote 6 of the introduction. There are, as yet, no comprehensive studies on this theme. Individual aspects are highlighted in: Walls, Andrew F., 2006, 'The Society for Promoting Christian Knowledge and the Missionary Movement in Britain', in Gross et al., *Halle and the Beginning of Protestant Christianity in India*, Vol. I, 107–28; O'Connor, Daniel, 2006, 'The Church of England and the Mission in India', in Gross et al., *Halle and the Beginning of Protestant Christianity in India*, Vol. I, 129–38; Gross, Andreas, 2006, 'Madras and the English-Halle Missionaries (1726–1836)', in Gross et al., *Halle and the Beginning of Protestant Christianity in India*, Vol. I, 311–44; Gross, 2006, 'Some Aspects of the English-Halle Mission in Cuddalore (1737–1829)', in Gross et al., *Halle and the Beginning of Protestant Christianity in India*, Vol. I, 381–405.

[222] *Annual Reports of the Portuguese Franciscans in India 1713–1833*, 1972, Collected and annotated by Fr. Achilles Meersman, Ordo Fratrum Minorum, Lisboa.

also began a broad mission campaign in India from 1542 onwards. The Jesuit epoch in India began with the mass conversions among Tamil fisher folk by Francisco de Xavier from 1542 till 1552, and this work in South India was continued by missionaries such as Henrique Henriques (1520–1600), Roberto de Nobili (1577–1656) and Constanzo Guiseppe Beschi (1680–ca. 1746).

In the immediate surroundings of the Tranquebar Mission there were Catholic missions that had been working since the second half of the seventeenth century. From 1663 onwards French Capuchin missionaries had been working in Pondicherry. The Jesuits came in 1689 and started their mission in the Carnatic in 1700 with its centre in Madurai.[223] Even after the French king, Louis XIV, announced the end of the Jesuit order in his territories in 1764, the missionaries remained there till their society was finally dissolved in 1773 bringing an end to their work in South India. The Capuchins and the French mission society, Missions Èntrangères de Paris, established between 1658 and 1663, considered themselves the successors of the Jesuit institutions. Many Jesuits, who did not return to Europe after their society had been dissolved, continued to work for other societies. The work of the Jesuit order was legalized again only in 1814 by the Papal bull *Sollicitudo Omnium Ecclesiarum* under Pope Pius VII (1742/in office: 1800–23).[224]

There were Catholic Christians in Tranquebar even when the Danes received permission to establish a trading settlement in 1620.[225] The Danish authorities counted the Catholics among that section of the population, which was easily accessible and which quickly developed a sense of loyalty towards the Danes. Catholic Christians were readily taken into the service of the Company, or employed in the personal service of a European. This situation naturally became complicated when the Protestant missionaries

[223] On the Jesuits in India see: Correia-Alfonso, John, 1997, *The Jesuits in India 1542–1773*, Gujarat Sahitya Prakash, Anand, Gujarat, India, 219; Thekkedath, *History of Christianity in India*, Vol. II; Županov, Ines G., 2005, *Missionary Tropics. The Catholic Frontier in India (16th and 17th centuries)*, The University of Michigan Press, Ann Arbor.

[224] Cf. Neill, *A History of Christianity in India*, 127–32.

[225] Exact figures for the Tranquebar region are not available. In 1771 Diogo reported that in a conversation a Catholic had named a figure of 38,000 Catholics for the entire Thanjavur region. NHB 7. St., 913–14.

sent by the Danish king arrived in Tranquebar and began to convert Indians to Protestant Christianity. Especially in the initial years of the parallel presence of Catholics and Protestants the former insisted on their earlier rights and emphasized their proven co-operation with the Danish colonial authorities.[226] The Danish trading company had had good experiences with the Catholic Indians working for it and, initially, did not appear to require the services of Protestant Indians brought up and educated by the Tranquebar Mission.[227] In addition, Catholic priests in Tranquebar were employees of the Company and received their salary from it. In the course of time, however, the tasks and spheres of work of the Catholics and Protestants in Tranquebar were separated, and this led to an easing of tensions between the priests of both confessions.[228]

The differences in beliefs of Protestants and Catholics were made very clear in the training of the Tamilian co-workers of the Tranquebar Mission. The manner of dealing with the Catholic population and Catholic missions was a problem that was often addressed during the teaching sessions that took place regularly. Local individuals who worked for the Tranquebar Mission as assistants, teachers, catechists and pastors were not only expected to talk about Hinduism as a 'false' religion, they also had to be in a position to articulate religious arguments against Catholic beliefs and practices. The personal instructions for catechists and Indian pastors contained concrete points for dealing with Catholic Christians. The situation in Thanjavur city till the middle of the 1750s was characterized, on the one hand, by the absence of European missionaries who could be addressed directly and, on the other hand, by a comparatively high percentage of Muslims and Catholics. For this reason the job instructions for Rajanayakkan, who was working in Thanjavur, contained the following additional points: Roman Catholics who wanted to convert to the Protestant faith would have to be introduced

[226] In 1710 Ziegenbalg wrote about the attitude of the commandant towards the Catholics: 'He is inimical towards us and the spread of our Protestant faith, but is very devoted to the papist priest and the spread of their papacy.' (translated from German), Ziegenbalg to Lange, 30 August 1710. See: Nørgaard, *Mission und Obrigkeit*, 17.

[227] Nørgaard, *Mission und Obrigkeit*, 52.

[228] Ibid., 176f.

to the missionaries prior to conversion. Rajanayakkan was also not allowed to enlist new catechists on his own.[229] In the description of Sattianaden's duties it was expressly stated that although conversations with Roman Catholics was desirable, no conversion efforts were to be made openly. This was because of an agreement that the Catholics too would not try to win over the converts of the Danish-English-Halle Mission.[230]

Presumably both sides did not keep to the agreement not to solicit or influence converts of the other side. In real terms, there was a constant hidden struggle for converts. As a former Catholic the catechist Rajanayakkan had to face the hostility of the Catholics. The Jesuit mission in Madurai viewed the onset of work by the Tranquebar missionaries in the kingdom of Thanjavur with deep suspicion. They considered Rajanayakkan to be a rival and, after unsuccessful attempts at winning him over,[231] they tried to hamper his work wherever possible. In a letter to the Mission Board in Copenhagen of 1749 Rajanayakkan reported about[232] the attacks by Roman Catholics against him and against the Lutheran Christians he had converted in Thanjavur.

In a reverse case in 1752 the missionaries stated with open satisfaction: 'The Catholic catechist Schawrinayagam is known to have a secret inclination towards our Church. He reads our books, one or the other of which he is said to have, and has also had things read out to him a few times by Rajanaicken [...]'[233] The missionaries also regarded it as a success when the Catholic 'Portuguese' priest Bento de Silvester converted to Protestantism in Calcutta and was later taken in by the Protestant mission in Madras.[234] On the

[229] HB 26. Cont., 12–16, 25 January 1728.

[230] HB 26. Cont., 1–3.

[231] Because he was so well known, and because of his rhetorical abilities Rajanayakkan apparently received an offer from the Catholics at the same time that a similar offer came from the Protestants. However, although he did not take up the former offer, he informed the missionaries in Tranquebar about it. HB 26. Cont., 12, diary of the missionaries in Tranquebar, 25 January 1728.

[232] RA Missionskollegiet 9b/1745–1750, translation of a Tamil palm-leaf letter from Rajanayakkan to the Mission Board, 6 October 1749.

[233] HB 78. Cont., report of the missionaries, 15 December 1752, (translated from German).

[234] HB 108. Cont., preface (339f.), 1798, 1802.

other hand, when Njanapragasam, a member of the Tamil mission congregation in Tranquebar, converted to Catholicism, they viewed his decision as despicable. Njanapragasam later even worked as a catechist for a Catholic mission.[235] In 1758 Muttu Schawri reported that some former Catholic Christians in Tiruppundurutti had returned to the Catholic Church after being part of the Protestant congregation for some years.[236]

Peaceful attempts at convincing the other side were not always sufficient, and attempts to win over converts of the other side were not always subtle. Sterner demands or prohibitions were also used. Catholic missionaries in the Cuddalore region prohibited members of their congregations from listening to the Protestant missionaries when they visited their places.[237] Personal attacks by Catholics on local co-workers of the Tranquebar Mission were mostly directed against those who originally came from Catholic families. Sarruwaien, assistant in Nattam in the Madurai region, was taken prisoner and carried off on the orders of a Catholic padre. The aim was to make him return to Catholicism.[238] As regards dealings with representatives of Catholic missions the Tranquebar missionaries also worked with instructions, admonitions, warnings, exhortations and prohibitions. In particular cases and with the help of special means direct missionary advances to Catholics were also permitted. Josua, the assistant in the Mahadevpattanam district, went with his wife to visit the Catholic relatives of some Christians of his congregation in order to talk to them separately from the others.[239]

However, there were also friendly encounters between Catholics and Protestants that were marked by mutual respect. Some official representatives of the Catholic clergy were, at times, very tolerant and open towards the Tranquebar Mission. In 1744 the Bishop of Mylapore (St. Thomé), Don Joseph Pinheiro, who, the Tranquebar missionaries felt, was tolerant and moderate in his attitude towards the Protestant mission, died at the age of 71. He had once even sent them Beschi's Tamil grammar.[240] In 1755 the junior catechist

235 NHB 52. St., 330.
236 HB 89. Cont., 572.
237 HB 90. Cont., 627, report, Cuddalore 1757.
238 HB 92. Cont., 863f.
239 HB 91. Cont., 788.
240 HB 61. Cont., 97.

Wallattu Muttu from Kuttanallur was asked to travel to the Maravar region to celebrate Christmas with the Christians of the *paḷḷar*-caste who had emigrated there. When he fell ill upon his arrival a Roman Catholic catechist gave him medical treatment.[241] The former Catholic Rajanayakkan, who had suffered under the enmity of the Catholics, also conversely enjoyed their respect. Thus, for example, the Catholics in Rautapaleiam[242] asked him to settle a dispute.[243] In times of trouble Christians asked their fellow-believers for help. When Catholic Christians had to flee Pondicherry in 1760 after the English occupied the city, 30 or 40 people asked the Tranquebar missionaries for permission to stay in the school in Porayar for some time.[244] While the Protestant missionaries helped lay-Catholics without any reservations, they viewed the appearance of Jesuit missionaries with suspicion: 'After the capture and destruction of the French place Ponticheri eight Jesuits gradually found their way here one after the other and they have hitherto used all imaginable cunning to be able to conduct their divine services in public, but, thank God, in vain.'[245] When increasing numbers of Jesuits and Roman Catholic Christians settled down in the villages of the Danish Company, and there was a danger of Protestant Christians being wooed away, the Tranquebar missionaries turned to the Danish authorities: 'We have submitted enough petitions, both in writing and orally, to the praiseworthy government to well and truly restrict the Jesuits.'[246]

In the 1780s Christoph Samuel John rejected conversion attempts among Catholics, since he regarded the conversion of a large number of Catholics as harmful and detrimental to the reputation of the Tranquebar Mission.[247] With his radical views John compared the Catholics to the 'untouchables'. Both groups, according to him, were difficult to really convert, since one always had to be prepared for reversions. It was better, he felt, to have one less convert than to harm the mission through disorderly and unreliable Christians addicted to

[241] HB 85. Cont., 30f.

[242] This was probably Rawutta-Paleiam, a suburb of Thanjavur.

[243] HB 98. Cont., 171.

[244] HB 93. Cont., 961.

[245] HB 96. Cont., 1303, joint letter from the missionaries in Tranquebar, 29 August 1761, (translated from German).

[246] HB 96. Cont., 1305, joint letter, 31 December 1761, (translated from German).

[247] NHB 31. St., 767.

alcohol.[248] He stated that he would prefer to be stricter with baptisms and only allow selected persons to become Christians in order to improve the reputation of the mission among Europeans.[249] This position did not, however, prevent John from making courtesy calls on Catholic priests while, at the same time, emphasizing his distance to them in his reports to the mission directors.[250]

Besides the direct encounters between co-workers of Catholic and Protestant missions, there were also indirect contacts. In a way, the Tranquebar missionaries profited greatly from the linguistic work done by their Catholic predecessors, even if they did not always acknowledge this openly. In the initial years, the Tranquebar Mission used the gospels as translated by the Catholics.[251] Ziegenbalg exchanged literature with the Catholics and used their texts after revising them and cleansing them of 'Papist leaven'.[252] He regularly asked his writer to read him books translated by the Catholics and, sometimes, expressed his appreciation of a good translation or a good style. He revised some parts of these translations, while others were rejected outright.[253] On 16 October 1739 the missionaries wrote that the 'Grammatica Latino-Tamulica', written by the Jesuit Constantin Joseph Beschi, was being printed on the mission printing press, since the Jesuits did not have their own press at that point of time. In return for this help, however, the Jesuits had to agree to a critical commentary, which was written by Ch. T. Walther and appended to the grammar.[254] Besides others also Catholic books were collected in the mission library.[255]

[248] NHB 32. St., 891, Ch. S. John to G.A. Freylinghausen, 10 September 1785.

[249] NHB 32. St., 887–98, Ch. S. John to G.A. Freylinghausen, 10 September 1785.

[250] NHB 33. St., 1094, May 1785.

[251] AB 68, letter (presumably from Ziegenbalg) of 12 October 1707. See also: Ziegenbalg, 'Kurze Beschreibung der Tätigkeit der Mission [...]', 42. On the ambivalence of these contacts see also: Sweetman, Will, 2006, 'Bartholomäus Ziegenbalg, the Tranquebar Mission and 'The Roman Horror'', in Gross et al., *Halle and the Beginning of Protestant Christianity in India*, Vol. II, 797–811.

[252] HB 4. Cont., 159.

[253] AB 171, Ziegenbalg to J. Lange, 22 December 1710.

[254] HB 50. Cont., 255; Walther, Christoph Theodosius, 1739, *Observationes grammaticae, quibus linguae tamulicae idioma vulgare, in usum operatiorum in messe Domini inter gentes vulgo malabares dictas, [...]*, Mission Printing Press, Tranquebar.

THE DUTCH AND THE TRANQUEBAR MISSION

In an open letter of 9 September 1715 Gründler had emphasized the usefulness of his correspondence in matters concerning the mission with English pastors in Madras and Bengal, as well as with Dutch pastors in Nagapattinam and Colombo.[256] While relations with the English priests were strongly influenced by the colonial policies of the trading company, the contacts with the Dutch predominantly concerned the religious care of the congregations.

From the time they captured the coastal city of Nagapattinam in 1658 the Dutch were in possession of an important trading base in the immediate vicinity of the Danish trade settlement in Tranquebar that had existed since 1620. The Calvinist priests, who had arrived in connection with Dutch trading activity, were mainly responsible for the pastoral care of the European employees of the VOC. Although some of these priests, such as Philipp Baldaeus (1632–72), or Abraham Roger (died 1649), were interested in meeting the local population and studying Hindu society, or in carrying out missionary activity among the local population, the Dutch as a whole did not lay claim to organized missionary work.[257] Between 1650 and 1690 the Dutch conquered a large number of Portuguese bases, reduced or put an end to the work of Catholic missionaries and expelled Franciscan monks and missionaries from these territories.[258] In the middle of the seventeenth century they were the largest economic power in Asia and their most important trading bases included, among others, Cochin and Craganore on the west coast of India. On the east coast they had important settlements in the seventeenth century in St. Thomé, Sadras, Pondicherry, Devanapatnam, Porto Novo, Karaikal and Nagapattinam. This situation continued till the beginning of the eighteenth century, when the English and French became the most important European powers in South India and the Dutch had to gradually give up important bases.

255 Cf. also HB 58. Cont., 1525.

256 HB 10. Cont., 850; 33. Cont., 912f.

257 Early forms of Protestant influence in India are dealt with in: Arasaratnam, 'Protestant Christianity and South Indian Hinduism'.

258 In 1658 the Dutch captured Nagapattinam and Tuticorin, in 1661 Quilon, in 1662 Craganore and in 1663 Cochin and Cannanore. Cf. *Annual Reports of the Portuguese Franciscans in India*, 6f.

When the Danish-English-Halle missionaries arrived, Nagapattinam, south of Tranquebar, was still an important Dutch base. The Tranquebar missionaries first visited the Dutch priests in 1708.[259] The Dutch gave them permission to use their church library in Nagapattinam. Thus, Ziegenbalg and Gründler had a copy made of the Portuguese translation of the Old Testament that was available there.[260] In the 1730s the number of members of the Tamil ('Malabarian') congregation in Nagapattinam, looked after by the Dutch, amounted to a little over thirty. Till the 1760s people from Nagapattinam were often given baptismal instruction and baptized in Tranquebar.[261] In 1782 Christian Wilhelm Gericke established himself for a few years in Nagapattinam, when the French had captured his main place of work—Cuddalore. With a few brief interruptions Gericke stayed in Nagapattinam till 1788 and looked after the Christian congregations set up by the Dutch there.[262] From Nagapattinam he also travelled to Pulicat (1785), another Dutch base.[263] In Nagapattinam Gericke worked with Rajappen (died 1785), who he had brought with him from Cuddalore, as well as with two local catechists who were paid by the Dutch Church.[264] When the missionary conference in Tranquebar decided in 1787 that Gericke would move to Madras, the Dutch asked him at the same time to take over their churches in Nagapattinam and to look after the congregations and social institutions linked with their Church. On 22 February 1787 Gericke wrote:

> But, yesterday the Dutch pastor of Nagapatnam and of this coast as well as members of the Church Council came to me and requested me to take over the management of a part of their church funds and to look after the spiritual and material welfare of the poor, who would

[259] Further visits followed, including in 1744, 1754 and 1772. HB 61. Cont., 144–76; 89. Cont., 538, 560.

[260] Ziegenbalg, 'Kurze Beschreibung der Tätigkeit der Mission', 42.

[261] HB 37. Cont., 69; 38. Cont., preface, 200, 205, 233; 40. Cont., 481, 485, 490; 42. Cont., preface; 47. Cont., 1331; 93. Cont., 931; 94. Cont., 1045; 95. Cont., 1105.

[262] C.F. Pascoe is wrong when he states that Gericke stayed there from 1782 to 1785. In 1825 the station was handed over to the SPG. Pascoe, *Two Hundred Years of the S.P.G.*, 518.

[263] NHB 33. St., 1077.

[264] NHB 33. St., 1086.

> have to remain here after all those working for the Dutch Company will have left for other places. They also asked me to look after the orphanage [...] and the hospital for lepers.[265]

In the meantime the English had captured Nagapattinam, and the Dutch employees of the Company moved to Paliacatta. Gericke was willing to run the former Dutch schools with English teachers. Indigent mothers, who had earlier received material support from the Dutch and who wanted to send their children to these schools, approached Gericke for help. The Dutch suggested that they would hand over their buildings with all fittings to him if he could organize a settlement from the English Company, which, however, the latter did not agree to.[266] Since Fabricius could not carry out all his duties in Vepery due to ill health, Gericke finally went there in the middle of 1788.[267] After this, the missionaries in Tranquebar visited Nagapattinam from time to time. Gericke placed one of his co-workers there—probably the catechist Santappen (died 1791).[268] He also continued to look after the Christian congregations in Pulicat.[269] In 1790 Gericke baptized a *śūdra* from Pulicat who had received baptismal instruction there and who was then taken into the service of the Dutch governor.[270] In 1790 Christoph Samuel John travelled to Nagapattinam in order, mainly, to look after the charity school set up by Gericke, and to help the two schoolteachers, Sandappen and Domingo de Rosario (died after 1804). In view of the fact that financial support for the Christian congregations there had almost completely collapsed after the Dutch left, Christian Friedrich Schwartz was able to procure a monthly payment of 40 pagodas for the poor-houses in Nagapattinam in 1794.[271] Later, John suggested that his nephew, who had studied theology in Halle and Berlin, and who was working for the SPCK, be appointed as a missionary in Nagapattinam.[272]

265 NHB 36. St., 1428, (translated from German).
266 NHB 36. St., 1428f.
267 NHB 37. St., 108f.
268 NHB 37. St., 109; 39. St., 295.
269 NHB 46. St., 939.
270 NHB 40. St., 379.
271 NHB 46. St., 938.
272 John, *On Indian Civilization*, 44.

The Mission regularly received donations from the Dutch living not only in India, but also in Ceylon and Indonesia. The governor of Nagapattinam, Lubbert Jan Baron de Eck (1719–65), sent the mission a sum of 100 *Pagodas* in January 1710 and 120 *Pagodas* a year later.[273] Antonia Adriana Lengele, wife of Director-General Pieter Rochus Pasques de Chavonnes in Batavia and a long-time benefactress of the mission, donated 400 Reichstaler (= 200 *Pagodas*) every year in the 1740s.[274] Jacob Klein and Johann Christian Breithaupt visited the Chavonnes during their stay in Batavia in 1745 and thanked them for their continuing support and publicity for the Tranquebar Mission.[275] The missionaries also received gifts and donations from the governor-general of Batavia, Gustaaf Willen Baron van Imhoff (1705–50), and other members of the 'Council of the Indies'.[276] Like the English or the Danes, wealthy Dutchmen also willed a part of their wealth to the mission. The governor-general, Jacob Mossel (1704–61), who died in Batavia on 15 May 1761, left the Mission 10,000 Dutch guilders.[277] The superintendent of Porto Noveo, Jacon Jacobs, donated five *Pagodas* for the poor.[278] Along with financial donations the mission also received help in the form of donations in kind. With the permission of Governor Falck the Dutchman Angelbeck had 300 palm trees felled to renovate the mission buildings and organized their transport from Jaffna to Cuddalore.[279] The governor of Ceylon, Julius Valentijn Stein van Gollenesse (in office 1743–54), promised wood for rafters and battens for the construction of a church near Porayar.[280]

[273] HB 93. Cont., 922; 95. Cont., 1109.

[274] HB 64. Cont., 593.

[275] HB 64. Cont., 746–57, Batavia diary of the missionaries Klein and Breithaupt.

[276] HB 64. Cont., 740. The VOC was headed by the 'High Government' with the 'Council of the Indies' and the governor-general. From 1619 onwards the official seat of the governor-general was in Batavia (Jakarta). Kubitschek, Hans Dieter and Ingrid Wessel, 1981, *Geschichte Indonesiens: Vom Altertum bis zur Gegenwart*, Akademie-Verlag, Berlin, 51, 77.

[277] HB 96. Cont., 1249, 1303.

[278] HB 93. Cont., 924.

[279] NHB 1. St., 106, Cuddalore diary, 19 April 1768. Angelbeck had been a student in Halle in the 1740s and was then a master-merchant and secretary of police in Colombo. NHB 2. St., 172.

[280] HB 61. Cont., 13; 64. Cont., 617.

Contacts also existed between the Tranquebar Mission and various Dutch settlements in Ceylon. In 1782 Klein travelled to Ceylon with Schawrirajen.[281] At the request of the Christians there Klein undertook another journey to Ceylon in 1785 where he was received by Dutch officials, the Resident, Maynaard, and the manager, Schröder (Schreuder).[282] With the help of a Dutch merchant friend König travelled to Ceylon in January 1785 and stayed there for four months.[283] König wanted to visit the Lutheran congregations in Ceylon. During the period of their stay Dutch pastors offered their church for divine services to the missionary and his unnamed Indian co-worker. In order to make his travels in Ceylon easier, the Dutch governor placed 20 'coolies' at his disposal and gave him official letters of introduction.[284] Similarly, Rottler went to Ceylon in 1788 with two unnamed mission employees.[285] Christian Friedrich Schwartz also visited Ceylon and stayed in Colombo and Jaffna.[286] Besides the official mission visits there was also co-operation in practical mission matters. On the orders of Governor Iman Willem Falck (in office 1765–85) the Dutch blacksmith Hendricks in Colombo made Tamil and Portuguese letters for the mission press in Tranquebar.[287] The Tamil translation of the Bible was sent to the theological seminary in Ceylon; the *Hallesche Berichte* to the governors in Ceylon and Nagapattinam.[288] With the permission of the Dutch pastor the Tamil catechist from Nagapattinam was present at the ceremonial ordination of the first Indian pastor of the Tranquebar Mission.[289] Occasionally, the missionaries took on tasks to oblige the Dutch. John baptized the child of a Dutch Resident who was staying with his family in Porto Novo in 1790.[290] If their co-workers were

[281] NHB 33. St., 1020.
[282] NHB 29. St., 499f.
[283] NHB 32. St., 908–44.
[284] NHB 32. St., 913, 932.
[285] NHB 37. St., 27–94.
[286] HB 93. Cont., 955–1022.
[287] NHB 29. St., 503.
[288] HB 61. Cont., 77f., diary of the missionaries in Tranquebar, 11 March 1744.
[289] HB 37. Cont., 171, ordination of the first country preacher, Tranquebar, 31 December 1731.
[290] NHB 42. St., 556.

unable to carry out their duties for a long time in regions where a quick replacement could not be found, the Dutch requested the Tranquebar missionaries for help in looking after the Christians living there. When the Indian pastor Rajappen was traveling with a catechist from Palayankottai in 1788 in order to visit Christians in various places, the Dutch Regent in Tuticorin asked them to spend a few months in his region to prepare people for baptism and to then baptize them. In Manappadu (Manapaar) alone 300 Hindus and Catholics were waiting for baptism. The catechist from Palayankottai stayed with the Dutch for nine months.[291] The Christians in Tuticorin and Manappadu, who were under Rajappen's care, were temporarily looked after by the Dutch when Rajappen was ill.[292]

Parallel to the official contacts informal co-operation developed between the Tamil employees of the Tranquebar Mission and the local co-workers of the Dutch. With the permission of the local pastor the Dutch local catechist, Andre, invited Ambrosius to Nagapattinam to give a talk there. Andre, who had been working in Nagapattinam since 1750, had originally been educated by the Halle missionaries in Cuddalore and had worked as a teacher there. On the orders of the governor, who felt responsible for the safety of the missionaries, he accompanied Johann Balthasar Kohlhoff (1711–90) and Jacob Klein on their journey to Nagapattinam in 1751.[293] Due to the lack of special schools in Nagapattinam the priests there sometimes sent local people to Tranquebar for baptismal preparation. In May 1751 the 'Portuguese' catechist, Pedro da Costa, and the Tamil assistant, Andre, accompanied slaves from Nagapattinam to Tranquebar and brought them back after a few days of instruction.[294] In 1753 the Tamil school teacher Packien (died 1791) was sent as a catechist from Tranquebar to Nagapattinam at the request of the Dutch pastor.[295]

[291] NHB 38. St., 197f.
[292] NHB 42. St., 553.
[293] HB 74. Cont., 201, 269; 75. Cont., 422; 78. Cont., (137), 888.
[294] HB 75. Cont., 392.
[295] HB 80. Cont., 1174.

THE MORAVIAN BRETHREN IN TRANQUEBAR

In the context of efforts to extend its territories in Asia the Danish Asiatic Company directed its attention in the 1750s to the Nicobar Islands. Representatives of the Company asked the Tranquebar missionaries for help in the attempt to set up a Danish colony there. In February 1756 the Danish government requested the missionaries to send one person to establish a mission station in the Danish colony on the Nicobar Islands. The choice fell on David Poltzenhagen who, however, like many other Danish soldiers and officials, died of a fever shortly after his arrival.[296] After the failure of these Danish missionary efforts, and after it was decided in Tranquebar that no further missionary would be sent out, the Asiatic Company took up the request from the Board of Directors of the Unitas Fratrum of Herrnhut for permission to carry out missionary work in a Danish colony. In 1760 a group of Moravian missionaries were granted the necessary privileges. In the same year a group of 14 Brethren came to Tranquebar and, with the permission of the Company, they set up a so-called Brüdergarten (Garden of the Brethren), from where they planned to begin their work on the Nicobar Islands.[297]

Against the backdrop of these political and economic constellations, equipped with permission and privileges from the Asiatic Company and the Danish king, the Moravian missionaries in Tranquebar enjoyed the goodwill and trust of the governors. The Danish-Halle missionaries feared the damage that their own missionary efforts might suffer through the presence of another group of Protestant missionaries in their immediate vicinity, even if the latter's work was to take place on the Nicobar Islands and not in Tranquebar.

[296] HB 85. Cont., 209–51.

[297] Nørgaard, *Mission und Obrigkeit*, 178–82; Krieger, *Kaufleute, Seeräuber und Diplomaten*. Beck, Hartmut, 1981, *Brüder in vielen Völkern: 250 Jahre Mission der Brüdergemeine*, Verlag der Ev.-Luth. Mission, Erlangen (= Erlanger Taschenbücher, Bd. 58); Ruhland, Thomas, 2006, 'The Moravian Brethren and the Danish-Halle Mission in Tranquebar—the 'Garden of the Brothers' at the Centre of a European Conflict', in Gross et al., *Halle and the Beginning of Protestant Christianity in India*, Vol. II, 743–66.

However, the planned work on the Nicobar Islands was delayed and did not begin for many years for economic and climatic reasons and because of a lack of personnel. After a five-year stay in Tranquebar there were still no developments in this direction. During this wait both sides spied on each other and repeatedly expressed their fears and their mutual suspicions. The constant postponement of a decision regarding the stay of the Moravian missionaries in Tranquebar made the Danish-Halle missionaries and the Mission Board in Copenhagen insecure and gave cause for speculations. In the meantime it was no longer certain whether the Brethren would decide between the option of going to the Nicobar Islands or returning to Europe, or whether they would not, in fact, risk going into Thanjavur and, in the worst-case scenario, taking over entire Danish-Halle congregations.[298]

For their part, the Moravian missionaries complained to the Mission Board in Copenhagen about the behaviour of their Halle colleagues in Tranquebar and they requested the Board to mediate on their behalf. According to instructions from their directors the Moravian Brethren were supposed to avoid all conflicts with the Danish missionaries, and they were not to take any converts from the Lutheran faith into their congregations.[299] After their permission to stay in Tranquebar was extended by another three years in 1766[300] the Mission board could only exhort its employees to be patient and understanding: 'Although we cannot say for certain what the decision concerning the Brethren will be, [...] we hope that our gracious

[298] In a joint letter to G.A. Francke in 1764 the missionaries expressed their initial conjectures: RA Miskolark 9c, joint letter from the missionaries to G.A. Francke, 26 September 1764. The Mission Board then formulated these fears openly in a letter to all the missionaries in Tranquebar as well as to Captain Jenner: RA Miskolark 4, 1765–89, letter from the Mission Board to all missionaries in Tranquebar, 13 November 1765.

[299] RA Miskolark 9c, *Pro Memoria* to the Mission Board in Copenhagen, Herrnhut 7 November 1765.

[300] RA Miskolark 4, 1765–89, letter from the Mission Board to all missionaries in Tranquebar, 13 November 1765; letter from the Mission Board to all missionaries in Tranquebar, 21 November 1765; letter from the Mission Board to G.A. Francke, 26 November 1765; letter from the Mission Board to G.A. Francke, 30 November 1765; letter from the Mission Board to Friedrich Michael Ziegenhagen, 7 December 1765; letter from the Mission Board to all missionaries, 7 December 1765; letter from the Mission Board to G.A. Francke, 14 December 1765.

God will let the matter be resolved in a manner that is best for the Church and that you will not have much cause to be unhappy with regard to them in the future.'[301] After another unsuccessful attempt at colonization and missionary work on the Nicobar Islands in 1768, the Moravian Brethren finally received permission in 1771 to settle down in other Danish colonies and this also legalized their 'Garden of the Brethren' in Tranquebar. Altogether, the Moravian Brethren lived and worked for 40 years in Tranquebar without going on the offensive and carrying out missionary work publicly. In 1800 they had to finally leave Tranquebar. In keeping with the instructions received, the Halle missionaries were initially very reserved towards the Brethren. Only at the end of the seventies, when it became clear that the Brethren would be there for a long time, did they begin to report about contacts with the missionaries in the 'Garden of the Brethren'. The last missionary of the Moravian Brethren left Tranquebar in 1802.[302]

The establishment of another mission station in the immediate vicinity aroused the interest and curiosity of the South Indian co-workers of the Tranquebar Mission. Since the Moravian Brethren did not build up an active mission system with their own churches and schools and did not go preaching among people from place to place, they hardly required any local employees. They were, however, interested in learning the language and in medical care by local experts. Although the Halle missionaries avoided public contact with the Brethren, private contacts were established and mutual help, when required, did not need to be justified. Contacts between the South Indian co-workers and the Brethren were, partly, more open and often against the wishes of their missionary superiors. Daniel Pullei and his brother, Peter Rajappen (died 1782), for example, worked closely with the Moravian Brethren. Daniel Pullei taught some of their missionaries Tamil, and this led to serious tensions in

[301] RA Miskolark 3, 1765–89, letter from the Mission Board to all missionaries, 25 November 1767, (translated from German).

[302] Lehmann, *Es begann in Tranquebar*, 281–89. Cf. also Fenger, *Geschichte der Tranquebarschen Mission*, 223f.; Niekamp, *Kurtzgefaßte Mißions-Geschichte*, II, 424f.; Römer, H., 1921, *Geschichte der Brüdermission auf den Nikobaren und des Brüdergartens bei Tranquebar auf Grund des handschriftlichen Materials im Unitäts-Archiv zu Herrnhut*, Missionsbuchhandlung, Herrnhut (=HMK 18); Germann, *Missionar Christian Friedrich Schwartz*, 86, 88, 101–07, 146–53.

the otherwise friendly relations between the Tranquebar mission and the 'Royal Government Interpreter'. Even Daniel Pullei's brother, who also had a good mastery over languages, envisaged a career for himself in the service of the Moravian Brethren, since the Danish governor had not appointed him as an interpreter.[303]

The story of Rajanayakkan's life, who worked for the Danish-Halle Mission for more than 40 years, is closely linked with the presence of the Moravian Brethren in Tranquebar.[304] As a result of intensive reflections concerning a comparison of religions Rajanayakkan was very keen as a young man to enter missionary service. In July 1727 he explained the motives behind this step:

> A long time ago, he said, St. Thomas came to this country and taught many people by preaching the gospel to them. After him their priests came [the Catholics, H.L.]. Now, we [the Tranquebar missionaries, H.L.] had also come for the same purpose. Were our teachings older or theirs? After our books came into the country some people slandered us by saying that we were priests who told lies. This induced him to get to know us better in order to find out whether this was true or not.[305]

Besides this comparative-religious aspect Rajanayakkan's identity as a *dalit* was probably also a reason to convert to the Lutheran faith. Whether, and to what extent, this identity also determined his consciousness as a non-commissioned officer of the Thanjavur army cannot be determined on the basis of the sources. However, it must be assumed that he saw a future for a *pa aiy r* in the Lutheran-Pietist faith. This belief was shattered when caste became the decisive hindrance for his ordination as a priest and it sharpened his understanding of the caste problems and the social disadvantages associated with them.

[303] NHB 28. St., 444; UH R 15 Tb N° 1b, diary Tranquebar 1768–82, 5 January 1776 and 27 August 1782; Daniel Pullei informed Missionary Klein about the death of his older brother on September 4, 1782 without mentioning his work with the Brethren; UH R 15 T N° 35, 129. St., letter from the missionary Gottfried Raabs, 27 August 1781.

[304] For the details of Rajanayakkan's life history see Liebau, 'Tamilische Christen im 18. Jahrhundert'.

[305] HB 25. Cont., 33f., diary of the missionaries in Tranquebar, 10 July 1727, (translated from German).

Usually, the Tamilians employed in the Danish-Halle Mission were under the regular control and supervision of the missionaries. They received instructions and were obliged to give regular written reports.[306] Disciplinary violations led to punishments including suspension. Because of the political conditions and because of the distance between Thanjavur and Tranquebar Rajanayakkan remained without this direct control for a long time. He had suggested that he would work independently in the region controlled by the king of Thanjavur.[307] Initially this meant that he was an indispensable support for the missionaries in a region inaccessible to them. As a *dalit*, however, he could not rise to the position of a pastor. Although Rajanayakkan always emphasized his position as a subordinate of the missionaries, he also, simultaneously, pointed out his own worth: 'although I am not worthy of serving the Lord's herd and becoming a servant of the missionaries, the Lord effects some masses through me.'[308]

In the 1760s the tensions between Rajanayakkan and the Halle missionaries increased. Therefore, the missionaries took umbrage at the fact that Rajanayakkan—accompanied by the Indian pastor Ambrosius—went for talks with the Moravian missionaries shortly after their arrival.[309] Rajanayakkan, who had informed himself about the articles of faith of this Pietist revival movement before his visit, asked the Moravian missionaries further substantial questions and took leave of them with the highly suggestive allegory: 'If a person has a washer man who does not wash his clothes clean, he should let him go and take another one. If he too does not wash well, he

[306] Some work-reports written on palm leaves and covering several months of the year 1743 have been preserved and are kept in the Royal Library in Copenhagen. Cf. also: Jeyaraj, *Inkulturation in Tranquebar*, 333f.

[307] HB 25. Cont., 35, diary of the missionaries in Tranquebar, 10 July 1727.

[308] RA Miskolark 9b, translation of a Tamil palm-leaf letter from the catechist Rajanayakkan to the Mission Board, 6 October 1749.

[309] UH, R 15 Tb, N° 1a, diary Tranquebar 1760–67, 7 and 21 February 1761; RA Miskolark 9e, excerpt of a letter from the missionaries in Tranquebar to G.A. Francke, 26 September 1764: 'Apart from this, Rajanaicken, who was here, went without our permission to the [Moravian, H.L.] missionary Voelckel and, as he later told us, asked him why they wouldn't go to Thanjavur. However, he didn't get a satisfactory reply [...],' (translated from German).

should give himself to another.'[310] Although the Brethren were initially skeptical about Rajanayakkan[311]—apparently because they suspected he might be spying for their rivals—a possible change of confession by the catechist was discussed after he had visited the missionaries a few more time.[312]

Rajanayakkan considered it his task in life not only to propagate the gospel on behalf of the Lutheran-Pietist missionaries ofTranquebar, but also to examine different European-Christian concepts with a view to their applicability to conditions in South India. He studied different forms of Christianity in order to find a religious dogma that would be acceptable and comprehensible to the Tamil people. He could only envisage social change taking place through religious change. Christian teachings had to be mediated in such a way that they did not contradict the feelings and norms of the people of the country. The idea of a crucified Jesus, for example, would not bring the religion closer to the Tamils. In contrast to this, Rajanayakkan felt that the method employed by the Moravian Brethren to talk primarily about the deeds and achievements of Jesus was much more promising.[313] The idea of an eternal life after death, as preached by the Christians, could also be ridiculed by Hindus who believed in the cycle of rebirths.[314] As a *paṟaiyār* he displayed a great degree of self-confidence when he assumed in his comparative analysis of religions that the Tamilians would have a say in determining the 'true' faith. Although the Tranquebar missionaries were his superiors and his employers, he did not accept their teachings uncritically.

For Rajanayakkan the move from Catholicism to Protestantism was already an active, self-determined process. His conviction about the correctness of Protestant teachings led to his break with the Catholic faith.[315] His attempt as a *dalit* to have a say in the creation of an Indian Christian Church made him an exception for his times

[310] UH, R 15 Tb, N° 1a, diary Tranquebar 1760–67, February 1761 (translated from German).

[311] UH, R 15 Tb, N° 1a, diary Tranquebar 1760–67, 5 March 1763; Lehmann, *Es begann in Tranquebar*, 289.

[312] UH, R 15 Tb, N° 1a, diary Tranquebar 1760–67, 3 May 1761.

[313] UH, R 15 Tb, N° 1b, diary Tranquebar 1768–82, 1 March 1771.

[314] HB 50. Cont., 273, November 1739.

[315] HB 34. Cont., 1083, letter from Rajanayakkan, 9 October 1732.

and his background. His failure was also due to the inability of the missionaries to transcend the social realities and to set an early benchmark in the Danish-English-Halle Mission in the form of a *dalit* priest. From the start of his missionary activity Rajanayakkan had made his position very clear: to look for a 'pure' religion in the interest of Indians—primarily of Indian Christians. In the final analysis this led him to distance himself critically from the missionaries. Based on his self-conceived task in life he felt that it was not only his duty, but also his right to weigh different variants of Christianity against one another without any consideration to his direct employers.

Rajanayakkan's growing doubts about the Lutheran faith, and his attempt to find the 'true' faith with the Moravian Brethren were important reasons for the catechist, who suffered from vision impairment in his old age,[316] to be transferred from Thanjavur to Arantangi.[317] Already in 1766 there had been an extensive public discussion of Rajanayakkan's comments on charges of disciplinary transgressions (not named) and his promise to improve.[318] Although the catechist continued to remain in contact with the missionaries when he was in Arantangi, the association was no longer an intensive one. After his death on 29 September 1771[319] the missionaries—in contrast to their normal practice—were not forthcoming in their report about the final hours of their long-term employee.[320] There were practically no obituaries for the Tamilian who had successfully represented the mission for 40 years and who the Europeans also regarded as a model for Indian Christians.[321] The mission offered the catechist's widow the post of a 'prayer leader', which she remained till her death.[322]

[316] NHB 4. St., 457, 4 October 1769.

[317] NHB 4. St., 422, report, 3 July 1769; 4. St., 482, report, 28 July 1769; NHB 8. St., 993, report from Tranquebar 1771.

[318] HB 106. Cont., 1230.

[319] NHB 5. St., preface, 122.

[320] NHB 8. St., 1025f., report from Tranquebar, 1771.

[321] HB 107. Cont., 314.

[322] NHB 10. St., 1347f., letter from the missionaries in Tranquebar, 7 October 1772. For his wife cf. also NHB 7. St., 891, diary, 23 February 1771; 7. St., 895, diary, 7 March 1771.

CHAPTER FIVE

The Role of Local Mission Employees in Education

> It would not, however, be an exaggeration to affirm that the Danes were the pioneers of modern educational system in India.[1]

The long-term effect and the success of a mission society depended on whether, and to what extent it was able to create a durable and recognizable network of multipliers and mechanisms of reproduction, which would help the spread of Christian teachings. The schools were the pillars of these functions. The structure and organization of the educational system of a mission determined its position in the local society to a high degree. As an essential instrument in the work of conversion it contributed to the spread and consolidation of Christian beliefs among the local population and to the rise of a local Christian elite. As a 'fertile bed of seeds'[2] for the spread of Christianity the schools also played a significant role in the work of the Danish-English-Halle Mission.[3] Since the schools were more strongly integrated in the local public sphere

[1] Rawat, Pyare Lal, 1981, *History of Indian Education*, Ram Prasad, Agra, Bhopal, 125.

[2] Cf. Ziegenbalg, 'Kurze Beschreibung der Tätigkeit der Mission', 21.

[3] For the development of the idea of education in the Tranquebar Mission cf.: Frykenberg, 'The Halle Legacy in Modern India'; Liebau, 'Über die Erziehung 'tüchtiger Subjekte' zur Verbreitung des Evangeliums'; Nehring, Andreas, 1999, 'Natur und Gnade: Zu Theologie und Kulturkritik in den Neuen Halleschen Berichten', in Bergunder, *Missionsberichte aus Indien im 18. Jahrhundert*, 220–45; Gensichen, Hans-Werner, 1975, "Dienst der Seelen' und 'Dienst des Leibes' in der frühen pietistischen Mission', in Heinrich Bornkamm et al. (eds.), *Der Pietismus in Gestalten und Wirkungen—Martin Schmidt zum 65. Geburtstag*, Luther-Verlag, Bielefeld, 155–78, (=Arbeiten zur Geschichte des Pietismus, Vol. 14.).

than other mission institutions, the structure of the educational system and the manner and course of teaching had to be adapted to these requirements.

Whether it was the early Jesuits in India, the Catholic missions of the eighteenth century or the Protestant missions of the nineteenth century, whether through forced mass conversions or through individual conversions, the change of religion was always linked with a transfer of knowledge—sometimes only of a religious-symbolic kind. At the latest with the advent of the Jesuits in the sixteenth century organized Christian missionary work in South India was accompanied by work in the sphere of education.[4] The educational work of the Jesuits in India was directed at the upper class Brahmins in order to establish a Catholic elite who would act as role-models for the masses, thus leading to further conversions.[5] On 15 January 1544 Francisco de Xavier reported to the society at Rome about a Jesuit school in Goa, in which about 500 Indians were being taught Latin, reading, writing and other subjects. Jesuit schools were also open to non-Christian Indians. The pupils in the school that Xavier describes were—without exception—Hindus. The school was financed through donations, but also through a regular grant from the Portuguese governor.[6] From the middle of the sixteenth century till the second half of the eighteenth century the Jesuits were actively engaged in the sphere of education in India. From the end of the eighteenth century onwards the importance of mission schools in many regions of South India grew considerably. It was only the middle of the nineteenth century that witnessed a compromise between public schools run by the state and mission schools, allowing both to co-exist. As a result of this, the earlier importance of the mission educational system declined.

[4] Cf. for this: Correia-Alfonso, *The Jesuits in India*, 43f.

[5] In Europe too, the educational work of the Jesuits was directed at the higher strata of society. While Catholic mendicant orders promoted primary education, the Jesuits concentrated on secondary schools. For education in the early modern period in general cf.: Kistenich, Johannes, 2001, *Bettelmönche im öffentlichen Schulwesen. Ein Handbuch für die Erzdiözese Köln 1600–1850*, Böhlau, Köln et al. (=Stadt und Gesellschaft, Vol. 1); von Dülmen, Richard, 1999, *Kultur und Alltag in der Frühen Neuzeit. Vol. 3: Religion, Magie und Aufklärung 16.-18. Jahrhundert*, Beck, Munich (First edition 1994), 122f.

[6] Cf. Sonntag, 1544, *Die Briefe des Francisco de Xavier*, 57.

There has been a marked increase in studies on the colonial educational system in India as also in studies on the connection between this system and the nascent national movement. Along with this there also appears to be a growing academic interest in the history of the mission educational system. The focus here is on the Anglican mission societies of the nineteenth century. Proceeding from their work in the field of educational policies Ingleby developed the following periodization for the 'long nineteenth century': He terms the period till 1850 as the revolutionary phase of developments in the missionary educational system, while the following period, till about 1920 when the new national Christian Churches in India came into existence, witnessed a 'more settled and developed approach' in the mission educational system.[7] Mathew follows a similar argument when he describes the mission educational system and the state educational system in the period between 1870 and 1930 as a development 'from dominance to compromise'.[8] These studies no longer perceive mission schools exclusively as institutions of conversion and, thus, as instruments in the struggle for converts. Their role in educating and disciplining those of the faith is no longer in the foreground. Missionary educational activities are increasingly being seen from the point of view of their role in identity change, but also with regard to their social and emancipatory role and, thus, as a factor of social and cultural change in the mission regions.[9]

[7] Ingleby, Jonathan C., 2000, *Missionaries, Education and India. Issues in Protestant Missionary Education in the Long Nineteenth Century*, ISPCK, Delhi, XIV.

[8] Mathew, *Christian Missions, Education and Nationalism.*

[9] Studies on the African mission educational system have progressed further than those on the Indian context. Cf. here especially the work of Adick, Christel, 1992, *Die Universalisierung der modernen Schule: eine theoretische Problemskizze zur Erklärung der weltweiten Verbreitung der modernen Schule in den letzten 200 Jahren mit Fallstudien aus Westafrika,* Schöningh, Paderborn et al.; Adick, C. (ed.), 1993, *Missions—und Kolonialpädagogik.* Themenheft der Zeitschrift 'Bildung und Erziehung' 46, 3; Adick, C., 1992, 'Koloniale Bildungspolitik: Universalisierung der modernen Schule oder ethnisch-nationale Diskriminierung?' in Wilfried Wagner (ed.), *Rassendiskriminierung, Kolonialpolitik und ethnisch-nationale Identität. Referate des 2. Internationalen Kolonialgeschichtlichen Symposiums 1991 in Berlin*, 457–468, Lit, Münster, Hamburg; Adick, C. and Wolfgang Mehnert in co-operation with Thea Christiani, 2001, *Deutsche Missions—und Kolonialpolitik in Dokumenten—eine kommentierte Quellensammlung aus den Afrikabeständen deutschsprachiger Archive 1884–1914*, IKO-Verlag für Interkulturelle Kommunikation, Frankfurt/Main [et

These issues have also been addressed with regard to the Tranquebar Mission, but, as yet, there has been no exhaustive study of the educational work of the first Protestant mission in Southeast India. While P.L. Rawat, in an overview of the history of education in India, evaluates the role of the Portuguese and French missions as insignificant, he calls the Danes the 'pioneers of modern educational system in India'.[10] Daniel Jeyaraj comments on the educational efforts in the initial years of the Tranquebar Mission and arrives at the conclusion that mission schools had a 'decisive influence on non-Christian schools'; they became 'the model for Hindu schools that were set up', and were 'beacons and pace setters for other local schools'.[11] R.E. Frykenberg gives the Danish-English-Halle Mission the credit for establishing a public school system. According to him, the mission schools contributed to a process that he calls the 'information revolution', through which information went from being a mainly private to a predominantly public matter.[12]

Viewed in the context of mission history the educational efforts of the Tranquebar Mission took place at a period of time when, on the one hand, Catholic activities were on the decline and, on the other, the Anglican interest in mission was growing stronger. The Jesuit order was banned in India in 1773. The Jesuits, who were working in India at that time, continued to work alone or joined other societies. From the last quarter of the eighteenth century onwards, Anglican revival movements began to have an increasing influence on the policies of the East India Company. Western influence on the Indian sub-continent increased noticeably in the eighteenth century, both in the political sphere as well as in culture and science. Through its network of schools in Southeast India the Tranquebar Mission also contributed to the acceleration of these processes.

---

al.], (= Historisch-vergleichende Sozialisations—und Bildungsforschung, Vol. 2); for the Catholic missions there is an interesting comparative study with the examples of three international mission societies in different local contexts: the Jesuits in Japan, the Steyler mission in Latin America and the White Fathers in Africa. Cf. Freitag, Christine, 1995, *Schule und Bildungshilfe in den Konzeptionen katholischer Missionsgesellschaften*, Böhlau, Köln et al.

[10] See the opening quote of this chapter.

[11] Jeyaraj, *Inkulturation in Tranquebar*, 287f.

[12] Frykenberg, Robert E., 'The Halle Legacy in Modern India', 7.

Frykenberg refers to this context and states that many ideas and concepts that had been worked out for India found their way into local structures through the social factor of education. According to him, the claim made by the Tranquebar missionaries, that they were putting August Hermann Francke's pedagogical ideas into practice in India, had an almost revolutionary character. 'Francke's dictum, that every human being in the world—every adult and child, regardless of age and gender—should be equipped with basic literacy and with a grasp of modern science, had revolutionary implications.'[13] According to Frykenberg, the Pietist concept of education, directed towards the masses and linking education with daily praxis, offered the best conditions for a broad-based transfer of Western concepts of education.[14] The importance of the social signals that emerged from this system of education increases when one takes their effects on the further development of the mission educational system in South India in the nineteenth century into account, as also when one considers that these structures brought forth a qualitatively and quantitatively important group of South Indian teachers who, for their part, also adapted and transmitted Western knowledge.

The work of Christian missions in the educational sector served fundamental goals of mission strategy: it was directed, first and foremost, at transmitting the contents and principles of Christianity to potential believers who could be thus directly prepared for the act of conversion. Religious teachings and, with them, important norms of a Western life style were meant to determine the thoughts and actions of the believers in future. The required transmission of knowledge occurred not only in sermons and conversations, but also in special mission schools and seminaries. The main goal of educational work gave rise to the second important thrust-area of the mission educational system: the education and care of Christian children who would have, besides religious instruction, classes in reading, writing and arithmetic. They constituted the base of the local Christian elite. The requirements for well-educated local teachers

[13] Frykenberg, 'The Legacy of Christian Friedrich Schwartz', 130.

[14] Frykenberg, 1996, 'Modern Education in South India 1784–1854: Its Roots and Its Role as a Vehicle of Integration under Company Raj', *American Historical Review* 91 (1): 37–65; Frykenberg, 'The Halle Legacy in Modern India'.

were met mainly from this group of loyal young people who were invested with a decisive function as role models.[15]

However, mission schools did not contribute only towards maintaining, reproducing and extending mission structures and towards the quantitative growth of local Christian congregations. Missionary educational work in India went far beyond this narrow, conversion-oriented direction. In fact, the goals and contents of education depended as much on the political, religious and cultural backgrounds of the relevant mission societies as on local practical requirements and the laws of the colonial state in the mission region. In their description of the mission educational system in 1744 the missionaries emphasized at the outset that their work among the Indian youth followed 'the model of the blessed institutions at Halle, the aim of the mission and the wishes of their esteemed superiors and benefactors in Europe.'[16] Since mission schools were open to non-Christians, they developed into sites of intercultural encounters and into indispensable instruments for establishing and maintaining contacts with the local population. The question in this context is to what extent the contents and methods of mission schools really fulfilled the requirements of the people, or whether, in fact, the foreign missionaries were trying to apply their pedagogic concepts and contents unchanged. As against the actual religious work of conversion, which was soon limited to particular groups of the population, the educational work of the mission was not oriented exclusively to these groups and made more far-reaching social offers.

THE EDUCATIONAL LANDSCAPE IN SOUTH INDIA

If in its daily work too, the Tranquebar Mission was forced to measure its methods and strategies against the social and religious conditions of its environment, the pressure of local conditions was even greater in the formation of the mission educational system. The competition from Catholic mission societies and the regulations of the colonial

[15] Cf. for this: Freitag, *Schule und Bildungshilfe in den Konzeptionen katholischer Missionsgesellschaften*, 133.

[16] HB 58. Cont., 1528.

powers were only two in an entire chain of reasons. If the Mission wished to ensure the existence of a stable network of schools in the long term, these would have to be of a kind that would appeal to large sections of the population independent of their religious and social background. Under prevailing conditions in the eighteenth century in South India this was only possible if, one the one hand, the growing need for a European-style education was taken into account, but, on the other hand, local cultural and religious norms were not disregarded. In view of the highly developed Tamil literary tradition and of an existing local school system the missionaries could not fully implement their ideas of a Christian educational system.[17]

Although the Tranquebar missionaries based their educational efforts on methods and trends taken from their European models,[18] they soon understood that it would also be necessary to incorporate elements of the existing educational system in South India. At the beginning of the eighteenth century the first missionaries were astonished to find various forms of a traditional—and not exclusively religious—mediation of knowledge. 'In all cities, small towns and villages there are schools in which the young people learn to read and write',[19] the missionaries wrote in 1709, not without a sense of surprise. This kind of school was the so-called *Patshala*, the (Hindu) village school, where children of different castes were given basic instruction in reading, writing and arithmetic. The schools sustained themselves through contributions—mainly in kind—that the parents had to give the teachers. However, the missionaries did not lay much store by the results of these educational avenues.

> However, only very few achieve any mastery in reading and writing, and even this has taken six years to achieve. That is why one hardly

[17] 'Wherever there were strong indigenous cultures with their own literary tradition, as in large parts of Asia and the Middle East, especially in the Islamic states and in regions under Hindu influence, there were initially very few possibilities for Europeans to gain influence over the educational system with the help of Christian missions, let alone reach the broad masses directly.' Cf. Mommsen, 'Europa und die außereuropäische Welt', 683, (translated from German).

[18] AB 89, letter from B. Ziegenbalg, 1 October 1708.

[19] HB 3. Cont., 111–48, here 127f. Replies of the missionaries to questions sent by A.H. Francke on the politics, economy, geography and religion of the Tamils.

> finds one among a thousand who can read and write, and among the thousand who can read and write there are very few who can write properly and with correct orthography, or who can read fluently.[20]

In a comment on the requirements of the Indian educational system at the beginning of the nineteenth century the Baptists William Carey (1761–1834), Joshua Marshman (1768–1837) and William Ward (1769–1823) stated that the number of local schools was so small that hardly one of a hundred Indians could read and write properly.[21] In these small schools children were trained for future employment in the local accounts and administrative system and earned their living later as *kaṇakkappiḷḷai*, *Dubash* or traders. Entry into these schools was restricted, but the system was self-regulatory in the sense that many children had to start working at a young age, or they were taught what they required for their future profession by the older generation in the family.

Sons from Brahmin families studied in the *Gurukula* (Sanskrit *gurukula*—family of the teacher), i.e. they often lived for ten years or more in close association with their teacher (*Guru*). They learnt the Veda and other holy books of Hinduism in Sanskrit, the classical high-language spoken by the Brahmins, which was not accessible to the majority of the population.[22]

The special features of the traditional teacher-student relationship were explained by a Tamilian in the fifteenth letter of the *Malabarische Korrespondenz*, which deals with the duties of parents, teachers and priests. The duty of the parents, the letter says, lies in taking care of and bringing up children till the age of five. From this point onwards the boys went to school and the girls were taught household work. Parents had to teach their children to support themselves and arrange their marriage. Children, for their part, were expected to respect and obey their parents, eat only after their father had eaten and look after their parents in their old age.[23]

Even among Indian Muslims education was restricted till

[20] HB 3. Cont., 111–48, here 127f., (tanslated from German).

[21] NHB 67. St., 601f. (1816).

[22] Vanina, Elena Ju., 1988, 'Nauka i obrazovanije v Indii posdnego srednevekovija i načala novogo vremeni (XVI-XVIII vv.)', in *Indija Ježegodnik 1987*, Moskva, 277–293.

[23] Cf. HB 7. Cont., 420–24.

the end of the nineteenth century to a select group of future religious office-bearers, who were either taught by home-tutors or in a mosque. Quran schools and Islamic educational institutions that were open to a broader section of Muslims only arose in the late nineteenth century.[24]

Generally, girls and women were excluded from all kinds of education. The exceptions to this were those girls who were meant to take up the life of a *devadasi* (temple dancer): 'Women are not educated, except for those who are meant to serve the idols in the temples and are called servants of the gods. These persons learn to read, write and sing; they are also taught the learned or Brahmin Malabarian, and there are often very clever persons among them.'[25] The twenty-second letter of the *Malabarische Korrespondenz* states the following about the *devadasis*: they were selected on the basis of their looks, learned to read when they were five years old and then went to a dance school. Their lives were dedicated to the gods and to work in the temple.[26] The following statement by Polycarpus Jordan shows how educated girls were viewed in the eighteenth century: 'Although there are schools everywhere, the girls are not sent to school. This is because girls who go to schools are seen as those who are to become dancing prostitutes.'[27] Daughters of enlightened Muslim princely families were sometimes the exception to this, whereas in Hindu Brahmin families, where men enjoyed an unrestricted access to education, women were not taught to read and write till the nineteenth century.[28] The twenty-third letter of the

[24] For the history of Muslim education in India see for instance: Kaur, Kuldip, 1990, Madrasa Education in India: A Study of its Past and Present. Centre for research in Rural & Industrial Development, Chandigarh.

[25] HB 3. Cont. 111–48, quote p. 127f., (translated from German).

[26] HB 7. Cont., 442–46.

[27] HB 4. Cont., 181, letter from P. Jordan, 4 October 1710, (translated from German).

[28] This fact is impressively articulated in the diary of a Brahmin woman, edited by Tanika Sarkar. At an advanced age, an unnoticed by the family, the woman had taught herself to read and write, and at the end of her life she wrote down her experiences. The reader is able to understand how the written word opened up new horizons for this formerly illiterate woman. Sarkar, Tanika, 1999, *Words to Win. The Making of Amar Jiban. A Modern Autobiography*, Kali for Women, New Delhi. See also: Sarkar, Tanika, 2001, 'A Book of Her Own, A Life of her Own. The Autobiography of a Nineteenth-Century Woman', in Tanika Sarkar (ed.), *Hindu Wife, Hindu Nation. Community, Religion and Cultural Nationalism*, 95–134, C. Hurst, London.

Malabarische Korrespondenz is devoted to the education of women in general: Till the age of five they were brought up in their families. From then on many girls worked for wealthy families. When they reached the age of seven, the girls learned cooking, weaving and spinning. They were often married off at the age of nine, whereupon they went to their marital house.[29]

The missionaries were disappointed and could not understand the lack of policies of the colonial powers with regard to education: 'It is surprising and a matter of regret that neither the English nor the Dutch have given any serious thought to setting up public schools in India. Although there is a seminary in Colombo, there is more talk of its decline than of its growth.'[30] In the plans of the English East India Company, oriented mainly towards its commercial interests and profits, the question of education played an almost negligible role in the eighteenth century. The Company followed a policy of non-interference in religious matters, which was officially accompanied by non-interference in the educational efforts of Christian missions. Accordingly, it neither had its own educational policy, nor did it officially provide financial support for a widespread network of schools. However, wherever Europeans undertook educational efforts, the lack of religious instructions in such schools was a major shortcoming in the eyes of the missionaries.[31]

After the British victory over Tipu Sultan in 1799 and after the Madras Presidency had been set up under English rule in 1801, the requirements of the colonial power in the field of education underwent a fundamental change. There was an increasing need for Indians who could be employed by the English administration. As British colonial educational policies took shape, the mission educational system found it increasingly difficult to maintain its dominant position in the field of education. Leading colonial officials and politicians reiterated the responsibility of the state for education in the colonies. In his draft-bill of 1793, William Wilberforce (1759–1833) pointed to the importance of education in the English colonies.

[29] HB 7. Cont., 447–48.

[30] NHB 32. St., 896, letter from Ch. S. John, 10 September 1787, (translated from German).

[31] Ibid.

In a report to the Board of Directors of the Company in 1811 the governor-general, Lord Minto (1751–1814), emphasized the role of education, after which this point was included in the charter of 1813. For the first time the charter of the East India Company contained direct statements about a special educational policy in the colonies: '... a sum of not less than one lac [100,000, H.L.] rupees in each year shall be set apart and applied to the revival and improvement of literature and the encouragement of the learned natives of India and for the Instruction and promotion of a knowledge of the sciences among the inhabitants of the British territories in India.'[32] In 1823 the English established the Committee of Public Instruction. The educational policies were continued even after the charter was changed in 1833; the sum of money earmarked for educational purposes was increased.[33]

In the Madras Presidency, where the Tranquebar Mission was situated since 1801, the conflicts in the educational sector increased from the 1820s onwards. In contrast to the policies of the colonial administrations in Bengal and Bombay, where the controversy between the Orientalists and the Anglicists dominated the educational policies for a long time, in Madras a policy of mass education in the local languages held sway under the governor, Sir Thomas Munro (1761–1827). His report on the situation of the educational system led to some changes in government policies. Besides the setting up of the Committee of Public Instruction an annual sum of Rs 50,000 was earmarked in the budget for education—a sum that was doubled by the 1850s.[34] In 1819 the government in Madras opened a schoolbook society as a counter-measure to the religious textbooks of the mission educational system.[35] As in every British

[32] Cited in: Aggarwal, J.C. and B.D. Bhatt (eds.), 1969, *Educational Documents in India (1831–1968)*, Arya Book Depot, New Delhi, 1.

[33] For the Indian educational system see, among others: Rawat, *History of Indian Education*; Ghosh, S. Ch., 1995, *The History of Education in Modern India 1757–1968*, Orient Longman, New Delhi.

[34] Cf.: *Imperial Gazetteer of India. Provincial Series. Madras, Vol. I*, 1985, (Reprint), New Delhi, 117–25.

[35] Mitchell, Lisa, 2009, *Language, Emotions, and Politics in South India. The Making of a Mother Tongue, Indiana University Press*, Bloomington, 281; Frykenberg, Robert Eric, 2008, *Christianity in India. From Beginnings to the Present*, Oxford University Press, New York, 311.

province, a director of public instruction was also appointed in the Madras Presidency.[36] The educational contents and goals of the mission schools were now increasingly in competition with colonial education, which was primarily concerned with introducing a Western educational system in order—in the long run—to train an indigenous, Western-oriented elite that would be loyal to the colonial power.[37] The missionaries also took note of the simultaneous establishment of 'Hindu colleges', where European languages and sciences were also taught and which were meant to counter the growing Christian educational system.[38]

The growing importance of the colonial educational system was documented in the nineteenth century in a series of reports and written comments. The milestones among them were the Wood Despatch of 1854, in which the political responsibility of the colonial power for the development of the educational system in India was emphasized,[39] or the report of the commission set up by Lord Ripon (1828–1909) in 1882 and named after William Wilson Hunter (1840–1900) who headed the commission.[40] After the Charles Wood Report on Education appeared in 1854 the government began to set up secular educational establishments—from primary schools to universities—whereupon the Protestant missions demanded recognition for their educational institutions and made every effort to maintain their pre-eminent position in the sphere of education. However, missionary educational establishments were now subordinated to the schools established by the government. Although the 'grant-in-aid-system' or the 'result system' ensured

[36] Fleisch, Paul, 1936, *Hundert Jahre lutherischer Mission*, Verlag der Evangelisch-Lutherischen Mission, Leipzig, 101.

[37] For the changes in the role of the mission educational system, see: Mathew, *Christian Missions, Education and Nationalism*.

[38] NHB 95. St., 1001, letter from Bernhard Schmid, 17 December 1847.

[39] In his report to the Court of Directors of the East India Company Sir Charles Wood (1800–85), president of the Board of Control (1852) and secretary of state (1859–66), demanded that the state take over responsibility for the educational sector. Cf. also: Zastoupil L. and M. Moir (eds.), 1999, *The Great Indian Education Debate. Documents Relating to the Orientalist-Anglicist Controversy, 1781–1843*, Introduction, Curzon, Richmond, Surrey (= London Studies on South Asia).

[40] *Report of the Indian Education Commission: Report of the Hunter Education Commission appointed by the Government of India in 1882*, 1883, printed by the Superintendent of Government Printing, Calcutta.

the continuance of government aid for the mission educational system,[41] it not only involved decisive compromises on the part of the mission, but it also indirectly offered the colonial power another possibility to have a voice in educational matters. The political rejection of mission schools increased after the report of the Hunter Commission, and this led to a sharpening of the conflict between the missions and the colonial authorities.

EUROPEAN EDUCATIONAL IDEALS AND INDIAN REALITY

The character of the educational system of the Danish-English-Halle Mission was shaped primarily by the pedagogical ideals that had arisen and were practiced in Halle, since almost every missionary associated his personal experiences in the field of pedagogy with the university and the Orphan House in Halle. The early educational policies of the Mission, especially, were completely indebted to the principles of Halle Pietism and its main representative, the pedagogue August Hermann Francke. Basic features of Francke's pedagogy determined the mission educational system till well into the nineteenth century, even though, in the course of time, corrections were made under the influence of ideas emanating from Enlightenment and rationalism, or new pedagogical approaches and types of schools were introduced.

August Hermann Francke's pedagogy was based on the cornerstones of Pietism, on the combination of inner faith and deeds, of Christian missionary zeal and social consciousness. In other words: it consisted of a synthesis of basic goals of education and upbringing—such as the spread of religious teachings and 'Christian virtues' of piety, punctuality and reliability—with scientific training

[41] The 'grant-in-aid-system' was introduced by the East India Company as a form of control through the state support for the promotion of education. By giving financial aid to educational institutions according to predetermined criteria the East India Company and, later, the colonial government tried to support private initiatives in the field of education. An important criterion was an orientation towards the curriculum laid down by the state. Cf. for this: Misra, Atmanand, 1973, *Grants in Aid of Education in India*, Macmillan, Delhi. The 'result system' envisaged financial and personnel support based on examination results, and this also pre-supposed the use of state-approved curricula. Cf. Fleisch, *Hundert Jahre lutherischer Mission*, 101.

and useful actions in this world. Determined by the eighteenth century-belief in the universal claim of Christian education[42] Francke's educational concepts too were characterized by a strong emphasis on religion, but they neglected to take into account either methods suitable for children or the need for children to play. Francke attached importance to a strictly regulated routine in which the children were expected to be constantly occupied under supervision. Leisure time and recreation were subordinated to this principle of useful activity. The precondition for the realization of these ideals was not only a strict schedule and proper use of time, but also a balance between intellectual, physical and musical activity. The goal of this education and upbringing was to produce pious, virtuous and hard-working young people who would live and work according to Pietist ideals, but who would also display qualities like independence, sense of responsibility, a strong will and good judgment.[43] Francke saw his educational institutions as a powerful instrument for the spread and consolidation of Christian faith in its Pietist form.[44]

[42] Steiger, Günter and Werner Flaschendräger (eds.), 1981, *Magister und Scholaren. Professoren und Studenten. Geschichte Deutscher Universitäten und Hochschulen im Überblick*, Urania Verlag, Leipzig et al.

[43] Francke's pedagogical understanding was determined by the effort to 'sow true piety'. Education served to develop qualities such as the love of truth, obedience and diligence. Lies, willfulness and laziness were to be thwarted. According to Francke corporal punishment was an effective and necessary means of upbringing. Cf. Francke, August Hermann, 1889, *August Hermann Franckes kurtzer und einfältiger Unterricht, wie die Kinder zur wahren Gottseligkeit und christlicher Klugheit anzuführen sind; zum Behuf christlicher Informatorum entworfen*, new edition of the 1748 edition by Otto Frick, Verlag der Buchhandlung des Waisenhauses, Halle/Saale. A concise description of Francke's pedagogic ideals is given in: Deppermann, Klaus, 1961, *Der Hallesche Pietismus und der preußische Staat unter Friedrich III (I.)*, 88–96, Vandenhoeck & Ruprecht, Göttingen. See also: Jacobi, Juliane, 2000, 'Der Blick auf das Kind. Zur Entstehung der Pädagogik des Halleschen Waisenhauses', in Josef N. Neumann and Udo Sträter (eds.), *Das Kind in Pietismus und Aufklärung*, 47–59, Verlag der Franckeschen Stiftungen Halle im Max-Niemeyer Verlag, Tübingen, (= Hallesche Forschungen, Vol. 5).

[44] An assessment of Francke's educational system in 1891 is respectful: 'One should not forget that Pietism, as Francke understood it, was a very aggressive movement, a continual and sharply carried out battle against the worldly activities and the complete lack of discipline and decorum in the Christian (Protestant) Church, and that his educational institutions were a decisive instrument in this struggle, since, basically, all these schools were meant to promote the study of theology.' Hansen, J., 1891, *August Hermann Franckes wichtigste pädagogische Schriften*, Schöningh,

The uncompromising emphasis on religious instruction was the path to this goal. Francke even used the children's mealtimes for readings from the Bible.[45]

Besides religion and languages subjects such as natural sciences, astronomy and hygiene were taught, as also music. A special feature of Francke's teaching methods, especially in the natural sciences, was the use of illustrative material. Apart from this, Francke's pedagogical concepts envisaged the link between learning and productive activity. Teaching was illustrative and practical; visits to workshops enhanced knowledge of the craft being taught.[46]

The extensive ensemble of schools and educational institutions, created by A.H. Francke in the 30 years of work in Halle, had links with North and South Europe, with Russia, England, North America and India. The experiences of the Halle Orphan House influenced the development of the educational system in Brandenburg-Prussia, Wuerttemberg, Saxony/Thuringia and beyond at a time when the economy and society had not yet recovered from the effects of the Thirty Years' War. In Berlin, the elementary schools run by the Huguenots were often situated in the teachers' houses. Besides the teachers, catechists were also involved in education; they revised what had been learned in arithmetic, writing and religion. In 1717 Frederick William I. proclaimed a common school law for the French colonies in Brandenburg-Prussia, which carried the threat of a penalty for refusing to attend school. Till about 1760 the schools were co-educational and there were 25–30 pupils to a teacher.[47] The effort to bring schools under state ownership, or to ensure a greater role of the state in education, continued to find expression in the promulgation of the Prussian General School Regulations of 1763,

Paderborn [et al.], 38, (= Schulz, B. et al., (eds.), *Sammlung der bedeutendsten pädagogischen Schriften aus alter und neuer Zeit. Mit Biographien, Erläuterungen und erklärenden Anmerkungen 1888–1914*, Vol. 8), (translated from German).

[45] Francke, *Segensvolle Fußstapfen*, 207f. This practice was done away with in the 1830s. See: Directorate of the Francke Foundations (ed.), 1863, *Die Stiftungen August Hermann Franckes zu Halle. Festschrift zur zweiten Säkularfeier seines Geburtstages*, Verlag der Buchhandlung des Waisenhauses, Halle, 10.

[46] Scharfe, *Die Religion des Volkes: kleine Kultur—und Sozialgeschichte des Pietismus*, Gütersloher Verlagshaus Mohn, Gütersloh, 141f. For the goals and methods of Pietist upbringing see also: von Dülmen, *Kultur und Alltag in der Frühen Neuzeit*, 127–35.

[47] Steiner, 'Das Schulwesen'.

or in the Austrian Common School Law of 1774. Special bodies were created for the administration of schools and teacher-training institutes were set up.

After the death of August Hermann Francke in 1727 the Francke Foundations continued to work in the manner he had established, even though the debates between representatives of Pietism, Rationalism and Enlightenment had an effect on the pedagogical contents of the schools run by the Foundation. Despite economic constraints Francke's successors made every effort to maintain the educational system. However, although the system was enlarged in the 1730s, economic and political developments since the 1750s led to difficulties. The effects of the Seven Years' War from 1756 to 1763, livestock death, fires, inflation, decline in the income of the Orphan House-pharmacy and of the schools made it difficult to provide for and maintain the institutions of the Foundations. Changes in pedagogical methods and in views on the philosophy of education also influenced developments. When, in the course of the eighteenth century, the critical and anti-dogmatic spirit of Pietism was increasingly subordinated to the idea of conversion, ideas propagated by the German educated bourgeoisie reached the university at Halle through Christian Thomasius, a representative of natural law, and through the rationalist Enlightenment philosopher Christian von Wolff (1679–1754). Along with Göttingen Halle was at that time one of the leading German universities that promoted mathematics, medicine and the natural sciences. Instead of the piety propagated by Pietism reason and humanity were sought to be developed.[48] When

[48] Flaschendräger, Werner, 1981,'Vernunft kontra Autoritäten. Universitäten im 'Jahrhundert der Aufklärung'', in Steiger and Flaschendräger, *Magister und Scholaren*, 55–71; on the role of science teaching in Halle see: Peterson, 'Science in the Tranquebar mission curriculum'. Up until the sixteenth century European universities had chiefly functioned as the pillars and mediators of the given truth in the Bible and in religious dogmas. In the sixteenth and seventeenth centuries the methods and tenets of scholastics supported by medieval monasteries were replaced by the spread of theology, philosophy, medicine etc. Professors and students wandered back and forth between the important European universities following the reputation of a school of thought. As opposed to this, the emerging bourgeois-capitalist system increasingly required science and education as instruments for social growth. The earlier schools in monasteries and cathedrals, which had only serviced a small part of the population, were not enough to cater to the increasing need for educated citizens.

the pedagogue August Hermann Niemeyer, a great-grandson of A.H. Francke, took over the preparatory school in Halle in 1784, the ideas of the Enlightenment also became a component of educational policy in the Francke Foundations. With this, teaching became more strongly oriented towards the world and the principles of usefulness.[49]

While Francke's ideas on education determined the direction for the formation of the educational network of the Tranquebar Mission, the pedagogical concepts developed in England and Scotland also influenced the mission schools in India, especially in the English stations run by Halle missionaries. Foremost among these was the Scottish Enlightenment, which contributed significantly to the development of the educational system and which, at the end of the eighteenth century, made the school and university system in Scotland better than in England. Many important missionaries sent out to India were Scots, for example, Alexander Duff (1806–78), John Wilson (1804–75), John Anderson (1805–55), Stephen Hislop (1817–63), or John Mack (1715–84).[50] By the time most of the Protestant missions started their work in the middle of the nineteenth century new contents had been identified in the Scottish and English educational sphere. Against the backdrop of Enlightenment and industrialization a bourgeois liberalization had set in with an unmistakable trend towards the secularization of education. The turn towards the material world was linked with a change in the demands made on the education of the new generation. Instead of devotedly submissive religious-minded officials without an opinion of their own, critical minds with the ability to form independent judgments were now in demand. All sections of society began to recognize the value of a school education, leading to an increased demand and, consequently, to a greater participation of rulers and governments in this area. As the state Church in England the

[49] August Hermann Niemeyer wrote the book *Grundsätze der Erziehung und des Unterrichts* in 1796. Cf. Directorate, *Die Stiftungen August Hermann Francke's in Halle*, 121f.; Cf. also Klosterberg, Britta, 2000, 'Bücher für Kinder und Jugendliche in den Glauchaer Anstalten', in Penelope Willard (ed.), *Die Franckeschen Stiftungen zu Halle im Jahre 2000*, 31–39, Verlag der Franckeschen Stiftungen, Halle.

[50] Cf. Laird, Michael Andrew, 1972, *Missionaries and Education in Bengal 1793–1837*, Clarendon Press, Oxford; Ingleby, *Missionaries, Education and India*, 35.

Anglican Church had a dominant social position and controlled schools and universities. Whereas in Scotland and Ireland the state began to play an important role in the educational system after the Reformation, in England there are hardly any indications of state intervention in the educational sphere before 1830. In 1833 and 1844 laws were promulgated making it compulsory for factory owners to allow children to attend school. Compulsory education for all was only introduced in England in 1876.[51]

THE EDUCATIONAL SYSTEM OF THE TRANQUEBAR MISSION

At the beginning itself Bartholomäus Ziegenbalg had been convinced that there was a causal connection between educational work and success of the missionary endeavour: 'If one wants to establish something of permanence among such heathens/then most of the efforts should be directed towards the young people.'[52] The close link between mission, education and upbringing was maintained throughout the existence of the Danish-English-Halle Mission. Translated into practice this meant that all possible incentives were created for the acceptance of the educational work of the mission. It was agreed 'to maintain all the children/who wanted to join the congregation with their parents/free of cost/so that their upbringing is in our hands/and so that we might always find such people among them/who can in future be used to propagate the Christian religion.'[53] This procedure corresponded to the intentions of the mission supervisory bodies and its promoters in Europe. Whereas later Christian missions in the nineteenth century often found themselves in conflict with the controlling and regulatory mechanisms of the British colonial administration, the Danish-English-Halle Mission profited from the policy of religious neutrality followed by the East India Company till the middle of the

[51] Schmale, Wolfgang and Nan L. Dodde (eds.), 1991, *Revolution des Wissens? Europa und seine Schulen im Zeitalter der Aufklärung (1750–1825). Ein Handbuch zur europäischen Schulgeschichte*, Dr Winkler, Bochum (for England cf. 97–136).

[52] HB, Vol. 1, ('Sendschreiben'), placed at the beginning of Cont. 1, Halle 1716, 16, (translated from German).

[53] Ibid., (translated from German).

nineteenth century. Even the Danes, as the local authorities in the mission region, did not have their own concepts of education, but used the mission schools to source well-educated young people for employment in their administration.

TYPES OF SCHOOLS AND FINANCING MODELS

The long-term considerations of mission strategy determined the educational policy of the DEHM and this meant that in the final analysis the most important organizational structures of the mission were reproduced in its educational system. Thus, the role of the local school co-workers also has to be envisaged along the coordinates: spatial organization, nationality, caste, religion and functional hierarchy. In 1706 Bartholomäus Ziegenbalg and Heinrich Plütschau kept 'their own schoolmaster with a small school'[54] in their house, got to know the local educational system, learned the local language and, at the same time, began their own work among the youth. Although the models of schools that were developed were based, to a great extent, on the European experiences of the missionaries, they were not simply a mere reproduction of these. The actual types of schools could only be developed as a synthesis of European models and the requirements of Indian reality.[55]

When the missionaries discovered that almost every large place had a 'heathen' school, they looked for ways to influence the teaching in these schools in the hope of arousing the interest of the teachers in Christianity and thus gaining access to the pupils. Constant contact with the local (Hindu) village schools was maintained through the methods of supervision and regular inspections. Representatives of the mission talked with the teachers and pupils, explained texts from the Bible, distributed songs and small prayers, on which the children were tested during subsequent visits. For the period around 1725 the work in the local schools is described in the following manner: In the forenoons one of the Tamil (mission) teachers read out from

[54] AB 42–46, B. Ziegenbalg to A.H. Francke, 1 October 1706, here p. 43.

[55] For the English missionary educational system in the nineteenth century Ingleby also ascertains that although the missionaries were influenced by ideas from home, these ideas were modified by the requirements and under the pressure of work in India. Ingleby, *Missionaries, Education and India*.

the Bible and explained the passages. In the afternoon he taught the children for an hour in the 'corrupt Portuguese'.[56] For the rest of the time the non-Christian teachers were responsible for teaching the children. Besides reading, writing and arithmetic Tamil books were also studied, but also the Biblical texts and Christian literature as desired by the mission.[57] Every Sunday Christian books and Bible passages were read in the six schools that were being supervised and financially supported by the mission at this point in time. However, this time-consuming supervisory programme, which also required a lot of personnel, did not lead to the desired results. Benjamin Schultze's attempt in 1725 to place all the 'heathen' schools in the Tranquebar district officially under mission supervision[58] did not noticeably promote interest in Christianity among the teachers and pupils, even though many teachers were, for a time, bound to the mission through its financial support. Although in 1726 this meant that 365 non-Christian children took part in the Easter examination of the mission schools, the actual interest in Christianity was in no way commensurable with the expenditure incurred. Drawing the logical conclusion from this the mission gave up this form of supervision of local schools in 1727, canceled the salary for the teachers and did not distribute any more materials to these schools.[59]

Although subsequent educational efforts by the missionaries were increasingly directed at setting up and maintaining their own educational institutions, some missionaries, even in later periods, returned to this method. With the intention of 'using the local schools as a means of getting to know the people of this place better'[60] Johann Ernst Geister and Johann Zacharias Kiernander took up the supervision of 'heathen' schools around 1740 in Cuddalore. Besides

[56] HB 33. Cont., 917f.

[57] Cf. HB 22. Cont., 905f., list containing 35 Bible passages used at schools.

[58] HB 23. Cont., 925, report from B. Schultze to the Danish king, Madras, 17 September 1726.

[59] HB 25. Cont., 15, daily register, 14 February 1727. Many years later Schultze accused Ch. T. Walther and Ch. F. Pressier of having closed down the 'schools set up by him' for personal reasons. RA Miskolark 9b, Letter from B. Schultze to Wiedebrock, Kohlhoff, Zeglin, Maderup, Klein, Poltzenhagen and Schwartz, Halle, 20 November 1750.

[60] HB 57. Cont., 1461, excerpt of a letter from Kiernander and Geister to G.A. Francke, 9 January 1742.

a 'Portuguese' and a 'Malabar' school run by the mission, there was also a 'heathen' school under its supervision. In order to intensify their contact with the local population, the missionaries felt that this school should be left in its original form and the children should 'learn to read, write and count in the manner of the country.'[61] Ten years later there was a Tamil school in the mission house in Cuddalore and one in Wandilpaleiam, as well as a 'Portuguese' school. In the local school that still existed, which was supervised by mission employees, but not financed by the mission, there were ten children from Madagascar, who were serfs of the Company. Their teacher was Johann Moite, a former pupil of the 'Portuguese' mission school in Cuddalore.[62]

In the beginning of the nineteenth century Daniel Schreyvogel tried once again to participate in the supervision of local non-Christian schools without placing them formally under the mission. Taking the experiences of the first Protestant missionaries into account he envisaged the setting up of a committee with a missionary as its member, which would look after all matters pertaining to schools: 'A century ago a similar attempt was made in Tranquebar that continued for 20 years, and later Dr John introduced this plan in the schools independent of the mission, which were then placed under the supervision of the Church Missionary Society.'[63]

The teaching of Christian children could be put into effect quickly and inexpensively in the house of a missionary. Introduced initially due to the lack of suitable space, the missionaries continued this form of teaching even after a well-developed network of schools was established. The children who were taught in the homes of missionaries and Indian co-workers were partly pupils who were to be given special training, especially in European languages. In addition, this form of teaching offered mission employees the possibility of a modest additional income. Some of these pupils were orphans, who were integrated into the families of mission employees, especially of European missionaries, and who received a major part of their education there. Around 1785 Christoph Samuel John's family took

[61] HB 57. Cont., 1461.
[62] HB 74. Cont., 262.
[63] NHB 84. St., 1248f., (translated from German).

in nine European children as 'boarders' in their house. John regretted that he had to refuse to take in some children of English parents, but his wife, he explained, could not look after a large number of children on her own and suitable Indian tutors were lacking.[64]

Wherever the financial situation of the mission and the local realities permitted it, the schools and the homes of mission employees were built as one complex. While building a house for the local catechist or assistant prayer-rooms and classrooms were included for reasons of cost and efficiency. This meant that even the Tamilian co-workers practiced a form of home schools. At the beginning of missionary work a school for non-Christian children was opened in Porayar. The classrooms were built as a wing of the house of the local catechist, so that he 'can visit the same every day and teach one or two hours daily in the school and help the teacher we have employed.'[65] In Nagapattinam the local catechists (who earlier had been associated with the Dutch) working with Christian Wilhelm Gericke had to teach children, slaves and Tamil servants in their own houses, since the mission had too few rooms.[66] In 1784 William Wheately, the teacher in the English school in Thanjavur, took in some school children, fed them and taught them at home, since they lived far away and wouldn't have been able to come to school on account of the heat.[67]

The model of home schools was one that the missionaries had experienced in Europe, where some of them had worked as private tutors for children of wealthy families. Here, too, very small groups were taught in a family-like atmosphere. This was, however, also similar to the Indian *gurukula*-tradition, which also provides for close contact between the teachers and the pupils, and where the pupils are not only given formal instruction, but where, through the proximity of the guru, they also imbibe important experiences of their teacher. Ch. S. John wanted to institutionalize this form of teaching in the framework of the mission and proposed that every (married) European missionary take in four to six children, who would then be taught in a group.[68] John received requests from Nagapattinam,

[64] NHB 32. St., 888.
[65] HB 14. Cont., 163f., (translated from German).
[66] NHB 33. St., 1086.
[67] NHB 30. St., 693.
[68] NHB 32. St., 889, letter from John, Tranquebar, 10 September 1785.

Ceylon, Batavia, Malacca and other European settlements to take their children into the mission schools, and this led him to set up a boarding school.[69]

The mission schools were attended by children of the mission congregations as well as by others who were being prepared for baptism. The first mission schools were house schools set up by Ziegenbalg and Plütschau as early as in 1707.[70] A separate school building was erected only two years later.[71] In 1736, of the 94 children in the three schools of the Tamil city congregation in Tranquebar nine had not been baptized.[72] In 1739 there were 173 school children in Tranquebar city, of whom 11 had not yet been baptized and whose parents or relatives were also undergoing baptismal preparation. Of these 173 children 57 were in the 'Portuguese' school, and of these 43 were mission children, while the remaining 14 were from outside.[73] Tranquebar offered the most extensive education, and children from other schools were often sent to Tranquebar for the higher classes. In 1752, for example, the pupils Gurupadam, Ṣinappen and Dewaprien were sent to Tranquebar from the English station Cuddalore for their further education.[74]

In 1707 already B. Ziegenbalg informed the Danish king, Frederick IV, about his intention of setting up a 'free school to teach mainly theology and true Christianity, but where there would also be an opportunity to deal with all kinds of sciences. The condition would be that everyone would have the freedom to decide whether they wanted to become Christians or not.'[75] These charity schools were also open to non-Christians and were established, financed and supervised by the mission.[76] In the first such charity school, set up on Johann Ernst Gründler's initiative, the children were given their school material free of

[69] John, *On Indian Civilization*, 6.

[70] HB, Vol. 1, ('Sendschreiben') placed at the beginning of Cont. 1, Halle 1716, 17f.

[71] HB 2. Cont., 92, letter from Gründler, 6 January 1710.

[72] HB 42. Cont., Vorrede, ('Kurtze Nachricht'), 5 October 1736.

[73] HB 49. Cont., 6.

[74] HB 78. Cont., 925, 930.

[75] AB 57, letter from Ziegenbalg to Frederick IV of Denmark, Tranquebar, 19 September 1707, (translated from German.

[76] HB 11. Cont., 864–69, letter from J.E. Gründler to the Mission Board in Copenhagen, Tranquebar, 16 August 1715.

cost.[77] Gründler opened this school with the permission of the Danish commandant, Hassius, who appealed to the people to allow their children to go to this school. It was pointed out that this would give the children a better chance in future to be employed by the Company.[78] The children would learn about the Christian faith and receive a Christian upbringing to prepare them for their future as employees of Europeans. Teaching encompassed reading, writing and arithmetic in Tamil and Portuguese, bible study, theological training and the study of Tamil poetry. Two years later the school had established itself and was accepted by the local population. Although hardly any of the pupils wanted to become Christians, the missionaries remained steadfast in their view that these young minds, even if their parents so not allow them to be baptized, should be taught the principles of Christian dogma along with other subjects, which will prove to be fruitful and useful, since one does not forget what one has learned in one's youth.[79]

After Gründler's death Benjamin Schultze continued the work in this charity school. In 1723 its development is described in the following manner:

> The charity school, he writes, [B. Schultze, H.L.] is only for the heathen children and is different from the Christian school, in which all the pupils are already Christians or are being prepared for holy baptism [...]. All the children have, at least, a general knowledge of God and Christ. Secondly, they do not shrink from us Christians as the rest of the nation does. Thirdly, because the gospel is read out to them every day for a whole hour, the children, as well as the adults, when they come by for this, get an opportunity to look into their hearts and their conscience, [...]. Fourthly, those who have learned to read, read our books on Sundays and are thus not only restrained from evil, but also receive some guidance for being good.[80]

[77] 'Even if high-ranking Malabarians do not wish to send their children to this school, the poor would probably use this institution and send their children to this school, since they do not have the money to send them to their Malabarian school.' (translated from German), HB 11. Cont., 864, J.E. Gründler to the Mission Board, 16 August 1715.

[78] HB 11. Cont., 864f., J.E. Gründler to the Mission Board, 16 August 1715.

[79] AB 471f., B. Ziegenbalg and J.E. Gründler to A.H. Francke, Tranquebar, 7 January 1717.

[80] HB 19. Cont., 344f., (translated from German).

On June 18, 1722 Schultze named this school 'The Royal Danish Lutheran Malabarian Charity-School',[81] and, five days later, the school was shifted to another place whose name Schultze did not mention.[82] These free schools enjoyed a good reputation among the local population because of their high standard of education, the only complaint often being that children of different castes were being taught together.[83] Charity schools financed and supervised by the English were also established.

Christoph Samuel John wrote his extensive treatise 'On Indian Civilization', which was published in 1813 in London and dealt with his model of free schools, as a contribution to the development of Indian civilization and to the 'civic education of Indians'.[84] John pleaded for co-operation between different missionary organizations with the English East India Company and proposed the establishment of a Separate Liberal Native School Society for all of India. He made this suggestion, on the one hand, to the East India Company, when it began to publicly debate its engagement with education in India and when it earmarked funds in its budget for the educational sphere. On the other hand, John also addressed this to the religious societies that were working in India at the beginning of the nineteenth century. Free schools, according to John, were meant to be supported by highly placed authorities and he named the schools set up by Christian Friedrich Schwartz as possible models.[85] The free schools that John established were taken over and run by the Church Mission Society after his death.[86]

After evaluating his long experience in teaching Indians and Europeans of different origin John developed his model of integrated schools. However, this international and intercultural experiment was based primarily on the intention of training South Indian children to be employed by Europeans. While, at first glance, this intercultural experiment and its combination of science with (general) education

[81] HB 20. Cont., 467, diary, B. Schultze, 18 June 1722.

[82] Ibid., 23 June 1722.

[83] HB 11. Cont., 957–59, 'Der Malabarischen Korrespondentz anderen Theil', 44th letter.

[84] John, *On Indian Civilization*.

[85] Ibid., 8.

[86] NHB 67. St., 592.

appeared far-reaching and far-sighted, it was ultimately born out of pragmatic needs and the pressing requirements of the time. Some reputed Hindu families sent their children to this school so that they could be trained for employment with Europeans. The basic idea of this school was to teach the local children the European way of life through this daily association with European children.[87] Prior to this, the European children had been taught separately from the Indians.

For the first time in 1775 the Mission Board directly entrusted the missionary Johann Wilhelm Gerlach with the setting up and supervision of a 'school of languages and sciences', which was to cater primarily to European Lutheran children in Tranquebar, but which would also be open to Tamil children.[88] There was a demand for a school of this kind among the Europeans living in South India. In February 1784 John thanked the Mission Board for permission to set up an 'educational institution for European children and Malabarian boys'.[89] When, at the end of the eighteenth century, Europeans living in India were increasingly sending their children to Europe for their education, John wanted Indian boys to also have this possibility. At this point in time John himself was thinking of returning to Europe because of his poor health. He requested that he be allowed to bring some Tamil boys with him for their further education. Other missionaries, he argued, could do the same, for example, Johann Daniel Mentel, who went back to Europe in 1784 for reasons of health. Daniel Pullei had also expressed the desire to send one of his sons to Europe for his education.[90] John's concept, which did not arouse the desired interest of the superiors in Europe, was basically to give talented Indian children the possibility of getting a further education in Europe after the age of 15.[91]

[87] NHB 32. St., 889, letter from John, Tranquebar, 10 September 1785. John names the 'handling of Malabarian boys' the 'main aim of the European school'. See also NHB 30. St., 705f., Letter from John, Tranquebar, 18 October 1784.

[88] RA Miskolark 3, 1765–1789, instruction for the missionary Johan Wilhelm Gerlach, 16 November 1775.

[89] RA Miskolark 9g, *Pro memoria* from Ch. S. John, Tranquebar, 12 February 1784.

[90] Ibid.

[91] NHB 32. St., 896, letter from John, Tranquebar, 10 September 1787.

The term 'provincial school' refers to those institutions that were either financed by the local rulers or supported by them through a donation of land. The first provincial schools were established in the 1780s through a co-operation between Christian Friedrich Schwartz, who had begun working for the SPCK in 1768 and who had settled down permanently in Thanjavur in 1778, and English colonial officials. According to Frykenberg, it is these schools that demonstrate Schwartz's importance as an 'educational innovator'.[92]

His, [Schwartz's, H.L.] scheme for a modern state-subsidized 'public' system of schools in India began with the rajas ofThanjavur, Shivaganga, and Ramnad. High schools that he established so impressed the East India Company's resident at Thanjavur that the company's directors in London and it's government at Fort St. George, in Madras, were persuaded to subsidize them, even though none of these schools lay within company territory.[93]

The local princes of the provinces would provide money or donate a village to finance the schools and to pay the teachers. Acting on behalf of the English, Schwartz had discussions in several provinces, among others, in Ramanathapuram and in Sivaganga. Some rulers agreed to donate a village and to give monthly financial support.[94] The provincial school in Ramanathapuram began with 10 pupils including the adoptive son of the ruler and some sons of ministers. The schoolmaster was Wheatley.[95]

Besides these institutionalized models that existed for a long time there were experiments, which did not prove successful for varying reasons. This included, for example, a separate private school with Catholics and Hindus run by Christoph Samuel John for a brief period.[96]

The expenditure incurred in maintaining the mission schools included funds for setting up and maintaining the buildings, funds for teaching material and money for feeding the children and providing

[92] Frykenberg, 'The Legacy of Christian Friedrich Schwartz', 130.
[93] Ibid., 132.
[94] NHB 30. St., 691.
[95] NHB 33. St., 1024, 1027.
[96] John, *On Indian Civilization*, 6.

for the teachers. The expenditure on each pupil included: cost of food, clothes, hygiene and teaching material. In reply to a question at the beginning of 1729 Christoph Theodosius Walther mentioned the annual costs for a grown-up school child as being 9 *Taler*, 3 *Fanam* and 60 *Kas*.[97] When the price of rice increased a few years later, it led to higher expenditure on the children[98] and in 1739 subsequently the expenditure on children of the first class (the older pupils) was 15 *Reichstaler*, 10 *Fanam* and 19 *Kas*; for children of the second class it was 12 *Reichstaler*, 8 *Fanam* and 20 *Kas*, while for the children of the third class (the youngest children) it was 8 *Reichstaler*, 9 *Fanam* and 21 *Kas*. With regard to the clothing provided to the children, the expenditure was determined not only by age, but mainly by the social background of the children: for children of the 'Portuguese' population larger sums of money were required for clothing.[99] In 1823 the monthly expenditure on a school child in Palayankottai was one *Taler* and six *Groschen*, which amounted to an annual sum of 15 *Taler*.[100]

Since the mission schools were self-supporting only to a very small extent, they were always dependent on willing sponsors. A regular system of state funding arose only in the second half of the nineteenth century when, with the introduction of the grant-in-aid-system, schools run by religious societies also had the possibility of applying for aid from public funds.[101] The missionaries of the Tranquebar Mission, however, were dependent on funds provided, to a large extent, by the Danish royal family, and also on additional support from European sponsors. Besides the regular donations the missionaries also established a network of private sponsorship. Individuals in Europe donated money to finance the education of

[97] AFSt/M 1 B 1 : 23, letter from Christoph Theodosius Walther to Georg Sarganeck, Tranquebar, 10 January 1729; HB 27. Cont., 225. The missionaries informed the crown prince of Denmark: 'The annual costs for a child, all things taken together, are, in a period of inflation, roughly 9 Rthlr.; when the cost of living is not so high, it is a little less.' (translated from German), HB 27. Cont., 207, letter from Dal, Bosse, Pressier and Walther, Tranquebar, 5 October 1728.

[98] HB 52. Cont., 680, letter from the missionaries to the editor, 19 December 1739.

[99] HB 52. Cont., 681f. Cf. also 58. Cont., 1544.

[100] NHB 72. St., 1263, report by G.E. Rhenius and L.B.E. Schmid, Palayamcottah 1823.

[101] Fleisch, *Hundert Jahre lutherischer Mission*, 78.

one or several school children in India and, in return, they received regular reports on the children's progress. Ninety-two European donors supported 150 children of the Tamil school in Tranquebar in 1765.[102]

The educational activities of the Tranquebar Mission were also supported by the Society for Promoting Christian Knowledge and by the English East India Company. In 1711 Bartholomäus Ziegenbalg thanked Anton Wilhelm Böhme in London for £60 that had been sent to the Mission for setting up a school for the poor.[103] From November 1726 onwards Benjamin Schultze got a 'certain subsidy' from the governor, who promised to give this sum for the entire period of Schultze's stay in Madras.[104] In 1738 Johann Anton Sartorius reported that the governor of Madras had made an annual sum of 100 pagodas available for the school in Cuddalore.[105] In 1788 the Company paid five Rupees per month for each of the 100 school children of the 'English' school in Madras.[106] In the 1780s the English East India Company asked Christian Friedrich Schwartz to set up three provincial schools in Thanjavur, Ramanathapuram and Sivaganga respectively. The costs were borne by the East India Company.[107] Sponsors for the English schools were also found among the officials of the Company in India, or from support movements in England. Sometimes, Europeans in India also took on personal sponsorships to finance the education of a particular child. In Cuddalore Kiernander taught a child whose entire education was financed by an alderman of Fort St. David.[108]

[102] AFSt/M 2 B 3 : 8, school catalogue of the children in the Tamil school who are receiving support from benefactors. January 1756, ??. 01. 1756. The information includes the name of the donor, the name and class of the child as well as a brief evaluation of the child's progress.

[103] AB 195, letter from Ziegenbalg to Böhme and Hoar in England, Tranquebar, 4, 5 December 1711.

[104] Lehmann, Arno, *Es begann in Tranquebar*, 227. In a letter to King George I. Schultze emphasizes that the school was established 'upon the earnest desire of the Governor'. SPCK ME/Cr 3 Letter from B. Schultze to King George, Madras, 16 December 1726.

[105] HB 46. Cont., 1318, letter from Sartorius, 3 February 1738.

[106] NHB 37. St., 111f.

[107] NHB, Preface to Vol. III, XI.

[108] HB 64. Cont., 713, 10 February 1745.

Besides the donations from Europe and from Europeans in India, the missionaries also looked for other ways and means of getting money for the mission schools. One of these was to conduct regular collections in the congregation.[109] Another source of income was through the sale of handicraft products and natural produce. The handicraft work done by the children was sold, and part of the income from this was used to help school graduates become financially independent. John gave the Indian teachers a part of the income from the sale of socks and mats in addition to their salary from the mission.[110] The mission also received income from lease-deeds, especially in the case of the so-called provincial schools. 'English' schools were set up in all the provinces of the *maṟavar*-region and of the Thanjavur kingdom, and these were financed, to a large extent, from the income of the districts. In February 1783 Schwartz reported that one of these schools had been set up in Ramanathapuram, with two more to follow, and that the king of Thanjavur had allocated 40 pagodas a month towards payment for a schoolmaster and for other expenses.[111] When the Raja of Thanjavur gave Schwartz a village to set up the school, the idea was to finance the schools with the income from the leases.[112]

Only very few parents paid school fees. The children in the mission schools were supported according to a graded system. They either did not pay fees, or they did not pay fees and were provided school material, or they did not pay fees and got free board and clothing. In some cases the children received a daily or a monthly allowance. Most of the children in the Tamil schools were fully supported by the mission. In the 'English' and 'Portuguese' schools there were generally always children whose parents paid for a part of the school education. In 1734, of the 50 children in the 'Portuguese' school at Tranquebar, 28 were maintained free of cost (19 boys and nine girls), while in the Tamil district congregation none of the 177 children paid for their education.[113] Of the 50 children enrolled in the 'English' school in Tiruchirappalli in 1771,

[109] HB 85. Cont., 1209 (1758)
[110] NHB 32. St., 890.
[111] NHB 30. St., Preface, 3.
[112] NHB, Preface to Vol. III, Xf.
[113] Cf. HB 37. Cont., Preface.

ten children received a free education.[114] In the years 1770/1772, of the 94 mission school children in Calcutta five did not pay any fees, 61 got free tuition and were given paper and books, 20 were financed by the 'city charity', and eight by their parents.[115] The monthly fees in Calcutta were four Rupees, and not all parents could pay this amount regularly. Around 1780 there were between 40–50 children being taught there, and it was difficult to pay the teachers regularly. The monthly salary of the 'Pomeranian' writer alone, who was working for the mission, amounted to Rs 150.[116] In the 1830s Daniel Schreyvogel proposed a credit model for the self-financing of the schools. A teacher who had been trained in a mission school would, once he started earning, give a certain amount from his salary to the person who had taught him. This amount could be one-fourth of his salary for a period of two years. If the person concerned became a catechist, he would only have to pay one-fourth of the higher salary for one year.[117]

RELIGIOUS AND SOCIAL FACTORS

In the initial years, the missionaries in Tranquebar assigned the children, on the basis of cultural and linguistic differences, to the 'Malabarian', the 'Portuguese' and the Danish schools. In 1711 already Ziegenbalg reported that there were three 'Malabarian', one 'Portuguese' and one Danish school in the city. The 'Malabarian' (Tamil) schools were divided into two boys' schools and one school for girls, while the 'Portuguese' and the Danish schools were co-educational. The Tamil boys were supervised by two Indian teachers, and the Tamil girls by an Indian widow. The teacher in the 'Portuguese' school was of Portuguese-Indian descent, had been brought up in the mission school, and spoke both Portuguese and Tamil. Both these languages were taught in the 'Portuguese' school. The Danish school was the only one where the Mission did not provide for the children, and where the parents paid fees.

[114] Cf. NHB 8. St., 1096.

[115] Cf. NHB 6. St., 771; 10. St., 1359.

[116] NHB 26. St., 173f.

[117] NHB 84. St., 1253. report of 1836.

Unlike the Tamil schools and the 'Portuguese' school, the pupils of the Danish school went home every evening, while the others, as a rule, were accommodated in the mission house.[118] Classes were held in their respective mother tongues, and the contents of instruction were partly adapted to the social and professional paths envisaged for the children.

As a rule, the Tranquebar Mission strictly separated children of European descent from Tamil children and had different curricula for each of the groups. Attempts to change this did not have lasting success. In November 1775, the Mission Board sent out Johann Wilhelm Gerlach with special instructions to look after the education of Europeans and Eurasians.[119] The royal instruction for Gerlach, dated 16 November 1775, enjoined upon him, first and foremost, to teach Christianity in the school and, beyond that, German and Latin. Suitable preceptors from the English school in Thanjavur were to be made available for teaching English.[120] At the request of the Mission Board the school 'would also be open to talented young people from among the local inhabitants.'[121]

Christoph Samuel John made a clear distinction between the education of the Tamils, i.e. the local population, and that of the 'Portuguese', i.e. the Indo-Europeans or Europeans. The criteria were differing abilities and differing needs based on their future paths in life. At the beginning of the 1780s Christoph Samuel John and Johann Peter Rottler developed a concept for a mixed European-Indian school, in which the appropriate social role of the children was clearly anchored in the school routine:

> After this Mr Rottler [...] conducts catechism with all of them, during which the Malabarian children stand behind the European children. This begins with a hymn and a prayer, for which the former

[118] Ziegenbalg, Gründler and Jordan give a detailed description of the early educational system in a letter to A.H. Francke, Tranquebar, 10 September 1712. Cf. AB 226f.

[119] Koilpillai, *The SPCK in India*, 19f. Koilpillai gives the following figures for the number of Eurasians in regions under British control: 40,000 in Madras, 50,000 in Bengal, 20,000 in Bombay.

[120] RA Miskolark 3, 1765–89, instruction for the missionary Johann Wilhelm Gerlach, 16 November 1775.

[121] NHB 18. St., 738, letter from Johann Wilhelm Gerlach, 20 January 1788.

kneel, while the latter remain standing with the teacher—a distinction that is necessitated by the clothes they wear.[122]

Lunch-time was used to teach the Tamilian children European eating habits, and

> [...] all Malabarian boys have to wait at table in order that they become skilled at serving Europeans and learning their way of life. They do, of course, break many glasses and plates before they learn to handle them. It also gives us a good opportunity to rid them of their stupid aversion to beef.[123]

The experiment was abandoned after some time, and the report do not provide any information about the reasons for this. Even when European and Tamil children were taught in the same school in this integration project, instruction in certain subjects was still conducted separately: The 20 Tamil children were mostly taught separately from the five European children by their Tamil teachers. They were only brought together for lessons in theology, even when these were in German.[124]

While developing the mission educational system in India the religious background of the children was also an important factor. The schools set up by the Danish-English-Halle Mission were not reserved for children of Christians. Even in the early years of the mission the charity school that was set up was a public school for non-Christians. In the further course of the mission the division according to religion was no longer carried out, and common schools, free of religious criteria, were established. In other words: the schools that were financed and supervised by the DEHM were, theoretically, open to adherents of all religions. With the exception of schools, or special classes, in which future employees of the mission were trained, and which were, therefore, meant exclusively for Christians, the

[122] NHB 30. St., 707, letter from Ch. S. John, Tranquebar, 18 October 1784. Cf. also: 30. St., 684f., letter from J.P. Rottler to G.A. Freylinghausen, 20 February 1784, (translated from German).

[123] NHB 30. St., 707, letter from Ch. S. John, Tranquebar, 18 October 1784, (translated from German).

[124] NHB 32. St., 888, letter from Ch. S. John to G.A. Freylinghausen, Tranquebar, 10 September 1785.

schools were open to all confessions.[125] There were many different kinds of motives for non-Christians to send their children to mission schools. Hindus, who were poor, sometimes sent their children to these schools for material considerations, since the schools often provided food and clothing. Members of socially higher groups had the professional opportunities for their children in mind. Around 1790 over 40 children were enrolled in the so-called English provincial school in Thanjavur, and they were all from Hindu families.[126] There is hardly any mention of Muslim or Catholic children in the context of these mission schools.[127] Some Brahmins, who sent their children to mission schools in the 1780s, expected advantages for their children from an English-medium education and were, therefore, willing to put up with the study of Christian texts.[128] 'Of my heathen seminarists, many display a better character, are more honest, sober and diligent than many professed Christians.'[129]

The caste differences created enormous difficulties when organizing the school routine. Contrary to the original intention of the missionaries, the caste problem had to be taken into account in the schools, for example, in the selection of teachers, in the organization of vocational training, or in the composition of classes. On 10 February 1731, Johann Anton Sartorius referred to this problem forcefully in a letter to Gotthilf August Francke, the editor of the *Hallesche Berichte*. High-caste parents would not send their children to a school, which had a *paṟaiyār* teacher.[130] The mission

[125] In the seventeenth century France practiced a strict confessional division; Protestant children did not go to Catholic schools. Steiner, Klaus, 2002, 'Das Schulwesen', in Gottfried Bregulla (ed.), *Hugenotten in Berlin*, 206–26, Union Verlag, Berlin.

[126] NHB 40. St., 387, Ch. F. Schwartz to Pasche in London, January 1791. Two years later 'children of about 12 Brahmins and children of some merchants' were being educated in the provincial school in Kumbakonam, also set up by Schwartz. NHB 47. St., 981.

[127] One of the few examples can be mentioned here: In 1770 a school was opened in Puleiarkuppam near Cuddalore, which began 'with three children from our congregation, one Catholic and several heathen children'. NHB 5. St., 649, report of the missionaries, 31 December 1770.

[128] NHB 36. St., 1395f., Ch. F. Schwartz to Johann Ludwig Schulze, 1 February 1788.

[129] John, *On Indian Civilization*, 22.

[130] HB 30. Cont., 673.

school regulations of the early 1740s made it obligatory for the teachers to ensure that *śūdra* children and *paṟaiyār* children were separated while studying, sleeping and eating.[131] Even while selecting children for special training the missionaries were forced to take the caste question into account. 'Recently we took in Parraier children for special classes, in order to make an attempt in this direction. We do not despise these people, but the Suttirer are better suited for the mission,'[132] John wrote in March 1787. A year later, in a joint letter, the missionaries lamented the lack of 'good national workers, especially of the higher (Suttirer) class'.[133] The contents of craft-lessons and the vocational training of the children required a heightened sensitivity for the caste question.[134]

The question of gender had always presented a special challenge to the formation of the mission educational system. Following the Halle model[135] the missionaries opened the first girls' school in Tranquebar in 1707. A widow supervised the girls. The contents of teaching were essentially similar to those of the boys, but consisted of different practical subjects such as stitching.[136] Whenever conditions allowed, boys and girls were taught separately like in Halle. Only in small places, where the number of school children was very small, and where there was only one teacher, girls and boys studied together. Taking into account the fact that girls in Tamil society of the eighteenth century

131 HB 58. Cont., 1532.

132 NHB 35. St., 1313, Ch. S. John to Johann Ludwig Schulze, Tranquebar, 29 March 1787, (translated from German).

133 NHB 35. St., 1323, letter from all the missionaries in Tranquebar, 8 February 1788.

134 NHB 30. St., 671f.

135 During Easter 1701 August Hermann Francke had opened a girls' school in Halle. Cf.: Francke, *Segensvolle Fußstapfen*, 474. In Bible-reading circles and in schools girls and women gained access to education and the possibility of engaging with questions of faith.

136 'The girls' school is separate. They have a widow, who is knowledgeable and loyal, to supervise them. She is with them during the day, and also sleeps alongside them at night in a closed room. Every morning the girls also pray together. After this, they are divided into their catechism-classes and learn their lessons, which consist of reading, writing and memorizing. They also have all the books of Christian teachings that the boys have [...]. They have their meals in the afternoon and evening separately in their room, and mealtimes are conducted in the same way as with the boys.' (translated from German), HB 6. Cont., 241.

only had access to education in exceptional cases, the percentage of girls in the larger schools was often astonishingly high. Girls comprised about one-third of the 190 school children of the Tamil district congregation in 1734. In the city schools the percentage of girls was often higher. In 1735 there were 61 boys and 43 girls being educated in the Tamil city congregation in Tranquebar.[137] The city had one 'Portuguese boys' school', one 'Portuguese girls' school', a 'Malabarian boys' school' and a 'Malabarian girls' school'. There was also a 'Portuguese boys' school' outside the city.[138] Schoolmistresses and teachers were trained to supervise the girls, and women were employed to teach 'needlework'.[139]

The mission schools were confronted with the connection between social questions and education when, for example, the children could not attend school regularly, because their parents were poor and they had to contribute to the family income by taking up work. In times of war and famine too, orphaned children initially came to school because of the meals provided. The number of children in the schools depended on various factors. On the one hand, the number of births and baptisms in the Christian congregation differed from year to year, and, on the other, natural catastrophes, wars and diseases contributed to fluctuations in the numbers. If there were infectious diseases these spread quickly due to the large number of pupils in each class. In 1739 the missionaries in Tranquebar reported, in reply to a query from the sponsors, that this was the reason for the decrease in the number of school children in 1737.[140] In the early years the mission found it difficult to win over children of the local population for its schools. Many parents did not find it necessary to allow their children access to education, and were skeptical towards the work of the missionaries.

The number of children being taught and supervised by a single teacher also fluctuated greatly. In small village schools, which were often hardly structured and, sometimes, consisted of only one class, there were, at times, no more than five to ten children. In the city

137 HB Preface to 40. Cont.
138 HB 40. Cont. 524.
139 HB 47. Cont., 1331.
140 HB 52. Cont., 680.

schools, in some years, there were 30–40 pupils to one teacher. In 1739 six teachers taught 88 children in the 'Malabarian boys' school' in Tranquebar, which meant that, on an average, there were 13 children to one teacher.[141] In 1756 there were 48 children with four teachers altogether in the four district schools.[142] In 1758 four male teachers and one female teacher were in charge of 80 boys and 65 girls respectively in the mission schools in Cuddalore.[143] The ratio was more unfavourable in the case of girls, since, often, not enough female teachers were trained and appointed, even tough the ratio of girls among the school children remained the same and constituted about 30 per cent. These figures become relative when one takes into account that the teachers had assistants, that, sometimes, additional women were employed for craft lessons, that a Tamil doctor taught selected children botany, and that the missionaries also took classes.

THE METHODS OF TEACHING

Against the backdrop of pedagogical developments in Europe as well as social changes in the mission region the missionaries periodically examined the contents and methods of education and modified them if necessary. A sensitive manner of dealing with local religious, cultural and social norms and traditions constituted a basic precondition for the acceptance of missionary educational work. In addition to this, educational policies of the British colonial power and the competition that arose from these between the mission schools and the state-run public schools forced the mission to make compromises in the school routine.

Prior to their appointment in South India most of the missionaries had gathered pedagogical experiences in Halle, where, as university students of advanced semesters, they were used for supervision or for teaching in the Royal Preparatory School, or in other schools, of the Francke Foundations.[144] The contents and methods of education

[141] HB 49. Cont., 3.

[142] HB 85. Cont., 4.

[143] HB 89. Cont., 527.

[144] From 1696 till 1749 altogether 3788 students of the Halle university worked as teachers in the Francke Foundations. Brieger, *Historisch=topographische Beschreibung der Stadt Halle*, 175.

in Halle, therefore, initially also constituted the yardstick of their pedagogical work in India. Often, the contact between teachers and students of the Halle preparatory school with the missionaries in India was maintained for some time after the latter's departure. Thus, in 1729, Christian Friedrich Pressier in Tranquebar wrote: '*Eine kleine schriftliche Ermahnung an die gegenwärtigen Scholaren des Pädagogii Regii zu Halle*' (A small written exhortation for the present scholars of the Royal Preparatory School at Halle).[145]

The missionaries developed an intensive exchange about educational methods and the contents of teaching with English officials in India, who had already shown a great interest in the pedagogical activities of the first missionaries. In a letter of 1713 to the English chaplain, George Lewis, at Fort St. George in Madras, Bartholomäus Ziegenbalg gave a detailed explanation of the pedagogical concepts used in the schools of the Danish-Halle Mission.[146] By writing this letter the missionary not only hoped to get financial support from the English (Ziegenbalg emphasized that the missionaries had very meagre funds),[147] but he was also aware of the changes in the English educational sector and assumed that the experiences of the mission would be interesting for English educational experts. The missionaries knew about the developments in the educational field in England and Scotland through the *Accounts of the Charity Schools*, published regularly in England, and which the missionaries asked to be sent to them. In his letter Ziegenbalg described the timetable and the teaching methods in detail, while emphasizing that the missionaries were also taking Indian traditions into account. As examples of this he mentioned how the younger children wrote in sand and how learning was done through the combined chanting of words and texts.[148]

[145] AFSt/M 1 B 1 : 33, letter from Christian Friedrich Pressier to the students of the Halle school, Tranquebar, 27 January 1729.

[146] Ziegenbalg, Bartholomäus, 1715, *A letter to the Reverend Mr Geo. Lewis. The Chaplain to the Honourable East-India Company, at Fort St. George: giving an account of the Method of Instruction used in the Charity-Schools of the Church, calle'd Jerusalem, in Tranquebar. [...] translated from the Portugueze-copy printed at Tranquebar*, printed and sold by J. Downing IV, London. The letter was originally printed in 1713 in the mission printing press in Tranquebar. HB 33. Cont., 928.

[147] Ziegenbalg, *A letter to the Reverend Mr Geo. Lewis*, foreword iif., 19.

[148] Ibid., 7, 19.

The main aim of the methods used for educating and bringing up the children was to shape pious and diligent Christians. Discipline, therefore, constituted the highest principle in the upbringing of the youth. This resulted primarily in a closely packed timetable. Classes generally began at 6 a.m. with prayer and catechization and ended with a prayer after dinner at 8 p.m. Free time in the course of the day was carefully measured out, it was strictly allotted and was always supervised. During meals and craft lessons the Bible, or other religious texts, were read out.

TABLE 5.1 The daily routine in the Tamil school in Tranquebar in 1709[149]

6.00–7.00 a.m.	Prayer and catechization with a missionary
7.00–9.00 a.m.	A chapter from the New Testament is read out to the children and discussed with them; in between breakfast at 8.00 a.m.
9.00–11.00 a.m.	Continuation of classes and repetition
11.00 a.m.–12.00 p.m.	Lunch
12.00–1.00 p.m.	Rest-hour under the supervision of a preceptor
1.00–2.00 p.m.	Writing exercises in the sand or on palm leaves
2.00–3.00 p.m.	Letter reading and writing
3.00–4.00 p.m.	Arithmetic
4.00–5.00 p.m.	A Tamilian assistant conducts catechization with all Tamil pupils and catechumen
5.00–6.00 p.m.	Repetition of topics and singing with the Tamilian teacher
6.00–7.00 p.m.	Dinner accompanied by readings from the New Testament by the preceptors
7.30 p.m.	Bedtime

[149] HB 4. Cont., 155–62, school regulations of 1709.

TABLE 5.2 The daily routine in the 'Portuguese' school in Tranquebar in 1709[150]

6.00–7.00 a.m.	Prayer and catechization in Portuguese
7.00–9.00 a.m.	Readings from the New Testament; in between breakfast at 8.00 a.m.
9.00–11.00 a.m.	Learning the alphabet and spelling exercises
11.00 a.m–12.00 p.m.	Lunch
12.00–2.00 p.m.	Knitting (socks)
2.00–3.00 p.m.	Catechism for boys
3.00–5.00 p.m.	The older children learn writing and arithmetic, the others learn the alphabet
5.00–6.00 p.m.	A 'Portuguese' co-worker conducts catechization
6.00–7.00 p.m.	Dinner, accompanied by readings from the New Testament by a preceptor
7.30 p.m.	Bedtime

TABLE 5.3 The daily routine in the 'Malabarian boys' school' in Tranquebar in 1726[151]

First class (the older pupils)	
6.00–7.00 a.m.	Catechization on the Bible by a missionary
7.00–8.00 a.m.	Reading practice with the New Testament
9.00–10.00 a.m.	'Aphorism hour', important passages from the Bible are memorized
10.00–11.00 a.m.	'Catechization hour', conducted by the Tamil teacher, based on theology, Large Catechism
11.00 a.m.–12.00 p.m.	Language instruction: Portuguese

(Contd...)

[150] Ibid.

[151] Cf. HB 22. Cont., 901–04.

Table 5.3 (contd.)

2.00–4.00 p.m.	Arithmetic and writing on palm leaves
4.00–5.00 p.m.	Reading and learning stories from the Old Testament
5.00–6.00 p.m.	Teachers explain 'some unobjectionable heathen books'; reading aloud from the 'Malabarian conversations'
6.00–7.00 p.m.	A Tamil teacher repeats the morning catechization; exception: on Mondays the pupils write a meditation or a prayer about the Sunday sermon
Second class (beginners)	
6.00–7.00 a.m.	Catechization on the Bible by a missionary
7.00–8.00 a.m.	Learning Tamil alphabets; first reading exercises
9.00–10.00 a.m.	'Aphorism hour', short passages from the Bible are memorized
10.00–11.00 a.m.	Catechization on the five main parts of the Small Catechism
11.00 a.m.–12.00 p.m.	Knitting (socks)
2.00–4.00 p.m.	Arithmetic and writing exercises in sand
4.00–5.00 p.m.	Reading hour
5.00–6.00 p.m.	Memorizing the Small Catechism
6.00–7.00 p.m.	A Tamil teacher repeats the morning catechization; exception: on Mondays the pupils write a meditation or a prayer about the Sunday sermon

The daily routine of the children in the 'Portuguese' and Danish schools was similar. Here, too, the children had to get up at 6.00 a.m. and—with the exception of a longish midday break—they were kept busy till about 8.00 p.m. This closely structured and intensive daily routine was practiced throughout in the educational work of the Danish-English-Halle Mission. In order that everyone could keep to the timings, the missionaries had a school bell made, which rang every hour.[152] The routine, which resembles the working day of an adult rather than the school day of a child, was surpassed in the Francke Foundations during this same period. Thomas Müller-Bahlke points out that children often ran away to escape the strict rules. However, excellent teaching compensated for the strict discipline and the meagre equipment—especially for the orphans—and, on the whole, it ensured the high social reputation of the Halle orphan house.[153]

Although the experiences in the Halle orphan house played an important role in determining the daily routine of the children in the mission schools in Southeast India, local advisors were consulted from the beginning. Bartholomäus Ziegenbalg and Johann Ernst Gründler asked their Tamil correspondents about the normal routine in local schools. The answer to their question, contained in the 34th letter of the *Malabarische Korrespondenz*, when viewed more closely, hardly contradicted the ideas and experiences they had brought from Europe. Brahmin school children had to get up before sunrise to bathe and pray. After three hours of learning they had breakfast and then studied again for three to four hours. They had lunch at 1 p.m., but were not supposed to rest after that. It was considered more important for the children to have one or two hours of physical activity every day. Dinner was served after 8 p.m.[154] Representatives of the Tamil Brahmin upper class also explained in the correspondence with Ziegenbalg and Gründler what kind of ceremonies were carried out in Tamil families when a child was admitted to school.[155] The missionaries learned that a boy's entry into school was an important event in which the entire family participated with various ceremonies. A unique aspect of this was that the schoolmaster concerned had to come with his entire class to the house of the new pupil, lead him to the school

[152] HB 58. Cont., 1529.

[153] Müller-Bahlke, 'Kinderleben in den Glauchaer Anstalten'. (here on p. 23 there is also the following timetable.) See also: Deppermann, *Der Hallesche Pietismus und der preußische Staat unter Friedrich III.*, 88–96.

[154] HB 7. Cont., 470–72.

[155] HB 7. Cont., 409–13, (Letter 11 of the *Malabarische Korrespondenz*).

TABLE 5.4 The daily routine in the Halle orphan house in 1719

4.45 a.m.	Wake-up call
5.00–6.00 a.m.	Morning prayers with the preceptors
6.00–6.45 a.m.	Breakfast, distributed by the preceptors
6.45–7.00 a.m.	Preparing for lessons, assembly
7.00–11.00 a.m.	Classes
11.00 a.m.–12.00 p.m.	Bath time, or silent independent work
12.00–1.00 p.m.	Lunch in the dining hall
1.00–about 1.15 p.m.	Free time in the school courtyard under the supervision of the preceptors. Silence to be observed
1.15–1.45 p.m.	Gymnastic exercises in the woodshed, or, in good weather, in the garden of the assistant director; in bad weather, distribution of paper and quills
1.45–2.00 p.m.	Preparation for lessons, assembly
2.00–6.00 p.m.	Classes
6.00–7.00 p.m.	Tea, consisting of half the breakfast portion; subsequently free choice of occupation under the supervision of the preceptors
7.00–8.00 p.m.	Dinner in the dining hall
8.00–8.30 p.m.	To be spent in the common room; opportunity for individual discussions with the preceptor or with one another
8.30–9.00 p.m.	Prayer time
9.00–10.00 p.m.	Short walk in the courtyard, then preparation for bedtime. Silence to be maintained except for brief individual exchanges with the preceptor; lights out.

and then bring him back home. The children and teachers were fed on this occasion.

The strict provisions of the children's daily routine in the mission schools could only be carried out through constant control and discipline. Disciplinary breaches, such as lack of punctuality, lack of cleanliness, or lack of the will to learn, were punished. The school regulations laid down the forms of punishment that could be applied: the teachers had to avoid indecent language and were told not to resort immediately to scolding and beatings in the case of minor offenses. The younger children, especially, should be made to learn through friendly encouragement, because they would easily lose the pleasure of learning if they were scolded and beaten. It was much more important to 'remind, exhort, warn'. Corporal punishment was to be avoided as far as possible. It was absolutely forbidden to hit a child on the chest and head. Important matters were to be brought to the notice of the inspectors; as much as possible was to be clarified in the class.[156] A method of punishing a child for not passing an examination was to not give it the usual gifts after examinations and on Christian festivals, since the distribution of gifts was linked to the child's academic performance.[157] Praise was seldom used as a pedagogical principle in the mission schools, but a child could receive recognition and encouragement through merit-based support.[158] He could be given a special task or selected for further education. A child could also enjoy recognition through special assistance on behalf of a European sponsor. In their reports the missionaries named children who were talented and deserved support, and individual sponsors often dedicated their donations directly for the support of a particular child. The progress of the children was periodically evaluated in reports and letters from the missionaries to friends and promoters of the Mission.[159]

The school children were examined in the different subjects

[156] HB 58. Cont., 1532, 1542. The *Malabarische Korrespondenz* describes the duties and the powers of the teachers: a schoolmaster should be able to explain intelligibly, should regard and treat all children as his own. He should not only mediate knowledge, but also practical wisdom. HB 7. Cont., 421f.

[157] NHB 25. St., Vorrede, 9 (1780).

[158] At the beginning of the nineteenth century, for example, weekly merit-based financial assistance was given in some village schools. This method was introduced, because the number of children in mission schools had, by now, exceeded the financial possibilities of the mission, and not all children could be given food and clothing. RA Miskolark 9i, report on the situation of the Royal Danish Mission in Tranquebar in the year 1803 by Ch. S. John, J.P. Rottler, A.F. Cämmerer.

[159] Criteria for the evaluation of the children by the missionaries included the discipline, piety and obedience as well as the intellectual abilities and the academic progress of the child. NHB 31. St., 749f.

at regular intervals. Under Ziegenbalg, each pupil was examined individually at the beginning of each month,[160] but later the number of examinations was reduced. At the beginning of the 1740s four examinations were conducted annually in the Tamil schools: the ceremonial annual examinations, which were attended by all the missionaries, South Indian pastors and catechists, and, sometimes, also by the Danish priests, took place in January and July. Each child was given some money for 'betel-areck' as a reward. Whereas these examinations were conducted jointly in a large room, individual examinations, conducted by the school inspectors, took place every April and October. On the basis of these examinations the inspectors decided which child would be promoted in the individual subjects.[161] For the subject 'reading' the children were divided into different classes according to the level of their skills. Thus, in 1744, the Tamil boys' school in Tranquebar had six reading classes, in which the boys were taught separately from 7–8 a.m.: the first class consisted of the 'seminarians' who had been selected for mission work, and of pupils who could read well; the second class comprised pupils who still required practice in reading; the third class consisted of those who could put word together; in the fifth were those who could spell the words, and in the sixth were those who were learning the alphabet. The best pupils sometimes had to copy texts or teach in the lower classes. The division of the children into these groups was reviewed every month, and the teachers then informed their superiors about which child should be promoted to which class.[162]

When viewing the different aspects of contact between the mission and the local population there was no other sphere, which presented so many daily problems and was so closely bound up with misunderstandings and prejudices as the entire complex of food and hygiene. While caste differences had to be taken into account in the preparation of food and the joint meals of the school children and teachers so that the traditional norms of ritual purity were adhered to, the regular practice of bathing and changing clothes (by the children) also required a sensitive approach from the missionaries. In order not

[160] Ziegenbalg, *A Letter to the Reverend Mr Geo. Lewis*, 19.

[161] HB 58. Cont., 1539f.

[162] Ibid. This system was used for the boys; for the girls there was only one reading class.

to go against existing conventions, and thereby possibly endanger the acceptance of the schools, but also in the interest of the children's health, the local norms were strictly observed from the beginning. The children who had their meals in the school received—as far as possible—food that was adapted to the local requirements.

The thirty-fourth letter of the *Malabarische Korrespondenz* contains a detailed description of local norms of hygiene as well as guidelines for healthy nutrition for children under the climatic conditions of South India.[163] For breakfast the children were given food cooked the previous day; from the mid-day meal onwards, the letter states, they got freshly prepared and well-spiced food. The additional component of buttermilk was important, as was a certain amount of fat content in the food. Once in four days the children were given a special digestive drink, and its preparation is described in detail. The children were given a laxative once a month.[164] The monthly expenses for purging in 1739 were quoted as being one *Fanam* per child, regardless of age.[165] The measures for personal hygiene, as Ziegenbalg and Gründler learnt from their correspondents, consisted in a weekly bath, after which the children had to rub oil on their body and wash it off with water again. Every day, before sunrise, they had to clean their teeth with a piece of special wood.[166] These rules of hygiene and nutrition were integrated into the mission routine in Tranquebar. The boys washed themselves at the river every morning under the supervision of a teacher, while the girls washed themselves in the courtyard.[167] The teachers took the children regularly to a pond, where they were supposed to 'bathe in the manner of the country'.[168] At the pond, the teachers were responsible for the children's safety; they were particularly meant to keep an eye on the younger children in the water, but they also decided whether one or the other child should refrain from washing his hair on a particular day for reasons of health. After the bath, oil was distributed, which the children

[163] HB 7. Cont., 470–72.
[164] Ibid.
[165] HB 52. Cont., 682.
[166] HB 7. Cont., 470–72.
[167] HB 58. Cont., 1534, 1538.
[168] HB 4. Cont., 159.

applied on their bodies.[169] They were given a haircut four times a year.[170]

All the children living in the mission house got new clothes thrice a year (at Christmas, in May and September), and the clothes were sent for a wash once a week.[171] Existing cultural specificities and customs were also taken into account in this regard: the clothes for the 'Portuguese' children differed from those of the Tamil children.[172] The children slept on mats that were replaced twice a year, and covered themselves with their clothes while sleeping.[173] In the mission schools outside the larger towns these rules were modified according to the local possibilities and requirements.

At all times, the schools of the DEHM were more than just places of learning, because wherever there were no church buildings the local Christians gathered regularly in the schools.[174] In times of war and famine the function of the schools in providing food and care to the children became even more important, since many children were in particularly bad health in such times and required special care. An infirmary was generally attached to a school and an attempt was always made to separate the sick children from the others. When the pupils of the Tamil boys' school in Tranquebar were suffering from an infectious disease, they were shifted to Porayar, where their classes continued.[175] Whenever necessary, sick children were put on a special diet and were looked after by the mission doctor along with a male and a female Indian helper. For the treatment of diseases that the mission doctor was not too familiar with, a local doctor was brought in.[176]

169 HB 58. Cont., 1531f.

170 HB 58. Cont., 1543.

171 AB 299, Ziegenbalg, P. Jordan and J.E. Gründler to A.H. Francke, Tranquebar, 10 September 1712.

172 The sources do not provide an exact description of the difference in the clothes, but indicate the difference in price for the children's clothing. HB 52. Cont., 681, letter from the missionaries in Tranquebar to the editor, 19 December 1739. Cf. also AFSt/M 2 B 5 : 1–8, coloured drawings by an unknown artist, commissioned by the missionary Nicolaus Dal, 1729, especially the school scenes. See also Liebau, *Geliebtes Europa//Ostindische Welt*, 139.

173 HB 58. Cont., 1543.

174 HB 78. Cont., 970. For example, in Tiruppappuliyur near Cuddalore (1752).

175 HB 58. Cont., 1528f.

176 HB 58. Cont., 1543.

As far as teaching material and text books were concerned, it was initially necessary to use the simplest available possibilities. The children carried out their first writing practice, according to the local tradition, in sand. Only the older children were taught to write on palm leaves.[177] Even in later years expensive paper was used very sparingly in the mission schools.[178] To learn the fundamentals of reading, writing and arithmetic the mission initially also used books by Tamil authors as school books, however, as Ziegenbalg emphasized, not without studying them carefully first and, if necessary, doing away with their 'mistakes'.[179] The mission authorities and friends of the mission in Europe also sent teaching material regularly. The SPCK sent a sufficient number of copies of the New Testament in Portuguese, and this took care of the teaching in the 'Portuguese' school.[180]

Once the technical possibilities were available from 1712 onwards[181] teaching material for different subjects was also printed in the mission printing presses. In 1716 the mission printing press in Tranquebar printed a Reader, or Spell Book in English.[182] In 1717

[177] The technique of writing on palm leaves is described very vividly in the *Malabarische Korrespondenz*: 'They are seated while writing and place the left hand, with which they hold the leaf, on the raised left knee; the hand rests on the knee and holds the leaf firmly: the right hand holds the stylus that should be long and heavy at the top. The leaves on which they write should have a double layer so that the stylus does not go through the surface.' (translated from German), HB 7. Cont., 409–13, The Eleventh Letter of the Malabarian Correspondence, footnote (h).

[178] Cf., for example, AFSt/M 1 B 32 : 23, writing specimens of Malabarian school children, enclosures to a letter from J.B. Kohlhoff to G.A. Francke, Tranquebar, 31 January 1744; AFSt/M 1 B 33 : 10, writing specimens of Malabarian school children, enclosures to a letter from J.B. Kohlhoff to G.A. Francke, Tranquebar, 22 December 1744.

[179] Germann, Wilhelm, 1880, 'Ziegenbalgs Bibliotheca Malabarica', *MNOIM* 32 (1/2): 1–20 and 62–94, here 8.

[180] HB 58. Cont., 1526.

[181] On the development of printing in the context of the DEHM see: Liebau, 'Translocal networks of the Tranquebar Mission Press in eighteenth century South Asia'; Liebau, Heike, 2008, 'Zur Beförderung des Missionswerks und zum Nutzen der East India Company. Die Druckerei in Vepery/Madras in der zweiten Hälfte des 18. Jahrhunderts', in: Michael Mann (ed.), *Aufgeklärter Geist und evangelische Missionen in Indien*, Draupadi Verlag, Heidelberg: 85–102; Muthiah, 'Giving India the Printed Word'.

[182] Cf. HB 13. Cont., 40; 33. Cont., 930, the title of this textbook is *A Guide to the English Tongue* by Thomas Dyche.

an ABC book in Portuguese was printed for the schools in English territories.[183] From 1725 till 1731 the mission printing press printed a grammar of Portuguese in four volumes written by Nicolaus Dal.[184] In 1733 the ABC-Book and School Book for Children was produced in the mission printing press in Tranquebar.[185] Besides this, the schools used simple religious texts or collections of Christian aphorisms, but they were not available in sufficient numbers.[186] From 1805 to 1809 the mission printing press in Vepery printed 600 copies of the New Testament (Tamil), 600 hymn-books (Tamil), several hundred copies of the Small and Large Catechism and 800 copies of a Tamil-English dictionary. The missionaries stated that Vepery had enough religious books for the use in schools.[187] Among the textbooks that were produced in Palayankottai at the beginning of the nineteenth century were a geography textbook in Tamil for the seminary (Part I—Introduction and Asia), an 'outline' of world history, a chronology of world history, a treatise on different natural phenomena, a treatise on the main religions and a Tamil grammar.[188]

The mission library, which was constantly expanded with important new publications in different fields of knowledge, was extremely important for shaping school lessons. Ziegenbalg and Plütschau had laid the foundation for the library, and this library was later expanded and systematized.[189] The missionaries collected books, journals, manuscripts and palm-leaf manuscripts of different religious origins and in different languages.[190] The older school

[183] HB 13. Cont., 3; 33. Cont., 930. Niekamp, *Kurzgefaßte Mißions-Geschichte*, 209.

[184] Dal, Nicolaus, 1728–31, *Grammatica portugueza para o uso da Escola Portugueza de Trangambar*, Parts 1–4, Mission Printing Press, Tranquebar. Cf. HB 21. Cont., 623; 23. Cont., 976; 25. Cont., 104; 32. Cont., 844; 33. Cont., 934f. Dal's name as author is mentioned on 8 October 1726 in connection with the completion of the second volume. Cf. HB 23. Cont., 976.

[185] HB 58. Cont., 1525.

[186] Kiernander also complained about the lack of textbooks. HB 92. Cont., 169f.

[187] NHB 66. St., 510, Madras 1812.

[188] NHB 72. St., 1277, report from G.E. Rhenius and L.B.E. Schmid, Palayamcottah 1823.

[189] Cf. Jeyaraj, *Inkulturation in Tranquebar*, 81–83.

[190] For the development of the library holdings see the catalogue of the mission library in: HB 11. Cont., 856; 13. Cont., 45. A new edition of the catalogue was prepared in 1721: HB 20. Cont., 510; 33. Cont., 932. Cf. further HB 58. Cont., 1525.

children were assigned the task, in turns, of regularly cleaning and removing dust and worms from the books.[191]

Developing arguments, learning by rote and meditating on biblical aphorisms[192] were the basic learning methods in the mission schools. Besides this, local forms of teaching that they encountered both in Muslim as well as in Hindu schools impressed missionaries like B. Ziegenbalg. These not only served to consolidate a particular component of learning, but also helped in the development of linguistic and rhetorical abilities. Singing helped to strengthen the children's vocal chords and improve intonation.[193] In the mission schools the frequent repetition and memorizing of doctrines and passages from the Bible served to anchor the knowledge that the children would always have to apply as Christians.[194] Classes in which these components were intellectually processed and assimilated in different contexts accompanied the mechanical memorizing of knowledge. This also included the meditation on the Sunday sermon at the beginning of each week, when the children wrote down their thoughts on what they had heard.[195] While learning in nature, i.e. during walks or while working in the mission—or school-garden, independent observation and the assimilation of experiences were promoted.

When the school children had to reproduce what they had learned, the teachers placed special emphasis on the demonstration of rhetorical skills. The children were meant to learn how to express their thoughts in a logical manner, and how to discuss a point independently. Staged disputes, or the attempt to initiate a conversation in any kind of situation served to develop rhetorical abilities. The extent to which the school and the mission constituted a single unit was amply demonstrated by the publicly-held classes that were arranged in such a way that the people of the place could listen to them and, indeed, were called upon to take active part in the discussions on the theme being dealt with. Teachers went with their class into a town/

[191] HB 58. Cont., 1536.

[192] Cf. for example, NHB 27. St., 259 (1781).

[193] Germann, 'Ziegenbalgs Bibliotheca Malabarica', 20.

[194] NHB 26. St., 173, excerpt from a letter from Johann Wilhelm Gerlach, 3 December 1781.

[195] HB 22. Cont., 901–04, Curriculum of the schools in Tranquebar. 1726.

village, sang Christian songs on the streets, carried out a public debate about questions of religion, or encouraged the children to use the opportunity for conversations with the local people.[196]

Towards the end of the eighteenth century the co-operation with the English in the field of pedagogy increased. The method of teaching developed by the cleric Andrew Bell (1753–1832)[197] and the Quaker Joseph Lancaster (1778–1838),[198] the so-called monitor-system, first practiced by Andrew Bell in Madras,[199] represented a comprehensive educational concept, which took up and developed many approaches used in the schools of the Danish-English-Halle Mission. Bell was a superintendent of the orphan school for boys, which was established in 1789 in Madras in conformance with a resolution of the Court of Directors of 1785. This school was intended to improve the education and upbringing of European and Indo-European orphans. Earlier, in 1784, the SPCK had already opened a school in Madras for Anglo-Indian children, which later became the Vepery Grammar School.[200] In 1786 Amalia Campbell, the wife of the governor, Archibald Campbell (1739–91), expressed the intention of setting up a girls' school for European orphans in Madras. She requested Christian Friedrich Schwartz for help in working out the concept of the school.[201] Shortly after the orphan

[196] HB 78. Cont., 969; 80. Cont., 1188.

[197] On his life see: *The Directory of National Biography. Founded in 1882 by George Smith. Edited by Sir Leslie Stephen and Sir Sidney Lee. From the Earliest Times to 1900*, published since 1717, Oxford University Press, London, Vol. II, 149–52.

[198] In his book 'Improvements in Education' published in 1803 Lancaster described his experiences with the monitor system, and referred to the book by A. Bell 'An Experiment in Education [...]' that had appeared in 1797. Cf. *The Directory of National Biography*, Vol. XI, 480–82; Lancaster, Joseph, 1803, *Improvements in education, as it respects the industrious classes of the community: [...]*, Darton and Harvey, London; Bell, Andrew, 1797, *An Experiment of Education, made at the Male Asylum of Madras. Suggesting a system by which a school or family may teach itself under the superintendence of the master or parent*, Cadell and Davies, London, Edinburgh, (2nd edition 1805; 3rd edition 1807).

[199] On the contacts between representatives of the Danish-English-Halle Mission and Andrew Bell see: Liebau, Heike, 2005, 'Von Halle nach Madras: Pietistische Waisenhauspädagogik und englische Appropriationen in Indien', in Jürgen Schriewer and Marcelo Caruso (eds.), *Nationalerziehung und Universalmethode. Frühe Formen schulorganisatorischer Globalisierung*, COMPARATIV, 15(2005), 1, 31–57.

[200] *History of Higher Education in South India*, Vol. I.

[201] NHB 34. St., 1165.

school for girls was set up, an orphan school for male children of military personnel was established.[202] Andrew Bell, who had come to India in 1787, accepted the post of superintendent of this orphan school in 1789, and developed his concept of pedagogical reform in the period till 1796 as director of the male orphan asylum. At around the same time the Quaker Joseph Lancaster in England worked according to the same, but slightly modified method.[203]

The Bell-Lancaster system was a tutor-system. Sponsorships were important; a less successful child was placed next to one who was good at studies and whose conduct was impeccable. Some boys were appointed tutors; they taught the younger children and received special benefits for their work. Exceptional pupils were placed for some time in a higher class and, depending on the results, they either went back to their earlier class or remained in the higher one. Each class had an assistant teacher who helped the teacher. A schoolmaster or a superintendent was responsible for the financial affairs of the entire school.[204]

In his pedagogical work in South India Bell profited from the long-standing experiences of the Halle missionaries with whom he maintained close contact, especially with Christian Wilhelm Gericke, Christian Pohle and Christoph Samuel John. John also introduced the methods that Bell had developed in India and that had gained worldwide recognition by the beginning of the nineteenth century in the mission schools. In his essay 'On Indian Civilization', published in London in 1813, John referred to the importance of this teaching method for the education of the younger generation in India. On a basis of a study of the works of Bell and Lancaster John pleaded for the use of this method in the free schools in India and demanded that a Liberal Native School Society be set up for India to put this into practice.[205] John got his information through books, newspapers and, probably, through the annual reports of the charity schools

[202] Bell, *An Experiment in Education*.

[203] Cf. NHB 67. St., Preface, VIII.

[204] Bell, *An Experiment in Education*. Even in the English schools set up by Lancaster the children's first attempts at writing were done in sand (like in India), which was given to them on flat tablets. The monitor-system also helped to train teachers. Cf.: *The Directory of National Biography*, Vol. XI, 480–82.

[205] John, *On Indian Civilization*, 2.

in England. He was also inspired to write his essay by Bell's book, published in 1797, in which the history of the orphan house in Madras was portrayed as an 'experiment of education'. Bell's book generated a great deal of interest and, time and again, it has been used for comparative pedagogical studies.[206]

The missionaries in Tranquebar also studied the experiences gathered by other missions in the use of this method. The Mission Reports also published reports of the London Missionary Society and the Church Missionary Society.[207] The Baptists William Carey, Joshua Marshman and William Ward gave a detailed description of their experiences with the Bell-Lancaster method in Serampore. They considered this method of teaching to be very suitable for Indian conditions. In Serampore, following the Bell-Lancaster method, the children first learned printed alphabets with the help of large tables and simple printed words, and these were repeated by spelling them out loudly and writing them down. Modifications of this method for Indian conditions were undertaken in the modeling of charts and books, in the manner in which the children were divided into classes and in the appointment of teachers and supervisors. Each class was meant to consist of about 10–12 pupils—all at roughly the same level of capability. The 'most mature' child was made the monitor, while the teacher was supposed to carry out mainly an administrative and regulatory function. He would determine the contents of teaching and choose the monitors. Arithmetic would be taught so that the children could make their way in life; the solar system could be explained, however only in simple terms. This method 'corresponded to the manner in which dogmas and rules are expressed in the Hindu Shastras and is, therefore, also in keeping with the ideas of even their scholars.'[208] Similarly, geography and history were also to be taught in a simple manner with special attention being devoted to Europe.

[206] Bell, *An Experiment of Education*. Cf.: *The Madras School, or Elements of tuition: comprising the analysis of an experiment in education made at […] Madras […] to which are added, extracts of sermons preached at Lambeth, a sketch of national institutions for training up the children of the poor, and a specimen of the mode of religious instruction at the Royal Military Asylum Chelsey.*—J. Murray, London, 1808.

[207] NHB 67. St., 597–620, report, written 1816 in Serampor, published 1818 in London and translated into German.

[208] Ibid., 606.

From about 1810 onwards the Bell-Lancaster method—also called the Madras method because of its origin in India—spread in England and the British colonies, but also in other European countries.[209] Thus, in 1829 there were 10,600 so-called Lancaster schools in Europe with 4.700,000 pupils; in Asia there were 1,600 schools with 5,00,000 pupils; in Africa there were 1,300 schools with 3,80,000 pupils, and in Australia there were 100 schools with 25,000 pupils.[210] In India, new charity schools were established, which were 'greatly improved for the needs of heathen children'[211] through the introduction of the Bell-Lancaster method. The Lancaster charts, especially, proved to be particularly suitable for language teaching. Developed by Lancaster for teaching English, they were used in India for different subjects. The rules of grammar were printed on large posters[212] and then used in class employing the monitor-teacher-system.[213] In the 1820s all the schools under Gottlieb Ewald Rhenius and Ludwig Bernhard Ehrengott Schmid in Palayankottai used this method.[214] Bernhard Schmid used the Bell-Lancaster method in different Tamil schools established by Rhenius in Madras and its vicinity. With very few exceptions, all the pupils were Hindus; some of the teachers were Christians, others were Hindus who accepted the school regulations.[215]

[209] For the significance of the method and the reasons for its spread see: Schriewer, Jürgen and Marcelo Caruso, 2005, 'Globale Diffusionsdynamik und kontextspezifische Aneignung: Konzepte historischer Internationalisierungsforschung', in Schriewer, *Nationalerziehung und Universalmethode*, 7–30; With special reference to the Indian context see: Tschurenev, Jana, 2011, "Pathsalas into Schools': Das monitorial system of education in Bengalen (ca. 1815–35)', in: *Jahrbuch Historische Bildungsforschung* 16, 2011, 11–38; Tschurenev, Jana, 2008, 'Diffusing Useful Knowledge: The Monitorial System of Education in Madras, London and Bengal, 1789–1840.' *Paedagogica Historica* XLIV, 3, 249–64.

[210] von Rönne, Ludwig, 1990, *Das Unterrichts-Wesen des Preußischen Staates, Vol. 1: Das Volksschul-Wesen des Preußischen Staates mit Einschluß des Privat-Unterrichts*, (Berlin 1855) Reprint: Böhlau, Köln, Wien, 26. See also NHB 67. St., Preface, VIII.

[211] NHB 67. St., Preface, VIII.

[212] NHB 67. St., 604.

[213] NHB 67. St., 607.

[214] In 1823 there were 12 schools with a total of 314 children. NHB 72. St., 1262f.

[215] NHB 83. St., 966, report from Ludwig Bernhard Ehrengott Schmid and his brother Deocar Schmid (1791–1828).

CHANGES IN THE SCHOOL CURRICULA

More than the methods, the curricula of the mission schools were constantly changing. The subjects to be taught and the concrete contents in these had to be re-examined time and again in view of the changing historical conditions and the political requirements arising from them, as well as in view of the development of knowledge in the eighteenth century. In addition to this, there were the varying pedagogical viewpoints and scientific ideas of the individual missionaries, who allowed their personal inclinations and interests flow into the educational work. The contents of education transported through the schools of the Tranquebar Mission represented a synthesis of the pedagogical ideals of the Halle missionaries that had been shaped by Pietism and Enlightenment, the development of the sciences in Europe and the practical requirements in India.

The central component of the curricula was constituted by those subjects, which—in the broadest sense—served to propagate the gospel. Around these were grouped the more praxis-oriented, linguistic, musical and natural science subjects, or physical education. Those pupils who were selected for a career in the mission also received extended theological training.

Literacy constituted the basis for all other classes. Since the medium of teaching was mainly the mother tongue, i.e. in most cases Tamil, the teachers first taught the children to read and write in Tamil. For the didactic of teaching the missionaries oriented themselves to the methods used in local schools, which they knew through their own observations, or which were explained to them by local informants.

> For the beginners, the teachers write out large letters of the alphabet, whose forms the pupils follow with their stylus till they get used to writing the letters of the alphabet on their own [...]. When a child has learned to write all the features of the letters of the alphabet given to him by the teacher, the latter writes out a line of words for him, and the boy writes the same words with his own letters on the following line. They practice this for a long time till they can write 3, 4, or 5 lines on a page, because then the letters get progressively smaller.[216]

216 HB 7. Cont., 409–13, 'Der Malabarischen Correspondenz Elfter Brief', footnote (h), (writing on palm leaves), (translated from German).

Whereas the curriculum of 1709 only talks of a study of translated Christian texts, in 1726 the teachers included some 'unobjectionable heathen books' in the curriculum. The children of the first class of the Tamil boys' school were not only supposed to know Christian literature, but they were also supposed to be familiar with the literary, moral and philosophical thoughts of Tamil literature.[217]

Religious instruction in its different forms was the central component of the curriculum. It consisted of prayer, catechizing, reading aloud, Bible reading and meditation.[218] A fundamental aspect of religious instruction was the catechism class, which was also held outside the school for potential converts, and served to prepare the neophytes for their entry into the Christian community. During the eighteenth century there was hardly any control by public school officials, which left the mission free to decide on the amount of religious instruction, what form it should take and where it should be placed in the curriculum. With increasing competition from public schools, or schools run by other mission societies, the question of the ration of religious instruction to secular subjects became important for the German missionaries. At the beginning of the nineteenth century some missionaries openly advocated a reduction in the proportion of religious instruction in the curriculum in order to make Christian missionary schools more competitive and more attractive for Hindus. The schools would be better attended, it was felt, 'if we were to exclude religious instruction',[219] a measure that would, however, contradict the original concerns of the missionary task. This dilemma between the requirements of the mission mandate, on the one hand, and the desire for a broad public acceptance of the mission schools, on the other, often forced the missionaries to make concessions and compromises. In 1816, the Baptist missionaries Marsham, Carey and Ward also stated that knowledge of the Bible should be mediated with careful thought, since, in any case, one could not expect to solve all the problems in the country through a study of the Bible.[220]

[217] HB 22. Cont., 901–04.

[218] Cf., among others, HB 4. Cont., 159.

[219] NHB 72. St., 1265, report from G.E. Rhenius and L.B.E. Schmid, Palayamcottah 1823.

[220] NHB 67. St., 597–620, here 608.

In the pedagogical understanding of leading Pietists training the children for work and preparing them for a profession were part of the duties of the school. The missionaries also followed this principle in the mission region, and it corresponded to the actual requirements of missionary educational work. The craft lessons and vocational training offered in the mission schools were oriented both to the mission infrastructure as well as to the requirements of possible employers of mission school graduates. The teaching of skills linked with a Christian upbringing and a responsible attitude towards work were important preconditions for a self-determined life after school. Girls and boys were trained separately in the crafts. The girls in the 'Tamil' school in Tranquebar learnt how to spin, to knit socks, to weave mats and to make thread from the fibres of coconut shells. They did kitchen work, watered the plants and fetched water. Some of the boys were trained in the same crafts. Others learned to weave baskets, to dye cloth, or were trained to become accountants, bookbinders or compositors.[221] The girls and boys who would later take up a trade were chosen at an early stage, and were then given additional lessons in the relevant vocational subjects.[222] Sometimes these children were sent to a smaller school where they were able to devote the forenoon to study, but could otherwise also be initiated into a trade by their family members.[223] The girls remained in the school till they were married off, while the boys were sent out as soon as they were admitted to Holy Communion, or were in a position to earn their own living.[224]

The upbringing towards a self-determined life also included training in medicine and hygiene. In 1712 the mission employed a Tamil doctor, who not only worked as a doctor, but who was also expected to

> 2) explain the Malabarian medical authors to the oldest school boys for one hour a day; 3) teach the school children botany and impart

[221] HB 4. Cont., 155ff.; preface to 42. Cont., § VIII. In the early years of missionary work the male pupils and catechumen also learnt to knit socks. This is not mentioned later. HB 25. Cont., 30; 33. Cont., 895; 42. Cont., Preface, § VIII; NHB 25. St., 8; 30. St., 671f.; 32. St., 889.

[222] NHB 32. St., 889.

[223] HB 58. Cont., 1580f.

[224] NHB 25. St., 8.

> a knowledge of herbs when they were taken out to the village every Monday, to bring these herbs back each time and store them in a designated room so that they could be used, whenever necessary, as medicine; 4) gradually collect all the material used in Malabarian medicine from different places, store them in the same room and familiarize selected boys with these medicines; [...][225]

The older boys were thus given instruction in medical questions once a day, and once every week the Tamil doctor went with them to collect herbs.[226] Later, too, the reports mention the appointment of local doctors with the mission. A report of 1775 states that a Tamil doctor was appointed for the schools.[227] In 1780 there is again a remark about the appointment of a Tamil 'graduate' doctor in the mission.[228]

Religious training, on the one hand, and praxis-oriented education, on the other, was linked to the natural sciences. Following the model of science instruction in the Francke Foundations visual aids for lessons were either made or brought from Europe. Sometimes, missionaries depended on their own initiative. When Johann Anton Sartorius and Johann Ernst Geister went from Madras to Cuddalore to work for the SPCK there, they made a copy of the globe for geography lessons in Cuddalore, since the globe was to remain in Madras. Sartorius entered the geographical terms in the Tamil script and added 'some geographical and astronomical aphorisms'.[229] In a memo of 1784 Christoph Samuel John and Johann Peter Rottler asked, among other things, for a globe, a microscope and a thermometer as well as for diverse utensils and a mirror for use in the schools and for research.[230]

In his schools Christian Friedrich Schwartz combined the study of Christian and Biblical texts with the principles of Enlightenment. He also taught English literature and European philosophy.[231]

225 HB 6. Cont., 313, report, 27 June 1712, (translated from German).

226 AB 229, letter from Ziegenbalg, Gründler and Jordan to A.H. Francke, Tranquebar, 10 September 1712.

227 NHB 15. St., 293.

228 NHB, Preface to the 25. St., 9.

229 HB 46. Cont., 1321.

230 RA Miskolark 9g, *Pro Memoria* for new missionaries from Ch. S. John, Tranquebar, 27 October 1784.

231 Frykenberg, 'The Legacy of Christian Friedrich Schwartz', 131.

Under his pedagogical influence Serfoji, the later Raja of Thanjavur, became 'an enlightened and highly educated young man', who set up a 'room of wonders' in the style of European natural history cabinets, and used globes, telescopes and laboratories.[232] Influential families sent their children to be educated in the provincial schools set up by Schwartz. 'The ruler of the country sent his adopted son.—The minister, who looks after the affairs of the country, did the same.'[233] Christoph Samuel John and Johann Peter Rottler, especially, displayed a marked interest in the natural sciences.[234] In particular, it was John who developed far-sighted ideas for the mission educational system. John considered it important to bring the children closer to their natural surroundings and to instill in them a love for nature. Books on the natural sciences published in Europe were important foundations for his teaching, such as Heinrich Sander's book on 'the wisdom and greatness and beauties of created things in Sea and Land, his economical natural history'.[235] Mission gardens were laid out in the schoolyards, and the children tended to the fruit trees and culinary herbs in these gardens.[236] In a memo addressed to the Mission Board in Copenhagen in 1796 John asserted the need for such teaching methods. As a representative of a generation whose concept of education had been determined by Enlightenment and rationalism, he considered the propagation of the (natural) sciences to be an integral concern of the mission. 'I prefer the gradual education of the youth and the nation and consider the promotion of the sciences to be a part of religion and mission, which it is my duty to promote.'[237]

In the teaching of mathematics the mission schools oriented themselves to the specificities of Tamil calculation methods, which

[232] Ibid., 134; cf. also Frykenberg, 'The Halle Legacy in Modern India'; Peterson, 'Science in the Tranquebar Mission Curriculum'.

[233] NHB 33. St., 1027.

[234] For the role of research in the natural sciences in the framework of the concept of mission of individual missionaries cf. Hommel,'Physico-Theology as Mission Strategy. Missionary Christoph Samuel John's Understanding of Nature', Hommel, 'Naturwissenschaftliche Forschungen'.

[235] John, *On Indian Civilization*, 38. Sander, Heinrich, 1779–1780, *Über Natur und Religion für die Liebhaber und Anbeter Gottes*, Weygandsche Buchhandlung, Leipzig.

[236] NHB 32. St., 889, John's letter to G.A. Freylinghausen, 10 September 1785.

[237] RA Miskolark 9h, *Pro Memoria* from Ch. S. John, Tranquebar, 3 March 1796, (translated from German).

differ from the European way in many aspects. For centuries local Tamil schools had attached great importance to the teaching of mathematics. Gründler and Ziegenbalg had learned from a Tamil correspondent that 'arithmetic is one of the most necessary arts amongst us and the children learn it in school before they even begin to write.'[238] In the tenth letter of the *Malabarische Korrespondenz* the special characteristics of Tamil arithmetic were explained in detail to the missionaries. The writer not only mentioned what was taught, but also how the children were taught mathematics. In this case, the missionaries had to be particularly willing to learn, since the structure of mathematical operations differed greatly from what was used in Europe. This is why they also had explicit questions in their correspondence about the methods for teaching mathematics. First, the numbers, especially those required for calculating grain, were learned in a singsong manner and written in sand. This was repeated till the children knew it by heart. This was followed by the multiplication tables and by addition and division. Those boys who were supposed to take up a job in this field were then taught the practical application of mathematical rules for dealing with finances, weights and measures. If they wanted to work as bookkeepers after finishing school, they need additional instruction for dealing with different currencies, or for calculating units of grain.[239] The fact that young people with good knowledge of mathematics had good employment opportunities became evident when parents took their children out of school even before they had finished their education, and placed them in jobs as accountants, so that they could contribute to the family's earnings.[240]

In contrast to the schools of the Francke Foundations[241] exercise and physical training did not constitute independent components of the curriculum in the schools of the DEHM. Physical activity, which primarily served to improve the health and well being of the children, but did not yield any concrete, measureable results, was not envisaged here. However, importance was given to physical

[238] Gründler, *Die Malabarische Korrespondenz*, 134, (translated from German).

[239] Gründler, *Die Malabarische Korrespondenz*, 128–34.

[240] NHB 72. St., 1264, report from G.E. Rhenius and L.B.E. Schmid, Palayamcottah 1823.

[241] Müller-Bahlke, 'Kinderleben in den Glauchaer Anstalten', 23.

activity in connection with certain practical results. The children regularly went on recreational outings, which were also used to learn about nature and to observe the country.[242] In accordance with the unity of body and soul as propagated by Pietism, forms of physical training were part of the curriculum from the beginning. In 1712 Ziegenbalg reported: 'Every week the children of the first class are taken out to the villages, where they are catechized in front of the heathens, after which they are given food in our church garden and told to move around.'[243] In 1712 Ziegenbalg also reported that all the school children worked in the mission garden in Porayar once a week.[244] In the course of the existence of the Danish-English-Halle Mission the network of school gardens was systematically extended and gardens were also laid in the vicinity of the city schools. 'The two long and large yards near the boys' and girls' schools were made into gardens and useful trees, flowers, but especially all kinds of vegetables have been planted there.'[245] These methods of 'physical exercise' also contributed to the self-sufficiency of the mission. When, as a result of the English-Mysore wars and the famines, many adults died and the mission had to provide for a greater number of children, those of them who were free of infectious diseases were looked after separately by a village catechist in the mission garden in Porayar. The day began with gardening, continued with some lessons in the forenoon as well as in the afternoon, and ended again with 'physical exercise' till sundown.[246] John later observed that through gardening and regular walks illnesses among the children, especially skin infections, decreased and that the children were, on the whole, more well-balanced. He reported euphorically: 'There is new life in our Malabarian children [...].'[247]

One of the most difficult problems to solve was the decision about the medium of instruction. Despite the fundamental intention of the

242 HB 4. Cont., 160, School regulations of 1709.

243 AB 227, letter from Ziegenbalg, Gründler and Jordan to A.H. Francke, Tranquebar, 10 September 1712, (translated from German).

244 Ibid.

245 NHB 30. St., 670, (translated from German).

246 Ibid.

247 NHB 32. St., 889, letter from Ch. S. John to G. A. Freylinghausen, 10 September 1785.

Tranquebar missionaries to acquire knowledge in the local languages so that even the school children could be taught in their mother tongue, this point had to be reassessed at regular intervals. The multilingual composition of the population in the mission region of the Danish-English-Halle Mission itself prevented a unified solution valid for all times. A basic principle of the Pietist approach was that the medium of instruction should be the mother tongue. At least in the first half of the eighteenth century the missionaries followed this principle. With the division of schools into a Tamil, a Danish and a 'Portuguese' school the intention of educating children in their mother tongue was emphatically underscored. Schultze also set up a school for children whose mother tongue was Telugu.

When the so-called English schools were set up on behalf of the SPCK the missionaries tried to appoint English-speaking teachers and have some subjects taught in English. Often, the percentage of children of English parents in these schools was not insignificant. Of the 25 children who Johann Zacharias Kiernander taught in 1758 in his school in Calcutta, there were 'five Portuguese, five Armenian, two Bengalis, one Hindustani and one Brahmin, the others were English children.'[248] Gerlach, who was sent to India in 1775 expressly for the educational work of the mission, and who was supposed to teach mainly Lutheran European children in his 'school of languages and sciences', also devoted a great deal of attention to the language question.[249] The importance of an English-medium education grew rapidly in the second half of the eighteenth century with the increasing consolidation of British colonial rule in South India. From about 1780 onwards the language question became one of the most pressing questions while framing the curriculum of mission schools.[250] R.E. Frykenberg is of the opinion that, at the very latest, at this point of time, but possibly earlier, the demand for an English-medium education and for the teaching of science

[248] HB 86. Cont., preface, 43.

[249] Cf. AFSt/M 1 B 67 : 22, letter from Johann Wilhelm Gerlach to Gottlieb Anastasius Freylinghausen, Tranquebar, 31 January 1778; AFSt/M 1 B 67 : 23, letter from Johann Wilhelm Gerlach to Sebastian Andreas Fabricius, Tranquebar, 31 January 1778; AFSt/M 1 B 67 : 24, letter from Johann Wilhelm Gerlach to Christian Gottlieb Kratzenstein, Tranquebar, 20 February 1778.

[250] Zastoupil, *The Great Indian Education Debate.*

and technology began to be raised by the Tamil people.[251] This increasing need for an English-medium education initially did not conform to the original ideals of the mission. An English-medium education undoubtedly offered better professional possibilities, but it contradicted the principle of Christian missions to impart knowledge in the local language in order to create the pre-conditions for a successful integration of Christianity in the local society. Yet, for all that, the need to increasingly teach in English gradually gained coinage. Christoph Samuel John was a supporter of the change to an English-medium education. However, since this could not be done in a comprehensive manner due to the lack of suitable co-workers, 'teaching in Trankenbar, especially in reading, writing and arithmetic, should be done, at least partially, in English, and a missionary who knows English should have only the English children in his house.'[252] New missionaries, he felt, should learn English in Europe, or, at the very least, use the long voyage to India for this purpose. The desire of young Indians, actively encouraged by their parents, to enter European service proved to be problematic. Many Indians, actually being trained for work in the mission, either left school early, or did not remain with the mission as planned. Because of this, the missionaries in Tranquebar, at one time, considered reducing lessons in European languages in favour of 'more natural history lessons in High Tamil'.[253]

Language instruction in the schools was subject to different criteria. Firstly, it was a principle of the Pietist approach to teach children in their mother tongue. Secondly, practical requirements played a role. Whatever the case, however, Tamil teaching constituted a fixed component of the curriculum. Especially in the first decades of missionary work it was also important to learn Portuguese to improve one's prospects for employment with Europeans.[254] Despite the

[251] Frykenberg, 'The Halle Legacy in Modern India', 15; Frykenberg, *Christianity in India*, 307–14.

[252] NHB 32. St., 897, letter from Ch. S. John to G.A. Freylinghausen, 10 September 1785, (translated from German).

[253] RA Miskolark 9i, report of the condition of the Royal Danish Mission in Tranquebar in the year 1803 by Ch. S. John, J.P. Rottler, A.F. Cämmerer (duplicate).

[254] 'For the schoolboys, especially those of a low caste, it is important that they learn to speak Portuguese, since many of them have to earn their living later with the

growing importance of English, which even the mission schools could not ignore, Portuguese played an important role in the syllabus for the Tamil children in Tranquebar till the 1780s. Besides Portuguese and English, lessons were also given in German.[255] John's suggestion of according priority to German over the other European languages was not carried through.[256] This idea was abandoned in favour of the systematic training of a few children in this language. Although German lessons were a part of the curriculum of the mission schools, it could not be taught in the desired and required manner. Therefore, children with a talent for and an interest in languages were given additional intensive language training in the house of a missionary. This was mainly done when a pupil was being expressly prepared for work in the mission and, particularly, for a career as a teacher.[257] The mission, it was said, should not spare additional costs in this case.[258] Local individuals trained in this way, among them, for example, Rangarajen, in turn taught German in the mission schools.[259] Njanaburanam was brought up and educated by John in the mission school in Tranquebar. Initially he worked as an assistant, and later taught German and arithmetic in the first class.[260] Attempts to teach Latin, Greek or Hebrew generally did not yield the desired results.[261] In the 1820s Bernhard Schmid in Palayankottai taught according to the following curriculum: the first course included Bible studies, arithmetic, geometry, history and geography. In the second course consisting of pupils who were being prepared for work as catechists, Sanskrit and the history of religion were taught in addition to the

blanques. [i.e. with the Europeans, H.L.]' (translated from German), HB 25. Cont., 30, diary of the missionaries in Tranquebar, 31 May 1727.

[255] HB 58. Cont., 1537; NHB 25. St., 134.

[256] NHB 30. St., 703. John was of the opinion: 'Without a European language, which, in the present situation means German, their [the Tamils, H.L.] intellect will never be properly enlightened and enriched with basic and necessary knowledge.' (translated from German).

[257] NHB 25. St., 134.

[258] RA Miskolark, 9g, some suggestions regarding the mission by Ch. S. John, Tranquebar, 20 February 1784.

[259] NHB 32. St., 992.

[260] NHB 46. St., 934.

[261] RA Miskolark 9g, some suggestions regarding the mission by Ch. S. John, Tranquebar, 20 February 1784.

above subjects. The third course consisted of the most talented pupils who were also taught the Bible languages.[262]

The shift from the original intention of teaching in the local language to a greater emphasis on English can be observed in different missions in the nineteenth century. For the Baptists Carey, Ward and Marshman in Serampore the following statements were the keynote of their missionary work: 'If, in addition, conversion is to achieve its true goal, it must make the people of a country happy in their own spheres and not take them out of these.'[263] They, therefore, arrived at the conclusion that sound knowledge could only be imparted in the mother-tongues of their pupils.[264] They felt that the wide use of English as the medium of instruction would alienate the children from their local and cultural roots. In the context of a pan-Indian educational policy this question triggered a fierce debate between the Orientalists and the Anglicists in the 1830s. Whereas the Anglicists were of the opinion that the local languages were not developed enough to serve as a medium for the transfer of Western knowledge, the Orientalists, including most of the representatives of Christian missions, fought to teach the Indian children in their respective mother tongues. The culminating point of this controversy was the position adopted by Thomas Babington Macaulay (1800–59) in 1853,[265] after which the role of English increased noticeably. In addition, the access to an English-medium education changed from being simply a question of prestige to becoming a political question, since the British, from the 1870s onwards, increasingly also appointed Indians to higher posts in the civil services.[266]

MISSION SCHOOL TEACHERS

The structural developments in the mission educational system as well as the changes in the contents and methods of teaching shaped

[262] NHB 83. St., 972.

[263] NHB 67. St., 603.

[264] NHB 67. St., 597–620.

[265] Macaulay, who was initially appointed as legal advisor in the executive council of the governor-general of India, was later given the responsibility for 'public affairs' and, in this function, had the task to work out a concept for the use of funds earmarked for educational purposes. Cf. Sharma, Ram Nath and Rajendra Sharma, 1996, *History of Education in India*, Atlantic Publishers & Dist., New Delhi, 79–87.

[266] Zastoupil, *The Great Indian Education Debate*.

the social, ethnic and religious composition of the teachers and the attendants. The schools were attended by members of different religious communities and social groups, which posed enormous challenges for the teachers, who had to integrate these groups and resolve conflicts in the daily routine of the schools. The Indian teachers trained especially for the schools of the Tranquebar Mission combined the European education they had gained in the framework of the Mission with their feeling of belonging to the local population based on a shared cultural background and an understanding of local society. Like the missionaries had done, almost every Indian mission employee worked for some time as a preceptor or a schoolteacher before being appointed to a higher post. Many remained mission schoolteachers their entire lives. Since the education of young people in reading, writing, arithmetic and other subjects was, besides religious instruction, an important concern of the mission from the beginning, teachers who could take over this work were always required. Some of them had been trained by the Mission and had often attended one of the mission schools. In addition to this, the Mission also 'borrowed' teachers—especially Europeans—from other professions such as the military or trade.

TEACHING PERSONNEL

The few European missionaries who were together in India at any given time could only teach in some central schools. In most of the villages classes were taken by South Indian schoolteachers and assistants who were regularly checked and guided by the catechists, local pastors or missionaries. They were the ones who had to translate the ideas, concepts and demands of the missionaries into the daily work with the children and youth. The management of the educational institutions lay with one of the missionaries. For important decisions like changes in the curriculum, preparation for examinations, or admitting and dismissing children, this missionary called for a conference of the teaching personnel. His duties also included the religious and moral instruction of teachers, regular supervision, and also ensuring that the schools were provided with teaching material, food, clothing and medicines.[267]

[267] HB 58. Cont., 1530.

The missionaries were convinced that it was necessary and appropriate to involve local teachers in the work of the schools. These men and women were not only reliable pillars of the mission network and thus guarantors for the reproduction and regeneration of the local Christian communities, but they also often commanded the respect of the villagers, and were thus a reliable link between the Mission and the local population. Although the missionaries sometimes entertained the ideal of increasing the number of Europeans employed in the schools, they invariably arrived at the opinion that the local co-workers were better suited to deal with the local children. They felt that the Indians could endure the hardships and struggles of teaching in India better than the Europeans.[268] However, the co-workers would have to be trained in the European way of thought and in the sciences.[269] One of the first Tamil mission school teachers was the poet Kanapati Vattiyar who taught in the Tamil school in Tranquebar under his baptismal name Christian Friedrich.[270] Decades later there was once again a famous Tamil poet who took up a career in the Mission—Vedanayakam Sastri. In the mission school in Tranquebar he learned, among other things, theology and astronomy, and after completing his studies he became a teacher in Thanjavur. Numerous pupils of Vedanayakam later became pastors, teachers, catechists or government employees.[271]

Considering the importance of the educational system for the strategy of the Mission it seems strange that the presence of teachers in the mission sources is less than that of the catechists and Tamil pastors. Whereas the monthly reports of the local pastors and catechists are, at least, mentioned regularly, are often paraphrased extensively, or are even reproduced in their entirety, there are no comparable sources with regard to the teachers. This also holds true for letters to European authorities; here too there are only letters from the Tamil pastors, or from one or the other catechist. One

[268] AB 226, Ziegenbalg, Gründler and Jordan to A.H. Francke, Tranquebar, 10 September 1712.

[269] NHB 32. St., 891, letter from Ch. S. John to G.A. Francke, 10 September 1785.

[270] 'The Malabarian school is now in good shape/and has a good preceptor/who was the most famous poet and schoolmaster among the Malabarians and the Moors in Tranquebar/and who had now been baptized.' (translated from German), Cf. HB 2. Cont., 98–102, letter from B. Ziegenbalg, 17 January 1719, here 99.

[271] Cf. Peterson, 'Science in the Tranquebar Mission Curriculum'.

reason for this source-situation seems to lie in the reporting system of the Tranquebar Mission, which clearly reflects the hierarchical organizational structure of the Mission. The monthly reports from the assistants, catechists and pastors dealt primarily with the actual work of conversion, i.e. conversations with the local people, baptismal preparations, statistics etc. The local schoolteachers were placed under a local catechist or pastor working in the vicinity. These catechists and pastors had to compile a written report every month and either read it out personally to the European missionaries, or have it read out by someone else. This latter task was often given to the schoolteachers who were not required to report in this detailed manner. The schoolmaster in Thanjavur, Dewanesen, regularly read out the reports written by Rajanayakkan and his assistant Arhagappen in Tranquebar, while his own reports are not mentioned.[272] Wallattu Muttu, a village schoolteacher in Kuttenallur around 1750, read out the monthly reports of the assistant Muttuschawri, with whom he worked.[273] The work of the schools was not emphasized in these reports. It constituted only one aspect of the work of conversion, and, therefore, only a few paragraphs were devoted to this work. The missionaries themselves wrote detailed reports about the condition of the schools on the basis of statistical information, examination results, assessments of the pupils and their own pedagogical work at irregular intervals.[274]

South Indian Christian schoolteachers constituted the majority of the teaching staff in the schools of the Tranquebar Mission. More than the assistants, catechists and pastors, whose main focus of work and whose knowledge lay in the religious sphere, the teachers had to deal with the latest (scientific) developments in the subjects they taught. Most of the catechists and assistants had worked as schoolteachers in the initial stages of their career as mission employees. Although some catechists also taught periodically, the two spheres of work were generally separated.[275] Some of the

[272] HB 70. Cont., 1620; 73. Cont. 125.

[273] HB 73. Cont., 41.

[274] HB 13. Cont., 19–38; 22. Cont., 901; 33. Cont., 891; 58. Cont., 1528–45.

[275] On the use of terms: Frykenberg calls the catechists and teachers 'pastor-teachers'. However, these functions were not always carried out by the same person; teachers were specially trained and their functions were different to those of the

South Indian catechists set up their own schools, as for example, Rajanayakkan in Thanjavur. In 1742, during the rule of Pratap Singh (1739–63), and in a period of frequent military attacks on Thanjavur, he was able to open a school. This school, which, on an average, had five to nine children, seems to have existed at least till 1757.[276] It cannot be ascertained to what extent political conditions, internal mission matters or the lack of schoolchildren contributed to the closure of the school. Rajanayakkan was also in charge of the mission schools in Tiruppalatturai, Rarasalam and Kawastalam and supervised the teachers there.[277] Christian David, who worked with John, Schwartz, Jänicke and Kohlhoff after graduating from the mission school in Tranquebar, was a catechist and schoolteacher for more than 10 years under Schwartz. When he went to Ceylon in 1800 as an ordained priest he was given the overall charge of the schools in Jaffna and Colombo. He also set up several new schools.[278] Even in Tranquebar itself some South Indian mission co-workers were appointed as inspectors of school. Thus, in the 1740s, the former catechist Schawrimuttu was made sub-inspector of the Tranquebar schools and was in charge of the supervision of these schools.[279] Frykenberg sees the Indian Christian teachers of the eighteenth century, who were trained in the framework of the mission and 'drilled in the latest most advanced ideas and methods of modern education developed at Halle', as 'harbingers of radical culturel and social change' in Tamil Nadu.[280]

Women were employed to supervise and take care of the girls. Even in the early years of the mission the missionaries handed over

---

pastors, catechists and assistants. Cf. Frykenberg, 'The Legacy of Christian Friedrich Schwartz'.

276 After this the school does not appear in the statistics. Whereas till 1758 the reports mention four district schools, from 1758 onwards (HB 89. Cont., 528) only three are mentioned. In 1763 there is a direct reference to the fact that the district school in Thanjavur existed only temporarily. HB 99. Cont., 304.

277 HB 66. Cont., 1068, translation of a letter from Rajanayakkan to the Mission Board, 15 January 1747.

278 NHB 60. St., 1091f.; 70. St., 999: cf. also Archives of the Gurukul Lutheran Theological College & Research Institute, Acc. No. 384, Autobiography of the Late Rev. Christian David (1771–1852).

279 HB 58. Cont., 1529f.

280 Frykenberg, 'The Legacy of Christian Friedrich Schwartz', 130.

the supervision of girls, or their lessons in certain crafts like spinning, knitting or mat weaving to women. One of the first female teachers of the Mission was Maria, who had been a pupil of the girls' school in Tranquebar. From 1712 onwards, as the oldest girl, she taught in the Tamil girls' school. Later, she officially became a schoolteacher there.[281] Around 1725 Barbara was a 'Portuguese' schoolteacher in Tranquebar.[282] Catharina was a supervisor and seamstress with the Portuguese girls under Plütschau. In the 1720s she became a seamstress in the 'Malabarian' girls' school in Tranquebar.[283] In the 1740s three female teachers and a female mat-weaver were employed in the Tamil girls' school in Tranquebar. A male teacher taught Bible history, but a schoolmistress conducted catechism.[284] Even around 1785 at least three female teachers worked in the girls' school in Tranquebar: Jesadial, Mariamuttu (born 1766) and Rahel (around 1730–1801).[285] There was also Ambei (around 1727–93), who had been teaching for many years. Rahel was the new teacher who had been specially appointed for the *paṟaiyār* girls and who had previously worked in Kawastalam for several years.[286] The women working in the mission schools were mostly those who were married to mission employees and who helped their husbands in their work. Therefore, they often took on independent functions only after the death of their husbands. Rahel, the widow of the catechist Ignasi in Kawastalam, had helped her husband during his lifetime. She had studied in the mission school and had distinguished herself by her knowledge of Tamil literature. After her husband's death she became a schoolteacher and the missionaries attested to her success with the children.[287] Ambei was the wife of the school caretaker Joseph

[281] HB 6. Cont., 331; 26. Cont., 82; AB 263. Maria is probably the same person as Metta Marya, who was one of the first children to be baptized by the Tranquebar missionaries and who later became a schoolteacher in Tranquebar under Plütschau. Cf. Staatsbibliothek Preußischer Kulturbesitz Berlin, Nachlass August Hermann Francke K 33, Fascicle B (H. Plütschau).

[282] AFSt/M 1 H 3 : 15, Letter from Nikolaus Dal to [Johann Georg v. Holstein, Johann Steenbuch, Johann Wilhelm Schröder, Jacob Lodberg] and [Wilhelm v. Munk], 7 July 1723 Tranquebar.

[283] AB 263, 267; HB 6. Cont., 331; 20. Cont., 408.

[284] HB 58. Cont., 1539.

[285] NHB 15. St., 276; 18. St., 679; 21. St., 1064; 32. St., 890; 38. St., 202.

[286] NHB 31. St., 751.

[287] NHB 59. St., 995–98, Rahel's biography.

(1717–95) who also worked in the house of the missionary Ole Maderup (1711–76). Their son Eliser also became a teacher. When Ambei died at the age of 66 she had completed 30 years of service as a schoolteacher in the 'Malabarian' girls' school.[288]

The Tamil employees in mission schools also included the *kaṇakkappiḷḷai* who, as copyists, writers and accountants, carried out their work in the framework of the schools. In 1709 seven writers were employed in the schools in Tranquebar, whose actual work involved making copies of (text) books, but who, when the need arose, were also made to supervise the children's learning.[289] Often, pupils of the higher classes took on the work of making copies, but generally there were copyists available, who were responsible for the accounts and transcript affairs of the mission. In 1751 two additional copyists were employed in Madras to deal with the large amount of work.[290]

Along with setting up and consolidating their own schools the first missionaries also regarded the inclusion of existing village schools as a possible way to impart religious instruction. This practice required skill in dealing with the 'heathen' teachers employed there who were expected to include short Christian texts, aphorisms and hymns in their teaching. In order to lay greater emphasis on their demands, the missionaries in the 1720s began to pay the village schoolteachers in the schools supervised by the Mission. Thus, in 1727, seven teachers received a small salary for their efforts on behalf of the mission.[291] This co-operative experiment with non-Christian teachers in the existing village schools was discontinued after a short while. However, from time to time, a non-Christian teacher was appointed in one or the other mission school, either because of his convincing pedagogical abilities, or because there was, as yet, no Christian congregation in that place. Thus, when he began work in Madras, Schultze had non-Christian teachers in the Telugu school there.[292] This method was also practiced in Cuddalore, as always accompanied by the unspoken wish that the teacher might one day become a

[288] NHB 18. St., 679; 46. St., 863, 906f. 927, 932; 50. St., 139.
[289] HB 4. Cont., 158f.
[290] AFSt/M 3 I 13; cf. also HB 33. Cont., 871 for the year 1730.
[291] HB 25. Cont., 15, daily Register, 14 February 1727.
[292] Lehmann, *Es begann in Tranquebar*, 227.

Christian, and by the hope that a large number of children would thus develop an interest in Christianity. In June 1742 the non-Christian teacher Porhani (born 1672), who had worked for three years as a 'Malabarian schoolmaster' in the 'heathen school' being supervised by the Mission in Cuddalore, was dismissed—officially on disciplinary grounds and because of his advanced age, but also because he had not converted to Christianity.[293]

For various reasons, the missionaries also appointed Europeans or descendants of mixed marriages. In the early years there were special so-called Portuguese and Danish schools. While the Danish school in Tranquebar was soon closed down, the 'Portuguese' school continued to exist. Polycarp Jordan, who had arrived from Europe as a non-ordained mission co-worker, worked briefly as a manager and accountant, but later became a teacher in the 'Portuguese' school. In 1714 he returned to Europe with Ziegenbalg.[294] During Ziegenbalg's and Gründler's time, when there were only a few missionaries, and when their own teachers had not yet been trained, Europeans from the Danish East India Company were allowed to work as preceptors for the schools of the Tranquebar Mission. Thus, in 1708, two employees of the East India Company worked as preceptors in the 'Portuguese' school in Tranquebar under Plütschau's supervision. They taught Danish and German there.[295] One of the two was a corporal who had served in Bengal.[296] The other was Jens Sievertsen (died 1741), of Danish origin, born in Copenhagen, who had probably come to South India with the Dutch East India Company. In 1709, at the age of nineteen, he began to work for the Tranquebar Mission and was a schoolteacher for Danish and Portuguese in Tranquebar for many years. After the Danish school was closed down, and mainly South Indian teachers trained by the mission were teaching in the 'Portuguese' school, Sievertsen was put in charge, among other things, of the mission accounts; he also transcribed the mission

[293] HB 52. Cont., 728; 57. Cont., 1448.

[294] Vorbaum, Reinhold, 1850–52, *Evangelische Missionsgeschichte in Biographien in 4 Bänden*, Vol. 1, No. 4, Schaub, Düsseldorf, Appendix, 61.

[295] Cf. HB, Vol. I, placed before 1. Cont., Halle 1716, 18, B. Ziegenbalg's report, 22 August 1708.

[296] Ibid.

diaries and took care of the correspondence, principally with the Dutch because of his knowledge of the language.[297] Georg, the son of a European father and an Indian mother, born in 1696, was one of the first in 1707 to be baptized by the Tranquebar missionaries. He became a pupil of the mission school, worked there as a tutor for Portuguese and was later appointed as a preceptor in the 'Portuguese' boys' school. From 1717 onwards Georg worked as a 'Portuguese' schoolteacher in the school established by Johann Ernst Gründler in Madras. In 1718 he was teaching 24 children there. When the school was closed down Georg probably returned to Tranquebar. In 1731 he is mentioned as a printer with the Mission in Tranquebar, where he had trained for some time as a young man under Johann Gottlieb Adler.[298]

Although it was better, especially for language instruction, to appoint Europeans, they were often too expensive for the Mission because of their higher salaries. For financial reasons Johann Wilhelm Gerlach appointed a non-European schoolteacher in his school in Calcutta in 1781, along with two grown-up boys who attended school, but also taught. Gerlach's staff, however, also included the German copyist Stark from Pomerania who, besides his work as a copyist, taught drawing, Latin and geography.[299] Many sons of missionaries worked in the provincial schools that were supervised by Ch. F. Schwartz. Born in India, and sometimes educated in Europe, they possessed the desirable knowledge of the country and its languages and were loyal to the mission. Schwartz intended to appoint the sons of Klein, Kohlhoff and Gericke in the new provincial schools to be established in Ramanathapuram and Sivaganga. His servant Joseph was also meant to become a schoolteacher there.[300] The Englishman Wheatley, who was earlier a schoolteacher in the English school in Tiruchirappalli, became the first teacher in the provincial school in Ramanathapuram.[301] Frequently, teachers of English were recruited

[297] HB 2. Cont., 77; 6. Cont., 236; 13. Cont., 2; 27. Cont., 16; 33. Cont., 893; 53. Cont., 891. See also Niekamp, *Kurtzgefaßte Mißions-Geschichte*, 491. Sievertsen died in 1741 at the age of 52.

[298] AB 227, 263f., 493, 500; HB 5. Cont., 186; 8. Cont., 624; 14. Cont., 164; 23. Cont., 973; 32. Cont., 818.

[299] NHB 26. St., 173f.

[300] NHB 30. St., 692.

[301] HB 103. Cont., 827; NHB 30. St., 693; 31. St., 787f.

from those English soldiers who had either been wounded and were unfit for service, or whose enlistment period had come to an end, but who, for various reasons, could not return to Europe. In the 1750s the two former English soldiers John Kare (died 1760) and Lewis Meade (died 1754) worked in Cuddalore as teachers.[302]

Christoph Samuel John attached great importance to European assistants in the educational system to train the South Indian teachers. However, even John could not imagine the actual work with Tamil school children without Tamil teachers. John realized that local parents often placed greater trust in their countrymen than in the Europeans, and this made it necessary to have local teachers in the educational system. The population did not trust the Europeans to teaching reading and writing in the local language. In Ch. S. John's opinion, however, the school inspectors who guided the teachers were, as far as possible, to be Europeans. European assistants would constitute a connection between the European missionaries and the South Indian teachers.[303] According to him, English had to be taught, in principle, by Europeans, or, at least, by Indo-Europeans. The optimal way of doing this would be to select these teachers from the graduates of the 'male asylum' in Madras.[304]

The teachers employed by the Mission received a meagre monthly salary. With this, the original Indian tradition whereby a teacher in the village community was supported by the parents of the children he taught was only partially followed.[305] It only existed where the Mission tried to involve local village schools in their strategy.[306]

[302] In 1754 Kare replaced Meade who was seriously ill. Kare himself died in 1760. HB 82. Cont., 1464f., 1488f., 1493; 84. Cont., 1747, 1756; 92. Cont., 902.

[303] John, *On Indian Civilization*, 29f.

[304] John, *On Indian Civilization*, 32. See pp. 392–94 of this study.

[305] According to Krishna Kumar, in the long term the practice of regular salary payments to the teachers led to the danger of their moral exclusion from the village community. Traditionally, the villagers were associated with 'their' teacher through constant direct contact, which also included control. Payment from external sources led to the development of a completely different relationship, which entailed a distance between the villagers and the teachers. Cf. Kumar, Krishna, 1991, *Political Agenda of Education. A Study of Colonialist and Nationalist Ideas*, SAGE, New Delhi, 76.

[306] HB 25. Cont., 15. The fifteenth letter of the *Malabarische Korrespondenz* states: The 'duties of the pupils towards their teachers is five-fold. 1) They must pay their teachers enough for these to feed themselves and their families [...].' (translated from German), HB 7. Cont., 422.

The missionaries always tried to find ways and means to pay the teachers working for them. J.Z. Kiernander took school fees of five Arcot Rupees from some of the parents, with which he could pay the schoolteachers and assistants as well as two older schoolboys who he had brought with him from Cuddalore (Tobias and Alphonso), and who he had been looking after privately in his home.[307] The six teachers and assistants who worked with Kiernander in Calcutta received between 10 and 40 Arcot Rupees every month. On the whole, the missionary had to raise 130 Arcot Rupees every month for the schools.[308]

The salary that the teachers got from the missionaries was relatively meagre, less than what soldiers were paid. Thus, teachers often gave up teaching and joined the army. Sometimes, teachers were involved in cases of misappropriation of funds. Phanuel (died 1779), who later became the junior catechist in the Kumbakonam district, began his career in the mission in 1776 as a teacher in Thanjavur after completing his education in the city-school in Tranquebar. However, he soon gave up this position and became a soldier. When he decided to return to the Mission, he was again appointed as a teacher, this time, at his own request, in Rarasalam. Due to financial problems among his relatives he misappropriated funds meant for the school children. For the rest of his life he tried to repay the money he owed the mission.[309] Arulappen, a teacher in Tranquebar, also misappropriated school funds during the period of his service.[310]

THE TRAINING OF LOCAL TEACHERS

The training of local co-workers as the basic precondition for a self-sufficient and self-perpetuating local Christian sector was one of the main concerns of the educational work of the Mission. The goal was to be able to appoint well-trained Christian personnel everywhere to look after and educate the children. Early on, the Tranquebar

[307] HB 85. Cont., Vorrede, 43; 92. Cont., Vorrede, 167f.
[308] HB 92. Cont., Vorrede, 168.
[309] HB 24. St., 1379–81.
[310] NHB 3. St., 275, 277.

missionaries created their own structures to train teachers and other mission co-workers.[311]

Every so often the missionaries selected 'suitable pupils' from the mission schools in order to train them for the teaching profession. Thus, they knew the future teachers (both male and female) from their childhood onwards and were clearly aware of each person's abilities and weaknesses. The missionaries also hoped that they would be unconditionally loyal and honest. In 1716, a special seminary was set up for selected pupils (selectans) of the higher classes.[312] The pupils of the seminary were first appointed as writers, then as teachers, assistants and catechists in the actual work of the mission.[313] A local intellectual elite was created through his purposeful training. Although the consolidation of Biblical teachings and the shaping of Christian-Pietist norms of behaviour dominated the training of teachers in the Tranquebar Mission, it was somewhat relativized by additional language training and instruction in the natural sciences.[314] With the growing influence of rationalism in Europe and against the backdrop of increasing requirements in colonial India the secular content in the training of the elite also increased. Thus, in the 1780s the training of selectans was revived[315] and some talented boys were 'also specially taught theology, history, geography, reading, writing and speaking in Portuguese and German by the missionaries, and thus prepared for service to the Church and for the general good.'[316] The selectans were taught exclusively by the

[311] In doing this they were following the traditions of the Francke Foundations in Halle, where a seminary for teachers (*Seminarium praeceptorum*) had been established in the initial years to give pedagogical training mainly to the students of theology of the Halle University who taught in the schools of the Orphan House. From among these students a few were selected to undergo further training in the *Seminarium Selectum Praeceptorum*. After the two-year training period they had to teach for at least another three years in the schools of the Foundations. Cf. Francke, *Segensvolle Fußstapfen*, IV, 185f.

[312] AB 471, Ziegenbalg to A.H. Francke, 7 January 1717. A few years earlier the missionaries had already mentioned the need for such an arrangement in a letter to Francke. AB 226, Ziegenbalg, Gründler and Jordan to Francke, 10 September 1712.

[313] HB 33. Cont., 893f.

[314] NHB 25. St., 134, daily routine in a school 1780, letter from Klein, 16 October 1780.

[315] NHB 26. St., 134.

[316] NHB 25. St., 8, letter from the missionaries in Tranquebar, 14 October 1780.

missionaries. Although, as Missionary Jacob Klein stated, most of them were *paraiyārs*, he also added that the children did not lack 'natural abilities'. They were taught church-history, geography, cosmography, Portuguese, German and arithmetic.[317] This form of talent promotion was linked to the selection of pupils for different professional fields both within and outside the mission. The selectans were not only trained for work in the mission, but also for work as merchants or accountants. Those who were to be taken into missionary service later had to undergo special additional practical training with one of the European missionaries.[318] Not enough pupils decided to go into the teaching profession because of the low salary. In 1783 there were only two who chose this career, while the rest of the selectans preferred other, better-paid jobs with Europeans.[319] In order to promote independence and a sense of responsibility from an early age, but also to relieve the teachers, and for financial reasons, older children were made to supervise the younger ones.[320] In the 1780s, for example, the selectans dealt with Bible stories with children of lower classes under the supervision of a missionary.[321]

For their work in the schools the teachers as well as the catechists and Indian pastors were given special instructions laid down in the relevant school regulations. The school regulations of the Tranquebar Mission of 1743 stated with regard to the duties of the sub-inspectors, the schoolmistresses and schoolmasters that they, first and foremost, had to be god-fearing. They were responsible for order and cleanliness in the schools and had to handle the available equipment with care. Each and every hour of class had to be carried out properly, i.e. other conversations were to be postponed till after the class. On no account would a class end early. It was compulsory for all teachers to participate in the morning prayer-hour at 6.00 a.m. During the class the teacher would, under no circumstance, sit quietly somewhere, but he was to walk back and forth between the children and deal with their problems. The sub-inspector was expected to check the teaching material regularly to ensure that books

317 NHB 26. St., 134, letter from Klein, 16 October 1780.

318 NHB 30. St., 672f., diary of the missionaries in Tranquebar, 1783.

319 NHB 30. St., 672.

320 NHB 26. St., 173, letter from Gerlach, 3 December 1781.

321 NHB 25. St., 134.

were available in sufficient quantity and in good condition. It was his job to see that each child had a book. His duties also included making sure that the children were provided food and water and that the rules of hygiene were being followed.[322]

When prospective teachers completed their training and were given their job instructions, their training did not end there. It was continued through diverse forms of further education. Regular meetings were conducted in the central mission stations for the co-workers. At these meetings, which were generally devoted to a particular religious topic, the European missionaries taught the schoolteachers and other Indian co-workers. Every Friday morning the teaching staff met for discussions. These meetings were also used to inform the South Indian co-workers about developments in Europe, and to read out letters from representatives and supporters of the Mission in Europe. A.H. Francke's pedagogical writings were among the books used to train the teachers. This was the case even in the 1750s in Cuddalore.[323] Such meetings for training purposes were not always organized by the European missionaries. Even South Indian co-workers in leading positions organized trainings and found forms whereby colleagues placed under them gave accounts of their work and shared their experiences. This guaranteed a constant flow of information; examination results were passed on and the possible educational path of individual pupils was discussed. At these meetings of the co-workers application were also presented for the transfer of talented children from small village schools to the city-school in Tranquebar for their further education.

One of the forms of regular further training also involved younger teachers sitting in and observing classes taken by the missionaries or by experienced local teachers. In this way they were familiarized with modern European teaching methods, contents and resources, and these ideas reached the most remote mission villages schools through the South Indian teachers. Johann Peter Rottler taught the children living with him and with Christoph Samuel John from Hoffmanns Kinderphysik, and the two Tamilian teachers Rangarajen

[322] HB 58. Cont., 1530.

[323] HB 80. Cont., 1229, 2 March 1753.

and Schawrirajen also sat in on these classes.[324] All assistants and teachers who were not busy elsewhere were expected to be present for reading lessons in the first class in the Tamil boys' school in Tranquebar, where a missionary read and explained Christian literature.[325] In the absence of a special teachers training institute, and because the public schools could not guarantee the relevant training for prospective teachers, individual missionaries often personally took on the training and further education of the teachers. They supervised some selected and, in their view, suitable young men who were allowed to assist them in their daily work and who spent the entire day with the missionaries. John suggested that local teachers be trained intensively in the homes of missionaries, on account of the German language, on the one hand, but on the other hand, also because of the advantages of constant contact and association. These young men, he felt, should also receive a good salary, so that others would not recruit them.[326] In order to prepare future teachers for their work even in the regular schools, the missionaries developed new methods of involving the assistants. Thus, Rottler made two assistants catechize daily under his supervision.[327]

In view of the combination of European and South Indian forms of teaching and learning, and in view also of the large demand for European-trained teachers it was obvious that the idea of training South Indian teachers in Europe would arise. This idea was already in play when Peter Maleiappen and Timotheus accompanied the missionaries Ziegenbalg and Plütschau on their journeys to Europe,[328] although the idea was, at that time, often overshadowed by the strategic compulsion to carry out propaganda for the Mission. No other Tamil mission pupil was sent following these two young men who could gather valuable experiences in Europe and who also received an education. Referring to the fact that in 1744 'two students of theology from the seminary in Colombo, two children of inter-racial parentage born in Ceylon, were sent to the University of Leiden in Holland, where they would study for three years at the

[325] HB 58. Cont., 1536.
[326] NHB 30. St., 703.
[327] NHB 30. St., 684.
[328] See also chapter 2, pp. 110f.

cost of the Dutch East India Company',[329] the missionaries indicated that this practice should also be considered in the context of the Tranquebar Mission. John was the first to point out the necessity of a stay in Europe for Indians. Towards the end of the eighteenth century it was possible for missionaries, but not yet very common, to send their children, who had been born and brought up in India, for a university education to Europe. Jacob Klein's son, Johann Gottfried, born in Tranquebar, studied with Dutch support in Halle and Copenhagen, and later worked as an English missionary in Tiruchirappalli.[330] Daniel Pullei, as a Tamilian co-worker, brought up the question again. He would have liked to send his sons to Europe for their further education.[331] Although the Tamilian received moral support from John, all further plans in this regard failed because of financial and organizational considerations.

[329] HB 61. Cont., 22f., letter from the missionaries in Tranquebar to Princess Charlotta Amalia, 31 December 1744.

[330] NHB 37. St., 114; 39. St., 256–63, 288; 44. St., 745; 58. St., 541.

[331] RA Miskolark 9g, *Pro Memoria* from Ch. S. John, Tranquebar, 12 February 1784. Cf. also Liebau, 'Tamilische Christen im 18. Jahrhundert'.

CHAPTER SIX

Women in the Tranquebar Mission

> Observant travellers noted the work of Asian women, how they earned their livelihood, their legal status and their freedom. These observations are, at most, mentioned only casually in the reports. They do not add up to a general impression that would question the image of the woman as a victim. An image of a peasant woman or a tradeswoman could not match up to the secret allure of scenes from the harem and the open horror of a widow burning.[1]

Like all spheres of public life in early modern times, even Christian missionary work was a male domain. The Protestant mission in the eighteenth century looked for independent young men who would not only devote themselves to the religious work, but who were also willing to leave behind their familial ties for an indefinite period, generally for ever.[2] The task of the Mission was the focus of all thought, and initially it left little space for thinking about the personal well being of the missionaries who, despite being conscious of their religious duty, also tried to establish a family life in their new surroundings. In the case of the Tranquebar Mission, in the course of time, the missionaries and the Mission Board together had to take decisions about the familial situation of the men in the field

[1] Osterhammel, *Die Entzauberung Asiens*, 368, (translated from German).

[2] For the role of women in different spheres of social life in early modern Europe see: Hufton, Olwen, 1998, *Frauenleben. Eine europäische Geschichte 1500–1800*, S. Fischer, Frankfurt/Main; Stedman, Gesa (ed.), 2001, *Englische Frauen der Frühen Neuzeit: Dichterinnen, Malerinnen, Mäzeninnen*, Wissenschaftliche Buchgesellschaft, Darmstadt; Köhle-Hezinger, Christel, 1994, "Frauen im Pietismus", *BWKG* 94 (1994), 107–21; Konrad, Dagmar, 2001, *Missionsbräute: Pietismus des 19. Jahrhunderts in der Basler Mission*, Waxmann, Münster [et al].

while keeping the concrete requirements of the Mission region in mind. These decisions included, for example, the search for suitable wives for the missionaries, the salary for married missionaries and, sometimes, the education of children of missionaries.

In view of the dominance of patriarchal structures, which were reflected in the religious sphere and thus also in the mission, it is not surprising that the role of women has, till now, seldom been included in a study of the history of missions in the eighteenth century.[3] Applied to the concrete history of the Tranquebar Mission there are some studies of the wives and daughters of the missionaries,[4] but the Indian women who contributed a great deal to the success of missionary work have been hitherto completely forgotten.[5]

In the middle of the nineteenth century a distinction arose between the European wives of missionaries who were primarily responsible for family and household, and the European women who came out on behalf of a mission society as missionaries, teachers or nurses. In many mission regions it was then the practice to send out unmarried men as missionaries, but to allow them to marry after a few years. When reading Alexander Merensky's (1837–1918) descriptions, a missionary of the Berlin Mission Society who worked in Transvaal (South Africa) from 1859 till 1882, it appears that the role of the missionary wives in Africa of the nineteenth century did not differ fundamentally from the position of the European wives in the Tranquebar Mission in the eighteenth century. The graphic

[3] Of the 2,500 biographies in the Biographical Dictionary of Christian Missions 280 are of women. Cf. Anderson, Gerald H. and William B. Eerdmans (eds.), 1998, *Biographical Dictionary of Christian Missions*, William B. Eerdmans Publishing, grand Rapids, Michigan, Cambridge.

[4] Erika Pabst has offered a first comprehensive portrayal on the role of women in the Tranquebar Mission with reference to the sources: Pabst, Erika, 2006, 'The Wives of Missionaries 1715–1838 (Short biographies)', in Gross, *Halle and the Beginning of Protestant Christianity in India*, Vol. III, 1529–42; Pabst, Erika, 2006, 'The Wives of the Missionaries: Their Experiences in India', in Gross, *Halle and the Beginning of Protestant Christianity in India*, Vol. II, 685–704.

[5] The biography of the Brahmin woman Clarinda who converted to Christianity is an exception. This will be dealt with in section 6.3.3. *Clarinda. A Historical Novel* by A. Madhaviah appeared in 1915 and was published again in 1992. For Clarinda see also: Packiamuthu, *Schwartz, Clarinda and Sathianathan*. The most recent study about this woman is the essay by Kent, 'Raja Clarinda—Widow, Concubine, Patroness: Women's Leadership in the Indian Church'.

description of the difficulties of bachelor life in South Africa is meant to show how necessary marriage was for a missionary. Merensky, however, felt that the bride of a German Africa-missionary should be a German herself. He found that alliances between German missionaries and African women always ended up with these families being excluded in many ways from mission life or from the life of the Europeans there, and that the offspring of such alliances suffered from identity problems even in the second and third generation. He also felt that as far as possible the bride should not be from another European nation, because only a German wife could create a typical German home for the missionary. Merensky had precise ideas about the duties of the wife: she would run the household, but would not take part in the actual work of the mission. It would be helpful if she were to train local children in her house to become domestic servants or teachers, and, especially, if she could teach the children the colloquial language. She, on the other hand, need not bother herself with learning the difficult local languages.[6]

Besides the women who sailed out as wives of missionaries, there was a growing need in the nineteenth century for women to work in different mission regions. From the middle of the nineteenth century Europe and America saw the rise of mission societies that focused specially on the conversion of women.[7] The areas targeted for such work were mainly India and Africa. Besides the health sector, educational work was one of the principal fields of activity of these organizations. These spheres gave rise to independent women's missions, which developed their own mission strategies and whose representatives worked independently of those mission societies that sent out mainly male co-workers.[8] In 1842 the Womens' Association for

[6] Heyden, Ulrich van der (ed.), 1996, *Alexander Merensky. Mein Missionsleben in Transvaal. Erinnerungen des Berliner Missionars in Südafrika 1859–1882*, [Berlin 1899], Edition Ost, Berlin, 207–17.

[7] Dana L. Roberts emphasizes the independent role of American women as wives of missionaries and teachers in the framework of Christian missions of the nineteenth century. The women were more than just assistants of the men, and, on no account, did they have only a marginal function. Roberts, Dana L., 1997, *American Women in Mission: A Social History of their Thought and Practice*, Mercer University Press, Macon, GA.

[8] These include, for example, *The Woman's Foreign Missionary Society of the Free Church of Scotland* or *Ladies' Society for Female Education in India and Africa.* Cf. also

the Christian Education of the Female Sex in the Orient (Frauenverein für christliche Bildung des weiblichen Geschlechts im Morgenlande) began its work in Berlin and chose East India as its focus. The task of this association was to prepare 'spinsters and widows' for work as teachers in a mission region, either as independent workers or as wives of missionaries.[9] Catholic missions for nuns also came into being, such as the Mission of the Sisters of Mercy of the Holy Cross (Mission der Barmherzigen Schwestern vom heiligen Kreuz), which carried out missionary work from 1894 in Bihar, Assam and Uttar Pradesh, or the Sisters of the Holy Cross Menzingen (Schwestern vom Heiligen Kreuz Menzingen), which worked in Kerala from 1906.[10]

WOMEN IN THE MISSION SOURCES

Whether it was European wives of missionaries who supported their husband's work—not only as housewives, but also as educators of the South Indian children living in their houses, or as administrators of mission funds—or whether it was local women who, in the case of the Tranquebar Mission, held official posts in contrast to their European counterparts: female players made a lasting imprint on the Mission in the eighteenth century.[11]

Ideas about the role of women in the daily work of the Mission and their share in the continued existence and the successes of

---

Savage, David W., 1997, 'Missionaries and the Development of a Colonial Ideology of Female Education in India', *Gender and History* 9 (2): 201–21.

[9] Lehmann, Hellmuth, 1974, *150 Jahre Berliner Mission*, Verlag der Evangelisch-Lutherischen Mission, Erlangen; Richter, *Indische Missionsgeschichte*; Richter, Julius, 1924, *Geschichte der Berliner Missionsgesellschaft 1824–1924*, Berliner ev. Missionsgesellschaft, Berlin.

[10] Pabst, Erika and Thomas Müller-Bahlke (eds.), 2005, *Quellenbestände der Indienmission 1700–1918 in Archiven des deutschsprachigen Raums*, Max Niemeyer Verlag, Tübingen (=Hallesche Quellenpublikationen und Repertorien; 9), 69–75; 90–98.

[11] The editors of the third volume of the 'Geschichte der Frauen' explore the hypothesis that the role of women in all spheres of life in early modern times was far greater than what is described in the sources. They speak of a broad presence of women players in all spheres and proceed on the assumption that early modern descriptions of the life of women were aimed at maintaining and asserting a male-dominated social order. Duby, Georges and Michelle Perrot (eds.), 1994, *Geschichte der Frauen. Vol. 3, Early Modern times*, Zweitausendeins-Verlag, Frankfurt/Main.

the Mission, which can be garnered from the observations of the European men, give rise to an image of women that is shaped by their own experiences in the family and by their educational background. In their biographies the missionaries first described the importance of their mothers who, as faithful and caring wives and self-sacrificing mothers, had an idealized function in their lives. During their school and university education the young men hardly came into contact with members of the other sex, and this only changed when they worked as private tutors. In this role, their opinion of their female pupils was positive if the daughters of the house were obedient, modest and quiet. The missionaries also based their choice of a wife on this image of the woman.

The family life of the missionaries was only mentioned in the mission reports when personal difficulties and problems directly affected the husband's work. Otherwise it was taken for granted that the household was harmonious and well organized. Since the wives seldom carried out their own correspondence, we have very few possibilities today to understand their state of mind and their views. Even if some did carry out a correspondence it was not published,[12] since the Mission sources primarily addressed a male readership and the sponsors, even in Europe, were mostly male. As far as the husbands were concerned, the life of the missionary wives belonged to the private sphere of the home and was, therefore, not part of their reports. Although it was different in the case of Indian women employed by the Mission, and their work was at least mentioned regularly, the reports about South Indian women were generally very brief when compared with those about their male colleagues. It is not clear whether the female co-workers also had to write monthly reports, or whether this was done only through their husbands or superiors. We must assume the latter, since the sources do not contain any references to the work-reports or diaries written by women.

Even when, as in some places, the work of a woman was described in great detail and praised, it was not always considered necessary

[12] That letters did exist is proven by the correspondence of Dorothea Ziegenbalg. Cf. Georgi, Lotte, 1958, *Maria Dorothea Ziegenbalg. Tatsachenberichte aus dem Leben der ersten deutschen evangelischen Missionarsfrau in Südindien*, Evangelische Verlagsanstalt, Berlin. Cf. also HB 16. Cont., Vorrede, letter from Dorothea Ziegenbalg, 30 September 1719.

to mention her name in this context. In a letter dated 15 February 1753 Johann Christian Breithaupt and Johann Philipp Fabricius gave a lengthy description of the life of a female teacher in the 'Portuguese' girls' school in Madras without mentioning her name: till she got married for the first time as a young girl she was working in the house of a 'Dutch-Portuguese' woman in Pulicat. After her husband died she returned to this family. The maidservant got to know the missionary Fabricius through church services in Pulicat where Fabricius stayed for a long time for political reasons. The woman learned to read and write Portuguese with the children of the mission school till Fabricius recommended her to a corporal as a wife. The couple took in an orphan girl and brought her up together. However, after even this second husband died and the woman was widowed yet again, the Mission gave her the charge of another child and accommodated all three of them in the mission house. In 1752 Fabricius took the woman with him when he returned to Vepery and appointed her as a teacher in the 'Portuguese' school.[13]

While it requires protracted research to reconstruct the work of male South Indian mission co-workers from the available sources, it is far more problematic to uncover the hidden world of local women in the daily work of the Mission.[14] Only in those cases where there are points of contact between the world of women and that of men, as in the mission schools, or where, as in the case of the Brahmin widow Clarinda who converted to Christianity, women broke through the barriers of the roles assigned to them, only then does the micro-history of the female mission co-workers become evident. Details and images beyond this can only be inferred indirectly. Although one can assume that apart from those Indian women whose names are known others worked in the mission, their biographies cannot be assembled like the missing pieces of a ceramic jug, and these women will probably always remain hidden.

A decisive reason for this is the nature of the sources. Women are always the silent actors in the mission sources: they do not report on their own and reports about them are not central to the mission

[13] HB 79. Cont., 1130f.

[14] Kent, Eliza F., 2004, *Converting Women: Gender and Protestant Christianity in Colonial South India*, Oxford University Press, New York, Oxford.

documents. With very few exceptions there are no biographies of female South Indian co-workers as are sometimes found for male co-workers published on different occasions.[15] The noticeable gaps in the sources of the Tranquebar Mission with regard to the situation of women are replicated in the reports of subsequent mission societies. Although reports about and by women are no longer a rarity in the Mission reports of the nineteenth century, it is the women missionaries and the wives who now get a voice in keeping with their new importance, not the local female mission co-workers. The mission reports now contain special pages for women and children. The texts by women in the nineteenth century were confined to particular genres; they were often texts for children and were directed at the young generation in Europe, or they were reports about institutions for girls within the Mission. These were texts by European women about women and children in India for women and children in Europe, which were used in the form of small propaganda booklets for the work in Europe. They reflect the change in the position of women in European society, which in turn influenced their view of women outside Europe.[16]

THE POSITION OF WOMEN IN MISSION REGIONS

If one proceeds from Ziegenbalg's perception of South Indian women in 1709, the latter were clearly visible in their daily routine with '[...] spinning wool, pounding rice, selling milk and butter, making pancakes, fetching water, working in other's houses, cooking, selling

[15] This also applies to the European missionary wives. Sometimes we learn where she comes from, but we seldom have a biography, let alone information about her education or her interests. Even in the case of Susanna König who was born on 27 April 1757 in Vepery/Madras and who married the missionary Johann Friedrich König in 1773, the reader is not told much about the young woman. After the death of her mother she was brought up by an aunt in Nagapattinam and died while giving birth to her first child. NHB 20. St., 957f.

[16] This is emphasized in: Jones, Adam, 1989, 'Schwarze Frauen, weiße Beobachter. Die Frauen der Goldküste in den Augen der europäischen Männer, 1600–1900', in Hans-Joachim König (et al.) (eds.), *Der europäische Beobachter außereuropäischer Kulturen. Zur Problematik der Wirklichkeitswahrnehmung*, 153–68, Duncker & Humblot, Berlin (=Zeitschrift für Historische Forschung, Supplement 7).

fish etc.'[17] The missionary also considered it important to mention the fact that the women, with the exception of the *devadāsi*, did not know how to read and write.[18] In the *Malabarische Korrespondenz* that the German missionaries Ziegenbalg and Gründler carried out with Tamilians the missionaries asked how the association between men and women was regulated in daily life. They learned why women should not eat with their husbands,[19] how the daughters were included in the rules of inheritance and to what extent the rules were unfavourable to them. Unlike the sons, the daughters did not have a claim to inheritance unless this was expressly decided and settled during the parent's lifetime. After the death of the parents unmarried daughters were dependent on the will of their brothers, and the latter were responsible for the upkeep of their sisters till they got married. Even the mothers did not get a share of the inheritance, but had to be looked after by the sons, in whose households they were generally made to work.[20]

The twenty-third letter of the *Malabarische Korrespondenz* is devoted to the educational and professional development of Tamil girls: the daughters were brought up at home till the age of five. In well-to-do families girls subsequently learned housework; daughters of poor families were sent out to work. At the age of seven daughters of wealthy families learned how to cook, weave mats and spin wool; by the time they were nine or ten years old they were of marriageable age and, from then on, they were not allowed to go out of the house unaccompanied. After marriage they went to their husband's house and did the housework there. Only daughters of princes and kings learned how to read and write. In poor families women had to pound rice and sell it to contribute to the family income.[21]

Many missionaries were aware of the difficult situation of South Indian women. The situation of widows was particularly precarious since they often did not get sufficient care from the family after the husband's death. This was also true for the Christian congregations.

[17] HB 3. Cont., 124.
[18] HB 3. Cont., 128.
[19] HB 7. Cont., 419, 14th letter of the *Malabarische Korrespondenz*.
[20] HB 7. Cont., 440f., 21st letter of the *Malabarische Korrespondenz*.
[21] HB 7. Cont., 447f., 23rd letter of the *Malabarische Korrespondenz*.

Through the practice of child marriage many young women were widowed at an early age and, generally, they were not married off again. In 1801 Immanuel Gottfried Holzberg presented his observations on the situation of widows among South Indian Christians: 'Soon after I arrived here I especially noticed the large number of widows in our congregation. Their numbers are so large because the children are married off early and because there is a lack of young men and widowers who could marry a widow.'[22] In order to reduce the problems of these women the missionary started a special fund for widows in Thanjavur. In 1820 Bernhard Schmid compared the situation of Indian women with the life of slaves.

> The Indian woman is, in the truest sense of the word, her husband's slave and is treated with the most humiliating distrust. She is not allowed to eat with him, but has to wait on her husband and children during meals. She is not allowed to sit down in her husband's presence without his permission, and when they go out together she has to walk a few steps behind him, generally a little to the side. She is not supposed to talk to any other man, and if she were to do so she would expose herself to the danger of punishment in the form of a beating. However, even the wives of Christians are normally not excluded from this slavery.[23]

THE WIVES OF MISSIONARIES

In its original stated intention the Christian mission directed its work at all sections of society independent of social hierarchy, religion and gender. Since the contemporary religious understanding in Europe believed that the propagation of the gospel and all the work relating to this was a job for men, the participation of women in the work of conversion was initially not provided for in the Tranquebar Mission. However, intercultural communication in the daily work of the Mission could not be limited to the world of men. Women, in fact, constituted a specially important target group, since it was assumed that they, as (Christian) mothers, would exert a great deal

[22] NHB 59. St., 1000f., (translated from German).
[23] NHB 72. St., 1205f., (translated from German).

of influence on the beliefs of future generations and that they thus had a decisive role to play as disseminators.

Even in the eyes of the early promoters of Protestant mission the conversion of non-Christian people was a job for men. On various occasions the mission directors found it difficult to reconcile themselves to sending out married missionaries or looking for brides for those in the field. This was not only on account of the dangers and hardships, or the costs, of the long voyage, but mainly because of the fear that missionary work would suffer if the missionaries were involved with their families.[24] The sensitive topic of marriage always brought the gender question to the attention of the mission directors. For a long time Europe subscribed to the view that wives would hamper the work of the missionaries rather than be of help to them. These perceived problems were then compounded by financial considerations and reservations about the ability of European women to endure the hardships of the voyage and the Indian climate to which they were not accustomed. Therefore, the institutions supporting the mission did not promote the marriage intentions of missionaries, but they also did not prevent them from getting married if they so wished.

The first missionaries of the Tranquebar Mission went out as young, unmarried men. After it became clear that they were not likely to return to Europe, Bartholomäus Ziegenbalg, Johann Ernst Gründler and Heinrich Plütschau decided in 1709 to look for brides at home who would be willing to share a life in the mission. How delicate this topic was at that time is evidenced by the fact that Ziegenbalg only talked about it in a letter to the director of the Friedrich-Werder High School in Berlin, Joachim Lange, and this letter was not published in the mission reports.[25] Ziegenbalg emphasized that wives were not only important for carrying out household duties and looking after the missionaries, but that the missionaries themselves would have a better reputation among the

[24] Witt, Ulrike, 1996, *Bekehrung, Bildung und Biographie: Frauen im Umkreis des Halleschen Pietismus*, Verlag der Franckeschen Stiftungen Halle im Max Niemeyer Verlag, Tübingen (=Hallesche Forschungen 2).

[25] AB 122, Ziegenbalg's letter of 7 October 1709 states: 'Therefore, I am now handing you the commission of this important matter that I can entrust to no one else in Germany other than my dearly loved friend.' (translated from German).

local population, especially among the Indian women, if they were married.[26] Ziegenbalg first proposed marriage to Juliane Pönicke from Lauchstädt.[27] When this alliance did not materialize he tried, during his trip to Europe in 1714/15, to get permission from the Salzmanns in Merseburg—whose children he had taught before leaving Europe in 1705—to marry their daughter Maria Dorothea (born 1693).

Since the search for a suitable wife in Europe not only involved greater financial expense and organization, but could also lead to unforeseen risks and unpleasant surprises, the missionaries tried to find wives among the Europeans living in the Danish colony in Tranquebar. On 21 December 1728 Christoph Theodosius Walther married Anna Christina Brochmann (1713–35), the daughter of the Privy Councillor in Tranquebar.[28] Samuel Gottlieb Richtsteig was married to the daughter-in-law of First-Lieutenant Matthias Luder (1679–1732) who was stationed in Tranquebar.[29] The practice that was established in the nineteenth century of an organized search and a sending out of mission brides on behalf of and according to the wishes of the missionaries in the field[30] was not common in the Tranquebar Mission except in some cases. Thus, the teacher in the mission school in Tranquebar, Wilhelm David Becker (1744–1817), asked the mission doctor, Johann David Martini (in mission service from 1777 till 1791), who went to Europe in 1784 for reasons of health and got married there, to bring a wife for him too.[31]

Since, as a rule, the missionaries of the Tranquebar Mission did not return to Europe, widespread branches of missionary families arose in India over the generations. Children of missionaries, born and brought up in India, possessed all the qualities that predestined them for the Mission: they knew the language of the country as well as European languages, they were accustomed to the climate,

[26] AB 123, Ziegenbalg's letter to J. Lange, 7 October 1709.

[27] AB 125–30, letter from Ziegenbalg to Juliane Pönicke, 7 October 1709.

[28] The couple had four sons and a daughter. All the children and his wife died before Walther's return to Europe in 1741.

[29] HB 38. Cont., 213f.

[30] Konrad, *Missionsbräute*.

[31] NHB 30. St., 707. RA Miskolark 9g, *Pro Memoria* from Ch. S. John, Tranquebar, 12 February 1784.

familiar with the customs and usages of the country and were, at the same time, trained in European modes of conduct. Newly arrived missionaries often married children of missionaries who had been living in India for a long time. Christian Wilhelm Gericke, who arrived in India in 1767, was married to a daughter of Georg Heinrich Conrad Hüttemann. In 1773, after having been in India for five years, Johann Friedrich König married a daughter of Johann Christian Breithaupt who had been in India since 1747. Breithaupt's daughter was born in 1757 in Vepery/Madras, and died as König's wife in 1777 while giving birth to her first child.[32]

Beginning with the second generation the children of missionaries often married among themselves. In 1811 one of the sons of Johann Balthasar Kohlhoff, Johann Caspar Kohlhoff, married Christina Magdalena Horst (born 1793), a daughter of Christoph Heinrich Horst. The missionaries Schnarre (died 1820) and Daniel Schreyvogel were related by marriage. It was not unusual for the widows of missionaries to marry another German missionary after their husband's death. In 1747, after a 17-year stay in Tranquebar, Daniel Zeglin married the widow of Gottfried Wilhelm Obuch who had been in Tranquebar since 1737 and had died in 1745. In 1736 Christian Friedrich Pressier, who had been in India since 1725, married the widow of the missionary Samuel Gottlieb Richtsteig, who had come to India in 1730 and had died in 1735.

Relationships between German missionaries and Indian women were considered to be improper and harmful to the reputation of the Mission. The few known examples of affairs between Europeans and Indians in the missionary sphere ended either with the missionary's return to Europe or, at the very least, with an official prohibition of the relationship and a refusal to marry the couple. Polycarp Jordan left India in 1714 after his intention to marry an Indian woman met with stiff resistance and a complete lack of understanding not only on the part of the mission directors in Europe but also on the part of his colleagues in India.[33] Later, Nicolaus Dal also found himself

[32] NHB 20. St., 957f.

[33] The published mission reports do not contain any reference to Jordan's marriage plans. However, early on Ziegenbalg pointed out that it was possible that Jordan intended to return to Europe. Cf. RA AsK 1397, 308, quoted from Nørgaard, *Mission und Obrigkeit*, 176, footnote 145.

in conflict with the mission directors when he wanted to marry an Indian woman.[34]

Towards the end of the eighteenth century it was no longer unusual for a missionary to set out from Europe with his wife. In his Memo for New Missionaries of 1784 Christoph Samuel John had made an impassioned plea for the advantages of such a practice:

> In this context I have to mention an important point, which I would have preferred to ignore had it not had serious consequences in the future for my missionaries. A future candidate would be well advised to choose a pious, skilled and social helper before he left Europe and bring her with him. Here, in this country, he would probably have to search long for such a person and might never find one like that if he decided to marry. I am aware of the objections that could be raised against such an early marriage, for example, that it is unsuitable, that it increases the costs for the voyage, interferes with the required focus of attention to learning the language in the beginning etc. However, the points in favour outweigh these objections. Those who know how children are usually brought up here will not expect much good from those that are born here. To marry a woman born in Europe is, however, a rare case here.[35]

According to this the wife was supposed to be 'a pious, skilled and social helper' of the missionary; she was meant to support him in his work and not take on independent duties. Whereas in the early years of the mission it was inconceivable to set out from Europe with a wife, this practice established itself in the last quarter of the eighteenth century. The mission doctor, Johann Gerhard König (1728–85) travelled to India with his wife, but she did not survive the hardships of the voyage.[36] The missionary Georg Gottlieb Bärenbruck (died 1833) spent a few months in England with his wife Anna Behrens learning English before they both set out for India in 1817. On the voyage to Madras his wife gave birth to a child who, however, died

[34] AFSt/M 2 G 6 : 1, letter from Benjamin Schultze to Gotthilf August Francke, 23 September 1727; cf. also Nørgaard, *Mission und Obrigkeit*, 176, footnote 145.

[35] RA Miskolark 9g, *Pro Memoria* for new missionaries from Ch. S. John and [J.P. Rottler], Tranquebar, 20 January 1784, (translated from German).

[36] HB 103. Cont., Vorrede, (190); 108. Cont., 1761f.; NHB 13. St., appendix, 107; 18. St., 674; 32. St., 886; 43. St., 674.

after a few hours.[37] In 1797 Immanuel Gottfried Holzberg also set out for India with his pregnant wife. His daughter was born on the ship.[38]

The European missionary wives were seldom given independent official duties in the mission since the care of their homes and families left them very little scope to also be active in the public domain. Their role was to be patient and self-sacrificing companions to their husbands. However, the families of the missionaries did not live in partitioned-off spheres of retreat like European bourgeois families generally did.[39] Besides the actual family members the families of missionaries temporarily housed newly-arrived missionaries and Indian children who received a special education. In addition, the work of administration and correspondence was carried out in the missionary's house and family members were involved in the work. Missionary wives were thus also members of the mission in a special way. Generally, the mission sources hardly contain any references to the familial circumstances of the missionaries, which often only became evident on the death of a missionary or of a family member.

There was a tacit agreement about the duties of missionary wives, which were essentially similar to the duties of Lutheran women of the lesser nobility and of the rising bourgeoisie in Europe.[40] While they had freedom in running the household and supported their husbands to the extent that they looked after other children placed in their families, only very few appeared in the public domain. The missionary wives of the eighteenth century were responsible for the household, for nursing the family in sickness and for the care of the children (their own and the other children who lived with them temporarily). It was very rare for the wives to work as teachers in one

[37] NHB 68. St., 794; 72. St., 1157f.

[38] NHB 49. St., 461.

[39] Described thus in an analysis of the affluent bourgeoisie in Basle in the eighteenth century. Cf. Trefzer, Rudolf, 1989, *Die Konstruktion des bürgerlichen Menschen. Aufklärungspädagogik und Erziehung im ausgehenden 18. Jahrhundert am Beispiel der Stadt Basel*, Chronos Verlag, Zürich, 44f.

[40] Hufschmidt, Anke, 2001, *Adlige Frauen im Weserraum zwischen 1570 und 1700: Status-Rollen-Lebenspraxis*, Aschendorff, Münster (= Veröffentlichungen der historischen Kommission für Westfalen, 12 A: Geschichtliche Arbeiten zur westfälischen Landesforschung, Vol. 15).

of the mission schools or, for example, as catechists among Indian women and girls. The wives, who generally came from bourgeois families and were educated, helped their husbands in dealing with administrative matters or with the correspondence in different languages. Bartholomäus Ziegenbalg, for instance, wanted his wife to learn French and Tamil in order to be able to help him with some of his extensive correspondence.[41]

Given these duties of the missionary wives John regretted the unmarried status of many missionaries. While missionary families could take in local children and thus promote the interests of the mission, it would be inappropriate for an unmarried man to do so. In 1779 when John began his schooling experiment for European children, he asked the supporting institutions in Europe to send him a new missionary, as far as possible a married one, so that his wife 'could help mine in our vast household and also in teaching the girls womanly skills.' He also asked for a European maid who would be willing to stay in India for three or four years.[42] John said that Johann Peter Rottler would also have taken in local children 'if he could have found a suitable wife here.'[43] John, therefore, strongly welcomed the fact that the doctor, Martin, was coming to India with a wife and was also bringing a bride for the teacher, Becker, who was working with John in his house.[44]

During their stay India very few of the missionary wives worked independently of their husbands in one of the mission institutions. John, who was very interested in developing the mission educational system and published works on this, pointed out in his most important treatise 'On Indian Civilization' that his wife shared this interest, but he did not elucidate further.[45] We only know that there were always several Tamil or Indo-European children being brought up in John's family. For some time his wife, Christina Sofia John, looked after seven children at home in addition to her own children and 'for the most part' she took care of the 'upbringing at home'.[46]

[41] AB 453, Ziegenbalg to Mr Wendt in Copenhagen, 20 August 1716.
[42] NHB 28. St., 388.
[43] RA Miskolark 9g, *Pro memoria* from Ch. S. John, Tranquebar, 12 February 1784.
[44] Ibid.
[45] John, *On Indian Civilization*, 5.
[46] NHB 28. St., 377.

Marianne Pohle was a remarkable exception who—however, only when she was widowed—helped in running the Female Asylum set up by the English East India Company in Madras. After the death of her husband, Christian Pohle, she first took over his work in the Tiruchirappalli congregation.[47] In December 1819 she vacated the family home for her husband's successor, David Rosen (1791–1857),[48] and went to Madras with her children—the youngest was born in 1811—where she supervised the Female Asylum along with Rottler who worked there as secretary and later as chaplain.[49] Johann Zacharias Kiernander's second wife contributed in a different way to the development of the mission in Calcutta. With the money that Kiernander inherited from her he built a church, a school and a mission house.[50]

The wives of missionaries began to play a more perceptible and socially recognized role as (mission) assistants to their husbands with independent responsibilities only at the beginning of the nineteenth century when the British East India Company became involved in the educational sector, which also meant the education of girls. While the East India Company primarily concentrated on the education and upbringing of European or Indo-European orphans and needy children, the wives of missionaries worked among Tamil girls in the mission schools. Thus, for example, the wife of the Leipzig missionary Carl Ochs, who worked in India from 1842 till 1859, was active in the orphan school for girls in Mayavaram. The wife of Heinrich Cordes (1813–92), the first missionary of the Leipzig mission, worked in the girls' school in Tranquebar. The wife of the Leipzig missionary Karl Friedrich Kremmer (1817–87) worked in the girls' school in Madras.[51] When India was opened up for English

[47] NHB 68. St., 778, communication from J.P. Rottler, 8 May 1818.

[48] NHB 71. St., 1164.

[49] NHB 71. St., 1161, Vepery, 1 August 1822, letter from E.A.G. Falcke to the editor G. Ch. Knapp. Cf. also Rottler's letter of 7 August 1822, NHB 71. St., 1102.

[50] NHB, Vol. 2, Vorrede VI. Cf. also Burkhardt, Gustav Emil, 1879, *Die evangelische Mission in Vorder-Indien*, Velhagen & Klasing, Bielefeld [et al.], (= G.E. Burkhardts Kleine Missions-Bibliothek von Reinhold Grundemann 3), 68f; Sandegren, Herman, 1928, *Johann Zacharias Kiernander—The First Swedish Missionary in India*, (translated from the Swedish original (1924) by E. Wimmercranz), National Missionary Society Press, Madras.

[51] Fleisch, *Hundert Jahre lutherischer Mission*, 79.

missions in 1813, missionary societies such as the CMS sent their own women delegates to India. The Berlin-educated Deocar Schmid, whose brother Ludwig Bernhard Ehrengott Schmid was working in Madras, ran the orphan-house for girls in Calcutta together with his wife. A Miss Cooke of the CMS was responsible for improving the conditions of teaching for girls and also had to supervise the high school for girls in Calcutta.[52]

WOMEN AS CO-WORKERS IN THE TRANQUEBAR MISSION

The presence of European women in the mission stations, or in other words, the presence of the wives of the missionaries, constituted an important moral pre-condition for the appointment of female local co-workers. Already in 1709 Bartholomäus Ziegenbalg mentioned this point as a justification for his own search for a wife: '… because we don't have wives we cannot employ women for them [the school children, H.L.], since the presence of so many men in the house could cause Satan to provoke a woman to be unchastely, which would make the enemy cheer.'[53]

From the point of view of mission strategy public conversations on the streets, in the fields and in public squares as well as sermons in the church were not enough to ensure the lasting success of the work of conversion. At least two other spheres therefore played a decisive role in the Tranquebar Mission. Firstly, the educational system became an important element of missionary work. The idea was to lay a stable foundation for a steady increase in the number of conversions through the work with children and young people. Secondly, it was considered necessary to create a basis of trust among the women in the region, since wives and mothers could influence not only an individual's decision for or against conversion, but also the general disposition towards the European missionaries. Male European missionaries were not suited for this task, and their European wives did not have enough access to the world of Tamil women.

[52] NHB 72. St., 1184f.

[53] AB 122, Ziegenbalg's letter to J. Lange, 7 October 1709, (translated from German).

Already when the first Tamil girls' school was opened in 1707 in Tranquebar it was evident that it would be necessary to involve local female co-workers in the work of the mission. Besides schoolmistresses and wardens for the girls, who then became part of the personnel in the schools, there was a constant need for female teachers in subjects that were only taught to girls such as housekeeping, cooking or tailoring. Throughout the eighteenth century the Tranquebar Mission did not envisage using the wives of missionaries for the work among women in South India. Rather, they specially selected and trained Indian women, who were indispensable in their function as a bridge between the European mission and the women and girls in the mission region. The Indian women worked in the housekeeping sector of the Mission, in the supervision of children as well as in actual missionary service. In the broad spectrum of the work of the Mission, however, women only occupied positions in the lower functions. Therefore, it seems almost revolutionary that at least two Indian women became catechists in the Tranquebar Mission.[54] For mothers who sent their daughters to mission schools, or for women who occupied a post in the Mission, this involved a departure from traditional bonds and existing moral norms. This sometimes resulted in a break with the family, since the women no longer fulfilled societal expectations.

It was also an advantage to have women working for the Mission, since they could look after the women members of the local Christian congregations. Apart from the fact that married women were not allowed to talk to other men and, for this reason alone, women employees represented more easily approachable partners for communication, women of a village could enter the house of a female co-worker or allow her into their houses. This was either not possible in the case of male co-workers, or only to a very limited extent.

> Since there was a large number of unmarried females or widows in the congregation who needed both schooling and supervision, and since the catechists cannot manage everything due to the growth of our work, we decided to appoint a sensible older woman with a

[54] The names of the two catechists are Maria and Regina. Both worked in the 1770s and 1780s in Tranquebar, NHB 51. St., 231.

> good character from the congregation as a schoolmistress. It is her job to teach especially the younger females—who include the as yet unmarried girls—to repeat the sermons with them, to lead them in prayer and to pay heed to their conduct. Sometimes, when a young married couple converts to Christianity, the catechists hesitate to go to their homes too often. In such cases a woman is useful and does not give offense. The monthly salary of this schoolmistress amounts to one Reichstaler.[55]

The inclusion of South Indian female co-workers in the work of the Mission thus arose from the requirements of mission strategy rather than from the desire of the missionaries to contribute to the emancipation of Indian women. These women were appointed as teachers, as 'Bible women' or 'prayer leaders' in places where they could work—in contrast to their male colleagues—without going against traditional moral and religious norms. Among the roughly 300 local employees of the Tranquebar Mission recorded by name there are about 25 women who worked officially as prayer leaders, assistants, teachers or catechists on behalf of the Mission. In addition, there were the wives of the male employees whose names do not always appear in the reports. Cooks, water-carriers, washerwomen, nurses and women in other similar functions are not counted among these.

Most of the Tamil women employees of the Mission were so-called prayer leaders or Bible women. Their duties included looking after the Christian women in the villages assigned to them, taking care of sick Christians, organizing a visit by the doctor, wherever necessary, or preparing the dying for death and calling a missionary or an Indian pastor at the required time. Bible women held regular Bible hours, which were attended by the Christian women of the area and which took place in a special room in the house of the prayer leader. She read from the Bible or went through the contents of sermons preached by the missionaries or the Indian pastors. These women also used these regular gatherings to narrate their difficulties and their worries to the representative of the Mission in the hope that these would be communicated to the European missionaries.

[55] HB 36. Cont., 1249, diary of the missionaries in Tranquebar, 5 October 1732., (translated from German). See also 39. Cont., 332, diary of the missionaries in Tranquebar, 3 May 1734.

Thus it is reported about the prayer leader Tawasai (in mission service from about 1740 till 1762) that she was worshipped and respected 'like a mother' in the congregation.[56] Tawasai stood not only by the women, but also by the male members of the congregation during illness and in their dying hours.[57] In 1761 the prayer leader Sebathal carried a sick and weak epileptic woman on her back to the missionaries in Tranquebar since this woman who had attended her Bible classes now wanted to be baptized.[58] Dewai, also a prayer leader, took in needy women temporarily in her house in Pudupaleiam and saw to their material and spiritual care.[59] If women were involved in legal disputes, women employees of the Mission occasionally proved to be their spokespersons. In 1783 an unnamed female catechist mediated between the mission and a European woman whose Christian slave, a Siamese by birth, had entered into a relationship with a Roman Catholic Tamilian, had left her job and was now meant to be severely punished.[60]

Women were indispensable for the work of the Mission primarily in the sphere of education. Following the model of the schools in the Halle Orphan House the missionaries established special schools or classes for girls in Tranquebar and in other mission stations. Besides the usual subjects like reading, writing and arithmetic the girls were taught household management and local crafts such as spinning, knitting and mat weaving. If possible, the girls remained in the schools till they were married and were then handed over into the care of their husband's family. Most of the local women who were employed by the Tranquebar Mission and whose life and work can be, at least partially, reconstructed, came from the girls' schools. Since the opening of the first girls' school in 1707 the need for South Indian women who would work as supervising tutors and teachers grew steadily. The history of female co-workers in these establishments demonstrates the efforts made by the missionaries for continuity in the education of girls and shows that the women were not selected

[56] HB 98. Cont., 210.
[57] HB 65. Cont., 879.
[58] HB 95. Cont., 1158.
[59] NHB 46. St., 933, A.F. Cämmerer to J.L. Schulze, 10 February 1794.
[60] NHB 30. St., 657f.

randomly, but that their participation in the work of the mission was systematically promoted and directed. By selecting suitable girls and preparing them for a job in the mission a new profession was created, which, for the first time, gave even women a chance to teach and bring up children outside the family.

Wherever the infrastructure was available the girls' school was separated from the boys' school. Boys and girls also ate separately, and a teacher supervised the girls at mealtimes. Since, for example in Tranquebar, some of the children coming from other places also spent the nights in the mission station, women employees were required to supervise the children day and night.[61] Widows who had no family responsibilities left and who could read and write appeared to be most suitable for this work. For these women, who were often still very young and who sometimes worked for decades in the Mission, the work in the mission also meant social security and stability.

Occasionally, even married women, whose husbands also worked for the Mission, worked for many years in the schools of the Mission. In the case of the teacher Ambei the entire family worked in the educational branch of the Mission. Ambei was a teacher in the Tamil girls' school in Tranquebar for more than 30 years; her husband Joseph was a doorman in one of the schools in Tranquebar, and their son Eliser, having been educated in the mission school, worked as a teacher in the Tamil school in Tranquebar.[62] In order to ensure the uninterrupted care of the girls Ambei was told to train her successor Mariamuttu, who also helped her.[63]

Generally, the missionaries devoted a lot of time and attention to selecting and preparing new teachers and supervising tutors. As with the boys they also made the older girls teach. One of the first pupils of the girls' school in Tranquebar was Maria. Born probably before 1705, she was baptized on 12 August 1708 and then put in the girls' school. From 1716 onwards, as the oldest girl, 'the big Maria' taught in the Tamil girls' school, initially under the supervision of the warden Tatschi who, besides the school, also looked after the women

[61] In the initial years an Indian widow carried out all these duties. HB 6. Cont., 241.
[62] NHB 18. ST., 679; 50. St., 139.
[63] NHB 40. St., 372.

and children of the Tamil congregation in Tranquebar. Later, Maria herself was officially made a schoolmistress.[64]

In 1785 the missionaries mentioned the names of three girls in the girls' school in Tranquebar who stood out because of their conduct and their knowledge. Mariamuttu, 19 years old at that point of time, came from a *śūdra* caste in Sandirapadi (Chandrapati). In 1783 she had lost her mother who had also been educated in the mission school.[65] Even Annamei, a 15–year-old orphan from a *paṟaiyār* family in Kumbakonam, was apparently a remarkably good pupil.[66] The family of the Christian woman Jesadial from Terehendur, also a *paṟaiyār*, had settled down in the territory of the Danish trading company after the mother's death and had sent the daughter to the mission school to be educated.[67] After some time all the girls were mentioned in the reports as co-workers of the Mission. Mariamuttu became Ambei's successor,[68] Annamei was Schawriammal's successor, probably as a prayer leader,[69] and Jesadial became a teacher in the Tranquebar girls' school.[70]

The female teachers employed in the Mission were required to know more than just to read and write. While there were often common classes for boys and girls in some subjects such as Bible history, which was taught by a male teacher, and that which had been learned was only repeated in separate classes by a male or a female teacher respectively, girls got separate training in some vocational subjects such as craft. Catharina, who had been married in July 1712 by the missionary Heinrich Plütschau, became a widow in September of the same year, worked as a supervisor and seamstress with the 'Portuguese' girls. From October 1724 onwards she was also the seamstress in the 'Malabarian' girls' school.[71]

[64] HB 6. Cont., 331; 26. Cont., 82; AB 263; for Tatschi (Tutschi) see also: Staatsbibliothek Preußischer Kulturbesitz Berlin, papers of August Hermann Francke K 33, fascicle B (H. Plütschau).

[65] NHB 31. St., 746f.

[66] NHB 31. St., 747f.

[67] NHB 31. St., 749.

[68] NHB 32. St., 890.

[69] NHB 46. St., 927, 50. St., 130.

[70] NHB 32. St., 890.

[71] AB 263, 267; HB 6. Cont., 331; 20. Cont., 408.

Only in a few instances, and that too in the later years of the Mission, were women appointed as catechists. Around 1780 two female catechists were working in the 'Portuguese' congregation in Tranquebar. Their duties involved visiting and taking care of the women of the congregation who were mainly domestic servants of Europeans, or female members of the Danish community.[72] One of these two catechists, Maria Cramer (died before 1784), had a son who first worked as a 'junior schoolmaster' and then as a schoolmaster after the 'Portuguese' schoolmaster had been dismissed for drunkenness.[73] In 1796 the two female catechists Maria and Regina worked in Tranquebar under Christoph Samuel John's direction.[74]

As with the male co-workers the missionaries took the social and religious specificities as well as the professional profile and the caste structure of the place and the concerned Christian congregation into account while appointing a female employee. The *paṟaiyār* woman Sebathal (died 1770) was a prayer leader in the village Itschiladi (Iccilati), which was inhabited mainly by *paṟaiyār*.[75] After her death in 1771 Rebeccal became her successor in the post.[76] In the 1770s Maria was prayer leader in the 'Portuguese' congregation in Tranquebar.[77] In the 1780s Schinna Schawriammal was the '*paṟaiyār*-assistant', or the 'first assistant' in Tranquebar. Around 1773, after her husband's death, she had been appointed as a prayer leader for the 'untouchables' in the city congregation and had worked as a cook before that. Her sons Schawrimuttu and Salomo attended the mission school and later also worked for the mission. Schinna Schawriammal worked in Tranquebar till her death in 1794.[78] At the same time Dewai also worked in the Tranquebar city congregation as the '*śūdra*-assistant' or the 'second-assistant' and prayer leader.[79]

[72] NHB 25. St., 7, Missionaries to the Learned Society of Batavia, Tranquebar, 14 October 1780.

[73] NHB 31. St., 744.

[74] NHB 51. St., 231.

[75] NHB 5. St., 623; 6. St., 703, 734, 738, 740, 760.

[76] NHB 7. St., 881.

[77] NHB 18. St., 679.

[78] NHB 12. St., 1577; 39. St., 233; 42. St., 507f.; 45. St., 838, 840; 46. St., 915.

[79] NHB 37. St., 103; 42. St., 479.

Some of the South Indian women worked independently within precisely defined parameters. Some were placed as assistants under one of the male mission co-workers, like Rahel who worked as an assistant and prayer leader in Kawastalam with Dewasagajam.[80] Muttunaiken (died around 1757), an assistant in the Tranquebar city congregation, had the help of a woman (prayer leader) to look after the women of the congregation.[81] Many women helped their husbands, who were employed by the Mission, even if they had not been directly instructed to do so. They accompanied their husbands on their journeys not, however, in the role of caring wives who had to cook or manage the housework. The wives worked alongside their husbands among the women of the places under their care. Some couples were employed together by the Mission; with other couples only the husband was officially in the employ of the Mission.

Josua, an assistant in the Mahadevpattanam district, and his wife Rahel, a schoolmistress, worked together since the 1730s. Josua was one of the few Indian co-workers who also had knowledge of medicine. His wife Rahel taught eight Hindu children. The couple, which belonged to a *śūdra*-caste, lived in Kuppachchikkottai (Kuppatschi-Kodtei). After Josua's death in 1763 Rahel worked for a few months with Dewanesen, the *śūdra*-catechist from Tiruchirappalli.[82] In the 1770s Maria worked in the girls' school in Tranquebar. Her husband Isaac, assistant in the 'Portuguese' congregation in Tranquebar, died in 1776. Rahel, the wife of the catechist Ignasi in Kawastalam, was the prayer leader in Rarasalam/Kawastalam till the 1770s.[83] After her husband's death (1770) she became a schoolteacher in Rarasalam; in 1784 she became the new schoolmistress of the girls' school in Tranquebar where she had great success with the children till her death in 1801.[84]

However, this joint missionary work of a Tamil couple over many years was an exception. Girls, who were taken into the service of the mission as young unmarried girls who were the older schoolgirls,

[80] NHB 39. St., 244.

[81] HB 58. Cont., 1517, Tranquebar 1744.

[82] HB 91. Cont., 788.

[83] NHB 59. St., V, 995.

[84] NHB 5. St., 612; 15. St., 276; 18. St., 679; 21. St., 1064; 32. St., 890; 38. St., 202; 46. St., 874.

for example, or just after completing their school education, were normally released from these functions when they got married, so that they could devote themselves entirely to their new duties in their young families. The further course of their lives depended not only on their husband's position, but also on the number of children, their health and on the expectations of their parents and in-laws. In this context, the caste affiliation was also decisive. While daughters of the higher castes were shielded from the outside world after the onset of menstruation, could not go out unaccompanied, and had to manage the household even after marriage, these norms were not applied strictly to women from *Dalit* families.[85]

Although joint missionary work by a couple was existent in some cases, a woman was usually officially taken into the service of the mission after her husband's death. Freed of her marital duties she could, if the children were grown up, use all the knowledge and experience she had gained in an area of her choice without deferring to a husband, children or family.[86] On the one hand, the status of a widow offered the necessary independence and the possibility of self-realization in whatever form it took. On the other hand, the lack of social security and of the necessities of life forced the women to look for employment. The widows of South Indian mission employees, who were mostly literate and well versed in Christian teachings, were welcome workers for the Mission. Among the female mission co-workers were widows who continued the work done by their husbands after the latter's death (generally as assistants), or were employed as prayer leaders in the place where their husbands had worked. Upon being widowed Schinna Schawriammal, for instance, who had been a cook till her husband's death in 1773, became a prayer leader of the *paṟaiyār* congregation in Tranquebar, a post she held till her death in 1794.[87]

[85] For the agency of women belonging to different social groups in colonial India see the collection of papers in: Ghosh, Anindita (ed.), 2008, *Behind the Veil. Resistance, Women and the Everyday in Colonial South Asia,* Palgrave Macmillan, England, New York.

[86] Even under European conditions widowhood was often the only chance for a woman to embark upon an independent intellectual or artistic path. As long as she was married she was bound to the family. Writing and publishing was, in any case, frowned upon. Cf. Stedman, *Englische Frauen der Frühen Neuzeit.*

[87] NHB 12. St., 1577; 39. St., 233; 42. St., 507f.; 45. St., 838, 840; 46. St., 915.

The female co-workers of the Mission were included in the mission social system. This meant being cared for when they were ill, but widowed women were also given support. When Tawasi was ill for nearly two years after being bitten by a rat (1752–54), the missionaries organized regular care and visits.[88] Sebathal, who was ill before her death in 1770, also received regular visits from the missionaries or from other South Indian employees.[89] The wives who were not employed by the Mission and, therefore, not paid for their work, received widow's alms every month after the death of their husbands. These alms were given to the widows of all former members of the congregation, but the amount was higher for widows of mission employees. In 1734/35 between 104 and 123 widows received alms from the Mission.[90] Widows who could still work were employed by the Mission and paid for their work. In 1772, after her husband's death, Rajanayakkan's widow was appointed as a prayer leader in the villages that her husband had looked after.[91] The women's work was made easier by the fact that the people of the villages already knew them from the work they had done with their husbands. The women themselves were often highly qualified and most of them had been educated in a mission school, but had not earlier worked independently because of the children and the family. They had, however, gathered experience while working with their husbands. For women employed by the Mission who had small children there was some sort of childcare. Thus, the children of one of the schoolmistresses in Madras, Anna (11) and Christian (6), were looked after in the local mission school while their mother was working.[92]

Direct co-operation between South Indian and European women in the mission region can only be seen in isolated cases beginning from the end of the eighteenth century. Barring some exceptions male missionaries were the superiors of the female co-workers. The presence and the work of local women was noted with interest and appreciated in Europe, and female European sponsors sent special

[88] HB 77. Cont., 758; 78. Cont., 850; 82. Cont., 1433f.

[89] NHB 5. St., 623; 7. St., 734, 738, 740.

[90] HB 38. Cont., preface, § XXIII; 40. Cont., preface, § X; 42. Cont., preface, § II. Cf. also: HB 38. Cont., 249f.

[91] NHB 10. St., 1347f.

[92] HB 36. Cont., 1235, Madras 1732.

gifts expressly for one or the other female co-worker. Thus, in 1732 an announcement was published that European women, who were friends of the Mission, had made a donation especially for girls and orphans in Madras.[93] European women sometimes donated money expressly for Indian widows.[94]

RAHEL: THE TEACHER

The prayer leader and schoolmistress Rahel, wife of the catechist Ignasi, displayed, according to the missionaries, a special talent for educating and bringing up children. After her husband's death in 1770 Rahel worked for another 20 years as a teacher in Kawastalam and Rarasalam and was often held up as a model to her male colleagues for her good work.[95] Considering the paucity of sources in general and of reports about women in particular the following impressive obituary for the widely respected schoolteacher, quoted in its entirety, gains a special significance as a unique biographical testimony.

> Brief biography of Rahel
> Rahel was the widow of our former catechist Ignasi in Kawastalam, with whom she led a Christian married life. She had three children who she had raised to be god-fearing and who gave cause for hope in our mission school, but who left this world before her with the exception of a married daughter who now lives in Mysore.
>
> In her youth she established a sound basis for salutary knowledge and piety, which she continued to nurture even after marriage. She asked her husband to read with her regularly and to pray with her, while she also practiced on her own. She especially helped him in teaching the young. From her husband she learned many choice passages from texts of heathen writers, especially the poets, where polytheism is rejected and the worship of a single god is recommended along with a virtuous conduct pleasing to Him. Thus, she became better and better not only at exhorting Christians, but also at talking to the heathens openly and in a well-founded manner

[93] HB 36. Cont., 1233f.

[94] On 1 August 1794, 'Mrs D.M. in St. [donated] 3 St. for four widows', NHB 45. St., 851.

[95] Cf. the short biography in NHB 59. St., 995–98.

about the teachings of Christianity. In this way she gained a lot of love and respect, more so because she led a pious life among Christians and Hindus. This was enhanced by beautiful natural talents that allowed her to talk fluently about whatever she knew. She combined a pleasant and friendly manner with a seriousness and zeal that suited her well. One could clearly see that she did not want to show off her knowledge and talent, but that she spoke about the excellence and the power of the holy gospel of Christ from the depths of her heart, from firm conviction and from experience.

After the death of her husband she was appointed as a schoolteacher in Rarasalam and came into her element. She dealt with the children in a very motherly fashion, knew how to win their love and confidence, discovered their individual abilities, came down to the level of the more simple-minded, encouraged the dull children and those who often missed school with a few Tuttu or pennies—often from her own money—and made more progress with the children than any schoolmaster before her. She always brought most of the children to the gathering where their knowledge would be tested, while others made excuses to stay away. The children followed her gladly because they had no reason to be afraid of the examination. During divine service in church Rahel's children stood out from the others with their pleasing demeanour and good behaviour. They were clearly distinguishable from the others through their erect posture, through the sincere gaze directed at the teacher and through their ready answers to questions of catechism. This was also the case during examinations. The rough, fearful, impolite conduct and the indecent gestures that are common among children of this country, who normally tend the cattle, were completely absent in her children. She had accustomed them to outward decorum and moderation, but also to a pleasing candour and cheerfulness, which made the examinations particularly pleasant and facilitated the work. A rolling of the eyes and other facial gestures, which indicate a false or misunderstood worship, were not part of her behaviour and neither did she allow it in her children, since she had learned from her teachers that an honest Christian does not only lift his heart in cheer, but also his head and his eyes and looks around him to see how everything is imbued with the goodness of the Lord. How much, therefore, the children's knowledge increased under such a pious and talented teacher and how far they surpassed the others is easy to comprehend. We were often surprised by their answers to the given question and by the wealth of their knowledge of passages from the Bible and from the Book of Hymns. The moral sayings and prayers that they had memorized in an uncomplicated manner also gave us a great deal of pleasure.

Just as she was a true blessing for her children, she was also a shining light for the other schoolteachers and catechists. Very recently, while presenting their reports, they spoke of her with admiration and respect and first one, and then the other narrated a pleasant anecdote about her. When they came with her for the festival celebrations, she had to lead the evening and morning prayers and singing, for which she chose the most beautiful songs, most of which she knew by heart. Among others, the hymns: Jesus my delight, My God, I bring you my heart, Be cheerful my soul, Jesus my sure defense after the trials of the days, were her favourites. She had a good voice for singing, which is so rare among the betel-chewing Malabarians. One gladly let her say the common prayer, since she did this not only with the greatest eloquence, but also with the most fervour and in a manner that was astonishing and moving for the others. She was never obtrusive, but if she was given an opportunity for a pious conversation she took it with pleasure, but without arrogance or conceit, which made her all the more popular.

This was also the manner in which she talked to the heathens. When required she spoke with great vigour about God's glory, which He has revealed in heaven and on earth in his wonderful and manifold works and benefactions as well as in the true word; about the general depravity of humans and about the need and the existence of a saviour; about the splendour of his salutary church and his teachings, which ensure spiritual reformation and true bliss. She would soon attract a large audience who would wonder how this poor *paritschi* had so much wisdom and could even quote many passages from their own books. By listening to her several heathens were actually inspired and encouraged to turn to Christianity. They subsequently came for baptismal preparation, were baptized and joined the congregation.

She retained her cheerful and active nature till the end. Even when she was over 70 years old she still came to the ceremonial examination with her children, who always got the best reports. In the end she had a diarrhea common in this country, which gradually sapped her strength. When one of us travelled to Thanjavur for reasons of health in September last year and spent the night in a rest house not far from Tiruppalatturai, he felt so ill and weak that he hardly thought he would be able to preach to the Christians who

> he knew would be waiting for him at night. They came, and he was astonished to see our good, pious, but deathly sick Rahel arriving there, carried by some Christians. She had not wanted to stay back, but begged and importuned to be taken along to see her teacher and be exhorted by him once more. This moving sight cheered and invigorated the missionary so much that he almost forgot himself and spoke till fairly late in the night about Jesus's question: Would you all also want to go away, and Peter's reply: Lord, where should we go? You have words of eternal life. The missionary exhorted the Christians not to act like those fickle people who left when their expectations of getting as much bread from Jesus as they wanted were not fulfilled, but to follow the disciples who were content with his care and his honest advice, who experienced in themselves the effects of his teachings as words of eternal life, who knew that they could not hope to find a better person and stood by him faithfully and resolutely. When the missionary continued his journey to Thanjavur the next morning, he heard on his arrival that Rahel had also had herself carried to some relatives there. After he had rested, he visited her. She was very happy to see him and testified to her wish to be free of this world so that she could be with Christ. Mr Kohlhoff and his catechist visited her often, and on the day she died she received the Holy Sacrament from him very emotionally and with affirmations of her faith and her longing for Christ. She exhorted the catechists and Christians present at her deathbed to grow in their knowledge and love of the Saviour and to be faithful to him with whom they had such a good life. She prayed and sang along with the hymn: Jesus, my sure defense, and remained fully conscious till the last minutes. She did not display any fear of death and slipped into the blessed abode of peace serenely, happily and gently, leaving behind a new, agreeable demonstration of the truth: Blessed are the poor in spirit, blessed even in death, for the kingdom of heaven is theirs.[96]

In this document, Rahel's strength is initially associated with her husband's influence, but later there is unqualified recognition of her personal abilities, achievements and successes in missionary work. This synthesis clearly demonstrates the attitude of the missionaries. They were not just surprised at the results of her work, they were literally taken aback at the manner in which Rahel—as

[96] NHB 59. St., 995–98, (translated from German).

a matter of course and with a quiet insistence—made her way as a schoolmistress and educator. Besides qualities like piety, discipline, selflessness and obedience it was mainly her comprehensive education and her outstanding pedagogical abilities and rhetorical talent which, in the eyes of the missionaries, made her a model even for her male colleagues.

CLARINDA: THE CHRISTIAN BRAHMIN WOMAN

Among the Indian women who are associated with the history of the Tranquebar Mission, the biography of the Brahmin widow Clarinda always evokes interest among historians, lay Christians and writers.[97] The story of her life, which is full of myths and legends, is, till today, linked with the rise of the Christian community in the Tirunelveli district where a small stone church bears the name of the Brahmin woman of the eighteenth century.[98] The church that was consecrated by Christian Friedrich Schwartz in 1785 and was in Clarinda's care, was renovated in 1959 and newly consecrated by a descendant of the first Indian Protestant priest, Aaron.[99] Celebratory mass is held regularly in honour of the founder of the Lutheran congregation in Palayankottai/Tirunelveli.[100]

The region in which Clarinda worked was, till well into the eighteenth century, a part of the Hindu kingdom of Madurai, which was ruled by a *Nāyaka* dynasty after the collapse of the Vijaynagar Empire in the middle of the sixteenth century. This dynasty also began to crumble towards the end of the seventeenth century and was propped up with the support of the Marathas. In 1743, when the Marathas were driven out of large parts of South India by the Nizām-ul-mulk, the *Subahdar* of the Deccan, Tirunelveli nominally came under the rule of the Nawab of Arcot. Since the days of the Vijaynagar Empire, which encompassed large regions of South India from 1336 till 1565, actual power, however, had been wielded by

[97] See footnote 5 in this chapter.

[98] *Conserve Monuments, Save Heritage, Research Club, Research Report, Possesing (sic!) Historical Interest & Conservation of Tombs and Monuments—Vol. III*, (place not mentioned) April 1999.

[99] Packiamuthu, *Schwartz, Clarinda and Sathianathan*, 61.

[100] Kadambavanam, *Tirunelveli attiyācatin ārampam*, 36.

some local feudal landlords, the *pāḷaiyakkārar*, who had military forces. Appointed at one time by the *Nāyaka* as administrators of conquered territories these landlords were able to consolidate their territorial influence and, till the advent of British rule, they could lend urgency to their demands through agitations and revolts. Since the middle of the 1750s the British began to extend their influence to the Tirunelveli region. From 1763 onwards the troops there were commanded by British officers, while actual administrative matters were dealt with by local officials on behalf of the Nawab. After 1781 the Nawab was forced to pay taxes to the East India Company. The British, despite being at war with Haider Ali, appointed special superintendents with the task of financial administration.[101]

Christian missionary activity had begun in Tirunelveli in the sixteenth century. In the first half of the 16th century the first Portuguese missionaries came to this region; in 1642 the famous Jesuit Francisco de Xavier visited the region and converted tens of thousands of *paravar*. From the seventeenth century till the ban on the Jesuit order in 1773 Tirunelveli was part of the Catholic Madurai Mission, for which, among others, Constanzo Guiseppe Beschi also worked from 1710 onwards. After the Jesuit order was reinstated in 1838 Tirunelveli continued to be a mission station of the French Jesuits with Tuticorin as the most important centre.[102]

It was only in the 1770s that the Tranquebar missionaries began to include the region south of Tiruchirappalli in their strategic considerations. From 1771 onwards the Indian catechist Schawrimuttu (born around 1752), who had been working in Tiruchirappalli, began working in Palayankottai, south of Tiruchirappalli, on the orders of Christian Friedrich Schwartz. Since he could read and write, he was asked to teach the Christians there.[103] This year is considered to be the beginning of Protestant missionary efforts in Tirunelveli.

[101] *Imperial Gazetteer of India Provincial Series*, Madras, Vol. 2., 1985, Usha Publications, New Delhi, 259–261. Cf. also Ramaswami, Nallathagudi Srinivasa, 1984, *Political History of the Carnatic under the Nawabs*, Abhimav, New Delhi, 84–121.

[102] *Imperial Gazetter of India Provincial Series*, Madras. Vol. 2., 1985, 264. For a short overview of the history of missionary activities in Tirunelveli see: Job, Thomas, 2006, 'History of Protestant Christianity in Tirunelveli', in Gross, *Halle and the Beginning of Protestant Christianity in India*, Vol. I, 497–525.

[103] NHB 8. St., 1101; Cf. also: Pascoe, *Two Hundred Years of the S.P.G.*, 531f.

The date on which an English officer turned to Schwartz with the request to baptize his South Indian mistress can no longer be ascertained. At this point of time Schwartz did not accede to the request on moral grounds, since they were living together without being married.[104] This story appears in the mission sources only at a later point of time when the young woman herself requested Christian Friedrich Schwartz to baptize her during his visit to Palayankottai in 1778. The English officer, Colonel Lyletton, who had died in the meanwhile, had initiated his mistress in the teachings of Christianity during the last years of his life, had taught her English and had bequeathed his entire estate to her. Schwartz, who now felt that the Brahmin widow had an 'open, solemn nature', baptized her, at her own request, as Clarinda. He also confirmed the private baptism given at birth to her adopted son.[105]

Little is known about Clarinda's parental home, her childhood and her youth. Born sometime between 1746 and 1750 in a Brahmin family Clarinda, whose original name was Kohila,[106] was brought up traditionally, married off early and became a widow at a young age after the death of her husband, a Maratha Brahmin who had been in the service of the *Raja* of Thanjavur.[107] According to Hindu tradition she was meant to become a *satī* and burn on her husband's funeral pyre. The English officer Lyletton, stationed in Thanjavur, who was apparently a witness to this ceremony, ordered the rescue of the young woman and she became his mistress. Saved from death as a *satī* Clarinda was rejected by her family and did not really have any alternative to a life with the person who had saved her. At first glance, the life story of the Brahmin widow Clarinda appears to be merely an early example of the numerous stories about Indian widows in the nineteenth century who, having been saved by Europeans from committing *satī*, became their concubines and then converted to Christianity after a period of time.[108] These women

[104] NHB 33. St., 1028f.

[105] NHB 21. St., 1095f; 31. St., 756f.; 33. St., 1028f.

[106] Cf. Kent, 'Raja Clarinda—Widow, Concubine, Patroness; Women's Leadership in the Indian Church'.

[107] NHB 31. St., 757.

[108] Cf. for instance: Hardgrafe, Robert L. Jr., 1998, 'The Representation of Sati: Four Eighteenth Century Etchings by Baltazard Solvyns', *Bengal Past and Present*, 117 (1998), 57–80.

were integrated into the world of Europeans in India, often inherited considerable wealth after the death of their admirers and sometimes went to Europe with the children born of such alliances. Although the circumstances under which Clarinda came into contact with the Christian world might resemble those of other Indian women, the further path of her life as a Christian and a missionary obviously differed greatly from them.

Life with an English officer in the company of Europeans not only meant a completely different lifestyle, different food habits, a different language and different social norms, it also meant a complete break with her past. One of the consequences of this new life was integration in the life of Europeans in South India, and the desire to become a Christian was only the logical course of events towards a new identity. Acquiring an education was also part of this process. As a member of an orthodox Maratha Brahmin family she had not been allowed to learn how to read or write.[109]

Palayankottai became the stage for Clarinda's life and work. Left on her own after the death of the English officer Clarinda used her inheritance and her contacts to the English to set up Christian missionary work in Palayankottai. With financial and moral help from English officials she first built a prayer house where interested people gathered daily for instruction. Clarinda, who had faithfully nursed her lover during his illness in his last years, probably inherited a considerable amount of money, which she used for her missionary work. Apart from setting up buildings for the work of conversion she also financed travels by the missionaries, paid local co-workers and helped the poor.[110] From time to time the German missionaries sent someone from Thanjavur or Tiruchirappalli to Palayankottai to help Clarinda or to baptize the catechumen who had undergone baptismal instruction.[111] When Christian Pohle visited her in 1779, i.e. one year after Clarinda had been baptized, he reported back that Clarinda had combined her Brahmin origin with the new faith and that she, 'because of her royal origins',

[109] Cf. the book edited and annotated by Tanika Sarkar about a Brahmin woman in the nineteenth century who secretly learned how to read and write under the constant fear of being discovered and punished. Sarkar, *Words to Win*.

[110] NHB 21. St., 1095; 31. St., 772; 33. St., 1028f.

[111] NHB 29. St., 592.

proudly called herself 'Rasa (Raja) Clarinda'.[112] It appears that Clarinda did not have children of her own, but she probably had two foster children, a daughter and a son. The foster daughter, Mariammal, was married in 1779 at the age of 18 to Clarinda's domestic servant who had been baptized on 29 June 1779 as Johann by Christian Pohle.[113]

At the end of 1778 and beginning of 1779 the Indian pastor Philipp travelled to the southern mission regions and also visited Clarinda in Palayankottai on this occasion.[114] In 1780 Schwartz tried to send Dewasagayam to Palayankottai and he, in turn, asked for Wisuwasi's help. Because of the unrest in this part of the country they took soldiers to accompany them. Dewasagayam stayed in Palayankottai for some time while Wisuwasi returned shortly thereafter to Ramanathapuram.[115] Njanapiragasam (born 1758), the catechist in Thanjavur, arrived in Palayankottai on 7 March 1783 and stayed till 12 May of the same year.[116] Clarinda herself maintained regular contact with the missionaries. At the end of 1783, Clarinda and some people she had taught had visited Thanjavur. Clarinda asked for co-workers and requested that a missionary or an Indian pastor be sent to Palayankottai. Since none were available Wisuwasi, who was then working in Ramanathapuram, was sent to Palayankottai.[117] When she left Thanjavur at the end of January 1784 Clarinda handed over her adopted son to be brought up by the missionaries in Thanjavur.[118]

Clarinda lived in Tereiwalli,[119] a village south of Palayankottai, and had appointed an assistant, Maria Schawri as a reader there.[120] Since Wisuwasi and Clarinda apparently could not work together in a harmonious manner, Wisuwasi went back.[121] On 7 March 1784

[112] NHB 24. St., 1432; 22. St., 1195; 31. St., 756f.
[113] NHB 24. St., 1433.
[114] NHB 23. St., 1302.
[115] NHB 26. St., 122.
[116] NHB 31. St., 761, 770.
[117] NHB 31. St., 757.
[118] NHB 21. St., 1095; 31. St., 757f.
[119] This probably refers to Tharuvai, south-west of Palayankottai.
[120] NHB 31. St., 761, 779.
[121] Packiamuthu, 'Schwartz, Clarinda and Sathianathan', 64.

Schwartz sent Njanapiragasam to take his place.[122] In July 1784 Schwartz again sent Njanapiragasam together with his father-in-law, the Indian pastor Rajappen (1742–97), to Palayankottai.[123] In February 1785 Schwartz sent Sathianathan there for the pastoral care of the congregation that had, in the meanwhile, grown to more than a hundred persons.[124] In the same year Schwartz consecrated the church that Clarinda had built and which was maintained with the help of the SPCK.[125] According to the reports, in October 1787 Sathianathan and the schoolmaster Samuel were working in Palayankottai and looking after a congregation of 120 persons.[126]

Clarinda's last meeting with the missionaries apparently took place in May 1792 when she visited Thanjavur, Tiruchirappalli and Tranquebar. She stayed for three days in Tiruchirappalli.[127] In connection with Jänicke's imminent journey to Palayankottai John reported on 14 January 1794 that the 'benevolent Clarinda of the Brahmin caste had died there recently'.[128] In a joint letter of 1 February 1794 to the editor of the mission reports, Johann Ludwig Schulze (1734–99), the missionaries König, John, Rottler and Cämmerer again expressed their sorrow at the passing away of the Brahmin woman: 'Mr Jänicke [...] will now set out on another journey to Paleiamkodtei where Clarinda of the Brahmin caste, a Christian who helped the congregation there in many ways, has now passed away'.[129] The exact date of her death is not known. It can only be narrowed down: according to the German mission sources, Clarinda died before 14 January 1794 after working for

[122] Ibid.

[123] NHB 31. St., 774f.

[124] NHB 31. St., 772. NHB 32. St., 1034; NHB 34. St., 1158, letter from Ch. F. Schwartz to F.W. Pasche, October 2, 1786.

[125] Kadambavanam, *Tirunelveli attiyācatin ārampam*, 39; NHB 32. St., 1028f.

[126] NHB 36. St., 1396. Eliza F. Kent quotes the list of baptisms from 1780 as published by Caldwell and analyses it in terms of caste and social composition of the congregation. Kent, 'Raja Clarinda—Widow, Concubine, Patroness: Women's Leadership in the Indian Church'. Cf. Caldwell, *Records of the Early History of the Tinnevelly Mission*, 11–12.

[127] See Pohle's diary entry, Tiruchirappalli, 13 May 1792, NHB 45. St., 785.

[128] NHB 45. St., 839.

[129] Cf. the relevant communications of the missionaries: NHB 46. St., 927, Tranquebar, 1 February 1794, (translated from German).

about 15 years to propagate Christianity in the region around Palayankottai. However, after her death, on 17 February 1794 Jänicke travelled to Palayankottai to enquire about the situation of the Christians who Clarinda had looked after till then. He worked in Ramanathapuram and set up a church there.[130] Beset by illnesses that regularly interrupted his work, he was still the only missionary available in this region,[131] which prompted Missonary Holzberg in 1798 to indicate the need for sending a missionary to Palayankottai since Jänicke's good work was no longer enough due to the constant growth of the congregation.[132] Besides Jänicke, Gericke also travelled to this region many times. At the beginning of 1800 Gericke was in Ramanathapuram and Palayankottai.[133] In 1802 Gericke went to the interior districts and to the southern mission areas. In 1803 Johann Caspar Kohlhoff went to Palayankottai for a few months.[134]

Thus, on the basis of the reports sent by the German missionaries the point of time at which Clarinda died can be localized fairly accurately. This means that the year 1806, which is still considered to be the year in which she died, has to be revised.[135] It was never possible to find sound evidence for this date on the basis of English-language sources. Robert Caldwell (1814–91), who in his 'History of Tinnevelly Mission' refers to a register in Thanjavur listing members of the congregation in 1780, in which Clarinda's name appears first, reiterated that registers for the period between 1803 and 1816 were no longer available.[136] Caldwell states however: '[...] the great movement among the Shanars which has led to such important results, and which originated in 1797, was totally unconnected with

129 Cf. the relevant communications of the missionaries: NHB 46. St., 927, Tranquebar, 1 February 1794, (translated from German).

130 NHB 49. St., 931.

131 NHB 49. St., 76; 52. St., 364, 386f., 387; 56. St., 714.

132 NHB 56. St., 711.

133 NHB 59. St., 966f.

134 NHB 60. St., 106, 1071.

135 Kadambavanam, *Tirunelveli attiyācatin ārampam*, 29, 36. For the story of Clarinda's life see also: Caldwell, *Records of the early History of the Tinnevelly Mission*, 7f; Appasamy, Paul, 1923, *The Centenary History of the C.M.S. in Tinnevelly*, Palamcottah Press, Palamcottah, 12f; Packiamuthu, 'Schwartz, Clarinda and Sathianathan'; Caldwell, *A political and general history of the District of Tinnevelly*, 244f.

136 Caldwell, *Records of the Early History of the Tinnevelly Mission*, 12.

Terivilai and Clorinda's people.'[137] We do not know why Caldwell's detailed description of Jänicke's work in Palayankottai does not include the reports of 1794. He refers to a remark by Schwartz of January 1794 and then skips an entire year to report about events of January 1795. It is this missing period which contains reports about the death of the Brahmin widow. Modern authors use Kohlhoff's reports for the SPCK when he wrote in 1808 'that Clarinda died a few years ago', and Paul Kadambavanam's conclusion from this remark that she died in 1806.[138] Basing himself on English-language sources D. Packiamuthu examines the co-operation between Schwartz, Sathianathan and Clarinda and the history of the Shanar mission in Tirunelveli, Palayankottai. Packiamuthu does remark that 'after the arrival of the Lutheran missionaries Jaenicke and Gericke sent by Schwartz on behalf of the SPCK, we do not hear about Clarinda's activities.' As an explanation for her absence in the reports he presumes: 'She must have been very happy that the Lord's work was being taken care of.'[139]

After the death of the charismatic and well-respected Brahmin widow, Clarinda, the care of the Christians living in Palayankottai and Tirunelveli was handed over to Sathianaden who supervised other South Indian co-workers carrying out the work. The missionaries exercised control through visits and stays at irregular intervals. Without the constant presence of a missionary Sathianathan, the three catechists and the three assistants working under him had to work independently.[140] Sathianathan, who had been going to Palayankottai regularly since 1785, and who was finally sent there in 1795, worked closely with Jänicke. In 1796, the 21–year-old Chinnamuth David Sundaram was sent as an assistant to Tirunelveli, and he played a leading role in the nascent Shanar Movement.[141]

[137] Ibid., 17. According to Caldwell Terivilai refers to the place where Clarinda lived. In the mission sources this place is mentioned as Teraiveli.

[138] Packiamuthu, 'Schwartz, Clarinda and Sathianathan', 66. Packiamuthu refers to: Kadambavanam, *Tirunelveli attiyācatin ārampam*, 13. Eliza F. Kent also uses these sources and thus arrives at the same conclusion regarding the year of Clarinda's death. Cf. Kent, 'Raja Clarinda', 660.

[139] Packiamuthu, 'Schwartz, Clarinda and Sathianathan', 65f.

[140] NHB 55. St., 651, around 1797.

[141] NHB 31. St., 784.

Clarinda was, like Rajanayakkan earlier, not only a bridge between her place of activities without a permanent missionary and the surrounding mission stations. Moreover, as a Brahmin woman, a widow and a former concubine of a British officer, she laid the foundations for the development of a Christian congregation which later lead to the Shanar Movement. Because of her background, however, she was also able to convert Brahmins.[142] The missionary work begun by Clarinda and other Indian co-workers was continued in the nineteenth century by European missionaries, first by Tobias Ringeltaube (1770–1816), then (1820) by Rhenius and Bernhard Ehrengott Schmid, who were transferred to Palayankottai from Madras where they had previously worked.[143]

[142] NHB 21. St., 1095f; 23. St., 1302.

[143] The final break with the CMS occurred in the 1830s. Rhenius and the other German missionaries left the CMS and went over to the LMS. SOAS LMS Deposit 1795–1940, Box N° 6, folder N° 5; NHB 70. St., 1010.

Concluding Observations

Indian Mission Employees and European-Indian Cultural Contact

The painting that decorates the crown of the 'India cupboard' in the art and natural history cabinet of the Francke Foundations in Halle/Saale depicts a Tamilian leaning over the top of the cupboard writing on a palm leaf. To his right and left inscribed palm leaves hang down. The Tamilian, perhaps a writer, or a poet, or perhaps a learned man, is concentrating on his work with apparent satisfaction. At the same time he appears to be watching over the objects displayed in the cupboard, which give an insight into daily life in southeast India in the eighteenth century. A visitor gets the feeling of being observed while he/she looks at the objects, almost as if someone is presenting his culture and is interested in seeing how it is being perceived by members of another culture.

Under the accession number AFSt/M 2 B 5 : 13 the archives of the Francke Foundations list a copper engraving with the title: 'Introducing the Evangelical-East-India Church'. In the centre is a depiction of a conversion scene framed by many smaller scenes of Christian missionary activity in daily life. The central figure is that of a missionary wearing a priestly robe and a turban, standing on a stage with his hand raised in a gesture of instruction and exhortation. He is surrounded by a large number of Tamilians who are listening to him reverentially.

These are two works created by European artists in the first half of the eighteenth century on a topic that would be described today with terms such as 'cultural encounter' and perception of the 'Other'. Two works of art that arose on the basis of information, reports and objects that reached Europe as a result of Protestant missionary

Painting that decorates the crown of the 'India cupboard' in the art and natural history cabinet of the Francke Foundations in Halle/Saale

Copper engraving: 'Introducing the Evangelical-East-India Church' (Archives of the Francke Foundations, Halle/Saala, AFSt/M 2 B 5 : 13)

efforts. Two works of art that seem to express different attitudes. The artist and engraver from Altenburg, Gottfried August Gründler (1710–75) painted the cupboard in the art and natural history cabinet. We do not know whether a historical personality served as a model for the artist, or which passages of the missionary reports, which he must have read carefully, served as an inspiration. In the work of the engraver from Augsburg, Johann Jacob Kleinschmidt (1687–1772), it is not the real representatives of the 'Evangelical Church in East India', the Tamils, who are in the foreground, as the title of the engraving suggests, but it is the messenger of the Christian faith, the European missionary, who is the main figure.

Today, three hundred years after the beginning of the Danish-English-Halle Mission, and almost 300 years after the painting and the copper engraving were created, there is a growing interest in studying Christian missionary activity in India from varying perspectives. The authors of studies on the history of the DEHM in numerous publications of the last ten years include not only theologians, scholars of religion and mission, but also historians, sociologists, linguists and scholars of South Asia in India, Europe and in other parts of the world. Their studies demonstrate that work on mission history can also give an insight into aspects of developments within local social structures.

In the framework of this study I have tried to explore the encounter between German missionaries and the Tamilians at the micro-level and to discover how the co-operation and co-existence between representatives of different religions and cultures functioned in the eighteenth century in southeast India. The study focuses on the Indian representatives of the Danish-English-Halle Mission and shows their role within the missionary intercultural encounter as well as in different spheres of work. What has emerged is that the missionary project conceived and financed by Copenhagen, Halle and London did not remain a European undertaking, but that in its local form in South India it became an intercultural project with important local players. What has also emerged is that there were continuities and ruptures, conflicts and crisis which can not only be explained by changes in the European attitude to mission, but which primarily reflected changing interests and changing power equations among the local players.

The 'offer' of conversion made by the European missionaries was not only tolerated and accepted in particular sections of society in southeast India, but it was also actively shaped by members of this society. Besides their specific abilities and contacts, which the Europeans urgently required, these people also brought their own interests and their personal expectations into their missionary work. This constellation influenced and changed the originally conceived mission strategy and, partly, even led to a reproduction of local social structures within the workings of the mission.

The space for intercultural encounters and negotiations linked with missionary work was extended to many spheres of life and, in this process, existing local networks were integrated into the work of the mission, were expanded and brought in contact with European networks. This required an adjustment to South Indian reality on the part of the European missionaries, but also demanded that Indian mission employees adjust to the rules of missionary work. As long as the participants in this encounter needed each other, as long as they were dependent on one another in one or the other way and did not deviate from the expected norms, the co-operation between them was marked by dialogue and negotiation. However, it was always clear who had the power to decide in case of a conflict.

The perspective chosen for this study was exciting, since it opened up new insights. It was surprising because the sources allowed greater scope for statements about the integration of local co-workers in the mission system than could be expected. This study could perhaps open the gates for similar, more detailed research in the future. At the end, however, questions remain, which I could not answer comprehensively, and avenues of research remain open, which I could only partially follow. I would like to highlight two points here.

THE SELF-PERCEPTION OF THE INDIAN MISSION EMPLOYEES

In view of the fact that the sources are decisively characterized by the European missionary perspective Stephen Greenblatt's demand that one resist the temptation to talk about or for the local people as if the mediation through a European perspective is not an important fact needs to be emphasized.[1] It is because of this approach and the necessary restraint in interpreting the documents that this study focuses on seemingly 'external' themes such as the composition, the rise, the structure, social position and efficacy of the 'national workers' as an intermediary group rather than on observations about the self-perception of the group. A comprehensive decoding of their inner views remains a task for future research. It has become apparent, however, that the situation of the sources—at least in the case of the Tranquebar Mission—cannot be used to justify the lack of research on South Indian mission employees. Compared to the number of texts by European missionaries the number of reports by the Tamilian co-workers may be small. But, not all the letters, reports, translations and other texts by the Tamilians have been discovered and evaluated as yet. Further focused research in this direction can contribute to opening up motives, strategies of action and the self-perception of these players.

THE BIOGRAPHIES OF THESE PLAYERS

The study of the self-perception of this group is closely linked with further work on the biographies of the Indian co-workers. The lives of most of the mission employees named in this study can be (at least partly) reconstructed extent from the sources. Their biographies not only help us to understand the daily life, the hierarchies and the functioning of Christian missionary work, but they also reflect village and caste structures as well as family circumstances over several generations. They can give us insights into the social and economic structures of South Indian villages in the eighteenth century, or provide information about gender roles. It has long been recognized that missionary sources contain innumerable statements about nature and about the society of the region. This refers primarily to the observations and research of the missionaries. A further reconstruction of the biographies of the Indian actors could open up a new dimension of insight into contemporary local society. They would offer a long-term anthropological survey of the players.

[1] Greenblatt, *Marvelous Possessions*, 7.

Biographies of South Indian Country Pastors[1]

Aaron (1698/9–1745)

Ordination: 28 December 1733

Aaron was born in the English colony of Fort St. David (Cuddalore) into the family of a *Veḷḷāḷar* merchant. He was brought up and educated in a strict Shaivite tradition. Against his father's will he attended the school set up in Cuddalore in 1717 by the SPCK with the help of the Danish-Halle missionaries. His teacher there was Schawrimuttu who had been trained in Tranquebar and who had been given leave of absence from Tranquebar in order to teach in Cuddalore. Aaron's contact with the Tranquebar missionaries was established through Schawrimuttu, who also gave this future pastor a first insight into Christianity. When Aaron's family had to leave Cuddalore on account of business losses and due to differences of opinion between his father and the local English authorities, Aaron went off on his own to the missionaries in Tranquebar and requested them to instruct him in the Christian religion. In 1718 he was baptized as Aaron by Ziegenbalg. He first became a teacher, and in 1719 he was made an assistant catechist in the congregation of the New Jerusalem church. In this function he regularly accompanied the Tranquebar missionaries on their journeys. In 1729 he became a catechist and

[1] These short biographies of the South Indian preachers of the Tranquebar Mission have been published for the first time in: Liebau, Heike, 2006, 'Indian Pastors 1733–1817 (Short biographies)', in Andreas Gross [et al.], (eds.), *Halle and the Beginning of Protestant Christianity in India, Vol. III*, 1543–49, Verlag der Franckeschen Stiftungen, Halle. I am thankful to the publisher for the permission to reprint them here.

began to train assistants and also to travel to surrounding places. Aaron was ordained on 28 December 1733 as the first Indian pastor in the Tranquebar mission, when he was 35 years old. He died on 25 July 1745 in Tranquebar and was buried in the Old Jerusalem church. Most of the members of Aaron's family remained Hindus. His father died in 1732 as a Hindu. His mother converted to Christianity on 9 April 1734 and, following this, other relatives of Aaron also converted. His mother died on 6 June 1738. Aaron married thrice. His first wife, Rahel, was a Christian of the Tranquebar congregation, daughter of a Tamilian who had converted from Hinduism. They had four children. After Rahel died in childbirth on 29 November 1731, Aaron married again in 1732 on the advice of the missionaries. His second wife, Ananday, was from a poor family and the daughter of a widow. Aaron had two more children with her. Ananday died on 18 May 1737. Aaron then married the daughter of the mission assistant Muttunayakkan. His children remained linked with the mission in different ways. One of his daughters got engaged on 1 June 1745 to Thomas, a son of the pastor Diogo. One of Aaron's sons, Gurupadam, worked with the mission in Madras. Sokkanaden, another son, was a schoolmaster in Tranquebar (1755) and was appointed assistant in 1763. Sadanaden was an assistant in the city congregation.

Diogo (1704?-1781)

Ordination: 28 December 1741

Diogo was born around 1704 in a Catholic family that had originally been of a high caste. In 1713 his mother converted to the Lutheran faith along with four children, Diogo being one of them. Diogo attended the mission school in Tranquebar and later taught there. Apart from Tamil he spoke good Portuguese. In April 1729 he was appointed catechist in the Tranquebar city congregation and from then on he constantly undertook journeys that took him to the Christians in the rural districts. In 1731 he went to Ramanathapuram as the first representative of the Tranquebar mission. He was sent on several journeys to the interior parts of the country in order to also win over local candidates for the post of catechist. From 1736 onwards Diogo was prepared for his ordination and for the post of a priest; on 28 December 1741 he was ordained and appointed pastor for the outlying districts of the village congregation. He died in October 1781 after having served the mission for more than 40 years. Diogo married four times; one of his wives was related to the pastor Rajappen. He had several children of whom some remained in the service of the mission after having completed their education. His son, Thomas, was sent as a teacher to Cuddalore in 1743. Nianapirasadam became the second city-catechist in Tranquebar in 1772.

Ambrosius (1711/13?-1777)

Ordination: 9 April 1749

Ambrosius was born in 1713 into a Catholic family which turned Protestant in 1717. Around 1720 he worked in the paper mill run by the mission in Porayar, where he also attended school. He then went on to become an apprentice with a weaver. However, he cut short his apprenticeship and tried his hand at seamanship which had been the family tradition. He took part in a journey to Colombo, after which he returned to the paper-mill and to the mission school. Among other things, Ambrosius learned German and Portuguese. When one of the school teachers died, Walther appointed him as an assistant in the mission school. In 1740 he was sent to Cuddalore as a catechist where he also continued his career as a teacher under the supervision of Johann Ernst Geister. When Aaron died in 1745 Ambrosius was proposed as his successor. With the permission of the Mission Board in Copenhagen and the SPCK in London Ambrosius was called back to Tranquebar, where he was prepared for his ordination and for the office of a priest. At this point of time he had a family of five children. Ambrosius was ordained during Easter of 1749 and appointed pastor in Mayuram (Mayavaram) district. In his last years he suffered from a disease of the lungs. He died on 8 February 1777.

Philipp/Pulleimuttu (1731/1743?-1788)

Ordination: 28 December 1772

Philipp was born around 1731 near Nagapattinam in a *Veḷḷāḷar* family. His original name was Pulleimuttu. After the early death of his father, his mother raised the children on her own. At the age of ten Philipp was captured by unknown slave-traders and abducted to the house of the Danish Commandant in Tranquebar. His mother fought to have him set free and demonstrated her gratitude for her son's freedom by not only converting to Christianity herself, but by sending her son and a daughter in 1741 to the Tamil mission school in Tranquebar. Johann Balthasar Kohlhoff was their first teacher there. Philipp later worked as a household help with Jacob Klein. In May 1751 he became a teacher, and in October 1757 he was appointed a city catechist in place of the late Muttunayakkan. He was ordained as pastor on 28 December 1772. In this function he had to travel a lot and was often accompanied by the assistant Schawrimuttu. On various occasions he also had to fulfill the role of a prison clergyman. Philipp died on 4 February 1788.

Rajappen (1742–1796/7)

Ordination: 7 May 1778

Rajappen was born in 1742 as the son of Christian parents. The family was originally of the *Vel̤l̤āl̤ar* caste. His grandfather had also converted to Christianity and had worked as a catechist. Rajappen grew up with him. In 1750 his grandfather enrolled him in the mission school. After the death of his father and grandfather Rajappen was first employed in the mission printing press and later appointed schoolmaster in Tranquebar. In 1769 the missionaries transferred him as schoolmaster and catechist to Tanjavur where he took up the position vacated by the assistant Dewanesen. In October 1777 Rajappen was recalled to Tranquebar, where he was appointed catechist. He was ordained on 7 May 1778 and was later transferred to Tanjavur again. In 1784 Schwartz sent him to Palayankottai with his son (in law?) Njanapiragasam to support the converted Brahmin woman Clarinda. When the pastor Philipp died in 1788, Rajappen was recalled to Tranquebar from Tanjavur to continue Philipp's work in the schools and the church there. From time to time he travelled from Tranquebar to Palayankottai (for example, in spring 1789). He probably spent his last years in Poraiyar, where he died in 1796. During his term of office Rajappen developed a strong interest in questions of medicine, and combined missionary work with medical work.

Sattianaden (Karpagam Sathiyanathan) (1750–1815)

Ordination: 26 December 1790

Sattianaden came from a high-caste Hindu family. As a young man he was taken by a mission assistant to Christian Friedrich Schwartz in Tiruchirappalli, where the missionary baptized him. Although his mother too became a Christian, his wife and mother-in-law were unwilling to do so. In his first years with the mission Sattianaden worked as a porter for Schwartz. Around 1770 he was appointed an assistant. After the Raja of Tanjavur had been deposed by the English and the Nawab, Sattianaden and Rajappen travelled in 1774/75 in the region of Tanjavur and kept the missionaries informed about political developments. On this basis Sattianaden accompanied the missionary Ch. F. Schwartz in 1799 to Srirangapatnam/ Seringapatnam for negotiations with Haider Ali. In the 1780s Sattianaden was a catechist with Ch. F. Schwartz in the English mission in Tanjavur. In 1784, after the end of the English-Mysore war, Schwartz sent him to Palayankottai to help the converted Brahmin woman, Clarinda, who was working for the mission. The catechist was ordained by Schwartz on 26 December 1790 and was appointed pastor in the southern regions of the mission, where he worked under Joseph Daniel Jänicke from 1791 onwards and where he continued the work after Jänicke's death. Sattianaden remained there till about 1804/05 and then returned to Tanjavur on account of differences of opinion with the local assistant and catechists. He probably died in 1815.

Abraham

Ordination: 17 March 1811

Abraham was ordained on 17 March 1811 by Christian Pohle and appointed pastor in Palayankottai. He could not stay there for reasons of health and returned to Tanjavur in 1812. Around 1822/23 he worked again in Tirunelveli/Palayankottai. At this point of time there was no European missionary working there. He received his pay from the interest from the estate of Christian Friedrich Schwartz.

Njanapiragasam (Njanapragasam or Gnanapiragasam) (1758–?)

Ordination: 17 March 1811

Njanapiragasam came from a *Chetti* family near Tillaiyadi. He attended the mission school in Tranquebar, but even as a child he had to contribute to the family income. After an illness he began to work in the paper mill run by the mission and, at the same time, he went to school and also worked in a missionary household. Njanapiragasam was supervised by Christoph Samuel John who taught him German and instructed him in the work of the mission. He was so successful in learning German that he could translate Biblical texts from German into Tamil. In 1772 he began to accompany Rajappen on his travels. The pastor Philipp and the catechist Rajappen suggested in 1774 that he be transferred to Tanjavur to take the place of the schoolmaster Gurupadam. While he was a teacher in Tanjavur he lived in Rajappen's house. Along with his work in the school he was also responsible for looking after the poor-house in Tanjavur. In 1784 Schwartz sent him to Palayankottai along with Rajappen to help the converted Brahmin widow Clarinda. In 1788 he went to Vellore for five months and subsequently worked again in Tanjavur as an assistant. In 1789 he became a catechist. After working for some years in Velur and Vepery, Njanapiragasam was sent by Gericke in 1792 to look after the Tamil congregation in Nagapattinam in place of the late Sandappen. He worked there for some years. On 17 March 1811 Christian Pohle ordained him in Tanjavur. Around 1820 he worked under J.C. Kohlhoff and Johann Georg Philipp Sperschneider in Tanjavur. His brother was the well-known Christian David (1771–1852) who worked in Ceylon. Rajappen was his father (in-law?).

Adeikalam (Adeikkalam)

Ordination: 17 March 1811

Around 1795 Adeikalam was a catechist and schoolmaster in the English school in Kumbakonam. At this point of time the school had twelve adult pupils, mainly from Brahmin families, some of whom were married. Around 1799 he was a catechist in Manapar. Around 1805 he worked under Kohlhoff. After being ordained by Christian Pohle on 17 March 1811, he was appointed pastor in Tanjavur where, in 1819, he continued to work under Kohlhoff and Sperschneider. Adeikalam's family consisted of five persons.

Wedanayagam (Vadanayakam) (roughly 1812)

Ordination 17 March 1811

Wedanayagam was ordained along with Adeikalam on 17 March 1811 by Christian Pohle in Tanjavur. There is no further information about him and his family in the mission reports. There is only an announcement of his death in a brief report about the years

1812–1814. It says that he died of a fever he had contracted in Palayankottai.

Schawrirajen (roughly 1755–1817)

Ordination: 1811?

Schawrirajen had studied under Christoph Samuel John in the mission school in Tranquebar and, throughout his life, he considered the missionary to be his ideal and his authority. In 1774 he was appointed as a co-worker in the mission and in 1776 as a teacher in Tranquebar. Later, however, he was suspended as a teacher for a breach of discipline. After this he worked for some months with Johann Peter Rottler before getting a job as a teacher again. Schawrirajen knew good German and, among other things, he taught Johann Caspar Kohlhoff's son German. To get practise in the language he carried on a correspondence in German with John. In 1782 Jacob Klein took him along on a journey to Colombo. Subsequently, Schawrirajen became a writer for the mission. For nine months he worked as a city catechist with Schwartz in Tanjavur. However, since he and his family were not able to adapt to the place, Schawrirajen returned to Tranquebar as a teacher where, from the 1790s onwards, he worked as a city catechist. His son-in-law, the catechist Njanamalei, sometimes accompanied him on his travels. He married around 1775; in 1785 he had a daughter, one son died soon after birth. His mother was the older sister of the catechist of the city church in Tranquebar, Arulappen (died 1795). Schawrirajen died in February 1817.

Pakkianaden

Ordination: 1817

Pakkianaden was a catechist under Johann Caspar Kohlhoff in Tanjavur. At his request he was ordained there in June 1817 by Christian Pohle.

Wisuwasanadan/Wisuwasi

Ordination: 1817

Wisuwasinaden was a catechist under J.C. Kohlhoff in Tanjavur and was ordained at his request by Pohle. Around 1822 he worked for the SPCK in Tirunelveli and lived in the village of Nazareth. It is unclear whether Wisuwasinaden and Wisuwasi refer to the same person. The latter, a former assistant and schoolmaster, appears in the Mission Reports from the 1770s. He was an 'untouchable' who was educated in the mission school in Tranquebar, then became a teacher in Kuttannalur and from 1774/75 was an assistant in Ramanathapuram. In the 1790s Rottler wrote about an assistant called Wisuwasi who collected snails and shells in Rameswaram for Rottler.

Nallatambi

Ordained: 1817

Nallatambi was ordained in 1817 along with Wisuwasinaden and Pakkianaden by Christian Pohle.

Abbreviations

JOURNALS AND PERIODICALS

AMZ	Allgemeine Missionszeitschrift
ELMB	Evangelisch-Lutherisches Missionsblatt
EMM	Evangelisches Missionsmagazin
EMZ	Evangelische Missionszeitschrift
EPW	Economic and Political Weekly
HB	(Hallesche Berichte) Der Königlich-Dänischen Missionarien (...)
HMK	Hefte zur Missionskunde
ICHR	Indian Church History Review
IESHR	The Indian Economic and Social History Review
MNOIM	Missionsnachrichten der Ostindischen Missionsanstalt zu Halle
MWF	Missionswissenschaftliche Forschungen
NHB	(Neue Hallesche Berichte). Neuere Geschichte der Evangelischen Missionsanstalten (...)
NZM	Neue Zeitschrift für Missionswissenschaft
VF	Verkündigung und Forschung
WB	Martin-Luther-University Halle-Wittenberg, Wissenschaftliche Beiträge
WZ	Martin-Luther-University Halle-Wittenberg, Wissenschaftliche Zeitschrift
ZDMG	Zeitschrift der deutschen Morgenländischen Gesellschaft
ZM	Zeitschrift für Missionswissenschaft

ZMR	Zeitschrift für Missionswissenschaft und Religionswissenschaft

INSTITUTIONS AND ORGANIZATIONS

AFSt	Archiv der Franckeschen Stiftungen zu Halle (Archives of the Francke Foundations at Halle)
ASAO	Association for Social Anthropology in Oceania
BFSt	Bibliothek der Franckeschen Stiftungen zu Halle (Library oft he Francke Foundations at Halle)
CHAI	Church History Association of India
CLS	Christian Literature Society
CMS	Church Mission Society
CWM	Council of World Mission
DEHM	Danish-English-Halle Mission
DHM	Danish-Halle Mission
KB	Det Kongelige Bibliotek Copenhagen (Royal Library Copenhagen)
LMS	London Mission Society
RA	Rigsarkivet Copenhagen (National Archives Copenhagen)
SPCK	Society for Promoting Christian Knowledge
UH	Unitätsarchiv der Evangelischen Brüder-Unität Herrnhut (Unitas Archives oft he Evangelical Unity of Brethren at Herrnhut)
UTC	United Theological College Bangalore

LITERATURE

AB	Ziegenbalg, Alte Briefe aus Indien
ADB	Allgemeine Deutsche Biographie
NDB	Neue Deutsche Biographie

MISCELLANEOUS

Cont.	Continuation, part of the Hallesche Berichte (HB)
St.	Stück, part of the NHB

Maps, Illustrations and Tables

MAPS

ILLUSTRATIONS

TABLES

Note on the Spelling of Indian Terms

This study contains the name of numerous Indian places, especially Tamil villages and towns. As far as the larger cities are concerned, the official names found in Indian atlases have been used. With the smaller places, especially the numerous villages, an attempt has been made to bring about uniformity in the different variations present in the sources. An example can illustrate how difficult this was at times. The place Kattumavadi appears in the sources in eleven different variations: Kadtumawatti, Kadtumawadi, Kuttumawadi, Kadtamawadi, Cattamawadi, Kattumawadi, Cadtumawadi, Kadteimawadi, Kadumawadi, Kadtanawadi, Kattunawadi. The list of villages of the Madras Presidency, compiled in 1930, offered a basic orientation.[1] In many cases an internet search helped to define the correct name of a place and its geographical location. The cities Chennai, Kolkatta and Mumbai appear in the text under the names that were in use at that time, i.e. as Madras, Calcutta and Bombay.

For various reasons I also had to compromise in the manner in which the names of Tamil co-workers are written. The names of Indian Christians are often a combination of Tamil translations of Christian terminology, Biblical names and caste or professional designations. Basically, I have oriented myself to the original sources, even when these spellings hardly match up to the demands of modern transliteration. I felt it was important to remain as close to the sources

[1] *Alphabetical list of villages in the taluks and districts of the Madras Presidency:* corrected up to September 1930.—Reprint: Asian Educational Services, New Delhi, Madras, 1992.

as possible but at the same time, to also bring about uniformity in the variations of spelling often found in the sources. The reference to the sources in future research is only possible in this way. This is also the reason why the English version of this study retains the German spelling of Tamil names (for example, Schawrirajen is not changed to Shawrirajen).

The transliteration of Tamil terms is based on the *Tamil Lexicon* published by the University of Madras in 1982.[2]

[2] *Tamil Lexicon*, six vols, [one] suppl. Reprinted: University of Madras, Madras 1982.

Glossary

The following abbreviations have been used to indicate the linguistic origin of terms:

A.	Arabic
E.	English
F.	Farsi/Persian
H.	Hindustani (Hindi or Urdu)
Kann.	Kannada
Lat.	Latin
Mal.	Malayalam
Nl.	Dutch
Pkt.	Prakrit
Port.	Portuguese
Singh.	Singhalese
Sk.	Sanskrit
Ta.	Tamil
Tel.	Telugu

References to resources and literature are given with the abbreviation, volume number and page number:

AMG	Kahnt, Helmut and Bernd Knorr, 1986, *Alte Maße, Münzen und Gewichte*, Bibliographisches Institut, Leipzig
CT	Thurston, Edgar, 2001, *Castes and Tribes of South India*, 7 vols., Asian Educational Services New Delhi, Madras, (Madras 1909).
DA	Šamatov, A.H., 1974, *Klassičeskij Dakkhini (Južnyj Hindustani)*, Nauka, Moskva.

FB	Duden, 2000, *Das große Fremdwörterbuch*, Dudenverlag, Mannheim [et al].
GA	Black, Jeremy, 2000, *Der große Atlas der Weltgeschichte*, RM-Buch-und-Medien-Vertrieb, Köln.
HL	Langenscheidt, *Handwörterbuch Latein-Deutsch*, 1971, Langenscheidt Verlag, Berlin [et al].
HR	*Hindi-Russkij Slovar*, 2 vols., 1972, Sowjetskaja Enciklopedija, Moskva.
LN	Fengler, Heinz [et al], 1976, *Lexikon der Numismatik*, VEB Verlag für Verkehrswesen, Berlin.
MA	MacLean, C.D., 1893, *Manual of the Administration of the Madras Presidency*, 3 vols., E. Keys, Madras.
SA	Mylius, Klaus, 1980, *Wörterbuch Sanskrit-Deutsch*, VEB Verlag Enzyklopädie Leipzig, Leipzig.
SU	Ansari, Zoe, 1964, *Urdu-Russkij Slovar*, Sowjetskaja Enciklopedija, Moskva.
TL	*Tamil Lexicon. 6 vols., 1 supplement*, 1982, University of Madras, Madras.
UH	Platts, John T., 1993, *A Dictionary of Urdu, Classical Hindi and English*, Munshiram Manoharlal Publ. New Delhi, (Oxford 1884).
Y/B	Yule, Henry and A.C. Burnell, 1995, *Hobson-Jobson*, Asian Educational Services, New Delhi, Madras, (London 1903).

A

aiyar	(Ta.) wise man, priest, Brahmin; term for ordained priests of the Protestant churches; (TL580)
akkiyāṉi	(Ta.) heathen, barbarian; (TL4)
Allack	(Ta.) āḻākku; measure for grain; 8 āḻākku =1 paṭi; (TL 253, MA 3/606)
Âna-tsuwadi	actually: (Ta.) āticuvaṭi; the first book that is read after learning the alphabet; refers to the 'Atticuṭi' of the poetess Auvaiyār
ammāṉai	(Ta.) a sub-genre of poetry, in which every verse has an ammāṉāy as a refrain (TL99)
āvaṇi	(Ta.) fifth month of the Tamil calendar, 12 August to 12 September (TL249, MA 1/610)
Arcot-Rupee	Rupee
atharvaveda	(Sk.) the fourth in the collection of → Vedas; consists of 20 books and 721 hymns, contains mainly spells and incantations; Vedas (SA 24, Y/B 961–63)

āyurveda	(Sk.) a form of medicine, ancient Indian collection of medical tracts, one of the four Vedas (SA 66, Y/B 961–63)

B

Balija	a Telugu speaking South Indian merchant → -jāti belonging to the 'right hand'; (CT 1/134–145)
Beri Chetti	(Ta.) pēri-ceṭṭi; a Tamilian merchant-jāti belonging to the 'left hand'; → ceṭṭi (TL 2901, CT 1/211–18)
Betel	from (Mal.) vetiḷḷa via (Port.) betle; leaf of the Piper betel, L. (Y/B89)
Betel-Areck	from → Betel and (Port.) areca; Areca nut; the areca nut is chopped and rolled in betel leaves along with lime, tobacco, cloves and cardamom (Y/B 89)
brāhmaṇa	(Sk.) Member of the priestly caste; → varṇa

C

Calico	cotton material, generally of reasonably fine weave; (Y/B 147f)
cāṇār	(Ta.) member of a → jāti; professional toddy-tappers; (TL 1359)
Cholas	(Sk.) coḷa; (Ta.) cōḻaṉ; dynasty in South India, first mentioned in the 3rd century BC. reached the zenith of its power between 854–1234; (TL 1676, GA/244)
cērvaikkāraṉ	(Ta.) also cērvaikāraṉ; 1. title of a member of the akampatiyar- → jāti working in the agricultural sector in Thanjavur as well as of some other → jāti; 2. captain, commander of a military unit; (TL 12, TL 1635, CT 6/362)
cheṭṭi	→ ceṭṭi
ceṭṭi	(Ta.) from (Pkt.) seṭṭi; 1. trader-→ jāti, 2. title for a member of this → jāti as well as, among others, of the → kōmaṭṭi and —balija (TL 1583, CT 2/91–97)
Courant	actually: term for standard (silver) coins to be accepted as payment, the metal content of which corresponds to the par value vouched for by the state in contrast to secondary coins and paper money; in the 18th century in Denmark the metal content of the (gold) ducats coins and of the (silver) Rigstaler coins continuously worsened; bank notes began to

	be used which were made out to both coins; (LN 191, AMG 154)

D

dakhinī	(H.) from (Sk.) dakṣiṇa; 'southern'; language, southern variant of Hindustānī; (DA 5–6, Y/B 302)
dalit	(Sk.) dalita; 'burst, exploded' also: subjugated, exploited; term for 'untouchables'; (SA 202, UH 524, SU 418)
devadāsi	(Sk.); (Ta.) tēvatāci; 'servant of God', temple-dancer; (TL 2064, Y/B 307)
Dravidian	(Sk.) drāviḍa; name of the people in the Deccan; here: joint term for the predominantly South Indian languages, among others, Tamil, Telugu, Malayalam, Kannada (SA 220)
dubash	(E.) for (H.) dubāšī; 'bi-lingual'; translator, interpreter, also: administrator in trading matters; (UH 529, Y/B 328)

F

Fanam	(Ta.) paṇam, from (sk.) paṇa; 'money'; a South Indian gold coin since the 9th century, later also a silver coin of differing value minted by colonial powers; around 1710: 24 Fanam were equal to 1 → Pagoda, 10 Fanam were 1 → Pardao, 1 Fanam equal to 80 → Kas (TL 2456, Y/B 348f)

G

Grantham	(Ta.) kirantam from (Sk.) grantha; 1. alphabet with which the Tamilians write Sanskrit, 2. the Sanskrit language; (TL 924, Y/B 397)
gurukula	(Sk.) 'house of a teacher'; classical Hindu school; (SA 142)

I

Iśvara	manifestation of the god Śiva popular in South India → Śiva
iṭaṅkai	(Ta.) 'left hand'; since the 11th century in the → Chola-region the separation of some → Dravidian

	craftsmen → jāti; the other group was the → valaṅkai; (TL 277)
iyer	→ aiyar

J

jāti	(Sk.) type, sort, class, family, here: caste

K

Kas	(Ta.) kācu; 'gold'; a small copper coin minted in South India till 1818, 80 Kas equal to 1 → Fanam (TL 846, Y/B 167f)
Kanakkappel	→ kaṇakkappiḷḷai
kaṇakkappiḷḷai	(Ta.) (village)-accountant, writer; (TL 701, Y/B 246)
karaiyar	(Ta.) 1. fishermen living near the seacoast, 2. colloquial for the paṭṭiṉavar in the Thanjavur district, a fishermen → jāti; (TL 769, CT 6/177–186)
Kattun	(A.) quṭun (Nl.) katoen; cotton canvas; (FB698, UH793)
Kirendum	→ Grantham
kōmaṭṭi	(Ta.) from (Tel.) kōmaṭṭi; a Telugu speaking South Indian merchant-jāti belonging to the 'right hand'; (TL 1189, CT 3/306–348)
kṣatriya	(Sk.) member of the second main social group → varṇa within Hinduism, traditionally members of the 'warrior class' (SA 128)

L

Lungi	(F.) lungi; coloured piece of cloth worn tied at the hips by a man, an article of clothing originally brought to South India by Muslims; → dhotī; (UH 966)

M

Malabarian	here: a common term for Tamil in the 18th century; (Y/B 541f)
maṇiyakāraṉ	(Ta.) leader, headman of a village; (TL 3044, Y/B 576f)
marakkāl	(Ta.) measure for grain with regional variations; in Madras 1 marakkāl=8 paṭi=64 āḻākku=12,291; at the beginning of the 18th century in Tranquebar 1

	marakkāl=4 medides=6 pounds of rice (TL 3082, MA 3/474, Y/B 567
Marrawer	→ maṟavar
Maṟavar	(Ta.) name of a caste, the population of a region south of Thanjavur ruled by rulers of this caste; (TL 3119, CT 22–48)
medide	(Port.) a measure for grain that was used in Tamil Nadu earlier, about 700–800 gms. of rice; also used in the mission reports as a measure;
mudaliyar	→ mutaliyār
mutaliyār	(Ta.) 1. Tamilian leader, 2. caste name of a sub-caste of the → veḷḷāḷar (TL 3260, Y/B 569f)
Mughal	member of the Mughal ruling dynasty (1526–1857)

N

nāṭṭaiyar	(Ta.) from nāṭu (country) and → aiyar (wise man, Brahmin, Protestant priest); Indian Christian priest, pastor, also: country pastor (TL 2207)
nawāb	(A) from nā'ib; 'representative'; vice-regent or governor under Mughal rule; (UH 1120, 1157, Y/B 610)
Nayak	→ nāyakaṉ
nāyaka	(Sk.) (Ta.) nāyakaṉ; leader, ruler, king; (TL 2222, Y/B 614)
nizām	(A.) actually: nizām-ul-mulk; administrator, governor; title of the Mughal vice-regents in the Deccan and the ruler of Hyderabad; (UH/1142, Y/B 628)
nizām-ul-mulk	→ nizām
njanigöl	→ ñāṉikaḷ
ñāṉikaḷ	(Ta.) pl. of (Ta.) ñāṉi; 1. wise person, philosopher, person with extensive religious knowledge, 2. according to Śaiva-devotees a person in the fourth (highest) stage on the path to salvation; (TL 1690)
nellu	(Ta.) nel, nellu; rice plant, rice without the husk (TL 2357, Y/B 623)

O

Oeles	→ ōlai
ōlai	(Ta.) 1. palm leaf, 2. a letter written on a palm leaf; a text was scratched with a stylus on a palm leaf, especially of the Borassus flabeliformis variety, and

	then dipped into a black paint in order to bring out the letters; (TL 629)

P

padroado	(Port.) 'Padroado real'; patronage of the Portuguese crown over the Catholic Church in Portugal and its colonies; the dioceses are not directly under the Pope, but under the king;
Pagoda	European term for 1. a temple, 2. South Indian gold coin that was called varāha or hūn by the Indians; the → star pagoda (named thus because of the star on one side) was a gold coin with a full weight of 3,4 gms and was the currency in South East India; (Y/B 652–657, MA 3/642–644)
Palanquin	(Port.) from (Sk.) paryaṅka; (Ta.) pallaku; sedan; (TL 2527, Y/B 659–61)
paḷḷar	(Ta.) Tamilian → jāti of agricultural workers; (TL 2551, CT 5/472)
pāḷaiyakkārar	(Ta.) military commander, commander of a fort, minor potentate, local ruler; → Polygar (TL 2638, Y/B 718f)
paṇṭāram	(Ta.) 1. Ascetic, 2. Śiva-monk, 3. non-Brahmin priest of the lower castes; (TL 2450, CT 6/45–52, Y/B 666)
Pandarattar	→ paṇṭārattar
paṇṭārattar	(Ta.) 1. caretaker of a treasure 2. government; here: high court judge; (TL 2450, CT 6/52)
paraṉ	(Ta.) 1. God as the highest being, 2. Stranger, Foreigner; (TL 2504)
paravar	(Ta.) fishermen's caste on the southern coast of Tamil Nadu; (TL 2502, CT 6/140–155)
Patshala	(Ta.) pāṭacālai from (Sk.) paṭh; school; here: traditional Hindu village school (ḤR 2/62, TL 2591, SA 261)
paṟaiyār	(Ta.) plural of paṟaiyaṉ; 1. collective term for Tamilian 'untouchables'; 2. drummer for temple processions; → jāti, often an agricultural worker; (TL 2564, CT 6/77–139, Y/B 678–80)
Paränese	(Lat.) persuasion, exhortation; a sermon of exhortation; (FB 988)
Pardao	(Port.) from (Sk.) pratāpa; 'splendour, sublimity';

	originally a gold coin minted mainly in Goa, later also a silver coin with a steadily decreasing value; at times term for a → pagode; (Y/B 673–678)
Pareier	→ paṟaiyār
Parängikarer	→ paraṉ
Parengi	→ paraṉ
Perdou	→ Pardao
Pertsuwadi	(Ta.) peyarccuvaṭi; dictionary (TL 2862)
poṅkal	(Ta.) a festival that takes place when the sun crosses the Tropic of Capricorn and continues in a northerly direction; this is the first day of the Tamil month tai (around 11 January); the festival is the Tamil harvest festival (TL 2910f)
Pro Memoria	(Lat.) in memory; aide memoire, memo; (FB 1094)

R

rāja	(Sk.) ruler, king
ṛgveda	(Sk.) one of the → Vedas
Rupie	initially an Indian silver coin introduced by Sher Shah (1539–1545) weighing 11,534g (till the advent of English colonial rule); the coins minted by the English in the 18th century were the Bengali Sicca-Rupie, the Sirat-Rupie in Bombay and the Arcot-Rupie in Madras; (LN 332f)

S

saluppaṉ cheṭṭi	→ caluppaṉ
caluppaṉ	(Ta.) member of a caste which deals with clothes made from linen; (TL 1331, CT 6/279)
sāmaveda	(Sk.) second → Veda; collection of chants and hymns used by priests in Vedic sacrificial rituals;
samhitā	(Sk.) anthology, literary collection; (SA 509)
samnyāsin	(Sk.) 'renouncing the world'; ascetic, believer, mendicant; (SA 502)
Sanskrit	classical Indo-European language
sarkār	(H) anglicized: Sircar, Circar; state, government, administration, (administrative) district; (UH 655, Y/B 840f)
sāri	(H.) dress of Indian women consisting of a piece of cloth draped around the body and pleated; (UH 625)

sastiram	(Ta.) cāstiram, from (Sk.) Śāstra; regulation, commandment, rule; doctrine, knowledge about a particular sphere, science, book of rules, holy book with divine authority; here: prophecy; (TL 1398, SA 480)
satī	(Sk.) satī; 'faithful wife'; wife who follows her deceased husband by self-immolation; the act of this self-immolation; (SA 512)
Sellingen	→ calaṅku
Sellinga	calaṅku (Ta.) coastal boat 10 to 12m long and 3m wide; (TL 1325)
setupati	(Ta) cētupati; hereditary title of the rulers of Ramnad as guardians of the Adam's bridge (islands in the straits between Sri Lanka and India); (TL 1630)
Shanar	→ cāṇār
Śāstra	→ sastiram
Śiva	(Sk.) an important deity of Hinduism; (SA 482)
śūdra	(Sk.) member of the fourth and socially lowest → varṇa within Hinduism; traditionally peasants and servants;
Sicca-Rupie	→ Rupie
sipāhī	(F.) via (H.) into (Ta.) cippāy; Sepoy, soldier (TL 1422, Y/B 809f)
Sternpagodas	→ pagode
subah	(H.) sūbā, (Ta.) cupai; district, province; (TL 1519)
subahdar	(H.) sūbedār, (Ta.) cupētār; governor of a province, a district, officer in the rank of a captain; (TL 1519)
Sutirer	→ śūdra
Swami	(Sk.) svāmin; lord, master; form of address for → Brahmins; (SA 571, Y/B 883)

T

takkacāstiram	(Sk./Ta.) takkacāstiram from takkam; Sanskrit book about the fundamentals of Hindu law; treatise on logics and dialectics; (TL 1702)
talaiyāri	(Ta.) a village and field guard; carried out police tasks and was also used as a soldier in military formations, among others, of the Danes (TL 1786, CT 7/2f)
tālūk	(A.), (Ta.) tālūka; administrative district, tax district; (TL 1849)

Tiruvaḷḷuvar	(Ta.) author of the tirukkuṟaḷ, of the 'Holy Kural'; this is considered the most important Tamil book on ethics; (TL 1916)

V

vaiśya	(Sk.) member of the third social → varṇa within Hinduism, traditionally merchants (SA 464)
valaṅkai	(Ta.) 1. right hand, 2. castes of the 'right hand'; → iṭaṅkai (TL 3532, MA 1/69)
vaṉṉiyar	(Ta.) plural of vaṉṉiyaṉ; a Tamilian → jāti also known as paḷḷi whose members find work especially as agricultural workers; (TL 3566, CT 6/1–28)
varṇa	(Sk.) 'outward appearance, colour'; term for a social class, family; according to the classical Brahmanic doctrine there are four main social groups: brāhmaṇa, kṣatriya, → vaiśya, → śūdra; (SA 424)
Vedas	→ veda
veda	(Sk.) '(Theological) knowledge'; the holy books of the Brahmins; → atharvaveda, → āyurveda, → ṛgveda, → sāmaveda (SA 461)
veḷḷāḷar	(Ta.) member of the quantitatively most important, predominantly peasant veḷāḷa → jāti in Tamil Nadu who are divided into numerous sub-groups according to their place of origin and their work; (TL 3798, CT 7/361–389)
vitānai	(Ta.) from (Singh.) vidāna; village official, especially in North Ceylon; (TL 3672)
Vijayanagar	kingdom in South India (1336–1646)
Viṣṇu	(Sk.) high-ranking god in Hinduism; (SA 452)
Vaishnava	denomination within Hinduism with the high-ranking god → viṣṇu

W

Warugian/Wardugian	(Ta.) vaṭuku; from (Kann.) baḍugu; German term used by the missionaries of the DEHM for Telugu; (TL 3479)

Z

zamorin	(Sk./Mal.) sāmūri 'sea-king'; title of the ruler of Calicut (Y/B 977)

Bibliography

Adas, Michael, 1989, *Machines as the Measure of Men, Science, Technology and Ideologies of Western Dominance*, Cornell University Press, Ithaca, London.

Adelung, Johann Christoph, 1806, *Mithridates oder allgemeine Sprachenkunde mit dem Vater Unser als Sprachprobe in bey nahe fünfhundert Sprachen und Mundarten*, Part I, Vossische Buchhandlung, Berlin.

Adick, Christel, 1992, 'Koloniale Bildungspolitik: Universalisierung der modernen Schule oder ethnisch-nationale Diskriminierung?', in Wilfried Wagner (ed.), *Rassendiskriminierung, Kolonialpolitik und ethnisch-nationale Identität. Referate des 2. Internationalen Kolonialgeschichtlichen Symposiums 1991 in Berlin*, 457–68, Lit; Münster, Hamburg.

Adick, Christel, 1992, *Die Universalisierung der modernen Schule: eine theoretische Problemskizze zur Erklärung der weltweiten Verbreitung der modernen Schule in den letzten 200 Jahren mit Fallstudien aus Westafrika*, Schöningh, Paderborn [et al.].

Adick, Christel (ed.), 1993, 'Missions- und Kolonialpädagogik', *Themenheft der Zeitschrift 'Bildung und Erziehung'*, 46 (3).

Adick, Christel and Wolfgang Mehnert in co-operation with Thea Christiani, 2001, *Deutsche Missions—und Kolonialpolitik in Dokumenten—eine kommentierte Quellensammlung aus den Afrikabeständen deutschsprachiger Archive 1884–1914*, IKO-Verlag für Interkulturelle Kommunikation, Frankfurt/Main [et al.], (= Historisch-vergleichende Sozialisations- und Bildungsforschung, Vol. 2).

Aggarwal, J.C. and B.D. Bhatt (eds.), 1969, *Educational Documents in India (1831–1968)*, Arya Book Depot, New Delhi.

Ahuja, Ravi, 1999, *Die Erzeugung kolonialer Staatlichkeit und das Problem der Arbeit. Eine Studie zur Sozialgeschichte der Stadt Madras und ihres Hinterlandes zwischen 1750 und 1800*, Steiner, Stuttgart.

Aiyar, R. Sathianatha and Sakkottai Krishnaswami Aiyangar, 2001, *History of the Nayaks of Madura*, (Madras 1924) Asian Educational Services, New Delhi.

Ali, Belagodu Sheikh, 2001, 'Cornwallis and the Mysore-Maratha War 1786–1787', in Irfan Habib (ed.), *Resistance and Modernization under Haidar Ali and Tipu Sultan*, 65–68, Tulika, New Delhi (=Confronting Colonialism).

Anderson, Gerald H. and William B. Eerdmans (eds.), 1998, *Biographical Dictionary of Christian Missions*, William B. Eerdmans Publishing, grand Rapids, Michigan, Cambridge.

Annual Reports of the Portuguese Franciscans in India 1713–1833, 1972, Collected and annotated by Fr. Achilles Meersman, Ordo Fratrum Minorum, Lisboa.

Ansari, Zoe, 1964, *Urdu-Russkij Slovar*, Sowjetskaja Enciklopedija, Moskva.

Appadurai, Arjun, 1974, 'Right and left hand castes in South India', *IESHR*, 11 (2/3): 216–59.

Appasamy, G.P., 1995, *Vedanayaka Sastriar: A Biography of the Suviseda Kavirayar of Thanjavur*, Madras.

Appasamy, Paul, 1923, *The Centenary History of the C.M.S. in Tinnevelly*, Palamcottah Printing Press, Palamcottah.

Arasaratnam, Sinnappah, 1981, 'Social History of a Dominant Caste Society. The Vellalar of North Ceylon (Sri Lanka) in the 18th Century', *IESHR*, 18 (3/4): 377–91.

Arasaratnam, Sinnappah, 1981, 'Protestant Christianity and South Indian Hinduism 1630–1730: Some Confrontations in Society and Beliefs', *ICHR*, 15 (1): 7–33.

Arasaratnam, Sinnappah, 1986, *Merchants, Companies and Commerce on the Coromandel Coast, 1650–1740*, Oxford University Press, New Delhi.

Arasaratnam, Sinnappah, 1989, 'Coromandel Revisited: problems and issues in Indian maritime history', *IESHR*, 26 (1): 101–10.

Arasaratnam, Sinnappah, 1995, 'Indian commercial groups and European traders, 1600–1800: Changing relationships in Southeastern India', in S. Arasaratnam, *Maritime Trade, Society and European Influence in Southern Asia 1600–1800*, 42–53, Variorum, Aldershot, Brookfield.

Arasaratnam, Sinnappah, 1995, 'Indian intermediaries in the trade and administration of the French East India Company in the Coromandel. (1670–1760)', in S. Arasaratnam, *Maritime Trade, Society and European Influence in Southern Asia 1600–1800*, 133–46, Variorum, Aldershot, Brookfield.

Arasaratnam, Sinnappah, 1995, 'Mare Clausum, the Dutch and Regional Trade in the Indian Ocean 1650–1740', in S. Arasaratnam, *Maritime Trade, Society and European Influence in Southern Asia 1600–1800*, 73–91, Aldershot, Brookfield.

Arasaratnam, Sinnappah, 1995, 'Pre-modern commerce and societies in Southern Asia. Inaugural lecture delivered at the University of Malaya, Kuala Lumpur on December 21, 1971', in S. Arasaratnam, *Maritime Trade, Society and European Influence in Southern Asia 1600–1800*, I, 1–22, Aldershot, Brookfield.

Arasaratnam, Sinnappah, 1995, 'The Dutch East India Company and its Cormandel Trade 1700–1740', in S. Arasaratnam, *Maritime Trade, Society and European Influence in Southern Asia 1600–1800*, VI, 325–46, Aldershot, Brookfield.

Arasaratnam, Sinnappah, 1995,'The politics of commerce in the coastal kingdoms of Tamil Nadu 1650–1740', in S. Arasaratnam, *Maritime Trade, Society and European Influence in Southern Asia 1600–1800*, II, 1–19, Aldershot, Brookfield.

Arasaratnam, Sinnappah, 1995, 'Factors in the rise, growth and decline of Coromandel ports circa 1650–1720', in S. Arasaratnam, *Maritime Trade, Society and European Influence in Southern Asia 1600–1800*, IX, 19–30, Aldershot, Brookfield.

Arasaratnam, Sinnappah, 1995, 'Society, power, factionalism and corruption in early Madras 1640–1746', in S. Arasaratnam (ed.), *Maritime Trade, Society and European Influence in Southern Asia 1600–1800*, 113–34, Aldershot, Brookfield.

Arasaratnam, Sinnappah, 1995, *Maritime Trade, Society and European Influence in Southern Asia, 1600–1800*, Variorum, Aldershot, Brookfield.

Aring, Paul Gerhard, 1987, *Christen und Juden heute—und die 'Judenmission'? Geschichte und Theologie protestantischer Judenmission in Deutschland, dargestellt und untersucht am Beispiel des Protestantismus im mittleren Deutschland*, Haag und Herchen, Frankfurt am Main.

Arnold, David and Stuart Blackburn (eds.), 2004, *Telling lives in India. Biography, Autobiography and Life History*, Indiana UP and Permanent Black, Bloomington.

Austen, Ralph A. and Jonathan Derrick, 1999, *Middlemen of the Cameroon Rivers. The Duala and their Hinterland c. 1600–c. 1960*, Cambridge University Press, Cambridge.

Baago, Kai, 1969, *Pioneers of Indigenous Christianity*, CLS, Madras.

Bachmann-Medick, Doris, 2002, 'Übersetzung im Spannungsfeld von Dialog und Erschütterung. Ein Modell der Auseinandersetzung zwischen Kulturen und Disziplinen', in Joachim Renn et.al., *Übersetzung als Medium des Kulturverstehens und sozialer Integration*, 275–91, Campus, Frankfurt, New York.

Baltzer, Justus (ed.), 1906, *August Hermann Francke*, Velhagen und Klasing, Bielefeld, Leipzig.

Bayly, Christopher Allan, 1983, *Rulers, Townsmen and Bazaars. North Indian Society in the Age of British Expansion 1770–1870*, Cambridge University Press, Cambridge [et al].

Bayly, Christopher Allan, 1990, *Indian society and the making of the British Empire*, Cambridge University Press, Cambridge [et al].

Bayly, Christopher Allan, 1996, *Empire & Information. Intelligence Gathering and Social Communication in India, 1780–1870*, Cambridge University Press, Cambridge [et.al.].

Bayly, Susan, 1989, *Saints, Goddesses and Kings. Muslims and Christians in South Indian Society 1700–1900*, Cambridge University Press, Cambridge.

Beck, Hartmut, 1981, *Brüder in vielen Völkern: 250 Jahre Mission der Brüdergemeine*, Verlag der Ev.-Luth. Mission, Erlangen (= Erlanger Taschenbücher, Vol. 58).

Bell, Andrew, 1797, *An Experiment of Education, made at the Male Asylum of Madras. Suggesting a system by which a school or family may teach itself under the superintendence of the master or parent*, Cadell and Davies, London, Edinburg, (2nd edition 1805; 3rd edition 1807).

Bergunder, Michael (ed.), 1999, *Missionsberichte aus Indien im 18. Jahrhundert. Ihre Bedeutung für die europäische Geistesgeschichte und ihr wissenschaftlicher Quellenwert für die Indienkunde*, Verlag der Franckeschen Stiftungen, Halle (=Neue Hallesche Berichte. Quellen und Studien zur Geschichte und Gegenwart Südindiens, Vol. 1).

Bayer, Theophil Siegfried, 1738, *Historia regni graecorum bactriani in qua simul graecarum in India coloniarum vetus memoris explicatur [...] accedit Christophori Theodosii Waltheri Doctrina Temporum Indica, cum paralipomenis*, Petersburg.

Beyreuther, Erich, 1952, *Bartholomäus Ziegenbalg: Aus dem Leben des ersten deutschen Missionars*, Evang. Verl.-Anst., Berlin.

Bitterli, Urs, 1986, *Alte Welt—neue Welt. Formen des europäisch-überseeischen Kulturkontakts vom 15. bis zum 18. Jahrhundert*, C.H. Beck Verlag, München.

Black, Jeremy, 2000, *Der große Atlas der Weltgeschichte*, RM-Buch-und-Medien-Vertrieb, Köln.

Bohnsack, Ralf and Winfried Marotzki (eds.), 1998, *Biografieforschung und Kulturanalyse. Transdisziplinäre Zugänge qualitativer Forschung*, Leske und Burdich, Opladen.

Boissevain, Jeremy, 1974, *Friends of Friends: Networks, Manipulators and Coalitions*, St. Martin's Press, New York.

Boyd, Robin, 1994, *An Introduction to Indian Christian Theology*, ISPCK, New Delhi.

Brecht, Martin and Klaus Deppermann (eds.), 1995, *Der Pietismus im achtzehnten Jahrhundert*, Vandenhoeck & Ruprecht, Göttingen (=Geschichte des Pietismus, vol. 2).

Brecht, Martin and Johannes van den Berg (eds.), 1993, *Der Pietismus vom siebzehnten bis zum frühen achtzehnten Jahrhundert*, Vandenhoeck & Ruprecht, Göttingen (=Geschichte des Pietismus, vol. 1).

Brentjes, Burchard, 1987, 'Meteorologische Beobachtungen des 18. Jahrhunderts in Madras', in Burchard Brentjes and Hans Joachim Peuke, *Wissenschaftsbeziehungen zwischen Halle und Indien in Tradition und Gegenwart*, 27–38, Halle (Saale) (=WB 1987/44 (I 42).

Brieger, Johann Georg, 1990, *Historisch-topographische Beschreibung der Stadt Halle im Magdeburgischen*, (im Verlag und zum Besten der evangelischen Schulanstalt, Grottkau, 1788), reprint, Fliegenkopf Verlag, Halle.

Brimnes, Niels, 1999, *Constructing the Colonial Encounter, Right and Left Hand Castes in Early Colonial South India*, Curzon Press, Richmond.

Brockington, John, 1992, *Hinduism and Christianity*, St. Martin's Press, New York.

Brown, Judith M., 2011, *Windows into the Past, Life Histories and the Historian of South Asia*, Oxford University Press, New Delhi.

Brown, Judith, 2009, 'Life Histories and the History of Modern South Asia', *American Historical Review*, June (2009) 587–95.

Brunner, Daniel, 1993, *Halle Pietists in England—Anthony William Boehm and the Society for Promoting Christian Knowledge*, Vandenhoeck & Ruprecht, Göttingen.

Bugge, Henriette, 1994, *Mission and Tamil Society: Social and Religious Change in South India (1840–1900)*, Curzon Press, Surrey, Richmond.

Burkhardt, Gustav Emil, 1879, *Die evangelische Mission in Vorder-Indien*, Velhagen & Klasing, Bielefeld [et al.], (= G.E. Burkhardts Kleine Missions-Bibliothek von Reinhold Grundemann).

Caland, Willem (ed.), 1926, *Ziegenbalg's Malabarisches Heidentum*, Koninklijke Akademie van Wetenschappen, Amsterdam (Verhandelingen der Koninklijke Akademie van Wetenschappen te Amsterdam/Afd. Letterkunde; N.R. 25.3).

Caland, Willem (ed.), 1930, *B. Ziegenbalg's kleinere Schriften*, Koninklijke Akademie van Wetenschappen, Amsterdam (Verhandelingen der Koninklijke Akademie van Wetenschappen te Amsterdam/Afd. Letterkunde; N.R. 29.2).

Caldwell, Robert, 1881, *Records of the Early History of the Tinnevelly Mission of the Society for Promoting Christian Knowledge and the Society for the Propagation of the Gospel in Foreign Parts*, Higginbotham and Co., Madras.

Caldwell, Robert A., 1982, *A political and general history of the District of Tinnevelly, in the Presidency of Madras, from the earliest period to its cession to the English Government in AD 1801*, (Government Press, Madras 1881) Reprint: *A History of Tinnevelly*, Asian Educational Services, New Delhi/Madras.

Caplan, Lionel, 1989, *Religion and Power: Essays on the Christian Community in Madras*, CLS, Madras.

Chatterjee, Ramakrishna, 1986, *Christian Missionaries and Labour Migration to Assam Tea Gardens in Colonial Times (Occasional Paper N⁰ 80)*, Centre for Studies in Social Sciences, Calcutta.

Conserve Monuments, Save Heritage, Research Club, Research Report, Possesing (sic!) Historical Interest & Conservation of Tombs and Monuments—Vol. III, (place not mentioned) April 1999.

Correia-Alfonso, John, 1997, *The Jesuits in India, 1542–1773*, Gujarat Sahitya Prakash, Anand, Gujarat, India.

Dal, Nicolaus, 1728–1731, *Grammatica portugueza para o uso da Escola Portugueza de Trangambar*, Parts 1–4, Mission Printing Press, Tranquebar.

Dansk Biografisk Leksikon, 1933–1944, Grundlagt af C.F. Bricka, Redigeret af Povl Engelstoft under Medvirkning af Svend Dahl, Schultz, København.

Das Gupta, Ashin, 1984, 'Indian Merchants in the Age of Partnership. 1500–1800', in Dwijendra Tripathi (ed.), *Business Communities of India. A Historical Perspective*, 27–39, Sage, New Delhi.

Das Gupta, Ashin Das and Michael Naylor Pearson (eds.), 1987, *India and the Indian Ocean 1500–1800*, Oxford University Press, Calcutta, New York.

Dausien, Bettina and Helga Kelle, 2005, 'Biographie und Kulturelle Praxis. Methodologische Überlegungen zur Verknüpfung von Ethnographie und Biographieforschung', in Bettina Völker, Bettina Dausien, Helma Lutz and Gabriele Rosenthal (eds.), *Biographieforschung im Diskurs*, 189–212, VS Verlag, Wiesbaden.

Denzler, Georg and Carl Anderson, 1993, *Wörterbuch der Kirchengeschichte*, Kösel, München.

Deppermann, Klaus, 1961, *Der Hallesche Pietismus und der preußische Staat unter Friedrich III (I.)*, Vandenhoeck & Ruprecht, Göttingen.

Dharampal-Frick, Gita, 1994, *Indien im Spiegel deutscher Quellen der frühen Neuzeit (1500–1750). Studien zu einer interkulturellen Konstellation*, Niemeyer, Tübingen.

Diller, Stephan, 1992, 'Tranquebar: Handelsplatz und Missionsstation (1620–1845)', *Forschungsforum (=Berichte der Otto-Friedrich-Universität Bamberg)*, Heft 4: 43–54.

Diller, Stephan 1999, *Die Dänen in Indien, Südostasien und China (1620–1845)*, Harrassowitz, Wiesbaden.

The Directors of the Royal Danish East India Company, Pvt. Ltd. hereby announce/... J. Holmste, 16 December 1727.

Directorate of the Francke Foundations (ed.), 1863, *Die Stiftungen August Hermann Franckes zu Halle. Festschrift zur zweiten Säkularfeier seines Geburtstages*, Verlag der Buchhandlung des Waisenhauses, Halle.

The Directory of National Biography. Founded in 1882 by George Smith. Edited by Sir Leslie Stephen and Sir Sidney Lee. From the Earliest Times to 1900, published since 1717 by the Oxford University Press, London

Dirks, Nicholas B., 2001, *Castes of Mind. Colonialism and the Making of Modern India*, Princeton University Press, Princeton.

Dodwell, Henry, 1986, *The Nabobs of Madras*, Asian Educational Services, New Delhi.

Downs, Frederick Sheldon, 1992, *History of Christianity in India, Vol. V, Part 5: North East India in the Nineteenth and Twentieth Centuries*, CHAI, Bangalore.

Dubois, Jean Antoine, 1978, *Hindu manners, customs and ceremonies*, (Madras 1906) Reprint, Oxford University Press, New Delhi.

Duby, Georges and Michelle Perrot (eds.), 2006, *Geschichte der Frauen. Vol. 3, Early Modern times*, Zweitausendeins-Verlag, Frankfurt/Main.

Duden, 2000, *Das große Fremdwörterbuch*, Dudeneverlag, Mannheim [et al].

Dutu, Alexander (ed.), 1989, *Brief und Briefwechsel in Mittel-und Osteuropa im 18. und 19. Jahrhundert*, Hobbing, Essen (=Brief und Briefwechsel im 18. und 19. Jahrhundert als Quellen der Kulturbeziehungsforschung, Vol. 1).

Duverdier, Gerald, 1977, 'Die 'Malabarische Correspondentz' und A.H. Francke', in Rosemarie Ahrbeck und Burchard Thaler (eds.), *August Hermann Francke 1663–1727*, 108–21, Halle (=WB 1977/37 (A 39).

Eaton, Richard Maxwell, 1984, 'Conversion to Christianity among the Nagas, 1876–1971', *IESHR*, 21 (1):1–44.

Eck, Werner, 1993, 'Überlieferung und historische Realität: Ein Grundproblem prosopographischer Forschung', in Werner Eck (ed.), *Prosopographie und Sozialgeschichte. Studien zur Methodik und Erkenntnismöglichkeit der kaiserzeitlichen Prosopographie*, 365–96, Böhlau, Köln [et al].

Feldbæk, Ole, 1984, 'The Development of an Indo-European Town in Mughal India: Tranquebar in the Seventeenth and Eighteenth

Centuries', in Kenneth Ballhatchet and David Taylor (eds.), *Changing South Asia: City and Culture*, 11–20, The Centre of South Asian Studies at SOAS, London.

Feldbæk, Ole,1986, *Danske Handelskompagnier 1616–1843*, Selskabet for Udgivelse af Kilder til Dansk Historie, København, Copenhagen.

Feldbæk, Ole, 1991, 'No Ship for Tranquebar for Twenty-Nine Years. Or: The Art of Survival of a Mid-Seventeenth Century European Settlement in India', in Roderich Ptak and Dietmar Rothermund (eds), *Emporia, Commodities and Entrepreneurs in Asian Maritime Trade, c. 1400–1750*, 29–36, Steiner, Stuttgart (=Beiträge zur Südasienforschung, vol. 14).

Fenger, J.F., 1845, *Geschichte der Tranquebarschen Mission nach den Quellen bearbeitet*, Gebhardt, Grimma.

Fenger, J.F., 1863, *History of the Tranquebar Mission: worked out from the original papers*, Evangelical Lutheran Mission, Tranquebar.

Fengler, Heinz [et al], 1976, *Lexikon der Numismatik*, VEB Verlag für Verkehrswesen, Berlin.

Fihl, Esther, 2009, 'Shipwrecked on the Coromandel: the First Indo-Danish contract, 1620', *Review of Development and Change*, XIV: 1–2.

Flaschendräger, Werner, 1981, 'Vernunft kontra Autoritäten. Universitäten im "Jahrhundert der Aufklärung"', in Günter Steiger and Werner Flaschendräger, *Magister und Scholaren. Professoren und Studenten*, 55–71, Urania-Verl., Leipzig, Jena, Berlin.

Fleisch, Paul, 1936, *Hundert Jahre lutherischer Mission*, Verlag der Evangelisch-Lutherischen Mission, Leipzig.

Forrester, Duncan B., 1974, 'Indian Christian's Attitude to Caste in the Nineteenth Century', *ICHR*, 8 (2): 131–47.

Forrester, Duncan B., 1975, 'Indian Christian Attitude to Caste in the Twentieth Century', *ICHR*, 9 (1): 3–21.

Förster, Stig, 1992, *Die mächtigen Diener der East-India Company: Ursachen und Hintergründe der britischen Expansionspolitik in Südasien, 1793–1849*, Steiner, Stuttgart.

Francke, August Hermann, 1727, Send=Schreiben an die Fünf Königl. Dänische Evangelische Herren Missionarios zu Tranquebar in Ost=Indien […], Waisenhaus, Halle.

Francke, August Hermann, 1705, *Pietas Hallensis: Being an Hitorical Narration Of the wonderful Foot-Steps Of Divine Providence In Erecting, Carrying on, and Building the Orphan-House*, […] at Glaucha near Hall in Saxony, Downing, London.

Francke, August Hermann 1708–1709, *Segens-volle Fußstapfen des noch lebenden und waltenden liebreichen und getreuen Gottes*, […], 3rd ed., in Verlegung des Wäysen-Hauses, Halle.

Francke, August Hermann, 1889, *August Hermann Franckes kurtzer und einfältiger Unterricht, wie die Kinder zur wahren Gottseligkeit und christlicher Klugheit anzuführen sind; zum Behuf christlicher Informatorum entworffen*, new edition of the 1748 edition by Otto Frick, Verlag der Buchhandlung des Waisenhauses, Halle/Saale.

Freitag, Christine, 1995, *Schule und Bildungshilfe in den Konzeptionen katholischer Missionsgesellschaften*, Böhlau, Köln.

Frenz, Matthias and Hansjürg Descher, 2006, "Das Werk der Bekehrung'—Überlegungen zum Verhältnis von Pietismus, Aufklärung und Mission im frühen 18. Jahrhundert', in Michael Mann (ed.), *Europäische Aufklärung und protestantische Mission in Indien*, 33–55, Draupadi Verlag, Heidelberg.

Fries, Wilhelm, 1913, *Die Stiftungen August Hermann Franckes*, Waisenhaus, Halle.

Fritz, Johann Friedrich, 1748, *Orientalisch- und Occidentalischer Sprachmeister*, Gessner, Leipzig.

Frykenberg, Robert Eric, 1996, 'Modern Education in South India 1784–1854: Its Roots and Its Role as a Vehicle of Integration under Company Raj', *American Historical Review* 91 (1): 37–65.

Frykenberg, Robert Eric, 1999, 'The Halle Legacy in Modern India: Information and the Spread of Education, Enlightenment and Evangelization', in Michael Bergunder (ed.), *Missionsberichte aus Indien im 18. Jahrhundert. Ihre Bedeutung für die europäische Geistesgeschichte und ihr wissenschaftlicher Quellenwert für die Indienkunde*, 6–29, Verlag der Franckeschen Stiftungen, Halle.

Frykenberg, Robert Eric, 1999, 'The Legacy of Christian Friedrich Schwartz', *International Bulletin of Missionary Research* 23 (3): 130–35.

Frykenberg, Robert Eric, 2008, *Christianity in India. From Beginnings to the Present*, Oxford University Press, New York.

Fuchs, Martin, 2002, 'Soziale Pragmatik des Übersetzens. Strategien der Interkulturalität in Indien', in Joachim Renn [et al.], *Übersetzung als Medium des Kulturverstehens und sozialer Integration*, 292–323, Campus, Frankfurt am Main, New York.

Füllberg-Stolberg, Katja and Heike Liebau, 1997, 'Einige Überlegungen zur Nutzung missionarischer Dokumente für historische Forschungen in Asien und Afrika. Eine vergleichende Quellenkritik', in Heike Liebau and Dietrich Reetz (eds.), *Globale Prozesse und 'Akteure des Wandels' in der Geschichte. Quellen und Methoden zu ihrer Untersuchung*, 169–96, Das Arabische Buch, Berlin.

Gäbler, Ulrich (ed.), 2000, *Der Pietismus im neunzehnten und zwanzigsten Jahrhundert*, Vandenhoeck & Ruprecht, Göttingen (=Geschichte des Pietismus, Vol. 3).

Gensichen, Hans-Werner, 1956, 'Die konfessionelle Stellung der dänisch-halleschen Mission', *EMZ*, 13: 1–19.

Gensichen, Hans-Werner, 1956, *Tranquebar Then and Now*, CLS, Madras.

Gensichen, Hans-Werner, 1959, 'Bartholomäus Ziegenbalg und der Islam', in Georg Hoffmann and Karl Heinrich Rengstorf (eds.), *Stat crux dum volvitur orbis. Eine Festschrift für Landesbischof D. Hanns Lilje, Abt zu Loccum, zum sechzigsten Geburtstag am 20. August 1959*, 140–46, Lutherisches Verlagshaus, Berlin.

Gensichen, Hans-Werner, 1961, *Missionsgeschichte der neueren Zeit*, Vandenhoeck & Ruprecht, Göttingen (=*Die Kirche in ihrer Geschichte. Ein Handbuch*, ed. by Kurt Dietrich Schmidt and Ernst Wolf, vol. 4. Lieferung T.).

Gensichen, Hans-Werner, 1962, 'Die deutsche Mission und der Kolonialismus', *Kerygma und Dogma*, 8: 136–49.

Gensichen, Hans-Werner, 1975, "Dienst der Seelen' und 'Dienst des Leibes' in der frühen pietistischen Mission', in Heinrich Bornkamm [et al.], (eds.), *Der Pietismus in Gestalten und Wirkungen—Martin Schmidt zum 65. Geburtstag*, 155–78, Luther-Verlag, Bielefeld (=Arbeiten zur Geschichte des Pietismus, Vol. 14.).

Gensichen, Hans-Werner, 1977, 'The social impact of the early Protestant missions in South India', *The Church in a Changing Society: Conflict—Reconciliation or Adjustment?* (International Commission on Comparative Ecclesiastical History), Uppsala, 430–35.

Gensichen, Hans-Werner, 1993, *Invitatio ad Fraternitatem. 75 Jahre Deutsche Gesellschaft für Missionswissenschaft (1918–1993)*, Lit., Münster, Hamburg.

Gensichen, Hans-Werner, 1999, 'Indienmission im Weltaspekt: Globale Perspektiven in den Halleschen Berichten', in Michael Bergunder (ed.), *Missionsberichte aus Indien im 18. Jahrhundert. Ihre Bedeutung für die europäische Geistesgeschichte und ihr wissenschaftlicher Quellenwert für die Indienkunde*, 30–43, Verlag der Franckeschen Stiftungen, Halle.

Georgi, Lotte, 1958, *Maria Dorothea Ziegenbalg. Tatsachenberichte aus dem Leben der ersten deutschen evangelischen Missionarsfrau in Südindien*, Evangelische Verlagsanstalt, Berlin.

Germann, Wilhelm, 1865, 'Die Geschichte der tamulischen Bibelübersetzung', *MNOIM*, 17: 86–119.

Germann, Wilhelm, 1865, 'Die wissenschaftliche Arbeit unserer alten Tamulen-Missionare mit Berücksichtigung neuerer Leistungen', *MNOIM*, 17 (1): 1–27.

Germann, Wilhelm, 1865, *Johann Philipp Fabricius: Seine fünfzigjährige*

Wirksamkeit im Tamulenlande und das Missionsleben des achtzehnten Jahrhunderts daheim und draußen, Deichert, Erlangen.

German, Wilhelm, 1867, [Bartholomäus Ziegenbalg] *Genealogie der Malabarischen Götter aus eigenen Schriften und Briefen zusammengetragen und verfaßt von Bartholomäus Ziegenbalg*, Higginbotham [et al.], Madras.

Germann, Wilhelm, 1868, *Ziegenbalg und Plütschau, Die Gründungsjahre der Tranquebarschen Mission*, Deichert, Erlangen.

Germann, Wilhelm, 1870, *Missionar Christian Friedrich Schwartz: Sein Leben und Wirken*, Deichert, Erlangen.

Germann, Wilhelm, 1880, 'Ziegenbalgs Bibliotheca Malabarica', *MNOIM* 32 (1/2): 1–20 and 62–94.

Germann, Wilhelm, 1886, 'Der Ausgang der Dänisch-Halleschen Mission in Indien', *AMZ*, 345–53.

Ghosh, Anindita (ed.), 2008, *Behind the Veil. Resistance, Women and the Everyday in Colonial South Asia,* Palgrave Macmillan, England, New York.

Ghosh, S. Ch., 1995, *The History of Education in Modern India 1757–1968*, Orient Longman, New Delhi.

Goel, Sita Ram, 1996, *History of Hindu-Christian Encounters AD 304 to 1996*, Voice of India, New Delhi.

Grafe, Hugald, 1967, 'The Relation between the Tranquebar Lutherans and the Tanjore Catholics in the First Half of the 18th Century', *ICHR*, 1: 41–58.

Grafe, Hugald, 1981, *Evangelische Kirche in Indien: Auskunft und Einblicke*, Verlag der Eveng.-Luth. Mission, Erlangen.

Grafe, Hugald, 1990, *History of Christianity in India, Vol. IV, Part 2: Tamilnadu in the Nineteenth and Twentieth Centuries*, Theological Publications in India, Bangalore.

Grafe, Hugald, 1999, 'Hindu Apologetics at the Beginning of the Protestant Mission Era in India', in Michael Bergunder (ed.), *Missionsberichte aus Indien im 18. Jahrhundert. Ihre Bedeutung für die europäische Geistesgeschichte und ihr wissenschaftlicher Quellenwert für die Indienkunde*, 69–93, Verlag der Franckeschen Stiftungen, Halle.

Graul, Karl, 1861, *Die Stellung der Evangelisch-Lutherischen Mission in Leipzig zur Ostindischen Kastenfrage*, Verlag de Evang.-Luth. Mission, Leipzig.

Greenblatt, Stephen, 1991, *Marvelous Possessions: The Wonder of the World*, The University of Chicago Press, Chicago.

Gross, Andreas [et al.], (eds.), 2006, *Halle and the Beginning of Protestant Christianity in India, Vol. I: The Danish-Halle and the English-Halle Mission. Vol. II: Christian Mission in the Indian Context. Vol. III:*

Communication between India and Europe, Verlag der Franckeschen Stiftungen, Halle.

Gross, Andreas, 2006, 'Madras and the English-Halle Missionaries (1726–1836)', in Andreas Gross [et al.], (eds.), *Halle and the Beginning of Protestant Christianity in India*, Vol. I, 311–44, Verlag der Franckeschen Stiftungen, Halle.

Gross, Andreas, 2006, 'Some Aspects of the English-Halle Mission in Cuddalore (1737–1829)', in Andreas Gross [et al.], (eds.), *Halle and the Beginning of Protestant Christianity in India*, Vol. I, 381–405, Verlag der Franckeschen Stiftungen, Halle.

Gründer, Horst, 1982, *Christliche Mission und deutscher Imperialismus. Eine politische Geschichte ihrer Beziehungen während der deutschen Kolonialzeit (1884–1914) unter besonderer Berücksichtigung Afrikas und Chinas*, Ferdinand Schöningh, Paderborn.

Gründer, Horst, 1992, *Welteroberung und Christentum. Ein Handbuch zur Geschichte der Neuzeit*, Gütersloher Verl.-Haus Mohn, Gütersloh.

Gründler, Johann Ernst und Bartholomäus Ziegenbalg, 1998, *Die Malabarische Korrespondenz: Tamilische Briefe an deutsche Missionare. Eine Auswahl*, (With an introduction and with explanations by Kurt Liebau), Thorbecke, Sigmaringen.

Habermas, Rebekka, 2008, 'Mission im 19. Jahrhundert. Globale Netze des Religiösen', *Historische Zeitschrift*, 56: 629–79.

Habib, Irfan, 1996, *An Atlas of the Mughal Empire: Political and Economic Maps with Detailed Notes, Bibliography and Index*, Oxford University Press, Delhi [et al.]

Habib, Irfan (ed.), 2002, *Resistance and Moderzination Under Haidar Ali and Tipu Sultan*, Anthem Press, London (=*Confronting Colonialism)*.

Hagedorn, Dieter, 1993, 'Eignet sich die prosopographische Methode zur Erforschung sozialer Strukturen in den Dörfern des Römischen Ägypten?', in Werner Eck, *Prosopographie und Sozialgeschichte*, 351–63, Böhlau, Köln, Wien, Weimar.

Hambye, Édouard René, 1997, *History of Christianity in India, Vol. III: During the Eighteenth Century*, CHAI, Bangalore.

Handmann, Richard, 1903, *Die Evangelische Lutherische Tamulen Mission in der Zeit ihrer Neubegründung: Ein Beitrag zur Geschichte der Evangelischen Mission im 19. Jahrhundert*, Hinrichs, Leipzig.

Hansen, C. Rise, 1980, *Sources of the history of North Africa, Asia and Oceania in Denmark*, The Danish National Archives, (Transl[ated] from Danish into Engl[ish]), München [et al] (=Sources of the history of North Africa, Asia and Oceania in Scandinavia, 1); (=Guides to the sources for the history of the nations, 3).

Hansen, J., 1891, *August Hermann Franckes wichtigste pädagogische Schriften*, Schöningh, Paderborn [et al.] (= Schulz, B. [et al] (eds.), *Sammlung der bedeutendsten pädagogischen Schriften aus alter und neuer Zeit. Mit Biographien, Erläuterungen und erklärenden Anmerkungen 1888–1914*, Vol. 8, Paderborn).

Hardgrafe, Robert L. Jr., 1998, 'The Representation of Sati: Four Eighteenth Century Etchings by Baltazard Solvyns', *Bengal Past and Present*, 117: 57–80.

Hausberger, Bernd (ed.), 2006, *Globale Lebensläufe. Menschen als Akteure im weltgeschichtlichen Geschehen*, Mandelbaum Verlag, Wien.

Hefner, Robert W., 1993, 'Of Faith and Commitment: Christian Conversion in Muslim Java', in Robert W. Hefner (ed.), *Conversion to Christianity: historical and anthropological perspectives on a great transformation*, 99–128, University of California Press, Berkeley.

Hefner, Robert William (ed.), 1993, *Conversion to Christianity: Historical and Anthropological Perspectives on a Great Transformation*, University of California Press, Berkeley.

Heidrich, Petra and Heike Liebau (eds.), 2001, *Akteure des Wandels. Lebensläufe und Gruppenbilder an Schnittstellen von Kulturen*, Das Arabische Buch, Berlin (=Studien des Zentrums Moderner Orient, 14).

Henry, Victor I., 1982, 'Tamil Translations of the Bible by the Danish-Halle Mission during the Eighteenth Century', *ICHR*, 16 (1): 72–85.

Heyden, Ulrich van der (ed.), 1996, *Alexander Merensky. Mein Missionsleben in Transvaal. Erinnerungen des Berliner Missionars in Südafrika 1859–1882*, [Berlin 1899], Edition Ost, Berlin.

Hindi-Russkij Slovar, 2 vols., 1972, Sowjetskaja Enciklopedija, Moskva.

Hinrichs, Carl, 1971, *Preußentum und Pietismus*, Vandenhoeck & Ruprecht, Göttingen.

Hinske, Norbert, 1989, *Zentren der Aufklärung. Vol I, Halle: Aufklärung und Pietismus*, Schneider, Heidelberg (=Wolfenbüttler Studien zur Aufklärung, Vol. 15).

Hjelm, Torben, 1988, *Fra det nu forsvundne Tranquebar. Billeder med en uddybende tekst, der beskriver historien om vor gamle handelskoloni, Tranquebar of logen Serampore samt Nikobar-øgruppen*, Strandberg, Copenhagen.

Holsten, Walter, 1949, *Johannes Evangelista Gossner. Glaube und Gemeinde*, Vandenhoeck und Ruprecht, Göttingen.

Hommel, Karsten, 2006, 'Naturwissenschaftliche Forschungen', in Heike Liebau, *Geliebtes Europa//Ostindische Welt. 300 Jahre interkultureller Dialog im Spiegel der Dänisch-Halleschen Mission. Katalog der Jahresausstellung der Frankeschen Stiftungen zu Halle*, 163–79, Franckesche Stiftungen, Halle.

Hommel, Karsten, 2006, 'Physico-Theology as Mission Strategy: Missionary Christoph Samuel John's (1746–1813) Understanding of Nature', in Andreas Gross [et al.] (eds.), *Halle and the Beginning of Protestant Christianity in India*, Vol. III, 1115–35, Verlag der Franckeschen Stiftungen, Halle.

Hommel, Karsten, 2010, "Für solche [Theologen] wolle Gott seine Ost-indische Kirche in Gnaden bewahren!' Physikotheologie und Dänisch-Englisch-Hallesche Mission', in Heike Liebau, Andreas Nehring and Brigitte Klosterberg, *Mission und Forschung: translokale Wissensproduktion zwischen Indien und Europa im 18. und 19. Jahrhundert*, 181–94, Verlag der Frankeschen Stiftungen, Halle.

Hoppe, Brigitte, 2010, 'Von der Naturgeschichte zu den Naturwissenschaften—die Dänisch-Halleschen Missionare als Naturforscher in Indien vom 18. bis 19. Jahrhundert', in Heike Liebau, Andreas Nehring and Brigitte Klosterberg, *Mission und Forschung: translokale Wissensproduktion zwischen Indien und Europa im 18. und 19. Jahrhundert*, 141–66, Verlag der Frankeschen Stiftungen, Halle.

Horton, Robin, 1975, 'On the Rationality of Conversion', Part I, *Africa*, 45 (3): 219–35.

Hourani, Albert, 1994, *Der Islam im europäischen Denken*, S. Fischer, Frankfurt am Main.

Hudson, Dennis D., 2000, *Protestant Origins in India: Tamil Evangelical Christians, 1706–1835*, William B. Eerdmans Pub., Grand Rapids, (=Studies in the History of Christian Missions).

Hufschmidt, Anke, 2001, *Adlige Frauen im Weserraum zwischen 1570 und 1700: Status-Rollen-Lebenspraxis*, Aschendorff, Münster (= Veröffentlichungen der historischen Kommission für Westfalen, 12 A: Geschichtliche Arbeiten zur westfälischen Landesforschung, Vol. 15).

Hufton, Olwen, 1998, *Frauenleben. Eine europäische Geschichte 1500–1800*, S. Fischer, Frankfurt am Main.

Imperial Gazetteer of India Provincial Series, Madras, Vol. 2, 1985, Usha Publications, New Delhi.

Ingleby, Jonathan C., 2000, *Missionaries, Education and India. Issues in Protestant Missionary Education in the Long Nineteenth Century*, ISPCK, Delhi.

Irschick, Eugene F., 1994, *Dialogue and History: Constructing South India, 1795–1895*, University of California Press, Berkeley.

Jacobi, Juliane and Thomas Müller-Bahlke (eds.), 1989, *'Man hatte von ihm gute Hoffnung ...' Das Waisenhausalbum der Franckeschen Stiftungen 1695–1749*, Verlag der Franckeschen Stiftungen Halle im Max Niemeyer Verlag, Tübingen.

Jacobi, Juliane, 1993, 'Das erste Waisenalbum des Halleschen Waisenhauses (1695–1749)', *Jahrbuch für historische Bildungsforschung*, vol. 6: 7–26, Klinkhardt, Bad Heilbrunn, Obb.

Jacobi, Juliane, 2000, 'Der Blick auf das Kind. Zur Entstehung der Pädagogik des Halleschen Waisenhauses', in Josef N. Neumann and Udo Sträter (eds.), *Das Kind in Pietismus und Aufklärung*, 47–59, Verlag der Franckeschen Stiftungen Halle im Max-Niemeyer Verlag, Tübingen (= Hallesche Forschungen, Vol. 5).

Jenkins, Paul, 1991, 'Missionsgeschichte: Ein Manifest', *ZM*, 3: 8–18.

Jeyaraj, Daniel, 1996, *Inkulturation in Tranquebar. Der Beitrag der frühen dänisch-halleschen Mission zum Werden einer indisch-einheimischen Kirche (1706–1730)*, Verlag der Evangelisch-Lutherischen Mission, Erlangen.

Jeyaraj, Daniel, 1997, 'Die Ordination des ersten protestantischen Pfarrers Aaron in Südindien, 28.12.1733', *ZM*, XXIII (2): 105–125.

Jeyaraj, Daniel, 1998, 'Ordination of the First Protestant Pastor Aaron—28.12.1733 and its Significance. A Contribution to Church History', in Daniel Jeyaraj (ed.), *Ordination of the First Indian Pastor Aaron*, 1–79, Lutheran Heritage Archives, Chennai.

Jeyaraj, Daniel (ed.), 1998, *Ordination of the First Indian Pastor Aaron*, Lutheran Heritage Archives, Chennai.

Jeyaraj, Daniel (ed.), 1999, *Christian Friedrich Schwartz: His Contributions to South India*, Lutheran Heritage Archives, Chennai.

Jeyaraj, Daniel, (ed.), 2003, *Bartholomäus Ziegenbalgs Genealogie der malabarischen Götter: Edition der Originalfassung von 1713 mit Einleitung, Analyse und Glossar*, Verl. der Franckeschen Stiftungen, Halle (=Neue Hallesche Berichte 3).

Jeyaraj, Daniel, 2005, *Genealogy of the South Indian Deities: an English translation of Bartholomäus Ziegenbalg's original German manuscript with a textual analysis and glossary*, Routledge, Curzon, London, New York (= studies in Asian religion).

Jeyaraj, Daniel, 2006, *A German Exploration of Indian Society: Ziegenbalg's 'Malabarian Heathenism' (an annotated English translation with an introduction and a glossary)*, The Mylapore Institute for Indigenous Studies et al., Chennai [et al.].

Job, Thomas, 2006, 'History of Protestant Christianity in Tirunelveli', in Andreas Gross [et al.], (eds.), *Halle and the Beginning of Protestant Christianity in India*, Vol. I, 497–525, Verl. der Franckeschen Stiftungen, Halle.

John, Christoph Samuel, 1813, *On Indian Civilization, or, report of a successful experiment made, during two years, on that subject, in fifteen Tamil and five*

English Native Free-Schools; with proposals for establishing a separate, liberal Native School Society, etc., F.C. and J. Rivington, London.

Jones, Adam, 1989, 'Schwarze Frauen, weiße Beobachter. Die Frauen der Goldküste in den Augen der europäischen Männer, 1600–1900', in Hans-Joachim König (et al.) (eds.), *Der europäische Beobachter außereuropäischer Kulturen: Zur Problematik der Wirklichkeitswahrnehmung*, 153–168, Duncker & Humblot, Berlin (=Zeitschrift für Historische Forschung, Supplement 7).

Jones, Adam, 1990, *Zur Quellenproblematik der Geschichte Westafrikas 1450–1900*, Franz Steiner, Stuttgart (=Studien zur Kulturkunde, vol. 99).

Juneja, Monica, 2006, 'Mission Encounters and Transnational History. Reflections on the Use of Concepts across Cultures', in Andreas Gross [et al.], (eds.), *Halle and the Beginning of Protestant Christianity in India*, Vol. III, 1025–45, Verlag der Franckeschen Stiftungen, Halle.

Jürgens, Hanco, 2006, 'German Indologists *Avant la Lettre*: Changing Horizons of the Halle Missionaries in Southern India' in Andreas Gross [et al.], (eds.), *Halle and the Beginning of Protestant Christianity in India*, Vol. III, 1047–89, Verlag der Franckeschen Stiftungen, Halle.

Justin, W., 1986, 'The Nature of a Mission Community: The Universities' Mission to Central Africa in Bonde', in Robert Bickers and Rosemary Seton (eds.), *Missionary Encounters: Sources and Issues*, 128–52, Routledge, London.

Kadambavanam, Paul S., 1960, *Tirunelveli attiyācatin ārampam* (Tamil), the Foundation of the Diocese of Tirunelveli, Chennai.

Kahnt, Helmut and Bernd Knorr, 1986, *Alte Maße, Münzen und Gewichte*, Bibliographisches Institut, Leipzig.

Karotemprel, Sebastian, 1994, *The Impact of Christianity on the Tribes of North East India*, Sacred Heart Theological College, Shillong.

Kaur, Kuldip, 1990, *Madrasa Education in India: A Study of its Past and Present*, Centre for Research in Rural & Industrial Development, Chandigarh.

Kent, Eliza F., 2004, *Converting Women: Gender and Protestant Christianity in Colonial South India*, Oxford University Press, New York, Oxford.

Kent, Eliza F., 2006, 'Raja Clarinda—Widow, Concubine, Patroness: Women's Leadership in the Indian Church', in Andreas Gross [et al.], (eds.), *Halle and the Beginning of Protestant Christianity in India*, Vol. II, 659–83, Verl. der Franckeschen Stiftungen, Halle.

Kelelear, John Joshua, 1743, 'De Lingua Hindustanica', in David Mill (ed.), *Dissertationes selectae: variae S. literarum capita exponentes et illustrantes. 455–88,* Lugduni Batavorum, Wishoff.

Kistenich, Johannes, 2001, *Bettelmönche im öffentlichen Schulwesen: Ein Handbuch für die Erzdiözese Köln 1600–1850*, Böhlau, Köln (=Stadt und Gesellschaft, Vol. 1).

Klosterberg, Britta, 2000, 'Bücher für Kinder und Jugendliche in den Glauchaer Anstalten', in Penelope Willard (ed.), *Die Franckeschen Stiftungen zu Halle im Jahre 2000*, 31–39, Verlag der Franckeschen Stiftungen, Halle.

Der Königl. Dänischen Missionarien aus Ost-Indien eingesandter Ausführlichen Berichten, Von dem Werck ihres Amts unter den Heyden, angerichteten Schulen und Gemeinen, ereigneten Hindernissen und schweren Umständen; Beschaffenheit des Malabarischen Heydenthums, gepflogenen brieflichen Correspondentz und mündlichen Unterredungen mit selbigen Heyden [...] Vols. 1–9 (Continuation 1–108), 1710–72, Waisenhaus, Halle, (HB—Hallesche Berichte).

Köhle-Hezinger, Christel, 1994, 'Frauen im Pietismus', *BWKG*, 94: 107–21.

Koilparampil, George, 1982, *Caste in the Catholic Community in Kerala: A Case Study of Caste Elements in the Inter Rite Relationship of Syrians and Latins*, Dept. of Sociology, St. Teresa's College, Cochin.

Koilpillai, Victor J., 1985, *The SPCK in India 1710–1985. An Account of the Work of the Society for Promoting Christian Knowledge*, ISPCK, London, Delhi.

Kolappa Pillay Kanakasabhapathi Pillay, 1957, *History of Higher Education in South India, Vol. I., University of Madras 1857–1957*, Associated Printers, Madras.

Konrad, Dagmar, 2001, *Missionsbräute: Pietismus des 19. Jahrhunderts in der Basler Mission*, Waxmann, Münster [et al].

Kooiman, Dick, 1989, *Conversion and Social Equality in India: the London Missionary Society in South Travancore in the 19th Century*, Manohar Publications, New Delhi.

Koschorke, Klaus, 1992, 'Kontextualität und Universalität als Problemstellung der Kirchengeschichte', *Evangelische Theologie: Synkretismus und Inkulturation*, München, 52 (3): 209–24.

Koschorke, Klaus (ed.), 1998, *'Christen und Gewürze' Konfrontation und Interaktion kolonialer und indigener Christentumsvarianten*, Otto Harrassowitz Verlag, Göttingen.

Krieger, Martin, 1998, *Kaufleute, Seeräuber und Diplomaten. Der dänische Handel auf dem Indischen Ozean (1720–1868)*, Böhlau, Köln (=Wirtschafts- und Sozialhistorische Studien 8).

Kubitschek, Hans Dieter and Ingrid Wessel, 1981, *Geschichte Indonesiens: Vom Altertum bis zur Gegenwart*, Akademie-Verlag, Berlin.

Kulke, Hermann and Dietmar Rothermund, 1982, *Geschichte Indiens*, Kohlhammer, Stuttgart et al.

Kulke Hermann and Dietmar Rothermund, 1998, *Geschichte Indiens von der Induskultur bis heute*, C.H. Beck Verlag, München.

Kumar, Krishna, 1991, *Political Agenda of Education. A Study of Colonialist and Nationalist Ideas*, SAGE, New Delhi.

La Croze, M.V., 1727, *Abbildung des Indianischen Christen-Staats.* [...] Translated and with comments by M. Georg Christian Bohnstedt, Spörl, Halle.

Laird, Michael Andrew, 1972, *Missionaries and Education in Bengal 1793–1837*, Clarendon Press, Oxford.

Lancaster, Joseph, 1803, *Improvements in education, as it respects the industrious classes of the community: [...]*, Darton and Harvey, London.

Landsberg, Hannelore, 2010, 'Eine Fischsammlung aus Tranquebar, die Berliner Gesellschaft Naturforschender Freunde und deren Mitglied Marcus Eliser Bloch', in Heike Liebau, Andreas Nehring and Brigitte Klosterberg, *Mission und Forschung: translokale Wissensproduktion zwischen Indien und Europa im 18. und 19. Jahrhundert*, 167–80, Verlag der Frankeschen Stiftungen, Halle.

Langenscheidt, *Handwörterbuch Latein-Deutsch*, 1971, Langenscheidt Verlag, Berlin [et al].

Larsen, Kay, 1940, *Guvernører, Residenter, Kommandanter og Chefer samt enkelte andre fremtrædende Personer i de tidligere Danske Tropekolonier*, Arthur Jensens Forlag, København.

Lehmann, Arno, 1952/53, 'Halle und die südindische Sprach- und Religionswissenschaft', *WZ*, II, *Gesellschafts-und Sprachwissenschaftliche Reihe*, Heft 3: 149–56.

Lehmann, Arno, 1955, 'Hallesche Mediziner und Medizinen am Anfang deutsch-indischer Beziehungen', *WZ*, V, *Mathematisch-Naturwissenschaftliche Reihe*, Heft 2: 117–32.

Lehmann, Arno, 1956, *Es begann in Tranquebar. Die Geschichte der ersten evangelischen Kirche in Indien*, Evangelische Verlagsanstalt, Berlin.

Lehmann, Arno, 1957, *Alte Briefe aus Indien, Unveröffentlichte Briefe von Bartholomäus Ziegenbalg 1706–1719*, (henceforth AB)), Evangelische Verlagsanstalt, Berlin,

Lehmann, Arno, 1959, 'Bibliotheca malabarica: Eine wieder entdeckte Handschrift', *WZ*, VIII, Heft 4/5: 903–06.

Lehmann, Arno, 1960, 'Der deutsche Anteil an der Dravidologie', *Forschungen und Fortschritte*, 34(10): 307–09.

Lehmann, Arno, 1961, 'The German Contribution to Tamil Studies', *Tamil Culture*, Vol. IX (2, Apr.-June): 109–16.

Lehmann, Arno, 1968, 'German Tamil Studies", *WZ*, XVII, Heft 6: 139–45.

Lehmann, Hellmuth, 1974, *150 Jahre Berliner Mission*, Verlag der Evangelisch-Lutherischen Mission, Erlangen.

Leipold, Aletta (ed.), 2007, *Vishnus Weltentraum. Geheimnisse des Indienschrankes in der Kunst- und Natralienkammer der Franckeschen Stiftungen*, Verlag der Franckeschen Stiftungen, Halle.

Lewis, R. Rambo, 1993, *Understanding Religious Conversion*, Yale University Press, New Haven.

Liebau, Heike, 1993, *Die Quellen der Dänisch-Halleschen Mission in Tranquebar in deutschen Archiven. Ihre Bedeutung für die Indienforschung*, Das Arabische Buch, Berlin.

Liebau, Heike, 1994, 'Missionsquellen als Gegenstand interdisziplinärer Forschungen', in Wilfried Wagner (ed.), *Kolonien und Missionen. Referate des 3. Internationalen Kolonialgeschichtlichen Symposiums 1993 in Bremen*, 380–92, Lit, Münster, Hamburg.

Liebau, Heike and Magret Liepach, 1994, 'Christliche Hindus—indische Christen? Die Nationalarbeiter der Dänisch-Halleschen Mission in Südindien im 18. Jahrhundert', in Joachim Heidrich (ed.), *Changing Identities: The Transformation of Asian and African Societies under Colonialism*, 307–22, Das Arabische Buch, Berlin.

Liebau, Heike, 1995, 'German Missionaries as Research Workers in India: Their Diaries as Historical Sources. Benjamin Schultze (1689–1760)—Exception or Norm?' *Studies in History*, 11 (1): 101–18.

Liebau, Heike, 1997, 'Indische Angestellte in der dänischen Kolonialadministration während der sozialen Unruhen in Tranquebar und Umgebung im Jahre 1787', *Asien, Afrika, Lateinamerika*, 25: 111–26.

Liebau, Heike, 1999, 'Der Islam in Südindien im Spiegel der dänisch-halleschen Missionsquellen', in Michael Bergunder (ed.), *Missionsberichte aus Indien im 18 Jahrhundert. Ihre Bedeutung für die europäische Geistesgeschichte und ihr wissenschaftlicher Quellenwert für die Indienkunde*, 153–74, Verlag der Franckeschen Stiftungen, Halle.

Liebau, Heike, 2001, 'Tamilische Christen im 18. Jahrhundert als Mitgestalter sozialer Veränderungen. Motivationen, Möglichkeiten und Resultate ihres Wirkens', in Petra Heidrich and Heike Liebau (eds.), *Akteure des Wandels. Lebensläufe und Gruppenbilder an Schnittstellen von Kulturen*, 19–44, Das Arabische Buch, Berlin.

Liebau, Heike, 2001, 'Zwischen Hinduismus und Christentum. Veränderung sozialer und religiöser Bindungen im Süden des vorkolonialen Indien', in Henner Fürtig (ed.), *Aneignung und Abgrenzung in der Globalisierung*, 107–18, Das Arabische Buch, Berlin.

Liebau, Heike, 2003, 'Country Priests, Catechists and Schoolmasters as Cultural, Religious and Social Middlemen in the Context of the Tranquebar Mission', in Robert Eroc Frykanberg and Alaine M Low, *Christians and Missionaries in India: cross-cultural communication since 1500, with special reference to caste, conversion, and colonialism*, 70–92, W.B. Eerdmans Pub., Grand Rapids, Mich.

Liebau, Heike, 2003, 'Über die Erziehung 'tüchtiger Subjekte' zur Verbreitung des Evangeliums: Das Schulwesen der Dänisch-Halleschen Mission als Säule der Missionsorganisation', in Artur Bogner et al. (ed.), *Weltmission und religiöse Organisationen Protestantische Missionsgesellschaften im 19. und 20. Jahrhundert*, 427–58, Ergon Verl., Würzburg.

Liebau, Heike, 2005, 'Von Halle nach Madras: Pietistische Waisenhauspädagogik und englische Appropriationen in Indien', in Jürgen Schriewer and Marcelo Caruso (eds.), *Nationalerziehung und Universalmethode. Frühe Formen schulorganisatorischer Globalisierung, COMPARATIV* 15(2005) 1, 31–57.

Liebau, Heike und Kurt Liebau, 2003, 'Der Missionar Benjamin Schultze: Eine Notiz zu seiner Korrespondenz und sein Beitrag zur Herausbildung der vergleichenden Sprachwissenschaft', in Heike Link and Thomas Müller-Bahlke, *Zeichen und Wunder. Geheimnisse des Schriftenschranks in der Kunst- und Naturalienkammer der Franckeschen Stiftungen*, 94–110, Verlag der Franckeschen Stiftungen, Halle.

Liebau, Heike, 2006, 'Indian Pastors 1733–1817 (Short biographies)', in Andreas Gross [et al.], (eds.), *Halle and the Beginning of Protestant Christianity in India, Vol. III*, 1543–49, Verlag der Franckeschen Stiftungen, Halle.

Liebau, Heike, 2006, 'The Indian Pastors in the Danish-Halle and the English-Halle Mission', in Andreas Gross [et al.], (eds.), *Halle and the Beginning of Protestant Christianity in India, Vol. II*, 719–34, Verlag der Franckeschen Stiftungen, Halle.

Liebau, Heike (ed.), 2006, *Geliebtes Europa//Ostindische Welt 300 Jahre interkultureller Dialog im Spiegel der Dänisch-Halleschen Mission, Jahresausstellung der Franckeschen Stiftungen zu Halle*, Verlag der Franckeschen Stiftungen, Halle.

Liebau, Heike, 2006, 'Das Hallesche Waisenhaus und die Tranquebarmission', in Michael Mann (ed.), *Europäische Aufklärung und protestantische Mission in Indien*, 125–142, Draupadi Verlag, Heidelberg.

Liebau, Heike, 2008, 'Zur Beförderung des Missionswerks und zum Nutzen der East India Company. Die Druckerei in Vepery/Madras in der zweiten Hälfte des 18. Jahrhunderts', in Michael Mann (ed.),

Aufgelärter Geist und evangelische Missionen in Indien, 85–102, Draupadi Verlag, Heidelberg.

Liebau, Heike, 2008, *Die indischen Mitarbeiter der Tranquebarmission (1706–1845), Katecheten, Schulmeister, Übersetzer,* Verlag der Franckeschen Stiftungen Halle im Max-Niemeyer Verlag, Tübingen, (=Hallesche Forschungen 26).

Liebau, Heike, Andreas Nehring and Brigitte Klosterberg (eds.), 2010, *Mission und Forschung. Translokale Wissensproduktion zwischen Indien und Europa im 18. und 19. Jahrhundert*, Verlag der Franckeschen Stiftungen, Halle (= Hallesche Forschungen 29).

Liebau, Heike, 2012, 'Alle Dinge, die zu wissen nötig sind.' Religiös-soziale Übersetzungsprozesse im kolonialen Indien', *Geschichte und Gesellschaft* (38): 1–29.

Liebau, Heike, forthcoming, 'Translocal networks of the Tranquebar Mission Press in eighteenth century South Asia', in Esther Fihl and A.R. Venkatachalapathy (eds.), *Grappling with Cultural Borders. Tranquebar—a place in South India,* Orient Blackswan, New Delhi.

Liebau, Kurt, 1996, 'Die ersten Tamilen aus der Dänisch-Halleschen Mission in Europa. Vom Objekt zum Subjekt kultureller Interaktion?', in Gerhard Höpp (ed.), *Fremde Erfahrungen: Asiaten und Afrikaner in Deutschland, Österreich und in der Schweiz bis 1945*, 9–28, Das Arabische Buch, Berlin.

Liebau, Kurt, 1997, 'Die 'Malabarische Korrespondenz' von 1712/1713 und das Bild der Tamilen vom Europäer', *asien, afrika, lateinamerika* (25): 53–73.

Liebau, Kurt (ed.), 1998, [Johann Ernst Gründler and Bartholomäus Ziegenbalg], *Die malabarische Korrespondenz: tamilische Briefe an deutsche Missionare; eine Auswahl. Eingeleitet und Erläutert von Kurz Liebau,* Thorbecke, Sigmaringen.

Liebau, Kurt, 2006, 'Benjamin Schultze—Childhood and Youth' in Andreas Gross [et al.], (eds.), *Halle and the Beginning of Protestant Christianity in India*, Vol. II, 567–94, Verlag der Franckeschen Stiftungen, Halle.

Liebau, Kurt, 2006, 'Buchdruck und Missionsbibliothek', in Heike Liebau (ed.), *Geliebtes Europa//Ostindische Welt 300 Jahre interkultureller Dialog im Spiegel der Dänisch-Halleschen Mission. Katalog der Jahresausstellung der Franckeschen Stiftungen zu Halle 2006*, 105–20, Verlag der Franckeschen Stiftungen, Halle.

Ludden, David, 1990, *Peasant History in South India*, Princeton University Press, Princeton.

Luig, Ulrich, 1997, *Conversion as a Social Process: A History of Missionary Christianity among the Valley Tonga, Zambia*, LIT, Hamburg.

Maclean, C.D., 1996, *Manual of the administration of the Madras Presidency, Vol. I-III (1885–1893)*, Asian Educational Services, New Delhi, Madras (E.Keys, 1893, Madras).

Madhaviah, A., 1992, *Clarinda. A Historical Novel*, (first ed. 1915), Nanbar Vattam, Tirunelveli.

The Madras School, or Elements of tuition: comprising the analysis of an experiment in education made at [...] Madras [...] to which are added, extracts of sermons preached at Lambeth, a sketch of national institutions for training up the children of the poor, and a specimen of the mode of religious instruction at the Royal Military Asylum Chelsey. J. Murray, London, 1808.

Majumdar, R.C. (ed.), 1984², *The Mughal Empire*, Bharatiya Vidya Bhavan, Bombay (=The History and Culture of the Indian People).

Mallampalli, Chandra, 2004, *Christians and Public Life in Colonial South India, 1863–1937*, Routledge Curzon, London, New York.

Mann, Michael, 2006, 'Südindien im 18. Jahrhundert: wirtschaftliche und politische Entwicklung', in Heike Liebau (ed.), *Geliebtes Europa// Ostindische Welt. 300 Jahre interkultureller Dialog im Spiegel der Dänisch-Halleschen Mission, Katalog der Jahresausstellung der Franckeschen Stiftungen zu Halle 2006*, 41–51, Verlag der Fanckeschen Stiftungen, Halle.

Maracci, Lodovico, 1698, *Alcorani textus universus: Ex correctionibus Arabum exemplaribus summa fide, atque pulcherrimis characteribus descriptus. Eademque fide, ac pari diligentia ex Arabico idiomate in Latinum translatus; Appositis unicuique capiti notis, atque refutatione: His omnibus praemissus est Prodromus Totum priorum Tomum implens, in quo contenta indicantur pagina sequenti, auctore Ludovico Marraccio*, Patavii.

Mathew, A., 1988, *Christian Missions, Education and Nationalism: From Dominance to Compromise, 1870–1930*, Anamika Prakashan, New Delhi.

Mehlig, Johannes (ed.), 1987, *Weisheit des alten Indien. Vol. I. Vorbuddhistische und nicht-buddhistische Texte*, Kiepenheuer, Leipzig, Weimar.

Mentel, Friedrich-Franz, 2001, 'Kirche, Schule, Mission. Die Wirksamkeit von Pietisten in Berlin (1701–1713)', *Jahrbuch für historische Bildungsforschung*, vol. 7., 109–30, Klinkhardt, Bad Heilbrunn/Obb.

Merkel, Franz Rudolf, 1921, 'Die Bedeutung der Mission für die Wissenschaft', *Mission und Wissenschaft*, in *HMK*, 17.

Mettele, Gisela, 2009, *Weltbürgertum und Gottesreich. Die Herrnhuter Brüdergemeine als globale Gemeinschaft 1727–1857*, Vendenhoeck & Ruprecht, Göttingen (=Bürgertum Neue Folge, 4).

Misra, Atmanand, 1973, *Grants in Aid of Education in India*, Macmillan, Delhi.

Mitchell, Lisa, 2009, *Language, Emotions, and Politics in South India. The Making of a Mother Tongue,* Indiana University Press, Bloomington.

Mohanavelu, C.S., 1993, *German Tamilology: German contributions to Tamil language, literature and culture during the period 1706–1945,* Saiva Siddhanta, Madras.

Mommsen, Wolfgang, 1994, 'Europa und die außereuropäische Welt', *Historische Zeitschrift* (258, June 3): 661–95.

Moritzen, Niels-Peter (ed.) 2002, *Von den Anfängen evangelischer Mission: zwei unbekannte Missionsschriften von 1713 und 1717,* 10–49, Verlag für Kultur und Wissenschaft, Bonn.

Mosse, David, 1994, 'Idioms of Subordination and Styles of Protest among Christians and Hindu Harijan Castes in Tamil Nadu', *Contributions to Indian Sociology,* 28 (1): 67–106.

Mylius, Klaus, 1980, *Wörterbuch Sanskrit-Deutsch,* VEB Verlag Enzyklopädie Leipzig, Leipzig.

Müller-Bahlke, Thomas, 2000, 'Kinderleben in den Glauchaer Anstalten zu Franckes Zeiten. Entsagung auf Teufel komm raus?' in Penelope Willard (ed.), *Die Franckeschen Stiftungen zu Halle im Jahre 2000,* 18–30, Verlag der Franckeschen Stiftungen, Halle.

Mundadan, Anthony Mathias, 1989, *History of Christianity in India, Vol. I: From the Beginning up to the Middle of the Sixteenth Century (up to 1542),* CHAI, Bangalore.

Muthiah, Subbiah, 2006, 'Giving India the Printed Word', in Andreas Gross [et al.], (eds.), *Halle and the Beginning of Protestant Christianity in India,* Vol. III, 1241–48, Verlag der Franckeschen Stiftungen, Halle.

Nebe, August, 1932, 'Die Missionsärzte der Dänisch-Halleschen Mission', *Die ärztliche Mission: Blätter zur Förderung der deutschen missionsärztlichen Bestrebungen,* 4: 98–101.

Nehring, Andreas, 1999, 'Natur und Gnade: Zu Theologie und Kulturkritik in den Neuen Halleschen Berichten', in Michael Bergunder (ed.), *Missionsberichte aus Indien im 18. Jahrhundert: Ihre Bedeutung für die europäische Geistesgeschichte und ihr wissenschaftlicher Quellenwert für die Indienkunde* , 220–45, Verlag der Franckeschen Stiftungen, Halle.

Nehring, Andreas, 2003, *Orientalismus und Mission. Die Repräsentation der tamilischen Gesellschaft und Religion durch Leipziger Missionare 1840–1940,* Harrassowitz, Wiesbaden.

Neild-Basu, Susan, 1984, 'The Dubashes of Madras', *Modern Asian Studies,* 18 (1): 1–31.

Neill, Stephen, 1985, *A History of Christianity in India 1707–1858,* Cambridge University Press, Cambrigde.

Neuere Geschichte der Evangelischen Missions-Anstalten zu Bekehrung der

Heiden in Ostindien, 1/1, 1770–8/95, 1848, Waisenhaus, Halle (NHB—Neue Hallesche Berichte).

Neumann, Josef N., 2006, 'Medizinische Forschungen', in Heike Liebau (ed.), *Geliebtes Europa//Ostindische Welt 300 Jahre interkultureller Dialog im Spiegel der Dänisch-Halleschen Mission. Katalog der Jahresausstellung der Franckeschen Stiftungen zu Halle 2006*, 180–93, Verlag der Franckeschen Stiftungen, Halle.

Neumann, Josef N., 2010, '*Malabarischer Medicus*—eine ethnomedizinisch-historische Quelle des frühen 18. Jahrhunderts', in Heike Liebau, Andreas Nehring and Brigitte Klosterberg (eds.), *Mission und Forschung: Translokale Wissensproduktion zwischen Indien und Europa im 18. und 19. Jahrhundert*, 195–203, Verlag der Franckeschen Stiftungen, Halle (= Hallesche Forschungen 29).

Neumann, Josef N., 2006, 'Tamil Medical Science as perceived by the Missionaries of the Danish-Halle Mission in Tranquebar', in Andreas Gross [et al.], (eds.), *Halle and the beginning of Protestant Christianity in India*, Vol. III, 1135–54, Verlag der Franckeschen Stiftungen, Halle.

Niekamp, Johann Lucas 1740, *Kurtzgefaßte Mißions-Geschichte Oder Historischer Auszug Der Evangelischen Mißions-Berichte aus Ostiniden [Teil I] von dem Jahr 1705 bis zu Ende des Jahres 1736*, in Verlegung des Waysen=Hauses, Halle.

Nielsen, Axel, 1933, *Dänische Wirtschaftsgeschichte*, G. Fischer, Jena.

Niemeyer, August Hermann 1796, *Grundsätze der Erziehung und des Unterrichts: Für Eltern, Hauslehrer und Erzieher*, Waysenhaus-Buchhandlung, Halle.

Nørgaard, Anders, 1977, 'Missionar Benjamin Schultze als Leiter der Tranquebarmission (1720–1726)', *NZM*, 33: 181–201.

Nørgaard, Anders, 1988, *Mission und Obrigkeit—Die Dänisch-hallische Mission in Tranquebar 1706–1845*, Gütersloher Verlagshaus Gerd Mohn, Gütersloh (=Missionswissenschaftliche Forschungen, 22).

Nørgaard, Anders, 2006, 'Secretaries of the Mission Board in Copenhagen 1714–1868', in Andreas Gross [et al.], (eds.), *Halle and the Beginning of Protestant Christianity in India*, Vol. III, 1565–67, Verlag der Franckeschen Stiftungen, Halle.

O'Connor, Daniel, 2006, 'The Church of England and the Mission in India', in Andreas Gross [et al.], (eds.), *Halle and the Beginning of Protestant Christianity in India*, Vol. I, 129–38, Verlag der Franckeschen Stiftungen, Halle.

Obst, Helmut, 1999, 'Missionsberichte aus Indien im 18. Jahrhundert: Eine Einführung in den missionsgeschichtlichen Kontext', in Michael Bergunder (ed.), *Missionsberichte aus Indien im 18. Jahrhundert. Ihre*

Bedeutung für die europäische Geistesgeschichte und ihr wissenschaftlicher Quellenwert für die Indienkunde, 1–5, Verlag der Frankeschen Stiftungen, Halle.

Oddie, Geoffrey A., 1991, *Hindu and Christian in South-East India*, Curzon Press, London (=London Studies on South Asia 6).

Oddie, Geoffrey A., 1995, *Popular Religion, Elites and Reform: Hook-Swinging and its Prohibition in Colonial India, 1800–1894*, Manohar, New Delhi.

Oddie, Geoffrey A., 1996, 'Missionaries as Social Commentators: The Indian Case', in Robert A Bickers and Rosemary E Seton, *Missionary Encounters: Sources and Issues*, 197–210, Curzon Press, Richmond, Surrey.

Oddie, Geoffrey A., 2000, 'India: Missionaries, Conversion and Change', in Kevin Ward and Brian Stanley (eds.), *The Church Mission Society and World Christianity 1799–1999*, 228–53, Curzon Press Ltd., Richmond, Surrey.

Osterhammel, Jürgen, 1998, *Die Entzauberung Asiens. Europa und die asiatischen Reiche im 18. Jahrhundert*, C.H. Beck Verlag, München.

Pabst, Erika and Thomas Müller-Bahlke (eds.), 2005, *Quellenbestände der Indienmission 1700–1918 in Archiven des deutschsprachigen Raums*, Max Niemeyer Verlag, Tübingen (=Hallesche Quellenpublikationen und Repertorien; 9).

Pabst, Erika, 2006, 'The Wives of Missionaries 1715–1838 (Short biographies)', in Andreas Gross [et al.], (eds.), *Halle and the Beginning of Protestant Christianity in India*, Vol. III, 1529–42, Verlag der Franckeschen Stiftungen, Halle.

Pabst, Erika, 2006, 'The Wives of the Missionaries: Their Experiences in India', in Andreas Gross [et al.], (eds.), *Halle and the Beginning of Protestant Christianity in India*, Vol. II, 685–704, Verlag der Franckeschen Stiftungen, Halle.

Packiamuthu, David, 'Schwartz, Clarinda and Sathianathan', in Daniel Jeyaraj (ed.), 1999, *Christian Friedrich Schwartz: His Contributions to South India*, 58–73, Lutheran Heritage Archives, Chennai.

Packiamuthu, David, 2000, 'The Beginnings of Protestant Mission in Madras', *ICHR*, XXXIV (2): 93–116.

Page, Jesse, 1921, *Schwartz of Tanjore*, SPCK, London.

Pankratova, Viktorija Aleksandrovna, 1982, *Christiane Keraly. Rol' v social'no-političeskoj žizni stata*, Nauka, Moskva.

Pascoe, Charles Frederick, 1901, *Two Hundred Years of the S.P.G. An Historical Account of the Society of the Propagation of the Gospel in Foreign Parts 1701–1900*, S.P.G., London.

Paul, Rayaiah D., 1961, *Chosen Vessels. Lifes of ten Indian Christian Pastors of the eighteenth and nineteenth Centuries*, Published for the Senate of Serampore College by the Christian Literature Society, Madras.

Pearson, Hugh, 1835, *Memoirs of Life and Correspondence of Christian Frederick Swartz,* D. Appleton & Co., New York.

Pelikan (Liebau), Heike, 1987, *Die 'Grammatica Hindostanica' des Benjamin Schultze (Quelle zur Erforschung des Dakkhini des 18. Jahrhunderts)*, ed. by Burchard Brentjes, Halle (=WB 35 [I 41] 1987).

Pelzer, Erich, 1998, *Die Wiederkehr des girondistischen Helden. Deutsche Intellektuelle als kulturelle Mittler zwischen Deutschland und Frankreich während der Französischen Revolution*, Bouvier, Bonn.

Peterson, Indira Viswanathan, 1999, 'Science in the Tranquebar Mission Curriculum: Natural Theology and Indian Responses', in Michael Bergunder (ed), *Missionsberichte aus Indien im 18. Jahrhundert: ihre Bedeutung für die europäische Geistesgeschichte und ihr wissenschaftlicher Quellenwert für die Indienkunde*, 175–219, Verlag der Franckeschen Stiftungen, Halle.

Peterson, Indira, 2003, 'Tanjore, Tranquebar and Halle: European Science and German Missionary Education in the Lives of two Indian Intellectuals in the Early Nineteenth Century', in Robert Eric Frykenberg (ed.), *Christians and Missionaries in India: Cross-Cultural Communication since 1500: With Special Reference to Caste, Conversion and Colonialism*, 93–126, W.B. Eerdmans, London.

Philipps, Thomas J., 1719, *Thirtyfour Conferences Between the Danish Missionaries and the Malabarian Brahmans (or Heathen Priests) in the East Indies, concerning the Truth of the Christian Religion: Together with some Letters written by the Heathens to the said Missionaries*, printed for H. Clements [...] W. Fleetwood [...] and J. Stephens [,,,], London.

Pillai, Ananda Ranga, 1985, *The Private Diary of Ananda Ranga Pillai: a record of matters political, historical, social and personal from 1736 to 1761*, Vol. I., (Madras, 1904), Asian Educational Services, New Delhi.

Platts, John T., 1993, *A Dictionary of Urdu, Classical Hindi and English*, Munshiram Manoharlal Publ. New Delhi, (Oxford 1884).

Podczeck, Otto, 1968, 'Die Arbeit am Alten Testament in Halle zur Zeit des Pietismus. Das Collegium Orientale theologicum A.H. Franckes', *WZ*, VII, *Gesellschafts- und Sprachwissenschaftliche Reihe*, Heft 5: 1059–1078.

Popley, Herbert A., 1987, *K.T. Paul. Christian Leader*, CLS, Madras (1938).

Pratt, Mary Louise, 1992, *Imperial Eyes: Travel Writing and Transculturation*, Routledge, London, New York.

Raghaviah, Jaiprakash, 1990, *Basel Mission Industries in Malabar and South Canara (1834–1914): A Study of its Social and Economic Impact*, Gyan Publishing House, New Delhi.

Rajan, Rekha Kamath, 2006, 'Johann Philipp Fabricius and the History of the Tamil Bible', in Andreas Gross [et al.], (eds.), *Halle and the Beginning of Protestant Christianity in India*, Vol. III, 1299–1308, Verlag der Franckeschen Stiftungen, Halle.

Rajaratnam, K., 1998, 'Foreword' in Daniel Jeyaraj (ed.), *Ordination of the First Protestant Indian Pastor Aaron*, V-VII, Lutheran Heritage Archives, Chennai.

Rajayyan, K.N., 1992, *History of Tamil Nadu 1565–1982*, Raj Publishers, Madurai.

Rajayyan, Kunjukrishnan Nadar, 1974, *History of Madurai (1736–1801)*, Madurai University, Madurai.

Ramaswami, Nallathagudi Srinivasa, 1984, *Political History of the Carnatic under the Nawabs*, Abhimav, New Delhi.

Ranger, Terence, 'The Local and the Global in Southern African Religious History', in Robert W. Hefner, *Conversion to Christianity: historical and anthropological perspectives on a great transformation*, 65–98, University of California Press, Berkeley.

Rasch, Aage, 1967, *Dansk Ostindien 1777–1845. Vore gamle Tropekolonier VII*, Fremad, Copenhagen.

Raulff, Ulrich, 1987, 'Vorwort', in U. Raulff, *Mentalitäten-Geschichte. Zur historischen Rekonstruktion geistiger Prozesse*, 7–20, Wagenbach, Berlin.

Rawat, Pyare Lal, 1981, *History of Indian Education*, Ram Prasad, Agra, Bhopal.

Raychaudhuri, Tapan, 1962, *Jan Company in Coromandel*, Nijhoff, The Hague.

Report of the Indian Education Commission: Report of the Hunter Education Commission appointed by the Government of India in 1882, 1883, printed by the Superintendent of Government Printing, Calcutta.

Richter, Julius, 1924, *Geschichte der Berliner Missionsgesellschaft 1824–1924*, Berliner ev. Missionsgesellschaft, Berlin.

Richter, Julius, 1924, *Indische Missionsgeschichte*, C. Bertelsmann, Gütersloh (1906).

Roberts, Dana L., 1997, *American Women in Mission: A Social History of their Thought and Practice*, Mercer University Press, Macon, GA.

Robinson, Rowena, 2000, "Taboo or Veiled Consent? Goan Inquisitorial Edict of 1736", *EPW* 35 (27): 2423–31.

Rodman, William L. and Dorothy Ayers Counts (eds.), 1982, *Middlemen and Brokers in Oceania*, The University of Michigan Press, Ann Arbor (=ASAO Monograph, No. 9).

Römer, H., 1921, *Geschichte der Brüdermission auf den Nikobaren und des Brüdergartens bei Tranquebar auf Grund des handschriftlichen Materials im Unitäts-Archiv zu Herrnhut*, Missionsbuchhandlung, Herrnhut (=HMK 18).

Rose, Frank, 1999, *The Economics, Concept, and Design of Information Intermediaries: A Theoretic Approach*, Physica Verlag, Heidelberg, New York.

Rotermund, Hermann, 1980, 'Alltagskultur—Kritische Literaturhinweise', in Wolfgang Fritz Haug and Kaspar Maase (ed.), *Materialistische Kulturtheorie und Alltagskultur*, 122–36, Argument-Verlag, Berlin.

Rothermund, Dietmar, 1989, *Indische Geschichte in Grundzügen*, Wissenschaftliche Buchgesellschaft, Darmstadt.

Ruhland, Thomas, 2006, 'The Moravian Brethren and the Danish-Halle Mission in Tranquebar—the 'Garden of the Brothers' at the Centre of a European Conflict', in Andreas Gross [et al.], (eds.), *Halle and the Beginning of Protestant Christianity in India*, Vol. II, 743–66, Verlag der Franckeschen Stiftungen, Halle.

Šamatov, A.H., 1974, *Klassičeskij Dakkhini (Južnyj Hindustani)*, Nauka, Moskva.

Sames, Arno, 2006, 'Beziehungen zwischen Kopenhagen, Halle und London', in Heike Liebau, (ed.), *Geliebtes Europa//Ostindische Welt. 300 Jahre interkultureller Dialog im Spiegel der Dänisch-Halleschen Mission, Jahresausstellung der Franckeschen Stiftungen zu Halle*, 29–34, Verlag der Franckeschen Stiftungen, Halle.

Sandegren, Herman, 1928, *Johann Zacharias Kiernander—The First Swedish Missionary in India*, (translated from the Swedish original (1924) by E. Wimmercranz), National Missionary Society Press, Madras.

Sander, Heinrich, 1779–1780, *Über Natur und Religion für die Liebhaber und Anbeter Gottes*, Weygandsche Buchhandlung, Leipzig.

Sangma, Milton S., 1987–1992, *History of the American Baptist Mission in North-East India 1836–1950*, 2 vols, Mittal Publications, Delhi.

Sanneh, Lamin, 1991, 'The Yogi and the Commissar: Christian Missions and the New World Order in Africa', in Wade Clark Roof (ed.), *World Order and Religion*, 173–92, State University of New York Press, New York.

Sarkar, Jadunath, 2001, 'Haidar Ali's invasion of the Eastern Carnatic, 1780', in Irfan Habib (ed.), *Resistance and Modernization under Haidar Ali and Tipu Sultan*, 21–34, Indian History Congress, New Delhi (=Confronting Colonialism), [First published in: Islamic Culture, XV (1941), 214–28].

Sarkar, Tanika, 1999, *Words to Win: The Making of Amar Jiban, a modern autobiography*, Kali for Women, New Delhi.

Sarkar, Tanika, 2001, 'A Book of Her Own, A Life of her Own. The Autobiography of a Nineteenth-Century Woman', in T. Sarkar (ed.), *Hindu Wife, Hindu Nation: Community, Religion and Cultural Nationalism*, 95–134, C. Hurst, London.

Satyanarayana, Adapa, 2006, 'The Contribution of Benjamin Schultze to Telugu Language and Learning', in Andreas Gross, *Halle and the Beginning of Protestant Christianity in India*, Vol. III, 1163–80, Verlag der Franckesche Stiftungen, Halle.

Satyanarayana, Adapa, 2010, 'Benjamin Schultze (1689–1760): The Foremost Telugu Linguist', in Heike Liebau, Andreas Nehring and Brigitte Klosterberg, *Mission und Forschung: translokale Wissensproduktion zwischen Indien und Europa im 18. und 19. Jahrhundert*, 239–55, Verlag der Frankeschen Stiftungen, Halle (= Hallesche Forschungen 29).

Savage, David W., 1997, 'Missionaries and the Development of a Colonial Ideology of Female Education in India', *Gender and History* 9 (2): 201–21.

Scharfe, Martin, 1980, *Die Religion des Volkes: kleine Kultur- und Sozialgeschichte des Pietismus*, Gütersloher Verlagshaus Mohn, Gütersloh.

Schicketanz, Peter, 1972, *Der Briefwechsel Carl Hildebrand von Cansteins mit August Hermann Francke*, DeGruyter, Berlin (= Texte zur Geschichte des Pietismus III, 1).

Schicketanz, Peter, 2001, *Der Pietismus von 1675 bis 1800*, Evangelische Verlagsanstalt, Leipzig (=Kirchengeschichtliche Einzeldarstellungen III/I).

Schmale, Wolfgang and Nan L. Dodde (eds.), 1991, *Revolution des Wissens? Europa und seine Schulen im Zeitalter der Aufklärung (1750–1825). Ein Handbuch zur europäischen Schulgeschichte*, Dr Winkler, Bochum.

Schmitt, Eberhard, 1988, *Wirtschaft und Handel der Kolonialreiche. Dokumente zur Geschichte der europäischen Expansion* (Vol. 4), C.H. Beck, München.

Schneiders, Werner (ed.), 2001, *Lexikon der Aufklärung: Deutschland und Europa*, C.H. Beck, München.

Schnitter, Helmut (ed.), 1994, *Gestalten um den Soldatenkönig: Biographische Skizzen*, Vol. I., Preußischer Militär-Verlag, Reutlingen.

Schriewer, Jürgen and Marcelo Caruso, 2005, 'Globale Diffusionsdynamik und kontextspezifische Aneignung: Konzepte und Ansätze historischer Internationalisierungsforschung', in Jürgen Schriewer and Marcelo Caruso, *Nationalerziehung und Universalmethode. Frühe Formen schulorganisatorischer Globalisierung*, *COMPARATIV*, 15 (2005), 1, 7–30.

Schröder, Wilhelm Heinz, 1985, 'Kollektive Biographie in der historischen

Sozialforschung. Eine Einführung', in Wilhelm Heinz Schröder (ed.), *Lebenslauf und Gesellschaft. Zum Einsatz von kollektiven Biographien in der historischen Sozialforschung*, 7–17, Klett-Cotta, Stuttgart (=Historisch-sozialwissenschaftliche Forschungen, 18).

Schultze, Benjamin, 1744, *Compendiaria Alcorani Refutatio Indostanice.* Autore Viro plur. Reverendo Benj. Schulzio Evangelico in India Missionario. Edidit Jo. Henr, Institutum Judaicum, Callenberg, Halae.

Schultze, Benjamin, 1745, [Grammatica Hindostanica] *Viri Plur. Reverendi Benjamini Schultzii Missionarii Evangelici Grammatica Hindostanica [...].* Edit Jo. Henr. Callenberg, Typographia Instituti Judaici, Halae. [Reprint: 1986, *Grammatica hindostanica von Benjamin Schultze*, ed. by B. Brentjes and C. Gallus, Univ. Halle-Wittenberg, Halle, WB 1986/38 (I 38)].

Schultze, Benjamin, 1747, *Psalmorum liber [...] in linguam Indostanicam*, translatus a Benj. Schulzio ... Edidit Jo. Henr. Callenbergius, Typographia orientali Instituti Judaici, Halae.

Schultze, Benjamin, 1750, Die auf der Küste Coromandel in Ost-Indien befindliche große und berühmte Stadt der Englischen Nation Madras oder Fort St. George [...], Waisenhaus, Halle.

Schultze, Benjamin, 1750, *The Large and Renowned Town of the English Nation in the East Indies upon the coast of Coromandel, Madras or Fort St. George, representing the Genius, the Manners, the Carriage, the Behaviour and the very Character of the natives: likewise their trade and house-Keeping, the Product of the country and usefullness of the Gardens, by way of thirty familiar Dialogues, written originally in the Waruga or Gentou Language; but afterwards translated into the English Tongue, for the benefit of some curious readers*, Waisenhaus,Halle.

Schultze, Benjamin, 1751, *Evangelium Matthaei in Linguam Indostanicam Translatum.* A Viro Plur. Reverendo Benj. Schultzio Evengelico in India Missionario. Edidit D.Jo. Henr. Callenbergius, Typographia orientali Instituti Judaici & Muhammedici, Halae.

Schultze, Benjamin, 1758, *Novum Jesu Christi Testamentum/In linguam Indostanicum translatum*, Typographia Orientali Instituti Judaici, Halae.

Schultze, Benjamin, 1778, *Pauli Apostoli Epistola Ad Hebræos, in Linguam Indostanicum Translata.* A Viro Plur. Reverendo Benj. Schultzio Evengelico in India Missionario. Edidit D.Jo. Henr. Callenbergius, Institutum Judaicum & Muhammedaicum, Halae.

Schultze, Benjamin, 1977, *Hindūstānī grāmar az Benğamin Šulze, A Grammar of Hindustani Language* by Benjamin Schultze, edited and translated into Urdu with Notes and Annotations by Abulais Siddiqi, mağlis-e tariqī-e adab, Lahore.

Scott, James C., 1977, 'Political clientelism: a bibliographical essay', in Steffen W. Schmidt et al., *Friends, Followers and Factions: A Reader in Political Clientelism*, 483–505, University of California Press, Berkeley et al.

Settgast, Ann-Charlott, 1981, *Der Mann in Tranquebar: Ein Portät des Bartholomäus Ziegenbalg*, Evang. Verl.-Anst., Berlin.

Sharma, Raj Bahadur, 1988, *Christian Missions in North India, 1813–1913. A Case Study of Meerut Division and Dehra Dun District*, Mittal Publications, Delhi.

Sharma, Ram Nath and Rajendra Sharma, 1996, *History of Education in India*, Atlantic Publishers & Dist., New Delhi.

Shobhanan, B. (ed.), 1996, *A History of the Christian Missions in South India*, Kerala Historical Society, Thiruvananthapuram.

Singh, Brijraj, 1999, *The First Protestant Missionary to India: Bartholomäus Ziegenbalg, 1683–1719*, Oxford, New Delhi, New York.

Singh, Gopal, 1976, *A Geography of India*, Atma Ram, Delhi (=A Geography of India. Delhi 1976).

Sixtieth Annual Report of the Evangelical Mission Establishments at Basel, 1 July 1895, The Experiences of a Native Traveling Pastor, 38–42.

Sonnerat, Pierre, 1784, *Reise nach Ostindien und China auf Befehl des Königs in den Jahren 1774–1781 unternommen. Aus dem Original in einen feinen Auszug gebracht*, Schneider, Frankfurt, Leipzig.

Sonntag, Franz Peter and Siegfried Foelz (eds.), 1977, *Die Briefe des Francisco de Xavier 1542–1552*, selected and translated by Elisabeth Gräfin von Vitzthum, with an introduction by Franz Peter Sonntag, Suhrkamp, Frankfurt am Main.

Spencer, Johann, 1732, [...] *De Legibus Hebræorum Ritualibus Earumque Rationibus, Libri Quator: Ad Nuperam Cantabrigiensem. In Qua Liber Quartus. Varia Capita & Dissertationes Aliaque Autoris Supplementa, Accesserre, Accurata, Efformata; Præmittitur Christoph Matthæi Pfaffi [...] Dissertation Præliminaris, Qua De Vita Spenceri, De Libri Pretio & Erroribus Quoque Disseritur, Autoresque, qui contra Spencerum scripsere, Enarrantur.* Tubingæ Sumtibus Johannis Georgi Cottæ.

Sprandel, Rolf, 1987, 'Erfahrungen mit der Mentalitätengeschichte', in Ulrich Raulff (ed.), *Mentalitäten-Geschichte. Zur historischen Rekonstruktion geistiger Prozesse*, 97–113, Wagenbach, Berlin.

Stampe, L., 1964, 'Missionskollegiet', *Nordisk Missionstidsktift*, 75: 225–41.

Stedman, Gesa (ed.), 2001, *Englische Frauen der Frühen Neuzeit: Dichterinnen, Malerinnen, Mäzeninnen*, Wissenschaftliche Buchgesellschaft, Darmstadt.

Steiner, Günter and Werner Flaschendräger (eds), 1981, *Magister und Scholaren. Professoren und Studenten. Geschichte Deutscher Universitäten und Hochschulen im Überblick*, Urania-Verlag, Leipzig [et al].

Stein, Burton, 1969, 'Integration of the Agrarian System', in Robert E. Frykenberg (ed.), *Land control and social structure in Indian history*, 175–216, The University of Wisconsin Press, Madison.

Stein, Jürgen, 2002, *Christentum und Kastenwesen: Zum Verhältnis von Religion und Gesellschaft in Indien*, Lembeck, Frankfurt/Main.

Steiner, Klaus, 1988, 'Das Schulwesen', in Gottfried Bregulla (ed.), *Hugenotten in Berlin*, 206–26, Union Verlag, Berlin.

Stephen, S. Jeyaseela, 1998, *Portuguese in the Tamil Coast: Historical Explorations in Commerce and Culture (1507–1749)*, Navajothi Pub. House, Pondicherry.

Stosch, Georg and Hilko Wiardo Schomerus, 1936, 'Die Bedeutung der dänisch-halleschen Mission', *Luthertum*, Leipzig, 11: 321–38.

Strandberg, Elisabeth, 1983, *The Modi Documents from Tanjore in Danish Collections*, Franz Steiner, Wiesbaden.

Struwe, Kamma, 1967, *Dansk Ostindien 1732–1776. Tranquebar under Kompagnistyre*, Fremad, København (=Johannes Brønsted (ed.): Vore gamle Tropekolonier. Vol. 6).

Subhramanian, N., 1989, *The Brahmin in the Tamil Country*, Ennes Publications, Madurai.

Subrahmanian, N., 1994, *Social and Cultural History of Tamilnad [AD 1336–AD 1984]*, Ennes, Udumalpet.

Subrahmanyam, Sanjay, 1990, *The political economy of commerce; Southern India 1500–1650*, Cambridge University Press, Cambridge.

Subramanian, P. 1978, 'Caste System in the Tamil Country in the 19th century', *Bulletin of the Institute of Traditional Cultures Madras*, 2: 34–44.

Sweetman, Will, 2006, 'Bartholomäus Ziegenbalg, the Tranquebar Mission and 'The Roman Horror'', in Andreas Gross [et al.], (eds.), *Halle and the Beginning of Protestant Christianity in India*, Vol. II, 797–811, Verlag der Franckeschen Stiftungen, Halle.

Tarlo, Emma, 1996, *Clothing Matters: Dress and Identity in India*, C. Hurst & Co. Publishers, London.

Thekkadath, Joseph, 1988, *History of Christianity in India, Vol. II. From the Middle of the Sixteenth Century to the End of the Seventeenth Century*, Theological Publications in India, Bangalore.

Thurston, Edgar, 2001, *Castes and Tribes of South India*, 7 vols., Asian Educational Services New Delhi, Madras, (Madras 1909).

Tiliander, Bror, 1974, *Christian and Hindu Terminology. A Study in their Mutual Relations with Special Reference to the Tamil Area*, Almquist & Wiksell, Uppsala.

Tiruwalluwer, 1803, *Gedichte und Gedenksprüche* (aus der Tamulischen Sprache übers. von August Friedrich Cämmerer), Raw, Nürnberg.

Trefzer, Rudolf, 1989, *Die Konstruktion des bürgerlichen Menschen. Aufklärungspädagogik und Erziehung im ausgehenden 18. Jahrhundert am Beispiel der Stadt Basel*, Chronos Verlag, Zürich.

Tschurenev, Jana, 2011,"Pathsalas into Schools': Das monitorial system of education in Bengalen (ca. 1815–35)', *Jahrbuch Historische Bildungsforschung*, 16: 11–38.

Tschurenev, Jana, 2008, 'Diffusing Useful Knowledge: The Monitorial System of Education in Madras, London and Bengal, 1789–1840.', *Paedagogica Historica* XLIV, 3, 249–64.

Ustorf, Werner, 1996, 'Dornröschen oder die Missionsgeschichte wird entdeckt', in Ulrich van der Heyden and Heike Liebau (eds), *Missionsgeschichte—Kirchengeschichte—Weltgeschichte: Christliche Missionen im Kontext nationaler Entwicklungen in Afrika, Asien und Ozeanien*, 23–38, Franz Steiner Verlag, Stuttgart.

van der Veer, Peter, 2001, *Imperial Encounters. Religion and Modernity in India and Britain*, Princeton University Press, Princeton.

Vanina, Elena Ju., 1988, 'Nauka i obrazovanije v Indii posdnego srednevekovija i načala novogo vremeni (XVI-XVIII vv.)', *Indija Ježegodnik 1987*, Moskva, 277–93.

Venkatachalapathy A.R., 2011, *The Province of the Book*, Permanent Black, New Delhi.

Vishvanathan, Gauri, 1998, *Outside the Fold: Conversion, Modernity and Belief*, Princeton University Press, Princeton.

Voges, Wolfgang, 1987, *Biographie und Gesellschaft. Methoden der Biographie- und Lebenslaufforschung*, Leske, Budrich, Opladen.

von Dülmen, Richard, 1999, *Kultur und Alltag in der Frühen Neuzeit. Vol. 3: Religion, Magie und Aufklärung 16.-18. Jahrhundert*, Beck, Münich (First edition 1994).

von Glasenapp, Helmut, 1986, *Indische Geisteswelt. Vol. I Glaube und Weisheit der Hindus*, Dausien, Hanau.

von Rönne, Ludwig, 1990, *Das Unterrichts-Wesen des Preußischen Staates, Vol. 1: Das Volksschul-Wesen des Preußischen Staates mit Einschluß des Privat-Unterrichts*, (Berlin 1855) Reprint, Böhlau, Köln, Wien.

von Stieglitz, Klaus, 1969, *Der unvollendete Auftrag*, Evangelischer Missionsverlag, Stuttgart.

Vorbaum, Reinhold, 1850–52, *Evangelische Missionsgeschichte in Biographien in 4 Bänden*, Vol. 1, No. 4, Verlag der Schaub'schen Buchhandlun, Düsseldorf.

Vormbaum, Reinhold, 1851, *Eingeborene Lehrer des Evangeliums in Ostindien*, Schaub, Düsseldorf (=Evangelische Missionsgeschichte in Biographien, vol. II).

Vriddagirisan, V., 1995, *The Nayaks of Tanjore*, (Annamalainagar 1942), Asian Educational Services, New Delhi.

Walls, Andrew F., 2006, 'The Society for Promoting Christian Knowledge and the Missionary Movement in Britain', in Andreas Gross [et al.], (ede.), *Halle and the Beginning of Protestant Christianity in India*, Vol. I, 107–28, Verlag der Franckeschen Stiftungen, Halle.

Walther, Christoph Theodosius, 1731, *Bibliotheca Tamulica consistens inrecensione librorum nostrorum, mscr-torum ad cognoscendam et linguam & res Tamulicas inseruientium*. [Royal Library, Copenhagen (KB) Ny.Kgl. Saml. 589C].

Walther, Christoph Theodosius, 1739, *Observationes grammaticae, quibus linguae tamulicae idioma vulgare, in usum operatiorum in messe Domini inter gentes vulgo malabares dictas, [...]*, Mission Printing Press, Tranquebar.

Ward, Kevin and Brian Stanley (eds.), 2000, *The Church Mission Society and World Christianity 1799–1999*, Grand Rapids.

Weber, Max, 1988, 'Die protestantische Ethik und der Geist des Kapitalismus', in M. Weber, *Gesammelte Aufsätze zur Religionssoziologie 1*, (first published 1922) Mohr/Siebeck, Tübingen.

Wendt, Reinhard, 1998, 'Allgemeine historische Perspektiven: Grundstrukturen des europäischen Interesses in Asien' in Koschorke, Klaus (ed.), *'Christen und Gewürze' Konfrontation und Interaktion kolonialer und indigener Christentumsvarianten*, 259–73, Otto Harrassowitz Verlag, Göttingen.

Werther, Gottfried, 1956, 'Die Briefe von Bartholomäus Ziegenbalg (1682–1719)', *WZ, Gesellschafts- und Sprachwissenschaftliche Reihe*, 5: 221–26.

Wilken, Christopher, 1721, *Venerable Communicant (Tamil). Translated by Peter Maleiappen, ed. by Benjamin Schultze*, Mission Printing Press, Tranquebar.

Wilken, Christopher, 1722, *Voerdige Comminicant. Translation from German into Danish by Benjamin Schultze*, Mission Printing Press, Tranquebar.

Winslow, M., 1996, *Winslow's A Comprehensive Tamil and English Dictionary*, Asian Educational Services, Madras, New Delhi.

Witt, Ulrike, 1996, *Bekehrung, Bildung und Biographie: Frauen im Umkreis des Halleschen Pietismus*, Verlag der Franckeschen Stiftungen Halle im Max Niemeyer Verlag, Tübingen (=Hallesche Forschungen 2).

Wohlrab-Sahr, Monika, 1998, 'Protestantische Ethik im islamischen Gewand. Habitusreproduktion und religiöser Wandel. Das Beispiel der Konversion eines Afroamerikaners zum Islam', in Ralf Bohnsack and Winfried Marotzki (eds.), *Biografieforschung und Kulturanalyse. Transdisziplinäre Zugänge qualitativer Forschung*, 183–201, Leske und Burdich, Opladen.

Wolf, Eric R, 1956, 'Aspects of Group Relations in a complex Society: Mexico', *American Anthropologist*, New Series 58 (6): 1065–78.

Young, Richard Fox and Daniel Jeyaraj, 2006, 'Singer of the 'Souvereign Lord': Hindu Pietism and Christian Bhakti in the conversion of Kanapati Vattiyar, a Tamil 'Poet'', in Andreas Gross [et al.], (eds.), *Halle and the Beginning of Protestant Christianity in India*, Vol. II, 951–72, Verlag der Franckenschen Stiftungen, Halle.

Yule, Henry and A.C. Burnell, 1995, *Hobson-Jobson*, Asian Educational Services, New Delhi, Madras, (London 1903).

Zastoupil Lynn and Martin Moir (eds.), 1999, *The Great Indian Education Debate. Documents Relating to the Orientalist-Anglicist Controversy, 1781–1843*, Curzon, Richmond, Surrey (= London Studies on South Asia).

Ziegenbalg, Bartholomäus and Heinrich Plütschau, 1709, *Propagation of the Gospel in the East: Being an Account of the Success Of Two Danish Missionaries, Lately sent to the East-Indies, For the Conversion Of The Heathens in Malabar*, ed. by Anton Wilhelm Böhme, Downing, London.

Ziegenbalg, Bartholomäus and Heikrich Plütschau, 1708, *Merckwürdige Nachricht aus Ost-Indien, Welche Zwey Evangelisch-Lutherische Prediger Nahmentlich, Herr Bartholomäus Ziegenbalg [...] Und Herr Heinrich Plütscho [...] gesandt*, Joh. Christoph Papen, Leipzig [et al.].

Ziegenbalg, Bartholomäus, 1715, *A letter to the Reverend Mr Geo. Lewis. The Chaplain to the Honourable East-India Company, at Fort St. George: giving an account of the Method of Instruction used in the Charity-Schools of the Church, calle'd Jerusalem, in Tranquebar. [...] translated from the Portugueze-copy printed at Tranquebar*, printed and sold by J. Downing IV, London.

Ziegenbalg, Bartholomäus and Johann Ernst Gründler, 2002, 'Kurze Beschreibung der Tätigkeit der Mission [...]', in Niels-Peter Moritzen (ed.), *Von den Anfängen evangelischer Mission: zwei unbekannte Missionsschriften von 1713 und 1717*, 10–49, Verlag für Kultur und Wissenschaft, Bonn.

Ziegenbalg, Bartholomäus, [*Genealogie der malabarischen Götter*], see German, Wilhelm, 1867 resp. Jeyaraj. Daniel, 2003, 2005.

Ziegebalg, Bartholomäus, [*Malabarisches Heidenthum*], see under Caland, Willem, 1926, resp. Jeyaraj, Daniel, 2006.

Županov, Ines G., 1999, 'Religious Conversion, Cultural Translation in Early Modern South India', *IIAS Newsletter* (19): 51.

Županov, Ines G., 2005, *Missionary Tropics. The Catholic Frontier in India (16th and 17th centuries)*, The University of Michigan Press, Ann Arbor.

Sources

Archiv der Franckeschen Stiftungen zu Halle (Archives of the Francke Foundations at Halle)[1]

AFSt/A 45/02/06	(anon.), probably Christian Friedrich Pressier: Plan of the city of Tranquebar, 1729, coloured drawing.
AFSt/H D 16 a	Diary written by Benjamin Schultze, from 1 January 1720 to 31 December 1721.
AFSt/H J 66 : 2	Benjamin Schultze: Vocabularium Telugo-Tamulo-Biblicum Novi Testamenti, 1728.
AFSt/H J 66a	Benjamin Schultze: Grammatica Telugica, Madras 1728.
AFSt/H J 69	Benjamin Schultze: Multilingual Conversation Book. 30 dialogues on everyday themes in Madras. Telugu-English. Manuscript, around 1730.
AFSt/M 1 B 1 : 9	Letter from Christoph Theodosius Walther to Ludwig Johann Cellarius, 30 January 1728.
AFSt/M 1 B 1 : 18	Excerpt of a letter from Christoph Theodosius Walther to Johannes Schrodt, 11 November 1728.
AFSt/M 1 B 1 : 23	Letter from Christoph Theodosius Walther to Georg Sarganeck, 10 January 1729.
AFSt/M 1 B 1 : 33	Letter from Christian Friedrich Pressier to the students of the Halle school, Tranquebar, 27 January 1729.

[1] Information about the archival material of the Danish-Halle Mission is available in an online database of the Archives of the Francke Foundations. http://192.124.243.55/cgi-bin/dhmeng.pl. The digital library of the Francke Foundations gives the reader access to the complete digitalized version of the Halle Reports. http://www.francke-halle.de/main/index2.php?cf=3_1_3_3_2.

AFSt/M 1 B 2 : 7	Diary and account of the taking over of the paper mill by the mission, written by Benjamin Schultze, 1 January 1725.
AFSt/M 1 B 2 : 13	[Benjamin Schultze`s] correspondence with Prince Rutturosirāsha, 21 January 1722.
AFSt/M 1 B 3 : 21	Letter from Christoph Theodosius Walther, Christian Friedrich Lange and Martin Bosse to Johann Joachim Lange, 8 October 1726.
AFSt/M 1 B 8 : 5	Essay by Christoph Theodosius Walther, Tranquebar, ??.??. 1730.
AFSt/M 1 B 12 : 7	Song: 'The established harmony between Zion and Jerusalem', Tranquebar, ??.??. 1729.
AFSt/M 1 B 13 : 29	Letter from Gotthilf August Francke to Nikolaus Dal, Martin Bosse, Christian Pressier, Christoph Theodosius Walther, Andreas Worm and Samuel Gottlieb Richtsteig, 24 January 1733.
AFSt/M 1 B 20 : 7	Letter from Martin Bosse to Gotthilf August Francke, 24 January 1735.
AFSt/M 1 B 32 : 17	Letter from the national preacher Diogo to Gotthilf August Francke, 20 January 1744.
AFSt/M 1 B 32 : 23	Letter from Johann Balthasar Kohlhoff to Gotthilf August Francke, 31 January 1744.
AFSt/M 1 B 32: 40	Letter from Gotthilf August Francke to the national preacher Aaron, 7 January 1745.
AFSt/M 1 B 32 : 41	Letter from Gotthilf August Francke to the national preacher Diogo, 7 January 1745.
AFSt/M 1 B 33 : 2	Letter from the national preachers Aaron and Diogo to the Mission Board in Copenhagen, 24 January 1745.
AFSt/M 1 B 33 : 10	Letter from Johann Balthasar Kohlhoff to Gotthilf August Francke, 22 December 1744.
AFSt/M 1B 33 : 36	Letter from Gotthilf August Francke to the national preachers Aaron and Diogo, 5 November 1745.
AFSt/M 1 B 43 : 13	Letter from Jacob Klein to Gotthilf August Francke, 8 October 1753.
AFSt/M 1 B 44 : 22	Letter from the national preachers Diogo and Ambros to Gotthilf August Francke, 1 February 1755.
AFSt/M 1 B 47 : 27	Letter from the Indian preacher Diogo to Gotthilf August Francke, 11 October 1756.
AFSt/M 1 B 48 : 11	Letter from Jacob Klein to Gotthilf August Francke, 16 October 1758.

AFSt/M 1 B 67 : 22	Letter from Johann Wilhelm Gerlach to Gottlieb Anastasius Freylinghausen, Tranquebar, 31.January 1778.
AFSt/M 1 B 67 : 23	Letter from Johann Wilhelm Gerlach to Sebastian Andreas Fabricius, Tranquebar, 31 January 1778.
AFSt/M 1 B 67 : 24	Letter from Johann Wilhelm Gerlach to Christian Gottlieb Kratzenstein, Tranquebar 20 February 1778.
AFSt/M 1 B 71 :35	Diary Sattianaden, December 1779.
AFSt/M 1 B 71 : 36	Diary Schawrimuttu 1780.
AFSt/M 1 B 75 : 26	Travel diary of the catechist Njanapiragaham of journeys to Ramanathapuram and Palayankottai, 2 February 1785.
AFSt/M 1 C 4 : 11	Letter from Bartholomäus Ziegenbalg and Johann Ernst Gründler to [unknown], 17 September 1712.
AFSt/M 1 C 4 : 13	Letter from Bartholomäus Ziegenbalg , Johann Ernst Gründler and Polycarp Jordan to Anton Wilhelm Boehme, 20 September 1712.
AFSt/M 1 C 6 : 103	Founding charter of the mission board by Friedrich IV, King of Denmark and Norway, 10 December 1714.
AFSt/M 1 C 31a : 30	Letter from Jacob Klein to Johann Ludwig Schulze, Tranquebar, 20 January 1790.
AFSt/M 1 C 32a : 35	Minutes of Sattianaden's examination.[Place not mentioned] 1791.
AFSt/M 1 H 3 : 15	Letter from Nikolaus Dal to [Johann Georg v. Holstein, Johann Steenbuch, Johann Wilhelm Schröder, Jacob Lodberg] and [Wilhelm v. Munk], 7 July 1723 Tranquebar.
AFSt/M 1 K 5 : 10	Biography of Aaron, June 1745.
AFSt/M 1 K 5 : 16	Brief curriculum vitae of Daniel Pullei by [Christoph Samuel John], ??. ??. 1803.
AFSt/M 2 A 2 : 5a	Information about Germans in the service of the king of Tanjore, ??. ??. 1750.
AFSt/M 2 A 2 : 7	List of names of the 'national workers' in the Portuguese congregations and the Tamil city and village congregations, ??.??.1746.
AFSt/M 2 A 2 : 8	List of names of the 'national workers' in the Portuguese congregations and the Tamil city and village congregations, ??.??.1743.
AFSt/M 2 A 2 : 9	List of names of all the 'national workers', ??.??.1749.

AFSt/M 2 A 2 : 10	List of names of the 'national workers' in the Portuguese congregations and the Tamil city and village congregations, 1 August 1763.
AFSt/M 2 A 2 : 11	Number of 'national workers' in Tranquebar in 1749, ??.??.1749.
AFSt/M 2 A 2 : 12	List of names of the 'national workers' in the Portuguese congregations and the Tamil city and village congregations, ??.??.1749.
AFSt/M 2 A 2 : 13	List of names of the 'national workers' in the Portuguese congregations and the Tamil city and village congregations, ??.??.1749.
AFSt/M 2 A 5 : 3	Translation of the Malabar book of edification for simple Christians, specially done in three volumes (till p. 20?) by Christoph Samuel John, 14 February 1793.
AFSt/M 2 A 5 : 21	Compendiaria Alcorani refutatio indostanice, Madras, 31 October 1741.
AFSt/M 2 B 1 : 8	Desription of the swingle festival of the fishermen by Johann Gerhard König, [Tranquebar] ??. ??. 1768.
AFSt/M 2 B 2 : 2	Wind- and weather observations 1732–1737, Madras, 20 October 1732.
AFSt/M 2 B 2 : 17	Meteorological observations in the year 1791, ??. ??. 1791.
AFSt/M 2 B 2 : 19	Some remarks and reflections on the Malabarian calendar, 30 December 1727.
AFSt/M 2 B 3 : 8	School catalogue of the children in the Tamil school who are receiving support from benefactors, January 1756, ??. 01. 1756.
AFSt/M 2 B 3 : 21	Index of the 'national workers' by Jacob Klein, ??. October 1776.
AFSt/M 2 B 3 : 22a	Tamil assistants in February 1777 by [Jacob Klein], ??.??.1777.
AFSt/M 2 B 5 : 1–8	Coloured drawings by an unknown artist, commissioned by the missionary Nicolaus Dal, 1729.
AFSt/M 2 B 5 : 13	Introducing the Evangelical-East-India Church, ??. ??. 1730.
AFSt/M 2 B 7 : 2	Some remarks for correction of spelling and pronunciation of Tamil words in the Mission Reports and in other historical and geographical texts, ??. ??. 1789.

AFSt/M 2 B 7 : 3a	Names commonly used by Tamil Christians and their meaning, by Christoph Samuel John, ??. ??. 1789.
AFSt/M 2 B 7 : 3b	Names that are common among the heathen Tamilians, by Christoph Samuel John, ??. ??. 1789.
AFSt/M 2 B 7 : 5	Translation of the Malabarian book of the morals Atusudi [Atticūti] written by Aweiar [Auvaiyār] by Christoph Samuel John, ??. ??. 1789.
AFSt/M 2 B 7 : 6	Translation of the Malabarian book of Morals Mūdurai [Mūturai] written by the famous philosopher Aweiar [Auvaiyār] by Christoph Samuel John, ??. ??. 1789.
AFSt/M 2 B 7 : 7	Translation of the Tamil book Ulagag a Nidi [Ulakanīti] by Ulakanatan by Christoph Samuel John, ??. ??. 1789.
AFSt/M 2 B 7 : 8	Translation [by Christoph Samuel John] of a small Tamil book of morals called Pottia mālei by Muttu-t Tāntavar, ??. ??. 1789.
AFSt/M 2 B 7 : 13	Catalogue of books in Telugu and Tamil available in Madras, Tranquebar, Copenhagen and Halle, 12. December 1744.
AFSt/M 2 B 8	The Lord´s Prayer in different Indian languages, ??. ??. 1730.
AFSt/M 2 B 11	'The Malabar Doctor', which gives a brief account of the heathen principles of medicine; of the manner in which they cure the sick and the medicines they use. Collected and translated for the information of doctors in Europe from the medical books of the Malabarians by J[ohann]. E[rnst]. G[ründler]. 1712.
AFSt/M 2 C 17 : 6	'On Indian civilization or report of a successful trial made sence two years on the subject in 15 tamil and 5 english men native free schools and proposals for establishing a[nd] separate liberal Native School Society, humbly submitted to the judgement & patronage of the honorable governments of the honorable East India Company, of the respectable religious societies & of the genereous & charitable public.' From Christoph Samuel John to Georg Christian Knapp, ??. 02. 1812.
AFSt/M 2 D 35 : 7	Report by Johann Zacharias Kiernander about the people of Madgascar and their language, Cuddalore, 31 January 1758.

AFSt/M 2 E 27 : 3	Memo from Christoph Samuel John to Gottlieb Anastasius Freylinghausen, 10 October 1785.
AFSt/M 2 E 27 : 8	News about the weather and the storm during the monsoon period 1794, by Christoph Samuel John, Tranquebar, 18 January 1795.
AFSt/M 2 E 37 : 1	Report on the ordination of the new country pastor Philipp by Johann Balthasar Kohlhoff, Daniel Zeglin, Oluf Maderup, Jacob Klein, Johann Friedrich König, Friedrich Wilhelm Leidemann, Christoph Samuel John, 28 December 1772.
AFSt/M 2 E 37 : 2a	Diary of the country pastor Philipp, of 19 December 1775 to 5 March 1776.
AFSt/M 2 E 37 : 3	Supplement to the diaries of 1777. About the country pastor Philipp's intended stay in the countryside by Johann Balthasar Kohlhoff, Daniel Zeglin, Johann Friedrich König, Christoph Samuel John, Johann Wilhelm Gerlach, Johann Peter Rottler, ??. ??. 1777.
AFSt/M 2 F 1	Reports and diaries from catechists and country pastors, 1782–85.
AFSt/M 2 F 2	Reports and diaries from catechists and country pastors, 1793–1805.
AFSt/M 2 F 3	Reports and diaries from catechists and country pastors, 1787–1805.
AFSt/M 2 G 6 : 1	Letter from Benjamin Schultze to Gotthilf August Francke, 23 September 1727.
AFSt/M 2 H 2 : 21	Account of the Mughals from 'Aureng-Sib', ??. ??. 1727.
AFSt/M 2 H 3 : 11	Information about the Mughals from 'Aurang-Sib' onwards, ??. ??. 1727
AFSt/M 2 H 3 : 15	Letter from Benjamin Schultze to [Gotthilf August Francke], ??. ??. 1728.
AFSt/M 3 I 3	Accounts from Tranquebar 1725–1764.
AFSt/M 3 I 11	Accounts from the Cansteinschen Bibelanstalt related to the Mission in India, 1746–1758.
AFSt/M 3 I 13	Accounts, 1715–1720; 1748–1828.
AFSt/P TAM 79	(anon.): 'Der Malabaren Sternkundigkeit und 12 Himmelszeichen'. Tranquebar 1719–1728 (Palm leaf manuscript).

Bibliothek der Franckeschen Stiftungen zu Halle (Library oft he Francke Foundations at Halle)

BFSt: Kt: 256	Plan and View of the Royal Danish Fort and City, Dansburg and Trankenbar, on the Coromandel Coast in East India according to the geometrical draft [...] Coloured engraving by Matthäus Seutter on the basis of the sketch provided by a missionary in Tranquebar. Augsburg, around 1745.
BFSt: Kt: 247	Accurate geographical plan of the Royal Danish city and fort Trankenbar or Tarangambadi and Dansburg on the Coromandel Coast in East India along with the places and villages belonging to it [...] Coloured engraving by Matthäus Seutter on the basis of the sketch provided by a missionary in Tranquebar. Augsburg, around 1745.

Rigsarkivet Copenhagen (National Archives Copenhagen)

RA Miskolark 3	Instruction for the missionary Johann Wilhelm Gerlach, 16 November 1775.
RA Miskolark 3	Letter from the Mission Board to all missionaries, 25 November 1767.
RA Miskolark 3b	Pro Memoria, by J. Klein, J.F. König, Ch. S. John and J.P. Rottler, Tranquebar, 20 July 1789.
RA Miskolark 4	Letter from the Mission Board to all missionaries in Tranquebar, 13 November 1765.
RA Miskolark 4	Letter from the Mission Board to all missionaries in Tranquebar, 21 November 1765.
RA Miskolark 4	Letter from the Mission Board to G.A. Francke, 26 November 1765.
RA Miskolark 4	Letter from the Mission Board to G.A. Francke, 30 November 1765.
RA Miskolark 4	Letter from the Mission Board to Friedrich Michael Ziegenhagen, 7 December 1765.
RA Miskolark 4	Letter from the Mission Board to all missionaries, 7 December 1765.
RA Miskolark 4	Letter from the Mission Board to G.A. Francke, 14 December 1765.
RA Miskolark 4	Letter from the Mission Board to all missionaries in Tranquebar, 24 November 1768.

RA Miskolark 4	Letter from the Mission Board to Ch. F. Schwartz, 29 October 1770.
RA Miskolark 4	Letter from Ch. S. John, 7 December 1785.
RA Miskolark 9b	Letter from Diogo to the Mission Board, 28 September 1748.
RA Miskolark 9b	Palm-leaf letter from Rajanayakkan to the Mission Board, 6 October 1749.
RA Miskolark 9b	Letter from Diogo to the Mission Board, 16 October 1749.
RA Miskolark 9b	Letter from Diogo to the Mission Board, 8 December 1750.
RA Miskolark 9c	Letter from Klein, Poltzenhagen and Schwartz to the Mission Board, 27 October 1751.
RA Miskolark 9c	Letter from Diogo and Ambrosius to the Mission Board, 20 October 1752.
RA Miskolark 9c	Letter from Diogo and Ambrosius to the Mission Board, 2 October 1753.
RA Miskolark 9c	Letter from Diogo and Ambrosius to the Mission Board, 10 October 1755.
RA Miskolark 9c	Joint letter from the missionaries to G.A. Francke, 26 September 1764.
RA Miskolark 9c	*Pro Memoria* to the Mission Board in Copenhagen, Herrnhut 7 November 1765.
RA Miskolark 9d	Letter from B. Schultze to a Counsellor of Justice, 23 March, 1759.
RA Miskolark 9e	Excerpt of a letter from the missionaries in Tranquebar to G.A. Francke, 26 September 1764.
RA Miskolark 9f	Letter from Ch. F. Schwartz to the Mission Board, Tiruchirappalli. 17 December 1766.
RA Miskolark 9f	Letter from Ch. F. Schwartz to the Mission Board, Tiruchirappalli, 26 October 1768.
RA Miskolark 9f	*Pro Memoria* for new missionaries from Ch. F. Schwartz, Tiruchirappalli, 12 October 1771.
RA Miskolark 9f	Letter from Ch. F. Schwartz to the Mission Board, Tiruchirappalli, 12 October 1771.
RA Miskolark 9g	*Pro Memoria* for new missionaries, from Ch. S. John and [J.P. Rottler] Tranquebar, January 20, 1784.
RA Miskolark 9g	*Pro Memoria* from Ch. S. John, Tranquebar, 12 February 1784.
RA Miskolark 9g	Some suggestions regarding the Mission by Ch. S. John, Tranquebar, 20 February 1784.

RA Miskolark 9g *Pro Memoria* from Christoph Samuel John, 12 December 1784.

RA Miskolark 9g *Pro Memoria* for new missionaries from Ch. S. John, Tranquebar, 20 January 1794.

RA Miskolark 9g *Pro Memoria* for new missionaries from Ch. S. John, Tranquebar, 27 October 1794.

RA Miskolark 9h *Pro Memoria* from the Tranquebar missionaries to the government, 24 November 1794.

RA Miskolark 9h *Pro Memoria* from Ch. S. John, Tranquebar, 3 March 1796.

RA Miskolark 9h Some preliminary thoughts for instructing new missionaries and assistants from Ch. S. John, J. P. Rottler, A. F. Cämmerer [1797],

RA Miskolark 9h Instruction for a future missionary in Tranquebar, 1798.

RA Miskolark 9h Instruction for a German catechist or teacher in Tranquebar, 1798.

RA Miskolark 9i *Pro Memoria*, 1800 [no date or signature].

RA Miskolark 9i Letter from Ch. S. John, J. P. Rottler and A. F. Cämmerer to the Mission Board, 6 August 1800.

RA Miskolark 9i Report on the situation of the Royal Danish Mission in Tranquebar in the year 1803 by Ch. S. John, J. P. Rottler, A. F. Cämmerer (duplicate).

RA Miskolark 9i Letter from J. P. Rottler to the Mission Board, 11 October 1806.

RA Miskolark 9i Letter from Daniel Schreyvogel, 2 February 1806.

RA AsK, N° 2183 c, Breve fra Tolken Daniel I Tanjore ang indløsning af pantsatte landsbyer 1783– 1784 (Tamil).

Royal Library (Det Kongelige Bibliotek), Copenhagen

KB Oriental Department. Cod Tamul 5 'Ulaga Nidi oder weltliche Gerechtigkeit', Ziegenbalg's translation of 3 September 1708.

Archives of the Gurukul Lutheran Theological College & Research Institute, Chennai

Acc. No. 384 Autobiography of the Late Rev. Christian David (1771–1852).

Staatsbibliothek Preußischer Kulturbesitz Berlin (Berlin State Library)

Nachlass August Hermann Francke K 33, Fascicle B (H. Plütschau).

Unitätsarchiv der Evangelischen Brüder-Unität Herrnhut (Unitas Archives oft he Evangelical Unity of Brethren at Herrnhut)

UH, R 15 Tb, N° 1a	Diary Tranquebar 1760–67.
UH R 15 Tb N° 1b	Diary Tranquebar 1768–82.
UH R 15 Tb, N° 1c	Diary Tranquebar 1783–99.
UH, R 15 T, N⁰ 35, 129.	St. Letter from Gottfried Raabs, Tranquebar, 27 August 1781.

Archive of the Society for Promoting Christian Knowledge, Cambridge

SPCK, ME/Cs 3	letter from H. Newman (1670–1743), secretary of the SPCK, to B. Schultze, London, 26 January 1742.
SPCK ME/Cr 3	Letter from B. Schultze to King George, Madras, 16 December 1726.

School of Oriental and African Studies (SOAS), London

SOAS/LMS	Deposit 1795–1940, Box N° 6, folder N° 5; NHB 70. St., 1010.
SOAS/CWM	South Indian (Tamil) Incoming Correspondence 1816–1860, Box no. 9, 1844– 1847, 'Short Account of all the Native Teachers here employed at the expense of kind friends in England'.

Glasgow University Library Special Collection, Manuscript Documents

GB 247	Bayer, Historia regni graecorum bactriani. Bayer's unpublished papers contain letters from other missionaries of the Tranquebar mission.

United Theological College Bangalore (UTC)
Microfilm collection SPCK reel 5, letter of 20 March 1802.

Names of Persons

Names of Places